Lecture Notes in Computer Science 12418

More information about this series at http://www.springer.com/series/7410

Jianying Zhou · Mauro Conti ·
Chuadhry Mujeeb Ahmed ·
Man Ho Au · Lejla Batina ·
Zhou Li · Jingqiang Lin ·
Eleonora Losiouk · Bo Luo ·
Suryadipta Majumdar · Weizhi Meng ·
Martín Ochoa · Stjepan Picek ·
Georgios Portokalidis · Cong Wang ·
Kehuan Zhang (Eds.)

Applied Cryptography and Network Security Workshops

ACNS 2020 Satellite Workshops
AIBlock, AIHWS, AIoTS, Cloud S&P, SCI, SecMT, and SiMLA
Rome, Italy, October 19–22, 2020
Proceedings

 Springer

Editors
Jianying Zhou (iD)
Singapore University of Technology
and Design
Singapore, Singapore

Chuadhry Mujeeb Ahmed (iD)
Singapore University of Technology
and Design
Singapore, Singapore

Lejla Batina (iD)
ICIS
Radboud University Nijmegen
Nijmegen, The Netherlands

Jingqiang Lin
University of Science and Technology
of China
Hefei, China

Bo Luo
University of Kansas
Lawrence, KS, USA

Weizhi Meng (iD)
Technical University of Denmark
Lyngby, Denmark

Stjepan Picek (iD)
Delft University of Technology
Delft, The Netherlands

Cong Wang (iD)
City University of Hong Kong
Hong Kong, China

Mauro Conti (iD)
University of Padua
Padua, Italy

Man Ho Au (iD)
The University of Hong Kong
Hong Kong, Hong Kong

Zhou Li
University of California
Irvine, CA, USA

Eleonora Losiouk (iD)
University of Padua
Padua, Italy

Suryadipta Majumdar (iD)
CIISE
Concordia University
Montréal, QC, Canada

Martín Ochoa (iD)
AppGate Inc.
Bogotá, Colombia

Georgios Portokalidis (iD)
Stevens Institute of Technology
Hoboken, NJ, USA

Kehuan Zhang
Chinese University of Hong Kong
Shatin, Hong Kong

ISSN 0302-9743 ISSN 1611-3349 (electronic)
Lecture Notes in Computer Science
ISBN 978-3-030-61637-3 ISBN 978-3-030-61638-0 (eBook)
https://doi.org/10.1007/978-3-030-61638-0

LNCS Sublibrary: SL4 – Security and Cryptology

This Springer imprint is published by the registered company Springer Nature Switzerland AG
The registered company address is: Gewerbestrasse 11, 6330 Cham, Switzerland

Preface

These proceedings contain the papers selected for presentation at the 18th International Conference on Applied Cryptography and Network Security (ACNS 2020) satellite workshops, which were held in parallel with the main conference.

ACNS 2020 was planned to be held in Rome, Italy, during June 22–25 2020. Due to the unexpected COVID-19 crisis, we first postponed the conference to October 19–22, 2020, but ended up deciding for the safety of all participants to have a virtual conference. The local organization was in the capable hands of Emiliano Casalicchio and Angelo Spognardi (Sapienza University of Rome, Italy) and Giuseppe Bernieri (University of Padua, Italy) as general co-chairs, and Massimo Bernaschi (CNR, Italy) as organizing chair. We are deeply indebted to them for their tireless work to ensure the success of the conference even in such complex conditions.

ACNS initiated four satellite workshops successfully in 2019. Each workshop provided a forum to address a specific topic at the forefront of cybersecurity research. In response to this year's call for workshop proposals, three new workshops were launched besides the four workshops launched last year.

- AIBlock: Second ACNS Workshop on Application Intelligence and Blockchain Security
- AIHWS: First ACNS Workshop on Artificial Intelligence in Hardware Security
- AIoTS: Second ACNS Workshop on Artificial Intelligence and Industrial IoT Security
- Cloud S&P: Second ACNS Workshop on Cloud Security and Privacy
- SCI: First ACNS Workshop on Secure Cryptographic Implementation
- SecMT: First ACNS Workshop on Security in Mobile Technologies
- SiMLA: Second ACNS Workshop on Security in Machine Learning and its Applications

This year, we received a total of 65 submissions. Each workshop had its own Program Committee (PC) in charge of the review process. These papers were evaluated on the basis of their significance, novelty, and technical quality. The review process was double-blind. In the end, 31 papers were selected for presentation at seven workshops, with an acceptance rate of 47.7%.

ACNS also gave the best workshop paper award. The winning papers were selected from the nominated candidate papers from each workshop. The following two papers shared ACNS 2020 Best Workshop Paper Award:

- Michael McCoyd, Won Park, Steven Chen, Neil Shah, Ryan Roggenkemper, Minjune Hwang, Xinyu Liu, and David Wagner, "Minority Reports Defense: Defending Against Adversarial Patches," from the SiMLA workshop
- Valence Cristiani, Maxime Lecomte, and Philippe Maurine, "Leakage Assessment through Neural Estimation of the Mutual Information," from the AIHWS workshop

Besides the regular papers being presented at the workshops, there were also six invited talks.

- "Computing on Encrypted Data: Hardware to the Rescue" by Farinaz Koushanfar from UC San Diego, USA, and "Fooling Smart Machines: Security Challenges for Machine Learning" by Simon Fricdberger from NXP, The Netherlands, at the AIHWS workshop
- "Adversarial Classification in IoT Applications Using Differential Privacy" by Alvaro Cardenas from University of California, Santa Cruz, USA, at the AIoTS workshop
- "Towards Building a Scalable Security Analytics Framework for Attack Detection on Ethereum" by Yajin Zhou from Zhejiang University, China, at the CLOUD S&P workshop
- "Cache-in-the-Middle (CITM) Attacks: Manipulating Sensitive Data in Isolated Execution Environments" by Kun Sun from George Mason University, USA, at the SCI workshop
- "Security and Privacy: The Sorrows of Young Droid" by Alessio Merlo from University of Genoa, Italy, at the SecMT workshop

ACNS 2020 workshops were made possible by the joint efforts of many individuals and organizations. We appreciate Springer's strong support on our new initiative. We sincerely thank the authors of all submissions. We are grateful to the program chairs and PC members of each workshop for their great effort in providing professional reviews and interesting feedback to authors in a tight time schedule. We thank all the external reviewers for assisting the PC in their particular areas of expertise. We also thank the organizing team members of the main conference as well as each workshop for their help in various aspects.

Last but not least, we thank everyone else, speakers and session chairs, for their contribution to the program of ACNS 2020 workshops.

We are glad to see the existing workshops are growing and new workshops on emerging topics are being launched. We hope this trend will continue in the coming years. We expect it could provide a stimulating platform to discuss open problems at the forefront of cybersecurity research.

September 2020

Jianying Zhou
Mauro Conti
ACNS 2020 Workshop Chairs

AIBlock 2020

Second ACNS Workshop on Application Intelligence and Blockchain Security

19 October 2020

General Chairs

Chunhua Su — University of Aizu, Japan
Xiapu Luo — The Hong Kong Polytechnic University, China

Program Chairs

Weizhi Meng — Technical University of Denmark, Denmark
Man Ho Au — The University of Hong Kong, China

Program Committee

Raja Naeem Akram — Royal Holloway, University of London, UK
Jintai Ding — University of Cincinnati, USA
Dieter Gollmann — Hamburg University of Technology, Germany
Debiao He — Wuhan University, China
Qiong Huang — South China Agricultural University, China
Georgios Kambourakis — University of the Aegean, Greece
Chhagan Lal — University of Padua, Italy
Romain Laborde — Paul Sabatier University, France
Wenjuan Li — The Hong Kong Polytechnic University, China
Jiqiang Lu — Beihang University, China
Felix Gomez Marmol — University of Murcia, Spain
Pantaleone Nespoli — University of Murcia, Spain
Jun Shao — Zhejiang Gongshang University, China
Jiangang Shu — Peng Cheng Laboratory, China
Andreas Veneris — University of Toronto, Canada
Qianhong Wu — Beihang University, China
Ding Wang — Nankai University, China
Guomin Yang — University of Wollongong, Australia

Additional Reviewers

Gu, Zhiqiang
Luo, Zhenqiu
Miao, Ying
Wang, Chenyu

AIHWS 2020

First ACNS Workshop on Articial Intelligence in Hardware Security

21 October 2020

Program Chairs

Lejla Batina	Radboud University, The Netherlands
Stjepan Picek	Delft University of Technology, The Netherlands

Program Committee

Lex Schoonen	Brightsight, The Netherlands
Fatemeh Ganji	Worcester Polytechnic Institute, USA
Liran Lerman	Thales Belgium, Belgium
Shahin Tajik	Worcester Polytechnic Institute, USA
Lukasz Chmielewski	Riscure, The Netherlands
Vincent Verneuil	NXP Semiconductors, Germany
Alan Jovic	University of Zagreb, Croatia
Luca Mariot	Delft University of Technology, The Netherlands
Chitchanok Chuengsatiansup	The University of Adelaide, Australia
Nele Mentens	Katholieke Universiteit Leuven, Belgium
Dirmanto Jap	Nanyang Technological University, Singapore
Shivam Bhasin	Nanyang Technological University, Singapore
Nikita Veshchikov	NXP, Belgium
Kostas Papagiannopoulos	NXP, Germany
Guilherme Perin	Delft University of Technology, The Netherlands

Publicity Chair

Marina Krcek	Delft University of Technology, The Netherlands

AIoTS 2020

Second ACNS Workshop on Articial Intelligence and Industrial IoT Security

20 October 2020

Program Chairs

Martin Ochoa   Cyxtera, Colombia
Chuadhry Mujeeb Ahmed   SUTD, Singapore

Organizing Chairs

Sridhar Adepu   SUTD, Singapore
John Henry Castellanos   SUTD, Singapore

Publicity Chair

Chhagan Lal   University of Padua, Italy

Program Committee

Anand Agrawal   NYU Abu Dhabi, UAE
Alvaro Cardenas   University of California, Santa Cruz, USA
Ding Ding   George Washington University, USA
Luis Garcia   University of California, Los Angeles, USA
Amrita Ghosal   University of Padua, Italy
Venkata Reddy   IIPE-Visakhapatnam, India
Subir Halder   University of Padua, Italy
Nandha Kumar Kandasamy   SUTD, Singapore
Eunsuk Kang   Carnegie Mellon University, USA
Elena Lisova   Mälardalen University, Sweden
Chhagan Lal   University of Padua, Italy
Junyu Lai   UESTC, China
Eleonora Losiouk   University of Padua, Italy
Chris Poskitt   SMU, Singapore
Rajib Ranjan Maiti   BITS-Hyderabad, India
Tohid Shekari   Georgia Tech, USA
Federico Turrin   University of Padua, Italy
Riccardo Taormina   Delft University of Technology, The Netherlands
Robin Verma   UTSA, USA

Cloud S&P 2020

Second ACNS Workshop on Cloud Security and Privacy

22 October 2020

Program Chairs

Suryadipta Majumdar	University at Albany, SUNY, USA
Cong Wang	City University of Hong Kong, China

Program Committee

Daniel Bastos	British Telecom, UK
Helei Cui	Northwestern Polytechnical University, China
Nora Cuppens	IMT Atlantique, France
Sabrina De Capitani di Vimercati	Universitá degli Studi di Milano, Italy
Yosr Jarraya	Ericsson Security, Canada
Kallol Krishna Karmaker	The University of Newcastle, Australia
Eduard Marin	University of Birmingham, UK
Ali Miri	Ryerson University, Canada
Makan Pourzandi	Ericsson Security, Canada
Indrakshi Ray	Colorado State University, USA
Pierangela Samarati	Universitá degli Studi di Milano, Italy
Paria Shirani	Concordia University, Canada
Lingyu Wang	Concordia University, Canada
Xingliang Yuan	Monash University, Australia
Yifeng Zheng	Data61, CSIRO, Australia

Additional Reviewers

Shirazi, Hossein
Karanfil, Mark
Cabana, Olivier

SCI 2020

First ACNS Workshop on Secure Cryptographic Implementation

21 October 2020

Program Chairs

Jingqiang Lin — University of Science and Technology of China, China
Bo Luo — The University of Kansas, USA

Publication Chair

Jun Shao — Zhejiang Gongshang University, China

Publicity Chairs

Le Guan — University of Georgia, USA
Debiao He — Wuhan University, China

Web Chair

Yuan Ma — Chinese Academy of Sciences, China

Program Committee

Bo Chen — Michigan Technological University, USA
Fu Chen — Central University of Finance and Economics, China
Junfeng Fan — Open Security Research, Inc., China
Johann Großschädl — University of Luxembourg, Luxembourg
Le Guan — University of Georgia, USA
Debiao He — Wuhan University, China
Linzhi Jiang — University of Surrey, UK
Fengjun Li — The University of Kansas, USA
Xiao Liu — Facebook Inc., USA
Zhe Liu — Nanjing University of Aeronautics and Astronautics, China
Yuan Ma — Chinese Academy of Sciences, China
Jun Shao — Zhejiang Gongshang University, China
Ruisheng Shi — Beijing University of Posts and Telecommunications, China
Juan Wang — Wuhan University, China
Jun Xu — Stevens Institute of Technology, USA

SecMT 2020

First ACNS Workshop on Security in Mobile Technologies

19 October 2020

Program Chairs

Eleonora Losiouk   University of Padua, Italy
Georgios Portokalidis   Stevens Institute of Technology, USA

General Chair

Olga Gadyatskaya   Leiden University, The Netherlands

Program Committee

Kevin Allix   University of Luxembourg, Luxembourg
Elias Athanasopoulos   University of Cyprus, Cyprus
Antonio Bianchi   Purdue University, USA
Yanick Fratantonio   EURECOM, France
Li Li   Monash University, Australia
Isabella Mastroeni   University of Verona, Italy
Guozhu Meng   Nanyang Technological University, Singapore
Kaveh Razavi   ETH Zurich, Switzerland
Andrea Saracino   National Research Council, Italy
Flavio Toffalini   SUTD, Singapore

SiMLA 2020

Second ACNS Workshop on Security in Machine Learning and its Applications

20 October 2020

Program Chairs

Zhou Li   University of California Irvine, USA
Kehuan Zhang   The Chinese University of Hong Kong, China

Program Committee

Kangkook Jee   The University of Texas at Dallas, USA
Baojun Liu   Tsinghua University, China
Wenrui Diao   Shandong University, China
Yinqian Zhang   The Ohio State University, USA
Di Tang   The Chinese University of Hong Kong, China
Zhe Zhou   Fudan University, China
Kai Chen   Institute of Information Engineering, Chinese Academy of Sciences, China
Chaowei Xiao   University of Michigan, USA

Additional Reviewers

Mingxuan Liu
Li Wang
Zhixiu Guo

Contents

AIoTS – Artificial Intelligence and Industrial IoT Security

Cloud S&P – Cloud Security and Privacy

SCI – Secure Cryptographic Implementation

SecMT – Security in Mobile Technologies

SiMLA – Security in Machine Learning and Its Applications

AIBlock – Application Intelligence and Blockchain Security

Towards a Formally Verified Implementation of the MimbleWimble Cryptocurrency Protocol

Gustavo Betarte[1], Maximiliano Cristiá[2], Carlos Luna[1(✉)], Adrián Silveira[1], and Dante Zanarini[2]

[1] InCo, Facultad de Ingeniería, Universidad de la República, Montevideo, Uruguay
{gustun,cluna,adrians}@fing.edu.uy
[2] CIFASIS, Universidad Nacional de Rosario, Rosario, Argentina
{cristia,zanarini}@cifasis-conicet.gov.ar

Abstract. MimbleWimble is a privacy-oriented cryptocurrency technology which provides security and scalability properties that distinguish it from other protocols of its kind. We present and briefly discuss those properties and outline the basis of a model-driven verification approach to address the certification of the correctness of an implementation of the protocol.

Keywords: Cryptocurrency · MimbleWimble · Idealized model · Formal verification · Security

1 Introduction

Cryptocurrency protocols deal with virtual money so they are a valuable target for highly skilled attackers. Several attacks have already been mounted against cryptocurrency systems, causing irreparable losses of money and credibility (e.g. [11]). For this reason the cryptocurrency community is seeking approaches, methods, techniques and development practices that can reduce the chances of successful attacks. One such approach is the application of formal methods to software implementation. In particular, the cryptocurrency community is showing interest in formal proof and formally certified implementations.

MimbleWimble (MW) is a privacy-oriented cryptocurrency technology encompassing security and scalability properties that distinguish it from other technologies of its kind. MW was first proposed in 2016 [29]. The idea was then further developed by Poelstra [37]. In MW, unlike Bitcoin [35], there exists no concept of address and all the transactions are confidential. In this paper we outline an approach based on formal software verification aimed at formally verifying the basic mechanisms of MW and (one of) its implementations [28][1].

---

[1] The methodology proposed in this work also applies to the *Beam* implementation: https://www.beam-mw.com.

© Springer Nature Switzerland AG 2020
J. Zhou et al. (Eds.): ACNS 2020 Workshops, LNCS 12418, pp. 3–23, 2020.
https://doi.org/10.1007/978-3-030-61638-0_1

We put forward a model-driven verification approach where security issues that pertain to the realm of critical mechanisms of the MW protocol are explored on an idealized model of this system. Such model abstracts away the specifics of any particular implementation, and yet provides a realistic setting. Verification is then performed on more concrete models, where low level mechanisms are specified. Finally the low level model is proved to be a correct implementation of the idealized model.

Security (idealized) models have played an important role in the design and evaluation of high assurance security systems. Their importance was already pointed out in the Anderson report [1]. The paradigmatic Bell-LaPadula model [4], conceived in 1973, constituted the first big effort on providing a formal setting in which to study and reason on confidentiality properties of data in time-sharing mainframe systems. *State machines* can be employed as the building block of a security model. The basic features of a state machine model are the concepts of state and state change. A *state* is a representation of the system under study at a given time, which should capture those aspects of the system that are relevant to the analyzed problem. State changes are modeled by a state transition function that defines the next state based on the current state and input. If one wants to analyze a specific safety property of a system using a state machine model, one must first specify what it means for a state to satisfy the property, and then check if all state transitions preserve it. Thus, state machines can be used to model the enforcement of a security policy.

Related Work. Developers of cryptocurrency software should not be scared of using mathematics as a tool to describe software. In fact, Nakamoto uses maths in his seminal paper on Bitcoin [35] and Wood uses it to describe the EVM [41]. However, these descriptions can not be understood as Formal Methods (FM) because they are not based on standardized notations nor on clear mathematical theories.

On the other hand, recently, the FM community has started to pay attention to cryptocurrency software. Idelberger et al. [27] proposed to use defeasible logic frameworks such as Formal Contract Logic for the description of smart contracts. Bhargavan et al. [8] compile SOLIDITY programs into a verification-oriented functional language where they can verify source code. Luu et al. [32] use the OYENTE tool to find and detect vulnerabilities in smart contracts. Hirai [25] uses LEM to formally specify the EVM; Grishchenko, Maffei and Schneidewind [24] also formalize the EVM but in F*; and Hildenbrandt et al. do the same but with the reachability logic system known as K. Pîrlea and Sergey [36] present a Coq [5,38] formalization of a blockchain consensus protocol where some properties are formally verified.

Additionally, Metere and Dong [34] present a mechanised formal verification of the Pedersen commitment protocol using EasyCrypt [2] and Fuchsbaue et al. [18] introduce an abstraction for the analysis of some security properties of MW. Our work assumes some of these results to formalize and analyze the MW protocol, to then propose a methodology to verify their implementations.

Finally, in [6] we outline some formal methods related techniques that we consider particularly useful for cryptocurrency software. We present some guidelines for the adoption of formal methods in cryptocurrency software projects. We argue that set-based formal modeling (or specification), simulation, prototyping and automated proof can be applied before considering more powerful approaches such as code formal verification. In particular, we show excerpts of a set-based formal specification of a consensus protocol and of the Ethereum Virtual Machine. We also exhibit that prototypes can be generated from these formal models and simulations can be run on them. By last, we show that test cases can be generated from the same models and how automated proof can be used to evaluate the correctness of these models. Our work follows the approach of Betarte et al. [6].

Contribution. In this paper, we present elements that constitute essential steps towards the development of an exhaustive formalization of the MW cryptocurrency protocol and the analysis of its properties. We also introduce and discuss the basis of a model-driven verification approach to address the certification of the correctness of a protocol's implementation. The proposed idealized model in this paper is key in the verification process and constitutes our main contribution, together with the analysis of its important properties. In particular, we determine sufficient conditions on our model to ensure the verification of relevant security properties of MW.

Organization of the Paper. The rest of the paper is organized as follows: Sect. 2 provides a very brief description of MW. Section 3 describes the building blocks of a formal idealized model (abstract state machine) of the computational behaviour of MimbleWimble. Section 4 provides a brief account of the verification activities we are putting in place in order to verify the protocol and its implementation. Final remarks and directions for future work are presented in Sect. 5. A preliminary version of this paper is available on arXiv [7].

2   The MimbleWimble Protocol

Confidential transactions [20, 33] are at the core of the MW protocol. A transaction allows a sender to encrypt the amount of bitcoins by using blinding factors. In a confidential transaction only the two parties involved know the amount of bitcoins being exchanged. However, for anyone observing that transaction it is possible to verify its validity by comparing the number of inputs and outputs; if both are the same, then the transaction will be considered valid. Such procedure ensures that no bitcoins have been created from nothing and is key in preserving the integrity of the system. In MW transactions, the recipient randomly selects a range of blinding factors provided by the sender, which are then used as proof of ownership by the receiver.

The MW protocol aims at providing the following properties [28, 29]:

- Verification of zero sums without revealing the actual amounts involved in a transaction, which implies confidentiality.
- Authentication of transaction outputs without signing the transaction.
- Good scalability, while preserving security, by generating smaller blocks—or better, reducing the size of old blocks, producing a blockchain whose size does not grow in time as much as, for instance, Bitcoin's.

The first two properties are achieved by relying on Elliptic Curves Cryptography (ECC) operations and properties. The third one is a consequence of the first two.

2.1   Verification of Transactions

If v is the value of a transaction (either input or output) and H is a point over an elliptic curve, then vH encrypts v because it is assumed to be computationally hard to get v from vH if we only know H. However, if w and z are other values such that $v + w = z$, then if we only have the result of encrypting each of them with H we are still able to verify that equation. Indeed:

$$v + w = z \Leftrightarrow vH + wH = zH$$

due to simple properties of scalar multiplication over groups. Therefore, with this simple operations, we can check sums of transactions amounts without knowing the actual amounts.

Nevertheless, say some time ago we have encrypted v with H and now we see vH, then we know that it is the result of encrypting v. In the context of blockchain transactions this is a problem because once a block holding vH is saved in the chain it will reveal all the transactions of v coins. For such problems, MW encrypts v as $rG + vH$ where r is a scalar and G is another point in H's elliptic curve, r is called *blinding factor* and $rG + vH$ is called *Pedersen commitment*. By using Pedersen commitments, MW allows the verification of expressions such as $v + w = z$ providing more privacy than the standard scheme. In effect, if $v + w = z$ then we choose r_v, r_w and r_z such that $r_v G + r_w G = r_z G$ and so the expression is recorded as:

$$\overbrace{(r_v G + vH)}^{v} + \overbrace{(r_w G + wH)}^{w} = \overbrace{r_z G + zH}^{z}$$

making it possible for everyone to verify the transaction without knowing the true values.

2.2   Authentication of Transactions

Consider that Alice has received v coins and this was recorded in the blockchain as $rG + vH$, where r was chosen by her to keep it private. Now she wants to transfer these v coins to Bob. As a consequence, Alice looses v coins and Bob receives the very same amount, which means that the transaction adds to zero: $rG + vH - (rG + vH) = 0G - 0H$. However, Alice now knows Bob's blinding factor because it must be the same chosen by her (so the transaction is balanced). In order to protect Bob from being stolen by Alice, MW allows Bob to add his blinding factor, r_B, in such a way that the transaction is recorded as:

$$(r + r_B)G + vH - (rG + vH) = r_B G - 0H$$

although now it does not sum zero. However, this *excess value* is used as part of an authentication scheme. Indeed, Bob uses r_B as a private key to sign the empty string (ϵ). This signed document is attached to the transaction so in the blockchain we have:

- Input: I.
- Output: O.
- Bob's signed document: S.

This way, the transaction is valid if the result of decrypting S with $I - O$ (in the group generated by G) yields ϵ. If $I - O$ does not yield something in the form of $r_B G - 0H$, then ϵ will not be recovered and so we know there is an attempt to create money from thin air or there is an attempt to steal Bob's money.

3 Idealized Model of MimbleWimble-Based Blockchain

The basic elements of our model are transactions, blocks and chains. Each node in the blockchain maintains a local state. The main components are the local copy of the chain and the set of transactions waiting to be validated and added to a new block. Moreover, each node keeps track of unspent transaction outputs (UTXOs). Properties such as zero-sum and the absence of double spending in blocks and chains must be proved for local states. The blockchain global state can be represented as a mapping from nodes to local states. For global states, we can state and prove properties for the entire system like, for instance, correctness of the consensus protocol.

3.1 Transactions

Given two fixed generator points G and H on the elliptic curve C of prime order n (whose discrete logarithms relative to each other are unknown), we define a single transaction between two parties as follows:

Definition 1 (Transaction). *A single transaction t is a tuple of type:*

$$Transaction \stackrel{\text{def}}{=} \{i : I^*, \ o : O^*, tk : TxKernel, tko : KOffset\}$$

with X^* representing the lists of elements of type X and where:

- $i = (c_1, ..., c_n)$ *and* $o = (o_1, ..., o_m)$ *are the lists of inputs and outputs. Each input c_i and output o_i are points over the curve C and they are the result of computing the Pedersen commitment $r.G + v.H$ with r the blinding factor and v the transactional value in the finit field $\mathbb{F}_n$.*

- $tk = \{rp, ke, \sigma\}$ is the transaction kernel where:
  - rp is a list of range proofs of the outputs.
  - ke is the transaction excess represented by $(\sum_1^m r' - \sum_1^n r - tko).G$.
  - σ is the kernel signature[2].
- $tko \in \mathbb{F}_n$ is the transaction kernel offset.

The transaction kernel offset will be used in the construction of a block to satisfy security properties.

Definition 2 (Ownership). *Given a transaction t, we say S owns the output o if S knows the opening (r, v) for the Pedersen commitment $o = r.G + v.H$.*

The strength of this security definition is directly related to the difficulty of solving the logarithm problem. If the elliptic curve discrete logarithm problem in C is hard then given a multiple Q of G, it is computationally infeasible to find an integer r such that $Q = r.G$.

Definition 3 (Balanced Transaction). *A transaction $t = \{i, o, tk, tko\}$, with transaction kernel $tk = \{rp, ke, \sigma\}$, is balanced if the following holds:*

$$\sum_{o_j \in o} o_j - \sum_{c_j \in i} c_j = ke + tko.G$$

A balanced transaction guarantees no money is created from thin air and the transaction was honestly constructed.

Property 1 (Valid Transaction). A transaction t is valid ($valid\_transaction(t)$) if t satisfies:

  i. The range proofs of all the outputs are valid.
 ii. The transaction is balanced.
iii. The kernel signature σ is valid for the excess.

These three properties have a straightforward interpretation in our model. Due to limitations of space, we formalize and analyze in this paper only some of the properties mentioned throughout the document.

3.2   Unconfirmed Transaction Pool

The unconfirmed transaction pool (mempool) contains the transactions which have not been confirmed in a block yet.

Definition 4 (Mempool). *A mempool mp is a list of type:*

$$Mempool \overset{\text{def}}{=} Transaction^*$$

---

[2] For simplicity, fees are left aside.

3.3   Blocks and Chains

Genesis block *Gen* is a special block since it is the first ever block recorded in the chain. Transactions can be merged into a *block*. We can see a block as a big transaction with aggregated inputs, outputs and transaction kernels.

Definition 5 (Block). *A Block b is either the genesis block Gen, or a tuple of type:*

$$Block \stackrel{\text{def}}{=} \{i : I^*, \ o : O^*, \ tks : TxKernel^*, ko : KOffset\}$$

where:

- *$i = (c_1, ..., c_n)$ and $o = (o_1, ..., o_m)$ are the lists of inputs and outputs of the transactions.*
- *$tks = (tk_1, ..., tk_t)$ is the list of t transaction kernels.*
- *$ko \in \mathbb{F}_n$ is the block kernel offset which covers all the transactions of the block.*

We can say a block is balanced if each aggregated transaction is balanced.

Definition 6 (Balanced Block). *Let b be a block of the form $b = \{i, o, tks, ko\}$ with $tks = (tk_1, ..., tk_t)$ the list of transaction kernels and where the j-th item in tks is of the form $tk_j = \{rp_j, ke_j, \sigma_j\}$. We say the block b is balanced if the following holds:*

$$\sum_{o_j \in o} o_j - \sum_{c_j \in i} c_j = ko.G + \sum_{ke_j \in tks} ke_j$$

We assume the genesis block *Gen* is valid. We define the notion of block validity as follows:

Property 2 (Valid Block). A block b is valid ($valid\_block(b)$) if b is the genesis block *Gen* or it satisfies:

i. The block is balanced.
ii. For every transaction kernel, the range proofs of all the outputs are valid and the kernel signature σ is valid for the transaction excess.

Blocks can be constructed by aggregating transactions as follows:

Definition 7 (Block Aggregation). *Given a valid transaction t_0 and a valid block b as follows:*

$$t_0 = \{i_0, o_0, tk_0, tko_0\} \ and \ b = \{i, o, tks, ko\}$$

a new block can be constructed as:

$$b' = \{i_0 \ || \ i, o_0 \ || \ o, tk_0 \ || \ tks, tko_0 + ko\}$$

where $||$ is the list concatenation operator and $+$ is the scalar sum.

Block aggregation preserves the validity of blocks; i.e. block validity is invariant w.r.t. block agreggation.

Lemma 1 (Invariant: Block Validity). *Given a valid transaction t_0 and a valid block b as in Definition 7. Let b' be the result of aggregating t_0 into b. Then, b' is valid.*

Proof. Let t_0 be the transaction $t_0 = \{i_0, o_0, tk_0, tko_0\}$ with $tk_0 = \{rp_0, ke_0, \sigma_0\}$. Let b be the block $b = \{i, o, tks, ko\}$, with $tks = (tk_1, ..., tk_t)$, the list of transaction kernels.

Applying Definition 7, we have that the resulting b' is of the form:

$$b' = \{i', o', tks', ko'\}$$

with $i' = i_0 \,\|\, i$, $o' = o_0 \,\|\, o$, $tks' = (tk_0, tk_1, ..., tk_t)$, $ko' = tko_0 + ko$

According to Definition 6, we need to prove the following equality holds for the block b':

$$\sum_{o_j \in o'} o_j - \sum_{c_j \in i'} c_j = ko'.G + \sum_{ke_j \in tks'} ke_j$$

Each term can be written as follows:

$$\left(\sum_{o_j \in o_0} o_j + \sum_{o_j \in o} o_j\right) - \left(\sum_{c_j \in i_0} c_j + \sum_{c_j \in i} c_j\right) = (tko_0 + ko).G + ke_0 + \sum_{ke_j \in tks} ke_j$$

Rearranging the equality and using algebraic properties on elliptic curves, we have:

$$\left(\sum_{o_j \in o_0} o_j - \sum_{c_j \in i_0} c_j\right) + \left(\sum_{o_j \in o} o_j - \sum_{c_j \in i} c_j\right) = (ke_0 + tko_0.G) + \left(ko.G + \sum_{ke_j \in tks} ke_j\right)$$

Now, we apply the hypothesis concerning the validity of t_0 and b. In particular, applying Definition 3 for t_0 and Definition 6 for b, we have the following equalities are true:

$$\sum_{o_j \in o_0} o_j - \sum_{c_j \in i_0} c_j = ke_0 + tko_0.G$$

and

$$\sum_{o_j \in o} o_j - \sum_{c_j \in i} c_j = ko.G + \sum_{ke_j \in tks} ke_j$$

That is exactly what we wanted to prove.   □

Definition 8 (Chain). *A chain is a non-empty list of blocks:*

$$Chain \overset{\text{def}}{=} Block^*$$

For a chain c and a valid block b, we can define a predicate $validate(c, b)$ representing the fact that is correct to add b to c. This relation must verify, for example, that all the inputs in b are present as outputs in c, in other words, they are unspent transaction outputs (UTXOs).

3.4 Validating a Chain

The model formalizes a notion of valid state that captures several well-formedness conditions. In particular, every block in the blockchain must be valid. A predicate $validChain$ can be defined for a chain $c = (b_0, b_1, \ldots b_n)$ by checking that:

- b_0 is a valid genesis block
- For every $i \in \{1, \ldots n\}$, $validate((b_0, \ldots, b_{i-1}), b_i)$

The axiomatic semantics of the system are modeled by defining a set of transactions, and providing their semantics as state transformers. The behaviour of transactions is specified by a precondition Pre and by a postcondition $Post$:

$$Pre \subseteq State \times Transaction$$

$$Post \subseteq State \times Transaction \times State$$

This approach is valid when considering local (nodes) or global (blockchain) states (of type $State$) and transactions (of type $Transaction$). Different sets of transactions, pre and postcondition are defined to cover local or global state transformations. At a general level, $State$ is $Chain$.

3.5 Executions

There can be attempts to execute a transaction on a state that does not verify the precondition of that transaction. In the presence of such situation the system answers with a corresponding error code (of type $ErrorCode$). Executing a transaction t over a valid state s $(valid\_state(s))$[3] produces a new state s' and a corresponding answer r (denoted $s \xrightarrow{t/r} s'$), where the relation between the former state and the new one is given by the postcondition relation $Post$.

$$\frac{valid\_state(s) \quad Pre(s,t) \quad Post(s,t,s')}{s \xrightarrow{t/ok} s'}$$

$$\frac{valid\_state(s) \quad ErrorMsg(s,t,ec)}{s \xrightarrow{t/error(ec)} s}$$

Whenever a transaction occurs for which the precondition holds, the valid state may change in such a way that the transaction postcondition is established. The notation $s \xrightarrow{t/ok} s'$ may be read as *the execution of the transaction t in a valid state s results in a new state s'*. However, if the precondition is not satisfied, then the valid state s remains unchanged and the system answer is the error

---

[3] When dealing with global states, $valid\_state$ is $validChain$.

message determined by a relation $ErrorMsg^4$. Formally, the possible answers of the system are defined by the type:

$$Response \overset{\text{def}}{=} ok \mid error \ (ec : ErrorCode)$$

where ok is the answer resulting from a successful execution of a transaction.

One-step execution with error management preserves valid states.

Lemma 2 (Validity is invariant).
$\forall \ (s \ s' : State)(t : Transaction)(r : Response),$
$valid\_transaction(t) \rightarrow s \xrightarrow{t/r} s' \rightarrow valid\_state(s')$

The proof follows by case analysis on $s \xrightarrow{t/r} s'$. When $Pre(s, t)$ does not hold, $s = s'$. From this equality and $valid\_state(s)$ then $valid\_state(s')$. Otherwise, $Pos(s, t, s')$ must hold and we proceed by case analysis on t, considering that t is a valid transaction and s is a valid state.

System state invariants, such as state validity, are useful to analyze other relevant properties of the model. In particular, the properties in this work are obtained from valid states of the system.

4   Verification of MimbleWimble

We now detail some relevant properties that can be verified in our model. In addition to some of the properties mentioned in previous sections, we include in our research other properties such as those formulated in [36], and various security properties considered in [18,19,30].

4.1   Protocol Properties

The property of *no-coin-inflation* or *zero-sum* guarantees that no new funds are produced from thin air in a valid transaction. The property can be stated as follows.

Lemma 3 (No Coin Inflation). *Given a valid transaction $t = \{i, o, tk, tko\}$ with transaction kernel $tk = \{rp, ke, \sigma\}$, it can be proved that no money is created from thin air; i.e. the transaction excess only contains the blinding factor and the kernel offset.*

Proof We know the transaction t is valid, in particular, the transaction is balanced. Applying Definition 3, we know that:

$$\sum_{o_j \in o} o_j - \sum_{c_j \in i} c_j = ke + tko.G$$

---

[4] Given a state s, a transaction t and an error code ec, $ErrorMsg(s, t, ec)$ holds iff error ec is an acceptable response when the execution of t is requested on state s.

Using Definition 1, we start to unfold the terms in the equality:

$$\sum_1^m r'.G + v'.H - \sum_1^n r.G + v.H = (\sum_1^m r' - \sum_1^n r - tko).G + tko.G$$

Applying algebraic properties on elliptic curves, we have:

$$\sum_1^m v'.H - \sum_1^n v.H = (\sum_1^m r'.G - \sum_1^n r.G) - (\sum_1^m r'.G - \sum_1^n r.G) - tko.G + tko.G = 0$$

Therefore,

$$(v_1' + ... + v_m').H - (v_1 + ... + v_n).H = (v_1' + ... + v_m' - v_1 - ... - v_n).H = 0.H = 0$$

It means that all the inputs and outputs add to zero. In other words, they summed to the commitment to the excess blinding factor and the kernel offset.

□

Thus, we have proved no money was created from thin air and the only ones who knew the blinding factors were the transacting parties when they created the transaction. This means the new outputs will be spendable by them.

An important feature of MW is the *cut-through* process. The purpose of this property is to erase redundant outputs that are used as inputs within the same block. Let C be some coins that appear as an output in the block b. If the same coins appear as an input within the block, then C can be removed from the list of inputs and outputs after applying the cut-through process. In this way, the only remaining data are the block headers, transaction kernels and unspent transaction outputs (UTXOs). After applying cut-through to a valid block b it is important to ensure that the resulting block b' is still valid. We can say that the validity of a block should be invariant with respect to the cut-through process. Basically, this invariant holds because the matching inputs and outputs cancel each other in the overall sum.

4.2   Privacy and Security Properties

In blockchain systems the notion of privacy is crucial: sensitive data should not be revealed over the network. In particular, it is desirable to ensure properties such as confidentiality, anonymity and unlinkability of transactions. Confidentiality refers to the property of preventing other participants from knowing certain information about the transaction, such as the amounts and addresses of the owners. Anonymity refers to the property of hiding the real identity from the one who is transacting, while unlinkability refers to the inability of linking different transactions of the same user within the blockchain.

In the case of MW no addresses or public keys are used; there are only encrypted inputs and outputs. Privacy concerns rely on *confidential transactions*, *cut-through* and *CoinJoin*. *CoinJoin* combines inputs and outputs from different transactions into a single unified transaction. It is important to ensure that the resulting transaction satisfies the validity defined in the model.

The security problem of double spending refers to spending a coin more than once. All the nodes keep track of the UTXO set, so before confirming a block to the chain, the node checks that the inputs come from it. If we refer to our model, that validation is performed in the predicate *validate* mentioned in Sect. 3.3.

4.3 Zero-Knowledge Proof

The goal is to prove that a statement is true, without revealing any information beyond the verification of the statement. In MW we need to ensure that in every transaction, the amount is positive, so that users cannot create coins. The key here is to prove that, without revealing the amount. As we defined in the model, the output amounts are hidden in the form of a Pedersen commitment, and the transaction contains a list of range proofs of the outputs to prove that the amount is positive. MW uses *Bulletproofs* to achieve this goal. In our model, this verification is performed as the first step of the validation of the transaction.

4.4 Unlinkability and Untraceability

MW does not use addresses, the protocol relies on confidential transactions to hide the identity of the sender and the recipient. It means that users have to communicate off-chain to create the transactions.

As we specified in our model, each node has a pool of unconfirmed transactions in the *mempool*. This transactions are waiting for the miners in order to be included in a block. We can distinguish two security properties of the transactions. Untraceability refers to the transactions in the mempool and unlinkability to the transactions in the block. In our model, this two notions are described as follows:

Property 3 (Transaction Unlinkability). Given a valid block b, it should be computationally infeasible to know which input cancels which output.

The following lemma captures the semantics of this property. Moreover, the operations *cut-through* and *CoinJoin*, which were described above, contribute to this property.

Lemma 4 (Transaction Unlinkability). *It is said a valid block b is transaction-unlinkable if for any polinomial probabilistic time adversary $\mathcal{A}$, the probability of finding a balanced transaction within the block is negligible.*

Proof. Let $b = \{i, o, tks, ko\}$ be a valid block with $tks = (tk_1, ..., tk_t)$ the list of transaction kernels. The j-th item in tks is of the form $tk_j = \{rp_j, ke_j, \sigma_j\}$.

The goal of the adversary $\mathcal{A}$ is to find a tuple of the form $\{i', o', ke'\}$ in b where the list of inputs i' is a subset of i and the list of outputs o' is a subset of

o, which satisfies the Definition 3 of a balanced transaction. It means that, the following equality must be true for the tuple:

$$\sum_{o_j \in o'} o_j - \sum_{c_j \in i'} c_j = ke' + tko'.G$$

If we refer to the process construction in Definition 7, the transaction kernel offsets were added to generate a single aggregate offset ko to cover all transactions in the block. It means that, we do not store the individual kernel offset tko' of the transaction in b once the transaction is aggregated to the block.

The challenge is trying to solve the adversary $\mathcal{A}$, could be seen as the subset sum problem (*NP-complete*) but, in this case, tko' is unrecoverable. So, although many transactions have few inputs and outputs, it is computationally infeasible, without knowing that value, to find the tuple.

$\square$

Property 4. (Transaction Untraceability). For every transaction in the mempool, it should not be possible to relate the transaction to the IP address of the node which originated it.

In regards to this property, we should refer mainly, to the broadcast of the transactions. Once the transactions are created, they are broadcasted to the network and they are included in the mempool. Each node could track the IP address from the node which received the transaction. At that point nodes could record the transactions, allowing them to build a transaction graph.

We define that the broadcast of a transaction can be performed with or without confusion. Without confusion means that, once the transactions are created, they are broadcasted immediately to all the network. However, if someone controls enough nodes on the network and discovers how the transaction moves, he could find out the IP address node from which the transaction comes from.

On the other hand, we define the broadcast with confusion as a way to obscure the IP address node.

Property 5. (Broadcast with confusion). Let's say node A sends a transaction to node B. We say B receives the transaction with confusion if given the IP address of node A, the node B does not know if the transaction was originated by the node A or not.

In other words, it can be said that if some malicious nodes, working together, construct a graph of the pairs (*transaction, IP address node*), the IP address node will not convey information about what node originated the transaction. Therefore, in our model, we define that the Property 5 must hold before the broadcast takes place. In order to achieve this, we can establish that the node broadcasting the transaction, should be far enough from the one which originated it. Moreover, *CoinJoin* could be performed before the broadcast.

Dandelion, proposed by Fanti et al [39], is a protocol for broadcasting transaction that intends to defend that deanonymization attack. Dandelion is not part of the MW protocol, however this kind of protocols should be implemented by each node to lower the risk of creating the transaction graph. The spreading propagation consists of two phases: the "steam" phase and the "fluff" phase. In the "steam" phase the transaction is broadcasted randomly to one node, which then randomly sends it to another, and so on. This process finishes when the "fluff" phase is reached, and the transaction is broadcasted to the network.

The following routines capture the semantic of the phases:

subroutine steam(tx : Transaction){

$c \leftarrow \{0, 1\}$ (* random decision *)

if c == 0 then

> *node ← select_random_node()*
>
> *node.steam(tx)*

else

> *this.fluff(tx)*

}

subroutine fluff(tx : Transaction){

broadcast(tx)

}

Each node, besides having the local state, should implement these two routines. Once the transaction is created and is ready to be included in the mempool, its broadcasting start in the "steam" phase. When it reaches the "fluff" phase, it is broadcasted to the network and added in the mempool.

Dandelion relies on the following three rules: all nodes obey the protocol, each node generates exactly one transaction, and all nodes on the network run Dandelion. The problem is that an adversary can violate them. For that reason, Grin implements a more advanced protocol called Dandelion++ [17] which intends to prevent that [23]. However, it is believed that Dandelion++ is not good enough to guarantee the privacy of a virtual coin [22]. For instance, the flashlight attack [26] is an open problem to research [21]. The scenario here is when an 'activist' want to accept donations but he cannot reveal his identity. At some point, he will deposit those payments to an exchange and his identity would be compromised. The adversary injects 'tainted coins' and could build a 'taint tree' looking through all deposits to the exchange. This way, he could link those deposits to the 'activist'.

The combined use of the MW protocol with a Zerocash-style commitment-nullifier scheme has been put forward in [40] as a countermeasure to the above attack. In the case of *Zcash*, every shielded transaction has a large anonymity set, namely, the set of transactions form which the transaction is indistinguishable from. In the case of Spectrecoin [16] the main idea is the use, only once, of public addresses (XSPEC) to receive the payments combined with an anonymous staking protocol.

4.5   Model-Driven Verification

MW is built on top of a consensus protocol. In that direction, we have developed a Z specification of a consensus protocol (see Appendix A). Z specifications in turn can be easily translated into the $\{log\}$ language [13], which can be used as both a (prototyping) programming language and an automated theorem prover for an expressive fragment of set theory and set relation algebra. We present an excerpt of the $\{log\}$ prototype of a consensus protocol in Appendix B. This $\{log\}$ prototype can be used as an executable model where simulations can be run. This allows us to analyze the behavior of the protocol without having to implement it in a low level programming language.

We also plan to use $\{log\}$ to prove some of the basic properties mentioned above, such as the invariance of *valid_state*. However, for complex properties or for properties not expressible in the set theories supported by $\{log\}$ we plan to develop a complete and uniform formulation of several security properties of the protocol using the Coq proof assistant [38]. The Coq environment supports advanced logical and computational notations, proof search and automation, and modular development of theories and code. It also provides program extraction towards languages like Ocaml and Haskell for execution of (certified) algorithms [31]. Additionally, Coq has an important set of libraries; for example [3] contains a formalization of elliptic curves theory, which allows the verification of elliptic curve cryptographic algorithms.

The fact of first having a $\{log\}$ prototype over which some verification activities can be carried out without much effort helps in simplifying the process of writing a detailed Coq specification. This is in accordance with proposals such as QuickChick whose goal is to decrease the number of failed proof attempts in Coq by generating counterexamples before a proof is attempted [15].

By applying the program extraction mechanism provided by Coq we would be able to derive a certified Haskell prototype of the protocol. This prototype can be used as a testing oracle and also to conduct further verification activities on correct-by-construction implementations of the protocol. In particular, both the $\{log\}$ and Coq approaches can be used as forms of model-based testing. That is, we can use either specification to automatically generate test cases with which protocol implementations can be tested [14,15].

5   Final Remarks

We have highlighted elements that constitute essential steps towards the development of an exhaustive formalization of the MimbleWimble cryptocurrency protocol, the analysis of its properties and the verification of its implementations.

The proposed idealized model is key in the described verification process and constitutes our main contribution. We have also identified and precisely stated sufficient conditions for our model to ensure the verification of relevant security properties of MimbleWimble.

We plan to continue working on the lines presented in Sect. 4, also considering tools oriented towards the verification of cryptographic protocols and implementations, such as `EasyCrypt` [2], `ProVerif` [10], and `CryptoVerif` [9]. In particular, we are especially interested in using `EasyCrypt`[5], an interactive framework for verifying the security of cryptographic constructions in the computational model.

A   Excerpt of a Z Model of a Consensus Protocol

The following are some snippets of a Z model of a consensus protocol based on the model developed by Pîrlea and Sergey [36]. For reasons of space we just reproduce a little part of it.

The time stamps used in the protocol are modeled as natural numbers. Then we have the type of addresses (*Addr*), the type of hashes (*Hash*), the type of proofs objects (*Proof*) and the type of transactions (*Tx*). Differently from Pîrlea and Sergey's model[6] we modeled addresses as a given type instead as natural numbers. In PS the only condition required for these types is that they come equipped with equality, which is the case in Z.

$Time == \mathbb{N}$

$[Addr, Hash, Proof, Tx]$

The block data structure is a record with three fields: *prev*, (usually) points to the parent block; *txs*, stores the sequence of transactions stored in the block; and *pf* is a proof object required to validate the block.

$$
\begin{array}{|l}
\hline
\_Block _____ \\
prev : Hash \\
txs : \text{seq } Tx \\
pf : Proof \\
\hline
\end{array}
$$

The local state space of a participating network node is given by three state variables: *as*, are the addresses of the peers this node is aware of; *bf*, is a block forest (not shown) which records the minted and received blocks; and *tp*, is a set of received transactions which eventually will be included in minted blocks.

$$
\begin{array}{|l}
\hline
\_LocState _____ \\
as : \mathbb{P}\,Addr \\
bf : Hash \nrightarrow Block \\
tp : \mathbb{P}\,Tx \\
\hline
\end{array}
$$

---

[5] See http://www.easycrypt.info.
[6] From now on we will refer to Pîrlea and Sergey model simply as PS.

The system configuration is represented by two state variables: *Delta*, which establishes a mapping between network addresses and the corresponding node (local) states (in PS this variable is referred to as the *global state*); and *P*, a set of packets (which represent the messages exchanged by nodes).

```
┌─ Conf ─────────────────────────────────────────────────
│ Delta : Addr ⇸ LocState
│ P : ℙ Packet
└────────────────────────────────────────────────────────
```

Packets are just tuples of two addresses (origin and destination) and a message.

$$Packet == Addr \times Addr \times Msg$$

The model has twelve state transitions divided into two groups: *local* and *global*. Local transitions are those executed by network nodes, while global transitions promote local transitions to the network level. In turn, the local transitions are grouped into *receiving* and *internal* transitions. Receiving transitions model the nodes receiving messages from other nodes and, possibly, sending out new messages; internal transitions model the execution of instructions run by each node when some local condition is met. Here, we show only the local, receiving transition named *RcvAddr*.

```
┌─ RcvAddr ──────────────────────────────────────────────
│ ΔLocState
│ p? : Packet
│ ps! : ℙ Packet
├────────────────────────────────────────────────────────
│ p?.2 = this
│ ∃ asm : ℙ Addr •
│       p?.3 = AddrMsg asm
│       ∧ as' = as ∪ asm
│       ∧ bf' = bf
│       ∧ tp' = tp
│       ∧ ps! = {a : asm \ as • (p?.2, a, ConnectMsg)} ∪
│           {a : as • (p?.2, a, AddrMsg as')}
└────────────────────────────────────────────────────────
```

As can be seen, *RcvAddr* receives a packet (*p?*) and sends out a set of packets (*ps!*). The node checks whether or not the packet's destination address coincides with its own address. In that case, the node adds the received addresses to its local state and sends out a set of packets that are either of the form (*p?.2, a, ConnectMsg*) or (*p?.2, a, AddrMsg as'*). The former are packets generated from the received addresses and sent to the new peers the node now knows, while the latter are messages telling its already known peers that it has learned of new peers.

B   Excerpt of a {*log*} Prototype of a Consensus Protocol

In this section we show the {*log*} code corresponding to the Z model presented
in Appendix A. {*log*} code can be seen as both a formula and a program [13].
Thus, in this case we use the code as a prototype or executable model of the Z
model. The intention is twofold: to show that passing from a Z specification to a
{*log*} program is rather easy, and to show how a {*log*} program can be used as
a prototype. The first point is achieved mainly because {*log*} provides the usual
Boolean connectives and most of the set and relational operators available in Z.
Hence, it is quite natural to encode a Z specification as a {*log*} program.

Given that {*log*} is based on Prolog its programs resemble Prolog programs.
The {*log*} encoding of *RcvAddr* is the following:

```
rcvAddr(LocState,P,Ps,LocState_) :-
LocState = {[as,As] / Rest} &
P = [_,this, addrMsg(Asm)] & un(As,Asm,As_) & diff(Asm,As,D) &
Ps1 = ris(A in D,[],true,[this,A,connectMsg]) &
Ps2 = ris(A in As,[],true,[this,A,addrMsg(As_)]) & un(Ps1,Ps2,Ps) &
LocState_ = {[as,As_] / Rest}.
```

As can be seen, `rcvAddr` is clause receiving the before state (`LocState`), the
input variable (`P`), the output variable (`Ps`) and the after state (`LocState_`).
As in Prolog, {*log*} programs are based on unification with the addition of set
unification. In this sense, a statement such as `LocState = {[as,As]/Rest}` (set)
unifies the parameter received with a set term singling out the state variable
needed in this case (`As`) and the rest of the variables (`Rest`). The same is done
with packet P where _ means any value as first component and `addrMsg(Asm)`
gets the set of addresses received in the packet without introducing an existential
quantifier.

The set comprehensions used in the Z specification are implemented with
{*log*}'s so-called Restricted Intentional Sets (RIS) [12]. A RIS is interpreted as
a set comprehension where the control variable ranges over a finite set (D and
As).

Given `rcvAddr` we can perform simulations on {*log*} such as:

```
S = {[as,{}] / R} &
rcvAddr(S,[_,this,addrMsg({a1,a2})],P1,S1) &
rcvAddr(S1,[_,this,addrMsg({a1,a3})],P2,S2).
```

in which case {*log*} returns:

```
P1 = ris(A in {a1,a2/_N2},[],true,[this,A,connectMsg],true),
S1 = {[as,{a1,a2}]/R},
P2 = {[this,a3,connectMsg],[this,a1,addrMsg({a2,a1,a3})],
      [this,a2,addrMsg({a2,a1,a3})] /
         ris(A in _N1,[],true,[this,A,connectMsg],true)},
S2 = {[as,{a2,a1,a3}]/R}
Constraint: subset(_N2,{a1,a2}), subset(_N1,{a1,a3}),
            a1 nin _N1, a2 nin _N1
```

That is, {*log*} binds values for all the free variables in a way that the formula is satisfied (if it is satisfiable at all). In this way we can trace the execution of the protocol w.r.t. states and outputs by starting from a given state (e.g. S) and input values (e.g. | [_,this,addrMsg(a1,a2)]), and chaining states throughout the execution of the state transitions included in the simulation (e.g. S1 and S2).

References

1. Anderson, J.: Computer Security technology planning study. Technical report, Deputy for Command and Management System, USA (1972)
2. Barthe, G., Dupressoir, F., Grégoire, B., Kunz, C., Schmidt, B., Strub, P.-Y.: EasyCrypt: a tutorial. In: Aldini, A., Lopez, J., Martinelli, F. (eds.) FOSAD 2012-2013. LNCS, vol. 8604, pp. 146–166. Springer, Cham (2014). https://doi.org/10.1007/978-3-319-10082-1_6
3. Bartzia, E.-I., Strub, P.-Y.: A formal library for elliptic curves in the coq proof assistant. In: Klein, G., Gamboa, R. (eds.) ITP 2014. LNCS, vol. 8558, pp. 77–92. Springer, Cham (2014). https://doi.org/10.1007/978-3-319-08970-6_6
4. Bell, D.E., LaPadula, L.J.: Secure computer systems: Mathematical foundations. Technical report MTR-2547, vol. 1, MITRE Corp., Bedford, MA (1973)
5. Bertot, Y., Castéran, P., (informaticien) Huet, G., Paulin-Mohring, C.: Interactive theorem proving and program development: Coq'Art : the calculus of inductive constructions. Texts in theoretical computer science. Springer, Berlin, New York (2004). Données complémentaires http://coq.inria.fr
6. Betarte, G., Cristiá, M., Luna, C., Silveira, A., Zanarini, D.: Set-based models for cryptocurrency software. CoRR, abs/1908.00591 (2019)
7. Betarte, G., Cristiá, M., Luna, C., Silveira, A., Zanarini, D.: Towards a formally verified implementation of the mimblewimble cryptocurrency protocol. CoRR, abs/1907.01688 (2019)
8. Bhargavan, K., et al.: Formal verification of smart contracts: short paper. In: Proceedings of the 2016 ACM Workshop on Programming Languages and Analysis for Security, PLAS 2016, pp. 91–96. ACM, New York (2016)
9. Blanchet, B.: CryptoVerif: a computationally sound mechanized prover for cryptographic protocols. In Dagstuhl seminar "Formal Protocol Verification Applied", October 2007
10. Blanchet, B.: An efficient cryptographic protocol verifier based on prolog rules. In: 14th IEEE Computer Security Foundations Workshop (CSFW-14 2001), 11–13 June 2001, Cape Breton, Nova Scotia, Canada, pp. 82–96. IEEE Computer Society (2001)
11. Buterin, V.: Critical update re: Dao vulnerability, June 2016
12. Cristiá, M., Rossi, G.: A decision procedure for restricted intensional sets. In: de Moura, L. (ed.) CADE 2017. LNCS (LNAI), vol. 10395, pp. 185–201. Springer, Cham (2017). https://doi.org/10.1007/978-3-319-63046-5_12
13. Cristiá, M., Rossi, G.: Solving quantifier-free first-order constraints over finite sets and binary relations. J. Automated Reasoning **64**, 295–330 (2019). https://doi.org/10.1007/s10817-019-09520-4
14. Cristiá, M., Rossi, G., Frydman, C.: log as a test case generator for the test template framework. In: Hierons, R.M., Merayo, M.G., Bravetti, M. (eds.) SEFM 2013. LNCS, vol. 8137, pp. 229–243. Springer, Heidelberg (2013). https://doi.org/10.1007/978-3-642-40561-7_16

15. Dénès, M., Hritcu, C., Lampropoulos, L., Paraskevopoulou, Z., Pierce, B.: Quickchick: Property-based testing for coq. In: The Coq Workshop (2014)
16. Korsell, E., Mueller, P., Schumann, Y.: Spectrecoin. https://spectreproject.io/Spectrecoin_White-Paper.pdf, June 2019
17. Fanti, G.C., et al.: Dandelion++: lightweight cryptocurrency networking with formal anonymity guarantees. CoRR, abs/1805.11060 (2018)
18. Fuchsbauer, G., Orrù, M., Seurin, Y.: Aggregate cash systems: a cryptographic investigation of mimblewimble. In: Ishai, Y., Rijmen, V. (eds.) EUROCRYPT 2019. LNCS, vol. 11476, pp. 657–689. Springer, Cham (2019). https://doi.org/10.1007/978-3-030-17653-2_22
19. Garay, J., Kiayias, A., Leonardos, N.: The bitcoin backbone protocol: analysis and applications. In: Oswald, E., Fischlin, M. (eds.) EUROCRYPT 2015. LNCS, vol. 9057, pp. 281–310. Springer, Heidelberg (2015). https://doi.org/10.1007/978-3-662-46803-6_10
20. Gibson, A.: An investigation into confidential transactions (2018). https://github.com/AdamISZ/ConfidentialTransactionsDoc/blob/master/essayonCT.pdf
21. Grin Community. Grin: Open Research Problems (2020). https://grin.mw/open-research-problems
22. Grin Team. Privacy Primer, November 2018. https://github.com/mimblewimble/docs/wiki/Grin-Privacy-Primer
23. Grin Team. Dandelion++ in Grin: Privacy-Preserving Transaction Aggregation and Propagation, July 2019. https://github.com/mimblewimble/grin/blob/master/doc/dandelion/dandelion.md
24. Grishchenko, I., Maffei, M., Schneidewind, C.: A semantic framework for the security analysis of ethereum smart contracts. In: Bauer, L., Küsters, R. (eds.) POST 2018. LNCS, vol. 10804, pp. 243–269. Springer, Cham (2018). https://doi.org/10.1007/978-3-319-89722-6_10
25. Hirai, Y.: Defining the ethereum virtual machine for interactive theorem provers. In: Brenner, M., et al. (eds.) FC 2017. LNCS, vol. 10323, pp. 520–535. Springer, Cham (2017). https://doi.org/10.1007/978-3-319-70278-0_33
26. Miers, I.: Blockchain Privacy: Equal Parts Theory and Practice, February 2019. https://www.zfnd.org/blog/blockchain-privacy/#flashlight
27. Idelberger, F., Governatori, G., Riveret, R., Sartor, G.: Evaluation of logic-based smart contracts for blockchain systems. In: Alferes, J.J.J., Bertossi, L., Governatori, G., Fodor, P., Roman, D. (eds.) RuleML 2016. LNCS, vol. 9718, pp. 167–183. Springer, Cham (2016). https://doi.org/10.1007/978-3-319-42019-6_11
28. Jedusor, T.: Introduction to MimbleWimble and Grin (2016). https://github.com/mimblewimble/grin/blob/master/doc/intro.md
29. Jedusor, T.: Mimblewimble (2016). scalingbitcoin.org/papers/mimblewimble.txt
30. Kiayias, A., Russell, A., David, B., Oliynykov, R.: Ouroboros: a provably secure proof-of-stake blockchain protocol. In: Katz, J., Shacham, H. (eds.) CRYPTO 2017. LNCS, vol. 10401, pp. 357–388. Springer, Cham (2017). https://doi.org/10.1007/978-3-319-63688-7_12
31. Letouzey, P.: A new extraction for coq. In: Geuvers, H., Wiedijk, F. (eds.) TYPES 2002. LNCS, vol. 2646, pp. 200–219. Springer, Heidelberg (2003). https://doi.org/10.1007/3-540-39185-1_12
32. Luu, L., Chu, D., Olickel, H., Saxena, P., Hobor, A.: Making smart contracts smarter. In: Weippl, E., Katzenbeisser, S. Kruegel, C., Myers, A., Halevi, S. (eds.) Proceedings of the 2016 ACM SIGSAC Conference on Computer and Communications Security, Vienna, Austria, 24–28 October, 2016, pp. 254–269. ACM (2016)

33. Maxwell, G.: Confidential transactions write up (2020). https://people.xiph.org/ ~greg/confidential_values.txt
34. Metere, R., Dong, C.: Automated cryptographic analysis of the pedersen commitment scheme. In: Rak, J., Bay, J., Kotenko, I., Popyack, L., Skormin, V., Szczypiorski, K. (eds.) MMM-ACNS 2017. LNCS, vol. 10446, pp. 275–287. Springer, Cham (2017). https://doi.org/10.1007/978-3-319-65127-9_22
35. Nakamoto, S.: Bitcoin: A peer-to-peer electronic cash system, March 2009. Cryptography Mailing list at https://metzdowd.com
36. Pîrlea, G., Sergey, I.: Mechanising blockchain consensus. In: Proceedings of CPP 2018, pp. 78–90. ACM, New York (2018)
37. Poelstra, A.: Mimblewimble, October 2016. https://download.wpsoftware.net/ bitcoin/wizardry/mimblewimble.pdf
38. The Coq Dev. Team. The Coq Proof Assistant Reference Manual - V. 8.9.0 (2019)
39. Venkatakrishnan, S.B., Fanti, G.C., Viswanath, P.: Dandelion: Redesigning the bitcoin network for anonymity. CoRR, abs/1701.04439 (2017)
40. Wanseob-Lim. Ethereum 9 3/4: Send ERC20 privately using Mimblewimble and zk-SNARKs, September 2019. https://ethresear.ch/t/ethereum-9-send-erc20-privately-using-mimblewimble-and-zk-snarks/6217
41. Wood, G.: Ethereum: A secure decentralised generalised transaction ledger eip-150 revision (759dccd - 2017-08-07) (2017). Accessed 03 Jan 2018

Secure Management of IoT Devices Based on Blockchain Non-fungible Tokens and Physical Unclonable Functions

Javier Arcenegui[✉], Rosario Arjona[✉], and Iluminada Baturone[✉]

Instituto de Microelectrónica de Sevilla (IMSE-CNM), Universidad de Sevilla, CSIC,
C/Américo Vespucio 28, 41092 Seville, Spain
{arcenegui,arjona,lumi}@imse-cnm.csic.es

Abstract. One of the most extended applications of blockchain technologies for the IoT ecosystem is the traceability of the data and operations generated and performed, respectively, by IoT devices. In this work, we propose a solution for secure management of IoT devices that participate in the blockchain with their own blockchain accounts (BCAs) so that the IoT devices themselves can sign transactions. Any blockchain participant (including IoT devices) can obtain and verify information not only about the actions or data they are taking but also about their manufacturers, managers (owners and approved), and users. Non Fungible Tokens (NFTs) based on the ERC-721 standard are proposed to manage IoT devices as unique and indivisible. The BCA of an IoT device, which is defined as an NFT attribute, is associated with the physical device since the secret seed from which the BCA is generated is not stored anywhere but a Physical Unclonable Function (PUF) inside the hardware of the device reconstructs it. The proposed solution is demonstrated and evaluated with a low-cost IoT device based on a Pycom Wipy 3.0 board, which uses the internal SRAM of the microcontroller ESP-32 as PUF. The operations it performs to reconstruct its BCA in Ethereum and to carry out transactions take a few tens of milliseconds. The smart contract programmed in Solidity and simulated in Remix requires low gas consumption.

Keywords: IoT devices · Blockchain technology · Non fungible tokens · Physical Unclonable Functions

1 Introduction

The Internet of Things (IoT) and blockchain are nowadays two technologies that are attracting a great interest. In general, IoT is a set of interconnected devices that exchange data and offer services to citizens, industries, businesses, and governments. IoT devices make smart the area where they are deployed (factories, hospitals, cities, etc.). Among the features that IoT devices must provide, security is one of the most important since they are the link between the physical world and Internet. An attacker may control either the actuators or sensors of an IoT device to carry out malicious actions. For example, a device with an insulin pump can be attacked to inject a lethal dose to the

© Springer Nature Switzerland AG 2020
J. Zhou et al. (Eds.): ACNS 2020 Workshops, LNCS 12418, pp. 24–40, 2020.
https://doi.org/10.1007/978-3-030-61638-0_2

patient or a blood pressure meter can be attacked to provide false readings. Secure IoT devices must prove that their hardware and software are trusted and that they behave in a trustworthy way. Similarly, they must trust the other devices or users with whom they interact [1, 2].

In the other side, a blockchain is a network of participants that take part in a distributed, synchronized and cryptographically secure data structure (ledger) composed of chained blocks that can be tracked by any participant. A block contains information about transactions (typically the exchange of digital currency or generic assets, date, time, etc.), participants involved in the transactions, data identifying the block univocally, and how the block is linked to the previous one. A new block is added if participants with the role of miners demonstrate (by a proof of work, stake, authority, etc.) that the new block is secure and most of the miners (typically 51% at least) agree to link the block (applying a consensus algorithm). Since not only the inclusion of a new block is based on a consensual agreement but also many of the participants (nodes) have an updated copy of the blockchain, it is very costly for hackers to manipulate any block [3].

Combining IoT and blockchain is very interesting because many transactions in smart areas involve IoT devices [4–6]. While it is not convenient for IoT devices to participate with the role of nodes or miners since they do not have enough memory and computing resources, it is practical they can participate with their own blockchain accounts (BCAs) associated with their cryptographic public keys so that they can take part in transactions and can sign them. This way, traceability of both devices and their data/actions is provided to the rest of blockchain participants, greatly increasing their security. The well-known blockchain Scalability Trilemma, which is to offer security, decentralization and scalability simultaneously, appears when many blocks and participants (being IoT devices or not) have to be handled [7]. In this work, we assume that there are other participants (apart from IoT devices) acting as nodes and miners that guarantee security and decentralization and that only the summary of many transactions carried out off-chain are stored in the blockchain to guarantee scalability.

The new generation of blockchain technologies allows smart contracts as a way to formalize agreements between participants. Typical agreements are to represent a cryptocurrency by a fungible token with a set of specifications (like its owner) and functions (like the way to change of owner). Fungible tokens of the same type are identical (like coins are identical) and are divisible into smaller units (like coins of different values). More recently, non-fungible tokens (NFTs) have been employed to represent unique assets (like collectables, certificates of any kind, any type of access rights, objects, etc.). An NFT is unique, indivisible, and different from another token of the same type. In particular, the ERC-721 standard describes how to build non-fungible tokens in the Ethereum blockchain [8]. Standard attributes of ERC-721 NFTs are: (a) the token identifier (tokenId), (b) the BCA of the NFT owner, and (c) the approved BCA by the owner to transfer the token to another owner. The digital and unique identifier, tokenId, allows recording and tracking a NFT in the blockchain. However, the token identifier does not have to be associated with a physical property of the device. In fact, it is generated automatically when the ERC-721 NFT is created.

In this work, we propose the use of NFTs to represent IoT devices. In particular, we base our development on the ERC-721 standard of Ethereum. The novelty of our proposed NFTs is that they represent IoT devices that participate in the blockchain and, hence, have a unique BCA. Then, we incorporate the BCA of the IoT device as an NFT attribute. Another novelty of our proposal is that, since the BCA of an IoT device is naturally associated with the physical device, the IoT device generates its BCA from a PUF response. PUFs allow generating unique, intrinsic, unpredictable and distinctive identifiers for each device by exploiting the random variations of the device manufacturing process [9]. The BCA is associated with a cryptographic public key, which in turn is associated with a cryptographic secret key. Our proposal is that IoT devices prove their authenticity if, firstly, any content stored in its memory is removed, and, secondly, they are programmed with a trustworthy firmware that does not contain its secret key. If the IoT device is able to reconstruct its secret key and, hence, its BCA, is because its PUF response is authentic.

In addition, we incorporate the BCA of the user of the IoT device as another NFT attribute in order to distinguish between users, who employ the IoT device for an application, and owners, who assign IoT devices to users and can transfer the token to new owners. Owners can also approve others (approved BCAs) to transfer tokens to other owners.

Our proposal allows a secure management of IoT devices since any participant in the blockchain (including the IoT device itself or another) can verify their manufacturers, managers (owners and approved), users, and the actions or data they are taking. Besides, the IoT device and its physical owner, approved, and user can be subscribed to the events of its associated NFT so that they can receive notifications about the situation of the NFT and behave accordingly.

In summary, the contributions of this work are the following:

- The proposal of an NFT based on the ERC-721 standard of Ethereum that includes as new attributes the BCA of the IoT device and the BCA of the user of the IoT device. Since the IoT device has a BCA, it can take part in blockchain transactions and can sign them. Since the BCA of the user of the IoT device is included, user and owner roles are distinguished.
- The use of PUFs to guarantee that only the IoT device able to provide the required PUF response is the only one able to generate its BCA.
- A solution that merges the IoT and blockchain paradigms to allow the secure traceability of the data generated and the operations performed by IoT devices in scenarios of remote management.
- A proof of concept of the proposed solution by using a Pycom Wipy 3.0 as IoT device that generates its BCA in the blockchain Ethereum from the response of its SRAM PUF.

The paper is structured as follows. Related work is included in Sect. 2. Section 3 presents the proposal of NFTs for secure devices. The extension of the ERC-721 standard for NFTs that not only considers the BCA of the owners (managers) but also the BCAs of the device and its user is described. The process to generate the device BCA from a secret seed obfuscated by the response of a SRAM PUF as well as the device management are explained. Section 4 includes a proof of concept based on the Pycom Wipy 3.0 board. In the one side, the feasibility of obfuscating and recovering 256-bit secret seeds from the use of internal SRAM PUFs is proven. In the other side, the implementation of the NFT with the SRAM PUF-based BCA by considering the Ethereum blockchain is shown. Section 4 also provides the execution times of the operations required to complete a transaction and the gas consumption of the smart contract functions programmed in Solidity and simulated in Remix [10]. Results are compared to other proposals in the literature. Finally, Sect. 5 concludes the work and adds future research directions.

2 Related Work

In the literature, ERC-721 NFTs are employed for several applications. The works [11] and [12] describe how the traceability of manufactured products can be performed using ERC-721 NFTs. The use of ERC-721 NFTs is also mentioned in [13] and in [14] for car sharing and event reselling applications, respectively. The management of IoT devices through the blockchain is extensively based on the use of smart contracts. However, the tokens used in many applications are not standard. In [15], tokenization is not directly related to the IoT devices. Instead, tokenization is employed through a task manager to ensure that all participants have something to lose if they misbehave. In [16], the IoT devices are grouped into IoT systems (like smart homes, smart hospitals, etc.) and each system is associated with the nearest blockchain-enabled fog node. A smart contract is defined on top of the blockchain-enabled fog nodes to support authentication and authorization of the IoT devices in a distributed fashion. In this proposal, IoT devices can communicate among them if they are registered and authenticated by blockchain-enabled fog nodes. The tokens are considered as certificates that include the device identifier, the device public address and the IoT system identifier. Therefore, the token involves two devices: the fog node and the IoT device. The solution proposed in [17] uses the principle of ERC-721 NFTs to implement a capability-based access control model in a decentralized IoT architecture. In this proposal, the tokens store the access rights for the resources/services available. A device in possession of one of these access tokens can access the resource/service according to the access control rules defined within the token. This solution is tested on a private Ethereum blockchain node.

None of the above commented solutions stablishes a physical link between a device and an NFT logical identifier. In [11], the digital and unique identifier, tokenId, which is a standard attribute of ERC-721 NFTs that allows recording and tracking an NFT in the blockchain, is a randomly selected string assigned to the device and stored in its RFID or QR code. In [15], the tokenId is the hash of a concatenation of the serial number embedded in the device chipset and a randomly generated salt. This can be also replaced by any random string that is not already in use when the device is registered. In [16], IoT devices are identified by certificates generated from a private key. In [17], tokenId is obtained by hashing three logical identifiers (the identifier of the device in possession of the token, the identifier of the resource/service, and the identifier of the resource as per the communication protocol).

Other works that employ the blockchain framework to provide supply chain integrity use PUFs to stablish a physical link between the devices and their logical identifiers [18–21]. The PUFs embedded in the products introduce a higher security level that reduces the risk of counterfeit and tampered electronic devices. However, these works do not employ explicitly the concept of NFTs.

To the best of our knowledge, there are no works in the literature using PUFs in ERC-721 NFTs as presented in the following.

3 Proposed NFTs for Secure Devices

The application scenarios of our proposal are smart areas with IoT devices that must be secure. The combination of IoT and Blockchain technologies enhances security. The main agents in these scenarios are: (a) the IoT devices (referred to as SDs, secure devices); (b) the users of the IoT devices; and (c) the application managers (referred to as owners), who assign devices to users and can transfer the devices to other managers. These three agents take part in the blockchain transactions through their BCAs (BCA_SD, BCA_user, and BCA_owner, respectively). Hence, they can authenticate each other and their messages in scenarios of remote management. A relevant amount of messages can be interchanged off-chain, to improve scalability, but the important transactions are registered to allow traceability in the blockchain. The owner (manager) and user can reset the device to ensure their firmware is trustworthy, avoiding the execution of malware. Conversely, the device allows reset if the request is from the owner or the user. In a smart hospital, for example, the owner can be the technical supervisor that assigns devices to doctors. In a smart infrastructure, the owner can be the manager of the technical workers who, depending on the scheduled tasks, assign the devices to one technician or another.

3.1 Main Features of the Proposed NFT

An IoT device becomes SD after being bound to our proposed NFT. The structure of the proposed token has the attributes shown in Table 1. The variables tokenId and BCA_owner are defined by the standard ERC-721. The standard also defines other variables (approved and operator) to help the owner to transfer NFTs to other owners, but this is not in the scope of this work, so that we omit them. The important variables added in this work are BCA_SD, which binds a device to the NFT, and BCA_user, which binds the device of the NFT to a user.

Table 1. Structure of the non fungible token

Type	Name of variable	Defined by the standard
TokenId_Type	tokenId	Yes
Address	BCA_owner	Yes
Address	BCA_SD	No
Address	BCA_user	No

The standard ERC-721 only declares functions related to the ownership of the token. A summary of them are included in the upper part of Table 2. They return which are the tokenIds of an owner (function "balanceOf"), who is the owner of a tokenId (function "ownerOf"), and how to transfer the tokenId to another address (function "transferFrom" detailed in Table 3).

Table 2. Functions employed in the proposed NFT

Defined by the standard
function balanceOf(address _owner) external view returns (uint256);
function ownerOf(uint256 _tokenId) external view returns (address);
function transferFrom(address _from, address _to, uint256 _tokenId) external payable;

Defined for this work
function createToken(address _owner, address _BCA_SD) external returns (uint256)
function userTransfer(uint256 tokenId, address _BCA_user) external;
function completeTransfer(uint256 _tokenId) external;
function tokenFromBCA(address _BCA_SD) external view returns (uint256);
function ownerOfFromBCA(address _BCA_SD) external view returns (address);
function userOf(uint256 _tokenId) external view returns (address);
function userOfFromBCA(address _BCA_SD) external view returns (address);
function userBalanceOf(address _BCA_user) external view returns (uint256);
function userBalanceOfAnOwner(address _BCA_user, address _owner) external view returns (uint256);

Table 3. Pseudo-code of the standard function "transferFrom"

Transfers a token from an owner to a new owner
Input: old_Owner, new_Owner, tokenId
Require (owner, operator, approved) = msg.sender
Require owner of tokenId = old_Owner
Change owner of tokenId to new_Owner
Send event Transfer

The functions needed in our case are shown in the bottom of Table 2. Given the BCA_SD, the functions "tokenFromBCA", "ownerOfFromBCA" and "userOf-FromBCA" return, respectively, the tokenId, the BCA_owner and the BCA_user. Given the tokenId, the function "userOf" returns the BCA_user. The tokenIds of any owner assigned to a user are returned by the function "userBalanceOf" and the tokenIds of a particular owner assigned to a user are returned by the function "userBalanceOfAnOwner".

The pseudo-codes of the functions added to the proposed token are shown in Table 4. A token is created by the manufacturer of the IoT device with the function "createTo-ken". It is assumed that the manufacturer creates the token when an "owner" buys the IoT device. The owner of the token can assign a user to the token with the function "userTransfer". If the owner of the token assigns it to the address "0", the token cannot be used by anyone, since this address is reserved in Ethereum. This is the way how an owner sets a device to a non-operative state.

Table 4. Pseudo-codes of the added functions

"createToken": Creates a new token linking BCA_SD to a tokenId
Input: _owner, BCA_SD Output: tokenId Require (manufacturer) = msg.sender Generate new tokenId Set tokenId to token Set owner of tokenId = _owner Set BCA_SD of tokenId = _BCA_SD Return tokenId
"userTransfer": The owner assigns a user to the token
Input: tokenId, _BCA_user Require (owner) of _tokenId = msg.sender Set BCA_user from _tokenId = _ BCA_user Send event UserTransfer
"completeTransfer": Notifies that the token is already operative
Input: _tokenId Require (user) of _tokenId = msg.sender Send event TransferCompleted

3.2 Binding the IoT Device to Its Associated NFT

The manufacturer challenges the PUF inside the IoT device and receives from the IoT device the public key generated and the BCA_SD associated, as well as the helper data and masks that the device PUF needs to reconstruct its public key and BCA_SD. The steps of this process are detailed in Fig. 1 for the case of SRAM PUFs that use Static Random Access Memories (SRAMs). The manufacturer creates the token for the first owner, and includes the tokenId, PUF challenge, masks and helper data in the firmware associated to the device. Hence, only that device will be able to reconstruct its public key from that firmware because only its PUF will be able to provide the adequate response to the challenge received. Any other device will be unable to reconstruct BCA_SD from that firmware.

Among the electronic circuits that can be employed as PUFs, in this work, we select SRAM PUFs because most of IoT devices include SRAM in its hardware. SRAM PUFs are based on the start-up values obtained by powering up the memory [9]. Each SRAM bit cell is a bistable circuit whose logic memory functionality comes from two cross-coupled inverters. A write operation forces the SRAM cell to transition towards one of the two stable states ('0' or '1'). If the cell is powered-up and no write operation is carried out, the positive feedback between the two inverters leads the cell to the start-up value imposed by the inverter that begins to conduct. Ideally, the two inverters are identical, but the random variations in the manufacturing process make them different so that one of them is the first to conduct in each cell. Flipping bits can appear in the PUF response since the inverters of some bit cells are so similar that their start-up values change due

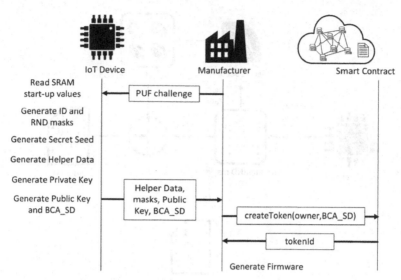

Fig. 1. The manufacturer binds the device to the NFT.

to noise. Particularly, those cells that change their value in half of the measurements, named herein as RND cells, are not adequate to identify the SD but are good to generate true random seeds. In the other side, the cells that provide generally the same start-up value, named herein as ID cells, are good to generate the PUF response. The use of the SRAM PUF inside the IoT device to generate the BCA_SD is illustrated in Fig. 2.

The first step of the token creation is to classify the SRAM cells addressed by the PUF challenge into ID and RND cells. For that purpose, the simple cell classification proposed in [22] is carried out. It consists in obtaining several measurements of start-up values by powering up and down the SRAM several times. For each measurement, the start-up values of all cells are compared. If the cell values do not change for all the measurements, the cells are registered as ID cells by an ID mask. If the cells change in half of the measurements, the cells are registered as RND cells in an RND mask. The second step of the token creation is to generate a true random Secret Seed from the start-up values of a set of RND cells selected by the RND mask. Since the Secret Seed are quite sensitive data because they identify cryptographically the SD, and the SRAM PUF response are also quite sensitive data because they identify physically the SD, the third step of the token creation is to generate non-sensitive data, known as Helper Data, from the Secret Seed and PUF response. The PUF response is obtained from the start-up values of a set of ID cells selected by the ID mask. Then, the Code Offset-based Helper Data algorithm described in [23] is used. It employs an Error Correcting Code to cope with flipping bits in the PUF response. Since the PUF response will show small bit flipping, a simple repetition Error Correcting Coder is employed. The steps of this process are detailed in Fig. 2a. The Secret Seed is not stored anywhere but is recovered from the response of the ID cells and the Helper Data, as illustrated in Fig. 2b. The Private and Public Keys of the device are obtained from the Secret Seed. Finally, the BCA_SD is computed from the Public Key. This is illustrated in Fig. 2c.

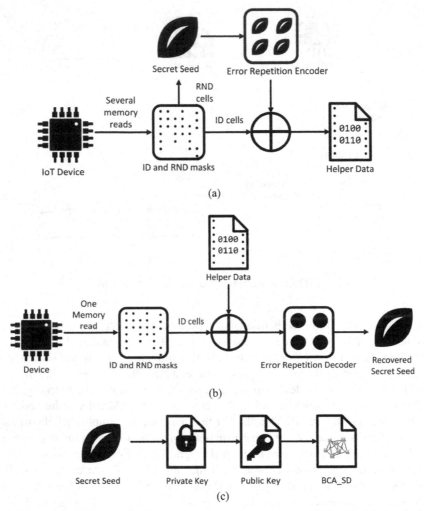

Fig. 2. Using the PUF inside the SD to generate and reconstruct the BCA_SD. (a) Generation of Secret Seed, masks, and Helper Data. (b) Secret Seed reconstruction. (c) Generation of Private Key, Public Key and BCA_SD from Secret Seed.

The manufacturer also programs in the device firmware that the device is subscribed to events "Transfer" (see Table 3), "UserTransfer", and "TransferCompleted" (see Table 4). With the two first events, the IoT device changes its state to "blocked" (non-operative) and can know its owner and user. This is important because the device will verify the BCAs and signatures of owner and user through their public keys if they request the device to update its firmware. The device does not need to store anything so the content of their memories can be deleted and a trustworthy firmware can be updated by its owner or user to ensure that the hardware and software of the device are trusted. Besides, the device will verify also the BCAs and signatures of the owner and user through their public keys when it is activated by them. The event TransferCompleted notifies that the user and device have authenticated each other successfully so that the device becomes operative for the application. Although being "activated", the IoT device is not ready to work ("operative") until this notification is received. Details of these steps related to user and device are shown in Fig. 3.

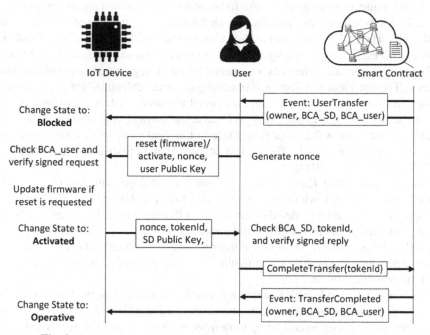

Fig. 3. States of the IoT device depending on events and user messages.

4 Implementation of the Proof of Concept

In this work, we employ a Pycom Wipy 3.0 board composed of an Espressif ESP32 chipset as IoT Secure Device (SD). This is a tiny development platform that allows ultra-low power usage and is very suitable to create IoT devices. The microcontroller ESP-32, which is the hardware core of the SD, contains an internal SRAM of 520 MB. This internal SRAM can be powered down and up without powering off the board completely so that it can be used as SRAM PUF.

4.1 SRAM PUFs from the IoT Device for Secret Obfuscation

One of the contributions of this work is the use of PUFs to obfuscate secret seeds employed to generate BCAs. In order to characterize the SRAM PUF, a specific firmware was developed to carry out the measurements by powering down and up the internal SRAM so as to extract automatically the start-up values. The internal SRAM is divided into three memories. In this work, the first 29,665 bytes (237,320 bits) of the last 100 KB

of the second memory were evaluated since they are enough for a statistical characterization. These bytes were not written or employed by the compiler to store execution
variables. Three different boards and 120 measurements were considered. The ID and
RND masks for each board were created with the first 20 measurements. The resting
100 measurements were employed for evaluation.

The minimum percentage of ID cells found was 84.07% (which means a minimum of
199,514 ID cells for the cells evaluated in each SRAM). Usually, most of the SRAM cells
are ID cells. The PUF responses considered have a size of 2048 bits, so that 97 different
responses per each board (291 responses in total) were evaluated. The similarity between
PUF responses from the same cells is evaluated by the average intra fractional Hamming
distance. The distribution of fractional Hamming distances calculated for responses from
the same SRAM cells is known as intra fractional Hamming distance distribution in the
PUF literature. For the measurements performed, the average intra fractional Hamming
distance calculated was 0.25% (a value close to the ideal value of 0, which means that
the PUF responses are equal). The number of intra Hamming distances calculated was
1,440,450 (100 · 99 · 291/2).

The decoder of the Error Correcting Code should cope with the noise of PUF
responses to reconstruct, with no errors, the secret from the Helper Data. The bit flipping
of a start-up value can be modeled essentially as a Bernoulli trial, which takes value '1'
(if the bit changes) with probability p and a value of '0' (if the bit does not change) with
probability $1 - p$. If the n bits obtained from the start-up values of n cells are assumed
to be independent, the probability of finding t flipping bits (or errors) in them is given
by a binomial distribution.

The $binocdf(t, n, p)$ Matlab function was employed to compute the failure probability in reconstructing a bit of the secret when using an Error Correcting Code with n-bit
codewords and capacity to correct up to t errors, with p estimated as the average intra
fractional Hamming distance. An 8-bit repetition Error Correcting Code (with $n = 8$
and $t = 3$) gives a probability of failure in reconstructing a bit of the secret of 2.71e-9
(according to the operation 1-binocdf(3, 8, 0.0025)). The 8-bit repetition Error Correcting Code is selected since an error rate of 10^{-6} is considered by many authors as a
conservative value that fulfills the requirements of most of typical security applications
[23, 24]. The results shown herein have been obtained for nominal operation conditions
(that is, nominal power supply voltage and ambient temperature). Of course, repetition
Error Correction Codes with bigger words can be employed to ensure the adequate
reconstruction of the secrets in any operation condition.

4.2 Development of an NFT with an SRAM PUF-Based BCA

In this work, we used Kovan, which is an Ethereum public testnet, as Ethereum Virtual
Machine (EVM) network. Ethereum is one of the most extended public blockchain
and is part of the third generation of blockchains (which employs smart contracts). In
Ethereum, secure transactions are based on the Elliptic Curve Cryptography (ECC). The
Elliptic Curve Digital Signature Algorithm (ECDSA) represents a robust and lightweight
signature scheme for constrained devices (such as IoT devices).

Several environments were employed to create the NFT. In the one side, the ESP-IDF
(Espressif IoT Development Framework), which is the official development framework

for ESP32 microcontrollers, was employed to use the Pycom Wipy as the core of an IoT secure device based on SRAM PUFs. In the other side, the blockchain functionalities were performed by using the Web3E-alphawallet library to create a BCA and carry out transactions in PlatformIO; Remix to program in Solidity language and deploy smart contracts; and Etherscan to check transactions. Figure 4(a) shows the Wipy board which is connected to a laptop. Figure 4(b) shows a screenshot of a transaction which is executed and checked by using the development environments.

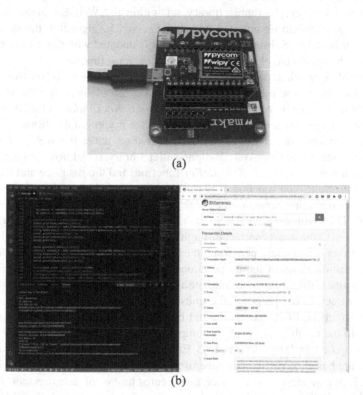

(a)

(b)

Fig. 4. (a) Real picture of the Wipy board. (b) Screenshot of a transaction performed through PlatformIO and checked through Etherscan.

The BCA of the SD is generated from a 256-bit secret seed obfuscated by the SRAM PUF response as explained above. Previously to the obfuscation, SRAM cells are classified to obtain the ID mask. Then, the seed obfuscation leads the ID mask application to obtain 2048 ID cells. The start-values of these cells are XOR-ed with the encoded Secret Seed (using the 8-bit repetition error correction encoder). The result is the 2048-bit Helper Data. The secret seed reconstruction needs the ID mask application to obtain the 2048 ID cells, the XOR operation with the Helper Data to obtain the 2048-bit coded seed and the 8-bit repetition error correction decoding to obtain the 256-bit decoded seed.

In order to create a BCA, private and public keys should be generated. A 256-bit private key is generated by applying a hash operation to the seed. A 64-byte public key results from applying the corresponding Elliptic Curve operation to the private key. In this work, we employ the *secp256k1* curve, which is the elliptic curve used in Ethereum. The BCA is obtained by applying the *Keccak256* operation to the public key and taking the most significant 20 bytes.

The different functions considered are performed by using the libraries provided by the development environments. The *Keccak256* function is obtained by using the *sha3.h* library from Trezor cryptographic library set within the Web3E-alphawallet library. A SHA3 context should be initiated with the *Keccak256* algorithm through the *keccak_256_Init* function. Subsequently, the context is updated with the data to be hashed and, finally, the results are obtained with the *keccak_final* function.

For the BCA creation, the *secp256k1* curve is obtained by using *contract.h* library from the Web3E-alphawallet library. The public key is obtained with the *PrivateKey-ToPublic* function. The BCA is obtained with the *PublicKeyToAddress* function. ECDSA is obtained by using *ecdsa.h* library within the Trezor cryptographic library.

The transactions are performed as JSON structures under the Web3E framework. A contract context from the Web3E-alphawallet library is defined by indicating the private key, a nonce with the *SetPrivateKey* function, and the gas price and limit by the *EthGetTransactionCount* function. The transaction is launched by the *SendTransaction* function. This operation generates the JSON structure associated, the transaction signed by using ECDSA with the private key, and a transaction hash as output. The transaction message is sent to the smart contract through a blockchain transaction. The realization of a smart contract is a similar operation but employing the *SetupContractData* function.

The execution times of these operations are included in Table 5. The transaction completion time is the total time to generate a transaction and its transfer to the blockchain or smart contract. In our proposal, the transaction completion time is composed of the seed reconstruction, BCA generation and blockchain transaction times. This value is compared to the resulting transaction completion time obtained in [16] and [20]. The solution proposed in [16] also employs Ethereum blockchain. However, IoT device identifiers are based on certificates generated from a private key that is not obfuscated by PUFs. [20] considers an IoT device that creates hashes of data together with a key generated by a PUF for mining purposes. In contrast to our proposal, this solution does not employ a public and standard blockchain.

Through the simulation of the smart contract functions "createToken", "transfer-From", "userTransfer" and "completeTransfer", the transaction gas consumption was evaluated. Table 6 illustrates the results obtained and shows a comparison with other similar functions proposed in [15] and [21]. The solution proposed in [15] does not employ PUFs and the device identifier is stored in the device-manager smart contract. The manager smart contracts verify information and decide whether a process can continue or not. Tokens are not directly related to the devices but to the tasks. Tokenization (which is not performed under the ERC-721 standard) is implemented by using a token-manager smart contract which is included in the task-manager smart contract. The task-manager smart contract provides a public register of available tasks related to the user, device, and tokens. Instantiations of users and devices are performed through the corresponding

Table 5. Execution times of the operations of a Secure Device based on PUFs

Operation		Execution time (ms)
Seed Obfuscation	SRAM cells classification	$3.8 \cdot 10^5$
	ID mask application, repetition error correction code and XOR operation	2.02
Seed Reconstruction	ID mask application, XOR operation and repetition error correction code	1.60
BCA Generation	256-bit private key generation (Keccak256 operation)	0.45
	64-byte public key generation (secp256k1 operation)	21.15
	20-byte BCA creation (Keccak256 operation)	0.45
Blockchain Transaction	Message preparation (configuration, ECDSA operation)	26.10
	Transfer to blockchain or smart contract	2.90
Transaction Completion in our proposal		52.65
Transaction Completion in [16]		69.0
Transaction Completion in [20]		192.30

manager smart contracts. In this way, manager smart contracts are only instantiated once, while the child (user and device smart contracts) are instantiated for each use. The gas values associated to the smart contract instantiation are included in Table 6. The solution in [21] provides a method for device traceability by using device authentication and ownership via blockchain smart contracts that do not employ NFTs explicitly. Device authentication is performed by PUF identifiers. However, the device has not capability to interact to the blockchain by a BCA associated to the PUF. The "createToken" function of our proposal, which can be compared to the *registerDevice* function of [21], consumes less gas. The standard "transferFrom" function of the ERC-721 NFT can be compared to the *transferOwnership* function of [21].

5 Conclusions

A solution for the secure management of IoT devices has been proposed. IoT devices are considered as Non Fungible Tokens (NFTs) based on the ERC-721 standard, which additionally include the BCA of the device user (not only the BCA of the device owner or manager) and the BCA of the IoT device. Device BCAs are generated from secret seeds obfuscated by Physical Unclonable Functions (PUFs). Any participant in the blockchain (including the IoT devices themselves because of their BCAs) can verify their manufacturers, owners, users, and the actions or data they are taking. Besides, the IoT devices, owners, and users are subscribed to the events of their associated NFTs so that they receive notifications about the situation of the NFT and behave accordingly.

Table 6. Gas consumption of smart contract functions

Proposal	Function	Gas consumption
Our	createToken	112,510
	transferFrom	34,272
	userTransfer	47,683
	completeTransfer	23,770
[15]	User	273,931
	User manager	530,579
	Device	446,652
	Device manager	1,097,206
	Token manager	413,560
	Task	554,883
	Task manager	3,052,709
[21]	registerDevice	121,478
	transferOwnership	30,365

The proposed device was implemented in a Pycom Wipy 3.0 board, proved with Kovan Ethereum testnet interacting with a smart contract programmed in Solidity, and verified with Remix. The SRAM PUF response employed has a size of 2048 bits to reconstruct secret seeds of 256 bits. The operations carried out by the Wipy board to generate the IoT device BCA and its employment in a transaction are carried out in a few tens of milliseconds. Smart contract functions are very simple. In fact, the gas consumption of the functions employed is low. A comparison is performed to other proposals in the literature in terms of execution times and gas consumption.

As future work, we plan to extend the proposal to provide security to the data generated by the IoT device, in terms of integrity, confidentiality, privacy, authentication, and provenance. In this way, not only the management of the IoT devices will be secure but also the storage and transmission of the data generated by these devices.

Acknowledgements. This work was supported in part by the Spanish Agencia Estatal de Investigación and Fondo Europeo de Desarrollo Regional (FEDER) under Projects TEC2017-83557-R and RTC-2017-6595-7, and Consejería de Economía, Conocimiento, Empresas y Universidad de la Junta de Andalucía under Projects AT17_5926_USE and US-1265146. The work of Rosario Arjona was supported by a Post-Doc Fellowship from the Spanish National Cybersecurity Institute (INCIBE).

References

1. Khan, M.A., Salah, K.: IoT security: review, blockchain solutions, and open issues. Future Gener. Comput. Syst. **82**, 395–411 (2018)

2. Stoyanova, M., Nikoloudakis, Y., Panagiotakis, S., Pallis, E., Markakis, K.: A survey on the Internet of Things (IoT) forensics: challenges, approaches, and open issues. IEEE Commun. Surv. Tutor. **22**, 1191–1221 (2020)
3. Buterin, V.: Ethereum whitepaper (2013). https://ethereum.org/whitepaper/. Accessed 19 Aug 2020
4. Christidis, K., Devetsikiotis, M.: Blockchains and smart contracts for the Internet of Things. IEEE Access **4**, 2292–2303 (2016)
5. Popov, S.: IOTA: feeless and free. IEEE Blockchain Technical Briefs (2019)
6. Prada-Delgado, M.A., Baturone, I., Dittmann, G., Jelitto, J., Kind, A.: PUF-derived IoT identities in a zero-knowledge protocol for blockchain. Internet Things **9** (2020)
7. Raiden Network. https://raiden.network/. Accessed 19 Aug 2020
8. ERC-721. http://www.erc721.org. Accessed 19 Aug 2020
9. Maes, R.: PUF-based entity identification and authentication. In: Maes, R. (ed.) Physically Unclonable Functions, pp. 117–141. Springer, Heidelberg (2013). https://doi.org/10.1007/978-3-642-41395-7_5
10. Remix. https://remix.ethereum.org. Accessed 19 Aug 2020
11. Westerkamp, M., Victor, F., Küpper, A.: Tracing manufacturing processes using blockchain-based token compositions. Digit. Commun. Netw. **6**, 167–176 (2020)
12. Hasan, M., Binil, S.: Decentralized cloud manufacturing-as-a-service (CMaaS) platform architecture with configurable digital assets. J. Manuf. Syst. **56**, 157–174 (2020)
13. Valaštín, V., et al.: Blockchain based car-sharing platform. In: IEEE International Symposium ELMAR (2019)
14. Le, T., Yoohwan, K., Ju-Yeon, J.: Implementation of a blockchain-based event reselling system. In: 6th IEEE International Conference on Computational Science/Intelligence and Applied Informatics (CSII) (2019)
15. Wickström, J., Magnus, W., Göran, P.: Rethinking IoT security: a protocol based on blockchain smart contracts for secure and automated IoT deployments. arXiv preprint arXiv:2007.02652 (2020)
16. Khalid, U., Asim, M., Baker, T., Hung, P.C.K., Tariq, M.A., Rafferty, L.: A decentralized lightweight blockchain-based authentication mechanism for IoT systems. Cluster Comput. **23**, 2067–2087 (2020). https://doi.org/10.1007/s10586-020-03058-6
17. Sghaier Omar, A., Basir, O.: Capability-based non-fungible tokens approach for a decentralized AAA framework in IoT. In: Choo, K.-K.R., Dehghantanha, A., Parizi, R.M. (eds.) Blockchain Cybersecurity, Trust and Privacy. AIS, vol. 79, pp. 7–31. Springer, Cham (2020). https://doi.org/10.1007/978-3-030-38181-3_2
18. Cui, P., Dixon, J., Guin, U., Dimase, D.: A blockchain-based framework for supply chain provenance. IEEE Access **7**, 157113–157125 (2019)
19. Xu, X., Rahman, F., Shakya, B., Vassilev, A., Forte, D., Tehranipoor, M.: Electronics supply chain integrity enabled by blockchain. ACM Trans. Des. Autom. Electron. Syst. **24**, 1–25 (2019). Article 31
20. Mohanty, S.P., Yanambaka, V.P., Kougianos, E., Puthal, D.: PUFchain: A hardware-assisted blockchain for sustainable simultaneous device and data security in the Internet of Everything (IoE). IEEE Consum. Electron. Mag. **9**, 8–16 (2020)
21. Islam, M.N., Kundu, S.: Enabling IC traceability via blockchain pegged to embedded PUF. ACM Trans. Des. Autom. Electron. Syst. **24**, 1–23 (2019). Article 36
22. Baturone, I., Prada-Delgado, M.A., Eiroa, S.: Improved generation of identifiers, secret keys, and random numbers From SRAMs. IEEE Trans. Inf. Forensics Secur. **10**, 2653–2668 (2015)
23. Guajardo, J., Kumar, S.S., Schrijen, G.-J., Tuyls, P.: FPGA intrinsic PUFs and their use for IP protection. In: Paillier, P., Verbauwhede, I. (eds.) CHES 2007. LNCS, vol. 4727, pp. 63–80. Springer, Heidelberg (2007). https://doi.org/10.1007/978-3-540-74735-2_5

24. Bösch, C., Guajardo, J., Sadeghi, A.-R., Shokrollahi, J., Tuyls, P.: Efficient helper data key extractor on FPGAs. In: Oswald, E., Rohatgi, P. (eds.) CHES 2008. LNCS, vol. 5154, pp. 181–197. Springer, Heidelberg (2008). https://doi.org/10.1007/978-3-540-85053-3_12

Bitcoin Blockchain Steganographic Analysis

Alexandre Augusto Giron[1,2]([⊠]), Jean Everson Martina[1],
and Ricardo Custódio[1]

[1] Programa de Pós-Graduação em Ciência da Computação, Departamento de
Informática e Estatística, Universidade Federal de Santa Catarina, Florianópolis,
Santa Catarina, Brazil
alexandre.giron@posgrad.ufsc.br, {jean.martina,ricardo.custodio}@ufsc.br
[2] Universidade Tecnológica Federal do Paraná, Toledo, Paraná, Brazil

Abstract. Steganography has been used as a way to hide data in files
or in messages traveling on communication channels. Its use can be
worrisome when it is used without proper authorization. Recently, it
has been detected that there are arbitrary files included in the public
blockchain of the Bitcoin cryptocurrency. The main concern arises when
such data inserted contains objectionable content, thus compromising
blockchain platforms. In this context, this paper presents an analysis of
the Blockchain of Bitcoin, based on some proposals for the use of steganography in blockchains and on detection methods of steganographic
data. Additionally, it is shown that we found no evidence of steganography data in Bitcoin using these techniques. We conclude by showing that
there is no specific approach, so far, for steganalysis in blockchains.

Keywords: Blockchain · Steganography · Hash channels · Nonces

1 Introduction

Not only financial services but, currently, almost all electronic services are beginning to explore the benefits of using blockchains in their infrastructure. New protocols, new applications, and solutions are announced every day with the incor-
poration of blockchain. Applications such as smart contracts, supply chains,
proof of existing services, and, recently, for secret communication are examples [3,12,14,26,28,29,32,38]. It is argued that blockchains make it possible for
applications to be more secure and less dependent on third parties.

The term blockchain can be defined as a decentralized digital registry cryptographically protected from tampering [17]. The use of blockchain in information systems became famous in 2008 when the cryptocurrency Bitcoin was
proposed [24]. Two of the main benefits of incorporating a blockchain in applications are the guarantee that data cannot be changed once registered and the
need not rely on a third party for this purpose.

© Springer Nature Switzerland AG 2020
J. Zhou et al. (Eds.): ACNS 2020 Workshops, LNCS 12418, pp. 41–57, 2020.
https://doi.org/10.1007/978-3-030-61638-0_3

However, blockchains are subject to entering questionable data. The work of Matzutt et al. [21] showed that at least 1600 arbitrary files were inserted, exploring different "spaces" inside of the Bitcoin blockchain. The authors argued that some of these files contain links to objectionable content [21]. This fact becomes particularly worrying since, on the blockchain, all data is made available to network participants, and that data cannot be deleted. This threat can, for instance, compromise the use of public blockchains. Countermeasures for this threat include content filters, editable blockchains, and increased transaction rates [1].

Although the insertion of inappropriate data into the blockchain may itself be a potential problem, an additional difficulty occurs when that data is somehow hidden in the blockchain, without being able to detect it a priori. Unfortunately, this inclusion can be done, for example, through a technique known as steganography. Steganography is a technique that can be used to camouflage data so that it is difficult to observe in files or communication channels [11]. In 2002, Hopper et al. formalized provably safe steganography [18]. Using Hopper terminology, it appears that Partala was the first to link steganography to blockchain, in 2018 [26]. Going back to the example of Matzutt et al. [21], they haven't analyzed the blockchain in the context of the well-known steganography techniques. Even though the data insertion methods in the blockchain can be a potential problem, hiding data steganographically can be also a potential problem, especially in public blockchains, accessible by any participant in the network.

Historically, there are reports of the use of steganography by the military and secret service agencies. In addition to the transport of confidential messages, it has also been used to track the spread of images or to guarantee the rights to use such images, through watermark schemes [16]. Another use would be the possibility to send and receive messages in situations where there are restrictions that prevent people from communicating, as in a dictatorial regime where censorship prevails [9].

On the other hand, Raggo and Hosmer show the use of steganography by terrorists with the seizure of a memory card by the German police in 2011 [30]. It contained terrorist training manuals and plans to attack Europe, steganographically hidden in a video. Another misuse of steganography techniques, which is common in practice, is by malware trying to exfiltrate data over the network [7] or to hide its presence in a system [4]. Besides, when Edward Snowden publicized NSA documents in 2013, it brought several concerns to the public about their privacy. Those documents leaked the NSA research about an attack on encryption algorithms in a way that the output also has covert information. For example, the NSA would use this information to reconstruct the encryption key of the user. This type of attack is called Algorithm Substitution Attack (ASA) [9], or Kleptography attack [1].

In this context, the detection of the presence of steganography in a communication channel (called steganalysis) is important to avoid some of those threats or to trigger countermeasures against it. Using blockchains as a steganographic channel have some "attracting" advantages compared to other cover mediums [26]:

- It has free access with a degree of anonymity;
- There is no central authority controlling the blocks stored on the blockchain; and
- Once the block is published, the data cannot be deleted, which means that it is not susceptible to censorship (i. e. an authoritarian regime).

Therefore, this paper aims to evaluate how steganography can be detected, if possible, in the blockchain. As a secondary goal, the Bitcoin blockchain will be analyzed in order to find if there is evidence of steganographic messages in it. Most of the related works evaluate its proposals using synthetic data or fictitious steganographic messages. In this paper, the focus is to find evidence of steganography use (if there is any) considering the Bitcoin's blockchain as a real case scenario. Bitcoin was chosen due to its high popularity and market share by the time of writing of this paper. The main contributions are summarized below:

- An overview of the available techniques for data insertion and hiding in the Bitcoin's blockchain;
- A search for steganographic evidence in Bitcoin, considering the first **253.38** GiB of blocks of the blockchain; and
- A discussion about the difficulty of this problem and the absence of positive findings (i.e. steganographic evidences) by our experiments, derived mostly from the lack of an specific steganalysis approach for the blockchain.

This paper is structured as follows. Section 2 presents the Related Work. Section 3 brings the necessary background on data hiding in blockchain and steganography. In Sect. 4 it is presented the methodology of the analysis performed in this work. Section 5 discuss the results of the experiments. Section 6 presents the conclusions and further research directions.

2   Related Work

Juha Partala [26] proposed a method of embedding and extracting covert information on the blockchain, called BLOCCE (**Blo**ckchain **C**overt **C**hannel). Although not implemented in practice, the author performed a security analysis of BLOCCE in the context of provably secure stegosystems. In summary, the method defines the embedding of a ciphered message m by choosing the payment addresses such that the Least Significant Bits (LSBs) form m. To extract it, the method defines a start indicator of the encrypted message.

Alsalami and Zhang [1,2] further advance in this line of research by presenting steganography attacks against blockchain platforms. They explored the uncontrolled randomness in blockchains and showed how this could be manipulated to enable covert communication and hidden persistent storage. They implemented their approach in Bytecoin and Monero cryptocurrencies. In addition, they examined the existing countermeasures to thwart this threat in the context of blockchains. However, there is no comment on the detection methods from a steganalysis point of view.

Fionov [15] also discuss covert channels for blockchains. He proposes seven channels in blockchains: two of them use uncontrolled randomness to hide data (similarly to Alsalami and Zhang); four channels are based on permutations of transactions (inputs and outputs); and the last channel is based on distribution of payments in a transaction. In his work, the channels are analyzed theoretically, in terms of capacity and detectability, but no practical experiment was conducted.

There are works in the same line of Matzutt et al. [21] about searching for arbitrary content inserted in blockchains and how to prevent such content of being inserted [6,20]. However, these works do not discuss it in a steganographic point of view. On the other hand, understanding how data can be inserted in the blockchain is the first step to use blockchain as a channel for steganography. Data insertion methods are covered in the next section.

It is important to note that these works we just presented do not focus on the steganalysis of a real blockchain. More than that, they focus on hiding information and not how to find out what may have actually been hidden. Our work, on the other hand, knowing these techniques, focuses on applying best-of-knowledge steganography detection techniques in order to try to identify if there is hidden content in the Bitcoin Blockchain.

3   Data Insertion and Hiding

To be able to adequately discuss later the techniques we applied to the Bitcoin Blockchain, it is essential to revise some of the known data insertion techniques for this blockchain, as well as revise some well-known steganography techniques for general data hiding. In this section, the data insertion methods for the Bitcoin's blockchain are introduced first (Sect. 3.1), followed by steganography concepts and the state-of-the-art proposals for covert communication using blockchain (Sect. 3.2).

3.1   Data Insertion in Bitcoin's Blockchain

We start with the work by Matzutt et al. which describes the methods for data insertion in the blockchain of Bitcoin, classified as follows [21]:

– In **Coinbase**: coinbase is the name of the first transaction input of each block in Bitcoin, used by the miners to collect rewards and additional fees. The transaction allows near to 100 bytes of arbitrary data in *ScriptSig* field. The typical example is the message in the coinbase transaction of the Bitcoin genesis block: "The Times 03/Jan/2009 Chancellor on the brink of second bailout for banks".
– Using **OP_RETURN**: since 2014, this is the Bitcoin standard way of adding extra data (limited to 83 bytes) to transactions. This opcode in a single output marks the transaction as invalid, and the outputs are unspendable.

- In **Standard transactions**: these transactions can be misused to insert data in output scripts. Two standard transaction types are Pay-to-PubkeyHash (P2PKH) and Pay-to-Script-Hash (P2SH). There is the obsolete Pay-to-Pubkey (P2PK) transaction, commonly found in coinbase transactions from the earlier blocks of the blockchain. Regarding P2PKH and P2SH, the respective public keys or script hash values can embed arbitrary data as miners do not verify it. The main problem is that the user must "burn coins" due to the receiver address be replaced by the data inserted. The amount of data that can be inserted varies from 57.34 KiB to 96.7 KiB.
- In **Non-standard transactions**: in this case, there is an additional difficulty because miners often ignore them, and therefore the data will not be inserted on the blockchain. The amount of data that can be inserted reaches near to 100 KiB.

3.2 Data Hiding in Blockchains

Before presenting the state-of-the-art approaches for data hiding using blockchain, some concepts will be defined below. We will start with some basic Steganography concepts in order to allow the reader to understand the following state-of-the-art approaches we present later.

Steganography is part of the information hiding methods used to make data harder to notice [22]. Typically, it is used to hide the fact that a (secret) communication is taking place. The following components are present in a stegosystem: the important message (the *hidden text*) m; the unsuspicious document d, which is called *covertext* if it contains m embedded into; and the *history* h, composed by the already transmitted documents in a communication *channel* C.

The main difference between the security notion of a cryptosystem and a stegosystem **is the presence of the communication channel**. The channel C is formalized as a probability distribution, and the communication can be viewed as a sampling from this distribution. In this sense, the security of a stegosystem relies in the fact that an observer is not able to distinguish the stegotext from objects randomly picked from the channel distribution [9].

Formally, Berndt [9] defines a secret-key stegosystem in a triple $StS = (StS.Gen, StS.Enc, StS.Dec)$. The stegoencoder $StS.Enc$ takes as input the *hidden text* m, the key k, generated by $StS.Gen(1^k)$, and the history $h \in (\sum^{dl(k)})^*$. $StS.Enc$ outputs a single document (the stegotext) d. On the other hand, the stegodecoder $StS.Dec$ requires k and a sequence of documents to return the original message m. Modern steganography security principles are then similar to Kerckhoffs' principle in cryptography, i. e. the security should rely only on the secret information: the key(s) [27].

In the design of secure stegosystems, a common technique is called *Rejection Sampling* [10]. This technique is based on taking samples d from the channel: if d already encodes the hidden text (i.e., by chance), then output d; otherwise, discard d and continue the sampling step. Depending on the channel, if the sampling of bits from the channel is close to the standard uniform distribution, it may be easier to find d that already encodes m, especially when m is an encrypted message. Another common technique (not necessarily in the security notion described) is by embedding in the Least Significant Bit (LSB). This technique takes advantage of (pseudo) random noise present in the acquired media data, such as images, video, and audio [11]. In addition, both techniques can be combined (rejection sampling plus LSB embedding).

We can now move to State-of-the-art approaches that redirected to blockchain data hiding, and we will cover here any approach for data hiding, which considers the specific characteristics of the channel, in this case, the blockchain. By the time of writing this paper, there are three specific approaches for hiding data in the blockchain.

The approach of Partala [26] (BLOCCE) follows the terminology of provably secure steganography (by Hopper et al. [18]). The technique is based on the LSB of the payment addresses. First, the message m is encrypted with a pseudorandom ciphertext function. Then, the addresses are ordered in a way that the LSBs form m. The extraction is based on a secret start indicator of m in the covertext. The formal specification given by Partala allows embedding of one bit per block of the blockchain. If a pre-computed list of L addresses are significantly greater than N (the size of the m), than it is easier to sample these addresses in order to match the LSB with the bits of m. In practice, **Partala's approach hides information in hashes** (or public keys), which represent addresses in a blockchain.

The approach of Alsalami and Zhang [1] exploits subliminal channels in cryptographic primitives. Their approach embeds information using the random numbers (c_j, r_j) of the ring signatures of the CryptoNote protocol. This protocol uses ED25519 Edwards-curve with group order of prime p equals to 253 bits. The approach uses the least significant 252 bits of c_j, r_j, presented in Fig. 1. There is a 128-bit IV where 64-bit are random bits and the rest are zero to indicate the presence of a message. The remaining 376 bits (or 47 bytes) are used to embed an encrypted m with a secret key k and the IV. In summary, **their approach hides information in a digital signature**, by using the random numbers of the signature generation process.

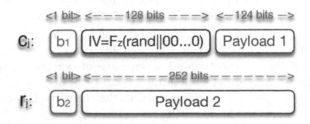

Fig. 1. Steganographic approach proposed by Alsalami and Zhang [1].

The combinatorial channels proposed by Fionov [15] have some conditions to hide data. His work treats input or output addresses as numbers. Then, a permutation of the addresses is selected in a way that it matches the data to be hidden (represented also as a number), similarly to a rejection sampling process. However, not enough details are provided on the security and on how to extract the hidden data from these channels.

The main drawback of BLOCCE is the low throughput. The approach can be viewed as a theoretical construction; it was not implemented in practice. In addition, no steganalysis technique was proposed to detect the hidden text in BLOCCE. Considering the approach of Alsalami and Zhang, a premise of an Initialization Vector as a cryptographic primitive is to be random [35]. Since their approach needs 64 bit zeros for the message indicator in the IV, the drawback is that it could low down the security factor of the original digital signature scheme.

Another important way of hiding information could be the use of Covert Communication in Hash Channels. The term "Hash Channels" was coined by Wu [39] in 2005. Similarly to Alsalami and Zhang, Wu shows that the digital signature protocols that use hashes allow covert communication due to the randomness (or pseudorandomness) observed in hashes. As hashes represent addresses in blockchain transactions, they can be used for covert communication in blockchains. In Wu's work, no detection techniques neither a steganalysis approach was proposed.

It seems that there are only few detection methods for covert communication in hash channels proposed so far. In the work of Kucner [19], followed by Teşeleanu [36], a side-channel attack is proposed to detect a hidden message, but in the context of kleptography. Their detection is based on the execution time to distinguish between "honest devices" (the ones that do not embed information) and "backdoored devices" (the ones that do). Since the information of the execution time is not available in the blocks already published in the blockchain, this method cannot be applied to detect hidden information in this case. So far, the steganalysis in hash channels seems to be an open problem. Other approaches exist, like the controlled randomness [1], but they are countermeasures to prevent covert communication, not to detect its presence.

4   Methodology

Knowing the data insertion points for the Bitcoin Blockchain, and also having revised classical steganography techniques and blockchain applied ones, we set to answer the following research question:

– Are there hidden messages in the Bitcoin Blockchain that use classical stenography techniques, and that could be detected with standard steganalysis?

The methodology followed in this paper is based on steganalysis experiments on the Bitcoin's blockchain, which can be obtained at https://bitcoin. org/en/download. The experiments aim to find evidence of the presence (or not) of steganographic messages in the blockchain. In addition, the blockchain

Table 1. Description of the Dataset of the Bitcoin's blockchain analyzed in this work.

Chunk number	Dataset (timestamp of the last block)	Approx. size (MiB)	Block count interval
1	2009-01-03 16:15:00 to 2009-07-02 23:42:50	3,95	Block #0 to #18007
2	2010-01-02 23:53:05	3,12	Block #18608 to #32747
3	2010-07-02 23:48:12	10,19	Block #32748 to #63939
4	2011-01-02 23:58:10	40,50	Block #63940 to #100765
5	2011-07-02 23:58:47	267,32	Block #100766 to #134463
6	2012-01-02 23:49:53	502,15	Block #134464 to #160340
7	2012-07-02 23:56:08	1085,34	Block #160341 to #187257
8	2013-01-02 23:52:07	2560,40	Block #187258 to #214877
9	2013-07-02 23:44:23	4339,41	Block #214878 to #244469
10	2014-01-02 23:59:25	4628,57	Block #244470 to #278334
11	2014-07-02 23:48:30	6217,90	Block #278335 to #308941
12	2015-01-02 23:57:48	7653,73	Block #308942 to #337190
13	2015-07-02 23:54:00	10028,16	Block #337191 to #363551
14	2016-01-02 23:56:10	14877,21	Block #363552 to #391461
15	2016-07-02 23:54:19	19492,93	Block #391461 to #419026
16	2017-01-02 23:55:50	21218,05	Block #419027 to #446347
17	2017-07-02 23:49:46	24858,20	Block #446348 to #473944
18	2018-01-02 23:50:33	25693,64	Block #473945 to #502287
19	2018-07-02 23:31:50	22848,60	Block #502288 to #530254
20	2019-01-02 23:53:08	22844,33	Block #530255 to #556758
21	2019-07-02 23:57:49	28409,40	Block #556759 to #583537
22	2020-01-02 23:41:39	26933,42	Block #583538 to #611005
23	2020-04-14 11:54:21	14951,96	Block #611006 to #625941

parser (available at: https://github.com/alecalve/python-bitcoin-blockchain-parser) was used to retrieve information of the blocks, such as addresses.

The first **253.38 GiB** of blocks (synchronized until 14/04/2020) were considered in this work, analyzed in data chunks. Its description is presented in Table 1. The chunks were created by using the timestamp information in the block headers. Each chunk of data is divided by semesters (using the timestamp information in each block). This division by time (instead of fixed size) would help to relate the findings with real-world events.

We executed two experiments: Checking LSB of addresses (Sect. 4.1) and Checking the Nonces (Sect. 4.2). The tools developed for each experiment are available at https://github.com/AAGiron/steganalysis-tool-blockchain.

4.1   Checking the LSB of Addresses

The work of Partala [26] inspires this experiment. It consists of uncompressing addresses of transactions in the blockchain and then extracts the LSB for analysis. In practice, since an address in Bitcoin can be viewed as an encoded hash, the problem of this analysis is how to detect covert information in Hash Channels.

A Bitcoin address is a Base-58 encoded version of a RIPEMD-160 hash. In summary, to generate an address, first, the ECDSA public key pk of a wallet is hashed through SHA256, producing the hash of the public key h_1. Then, h_1 is hashed again with RIPEMD-160 hash algorithm [13], producing a second hash h_2. The version byte (i.e., *0x00* for the main Bitcoin network) is added in front of h_2. In addition, four bytes from a double SHA-256 hash of h_2 are appended in the end of h_2. The last step is the encoding of h_2 using Base-58 encoding.

In a practical scenario, it would be easier to hide a message in the LSB of h_1 through rejection sampling, unless the user had a pre-computed list of final addresses. Therefore, in this experiment, the LSB of each of the addresses analyzed is the one from hash h_1.

The metrics for the evaluation are derived from statistical analysis. Shannon's entropy [33] is used as a measure of unpredictability of the values. The distribution of the Arithmetic Mean (AM) is used to analyze if the samples are close to a normal distribution. In addition, if the AM of all samples is close to 127.5, it is a possible indicator that the bytes were generated randomly. Lastly, the Monobit test compares if the number of 0 s and 1 s in a set is approximately the same.

The objective is to detect if the LSB of addresses in the transactions is generated by SHA256. The result statistics are expected to match a synthetic set of LSB hashes, with high entropy, close to a normal distribution, and with a low percentage of monobit failures. If the result statistics are not compatible with the expected result, it could be an indicator that the LSB has been manipulated to hide a message. In this cases, the extracted LSB data will be searched to find the presence of hidden data (file documents, images, and other types of data).

However, these metrics will probably fail to detect the presence of hidden-texts if the hidden-texts are encrypted before being hidden. In this case, this detection will be effective only if a "fingerprint" was left, like a message start indicator; or, if a known protocol was used, for example, the fingerprint string "Salted" in OpenSSL [25].

In order to compare the distribution of the LSB of the addresses extracted from the blockchain, a synthetic set of 1 Gigabit of SHA256 LSB data was generated. The synthetic data was produced using the SHA256 implementation of OpenSSL, with seeds provided by the /dev/urandom generator of Linux kernel 4.15.0-20-generic.

It is worthy to state that there is a chronological gap between the blocks in the chunks 1–18 (until 2017) and the BLOCCE publication (2018), which inspired this experiment. This chronological gap could low down the expectation of finding evidence in those chunks. Still, the experiment is required to corroborate this statement.

4.2 Checking the Nonces

The second experiment is realized by analyzing the Nonces of a block. The idea came from the website *bitslog.com*[1] which detected patterns on the mining process and also in the LSByte (Least Significant Byte) values of the nonces. One hypothesis raised on the website was that the nonces could contain a hidden message.

The 32-bit nonce in the block header is the value adjusted by miners for the Proof-of-Work consensus algorithm. The nonce is incremented in order to make the hash of the block header less or equal to an expected target [24]. Although miners control the nonce, it is unpredictable which nonce will produce the desired hash. Therefore, this experiment aims at first to verify the results from the website *bitslog.com*. If confirmed, the second step is to analyze the extracted data (e.g. LSBytes) of the nonces. The same metrics of the previous experiment (Sect. 4.1) will be used.

In addition, since the blockchain can be used for arbitrary data, it could store an image with a hidden message in it, for example. The work of Matzutt et al. [21] has found 144 images inserted via known services (Apertus for images, Satoshi Uploader for files) and 2 images without it. The steganalysis, in this case, would be done using traditional steganalysis techniques for images (i.e., analysis of the histogram of the image), which was out of the scope of this work.

5 Results and Discussion

5.1 Checking LSB of Addresses

The results of the experiment of Sect. 4.1 for the first chunk of data are summarized in Table 2. The addresses of transactions are grouped by transaction type: *coinbase*, *pubkey*, *Pay-to-Public-key-Hash* (P2PKH) and *Pay-to-Script-Hash* (P2SH). The *coinbase* here is the address (or addresses) in the output of first transaction of each block. The LSB of the extracted addresses are compared to the LSB of the synthetic dataset of 1 Gbit of SHA256 hashes.

The statistical metrics presented in Table 2 are: the Entropy (bits-per-byte), the AM of the data bytes, both calculated with ENT software [37]; and the percentage of failures regarding the Monobit test [8]. In the Monobit test used in this paper, each set of bits has 20000 bits, and the percentage of failures is defined by the number of sets that fails over the total number of sets.

The comparison in Table 2 shows that there is a difference of the LSBs in the addresses when compared to the expected output (the first line in Table 3). The results for P2PKH are not compatible with the synthetic data set, but the dataset was too small to compare. The monobit test was not computed for the datasets that have size smaller than 20000 bits.

The extracted LSB were appended together in four files (for each transaction type), and then the files were checked with Scalpel [31], a *file carving* tool.

---

[1] https://bitslog.com/2013/09/03/new-mystery-about-satoshi/.

Table 2. Results of the statistical analysis of the LSB of the first chunk of blocks.

Transaction type	Dataset	Entropy	Arithmetic mean (AM)	Monobit failures
SHA256 LSB	1 Gbit	7.999998	127.5034	~0.012%
coinbase LSB	2.3 KiB	7.908350	126.5942	–
pubkey LSB	2.3 KiB	7.923754	124.8914	–
P2PKH LSB	9 bytes	2.641604	179.6667	–
P2SH LSB	–	–	–	–

However, no meaningful data representation (ASCII, images or documents) were found. A RPM file (fingerprint *"0xEDAB EEDB"*) was found by scalpel, but later it turned out to be a false positive.

The results of the analysis of chunk 9 of the blockchain are presented in Table 3. Possibly, the presence of repeated addresses in the transactions was the cause of the high rate of failures in the Monobit test, low AM and low byte entropy. It was found that the data extracted from *pubkey* transactions is composed mostly of zeros, which explains the low entropy and low AM. For completeness, scalpel was executed to check the extracted data for each transaction type and no meaningful message was found. In the LSBs of the *pubkey* transaction, scalpel did not find any files. In the P2PKH transaction, scalpel found 290 files, composed by PGP (i.e. fingerprint *"0xA600"*) and RPM files, all of them false positives.

Table 3. Results of the statistical analysis of the chunk number 9.

Transaction type	Dataset	Entropy	Arithmetic mean (AM)	Monobit failures
coinbase LSB	16.4 KiB	7.973333	133.7690	~66.67%
pubkey LSB	18.7 KiB	0.761906	3.4775	100%
P2PKH LSB	3.0 MiB	7.921173	118.9001	86.51%
P2SH LSB	1.8 KiB	7.876623	130.4107	–

Regarding the last chunk of data (number 23), the results are presented in Table 4. Similar behavior was found considering the *pubkey* transaction type but in this case the data was composed mostly by ones. Scalpel returned 356 files (all false positives) considering P2PKH extracted data and 281 files (also false positives) considering P2SH data, composed mostly of PGP and RPM fingerprints, but also MPG, WPC and one OST fingerprint.

All of the statistical results can be found in the Github repository previously mentioned. Scalpel was also executed for all chunks of data and no meaningful message was found. This indicates that there are no hidden steganographic messages or, if they exist, they could not be detected with this experiment.

Table 4. Results of the statistical analysis for the last chunk of blocks.

Transaction type	Dataset	Entropy	Arithmetic mean (AM)	Monobit failures
coinbase LSB	1.7 KiB	7.481999	162.3399	–
pubkey LSB	26.4 KiB	1.915187	142.0985	90%
P2PKH LSB	4.1 MiB	7.965501	124.4108	40.85%
P2SH LSB	3.8 KiB	7.992155	128.2559	6.94%

5.2   Checking the Nonces

From the experiment described in Sect. 4.2, firstly, the nonces were verified in terms of the AM frequencies. Figure 2 shows the distribution of the first chunk blocks, which is not very close to a normal distribution. The tables for the computed metrics and histograms computed for the AM of all of the chunks are available at https://github.com/AAGiron/steganalysis-tool-blockchain/tree/master/results. The AM histograms have similar shape as in Fig. 2.

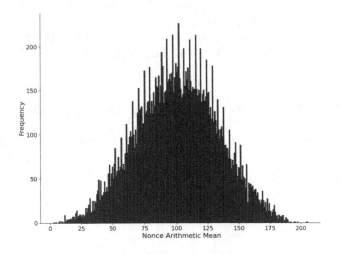

Fig. 2. Distribution of the AM of the Nonces in the First chunk of blocks.

However, there are differences perceived when comparing the values of the Most-Significant-Byte (MSByte) with the LSByte values of Nonces. Figure 3b shows MSByte values biased towards zero, probably due to the incremental nature of the nonces. On the other hand, in Fig. 3a the gap observed on the value interval 10 to 19, for example, regarding the LSByte values is intriguing. This result corroborates with the results pointed out by *bitslog.com*.

Similar behavior was perceived in the chunks 2,3 for LSBytes presented in Fig. 3a, which has gradually changed until chunk 11 (Fig. 3c). Regarding

MSBytes, the bias towards zero stop to occur in chunk 5 and kept this behavior until chunk 14, which can be observed in Fig. 3d. But in the remaining chunks, starting in the year 2016, the MSBytes had another pattern, presented in Fig. 3f. Interestingly, both LSBytes and MSBytes have changed their behavior among the years and there are different patterns that can be observed.

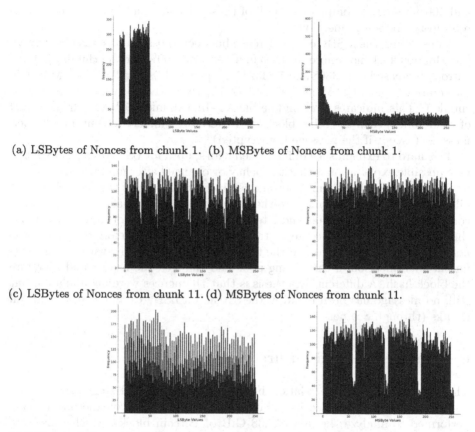

(a) LSBytes of Nonces from chunk 1. (b) MSBytes of Nonces from chunk 1.

(c) LSBytes of Nonces from chunk 11. (d) MSBytes of Nonces from chunk 11.

(e) LSBytes of Nonces from chunk 21. (f) MSBytes of Nonces from chunk 21.

Fig. 3. Comparison of the LSBytes and MSBytes of the Nonces from the chunks 1,12 and 21.

The evaluation metrics were also applied to the extracted data, and they show that its data is not random. The byte entropy calculated for the LSBytes of the first chunk was 6.779773 bits per byte, with AM equal to 56.4422. For the MSBytes, the byte entropy calculated was 7.640788 and AM metric was 96.5922. In addition, Monobit test failures reached 100%, both for LSBytes and for MSBytes. Although this result indicates the non-random nature of the LSBytes and MSBytes of the nonces, no meaningful message has been found in the extracted data. In the first chunk, $18, 6$ KiB of LSBytes were extracted from nonces (and the same amount of MSBytes). Scalpel was also used for this verification and similar false positives of the previous experiment were identified.

The evaluation metrics changed for the other chunks. The byte entropy of the extracted LSBytes increased to 7.973855 (chunk 11, 30, 6 KiB) and to 7.943257 (chunk 21, 26, 7 KiB), compared to the first chunk. AM also increased (123.0151 and 122.2475, respectively). Monobit test result in 91, 6% failures for chunk 11 and 100% for 21. A compilation of all of these metrics is available in the github repository previously mentioned.

Considering the MSBytes, a difference between those chunks was observed in the Monobit test: no failure for the chunk 11 and 100% for the chunk 21. Byte entropy increased (7.993308 and 7.943257, respectively) as well as the AM metric for chunk 11 and 21 (127.2097 and 122.2475, respectively), when compared to chunk 1. This indicates that middle blocks (like chunk 11) have a higher level of randomness than the other blocks and therefore unlikely to contain a hidden message (except if the message is encrypted).

It is hard to explain such different behaviors, both for LSBytes and MSBytes. One possible explanation is that the behavior changed after mining pools started to operate in the blockchain. Coordinate miners could iterate through all of the 4 billion possibilities of the nonce without finding the target hash. Since 2012, the consequence of mining pools and later the ASIC hardware for mining is the use the "extra nonce" in the coinbase transaction [5], and therefore the nonce was not the only factor used to find the target hash. Additionally, with mining tags for the identification of the mining pool also changed the header and therefore the block hash. A different hypothesis is that the nonces were manipulated, but still, no message has been found in the extracted LSBytes and MSBytes for all chunks (through Scalpel).

6   Conclusions and Future Work

This paper aimed at the relation between blockchain and steganography, on how the last can be applied in and on how to detect it. Two experiments were performed to analyze the first 253.38 GiB of Bitcoin blocks, which constitute a significant part of the entire network (by the time of writing this paper). No steganographic evidence could be found within these blocks, considering that hash channels (of Partala's approach [26]) and the block nonces were investigated.

The main difficulty of the detection is that it could not be found any steganalysis approach that is specific for the blockchain. Such approach should consider the characteristics of the underlying structure of the blockchain, in order to increase the detectability level of covert channels in this scenario. It seems that it remains an open research problem that will be considered for future work.

The results corroborate with the observation made in *bitslog.com*, regarding the behaviour of the nonces. However, after extracting the LSBytes and MSBytes, no hidden message or meaningful content could be found in this data, by using statistical analysis and Scalpel for file carving. It is worthy to note that other blockchains could be also subject for analysis, in particular for blockchains that might have lower transaction costs than Bitcoin or higher anonymity levels.

An approach that will be considered for future work is the redesign of the LSB experiments using clustering techniques [23, 34]. The objective is to extract the LSB from addresses that belong to the same cluster. In the context of blockchain applications, the importance of steganalysis lies on the fact that it would help to prevent misuse of public blockchains. Blockchains constitute a promising architecture for many financial and non-financial applications, which cannot afford to be jeopardized by steganography.

References

1. Alsalami, N., Zhang, B.: Uncontrolled randomness in blockchains: Covert bulletin board for illicit activity. Cryptology ePrint Archive (2018). ia.cr/2018/1184
2. Alsalami, N., Zhang, B.: Utilizing public blockchains for censorship-circumvention and iot communication. In: 2019 IEEE Conference on Dependable and Secure Computing (DSC), pp. 1–7. IEEE (2019)
3. Andoni, M., et al.: Blockchain technology in the energy sector: a systematic review of challenges and opportunities. Renew. Sustain. Energy Rev. **100**, 143–174 (2019)
4. Andriesse, D., Bos, H.: Instruction-level steganography for covert trigger-based malware. In: Dietrich, S. (ed.) DIMVA 2014. LNCS, vol. 8550, pp. 41–50. Springer, Cham (2014). https://doi.org/10.1007/978-3-319-08509-8_3
5. Antonopoulos, A.M.: Mastering Bitcoin: Programming the Open Blockchain. O'Reilly Media Inc., Newton (2017)
6. Ateniese, G., Magri, B., Venturi, D., Andrade, E.: Redactable blockchain-or-rewriting history in bitcoin and friends. In: 2017 IEEE European Symposium on Security and Privacy (EuroS&P), pp. 111–126. IEEE (2017)
7. Bąk, P., Bieniasz, J., Krzemiński, M., Szczypiorski, K.: Application of perfectly undetectable network steganography method for malware hidden communication. In: 2018 4th International Conference on Frontiers of Signal Processing (ICFSP), pp. 34–38. IEEE (2018)
8. Bassham, L.E., et al.: A statistical test suite for random and pseudorandom number generators for cryptographic applications. Technical report, National Institute of Standards and Technology (NIST) (2010)
9. Berndt, S., Liśkiewicz, M.: Provable secure universal steganography of optimal rate: Provably secure steganography does not necessarily imply one-way functions. In: Proceedings of the 4th ACM Workshop on Information Hiding and Multimedia Security, pp. 81–92. ACM (2016)
10. Cachin, C.: An information-theoretic model for steganography. In: Aucsmith, D. (ed.) IH 1998. LNCS, vol. 1525, pp. 306–318. Springer, Heidelberg (1998). https://doi.org/10.1007/3-540-49380-8_21
11. Cole, E.: Hiding in Plain Sight. Wiley, Hoboken (2002)
12. Crosby, M., Pattanayak, P., Verma, S., Kalyanaraman, V., et al.: Blockchain technology: Beyond bitcoin. Appl. Innov. **2**(6–10), 71 (2016)
13. Dobbertin, H., Bosselaers, A., Preneel, B.: RIPEMD-160: a strengthened version of RIPEMD. In: Gollmann, D. (ed.) FSE 1996. LNCS, vol. 1039, pp. 71–82. Springer, Heidelberg (1996). https://doi.org/10.1007/3-540-60865-6_44
14. Fernández-Caramés, T.M., Fraga-Lamas, P.: A review on the use of blockchain for the internet of things. IEEE Access **6**, 32979–33001 (2018)

15. Fionov, A.: Exploring covert channels in bitcoin transactions. In: 2019 International Multi-Conference on Engineering, Computer and Information Sciences (SIBIRCON), pp. 0059–0064. IEEE (2019)
16. Von zur Gathen, J.: Cryptoschool. Springer, Heidelberg (2015). https://doi.org/10.1007/978-3-662-48425-8
17. Henry, R., Herzberg, A., Kate, A.: Blockchain access privacy: challenges and directions. IEEE Secur. Priv. **16**(4), 38–45 (2018). https://doi.org/10.1109/MSP.2018.3111245
18. Hopper, N.J., Langford, J., von Ahn, L.: Provably secure steganography. In: Yung, M. (ed.) CRYPTO 2002. LNCS, vol. 2442, pp. 77–92. Springer, Heidelberg (2002). https://doi.org/10.1007/3-540-45708-9_6
19. Kucner, D., Kutylowski, M.: Stochastic kleptography detection. In: Public-Key Cryptography and Computational Number Theory, pp. 137–149 (2001)
20. Matzutt, R., Henze, M., Ziegeldorf, J.H., Hiller, J., Wehrle, K.: Thwarting unwanted blockchain content insertion. In: 2018 IEEE International Conference on Cloud Engineering (IC2E), pp. 364–370. IEEE (2018)
21. Matzutt, R., et al.: A quantitative analysis of the impact of arbitrary blockchain content on bitcoin. In: Meiklejohn, S., Sako, K. (eds.) FC 2018. LNCS, vol. 10957, pp. 420–438. Springer, Heidelberg (2018). https://doi.org/10.1007/978-3-662-58387-6_23
22. Mazurczyk, W., Caviglione, L.: Information hiding as a challenge for malware detection (2015). arXiv preprint arXiv:1504.04867
23. Meiklejohn, S., et al.: A fistful of bitcoins: characterizing payments among men with no names. In: Proceedings of the 2013 Conference on Internet Measurement Conference, pp. 127–140. ACM (2013)
24. Nakamoto, S.: Bitcoin: A peer-to-peer electronic cash system (2008). https://bitcoin.org/bitcoin.pdf
25. OpenSSL.org.: OpenSSL Cryptography and SSL/TLS Toolkit. https://www.openssl.org/
26. Partala, J.: Provably secure covert communication on blockchain. Cryptography **2**(3), 18 (2018)
27. Provos, N., Honeyman, P.: Hide and seek: an introduction to steganography. IEEE Secur. Priv. **1**(3), 32–44 (2003)
28. Puthal, D., Malik, N., Mohanty, S.P., Kougianos, E., Das, G.: Everything you wanted to know about the blockchain: its promise, components, processes, and problems. IEEE Consum. Electron. Mag. **7**(4), 6–14 (2018)
29. Radanović, I., Likić, R.: Opportunities for use of blockchain technology in medicine. Appl. Health Econ. Health Policy **16**(5), 583–590 (2018)
30. Raggo, M.T., Hosmer, C.: Data hiding: exposing concealed data in multimedia, operating systems, mobile devices and network protocols. Newnes (2012)
31. Richard III, G.G., Roussev, V.: Scalpel: a frugal, high performance file carver. In: DFRWS (2005)
32. Scott, B., Loonam, J., Kumar, V.: Exploring the rise of blockchain technology: towards distributed collaborative organizations. Strat. Change **26**(5), 423–428 (2017)
33. Shannon, C.E.: A mathematical theory of communication. Bell Syst. Tech. J. **27**(3), 379–423 (1948)
34. Spagnuolo, M., Maggi, F., Zanero, S.: BitIodine: extracting intelligence from the bitcoin network. In: Christin, N., Safavi-Naini, R. (eds.) FC 2014. LNCS, vol. 8437, pp. 457–468. Springer, Heidelberg (2014). https://doi.org/10.1007/978-3-662-45472-5_29

35. Stallings, W.: Cryptography and Network Security: Principles and Practice, 7th edn. Pearson, Upper Saddle River (2017)
36. Teşeleanu, G.: Subliminal hash channels. Cryptology ePrint Archive, Report 2019/1112 (2019)
37. Walker, J.: Ent: a pseudorandom number sequence test program. Software and documentation (2008). http://www.fourmilab.ch/random/
38. Williams, S.P.: Blockchain: The Next Everything. Scribner, New York (2019)
39. Wu, C.K.: Hash channels. Comput. Secur. **24**(8), 653–661 (2005)

Dynamic Group Key Agreement for Resource-constrained Devices Using Blockchains

Yaşar Berkay Taçyıldız[1], Orhan Ermiş[2]([⊠]), Gürkan Gür[3], and Fatih Alagöz[1]

[1] Department of Computer Engineering, Boğaziçi University, Istanbul, Turkey
{berkay.tacyildiz,fatih.alagoz}@boun.edu.tr
[2] EURECOM, Sophia Antipolis, France
orhan.ermis@eurecom.fr
[3] Zurich University of Applied Sciences (ZHAW), Winterthur, Switzerland
gueu@zhaw.ch

Abstract. Dynamic group key agreement (DGKA) protocols are one of the key security primitives to secure multiparty communications in decentralized and insecure environments while considering the instant changes in a communication group. However, with the ever-increasing number of connected devices, traditional DGKA protocols have performance challenges since each member in the group has to make several computationally intensive operations while verifying the keying materials to compute the resulting group key. To overcome this issue, we propose a new approach for DGKA protocols by utilizing Hyperledger Fabric framework as a blockchain platform. To this end, we migrate the communication and verification overhead of DGKA participants to the blockchain network in our developed scheme. This paradigm allows a flexible DGKA protocol that considers resource-constrained entities and trade-offs regarding distributed computation. According to our performance analysis, participants with low computing resources can efficiently utilize our protocol. Furthermore, we have demonstrated that our protocol has the same security features as other comparable protocols in the literature.

Keywords: Group key agreement · Blockchain · Hyperledger fabric · IoT

1 Introduction

The digitalization of daily life and human activities has become a reality via the emergence of more prevalent and high-performance communications and networking. With the advent of 5G networks, innovative and collective solutions which consist of different type of devices are now much more feasible. The envisaged use-cases and applications involve a huge number of devices and pervasive data sharing and dissemination such as massive Machine-Type Communications

© Springer Nature Switzerland AG 2020
J. Zhou et al. (Eds.): ACNS 2020 Workshops, LNCS 12418, pp. 58–76, 2020.
https://doi.org/10.1007/978-3-030-61638-0_4

(mMTC) and Multi-access Edge Computing (MEC) scenarios. Although some of these systems require ultra-reliable and real-time connectivity in rather preset conditions (e.g., telesurgery or industrial networks), many others require a dynamic environment where interaction between networked entities changes frequently and minor latency due to security functions can be tolerated (e.g., ad hoc data sharing or sensor-based monitoring scenarios). Moreover, IoT devices with low computing power and limited energy resources are expected to operate seamlessly and efficiently in future networks. In such systems, as the number of connected devices increases rapidly, decentralized and efficient secure communication frameworks are essential to meet the service requirements.

As a secure communication facilitator, group key agreement protocols where participants can agree on a common secret key in an insecure channel have gained significant importance. Starting with Diffie-Hellman [11] where two parties can agree on a secret key, several protocols have been developed which enable multiple parties to agree on a common key [18,19]. However, such protocols were mostly designed for static groups, where the members of the group do not change until the end of communication session. Therefore, if the members in the group change, the entire protocol should be executed from the beginning for all participants in the group. On the other hand, some protocols provide additional functionalities to handle that re-execution overhead. Such protocols are called Dynamic Group Key Agreement (DGKA) protocols [13,15–17,30]. Although DGKA protocols are more efficient compared to static ones, there exist some other several factors which affect their performance – the first one is the way of broadcasting key agreement parameters and the second being the validation of participant identities via verification of received parameters. To perform better in parameter distribution and verification stages, cluster-based approaches [14,17,21] and tree-based methods [13,20] have been proposed in the literature.

As a decentralized computing platform, blockchain technology has recently emerged starting with *Bitcoin* [24] as a monetary system based on cryptocurrency. The technology is later decoupled from cryptocurrencies and transformed into a wider domain with the concept of *Distributed Ledger Technology (DLT)* such as in Hyperledger Fabric (HF) [31]. Essentially, HF is a generic decentralized application development platform where transactions history is shared among peers as computation nodes in the network. DLT allows decentralization, greater transparency and easier auditability in a distributed setting.

In our work, we propose a dynamic group key agreement protocol called B-GKAP which is an improved version of KAP-PBC [16] protocol and integrates the HF platform to improve key computation performance while keeping important security properties of known DGKA protocols. The main rationale for using the blockchain technology is to offload computational burden in a trustworthy and distributed manner for resource-constrained environments. The HF provides capabilities, e.g., Fabric Channels, of a permission-based blockchain platform to realize this extension in an efficient and secure way. The relevant benefits of our implemented approach are shown with the complexity analysis carried out for different aspects such as communication and computation in our experiments.

Our main contributions in this work are as follows:

1. To reduce the number of parameter transmissions in the protocol, DGKA participants communicate with the blockchain network instead of communicating with each other in our proposal. In this way, the amount of network transmissions is decreased significantly.
2. We employ a blockchain application in HF to perform verification of group key agreement parameters. Therefore, instead of each participant performing verification of every other participant, we migrate those operations to the blockchain network. Our performance evaluation show that B-GKAP provides better results in terms of scalability when compared to conventional DGKA protocols.
3. We propose a detailed security analysis for B-GKAP by considering the the the well-known security attacks and properties. Our analysis shows that B-GKAP achieves the same level of security with the existing DGKA protocols. Furthermore, we extend our analysis for the use of blockchain network in group key computation based on the *honest-but-curious* security model.

The outline of this paper is as follows: in Sect. 3, we discuss the group key agreement solutions and blockchain platforms in the technical domain. Sect. 4 explains our proposed model B-GKAP in terms of its system model, protocol flow and functions. Then, in Sect. 5, we prove that our protocol has the same security features with known group key agreement protocols. In Sect. 6, we discuss performance of our model in terms of communication and computational costs, and simulation results. Finally, Sect. 8 summarizes our findings in this study, followed by a discussion of potential future work.

2   Preliminaries

In this section, we introduce general definitions and the security model of B-GKAP.

2.1   General Definitions

This section introduces the general definitions of B-GKAP based on [16].

Definition 1. *Participants:*

- *Each participant is an entity and is represented as U_i.*
- *Each participant U_i who fully follows the protocol is called as "honest participant".*
- *The participant list is represented as $\mathcal{U} = \langle U_1, U_2, \ldots, U_{N+M} \rangle$ which consists of two subgroups, network participants as $|\mathcal{U}_{net}| = M$, and group participants as $|\mathcal{U}_{grp}| = N$.*

$$\mathcal{U} = \mathcal{U}_{grp} \cup \mathcal{U}_{net}$$

- *The participant group $\mathcal{U}_{grp}$ is circular so that $U_{N+i} = U_i$ for some positive $1 \leqslant i \leqslant N$. The order of the participants is known by each participant.*

Definition 2. Public Parameters: *B-GKAP uses the following public parameters based on the definitions in [16]:*

- $p = 2q + 1$, *where both p and q are large prime numbers.*
- g *is a generator for $G_q = \{i^2 | i \in Z_p^*\}$, where G_q is a cyclic subgroup of quadratic residues in Z_p^*.*
- T *is the time-stamp against replay attack.*

Definition 3. Long-term Public Private Key Pair: *The protocol uses the following long-term key definitions based on [16]. Each entity in B-GKAP holds this key pair.*

- $x_i \in Z_q^*$ *is the private key and only the entity that holds the key knows it. This key is never shared with other entities in the network.*
- y_i *is the public key where $y_i = g^{x_i}$ mod p*

Since our solution is based on KAP-PBC in [16], we assume that long-term public keys of each participant are issued via a Certification Authority (CA). Before the transmission, each variable is signed with long-term private key. Thus, during signature verification stage, identities of the participants are authenticated.

Definition 4. Schnorr Signature Scheme: *Based on the definition in [27], a message M can be signed as $e, s = SS(x_i, y_i, M)$ and the signature products e, s can be verified using $SV(y_i(e, s), M) \stackrel{?}{=} True$. In these equations, SS stands for 'Schnorr Sign' and SV stands for 'Schnorr Verify'.*

Definition 5. Ledger Functions: *Each network participant U_i in $\mathcal{U}_{net}$ maintains its own blockchain ledger and has two functions called readLedger($\cdot$) and writeLedger($\cdot$). A variable x can be written to the ledger via writeLedger(x), and read from the ledger via $x = readLedger()$.*

2.2 Security Models

We consider *malicious* and *honest-but-curious* security models for the group participants and the network participants of B-GKAP, respectively. We assume that the potential entities for the malicious security model are as follows:

- *Group participants:* Participants that actively involve in the group key computation.
- *B-GKAP users:* Users that have valid certificates received from CA. They do not need to participate every group key computation.
- *Non-members:* Standard Internet users without a valid certificate.

Based on the entity definitions above, a DGKA protocol should provide security against the following threats: (i) violation of security properties (authentication, fault-tolerance and forward secrecy) (ii) security attacks (impersonation, eavesdropping and replay attacks) and (iii) secure dynamic group operations (backward and forward confidentiality properties). We refer the reader to Sect. 5 for further details.

On the other hand, B-GKAP differs from conventional DGKA protocols by including entities of HF into group key computation process. The main idea is to outsource the verification overhead of temporary public keys and exchanged secrets to the HF network for achieving a more scalable DGKA protocol. Network participants are powerful entities and they have access to all keying materials to compute the group key; in fact, these participants are computationally bounded by the B-GKAP algorithm and they cannot compute the group key. Therefore, we consider the *honest-but curious* security model for the network participants. Based on the definition in [26], we define *honest-but-curious* adversary for B-GKAP as follows:

Definition (Honest-But-Curious (HBC) Adversary). *The Honest-But-Curious (HBC) adversary is a legitimate network participant in B-GKAP that tries to learn the group key while honestly following the protocol [26].*

3   Related Work and Technical Background

In this section, we overview the literature with respect to DGKA protocols and blockchain technologies. In particular, we elaborate on the HF[1] platform which we have employed as the blockchain platform to implement and evaluate our protocol.

3.1   GKA Protocols

Diffie-Hellman key exchange protocol [11] is the first group key agreement protocol that is used for securing the communication among two parties using a common key computed by these participants. Later, the concept of two-party secure communication was extended by Ingamarsson et al. in [18] to multi-party setting. In addition, the protocol in [6] is also accepted as a pioneering work regarding the key agreement protocol research with the proposed efficient group key computation. Nevertheless, these protocols were designed specifically for static groups, which means any change in the set of communicating parties requires the re-execution of the group key agreement protocol for all communicating participants. In this work, our main focus is on the DGKA protocols that use some auxiliary functions to update the group key without re-executing the protocol from scratch for all participants as elaborated in [2, 10, 12, 13, 15–17, 28, 32]. These protocols have many application areas such as conference communication [15], secure file sharing systems [16], and secure communication in Mobile Ad Hoc Networks (MANETs) [17]. Although the listed protocols have proposed efficient group key computation approaches, novel solutions are necessary to overcome the overhead of verification operations during group key computation while dealing with large groups and resource-constrained devices.

3.2   HF Platform

HF is a permissioned blockchain platform that only allows identified participants [1]. Thus, with the identification of the network modules, Byzantine Fault Tolerant (BFT) [8] or Crash Fault Tolerant (CFT) [25] consensus protocols can be utilized. Another important feature of HF is that most of the HF components are designed to be modular such as Membership Service Provider (MSP) and consensus protocol. This modular

---

[1] https://www.hyperledger.org/projects/fabric.

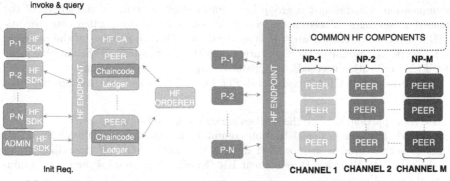

(a) B-GKAP block diagram.   (b) B-GKAP model. (P: Group Participant
                                       NP: Network Participant)

Fig. 1. B-GKAP block diagram and model.

design is made possible by its novel execute-order-validate architecture. In other applications [7,24], order-execute architecture is utilized where transactions are first ordered via a consensus protocol, and then they are executed by all peers sequentially. On the other hand, in HF, execution of the transactions is performed first to allow running non-deterministic applications and the ordering phase is separated from the validation step to isolate consensus logic from the peers. Therefore, the transactions can run in parallel without the necessity to keep the order. After the consensus is provided by ordering state, the final state of the transaction can be applied by all nodes individually. Therefore, in this work, our main motivation is to employ HF platform to perform necessary verification operations for increasing the group key computation performance. Accordingly, we propose an improved dynamic group key agreement protocol called B-GKAP based of KAP-PBC [16] protocol by integrating the HF platform. The most important feature of the proposed protocols is to improve the key computation performance particularly for the communication cost while providing the same security level with the existing protocols in the literature.

4   B-GKAP: Blockchain-Based Group Key Agreement Protocol

In this section, we introduce our Blockchain based Group Key Agreement Protocol (B-GKAP) which is deployed on HF as a blockchain platform. In the first section, we provide a system overview that explains the positioning of the HF components. Then, we introduce B-GKAP in more details.

4.1   System Overview

B-GKAP is based on the Key Agreement Protocol with Partial Backward Confidentiality, namely KAP-PBC [16], but extends and improves its performance with HF platform. Additionally, in B-GKAP, we migrate the communication among participants to communication between participants and the network, which in return reduces the communication cost during the group key computation in terms of the length of the transmitted messages. Moreover, to verify the variables of the participants, we utilize HF chaincodes. When a variable is received as an invoke request by the network, the chaincode first performs the verification operation depending on the variable type. Then if the verification succeeds, the chaincode approves the operation.

The overview of B-GKAP is shown in Fig 1a, which consists of the following main components:

1. B-GKAP participants are the entities which compute the group key.
2. B-GKAP admin sends initialization command to start up the HF platform and setup initial variables as specified in Sect. 2.1. Both B-GKAP participants and admin use HF Software Development Kit (SDK) which enables them to communicate with the network.
3. The peers are responsible for simulating incoming transactions by utilizing B-GKAP chaincode. Additionally, each peer maintains a blockchain ledger and latest ledger state. We have utilized HF ledger to store B-GKAP parameters.
4. HF Endpoint is a logical endpoint which can correspond peers or orderers.
5. B-GKAP Chaincode handles all ledger read-write requests of the participants, and performs the necessary verification operations.
6. HF Orderer performs the ordering of the produced transaction output sets as a block of transactions and it disseminates to all HF peers. Then peers update their ledger states.
7. HF CA maintains the identities of the HF components and B-GKAP participants.

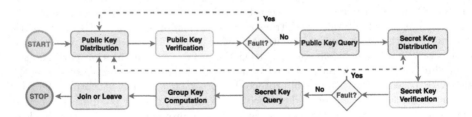

Fig. 2. B-GKAP flowchart

4.2 B-GKAP Protocol

As shown in Fig. 2, first, each participant $U_i \in \mathcal{U}$ executes *Public Key Distribution* step to distribute temporary public keys. Then, each network participant executes *Public Key Verification* and *Fault Correction* steps to remove dishonest participants from the group. Later on, remaining honest participants execute *Public Key Query* to fetch the temporary public key of the next participant in the group. Once this step is completed, each participant executes the *Secret Key Distribution* to send the secret keys to the network participants. Afterward, network participants perform *Secret Key Verification* and *Fault Correction* to exclude malicious participants from the group. Finally, each participant performs *Secret Key Query* and *Group Key Computation* steps to compute the common group key. Additionally, when a new participant joins the group or leaves the group, *Participant Join* or *Participant Leave* steps can be executed.

As illustrated in Fig. 1b, there are network participants which are not involved in the group key computation phase. Instead, they produce B-GKAP parameters except for the secret key. Therefore, network participants can verify the temporary public and secret keys of the participants who compute the group key. Each network participant has multiple peers and an isolated ledger via HF channels. In this way, secret key variables can be stored and validated separately by each network participant.

4.3 B-GKAP Protocol Steps

In this section, we give details of the protocol steps.

Public Key Distribution (sendPK($\cdot$)). *Each participant $U_t \in U$ executes the following to distribute temporary public keys. Group participants $U_i \in U_{grp}$ distribute their temporary public keys to each network participant $U_j \in U_{net}$.*

> *1: randomly select $t \in Z_q^*$*
> *2: $\omega = g^t mod p$*
> *3: Sign ω: $e, s = SS(x, y, \omega)$*
> *4: Send the message $M = \{\omega, e, s, T\}$*

Public Key Verification (verifyPK($\cdot$)). *Each network participant $U_j \in U_{net}$ executes the following to verify temporary public key of each group participant $U_i \in U_{grp}$. According to verification result, the key is written to the ledger of U_j.*

> *1: **for all** $U_i \in U_{grp}$ **do***
> *2:   Check the timestamp T*
> *3:   **if** $SV(y_i, (e_{1,i}, s_{1,i}), \omega_i)$ **then***
> *4:   writeLedger(ω_i)*
> *5:   **end if***
> *6: **end for***

Fault Correction (faultCorr($\cdot$)). *Each network participant $U_j \in U_{net}$ performs the following to remove any group participant $U_i \in U_{grp}$ whose verification of its temporary public key or secret key fails.*

> *1: **for all** $U_i \in U_{grp}$ **do***
> *2:   **if** U_i is faulty **then***
> *3: U_i is removed from the participant group, $U' = U - U_i$*
> *4:   Execute participantLeave($\cdot$)*
> *5:   **end if***
> *6: **end for***

Public Key Query (queryPK($\cdot$)). *In this step, each group participant $U_i \in U_{grp}$, requests for temporary public key of next group participant U_{i+1} in the group from the target network participant $U_j \in U_{net}$ (the selection of U_j is determined in a way to ensure equal distribution of workload).*

U_j *performs the following:*

 1: $\omega_{i+1} = readLedger()$
 2: *Sign temporary public key of* U_{i+1}, $e_j, s_j = SS(y_j, x_j, \omega_{i+1})$
 3: *Send message to* U_i, $M = (\omega_{i+1}, e_j, s_j, T)$

U_i *performs the following:*

 1: *Receive the message* M
 2: *Check timestamp* T
 3: *Verify signature of* U_j: $SV(y_j, (e_j, s_j), \omega_{i+1})$

Secret Key Distribution (sendSK($\cdot$)). *Each group participant* $U_i \in \mathcal{U}_{grp}$ *performs the following to generate and distribute secret key* (CK_i) *to the target network participant* $U_j \in \mathcal{U}_{net}$ *(the selection of* U_j *is determined in a way to ensure equal distribution of secret keys).*

 1: *Generate* CK_i: $CK_i = \omega_{(i+1)}^{t_i} \mod p = g^{t_i t_{i+1}} \mod p$
 2: *Randomly select an integer* $a \in Z_q^*$
 3: $k = (\omega_j^a \bmod p) \mod q$
 4: *Randomly select a line* $L(x)$, $L(x) = xc_i + CK_i \mod q$, $c_i = g^a \mod p$
 5: $d_i = L(k) \mod q$
 6: $d_i' = k \oplus d_i$
 7: $e_{2,i}, s_{2,i} = SS(x_i, y_i, CK_i)$
 8: *Send the message* $M = \{s_{2,i}, e_{2,i}, c_i, d_i', T\}$

Secret Key Verification (verifySK($\cdot$)). *Each network participant* $U_j \in \mathcal{U}_{net}$ *performs following to verify secret keys of group participants* $U_i \in \mathcal{U}_{grp}$.

 1: **for all** $U_i \in \mathcal{U}_{grp}$ **do**
 2:     *Receive message* $M = \{s_{2,i}, e_{2,i}, c_i, d_i', T\}$
 3:     *Recover* CK_i *and check* T
 4:     $k = (c_i^{t_j} \mod p) \mod q$
 5:     $d = d_i' \oplus k$
 6:     $CK_i = d - c_i * k \mod q$
 7:     *Check the signature of* U_i
 8:     **if** $SV(y_i, (e_{2,i}, s_{2,i}), CK_i)$ **then**
 9:         $writeLedger(CK_i)$
10:     **end if**
11: **end for**

Secret Key Query (querySK($\cdot$)). *After the fault correction step, each group participant* $U_i \in \mathcal{U}_{grp}$ *performs following to query secret keys from each network participant* $U_j \in \mathcal{U}_{net}$ $(CK_{1...N} = CK_1 || CK_2 || \ldots || CK_N)$.

U_j performs the following:

1: Randomly select an integer $a \in Z_q^*$
2: $c_j = g^a \mod p$
3: $k_i = (\omega_i^a \bmod p) \bmod q$
4: **for all** $U_k \in \mathcal{U}_{grp} - U_i$ **do**
5:     Randomly select a line $L(x) = xc_j + CK_k \mod q$
6:     $d_k = L(k_i) \mod q$
7:     $d_k' = k_i \oplus d_k$
8: **end for**
9: Sign $CK_{1...N}$: $e_{2,j}, s_{2,j} = SS(x_j, y_j, CK_{1...N})$
10: Send $M = \{s_{2,j}, e_{2,j}, c_j, \{d_1', d_2', \ldots, d_N'\}, T\}$

U_i performs the following:

1: $k_i = (c_j^{t_i} \mod p) \mod q$
2: **for all** $U_k \in \mathcal{U}_{grp} - U_i$ **do**
3:     $d_k = d_k' \oplus k_i$
4:     $CK_k = d_k - c_j * k_i \mod q$
5: **end for**
6: Check timestamp T
7: Check the signature of U_j: $SV(y_j, (e_{2,j}, s_{2,j}), CK_{1...N})$

Group Key Computation (compute($\cdot$)). Each group participant $U_i \in \mathcal{U}_{grp}$, computes the group key.

1: **for all** $U_i \in \mathcal{U}_{grp}$ **do**
2:     $CK = ((CK_1 CK_2 \cdots CK_{|\mathcal{U}_{grp}|}) \bmod p) \bmod q = (g^{t_1 t_2 + t_2 t_3 + \ldots + t_{n-1} t_n + t_n t_1} \bmod p) \bmod q$
3: **end for**

Participant Join (join($\cdot$)). Let $U_i \in \{U_{N+1}, U_{N+2}, \ldots, U_{N+K}\}$ be the participant that wants to join the group $U_{grp} = \{U_1, U_2, \ldots, U_N\}$. The join operations operate as follows:

1: **if** $U_i \in \{U_N, U_{N+1}, \ldots, U_{N+K}\}$ **then**
2:     U_i performs queryPK($\cdot$) and querySK($\cdot$)
3:     U_i performs sendPK($\cdot$)
4:     Network participants perform faultCorr($\cdot$)
5:     U_{i-1} performs sendSK($\cdot$)
6:     Network participants perform faultCorr($\cdot$)
7: **end if**
8: **for all** $U_i \in \{U_1, U_2, \ldots, U_{N+K}\}$ **do**
9:     U_i performs querySK($\cdot$) and compute($\cdot$) functions
10: **end for**

Participant Leave (leave($\cdot$)). Let $U'_{grp} = \{U_i, U_{i+1}, ..., U_{i+K}\}$, where $K < N$, be the set of leaving participants from U_{grp}. The leave operations operate as follows:

1: **if** $|U_{grp}| - |U'_{grp}| < 2$ **then**
2:     The group key computation is terminated
3: **end if**
4: **for each** leaving participant $U_j \subset U'_{grp}$ **do**
5:     non-leaving participant(s) $U_{j-1} \in U_{grp} - U'_{grp}$, performs sendPK($\cdot$)
6:     Network participants perform faultCorr($\cdot$)
7:     U_{j-1} and $U_{j-2} \in U_{grp} - U'_{grp}$ perform sendSK($\cdot$)
8:     Network participants perform faultCorr($\cdot$)
9: **end for**
10: **for all** $U_i \in U_{grp} - U'_{grp}$ **do**
11:     U_i performs querySK($\cdot$) and compute($\cdot$)
12: **end for**

---

5   Security Analysis

In this section, we provide a security analysis of B-GKAP. We consider the basic security properties as well as potential attacks for group key agreement protocols for our analysis.

5.1   Security Properties of GKA Protocols

In this section, we analyze B-GKAP with respect to the the basic security properties of group key agreement protocols such as authentication, fault tolerance and forward secrecy.

Authentication: This property is used for validating the identities of participants during the execution of the protocol. In B-GKAP, as an initial authentication mechanism, we assume that all participants are pre-identified with HF CA [31]. As a requirement of interacting with HF Network, all participants have to use TLS v1.3[2] certificate to provide identification. The TLS certificate is created by HF Admin prior to the network initialization. For the second level of authentication mechanism, long-term key pairs of the participants are used. All long-term public keys of the participants must be signed by a trusted CA. During variable exchange between the participants and the network, all message payloads is signed with the long-term private key of the sender entity. Eventually, receiving entity verifies the signature of the payload by sender's long-term public key using Schnorr's signature [27].

Fault Tolerance: In the course of group key agreement processes, malicious participants should be immediately detected and removed from the group. In B-GKAP, detection and elimination of faulty participants occurs during the execution of $verifyPK(\cdot)$, $verifySK(\cdot)$ and $faultCorr(\cdot)$ functions. If a malicious participant is detected in $verifyPK(\cdot)$ or $verifySK(\cdot)$ functions, the key of the malicious participant is not written to the ledger. Later, the $faultCorr(\cdot)$ function is used for removing this participant from the group.

---

[2] https://tools.ietf.org/html/rfc8446.

Forward Secrecy: This property is used for protecting the previous and subsequent group keys against the compromise of long-term private keys of participants in the group. Therefore, in B-GKAP, the long-term key pairs of participants are only used to authenticate these participants. Additionally, each entity in B-GKAP generates a new temporary public-private key pair using $sendPK(\cdot)$ function for each session. Thus, B-GKAP provides the forward secrecy property.

5.2   Protection Against Security Attacks

In this section, we provide the security analysis of B-GKAP against impersonation, eavesdropping and replay attacks.

Impersonation Attack: As mentioned in Sect. 2.2, the motivation of the impersonation attack is to take place of any group participant during the protocol execution. To do so, an attacker needs to be able to generate the signature of that entity. Since B-GKAP uses the Schnorr signature scheme [27] as an authentication mechanism and, as stated in [3] and [23], the Schnorr signature is secure against impersonation attacks, B-GKAP also provides security against the impersonation attack.

Eavesdropping Attack: The goal of the eavesdropping attack in group key agreement protocols is to capture the computed group key by eavesdropping the communication channels among entities. In order to generate a group key, the attacker must obtain secret keys (CK_i) of all participants $(CK_1, \ldots, CK_N)$. In B-GKAP, entities exchange secret keys in $sendSK(\cdot)$ and $querySK(\cdot)$ functions. In those functions, all secret key values are extracted using c, d' variables of the sender and temporary private key (t) of the receiver. Since only the participants in the key agreement group $\mathcal{U}$ knows their temporary private key (t), to compute $k = (c^t modp)$ equation, attacker should try to extract t_j from $\omega_j = g^{t_j} modp$ for each participant U_j in $\mathcal{U}$. Therefore, because solving this equation is as hard as the discrete logarithm problem, B-GKAP is secure against eavesdropping attack. Furthermore, as proved in [16] (Theorem 1), KAP-PBC is secure under the Decisional Diffie-Hellman Problem. Since B-GKAP uses the same functions ($sendSK(\cdot)$ and $querySK(\cdot)$) while distributing the short-term public keys and secret keys, it is also secure under the Decisional Diffie-Hellman Problem.

Replay Attack: During the communication between the B-GKAP entities, an attacker might capture and re-transmit messages in the network to degrade the availability of recipient parties such as in Distributed Denial-of-Service (DDoS) attack. Therefore, to provide a protection against such attacks, we also append timestamp variable (T) into the communication messages among participants during the execution of the protocol.

5.3   Security of Join and Leave Operations

Dynamic group operations enable group key agreement protocols to be more efficient during re-generation of group keys. In order to overcome security weaknesses stated in [22], a protocol must ensure forward and backward confidentiality properties. Forward confidentiality property assures that further group keys cannot be computed by a participant who has left the group. Conversely, backward confidentiality feature warrants that previous group keys cannot be computed by recently joined participants. In the following sections, we prove that Leave and Join operations in B-GKAP provide the same security features as [16] assures.

Prior to applying dynamic group operations, let the participant group be $\mathcal{U}_{grp} = \{U_1, U_2, U_3, \ldots, U_N\}$ and the group key be:

$$CK = ((g^{t_1 t_2 + \cdots + t_{i-1} t_i + t_i t_{i+1} + \cdots + t_N t_1}) modp) modq)$$

Lemma 1. *Under the difficulty of discrete logarithm problem, join operation does not violate backward confidentiality.*

Proof. The participant U_N and joining participants should run $join(\cdot)$ algorithm. Let the joining participants be $U' = U_{N+1}, U_{N+2}, \ldots, U_{N+k}$ and the new group key be $CK' = ((g^{t_1 t_2 + \cdots + t_{N-1} t'_N + t'_N t_{N+1} + \cdots + t_{N+k} t_1}) modp) modq$. We assume that any joining participant with malicious intent has the previous message exchanged during the computation of CK. In order to compute the previous group key, the malicious participant should obtain t_N from either using $g^{t_{N-1} t_N}$ or $g^{t_N t_1}$, which is as hard as solving the discrete logarithm problem. Thus, B-GKAP provides backward confidentiality under the difficulty of discrete logarithm problem.

Lemma 2. *Under the difficulty of discrete logarithm problem, leave operation does not violate forward confidentiality.*

Proof. Let $\mathcal{U}' = U_i, U_{i+1}, U_{i+2}, \ldots U_{i+k}$ be leaving participants where $U' \subseteq U$. As given in function $leave(\cdot)$ (Sect. 4.3), when participants in $\mathcal{U}'$ leaves the group, the group key is re-computed as $CK' = ((g^{t_1 t_2 + \cdots + t_{i-2} t'_{i-1} + t'_{i-1} t_{i+k+1} \cdots + t_N t_1}) modp) modq$. If there exist some malicious participants in the leaving ones and they want to compute the new group key CK' using the old keying materials, they have to obtain t'_{i-1} by either using $g^{t_{i-2} t'_{i-1}}$ or $g^{t'_{i-1} t_{i+k+1}}$. Since solving these equations is as hard as solving the discrete logarithm problem, B-GKAP provides forward confidentiality property.

5.4   Security of B-GKAP Hyperledger Fabric Network

In B-GKAP, the network participants store all keying material exhanged by the group participants. Such participants are involved in the execution of B-GKAP except for the secret key generation and key computation steps. During the network initialization step ($sendPK(\cdot)$), each network participant U_m network entities generate temporary public-private key pair (t_m, ω_m). Participants use these public keys to encrypt their secret keys before the submission. Thus, the network can unveil the secret keys of the participants using its temporary private key (t_m). Additionally, the network participants also hold its own long-term key pair (x_m, y_m). These keys are used for signing the protocol variables that are sent to the participants. Hence, participants ensure that they are receiving variables from a trusted entity. Moreover, the secret key verification step is distributed among the network entities. Since the ledger of each entity is isolated via the Fabric channels, the secret keys of the participants are also isolated[3]. Therefore, as described in Sect. 2.2, we consider the *honest-but-curious* security model for network participants. Although they have the keying material to compute the group key, all the network entities should work cooperatively to compute the key.

Furthermore, HF platform provides storage immutability via blockchain ledgers. The ledger is distributed among peers, and to change the ledger data, a subset of peers

---

[3] https://developer.ibm.com/tutorials/cl-blockchain-private-confidential-transactions-hyperledger-fabric-zero-knowledge-proof/.

needs to generate the same output. This feature is forced by endorsement policies. Finally, our design guarantees that even if a peer is compromised or failed, the system remains operational.

In B-GKAP protocol, prior to secret key distribution, identities of network participants are verified via $U_j \in \mathcal{U}_{network}$, $SV(y_j, e_{2,j}, s_{2,j}, \omega_j) \neq false$, and secret key CK_i of each participant $U_i \in \mathcal{U}_{grp}$ is encrypted via temporary public key ω_j of the network participant $U_j \in \mathcal{U}_{net}$. Thus, network participants can only receive intended parameters which are $\omega_i, s_i, e_i, d_i', c_i$ for $U_i \in \mathcal{U}_{grp}$. Moreover, in HF, the only way to interact with the ledger is via Fabric chaincodes. Because implemented chaincode has defined a set of functionality and is shared among the peers, the network has no other choice but to follow the B-GKAP protocol. Given these properties, B-GKAP fits the HBC adversary model.

6 Performance Analysis

In this section, communication cost and computational cost complexity of B-GKAP are analyzed and simulation results are presented. During our analysis, we only consider the participants which compute the group key. All simulations were carried out on a machine of Intel Core Broadwell Processor (2.5GHz x 8 cores), L1 Cache 32KB, L2 Cache 4MB, L3 Cache 16MB, and 32GB RAM. We have used Docker Engine v18.06.1-ce-mac73[4] and Hyperledger Fabric v1.4.3[5]. For both B-GKAP chaincode and B-GKAP participant implementations, we have used Go programming language v1.13.3[6]. Moreover, we have utilized the same environment for the implementation of other protocols for performance comparison.

6.1 Communication Cost Complexity $\mathcal{C}_t$

B-GKAP Functions: In B-GKAP, variable transmission occurs between participants $(U_i \in \mathcal{U}_{grp})$ and network participants $(U_j \in \mathcal{U}_{net})$. Since all transmitted variables are modular base of p and q, length of a variable is equal to its modular base. Table 1 indicates network transmission length of each function in B-GKAP.

Table 1. Transmission length of each B-GKAP function in bits.

Function	Transmission length
$sendPK(\cdot)$	$(2q + p)$
$queryPK(\cdot)$	$(2q + p)$
$sendSK(\cdot)$	$(3q + p)$
$querySK(\cdot)$	$(N + 1)q + p$

---

[4] https://docs.docker.com/engine/.
[5] https://hyperledger-fabric.readthedocs.io/.
[6] https://golang.org/project/.

Table 2. Computational and communication complexities for N participants.

Protocol	$C_c \times T_{exp}$	C_t
Protocol in [13]	$\leq O(\log_3 N)$	-
Protocol in [29]	$O(N)$	$(N+2)|q| + 4|p|$
Protocol in [15]	$O(N)$	$(N+2)|q| + 4|p|$
GKAP-MANET [17]	$O(N)$	$2|q| + 5|p|$
KAP-PBC [16]	$O(N)$	$(N+4)|q| + 2|p|$
B-GKAP	$O(1)$	$5|q| + 2|p|$

Key Computation: During key computation, several variable transmissions between participants and the network occur. For each participant $U_i \in \mathcal{U}_{grp}$, network transmissions are performed in $sendPK(\cdot)$ and $sendSK(\cdot)$ functions. In total, for the number of network participants M, $|(2M+3)q + (M+1)p|$ bits are transmitted for each DGKA participant. Therefore communication complexity of key computation is $C_t = O(M)$.

Join Operation: For the join operation, when K participants join the group, $K+1$ participants perform network transmission in $sendPK(\cdot)$ function, and $K+2$ participants perform network transmission in $sendSK(\cdot)$. In total, for K joining participants, $|(2M(K+1) + 3K + 6)q + (M + K + 2)p|$ bits are transmitted.

Leave Operation: In the leave operation, for the leaving participant U_i, participant U_{i-1} executes $sendPK(\cdot)$. Moreover, participants U_{i-1} and U_{i-2} execute $sendSK(\cdot)$. Therefore, $|(2M+6)q + (M+2)p|$ bits are transmitted.

6.2   Computational Cost Complexity C_c

In computational cost analysis, we consider modular exponential operations as the principal factor while calculating our results. The time cost of these operations can be stated as $T_{exp} = O(x^y \bmod z)$. In B-GKAP, group participants $U_i \in \mathcal{U}_{grp}$ performs verification for only network participants $U_j \in \mathcal{U}_{net}$. If we consider that M is negligible against the participant count N, the computational cost complexity of group key computation, join and leave operations is $C_c = O(1)T_{exp}$.

7   Discussion on the Performance of B-GKAP

In this section, we compare the communication cost and computational cost complexities of B-GKAP with some well-known GKA protocols by considering the total computational and communication costs of a single participant as the benchmark.

Comparison for the computational and communications costs of B-GKAP with other well-known dynamic group key agreement protocols [13,15–17,29] is given in Table 2. For instance, GKAP-MANET protocol relies on the most efficient group key agreement protocol proposed by Burmester and Desmedt (BD) in [6]. BD protocol has many other variants that improve the security of the original work against active attacks while achieving a constant round of communication and less computational overhead as introduced in Katz-Yung protocol [19]. However, such static protocols are computationally more expensive than the dynamic ones. Therefore, we only compare B-GKAP with other dynamic group key agreement protocols.

As shown in Table 2, B-GKAP is more efficient than most of the protocols regarding the communication and computational complexities for each participant. In terms of total communication complexity, the other protocols perform network transmission to every other participant in the key agreement group. On the other hand, B-GKAP participants only transmit messages to a limited number of network participants. Moreover, in B-GKAP, participants only perform verification for the network participants instead of performing verification for incoming parameters from other participants. As a cost of utilizing HF SDK, the lightweight client code in a B-GKAP participant needs to establish several connections to a limited number of HF peers and orderers for data transmissions, which is a slight additional overhead compared to the mentioned protocols. Moreover, this number becomes more negligible when the number of participants increases. Given these reasons, the overhead for participants in B-GKAP is significantly lower than counterparts. Due to these complexity advantages compared to other protocols, B-GKAP can be a good candidate for resource-constrained devices.

As a case study, we further investigate B-GKAP performance and compare it to KAP-PBC counterpart as a baseline scheme. Figure 3 illustrates the group key computation performance of KAP-PBC and B-GKAP for N group participants. As the orderer parameters, we set batch size as N/M for B-GKAP where M is number of network participants and batch timeout as five seconds. Since the solution is designed for several network participants such as large organizations, this simulation is performed with one and two network participants, which are represented as B-GKAP and B-GKAP$^+$ respectively. Additionally, each network participant maintains two HF peers.

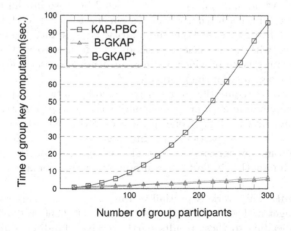

Fig. 3. B-GKAP and conventional model comparison.

The results show that, group key computation time of the conventional method increases exponentially as the participant count increases. In contrary, group key computation of B-GKAP increases linearly. First, the communication cost complexity of KAP-PBC is $O(N^2)$ whereas in B-GKAP, the communication cost complexity is $O(N)$. For the computational cost complexity, B-GKAP outperforms KAP-PBC with its constant computational cost $O(1)$. The reason of slight performance difference between B-GKAP and B-GKAP$^+$ is that in B-GKAP$^+$, the orderer needs to process submitted public variables in two transaction blocks. Moreover, in our simulations, we set batch size such that the HF network can process without an issue. For more participants, the network should process the transactions for multiple batches, which would affect the performance slightly.

8   Conclusion

In this study, we present B-GKAP which employs HF blockchain platform to partially offload the group key computation and thus alleviate the performance burden for resource-constrained environments. Our approach is specifically geared towards non-real-time scenarios such as ad hoc data sharing or group communications considering potential latency due to blockchain operations, albeit being minimal. With our protocol, the computation overhead of the group key agreement participants is decreased significantly by migrating the verification of the distributed parameters to the network participants. Thus, participants with low computation power and energy resource can conveniently adopt our GKA protocol. Additionally, we have reduced the number of network transmissions for group key computation, leave and join operations. Hence, for network environments such as connected IoT devices or edge network nodes where participant group changes frequently, our solution provides more efficient dynamic operations. Furthermore, we have distributed secret keys of the participants among the network participants via Fabric Channels. In this way, malicious network participants cannot generate group keys without colluding.

HF platform provides immutable storage property for stored variables via blockchain ledger. Additionally, in HF, not only valid but also invalid transactions are stored in the ledger. This feature makes our system auditable for further investigations. Another important feature of HF is its modularity. For instance, its consensus protocol can be replaced with more efficient methods as a future work. Moreover, with its modular membership service provider, various authentication schemes can be utilized depending on the usage area of the protocol.

Furthermore, to overcome the problem of colluding network participants, Fabric chaincode runtime environment, and ledger storage can be transferred to a Trusted Execution Environment (TEE) [5]. Consequently, even the network participants cannot access to secret keys of the participants. Investigation of the applicability of post-quantum secure group key agreement protocols such as [4,9] together with blockchain platforms can be an another important future work for this domain.

Acknowledgment. This work is partially supported by the Turkish Directorate of Strategy and Budget under the TAM Project number DPT2007K120610.

The research leading to these results partly received funding from the European Union's Horizon 2020 research and innovation programme under grant agreement no 871808 (5G PPP project INSPIRE-5Gplus). The paper reflects only the authors' views. The Commission is not responsible for any use that may be made of the information it contains.

References

1. Hyperledger Fabric. https://www.hyperledger.org/projects/fabric. Accessed 30 September 2019
2. Alwen, J., et al.: Keep the dirt: tainted treekem, adaptively and actively secure continuous group key agreement. Cryptology ePrint Archive, Report 2019/1489 (2019). https://eprint.iacr.org/2019/1489
3. Bellare, M., Palacio, A.: GQ and schnorr identification schemes: proofs of security against impersonation under active and concurrent attacks. In: Yung, M. (ed.) CRYPTO 2002. LNCS, vol. 2442, pp. 162–177. Springer, Heidelberg (2002). https://doi.org/10.1007/3-540-45708-9_11
4. Bobrysheva, J., Zapechnikov, S.: Post-quantum group key agreement scheme. Cryptology ePrint Archive, Report 2020/873 (2020). https://eprint.iacr.org/2020/873
5. Brandenburger, M., Cachin, C., Kapitza, R., Sorniotti, A.: Blockchain and trusted computing: problems, pitfalls, and a solution for hyperledger fabric. arXiv e-prints arXiv:1805.08541, May 2018
6. Burmester, M., Desmedt, Y.: A secure and efficient conference key distribution system. In: De Santis, A. (ed.) EUROCRYPT 1994. LNCS, vol. 950, pp. 275–286. Springer, Heidelberg (1995). https://doi.org/10.1007/BFb0053443
7. Buterin, V.: A next-generation smart contract and decentralized application platforme. https://github.com/ethereum/wiki/wiki/White-Paper
8. Castro, M., Liskov, B.: Practical byzantine fault tolerance and proactive recovery. ACM Trans. Comput. Syst. (TOCS) 20(4), 398–461 (2002)
9. Choi, R., Hong, D., Han, S., Baek, S., Kang, W., Kim, K.: Design and implementation of constant-round dynamic group key exchange from rlwe. IEEE Access 8, 94610–94630 (2020)
10. Chuang, Y.H., Tseng, Y.M.: An efficient dynamic group key agreement protocol for imbalanced wireless networks. Int. J. Net. Man. 20, 167–180 (2010)
11. Diffie, W., Hellman, M.: New directions in cryptography. IEEE Trans. Inform. Theor. 22, 644–654 (1976). https://doi.org/10.1109/TIT.1976.1055638
12. Dutta, R., Barua, R.: Constant round dynamic group key agreement. In: Zhou, J., Lopez, J., Deng, R.H., Bao, F. (eds.) Information Security (2005)
13. Dutta, R., Barua, R.: Dynamic group key agreement in tree-based setting. In: Boyd, C., González Nieto, J.M. (eds.) Information Security and Privacy, pp. 101–112. Springer, Berlin Heidelberg, Berlin, Heidelberg (2005)
14. Dutta, R., Dowling, T.: Secure and efficient group key agreements for cluster based networks. In: Gavrilova, M.L., Tan, C.J.K., Moreno, E.D. (eds.) Transactions on Computational Science IV. LNCS, vol. 5430, pp. 87–116. Springer, Heidelberg (2009). https://doi.org/10.1007/978-3-642-01004-0_6
15. Ermiş, O., Bahtiyar, Ş., Anarim, E., Çağlayan, U.: An improved conference-key agreement protocol for dynamic groups with efficient fault correction. Secur. Commun. Netw. 8(7), 1347–1359 (2015)
16. Ermiş, O., Bahtiyar, Ş., Anarim, E., Çağlayan, U.: A key agreement protocol with partial backward confidentiality. Comput. Netw. 129, 159–177 (2017)
17. Ermiş, O., Bahtiyar, Ş., Anarim, E., Çağlayan, U.: A secure and efficient group key agreement approach for mobile ad hoc networks. Ad Hoc Netw. 67, 24–39 (2017)
18. Ingemarsson, I., Tang, D., Wong, C.: A conference key distribution system. IEEE Trans. Inform. Theor. 28, 714–719 (1982)

19. Katz, J., Yung, M.: Scalable protocols for authenticated group key exchange. J. Cryptol. **20**(1), 85–113 (2007)
20. Kim, Y., Perrig, A., Tsudik, G.: Tree-based group key agreement. ACM Trans. Inform. Syst. Secur. **7**(1), 60–96 (2004)
21. Konstantinou, E.: Cluster-based group key agreement for wireless ad hoc networks. In: 2008 Third International Conference on Availability, Reliability and Security, pp. 550–557, March 2008. https://doi.org/10.1109/ARES.2008.106
22. Lee, S., Kim, J., Hong, S.: Security weakness of Tseng's fault-tolerant conference key agreement protocol. J. Syst. Softw. **82**, 1163–1167 (2009)
23. Morita, H., Schuldt, J.C.N., Matsuda, T., Hanaoka, G., Iwata, T.: On the security of the schnorr signature scheme and DSA against related-key attacks. In: Kwon, S., Yun, A. (eds.) ICISC 2015. LNCS, vol. 9558, pp. 20–35. Springer, Cham (2016). https://doi.org/10.1007/978-3-319-30840-1_2
24. Nakamoto, S.: Bitcoin: a peer-to-peer electronic cash system. Technical report, Manubot (2008)
25. Ongaro, D., Ousterhout, J.: In search of an understandable consensus algorithm. In: 2014 USENIX Annual Technical Conference (ATC), pp. 305–319 (2014)
26. Paverd, A., Martin, A., Brown, I.: Modelling and automatically analysing privacy properties for honest-but-curious adversaries. Uni. of Oxford, Technical report (2014)
27. Schnorr, C.P.: Efficient identification and signatures for smart cards. In: Quisquater, J.J., Vandewalle, J. (eds.) EUROCRYPT 1989. LNCS, vol. 434, pp. 688–689. Springer, Heidelberg (1990). https://doi.org/10.1007/3-540-46885-4_68
28. Steiner, M., Tsudik, G., Waidner, M.: Key agreement in dynamic peer groups. IEEE Trans. Parallel Distrib. Syst. **11**(8), 769–780 (2000)
29. Tseng, Y.M.: An improved conference-key agreement protocol with forward secrecy. Informatica Lith. Acad. Sci. **16**(2), 275–284 (2005)
30. Tseng, Y.M.: A communication-efficient and fault-tolerant conference-key agreement protocol with forward secrecy. J. Syst. Softw. **80**(7), 1091–1101 (2007)
31. Vukolić, M.: Hyperledger fabric: towards scalable blockchain for business. Technical report, Trust in Digital Life 2016. IBM Research (2016)
32. Zhang, Q., et al.: A hierarchical group key agreement protocol using orientable attributes for cloud computing. Inform. Sci. **480**, 55–69 (2019)

Tokenization of Real Estate Using Blockchain Technology

Ashutosh Gupta[1]($\boxtimes$), Jash Rathod[1]($\boxtimes$), Dhiren Patel[1]($\boxtimes$), Jay Bothra[2]($\boxtimes$), Sanket Shanbhag[1]($\boxtimes$), and Tanmay Bhalerao[3]($\boxtimes$)

[1] VJTI Mumbai, Mumbai, India
{avgupta_b17,jsrathod_b17}@ce.vjti.ac.in, dhiren29p@gmail.com,
sanketshanbhag@gmail.com
[2] HSBC, London, UK
jb202038@gmail.com
[3] Autodesk India Pvt. Ltd., Mumbai, India
tsb2127@gmail.com

Abstract. Real estate is by far one of the most trusted investments that people have preferred, being a lucrative investment it provides a steady source of income in the form of lease and rents. Although there are numerous advantages, one of the key downsides of real estate investments is lack of liquidity. Thus, even though global real estate investments amount to about twice the size of investments in stock markets, the number of investors in the real estate market is significantly lower. Blockchain technology has real potential in addressing the issues of liquidity and transparency, opening the market to even retail investors. Owing to the functionality and flexibility of creating Security Tokens, which are backed by real-world assets, real estate can be made liquid with the help of Special Purpose Vehicles. Tokens of ERC 777 standard, which represent fractional ownership of the real estate can be purchased by an investor and these tokens can also be listed on secondary exchanges. The robustness of Smart Contracts can enable the efficient transfer of tokens and seamless distribution of earnings amongst the investors. This work describes Ethereum blockchain-based solutions to make the existing Real Estate investment system much more efficient.

Keywords: Blockchain · Real estate · Ethereum · Tokenization · Security token · Special purpose vehicle

1 Introduction

Real estate is a unique and complex asset class. The commercial real estate market makes up a significant economic global segment in terms of the asset base and the transactional activity. Although the investment market for real estate is huge, it has been dominated by a relatively closed network of firms and organizations able to make large investments which are not liquid. Real estate is different from various other asset classes as it involves high transaction

J. Zhou et al. (Eds.): ACNS 2020 Workshops, LNCS 12418, pp. 77–90, 2020.
https://doi.org/10.1007/978-3-030-61638-0_5

costs, land use regulations and other barriers to entry. These characteristics of real estate have implications for the overall efficiency of the market. While there have been improvements in the information flow and transaction set up and completion – we are only at the initial few steps in terms of digitization [14]. A significant portion of the digitized information is hosted on disparate systems, which results in a lack of transparency and efficiency, and a higher incidence of inaccuracies that creates a greater potential for fraud. There is still a lot of improvement that can be made in real estate when it comes to the use of digital technology and the representation of physical assets in digital forms.

Blockchain technology could enable the real estate industry to address these inefficiencies and inaccuracies. Simply said, a blockchain is essentially a shared and distributed database or ledger. Transactions are processed and bundled in blocks and the blocks encrypted and cryptographically linked in a chain. The processing takes place within a network of nodes – either public or private – with a consensus design intended to decentralize authority such that no single source is the sole decider of transactional integrity. Rather authority is decentralized across the operators of the nodes, with each node validating and maintaining verified copies of the ledger [18]. By recording and combining transactions into a decentralized, secure ledger, a blockchain network creates a "chain" of chronological data that no one party has control of or can change and such that each block and the individual transaction can be verified via cryptography. The transaction records are further protected by the replication of the data across nodes allowing for multiple and verifiable sources of truth. The main contributions of this paper are:

- Providing an approach for Real Estate Asset tokenization by using Ethereum, thus making it liquid, secure and efficient.
- Extend the approach to provide an automated solution for the transfer of tokens and distribution of earnings to investors.

The remainder of this paper is organized as follows: Section 2 describes the existing system and its flaws. Section 3 discusses the preliminaries for this work. Section 4 describes the proposed workflow and Sect. 5 elaborates on the implementation architecture. Finally, Sect. 6 concludes the paper and suggests directions for future scope.

2   Existing System and Its Flaws

Real estate is real and tangible property made up of land as well as anything on it including natural resources, flora and fauna, and buildings. Any real estate falls into one of the three categories - Residential, Commercial, and Industrial. One of the traditional methods to invest in real estate is to buy land or property directly through a real estate broker. Some of the advantages of real estate investments are competitive risk-adjusted returns, high tangible asset value, and attractive and stable income returns in the form of rent and leasing fees. Figure 1 depicts the various ways to invest in real estate.

There are numerous drawbacks to traditional real estate investment. First of all, the initial cost required to buy property is very high. Most of the investors are not able to meet this required amount and hence cannot invest in real estate. The system also suffers from a lack of liquidity. Real estate investments are highly illiquid. To keep earning rental income from the underlying property, the owner also has to find suitable tenants. One cannot sell a fraction of their asset and have to sell the entire underlying asset. Moreover, there are generally numerous intermediaries such as brokers, lawyers, etc. involved in the system. The transaction costs associated with the real estate market are high and it takes a lot of time for a real estate deal to get finalized. All these factors make the system cumbersome and unattractive to a retail investor [2].

Another alternate method to invest in real estate is through Real Estate Investment Trusts (REIT). A REIT is a trust, corporation or an association that owns, or finances income-producing real estate and can be publicly listed or privately owned [6]. The income of a REIT is generated through rent earned from its owned-asset portfolio, interest earned by financing real estate assets or sale proceeds upon sale of assets under management.

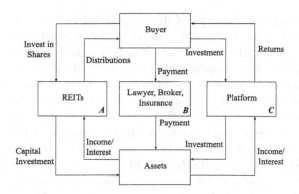

Fig. 1. Investment through **A.** REITs **B.** Traditional System **C.** Crowdfunding

Although REITs help to mitigate the problem of illiquidity in real estate, they have several disadvantages. Historically, public REITs have had lower returns than private REITs. They also trade on an average at a premium to the underlying Net Asset Value. The total value of the commercial real estate assets value captured by the REITs is significantly smaller than the total Commercial Real Estate market. Hence, a large number of commercial real estate is out of reach for investors. Moreover, the retail investors are also dependent upon the REIT managers and do not have the option of customizing their real estate exposure. An investor might want access to a specific type of asset in a specific geography and currently, REITs do not provide the benefit of such a granular level of investment. Some REITs also incur high management and transaction fees, leading to lower payouts for investors [13].

Crowdfunding is defined as a collection of equity and debt to be invested in several kinds of projects through a web-based platform able to create opportunities by matching lenders and sponsors. The capital raised in real estate crowdfunding is used in order to purchase, develop or refurbish a Real Estate asset with the aim of subsequent use or transaction [1].

Real estate crowdfunding has failed to take off for multiple reasons. One of the biggest reasons is the quality of assets listed on the crowdfunding platform. When assets that were unable to raise capital through traditional means of the financing end up on crowdfunding platforms. Other issues with crowdfunding are multi-year lock-in periods required. This locks investor capital and even with some platforms providing a secondary market for these assets this reduces overall liquidity. Certain platforms allow investors to sell their holdings after one year but these secondary markets are siloed [13]. All these factors make REITs and crowdfunding undesirable for retail investors.

3   Preliminaries

3.1   Blockchain

Blockchain technology is a type of distributed ledger technology that uses a Peer-to-Peer (P2P) network model consisting of immutable and time-stamped records of data. This work employs the use of Ethereum blockchain. As the name suggests, Blockchain is an append-only chain of blocks that are back-linked. It was first introduced by Satoshi Nakamoto in [11]. Some of the main advantages of this technology are security, immutability, decentralization, and transparency. It uses public-key cryptography as the base for identifying users and granting them access to their assets on chain stored in these wallets. Cryptographic hash functions, or simply hash functions, are known to be one way, i.e., the input cannot be deciphered from the hash value of the input. These are used to create a tamper-proof record of any form of transactions on the ledger.

A blockchain system consists of users or computers which are called nodes [11]. These nodes form the peers in the network. Any communication or sharing of resources between two peers is called a transaction, like, in Bitcoin blockchain, the transfer of bitcoins is called a transaction. A block is a collection of transactions that are verified and added to the blockchain. A block consists of a block header and a block body. The block header consists of a previous block hash as one of its elements, which serves as a link to the previously added block and the block body consists of the transactions. The validation of the transaction is done by miners on the blockchain. These miners contend to solve a cryptographic hash algorithm-based difficult mathematical puzzle. A consensus protocol enables all the nodes of the network to reach a common agreement and ensures that there is only one version of the truth that is agreed upon by all the nodes in the Blockchain.

When a transaction occurs, it is broadcasted to the entire network. The nodes in the network validate the transaction and the user's status. A set of verified transactions is considered to be added to the block. Miners solve the mathematical puzzle and the one who solves it first broadcasts it to the entire network and mines the new block on the blockchain. This new block is permanent and unalterable. The new state of the blockchain is updated in the ledger present with each node, and it is distributed to each and every node on the network, it makes it decentralized.

3.2 Ethereum

Ethereum is a global, open-source platform for decentralized applications. It is a specific blockchain-based software platform that enables the possibility of building and running smart contracts and Distributed Applications (DApps) [10]. Ether is the cryptocurrency asset employed in the Ethereum blockchain. In some extent, Ether is the fuel for operating distributed applications over Ethereum. Using this cryptocurrency, it is possible to make payments to other accounts or to the machines executing some requested operation. Ether thus enables running DApps, enabling smart contracts, generating tokens during Initial Coin Offering (ICOs), i.e., a type of funding using cryptocurrencies, and also for making standard P2P payments.

A transaction on Ethereum consists mainly of five elements [17], namely, From (sender), To (Receiver), Gas (fees to be paid for performing operations), Data/Input (message), and Value (amount transferred in Wei). A consensus algorithm is a procedure through which all the peers of the Blockchain network reach a common agreement about the present state of the distributed ledger. Consensus algorithms hence achieve reliability in the Blockchain network and establish trust between unknown peers in a distributed computing environment. Proof of Work (PoW) is a consensus algorithm that aims at solving a costly and time-consuming mathematical puzzle for a new block to be added to the blockchain and at the same time easy for other nodes to verify it. Proof of Stake (PoS) concept states that a person can mine or validate block transactions according to how many coins he or she holds. This means that the more cryptocurrency owned by a miner, the more mining power he or she has. At present, Ethereum is using Proof of Work. But, it is transitioning into using Proof of Stake eventually.

3.3 Smart Contracts

Smart contracts are portions of codes where the logic is implemented. Ethereum provides a Turing complete programming language e.g. Solidity that allows creating programs and running them on the blockchain. When users send the transactions, the portion of code is executed [8]. The execution of a smart contract occurs when a miner includes a transaction in a block and re-run by every recipient of this block upon arrival. These are open to all other users and once the transactions are completed, they cannot be reversed. In this way, the merits of the blockchain of immutability and cryptographically provided security are further strengthened by the efficacy of smart contracts. Smart Contracts on the Ethereum Network are generally written using the programming language

Solidity. This Solidity-based smart contract is compiled using Ethereum Virtual Machine (EVM) bytecode and subsequently executed and deployed on the Ethereum Blockchain [16].

3.4 Tokenization

The tokenization of assets refers to the process of issuing a blockchain token (specifically, a security token) that digitally represents a real tradable asset [7]. Tokenization is in many ways similar to the traditional process of securitization. These security tokens are created through a type of initial coin offering (ICO) sometimes referred to as a security token offering (STO) to distinguish it from other types of ICOs, which can produce different tokens such as equity, utility, or payment tokens. An STO can be used to create a digital representation— a security token—of an asset, meaning that a security token could represent a share in a company, ownership of a piece of real estate, or participation in an investment fund. These security tokens can then be traded on a secondary market. The main benefits of tokenization of assets are:

- Liquidity - By tokenizing assets, the tokens can be then traded on a secondary market of the issuer's choice. This access to a broader base of traders increases the liquidity [9].
- Faster and cheaper transactions - Because the transaction of tokens is completed with smart contracts, certain parts of the exchange process are automated. This automation can reduce the administrative burden involved in buying and selling, with fewer intermediaries needed, leading to not only faster deal execution but also lower transaction fees.
- Transparency - A security token is capable of having the token holder's rights and legal responsibilities embedded directly onto the token, along with an immutable record of ownership. These characteristics promise to add transparency to transactions, allowing you to know with whom you are dealing, what your and their rights are, and who has previously owned this token.
- Accessibility - Importantly, tokenization could open up investment in assets to a much wider audience thanks to reduced minimum investment amounts and periods. Tokens are highly divisible, meaning investors can purchase tokens that represent incredibly small percentages of the underlying assets.

3.5 Special Purpose Vehicle

A Special Purpose Vehicle is a separate legal entity created by an organization. The Special Purpose Vehicle is a distinct company with its own assets and liabilities, as well as its own legal status. Usually, a Special Purpose Vehicle is created for a specific objective [3]. Special Purpose Vehicles can be viewed as a method of distributing the risks of an underlying pool of exposures held by the Special Purpose Vehicle and reallocating them to investors who want to take those risks. This allows investors to be able to invest in those opportunities which would not otherwise exist and provides an additional source of revenue generation for the firm sponsoring the Special Purpose Vehicle. Some of the most common uses of a Special Purpose Vehicle are:

- Securitization - Special Purpose Vehicles are the key characteristic of securitization and are commonly used to securitize loans and other receivables.
- Asset Transfer - Many assets are either non-transferable or difficult to transfer. By having a Special Purpose Vehicle own a single asset, the Special Purpose Vehicle can be sold as a self-contained package, rather than attempting to split the asset or assign numerous permits to various parties.
- Financing - A Special Purpose Vehicle can be used to finance a new venture without increasing the debt burden of the firm sponsoring the Special Purpose Vehicle and without diluting existing shareholders. The sponsor may contribute some of the equity with outside investors providing the remainder.

3.6   Legal Aspects of Security Tokens, Smart Contracts, and Special Purpose Vehicle

The Securities and Exchange Commission (the "SEC") has regulatory authority over the issuance or resale of any ethereum token or other digital asset that has the characteristics of an "investment contract". Under Securities Act § 2(a)(1) and Securities Exchange Act § 3(a)(10), a security includes "an investment contract.". An "investment contract" has been defined by the U.S. Supreme Court as an investment of money in a common enterprise with a reasonable expectation of profits to be derived from the entrepreneurial or managerial efforts of others. On September 11, 2018, the U.S. District Court for the Eastern District of New York held that a digital token can be deemed to be a security under the Howey test [5].

According to the Financial Conduct Authority (FCA) in their Policy Statement 19/22, the security tokens are within the regulatory parameter [4]. This means that firms carrying on specified activities involving security tokens need to ensure that they have the correct permissions and are following the relevant rules and requirements.

To make the smart contract associated with the platform legally binding, we can use the approach as suggested in [12]. The approach involves digitally signing the legal contract by the different entities involved in the transaction. Once the legal contracts have been signed, they are added to an immutable distributed database such as the InterPlanetary File System (IPFS) and the hashes of these legal documents are added to the smart contract. This ensures that the smart contract was legally agreed upon by every party in the transaction and any disputes can be upheld in a court of law.

The Special Purpose Vehicle owning the asset would be tokenized and the shares of the Special Purpose Vehicle would be distributed to the token holders. The Special Purpose Vehicle is treated as a corporation and is subject to laws pertaining to the respective jurisdictions. A shareholder certificate can be provided to token holders. The token holders will have to comply with the respective KYC/AML norms.

4   Proposed Workflow for Tokenizing Real Estate

The process involves background verification of users (asset owners and investors) and registering them on the platform. Later, a Special Purpose Vehicle is created which holds the title of the asset and is tokenized. The tokens are issued initially through a security token offering and using smart contracts the monthly distribution of the income generated by the asset is done to the investors. These processes are described in detail below:

4.1   Registration of Entities

We propose a common platform where the asset owners can be connected with the investors. Every Real estate owner, as well as the investors, will have to register on the platform. A Know Your Customer (KYC) and Anti Money Laundering (AML) verification for every user registered on the platform would be conducted through a third-party provider. Basic details regarding the User's identity would need to be submitted by the user electronically to the platform. Once the KYC and AML requirements are satisfied, the user can be able to access the services of the platform.

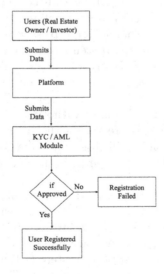

Fig. 2. Registration of users on platform

4.2   Creation of Special Purpose Vehicle

Once an Owner of the property is registered, he/she can now submit the necessary documents and paperwork in accordance with the local jurisdiction. A

Special Purpose Vehicle is created. The Special Purpose Vehicle would serve as the legal owner of a real estate. Also, the Special Purpose Vehicle would be responsible for the operation of the real estate or, in general, the underlying assets. These operations can be the functioning of a hotel or renting the property for commercial purposes. It is the Special Purpose Vehicle that would be responsible to verify the documents with the concerned authorities. The Special Purpose Vehicle is only created upon successful verification of the paperwork. In case of any inconsistency with either the information of the asset or the Special Purpose Vehicle, the entire deal is called off, on grounds of not complying with legal formalities. The reason for opting for a Special Purpose Vehicle instead of direct tokenization of an asset is that in most countries, directly tokenizing the underlying asset is not possible due to the lack of legal and technical frameworks for enabling the tokenization of property rights [15].

4.3   Tokenization and Smart Contract

Once everything is verified, the Special Purpose Vehicle is successfully created and the process of tokenization can be proceeded with. It is the Special Purpose Vehicle and not the underlying asset which would be tokenized. The tokens generated would represent shares of the Special Purpose Vehicle. It means that every token holder would have some percentage of ownership in the Special Purpose Vehicle based on the number of tokens they hold. From the legal perspective, the ownership of these Security Tokens is guaranteed owing to an Special Purpose Vehicle that we establish for each of our clients. The Security Tokens issued are an economic right to share the profits of the Special Purpose Vehicle.

It is at this stage that the crypto tokens are actually minted on the Ethereum blockchain of ERC 777 standard. These security tokens, which are blockchain native, are now a representation of the fractional ownership of the Special Purpose Vehicle and by extension the asset. Subsequently, these tokens must be embedded with subjected regulation on a Smart Contract. The underlying Smart Contract would contain the entire business logic of transfer of ownership and validating the users and transactions. Moreover, the use of a Smart Contract can be further extended to incorporate additional features of the token.

4.4   Security Token Offering (STO)/Initial Coin Offering (ICO)

Once the Special Purpose Vehicle has been tokenized, the tokenized securities will be issued to the investors through a Security Token Offering. Unlike the tokens issued through an ICO, Security tokens are backed by an asset. Hence, the tokens of Special Purpose Vehicle would be issued through an STO. The asset would be listed on the platform. Target price and the number of tokens would be set based on the value of the asset. The registered user will be able to view all the asset features such as the location, cost, expected returns and other details of the asset on the platform. Once the user decides to purchase the token of the given asset, they will pay the required amount based on the number of tokens purchased.

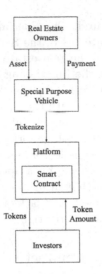

Fig. 3. Tokenization of real estate

If the STO is successful, which means if the STO is able to raise the required target amount of funds, the investors will receive their corresponding tokens and the asset title would transfer in the name of the Special Purpose Vehicle offline. Whereas, if the STO is not successful and is unable to raise the required amount necessary to purchase the asset, the amount paid by the existing investors would be refunded and the title ownership would still lie in the name of the original asset owner.

Once the investors have received their tokens, they would be able to benefit from the monthly returns of the tokens as well as from the capital appreciation due to the rise in token value. Since the implemented token is based on Ethereum and is of the ERC 777 standard, the investors can also freely sell these tokens in the secondary market via different exchanges where the tokens can be traded. This ability of trading the tokens ensures liquidity to the investors.

4.5   Distribution of Dividends to the Investors

As discussed earlier, the real estate can be used for various purposes. It could be rented for commercial or residential purposes or it could be a hotel business. In any case, revenue can be generated from the asset. The profits can be distributed to the investors in the proportion of the number of tokens they own. This system can be automated and efficiently implemented using a smart contract. The smart contract can have the functionality of calculating the percentage of ownership and smoothly transfer the proportion of profits to the investor without any scope for frauds or discrepancies. Along with functionality for dividends' distribution, additional features for voting of investors in case of any decision taking can also be implemented.

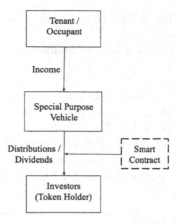

Fig. 4. Distribution of dividends to ivestors

5 Implementation Architecture of the Proposed System

The platform will be based on the ethereum blockchain which allows us to use smart contracts. The security tokens which are backed by the shares of the Special Purpose Vehicle will be embedded in the smart contract. The tokens will follow the ERC 777 standard protocols. ERC 777 standard defines a common list of rules which all ethereum tokens must adhere to.

ERC 777 defines 13 different functions for the benefit of other tokens within the Ethereum system. The Thirteen functions defined by the ERC 777 are:

- name() - This function returns the name of the token in string format
- symbol() - This function returns the symbol of the token in string format
- totalSupply() - This function identifies the total number of tokens created
- balanceOf() - The balanceOf function returns the number of tokens that a particular address, in this case, the contract owner, has in their account.
- granularity() - This function gets the smallest part of the token that's not divisible. The granularity is the smallest amount of tokens (in the internal denomination) which may be minted, sent or burned at any time.
- defaultOperators() - It gets the list of default operators as defined by the token contract
- isOperatorFor() - This function indicates whether the operator address is an operator of the holder address.
- authorizeOperator() - This function sets a third party operator address as an operator of the sender to send and burn tokens on its behalf.
- revokeOperator() - This function removes the right of the operator address to be an operator for sender and to send and burn tokens on its behalf.
- send() - This function sends the amount of tokens from the address of the sender to the address of the recipient.
- operatorSend() - This function sends the given amount of tokens on behalf of the address of sender to the receiver.

- burn() - This function burns the given amount of tokens from the address of the sender.
- operatorBurn() - This function burns the amount of tokens on behalf of the address given.

Altogether, this set of functions and signals ensures that Ethereum tokens of different types will uniformly perform in any place within the Ethereum system. As such, nearly all of the digital wallets which support the ether currency also support ERC 777 compliant tokens. Following the ERC 777 standard for the tokens would allow the tokens to be listed and traded in numerous secondary market exchanges that are compatible with ERC 777 tokens.

Algorithm 1. Transfer Tokens

Input: recipient_address
    tokens
function *transfer*:
1: **if** (recipient_address $\neq$ stakeholder **or**
    Balance of $msg.sender$ < tokens) **then**
2:    Abort session
3: **else**
4:    Debit tokens from account of $msg.sender$
5:    Credit tokens to account of recipient_address
6:    Emit tokens is transferred from $msg.sender$ to
    recipient_address
7: **end if**

On top of these above listed six functions, a function for Asset income distribution is also implemented in the smart contract. The algorithm takes as input the accumulated_wealth which denotes the income accumulated by the Special Purpose Vehicle over the years and the income which denotes the income of the Special Purpose Vehicle during the current month. The algorithm is invoked by the Special Purpose Vehicle at the end of each month. The algorithm first verifies whether the account which invoked the contract is the Special Purpose Vehicle. Then for every token holder it calculates the proportion of tokens that the token holder owns and calculates the dividend distributed to them accordingly. The contract then credits the dividend into each token holders account. A transaction is emitted to the blockchain stating the respective dividend has been credited in the Tokenholder's account.

Algorithm 2. Distribution of Dividends

Input: accumulated_wealth
    income
function *distribute*:
1: **if** $(msg.sender \neq$ Special Purpose Vehicle) **then**
2:    Abort session
3: **else**
4:    **for** every token holder **do**
5:      Calculate Percentage of ownership (percent_own)
6:      dividend = income * percent_own
7:      accumulated_wealth - dividend
8:      Balance of token_holder = Balance of token_holder + dividend
9:    **end for**
10:    Emit dividends distributed to token holders
11: **end if**

---

6   Conclusion

In this paper, we present an approach to introduce liquidity in a real estate investment by leveraging the use of Blockchain technology. We have used a Special Purpose Vehicle for the purpose of holding the underlying asset. Special Purpose Vehicle is tokenized and is providing the investors the flexibility to purchase ERC 777 standard security tokens as per their convenience. A Smart Contract is developed for the transfer of tokens and also an automated solution for distribution of dividends is implemented.

The future directions for this work focus on using a Decentralized Autonomous Organization (DAO) instead of a Special Purpose Vehicle to further improve decentralization. We can also provide functionality for additional features like voting and loyalty rewards for token holders. Moreover, each token can also be structured to represent ownership in the Special Purpose Vehicle which not only owns a single asset but holds the title for multiple assets belonging to the same class. For example, tokens can be made to represent shares of a Special Purpose Vehicle which holds two or more assets.

References

1. Ey-real   estate   crowdfunding-march   2019.pdf.   https://www.ey.com/Publication/vwLUAssets/Real_Estate_Crowdfunding/$FILE/EY-Real%20Estate%20Crowdfunding-March%202019.pdf. Accessed 14 May 2020
2. Icorating.com. https://icorating.com/upload/whitepaper/yNnaV9f5nFjxrcMukahyrzKBBvdIEyufEC2AoAT0.pdf. Accessed 14 May 2020
3. The next chapter: creating an understanding of special purpose vehicles. https://www.pwc.com/gx/en/banking-capital-markets/publications/assets/pdf/next-chapter-creating-understanding-of-spvs.pdf. Accessed 14 May 2020
4. Ps19/22: Guidance on cryptoassets. https://www.fca.org.uk/publication/policy/ps19-22.pdf. Accessed 14 May 2020

5. Securities. https://blockchainlawguide.com/securities/. Accessed 14 May 2020
6. Tokenisation report.pdf. https://www.sbs.ox.ac.uk/sites/default/files/2020-01/Tokenisation%20Report.pdf. Accessed 14 May 2020
7. The tokenization of assets is disrupting the financial industry. https://www2.deloitte.com/content/dam/Deloitte/lu/Documents/financial-services/lu-tokenization-of-assets-disrupting-financial-industry.pdf. Accessed 14 May 2020
8. Atzei, N., Bartoletti, M., Cimoli, T., Lande, S., Zunino, R.: SoK: unraveling bitcoin smart contracts. In: Bauer, L., Küsters, R. (eds.) Principles of Security and Trust, vol. 10804, pp. 217–242. Springer, Cham (2018). https://doi.org/10.1007/978-3-319-89722-6_9. http://link.springer.com/10.1007/978-3-319-89722-6_9
9. Blankenship, M.J., Howard, C.B., Lopez, R.: The tokenization of real estate-how blockchain technology will impact real estate, p. 2. https://www.lockelord.com/-/media/files/newsandevents/publications/2019/07/fintech20190729the-tokenization-of-real-estatelope/fintech20190729the-tokenization-of-real-estatelope.pdf?la=en&hash=A784B2ACC54B61202956ECFE2CC27E7A
10. Buterin, V.: A Next Generation Smart Contract & Decentralized Application Platform, p. 36 (2009)
11. Nakamoto, S.: Bitcoin: a peer-to-peer electronic cash system, p. 9 (2009)
12. Patel, D., Shah, K., Shanbhag, S., Mistry, V.: Towards legally enforceable smart contracts. In: Chen, S., Wang, H., Zhang, L.-J. (eds.) ICBC 2018. LNCS, vol. 10974, pp. 153–165. Springer, Cham (2018). https://doi.org/10.1007/978-3-319-94478-4_11
13. Smith, J., Vora, M., Benedetti, D.H., Yoshida, K., Vogel, Z.: Tokenized securities & commercial real estate, p. 46. https://mitcre.mit.edu/wp-content/uploads/2019/11/Tokenized-Security-Commercial-Real-Estate2.pdf
14. Thota, S.: Blockchain for real estate industry. J. Soc. Sci. Re. (52), 53–56 (2019). https://doi.org/10.32861/sr.52.53.56. https://arpgweb.com/journal/10/archive/02-2019/2/5
15. Uzsoki, D.: Tokenization of infrastructure: a blockchain-based solution to financing sustainable infrastructure, p. 45. https://www.iisd.org/sites/default/files/publications/tokenization-infrastructure-blockchain-solution.pdf
16. Vujicic, D., Jagodic, D., Randic, S.: Blockchain technology, bitcoin, and Ethereum: a brief overview. In: 2018 17th International Symposium INFOTEH-JAHORINA (INFOTEH), pp. 1–6. IEEE, East Sarajevo (2018). https://doi.org/10.1109/INFOTEH.2018.8345547. https://ieeexplore.ieee.org/document/8345547/
17. Wood, D.G.: Ethereum: a secure decentralised generalised transaction ledger. eip-150 revision, p. 32 (2012)
18. Zheng, Z., Xie, S., Dai, H., Chen, X., Wang, H.: An overview of blockchain technology: architecture, consensus, and future trends. In: 2017 IEEE International Congress on Big Data (BigData Congress), pp. 557–564. IEEE, Honolulu, June 2017. https://doi.org/10.1109/BigDataCongress.2017.85. http://ieeexplore.ieee.org/document/8029379/

AIHWS – Artificial Intelligence in Hardware Security

Practical Side-Channel Based Model Extraction Attack on Tree-Based Machine Learning Algorithm

Dirmanto Jap[1], Ville Yli-Mäyry[2], Akira Ito[2], Rei Ueno[2], Shivam Bhasin[1(✉)], and Naofumi Homma[2]

[1] Nanyang Technological University, Singapore, Singapore
{djap,sbhasin}@ntu.edu.sg
[2] Tohoku University/CREST, Sendai, Japan
{ville,ito,ueno,homma}@riec.tohoku.ac.jp

Abstract. Machine learning algorithms have been widely applied to solve various type of problems and applications. Among those, decision tree based algorithms have been considered for small Internet-of-Things (IoT) implementation, due to their simplicity. It has been shown in a recent publication, that Bonsai, a small tree-based algorithm, can be successfully fitted in a small 8-bit microcontroller. However, the security of machine learning algorithm has also been a major concern, especially with the threat of secret parameter recovery which could lead to breach of privacy. With machine learning taking over a significant proportion of industrial tasks, the security issue has become a matter of concern. Recently, secret parameter recovery for neural network based algorithm using physical side-channel leakage has been proposed. In the paper, we investigate the security of widely used decision tree algorithms running on ARM Cortex M3 platform against electromagnetic (EM) side-channel attacks. We show that by focusing on each building block function or component, one could perform divide-and-conquer approach to recover the secret parameters. To demonstrate the attack, we first report the recovery of secret parameters of Bonsai, such as, sparse projection parameters, branching function and node predictors. After the recovery of these parameters, the attacker can then reconstruct the whole architecture.

1 Introduction

With the growing trend of machine learning (ML) across various fields and application, the security of ML has been thoroughly scrutinized. Recently, a new type attack against ML using side-channel attacks (SCA) have been reported [1,5,11]. These attacks have shown it is possible to recover the trained ML model which is usually intellectual property, and the leak of which leads to monetary losses. Attacks that enable the theft of ML intellectual property have only be shown for complex ML algorithms like multilayer perceptron (MLP) or convolutional neural network (CNN). However, security of other widely used algorithms for

© Springer Nature Switzerland AG 2020
J. Zhou et al. (Eds.): ACNS 2020 Workshops, LNCS 12418, pp. 93–105, 2020.
https://doi.org/10.1007/978-3-030-61638-0_6

resource constrained platforms is still highly unexplored. To highlight the importance, ML algorithm, such as decision trees are widely used in industrial environments, especially in Industrial internet of things (IIoT), for anomaly detection and quality assurance of the supply chain. Under industry 4.0, IIoT relies upon small edge devices deployed over industrial site to perform crucial tasks. For example, quality assessment of manufactured products is often done with in the supply line by small sensor modules running ML algorithms. Given the task, reaction time and available resources on sensors, simpler ML algorithms are often used like decision trees. Several optimizations of supply chain and smart manufacturing have been proposed based on decision trees [12]. The algorithms are highly optimized to improve the supply chain and thus remain crucial proprietary information. Thus, in this paper, we assess the security of decision tree ML algorithm against electromagnetic (EM) SCA. We investigate some public libraries for decision tree implementation, and analyze potential exploitable leakages in the implementation.

1.1 Related Works

As per the authors' best knowledge, there has been no work so far investigating the SCA vulnerabilities of decision tree algorithms. Indeed, SCAs on ML implementations are relatively new, and most of the reported attacks are focusing so far on more popular MLP or CNN implementations. For example, Hua et al. [5] demonstrate recovery of CNN secret parameters by targeting zero pruning using cache leakage. Another work, by Wei et al. [11], shows input recovery attack via EM side-channel targeting a special architecture called line buffers. Recently, Batina et al. [1] proposed a generic and systematic reverse engineering of deep neural networks via EM side-channel. The attack recovers parameters like number of layers, number of neurons in each layer, activation function, CNN kernel size etc. As such, these works illustrate the potential of SCA based attacks against ML in general.

1.2 Contributions

This work follows the attack methodology presented in [1], namely using divide-and-conquer approach to recover the parameters for each operation. In this paper, we investigate the security of *decision tree based ML algorithms* against SCA through EM emanation. With a divide-and-conquer approach, it is possible to recover different secret parameters, one at a time. In other words, the proposed methodology can be considered as a model extraction attack on tree-based algorithms. Thus, another important point is to first identify crucial targets to recover in the decision tree followed by practical demonstration of parameter recovery. To the best of our knowledge, this is the first work that targets a tree-based ML algorithm.

2   Background

In this section, we provide basic background about decision trees as well as Bonsai, which will be the main target for the investigation. We provide a brief description of the target algorithm and the attack methodology. For the attack, we consider variants of side-channel attacks (SCA) and recall general basics about profiling and non-profiling based SCA.

2.1   Decision Tree

Decision tree [2] is a classification, as well as regression algorithm, which can be illustrated as a tree structure with if-else rules, starting from top to bottom, based on the attributes or features split. In contrast to other more complex learning algorithm, decision tree is relatively simple, and is easy to understand. However, decision tree is also sensitive to small changes in the training data. The decision tree that is grown large enough will usually tend to overfit the training data, *i.e.*, having low bias, but with high variance trade-off. Hence, some post-processing methods such as pruning are sometimes required after construction of the decision tree.

2.2   Bonsai

Bonsai [8] is designed for efficient Decision Tree prediction on IoT devices. In the paper, the authors reported the implementation of Bonsai on Arduino Uno board, mounting an 8-bit ATmega328P microcontroller, operating at 16 MHz with no native floating point support, 2 KB RAM and 32 KB read-only flash. The implementation is reported to minimize the model size while still maintaining the prediction accuracy. To achieve the efficiency, the tree model is trained to learn a single, shallow, sparse tree with powerful nodes. To fit in the board, the model is also trained to sparsely project all data into a low-dimensional space in which the tree is learned. Both internal and leaf nodes in Bonsai are also tailored to make non-linear predictions, by summing individual node predictions along the path. This allows sharing of the parameters along paths to reduce the model size. Using these techniques, Bonsai can achieve the accuracy of non-linear classifiers while still maintaining the model size of a typical linear classifier.

The prediction for a point x are given by

$$y(x) = \Sigma_k I_k(x) W_k^\top Z x \circ tanh(\sigma V_k^\top Z x) \tag{1}$$

where $\circ$ denotes element-wise Hadamard product, σ denotes used defined hyper-parameter, Z is a sparse projection matrix from higher input dimension to lower space. I_k, W_k and V_k are Bonsai parameters, where $I_k(x)$ is an indicator function determining path taken by x, and W_k and V_k are sparse predictors learned at node k. The indicator function I_k is computed by learning sparse vector θ at each internal node. After the learning, the sign of $\theta^\top Z x$ determines whether point x should be branched to the node's left or right child. The pseudocode of Bonsai is presented in Algorithm 1.

2.3 Side-Channel Attacks (SCA)

Even though in theory the algorithm is secure, in practice, the implementation might leak some information physically (referred to as side-channel). Side-Channel Attacks (SCA) [7], widely used in physical security domain, can also be used to exploit leaked information from these models. SCA can be further classified as profiling or non-profiling based. In profiling based attacks, the attacker is assumed to have capability to learn from a similar device (clone device) and use the learned model when attacking the actual target device. For non-profiling based attack, the attacker only collects data/traces from the target device when sensitive computation is running, and then performs statistical analysis based on leakage models like Hamming weight or distance to recover the target secret.

Algorithm 1: Pseudocode of Bonsai

Data: Training Input: X, Parameter: Z, V, W, θ, depth
Result: Class label c

```
1  node = 0, n = 0, score = 0;
2  X = Z | * | X ;
3  X = X - mean;
4  while n < depth do
5  |   W_0 = W[node] * X;
6  |   V_0 = V[node] * X;
7  |   V_0 = tanh(V_0);
8  |   X_0 = W_0 ∘ V_0;
9  |   θ_0 = θ[node] * X;
10 |   node = (θ_0 >0)? ((2*node)+1):((2*node)+2);
11 |   score = score + X_0;
12 |   n = n+1;
13 end
14 c = argmax(score);
```

Correlation Power Analysis (CPA). With access to known inputs (or outputs), the adversary maps them to a function with a fixed unknown (or secret) constant. The adversary can then observe the side-channel leakage of the resulting computation. The adversary, assuming that the leakage is following specific leakage model, then builds a hypothetical leakage set for all possible value of the constant, given the knowledge of the inputs. For every hypothetical constant, the outputs are correlated with the actual observed side-channel leakage. The hypothetical constant value which leads to the highest (absolute) correlation value is then deemed to be the correct unknown recovered by the attack. In SCA, the attack is considered successful if the correct constant can be distinguished from the incorrect constant values. In other words, if the guessed values are ranked based on the correlation value, the attack is successful if the correct guess is ranked the highest. For the choice of leakage model, the most commonly used is Hamming weight or Hamming distance model [10]. In this work, Hamming weight leakage model is used, since it is the commonly observed leakage model in microcontroller or software implementation [9]. The model directly represents leakages due to loading on sensitive data into a pre-charged data bus.

Template Attacks (TA). In TA, the adversary is assumed to have full (or at least, some level of) control over the device similar to the target. The adversary then identifies some leakage points and builds a template for each possible values. The template for each value typically consists of sample mean vector and sample covariance matrix, computed based on the training data having that value. In the matching or attack phase, the adversary measures a new trace from the target device where secret is unknown and calculates the probability for each value, based on the built templates. The trace will be grouped to the value in which highest probability is achieved leading to recovery of the secret.

3 Attack Overview

In this section, the attack methodology will be detailed. To begin, the target implementation will be studied. Based on preliminary investigation, vulnerable operations will be identified, and different possibility of attacks will be investigated for each vulnerable operation. Finally, after recovering each secret parameters by targeting different parameters, the whole trained model can be reconstructed.

3.1 Measurement Setup and Target Library

As mentioned earlier, for the target implementation, we consider Bonsai, a publicly available library for tree-based ML algorithms which can be fitted into low-end IoT devices, such as AVR ATmega328p and ARM Cortex-M3. The model can be trained offline, and the resulting model can be exported to IoT device for deployment[1]. For the attacker model, the adversary is assumed to be a malicious client who legally acquires a copy (or few) of licensed ML models, and then relies on reverse engineering to recover the model to avoid paying for additional licences. As the target is a licensed copy, the adversary can feed known inputs and observe the side-channel leakage. As stated earlier, the reverse engineering is conducted by observing EM side-channel leakage, since it can achieve better precision and localization. For the following experiments, the target board is Arduino Due with ARM Cortex M3 as an IoT device with 512 KB flash, 96 KB SRAM and 84 MHz operating frequency. The choice of board is due to the reason that the board is more widely deployed and more powerful than the example given by the library, the Arduino Uno. Hence, the trained model can simply be adopted for the targeted platform. The measurements are captured using RF-U 5-2 near-field EM probe from Langer as shown in Fig. 1, on a Lecroy

---

[1] The source code is publicly available at: https://github.com/microsoft/EdgeML.

WaveRunner 610zi oscilloscope. A 30 dB pre-amplifier is also used for improving measurement quality. A preliminary investigation with known fixed data is conducted to find the best spot for attack. A grid search is performed, where different probe positions are tested. A single look up table operation is executed, and position which gives the highest SNR is chosen. Based on preliminary timing investigation, on average, one classification will take around 3–5 s, including the serial communication. Since there are conditional branching, the timing behavior is not constant. The strategy of the attacker is then to focus the attack on each individual layer, using the information recovered in one layer to attack the next layer. Due to time constraint, a total number of 100,000 traces are collected.

Fig. 1. Experimental setup depicting the placement of EM probe over targeted ARM Cortex-M3 microcontroller running Bonsai Library

For the training, a shallow decision tree will be trained on Bonsai with the USPS handwritten digit dataset [6]. This is the same dataset used in the demo example for Bonsai. The model is trained on this dataset, and then downloaded to ARM Cortex-M3. Thus, the key model parameters like depth, branching function, node predictors etc. for the deployed model are fixed. As the depth of the tree can be easily guessed by checking the inference execution time, we consider it to be a known parameter. For testing, the adversary will consider only random numbers as inputs, without limiting to a specific dataset, as it is not required for the analysis. In an attack against Bonsai, the adversary can assume that the trained parameters are secret, and the normalization factors are known for the input, and thus, the recovery targets can be identified.

3.2 Identification of Sensitive Parameters

Some of trained Bonsai parameters can be identified by analyzing the parameter description. The main secret parameters of the model are Z, θ, V, W, which are *sparse projection parameters, branching function and node predictors*. The sparse projection is to map higher dimensional features to lower dimension to allow better fit for IoT devices. The sparse projection matrix, Z, when implemented, can be split into Z_{val} and Z_{idx}, the value and index, rather than full matrix, to further reduce the overhead. As for the branching function, at each layer, the θ parameter determines which direction the node will branch. At each node in the path traversed by the input, a vector score for each class is computed using the learned parameter matrices V and W, so that each node predicts the vector $W_k^\top Z x \circ tanh(\sigma V_k^\top Z x)$ (see Eq. (1)). The predictions are then summed, and the class with highest score is returned as predicted label. As per Bonsai's documentation, the functional form of the node predictor was chosen empirically.

In general, these parameters are used in separate functions throughout the algorithm (refer to Algorithm 1). For example, the node predictor parameters are typically used in matrix multiplication, and hence, each individual multiplication can be individually targeted. Rather than showing the recovery of each parameter individually, we consider to report the attack for the critical operations, in which the parameters are involved. Hence, the operations are the main target to be reversed for recovering the model. We have identified three basic operations in which these parameters are used during the computations. These operations are: 1) fixed point multiplication (involving parameter V, W, Z_{val}, θ), 2) loading of the index (when loading the parameter Z_{idx}) and 3) conditional branching (to determine the path traversed by the input). For each operation, we analyse and adopt different side-channel methodology strategy to recover the corresponding parameter.

3.3 General Attack Flow

In general, after the adversary has identified the target operations, the adversary can initiate the attack in a top-down manner. The assumption is that adversary has control over the input data, either through test data similar to training set, or randomly chosen data, as the output label does not impact the attack process. Also, in this case, the attacker is assumed to know fixed data, such as normalization mean for the input, as well as the depth of the tree. For Bonsai, assuming that the procedure is executed sequentially[2], the attacker can then

---

[2] An example of a trained model can be found on: https://github.com/microsoft/EdgeML/tree/master/tools/SeeDot/seedot/arduino.

recover the parameter by attacking the operation starting from the root all the way to the leaf of the tree, based on the sequence in Algorithm 1.

In Fig. 2, we have illustrated the general flow of the attack. As mentioned earlier, we do the attacks as described previously starting from the root node. In this case, we can use all the traces collected, and we can first recover the sparse projection matrix (Z_{val} and Z_{idx}) and then recover the first row of the matrices (W, V, T). Afterwards, using this information, once we have recovered the branching, we can move on to the next row. However, due to the branching, not all of the traces or data can be used in the next layer. Due to the splitting of the data during the branching (when deciding the next node path), the dataset used will also be split normally. Hence, when treating the next branch node (left or right), the adversary can treat it as a new root node, and repeat the process, albeit with lesser number of traces. Note that for parameter W, V, T, there are 3 dimensions of interest: $2^{depth} - 1$ as number of rows, number of class labels, and projected features (28 for this dataset).

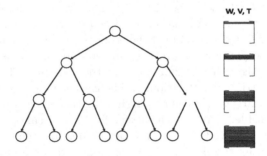

Fig. 2. Attack flow illustration

4   Experimental Results

In this section, we present the recovery process for each sensitive parameter individually in a divide-and-conquer manner. After each parameter has been recovered, the results can be combined in which finally leads to a full recovery of the model.

4.1   Recovering Sparse Projection Parameters and Node Predictors

The operation for node predictor is normally expressed as matrix multiplication. The matrix multiplication itself can be expressed as sequence of individual fixed-point multiplications, between known user defined input and secret targeted parameter. The user defined input could either be the chosen or random input to the tree. The secret target parameter is a constant value, an element of the targeted matrix (V, W, θ). This is indeed similar scenario to known plaintext attack method in SCA and we use correlation power analysis (CPA) analysis [3], but utilize electromagnetic emanations from the device instead of power consumption information as the information leakage source. We use CPA to statistically recover the secret node predictor over several EM measurements with known but varying inputs.

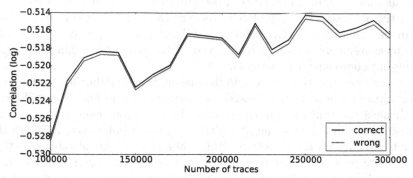

(a) CPA results on fixed point multiplication: The correct value is denoted with black, and the wrong one is denoted with red. In this case, after 100k traces, the correct one can be distinguished

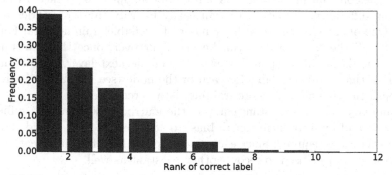

(b) The distribution of the correct label ranking on 3k traces test data.

Fig. 3. The results of attack on signed multiplication using CPA and attack on index loading using TA

CPA for Fixed-Point Multiplication. In Bonsai, the fixed point length can be of 8-bit or 16-bit, so the no. of hypotheses is either 2^8 or 2^{16}. The attack is successful if the correct values for each element in the matrix (sparse projection or node predictor) can be recovered. In terms of SCA, this can be achieved if each correct value achieves higher correlation in comparison to incorrect values. The attack results are shown in Fig. 3a for 16-bit data type (harder of the two cases). In this case, we only show the recovery of one constant. The procedure can be repeated until all constant values in the targeted matrices are recovered.

The black line depicts the correct value, which shows higher correlation than best of incorrect values, depicted in red (the incorrect values with highest correlation). Due to the property of fixed point multiplication, the correct weight and its logical complement will show same absolute correlation with opposite polarity, due to linearity of the multiplication operation. Thus, the attacker can either brute force for the polarity of the weights or bias the inputs carefully to recover the exact weight. In this case, 1,000 traces will be sufficient. However, in practice, the attacker usually prefers to recover the unique constant candidate. This can be achieved by introducing minor bias in the input data, and with 100,000 measurements, it is possible to recover the correct key candidate from its wrong but complement hypothesis.

The difference generally comes from the bias in data distribution. In this case, if the distribution is uniformly balanced, the correct constant and its complement will both have the same maximum (absolute) correlation, hence, by removing some positive (or in this case, negative) trace to cause imbalance, it allows the attacker to distinguish the correct constant values. The bias introduced is that there are more positives input than negatives to skew the correlation result. It can be done by removing few traces corresponding to negative input value to make the distribution imbalanced. Hence, in this case, each constant value can be recovered individually to partially reconstruct the matrices. For the matrix multiplication to speed up the operation, conditional branching might be introduced. If the constant in the matrix is 0, it can be skipped, and hence, by noting the timing difference, the adversary can easily identify the zero entries in the matrix. One of the challenges is the number of available training data. For the root node, all the training data can be used, however, once the branching is involved, the data will be split. For example, in the next layer, approximately only half of the data is available for each of the node (see Fig. 2). As such, the more depth the tree has, the more training data is required.

In summary, for each constant entry in the matrix, $1,000$ traces is sufficient for GE = 2, and by introducing small bias, to achieve GE = 1, around $100,000$ traces are typically required. Since each trace captured the full classification, the same trace set can be used to recover other constant as well.

4.2   Recovering Sparse Projection Index Parameters

When performing dimensionality reduction through the multiplication with sparse matrices, the constant (Z_{val}) and the target features (Z_{idx}) are pre-stored in the memory rather than the full matrix Z. The constant Z_{val} can be recovered when targeting the multiplication. The index loading can be targeted with Template Attack (TA) [4] on *load* operation. As *load* involves memory access, the operation perform memory access and leaks with higher signal to noise ratio (SNR) than other logical operations. Basically, since the loading operation in microcontrollers is known to leak information, this operation can be profiled.

TA for Index Recovery. To mount our attack, we should first find the timing when the index (Z_{idx}) is being loaded by the measured EM emanation. Basically, when the targeted index, Z_{idx}, is being fetch from the memory, we measure leakage. However, since this is a single loading operation, basic CPA or non-profiling based attack could not be performed, since it requires known user data. Hence, we adopted TA. However, this means a training/profiling will be required. In this case, we split the data for training and testing. We first apply pre-processing technique to determine the point of interest in the traces. We uniquely identified 3 points or features in the traces which contain useful information, and afterwards, for each label, we measure the template (the mean vector and covariance matrix). Then, on the testing phase, we calculate the probability of the test data, given the templates. To improve SNR for the experiments, we perform averaging 100 times. The train-test split is then set to 7:3, for a fairer evaluation.

In the given example for Bonsai, the USPS dataset is projected to 28 feature space. This projection can be also applied to any dimension, but for simplicity, the given feature dimension is used as default. We showed the results in Fig. 3b, measuring the GE of the index. With a profiling set of 7,000 averaged traces and the attack trace set of 3,000 traces, we report an accuracy of 38.9% and success rate of 95.5% for the correct index being in top-5 candidates (GE = 5). As observed from the figure, the success for first order rank is not that good (accuracy of 38.9%), meaning that the actual label is recovered around 38.9% of the time. However, it can also be observed the correct label is within top 5 prediction with high success rate (95.5%), meaning that in most cases, the attacker can brute force the top 5 prediction to recover the correct index. In this case, the first order and top 5 success rate will be highly dependent on the number of features used. In terms of number of input features, with more features more constants must to be recovered, and hence the success rate will likely decrease or more brute force required to reduce the number of candidates.

4.3   Recovering Branching Function

In general, in tree based algorithms, conditional branches are used to decide which path to transverse. In the case of Bonsai, if the previous parameters can be recovered, this step is trivial. However, we also investigate the alternative attack which might also be possible for this case. We target the *if-else* structure of conditional branching using timing side-channel. We measure the execution time of the following function which computes branching function as:

$$node1 = ((tmp > 0)?((2 * node0) + 1) : ((2 * node0) + 2));$$

The timing information is directly available on the EM measurements previously captured, accurate to nanosecond scale. Normally, the $node1$ is the target node, $node0$ is the original node, and tmp is the intermediate value. Our experiments reported successful recovery of tmp using timing information. We observed that the mean timing for first and second branches are 3.41 ns and 3.36 ns respectively. The variance in timing is only 0.01 ns, and hence, modelling this as TA with single feature, it allows the 100% recovery success. Hence, by building the timing profile, one can easily identify the path taken.

5   Conclusion

In this paper, we report side-channel based model extraction attack for tree-based algorithms running on IIoT. We target Bonsai, a public library, and identify crucial operations to target including sparse projection parameters, branching function and node predictors. Practical experiments on 32-bit ARM microcontroller using EM side-channel information were demonstrated for parameter recovery. Moreover, the target operations are also present in other learning algorithms, which make the proposed approach generic.

Acknowledgement. This work was performed in the Cooperative Research Project of the Research Institute of Electrical Communication, Tohoku University with Nanyang Technological University. This research was also supported in part by JST CREST Grant No. JPMJCR19K5, Japan.

References

1. Batina, L., Bhasin, S., Jap, D., Picek, S.: CSI NN: reverse engineering of neural network architectures through electromagnetic side channel. In: Heninger, N., Traynor, P. (eds.) 28th USENIX Security Symposium, USENIX Security 2019, Santa Clara, CA, USA, 14–16 August 2019, pp. 515–532. USENIX Association (2019). https://www.usenix.org/conference/usenixsecurity19/presentation/batina
2. Breiman, L., Friedman, J.H., Olshen, R.A., Stone, C.J.: Classification and Regression Trees. Wadsworth (1984)
3. Brier, E., Clavier, C., Olivier, F.: Correlation power analysis with a leakage model. In: Joye, M., Quisquater, J.-J. (eds.) CHES 2004. LNCS, vol. 3156, pp. 16–29. Springer, Heidelberg (2004). https://doi.org/10.1007/978-3-540-28632-5_2
4. Chari, S., Rao, J.R., Rohatgi, P.: Template attacks. In: Kaliski, B.S., Koç, K., Paar, C. (eds.) CHES 2002. LNCS, vol. 2523, pp. 13–28. Springer, Heidelberg (2003). https://doi.org/10.1007/3-540-36400-5_3
5. Hua, W., Zhang, Z., Suh, G.E.: Reverse engineering convolutional neural networks through side-channel information leaks. In: Proceedings of the 55th Annual Design Automation Conference, DAC 2018, San Francisco, CA, USA, 24–29 June 2018, pp. 4:1–4:6. ACM (2018). https://doi.org/10.1145/3195970.3196105
6. Hull, J.J.: A database for handwritten text recognition research. IEEE Trans. Pattern Anal. Mach. Intell. **16**(5), 550–554 (1994). https://doi.org/10.1109/34.291440
7. Kocher, P.C.: Timing attacks on implementations of Diffie-Hellman, RSA, DSS, and other systems. In: Koblitz, N. (ed.) CRYPTO 1996. LNCS, vol. 1109, pp. 104–113. Springer, Heidelberg (1996). https://doi.org/10.1007/3-540-68697-5_9
8. Kumar, A., Goyal, S., Varma, M.: Resource-efficient machine learning in 2 KB RAM for the internet of things. In: Precup, D., Teh, Y.W. (eds.) Proceedings of the 34th International Conference on Machine Learning, ICML 2017, Sydney, NSW, Australia, 6–11 August 2017. Proceedings of Machine Learning Research, vol. 70, pp. 1935–1944. PMLR (2017). http://proceedings.mlr.press/v70/kumar17a.html
9. Mangard, S., Oswald, E., Popp, T.: Power Analysis Attacks. Springer, Boston, MA (2007). https://doi.org/10.1007/978-0-387-38162-6

10. Messerges, T.S., Dabbish, E.A.: Investigations of power analysis attacks on smartcards. In: Guthery, S.B., Honeyman, P. (eds.) Proceedings of the 1st Workshop on Smartcard Technology, Smartcard 1999, Chicago, Illinois, USA, 10–11 May 1999. USENIX Association (1999). https://www.usenix.org/conference/usenix-workshop-smartcard-technology/investigations-power-analysis-attacks-smartcards
11. Wei, L., Luo, B., Li, Y., Liu, Y., Xu, Q.: I know what you see: power side-channel attack on convolutional neural network accelerators. In: Proceedings of the 34th Annual Computer Security Applications Conference, ACSAC 2018, San Juan, PR, USA, 03–07 December 2018, pp. 393–406. ACM (2018). https://doi.org/10.1145/3274694.3274696
12. Wu, D., Jennings, C., Terpenny, J., Gao, R.X., Kumara, S.: A comparative study on machine learning algorithms for smart manufacturing: tool wear prediction using random forests. J. Manufact. Sci. Eng. **139**(7) (2017)

Controlling the Deep Learning-Based Side-Channel Analysis: A Way to Leverage from Heuristics

Servio Paguada[1,2]([⊠]) [iD], Unai Rioja[1,2]([⊠]) [iD], and Igor Armendariz[2]([⊠]) [iD]

[1] Digital Security Group, Radboud University, Nijmegen, The Netherlands
{servio.paguadaisaula, unai.riojasabando}@ru.nl
[2] Ikerlan Technological Research Centre, Arrasate-Mondragón, Gipuzkoa, Spain
{slpaguada, urioja, iarmendariz}@ikerlan.es

Abstract. Deep neural networks have become the state-of-the-art method when a profiled side-channel analysis is performed. Their popularity is mostly due to neural nets overcoming some of the drawbacks of "classical" side-channel attacks, such as the need for feature selection or waveform synchronization, in addition to their capability to bypass certain countermeasures like random delays. To design and tune a neural network for side-channel analysis systematically is a complicated task. There exist hyperparameter tuning techniques which can be used in the side-channel analysis context, like Grid Search, but they are not optimal since they usually rely on specific machine learning metrics that cannot be directly linked to e.g. the success of the attack.

We propose a customized version of an existing statistical methodology called Six Sigma for optimizing the deep learning-based side-channel analysis process. We demonstrate the proposed methodology by successfully attacking a masked software implementation of AES.

Keywords: Cryptographic hardware · SCA · Six sigma · Deep learning · Hyperparameter tuning · Grid search · Guessing entropy

1 Introduction

The integration of countermeasures against side-channel analysis (SCA) attacks in small electronic devices and their validation has become a popular research topic in recent years. One approach for assessing the security of embedded systems against SCA (e.g. Common Criteria (CC) [13]) was to attack the device with different methods and techniques and quantify the resistance of the device based on whether the attacks are successful and the amount of resources needed. This approach is still used by entities like ANSSI [3] and BSI [1], but the amounts of time and resources needed for performing this kind of evaluations is constantly

---

S. Paguada and U. Rioja—These authors contributed equally to this work.

© Springer Nature Switzerland AG 2020
J. Zhou et al. (Eds.): ACNS 2020 Workshops, LNCS 12418, pp. 106–125, 2020.
https://doi.org/10.1007/978-3-030-61638-0_7

growing. Basically, the ever-increasing number of known SCA techniques, algorithms implemented, power models, etc. make this kind of evaluation infeasible for less experienced ones. To overcome the drawbacks, several leakage assessment techniques have arisen recently with the purpose of determining whether a device leaks information through side channels in a quick and simple way. The most popular one is the Test Vector Leakage Assessment (TVLA) methodology by Cryptography Research (CRI) [5]. The approach is using a statistical test (commonly Welch's t-test or Pearson's χ^2-test [33]) to distinguish whether two sets of data (e.g., random vs fixed) are significantly different. Those tests alone are not enough for evaluating a device security against SCA, since they do not quantify the leakage or give any clue about its exploitability, but are suitable for a preliminary ("black-box") evaluation. Thus, current certification processes like EMVCo [14] or Common Criteria (CC)[13] still require to evaluate the robustness of the Device Under Test (DUT) by directly attacking it with various side-channels techniques (e.g., differential power analysis [23], correlation power analysis [8], mutual information analysis [4,16], template attacks [10,12], deep learning-based attacks [27,31,36], etc.). However, the problem persists: the process of exploiting leakage with SCA techniques is a complex procedure in which not only the acquisition of hundreds of thousands or even millions of power traces is needed, but also the usage of signal processing techniques in combination with advanced statistical and mathematical tools is most of the times mandatory. In real-world experimental setups, the results are largely influenced by a huge amount of parameters that are not easily adjusted without trial and error and are heavily relying on the experience of professional security analysts.

The exploitation of SCA leakage using deep learning techniques is a promising approach since it addresses some of the problems of "classical" side-channel attacks, such as the need for preprocessing or feature (points-of-interest) selection. Also, related works on the topic show how neural networks can learn second-order leakages [27] and bypass desynchronization [37,45]. Conversely, the inclusion of deep neural networks in the equation implies adding even more complexity to an already difficult path, in which many decisions have to be taken with not much more clue, than the know-how of the people who have dealt with this kind of issues in the past. The usage of deep learning-based side-channel attacks (DL-SCA) is an unpredictable task, since the intrinsic stochasticity of neural networks causes that, even if we apply an architecture designed for a specific SCA data set, we can obtain bad results. Also, it is a non-repetitive task: a model that works properly for a certain data set can have terrible performance in a different one. Moreover, the selection of the proper values for the neural net's hyperparameters is not a trivial task. Therefore, it is important to use a suitable methodology to perform an experimentation process with those characteristics. Six Sigma is a well-known statistical methodology oriented to improve industrial processes (production and quality engineering) by reducing its variability. A customized Six Sigma methodology for reducing the uncertainty associated with the SCA process was introduced in [38]. In that work, we present a customized Six Sigma methodology, applicable to the different phases of the SCA process (acquisition optimization, attack optimization and leakage assessment). To the best of our knowledge, this is the only instance of considering Six Sigma for the SCA field until now. In this work, we go one step further by extending this methodology to the DL-SCA context and by using it for tuning both, architecture hyperparameters and optimizer hyperparameters [37].

Problem Statement: The design of a proper neural network architecture for DL-SCA evaluation is a cumbersome process as well as repetitive, not making it easy for SCA channel evaluators and researchers to fine-tune an architecture having many different data sets of leakage traces. There exist hyperparameter tuning techniques that may help to this task, but they are not optimal for the DL-SCA issues, as explained in Sect. 4.

Our Contribution: In addition to our previous work in [38], in which we applied Six Sigma in several SCA scenarios, we go deeper by extending this methodology to the DL-SCA context. Our approach is to develop a customized Grid Search using Six Sigma, in which it is possible to identify and quantify the effect of each hyperparameter in the DL-SCA process. Instead of trying all possible combinations of the finite set of hyperparameters, we search for the best combination of them in a more methodical and ordered way. This approach considerably reduces the number of possible hyperparameter combinations (as detailed in Sect. 5) and hence the huge amount of time needed in a regular Grid Search procedure. The search is performed by using our novel *score function* that is based on guessing entropy [44] allowing us to integrate Six Sigma and its hyperparameter tuning procedure into the SCA context (see Sect. 4 for detailed explanation). The score function is an important piece in the tuning process, as it establishes the score performance that we would like to achieve at the end of the procedure. To demonstrate our contributions in practice, we have conducted experiments showing an improvement in the score performance of a previously built architecture [48] (Sect. 5). All this in addition to the benefits of using our (simplified) methodology. A similar approach can be applied for an architecture that is built from scratch.

The rest of the paper is organized as follows: Sect. 2 reminds the main concepts of the Six Sigma methodology, explains its main steps and connects it to the practical use case (Sect. 5). Section 3 summarizes briefly the state-of-the art in deep learning-based side-channel analysis. Section 4 gives an overview of the existing hyperparameter tuning techniques and explains our guessing entropy-based score function. Finally, Sect. 6, concludes the paper.

2   Six Sigma Methodology

The Six Sigma (6σ) methodology was created in 1986 by Bill Smith, while working as an engineer at Motorola, as the company that registered the term as their trademark in 1993 [19]. The primary objective was to minimize the variability of the output of a process. To achieve this, different empirical quality management methods, along with statistical methods are used. In this improvement process some steps have to be repeated until a main goal is reached. In our

Fig. 1. Custom Six sigma methodology steps.

case, Six Sigma involves the DMAIC methodology implicitly (**Define-Measure-Analyze-Improve-Control**), which is based on the Deming's Plan-Do-Check-Act Cycle [11,43]. The steps of the methodology are shown in Fig. 1, pointing to how they could fit in an DL-SCA context and linking them to our use case (Sect. 5). More details can be found in [38].

- **Define** the system. Here the system's inputs are the client requirements and the project's goal. In our case, the "Define phase" consists of not only the definition of the experiments itself but also the main goal(s) and the OK-criterion. We interpret this OK-criterion as the quantification of the goal we want to achieve. In other words, the definition of a factor that enables us to decide if the experiments are conclusive or not. A more detailed explanation can be found in the "Define" section of the use case (Sect. 5.2).
- **Measure** the current process setup. To characterize the current state of the process, here one collects its parameters and outputs. In our case, the objective is to define the variables/parameters we are going to tune. We need to define the variables of the system (architectural hyperparameters, optimizer hyperparameters, etc.) that could affect the performance of the DL-SCA. For those variables, one prescribes a minimum and a maximum value and selects three of them. In the "Measure" section of our use case (Sect. 5.3) the reader can find a detailed explanation.
- **Analyze** the data obtained from the process, and determine its relationships with the problem. This step consists of experimentation e.g., crafting an experimental design or Design of Experiments (DoE). DoE is a branch of applied statistics, which is responsible for evaluating the factors (or variables) that influence a parameter or group of parameters. Note that in this paper we do not deeply explain DoE, but we refer interested readers to [32], and [15]. The objective is to quantify which variables have more influence over the experiment and adjust them to the proper values. To do that, a DoE with the 3 selected working variables to perform 8 experiments is chosen. The output of it gives the coefficient for each variable, which tells us if the effect is positive or negative (improves or not the result of the experiment) and how strong each one in comparison with the others is. In the "Analyze section" of use case 5.4 the output of each DoE can be observed in more detail.
- **Improve** the current process using the analysis of root causes done in the previous step to identify, test and implement a solution for the discovered problems. In this customized Six Sigma, this step consists of the analysis of the experimental design's results. Here one adjusts the identified working

variables that have more influence over the experiments. If the OK-Criterion is not reached after the 8 experiments, the process should be repeated from the previous step, considering to change the selected variables or readjust their minimum and maximum values. This is considered as one iteration. The idea is to perform several iterations between these two last steps until the main objective is reached. Practical examples of this analysis of the results and the readjustment of the DoE variables are shown in the "Improve" section of our use case (5.5).

- **Control** the newly improved process to correct any undesired deviations on it. Repeat the steps until obtaining the desired quality level. This step does not strictly apply to our problem, but it can be understood as the action of taking notes of the results to apply in future experiments.

3   Deep Learning-Based Side-Channel Analysis

DL-SCA belongs to the so-called profiling attacks, the dominant type in SCA nowadays. It is divided into two phases: the profiling phase and the attack phase. In the profiling phase, a leakage model of the targeted device is built by using standard classification techniques like in Template attacks [10,12], Support Vector Machine (SVM) [21,22,24], Random Forest (RF) [25], regression or the Stochastic models approach [39] or even recently introduced Deep learning techniques [9,27,36]. In the attack phase, the model is applied and the secret key is guessed. Template attacks and deep learning are the two most popular approaches [26]. Here we focus on deep learning-based attacks because of their popularity and the lack of a methodical approach for efficient analysis.

The main goal in a DL-SCA is to deduce the secret key used to perform cryptographic operations. Thus, the attacker has to first take measurements of some device's physical property (commonly the power consumption or the electromagnetic radiation emitted by the device) during the manipulation of some intermediate value $iv = f(p, k)$ related to the plain text p and the secret key k. In the profiling phase, the attacker uses a set of n_p profiling traces $(T_{p,k})$ to train a neural network to classify possible iv values. Then, in the attack phase, from a set of n_a real power traces and its input data (plain text), the attacker tries to guess the correct iv value (or its Hamming Weight) by using the trained neural network. Since $iv = f(p, k)$, knowing iv and p the secret key k can be recovered.

Multiple related works on DL-SCA have been developed in recent times. Most of them are based on two deep learning architectures: Multilayer Perceptron (MLP) and Convolutional Neural Networks (CNN). MLP was the first architecture used in DL-SCA due to its simplicity. Although the first proposal was using regression to characterize leakage [47], MLP are mostly used to classify the intermediate value of the traces (as explained above) [27,29]. Conversely, CNNs have also been applied to SCA because its spatial invariance property provides robustness against data distortions like environmental noise and countermeasures [9,20,27,46]. Several studies have also compared the performance of different profiling SCA techniques [36,37,48,50]. As mentioned above, one of the main drawbacks of classical SCA (profiled or non-profiled) is the need for pre-processing and feature selection, which require human engineering and therefore, the success of the attack strongly relies on the expertise of the evaluator. Although its usage increases the complexity of the attack, DL-SCA claims to overcome those difficulties since the features are selected automatically from traces by the neural network. Also, it has been shown that neural networks are capable of bypassing desynchronization [30,36,37] and dealing with masking countermeasures [17,27].

4   Hyperparameter Tuning

In this section, we give an overview of grid search among some other commonly used hyperparameter tuning techniques in order to pin down the hyperparameter tuning issue. Additionally, we formalize the score function that we use later in the experiments.

4.1   Grid Search and Other Techniques in the SCA Field

A well-known hyperparameter tuning procedure is grid search [18], which exhaustively search through a manually specified subset of hyperparameters space. In other words, for each hyperparameter a finite set of values is selected. Then, the grid search algorithm trains a net for each combination of hyperparameters and evaluates their performance on a validation data set. It uses what is usually called *score function* to evaluate the chosen hyperparameter set. Regarding the type of application (i.e. regression or classification), it is common to use the average accuracy score or mean square error as score function, but an alternative score function can be specified in order to adapt the search to a specific use case. Although exhaustive, grid search has been used widely in many applications that involve machine learning algorithms due to the need to find the hyperparameters that better performance has for the problem. In fact, its use is attributed to its easy software implementations available in many data analysis tools.Other procedures for tuning are *Hyperopt* [7] and *Hyperas* [6] that rely on randomly chosen trials of hyperparameter. Although it has been proven that random approaches are more efficient than grid search in general applications [18], we focus on grid search since we aim to connect currently used hyperparameter tuning procedures with SCA (by using a score function based on an SCA metric).

As mentioned above, machine learning metrics are commonly used as score functions in hyperparameter tuning procedures. This is not optimal since machine learning metrics are not reliable for evaluating the effectiveness of a deep learning architecture in the SCA context [35]. We speak in terms of general applications, as we argue that many of the contributions made in the deep learning field, and more specifically for hyperparameter tuning, are indeed applicable in the SCA field. An example can be found in publications such as [48], where grid search has been used as a procedure to find out the best set of hyperparameters.

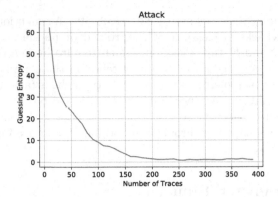

Fig. 2. Averaged guessing entropy plot from the attack using the baseline model in [48], where an score value of 0.65 was obtained using Eq. 1.

In any case, as demonstrated in [35], conventional machine learning metrics are not very informative for the side-channel analysis domain, concluding that the best metrics are SCA specific metrics like success rate (SR) and guessing entropy (GE) [44] which are directly linked to the success of the attack. Also, it worth mentioning a recent work that purposes a novel DL-SCA metric called Cross-Entropy Ratio (CER) [49], closely related to SR and GE. Anyhow, we focus on GE because it is a well-known and understood metric in the SCA field.

In essence, the GE of an attack (or a battery of attacks) measures the average number of key candidates an attacker needs to test in order to reveal the secret key. In other words, is a measure of the difficulty that an attacker has to guess the secret key. In a profiled SCA scenario, given a n_a number of power traces in the attack phase and being $|K|$ the size of the keyspace, the attack outputs a key guessing vector $\mathbf{g} = [g_1, g_2, ..., g_{|K|},]^1$ with decreasing order of probability. The GE is the average rank of the correct key candidate in $\mathbf{g}$ over several attacks. The higher GE value, the more difficult it would be for an attacker to guess the correct key. An example of a GE graphic can be found in Fig. 2 where it can be observed how the GE of the attack (y-axis) decreases as the number of traces employed for the attack increases (x-axis).

Nevertheless, to the best of our knowledge, there is no procedure specifically designed for SCA and thus, one of our contributions is to introduce a score function based on GE. Moreover, combining this with our customized Six Sigma methodology brings the possibility to quantify the impact of each hyperparameter on the performance of the DL-SCA. A standard implementation does not allow to analyze such an impact systematically.

Our customized Grid Search procedure allows us to find out an optimal combination of hyperparameters in a more ordered and methodical way (instead of trying all possible combinations of the finite set of hyperparameters). Such a

---

[1] The key guessing vector $\mathbf{g}$ (over n_a power traces) is computed using the log-likelihood principle $g_i = \sum_{j=1}^{n_a} \log(\hat{p}_{ij})$.

tuning process requires a score function as a way to quantify the effect of each hyperparameter. Moreover, the score function is the mathematical foundation for defining the *OK-criterion*. In the next subsection, we explain how this function is defined.

4.2   A Scoring Function Based on Guessing Entropy

For both Grid Search and our customized Six Sigma procedure, we need a quantification of the output of each experiment (namely hyperparameter combination), and this is achieved with the *score function*. In a nutshell, our score function quantifies the result of the experiment by taking into account three aspects: the final guessing entropy value (the guessing entropy of a successful attack will converge to 0), when the guessing entropy converges i.e. how fast the model reaches the minimal guessing entropy value, and the shape of the slope (we assess how far is the slope of the curve from an optimal shape). The formal expression of the function is shown in Eq. (1).

$$sf(ge) = \frac{trend}{2} \cdot \left(\frac{M - ge_{i=N}}{M} + \frac{N - \mathrm{argmin}(ge)}{N} \right) \tag{1}$$

where ge is the guessing entropy vector (of length N), M is the maximum GE value[2], $ge_{i=N}$ is the final guessing entropy value of the attack and $\mathrm{argmin}(ge)$ is the index of the minimum value of the guessing entropy vector. As $trend$, we understand a value between 0 and 1, which tells us whether the slope of the guessing entropy vector is optimal. We obtain it by computing the cumulative of the difference between the neighboring values, for all guessing entropy vector elements, that is divided by the max difference value (a.k.a MinMax scaler) as follows:

$$trend = \frac{\sum_{i=1}^{N-1}(ge_i - ge_{i+1}) - \min(ge)}{\max(ge) - \min(ge)} \tag{2}$$

For instance, if we apply Eq. 1 to the GE plot shown in Fig. 2 (which correspond to an attack over the ASCAD [37] dataset using the baseline model purposed in [48]) we obtain a baseline value of 0.65. The closest this value is to 1, the better performance the model has. We take this value of 0.65 as a starting point for our use case.

5   Use Case: Deep-Learning Based Side-Channel Attack over a Protected AES Implementation

In this section the proposed method is presented and explained step by step, giving as examples the procedures done with our experimental setup to optimize

---

[2] In SCA on software AES implementations, is common to target 8-bit intermediate values. In this case, since the size of the keyspace $|K|$ is 2^8, the maximum GE value (worst case) is 256.

the DL-SCA process. First, we briefly describe the presented use case and then we elaborate on the 5 steps following the DMAIC scheme.

Moreover, we show how the number of hyperparameter combinations employed in the tuning procedure is drastically reduced comparing it with a regular Grid Search procedure. As explained above, in a regular procedure a finite set of values for each hyperparameter is selected, and each combination of them is evaluated in order to select the optimal values. An example can be observed in [48], where grid-search optimization is performed using 40 320 hyperparameter combinations[3]. By combining our customized Six Sigma procedure with Grid Search optimization we have been able to improve the results obtained with the hyperparameter combination shown in [48] with only 32 hyperparameter combinations ($2^3 \cdot 4$ iterations), showing a significant improvement (99.92% fewer combinations).

5.1 Use Case Description

For the experiments, we have used ASCAD [37] as the first open database for DL-SCA. The target platform in this data set is an 8-bit AVR microcontroller (ATmega8515), implementing a masked AES-128 cipher [2,28] and the traces are obtained by measuring the electromagnetic emanation of the device. The data set provides 60 000 traces where 50 000 are used for profiling and 10 000 for the attack. These traces are a window of 700 relevant raw samples per trace, representing the third byte of the first round masked S-Box operation. For a deeper explanation of the ASCAD dataset we refer to [37]. As the sensitive intermediate value we use an S-box output: $Y^{(i)}(k^*) = \mathrm{Sbox}[P_3^{(i)} \oplus k^*]$.

5.2 Define

In this step, we specify our experiments. We use a CNN to perform an attack over the aforementioned traces. The amount of traces used for the profiling phase is a variable included in the system's variables, its range values should be determined in the measure step. It is a good practice to include a validation set in the training phase, and it could be anything from 20% to 25% of the number of traces (for training). In the attack phase, a random choice from a subset of the total traces is conducted, Table 1 summarize all these values. After the attack, the guessing entropy is computed and used by the score function. The resulting value represents the evaluation of the performance produced by the chosen hyperparameters set.

Main goal: Here the goal that we want to achieve is defined. For our experiment we set the following goal: successfully attack a masked AES implementation with a DL-SCA, increasing the baseline score (Fig. 2, Eq. 1) from 0.65 to 0.70 and hence improving the performance of the CNN model purposed in [48].

---

[3] In [48], if we analyze the possible combinations of the specified subset of hyperparameters for Grid search optimization, we obtain $3^2 \cdot 4^2 \cdot 8^1 \cdot 7^1 \cdot 5^1 = 40\,320$ possible combinations

Table 1. Values of variables for the profiling and attack phase

Variable	Value and description
# profiling traces	To be set in the measure step
# validation traces	20% to 25%
# attack traces	400 random chosen (from 10 000 subset) in 50 attack trials

OK-criterion: The quantification of the goal, a factor that indicates whether the experiments are conclusive or not. During the experiments, one tries to tune several parameters obtaining different results through iterations, so the *OK-criterion* indicates when to stop Six Sigma running. Also, it tells us when we have reached our objectives. In this use case, since we measure the performance of each experiment with the score function (Sect. 4.2), our *OK-criterion* is to obtain a score greater than or equal to 0.70 using that function. As explained before, after conducting several attacks over the ASCAD fixed key data set using the CNN architecture proposed in [48] (which has shown competitive performance in that dataset) and computing the averaged guessing entropy, we have obtained the results depicted in Fig. 2 and an averaged score value around 0.65. Thus, we take 0.65 as baseline value and establish a value of 0.70 as good enough to consider an improvement in the results i.e. **OK-Criterion** $= sf(ge) \geq 0.70$

5.3 Measure

The purpose of this step is to define the system's variables that we are going to study. The parameters can be different in nature (architectural hyperparameters, optimizer hyperparameters, preprocessing parameters, etc.). Also, there are some parameters that can be considered in most of the cases (optimizer, batch size, epochs, n° of neurons, n° of layers, etc.) while other parameters will depend on the specific use case. After prompting all the possible parameters that need further tuning, the three variables that are more likely to affect the results of the experiment have to be chosen. Thus, the parameters must be sorted by relevance. An expert evaluator would do that based on his own intuition, but they can also be ranked randomly. Although this could imply more iterations, it is a good solution whenever the evaluator is not sure how to rank them.

For each parameter a minimum and a maximum value has to be specified, although some parameters will be Boolean others will have a range of possible values. Also, this list must be analyzed to avoid the selection of parameters that can be dependent on each other. Table 2 gives the parameters with their descriptions and ranges. The top three variables will be analyzed in the next step, performing a DoE on them (Table 4). The rest of the parameters have to be fixed in values between their minimum and maximum. It should be noticed that there are some parameters that can be set apart from the experimental design (see Table 3). Here we consider variables that could be included in the previous list, but can be fixed by the evaluator, or there could be another method

Table 2. Defined variables that will be used in the experimental design

Rank	Parameter	Description	Range	Fixed Value
1	# traces (profiling)	The 45k training traces can be used in the profiling phase or only a subset of them	20k vs 45k	
2	# epochs	A trade-off to avoid overfitting and underfitting	25 vs 50	
3	Optimizer	Different optimizers can be used (SGD, RMSprop, Adam, etc)	RMSprop vs Adam	
4	Batch normalization	Technique for improving the speed, performance, and stability of artificial neural networks	NO vs YES	**YES**
5	Dropout	A trade-off to avoid slowing down training process	NO vs YES	**NO**
6	Kernel size	According to state of the art methodologies [48]	1 vs 3	**1**
7	Activation function	ReLu and SeLU avoid convergence problems of the optimizer	ReLU vs SeLU	**SeLU**
8	Weight initialization	He uniform and Glorot uniform have proved to provide good results	Glorot uniform vs He uniform	**He uniform**
9	Dim of internal FC layers	A trade-off avoiding a too complex model	10 vs 20	**10**
10	# Conv Layers	A trade-off avoiding a too complex model	1 vs 2	**1**
11	# FC Layers	A trade-off avoiding a too complex model	3 vs 5	**3**

for tuning them, e.g., the learning rate, can be tuned using *One Cycle Policy* [40–42]. This also allows for reducing the number of variables involved.

As a starting point, range values in Table 2 are chosen according to the state-of-the-art proposals in the SCA context, as well as deep learning general recommendations. One of the main reasons for the latter is to avoid underfitting and overfitting as well as class biases [18,34,35]. Hyperparameters like number of epochs, number of traces, dropout, batch normalization, weight initialization are just a few of them which have to be properly tuned to achieve a good classification. Keep in mind that almost always a trade-off between variables has to be found, by instances dropout can reduce overfitting but could also slow down the training process, being necessary to increase the number of epochs. Currently,

Table 3. Fixed Parameters (not considered in the experimental design)

Rank	Parameter	Description	Range	Fixed value
12	Learning Rate	The LR will be tuned with the One Cycle Policy	One Cycle Policy	**One Cycle Policy**
13	Stand-ardization	Zero mean and regularization are mandatory in almost every SCA scenario	YES	**YES**
14	Desynchr-onization	For this use case we do not consider desynchronization	NO	**NO**
15	Batch size	We fix the batch size to 50 following the state-of-the art suggestions	50	**50**
16	Max Pool	Max Pooling according to state-of-the-art approaches	YES	**YES**
17	Loss Function	*Categorical Cross-Entropy* because of the intrinsic nature of the classification problem addressed by the learning algorithm	cross-entropy	**cross-entropy**

kernel size of 1 has been proved to be an optimal value for the first convolutional block [48]. Nevertheless, to show the effect of applying the suggested methodology, we established a range value of 1 vs 3. For the following range values, *he uniform* and *glorot uniform* have proved to achieve good result for classification, similar case apply for *ReLU* and *SeLU* activation functions for the hidden layers of the deep learning model. Since DL-SCA could be described as a classification problem, the loss function to be used is a *Categorical Cross-Entropy*. Such function aims to minimize the cross-entropy, which is equivalent to maximize the lower bound of the mutual information between traces and secret key [31].

5.4   Analyze

From the ordered list, the three top parameters are chosen (Table 4), and a simple Design of Experiments (DoE [15]) process is carried out. We choose the 3 variables factorial DoE for its simplicity and reliability. Therefore, we perform 2^3 experiments following the process described in [38] (Sec. 3.4.).

The DoE as explained above was applied to create 8 experiments with the limit in the values as shown in Table 5. Note that the order of the experiment must follow exactly the one given in the table. After the experiments the "Round 1" column in Table 5 was filled with the obtained scores. The set of 8 experiments has been repeated using cross-validation [18] (with different subsets of traces, column "Round 2") to ensure that the results are consistent and are not altered by the intrinsic randomness of the neural networks. The coefficients are

Table 4. Working variables and values (1st DoE iteration)

Factor letter	Factor name	Low settings	High settings
A	# traces (profiling)	20k	45k
B	# epochs	25	50
C	optimizer	RMSprop	Adam

calculated with the averaged data (column "Average"). The number of rounds can be increased for better confidence but it will also increase the computing time. At this point, we have one set of results and hence the factors of Eq. (3) given by DoE. The parameters A, B, and C in Fig. 3 mean that our experiment has better results when the **Number of traces for profiling** is **45k**, and we train with **50 epochs** using the **Adam optimizer**.

$$DoE = 0.425 + 0.165 * A + 0.022 * B + 0.0282 * C \\ + -0.069 * AB + -0.019 * AC + 0.109 * BC \tag{3}$$

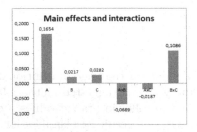

Fig. 3. Coefficients and interactions (1st DoE iteration)

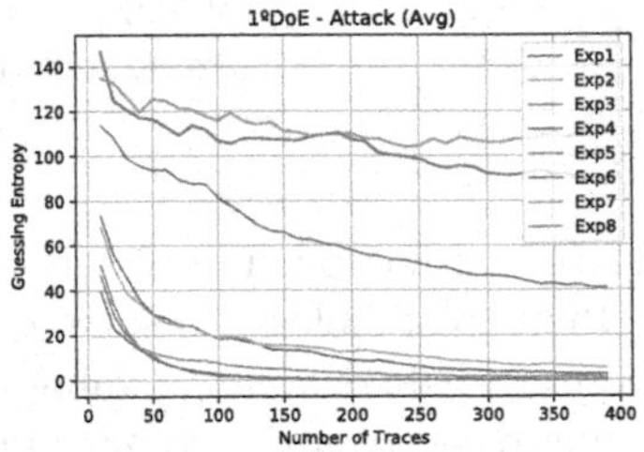

Fig. 4. Averaged Guessing entropy of the 8 experiments (1st DoE iteration)

Table 5. First DoE iteration with results

Execution order	Number of traces (profiling)	Num of Epoch	Optimizer	Round 1	Round 2	AVG
1	20k	25	RMSprop	0.2341	0.3381	0.2861
2	20k	25	Adam	0.0494	0.0546	0.0520
3	20k	50	RMSprop	0.1384	0.1403	0.1393
4	20k	50	Adam	0.6238	0.4981	0.5610
5	45k	25	RMSprop	0.6375	0.7250	0.6813
6	45k	25	Adam	0.6000	0.5875	0.5938
7	45k	50	RMSprop	0.4889	0.4721	0.4805
8	45k	50	Adam	0.7125	0.4989	0.6057

5.5   Improve

After performing DoE, in this step the evaluator should analyze the results, interpret them and apply the necessary changes. If the impact of one parameter is clear, its value can become fixed in its maximum/minimum value. Otherwise, the range of the variable can be modified and used in another DoE iteration. After fixing the values of the tuned variables, the evaluator may add the next parameters in the table and perform another iteration of the DoE, until we reach the OK-criterion. Conversely, one can derive from the results that certain combinations of parameters work better than others (the effect of the interactions can be very relevant to make a decision) and select the 3 variables for the next iteration accordingly. For a better interpretation of the results, the evaluator should observe the Guessing Entropy plot of each one of the 8 experiments (Fig. 4) apart from the scores shown in Table 5. We observe that the best performance is for experiment number eight, and thus, it has the highest score of the 8 experiments. The OK-Criterion has not been reached in any of the experiments but we can clearly see that we obtain better results with 45k traces, 50 epochs and Adam optimizer. Thus, we fix these 3 variables and select the next three from the list (Table 6).

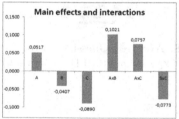

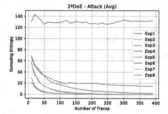

Fig. 5. Coefficients and interactions (2nd DoE iteration)

Fig. 6. Averaged Guessing entropy of the 8 experiments (2nd DoE iteration)

Table 6. Second DoE Iteration with results

Execution order	Batch normal-ization	Dropout	Kernel size	Round 1	Round 2	AVG
1	NO	NO	1	0.7500	0.4988	0.6244
2	NO	NO	3	0.5499	0.7500	0.6499
3	NO	YES	1	0.7000	0.6875	0.6938
4	NO	YES	3	0.0509	−0.0322	0.0093
5	YES	NO	1	0.5731	0.5720	0.5726
6	YES	NO	3	0.3256	0.6747	0.5001
7	YES	YES	1	0.5371	0.7625	0.6498
8	YES	YES	3	0.6375	0.7000	0.6688

Second DoE Iteration

Results of the second iteration are shown in Table 6 and Figs. 5 and 6. The OK-Criterion has not been reached yet but we can see a clear gain concerning the previous iteration. From observing the coefficients of each variable (Fig. 7) we notice **Batch Normalization** has a clear good effect on the attack, while **Dropout** is not so clear. Some experiments using Dropout have good results but in general, it slows down the learning process by reducing the chance to achieve good performance with the chosen number of epochs, so we decide to fix it to its minimum value (**no dropout**). Nevertheless, the variable can be considered again in the next iterations if necessary. Related to **kernel size**, in this case we obtain better results with a kernel size of **1**. The three variables are fixed to their maximum/minimum value taking into account the effects and a third DoE iteration is performed.

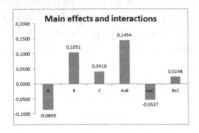 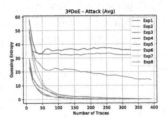

Fig. 7. Coefficients and interactions (3rd DoE iteration)

Fig. 8. Averaged Guessing entropy of the 8 experiments (3rd DoE iteration)

Table 7. Third DoE iteration with results

Execution order	Num epochs	Activation function	Weight initialization	Round 1	Round 2	AVG
1	50	ReLU	Glorot	0.5430	0.6125	0.5777
2	50	ReLU	He	0.6375	0.6750	0.6563
3	50	SeLU	Glorot	0.3490	0.4209	0.3850
4	50	SeLU	He	0.7000	0.6750	0.6875
5	75	ReLU	Glorot	0.1205	0.2003	0.1604
6	75	ReLU	He	0.0936	0.2062	0.1499
7	75	SeLU	Glorot	0.6000	0.7500	0.6750
8	75	SeLU	He	0.5621	0.7125	0.6373

Third DoE Iteration

The results of the third iteration are shown in Table 7, Fig. 8 and Fig. 7. In this iteration, we have added again the **number of epochs** variable to assess if a larger number of epochs improves the outcomes. The results show clearly that we obtain better performance with 50 epochs. We observe that, in general, **SeLU activation function** and the **Glorot weight initialization** provide better results, although we obtain similar performance using SeLU + Glorot (Table 7, Exp 7) and Selu + He (Table 7, Exp 4). Since the OK-Criterion has not been reached we add the next 3 variables (Dimension of the fully-connected layer, Number of convolution layers and Number of fully-connected layers), and perform another iteration.

Fourth DoE Iteration

The results of the fourth iteration are shown in Table 8 and Figs. 9 and 10. Analyzing the results, adding more **convolution layers** or **fully-connected layers** does not produce any improvement (actually the results are slightly worse). Nevertheless, we see a clear improvement while increasing the **number of neurons** in the fully-connected layers. Since we have reached the OK-Criterion in several experiments (2, 4 and 6), we consider the Six Sigma process concluded.

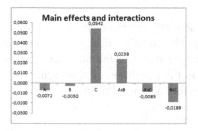

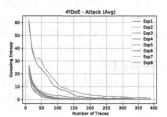

Fig. 9. Coefficients and interactions (4th DoE iteration)

Fig. 10. Averaged Guessing entropy of the 8 experiments (4th DoE iteration)

Table 8. Fourth DoE iteration with results

Execution order	Dim of fc layer	Num of Conv layers	Num of fc layers	Round 1	Round 2	AVG
1	10	1	3	0.6687	0.6125	0.6406
2	10	1	4	0.7125	0.7750	0.7438
3	10	2	3	0.5875	0.5421	0.5648
4	10	2	4	0.7750	0.6500	0.7125
5	20	1	3	0.5106	0.5607	0.5356
6	20	1	4	0.7500	0.7000	0.7250
7	20	2	3	0.6625	0.6875	0.6750
8	20	2	4	0.6375	0.7000	0.6687

6   Conclusion and Perspectives

The experimental results demonstrate the suitability of this method for improving the DL-SCA process. Our customized Six Sigma methodology not only optimizes the Grid Search procedure by reducing the number of hyperparameter combinations to try (and hence the computation time) but also allow evaluators to systematically track and quantify the impact of each hyperparameter in the guessing entropy of the attack, making it easier to adjust them to an optimal value.

The methodology steps proposed are simple, methodical and very helpful while dealing with the analysis of those characteristics. This approach can be helpful to any researcher or evaluator in a testing laboratory; it allows technicians without a deep knowledge of all the basics involved in these methods to implement and interpret DL-SCA evaluations properly. The methodology can also be used by experts when they have to come up with a new architecture for an alternative testing platform (e.g., new devices, attacks). Our recommendation for them is to run the proposed method at least once, so they can find out the best hyperparameters as a starting point.

Even though for this work we decided to show the effects of using Six Sigma to optimize the grid search procedure, we argue that all the aforementioned procedures and techniques (i.e. random approaches) are potential candidates to be optimized for DL-SCA, and these are taken as futures lines of research. Additionally, more complex data set from 32-bit platforms, and HW implementations will be considered for future works.

References

1. Federal Office for Information Security (BSI) - Common Criteria for examination and evaluation of it security. https://www.bsi.bund.de/EN/Topics/CommonCriteria/commoncriteria.html. Accessed 17 June 2020
2. FIPS 197: Announcing the Advanced Encryption Standard (AES), November 2001. https://nvlpubs.nist.gov/nistpubs/FIPS/NIST.FIPS.197.pdf
3. Agence Nationale de la Sécurité des Systèmes d'information - Certified products (2019). https://www.ssi.gouv.fr/en/products/certified-products/. Accessed 17 June 2020
4. Batina, L., Gierlichs, B., Prouff, E., Rivain, M., Standaert, F.X., Veyrat-Charvillon, N.: Mutual information analysis: a comprehensive study. J. Cryptology **24**(2), 269–291 (2011)
5. Becker, G., et al.: Test vector leakage assessment (TVLA) methodology in practice (extended abstract) (2013)
6. Bergstra, J., Bengio, Y.: Random search for hyper-parameter optimization. J. Mach. Learn. Res. **13**, 281–305 (2012)
7. Bergstra, J., Komer, B., Eliasmith, C., Yamins, D., Cox, D.D.: Hyperopt: a python library for model selection and hyperparameter optimization. Comput. Sci. Discov. **8**(1), 014008 (2015)
8. Brier, E., Clavier, C., Olivier, F.: Correlation power analysis with a leakage model. In: Joye, M., Quisquater, J.-J. (eds.) CHES 2004. LNCS, vol. 3156, pp. 16–29. Springer, Heidelberg (2004). https://doi.org/10.1007/978-3-540-28632-5_2

9. Cagli, E., Dumas, C., Prouff, E.: Convolutional neural networks with data augmentation against jitter-based countermeasures. In: Fischer, W., Homma, N. (eds.)
   CHES 2017. LNCS, vol. 10529, pp. 45–68. Springer, Cham (2017). https://doi.org/
   10.1007/978-3-319-66787-4_3
10. Chari, S., Rao, J.R., Rohatgi, P.: Template attacks. In: Kaliski, B.S., Koç, K.,
    Paar, C. (eds.) CHES 2002. LNCS, vol. 2523, pp. 13–28. Springer, Heidelberg
    (2003). https://doi.org/10.1007/3-540-36400-5_3
11. Cheng, C.S., Lee, S.C., Chen, P.W., Huang, K.K.: The application of design for
    Six Sigma on high level smart phone development. J. Q. 19, 117–136 (2012)
12. Choudary, M.O., Kuhn, M.G.: Efficient, portable template attacks. IEEE Trans.
    Inf. Forensics Secur. 13(2), 490–501 (2018)
13. Common Criteria: Common Criteria v3.1. Release 5, April 2017. https://www.
    commoncriteriaportal.org/cc/index.cfm?. Accessed 17 June 2020
14. EMVCo: EMV specifications (2001). https://www.emvco.com/. Accessed 17 June
    2020
15. Fisher, R.A.: The Design of Experiments, 9th edn. Macmillan (1935)
16. Gierlichs, B., Batina, L., Tuyls, P., Preneel, B.: Mutual information analysis. In:
    Oswald, E., Rohatgi, P. (eds.) CHES 2008. LNCS, vol. 5154, pp. 426–442. Springer,
    Heidelberg (2008). https://doi.org/10.1007/978-3-540-85053-3_27
17. Gilmore, R., Hanley, N., O'Neill, M.: Neural network based attack on a masked
    implementation of AES. In: Proceedings of the 2015 IEEE International Sympo-
    sium on Hardware-Oriented Security and Trust, HOST 2015, pp. 106–111, June
    2015
18. Goodfellow, I., Bengio, Y., Courville, A.: Deep Learning. The MIT Press, New
    York (2016)
19. Gordon, J. (ed.): Six Sigma Quality for Business and Manufacture. Elsevier Science,
    October 2002, hardcover ISBN: 9780444510471
20. Hettwer, B., Gehrer, S., Güneysu, T.: Profiled power analysis attacks using con-
    volutional neural networks with domain knowledge. In: Selected Areas in Cryp-
    tography - SAC 2018–25th International Conference, Calgary, AB, Canada, 15–17
    August 2018, pp. 479–498 (2018)
21. Heuser, A., Zohner, M.: Intelligent machine homicide. In: Schindler, W., Huss, S.A.
    (eds.) COSADE 2012. LNCS, vol. 7275, pp. 249–264. Springer, Heidelberg (2012).
    https://doi.org/10.1007/978-3-642-29912-4_18
22. Hospodar, G., Gierlichs, B., De Mulder, E., Verbauwhede, I., Vandewalle, J.:
    Machine learning in side-channel analysis: a first study. J. Cryptographic Eng.
    1, 293–302 (2011)
23. Kocher, P., Jaffe, J., Jun, B.: Differential power analysis. In: Wiener, M. (ed.)
    CRYPTO 1999. LNCS, vol. 1666, pp. 388–397. Springer, Heidelberg (1999).
    https://doi.org/10.1007/3-540-48405-1_25
24. Lerman, L., Bontempi, G., Markowitch, O.: Side channel attack : an approach
    based on machine learning. In: Constructive Side-Channel Analysis and Secure
    Design, COSADE (2011)
25. Lerman, L., Bontempi, G., Markowitch, O.: A machine learning approach against
    a masked aes. J. Cryptograph. Eng. 5(2), 123–139 (2015)
26. Lerman, L., Poussier, R., Markowitch, O., Standaert, F.X.: Template attacks versus
    machine learning revisited and the curse of dimensionality in side-channel analysis:
    extended version. J. Cryptograph. Eng. 8(4), 301–313 (2018)

27. Maghrebi, H., Portigliatti, T., Prouff, E.: Breaking cryptographic implementations using deep learning techniques. In: Carlet, C., Hasan, M.A., Saraswat, V. (eds.) SPACE 2016. LNCS, vol. 10076, pp. 3–26. Springer, Cham (2016). https://doi.org/10.1007/978-3-319-49445-6_1

28. Mangard, S., Oswald, E., Popp, T.: Power Analysis Attacks: Revealing the Secrets of Smart Cards. Springer, Boston (2007). https://doi.org/10.1007/978-0-387-38162-6

29. Martinasek, Z., Malina, L.: Comparison of profiling power analysis attacks using templates and multi-layer perceptron network, January 2014

30. Martinasek, Z., Malina, L., Trasy, K.: Profiling power analysis attack based on multi-layer perceptron network. In: Mastorakis, N., Bulucea, A., Tsekouras, G. (eds.) Computational Problems in Science and Engineering. LNEE, vol. 343, pp. 317–339. Springer, Cham (2015). https://doi.org/10.1007/978-3-319-15765-8_18

31. Masure, L., Dumas, C., Prouff, E.: A comprehensive study of deep learning for side-channel analysis. Trans. Cryptographic Hardware Embed. Syst. **2020**, 348–375 (2019)

32. Montgomery, D.C.: Design & Analysis of Experiments. Wiley, USA (2019)

33. Moradi, A., Richter, B., Schneider, T., Standaert, F.X.: Leakage detection with the $\mathcal{X}^2$-test. IACR Trans. Cryptographic Hardware Embed. Syst. **2018**(1), 209–237 (2018)

34. Perin, G., Buhan, I., Picek, S.: Learning when to stop: a mutual information approach to fight overfitting in profiled side-channel analysis. IACR Cryptol. ePrint Arch. **2020**, 58 (2020)

35. Picek, S., Heuser, A., Jovic, A., Bhasin, S., Regazzoni, F.: The curse of class imbalance and conflicting metrics with machine learning for side-channel evaluations. IACR Trans. Cryptographic Hardware Embed. Syst. **2019**(1), 209–237 (2018)

36. Picek, S., Samiotis, I.P., Kim, J., Heuser, A., Bhasin, S., Legay, A.: On the performance of convolutional neural networks for side-channel analysis. In: Chattopadhyay, A., Rebeiro, C., Yarom, Y. (eds.) SPACE 2018. LNCS, vol. 11348, pp. 157–176. Springer, Cham (2018). https://doi.org/10.1007/978-3-030-05072-6_10

37. Prouff, E., Strullu, R., Benadjila, R., Cagli, E., Canovas, C.: Study of deep learning techniques for side-channel analysis and introduction to ascad database. IACR Cryptol. ePrint Arch. **2018**, 53 (2018)

38. Rioja, U., Paguada, S., Batina, L., Armendariz, I.: The uncertainty of side-channel analysis: a way to leverage from heuristics. Cryptology ePrint Archive, Report 2020/766 (2020). https://eprint.iacr.org/2020/766

39. Schindler, W., Lemke, K., Paar, C.: A stochastic model for differential side channel cryptanalysis. In: Rao, J.R., Sunar, B. (eds.) CHES 2005. LNCS, vol. 3659, pp. 30–46. Springer, Heidelberg (2005). https://doi.org/10.1007/11545262_3

40. Smith, L.N.: Cyclical learning rates for training neural networks. In: IEEE Winter Conference on Applications of Computer Vision (WACV), pp. 464–472 (2017)

41. Smith, L.: A disciplined approach to neural network hyper-parameters: Part 1 - learning rate, batch size, momentum, and weight decay, March 2018

42. Smith, L.N., Topin, N.: Super-convergence: very fast training of residual networks using large learning rates. CoRR abs/1708.07120 (2017)

43. Srinivas, S.S., Sreedharan, V.R.: Failure analysis of automobile spares in a manufacturing supply chain distribution centre using Six Sigma DMAIC framework. Int. J. Serv. Oper. Manage. **29**(3), 359–372 (2018)

44. Standaert, F.-X., Malkin, T.G., Yung, M.: A unified framework for the analysis of side-channel key recovery attacks. In: Joux, A. (ed.) EUROCRYPT 2009. LNCS, vol. 5479, pp. 443–461. Springer, Heidelberg (2009). https://doi.org/10.1007/978-3-642-01001-9_26
45. Tubbing, R.: An analysis of deep learning based profiled side-channel attacks: custom deep learning layer, CNN hyperparameters for countermeasures, and portability settings (2019)
46. Yang, G., Li, H., Ming, J., Zhou, Y.: Convolutional neural network based side-channel attacks in time-frequency representations. In: Bilgin, B., Fischer, J.-B. (eds.) CARDIS 2018. LNCS, vol. 11389, pp. 1–17. Springer, Cham (2019). https://doi.org/10.1007/978-3-030-15462-2_1
47. Yang, S., Zhou, Y., Liu, J., Chen, D.: Back propagation neural network based leakage characterization for practical security analysis of cryptographic implementations, pp. 169–185, November 2011
48. Zaid, G., Bossuet, L., Habrard, A., Venelli, A.: Methodology for efficient CNN architectures in profiling attacks. IACR Trans. Cryptographic Hardware Embed. Syst. **2020**(1), 1–36 (2019)
49. Zhang, J., Zheng, M., Nan, J., Hu, H., Yu, N.: A novel evaluation metric for deep learning-based side channel analysis and its extended application to imbalanced data. In: CHES 2020, pp. 73–96 (2020)
50. Zotkin, Y., Olivier, F., Bourbao, E.: Deep learning vs template attacks in front of fundamental targets: experimental study. IACR Cryptol. ePrint Arch. **2018**, 1213 (2018)

A Comparison of Weight Initializers in Deep Learning-Based Side-Channel Analysis

Huimin Li[(✉)], Marina Krček[(✉)], and Guilherme Perin[(✉)]

Delft University of Technology, Delft, The Netherlands
{h.li-7,m.krcek,g.perin}@tudelft.nl

Abstract. The usage of deep learning in profiled side-channel analysis requires a careful selection of neural network hyperparameters. In recent publications, different network architectures have been presented as efficient profiled methods against protected AES implementations. Indeed, completely different convolutional neural network models have presented similar performance against public side-channel traces databases. In this work, we analyze how weight initializers' choice influences deep neural networks' performance in the profiled side-channel analysis. Our results show that different weight initializers provide radically different behavior. We observe that even high-performing initializers can reach significantly different performance when conducting multiple training phases. Finally, we found that this hyperparameter is more dependent on the choice of dataset than other, commonly examined, hyperparameters. When evaluating the connections with other hyperparameters, the biggest connection is observed with activation functions.

Keywords: Weight initialization · Deep learning · Side-channel analysis

1 Introduction

There has been rapid progress in profiled side-channel attacks (SCAs) based on machine learning techniques in recent years. These techniques proved to be very successful by outperforming some of the classical attacks [3,14], like template attacks [4]. Around a decade ago, machine learning algorithms like SVM [9] and Random Forest [15,19] represented the standard choice for machine learning-based SCA.

More recently, deep learning-based SCAs started when Maghrebi et al. demonstrated the strong performance of several neural network types, most notably, convolutional neural networks [16]. Despite many successes, there are still many difficulties (and unanswered questions) when training deep neural networks, especially those related to how to tune hyperparameters. This tuning phase can highly influence the model's performance, so it is important to

© Springer Nature Switzerland AG 2020
J. Zhou et al. (Eds.): ACNS 2020 Workshops, LNCS 12418, pp. 126–143, 2020.
https://doi.org/10.1007/978-3-030-61638-0_8

properly address the issue and have a good strategy for selecting the hyperparameters. Hyperparameters are all those configuration variables external to the model, like the number of hidden layers in a neural network. The parameters are the configuration variables internal to the model and estimated from data (e.g., the weights in a neural network).

As there are many hyperparameters, and numerous possible combinations that can be explored, selecting proper hyperparameters can be a very time-consuming process. Researchers commonly approach this problem by selecting the hyperparameters they deem relevant and then conducting a grid search. While such an approach works well (as confirmed by successful attacks on various AES implementations), there are also potential drawbacks. Most notably, grid search skips many possible values while limiting the setup to only certain hyperparameters, completely disregards other hyperparameters' influence. In [23], the authors proposed a methodology to select hyperparameters that are related to the size (number of learnable parameters, i.e., weights and biases) of layers in CNNs. This includes the number of filters, kernel sizes, strides, and the number of neurons in fully-connected layers. In [1], the authors conducted an empirical evaluation for different hyperparameters for CNNs on the ASCAD database. Kim et al. investigated how adding noise to the input (thus, serving as regularization) improves the performance of profiled SCAs [11], which is a technique that can be used with any neural network architecture.

In this work, we focus on the weight initialization strategies for CNNs in SCA, and we explore its influence on the performance of the attacks. Thus, we investigate a hyperparameter, i.e., selecting different weight initializers directly responsible for weights parameter. Our experiments show that most of the weight initializers work well. More precisely, there is a decent selection of weight initializers one can use in deep learning-based SCA and expect good results. Next, our experiments show significant differences concerning key rank results, as within one guessing entropy experiment, it is common to obtain both perfect attack and attack that does not work at all. Interestingly, our results indicate that independent training phases result in significantly different guessing entropy performances. This means that it is not enough to consider only one training experiment, but one must conduct a proper statistical analysis for training and testing phases. We evaluate the evolution of weights and biases concerning the progress of epochs, and we observe most changes in Convolutional and Batch Normalization layers. In contrast, the fully-connected layers (those responsible for classification) remain almost constant throughout the training phase. Finally, we examine the connection between weight initializers and other hyperparameters, and we determine that the biggest influence comes from the combination of activation functions and weight initializers. This indicates that future experiments should consider both hyperparameters.

2   Background

2.1   Side-Channel Analysis

Side-channel analysis is a type of implementation attacks, where instead of attacking the algorithm itself, adversary attacks the physical device that implements the algorithm [17]. Profiled side-channel attacks are the most powerful type of side-channel attacks as they assume that the attacker has access to an identical copy of a device to build a profile. These attacks have two phases, namely, profiling and online attack. The profiling phase is a modeling problem, for which machine learning algorithms perform well. The online phase is the actual attack on a similar device to recover the secret information and is done using the profiling phase's model.

2.2   Machine Learning and Side-Channel Analysis

Machine learning is a subset of artificial intelligence and is based on learning specific patterns from given data. Since this approach is data-driven, it does not require explicit instructions and rules. Therefore, such algorithms work well in modeling problems. Currently, neural networks are a prevalent machine learning technique in SCA, and in our experiments, we investigate deep learning. Deep learning represents methods based on artificial neural networks, and some of the deep learning architectures are multilayer perceptrons (MLPs), recurrent neural networks (RNNs), and convolution neural networks (CNNs). In our experiments, we concentrate on CNNs from [23] and [11]. We opt not to consider MLP as there are less "accepted" MLP architectures in the literature, and the number of hyperparameters is more limited, which makes it possible to include weight initialization in the hyperparameter tuning phase.

To understand weight initializers, we first explain neurons, the base building block of artificial neural networks. Neuron takes input values and calculates the weighted sum using the weight matrix. For a neural network to learn nonlinear functions and models, nonlinear activation functions are applied to the weighted sum. Output of one neuron is described with the equation $y = f(b + \sum_{i=1}^{n} x_i w_i)$, where, the input x is of size n, w are the weights, b the bias and f is the activation function. Bias is also a weight for an input x_0 with an assigned value of 1. The equation takes a form $y = f(\sum_{i=0}^{n} x_i w_i)$ where $x_0 = 1$ and $w_0 = b$. This calculation is done in all neurons of one layer, so we can describe it with matrices, where features of the input samples can be arranged as columns or rows. In Keras, the features are arranged as columns, and in this setting the equation equals:

$$\mathbf{Y} = \mathbf{X} * \mathbf{W} + \mathbf{B}, \tag{1}$$

where $\mathbf{X}$ is the input, $\mathbf{W}$ is the weight, and $\mathbf{B}$ is the bias matrix. The weight matrix of a layer l is a matrix of dimension (size of layer $l-1$, size of layer l), while the bias matrix is (1, size of layer l), with the size of the layer being the number of neurons in the layer. Weight initializers are strategies for setting the initial values of a weight matrix for a neural network layer. Later, in the training phase during back-propagation, the weights in the weight matrix are adjusted with the selected optimization algorithm. Commonly used optimization algorithms are Stochastic Gradient Descent, RMSprop, and Adam [12], which we use in our experiments. Here, we explore different weight initialization strategies and how they impact the performance of deep learning-based SCA.

2.3   Weight Initializers

As mentioned, weight initializers represent how the initial values of a neural network layer's weight matrix are set. It is believed that neural networks are very sensitive to the initial weights [18]. When the deep learning algorithm was first successfully proposed, it was common to initiate weights with Gaussian noise, setting the mean equal to zero, and the standard deviation to 0.01. This way of initializing weights was not enough to train deep neural networks because of problems, such as *vanishing gradients*, *exploding gradients*, or *dead neuron* [13,18], which significantly hampered its development. In 2010, Glorot and Bengio [22] analyzed the problem systematically and proposed a formula to initialize weights depending on the number of input and output units (neurons). Glorot initializer works well in many cases and is still popular today. In 2015, He et al. [8] put forward that Glorot initializer does not work with well ReLU activation function, and extended the formula to meet ReLU based neural networks through only using the number of input units and increasing the scaling by $\sqrt{2}$. As more people have devoted themselves to the study of weight initialization, various methods have appeared. In general, these methods can be divided into two categories: Zeros and Ones initialization, and Random initialization.

Zeros and Ones Initialization. With all weights initialized to 0 (1), all weights are the same, and the activation in all neurons is also the same. That way, the loss function's derivative is the same for every weight in a weight matrix of a layer. When all weights have the same value, in all iterations, this makes hidden layers symmetric. Every neuron of the layer computes the same function, so the model behaves like a linear model.

Random Initialization. All weight matrix values are set to random numbers, usually from a normal or uniform distribution. As mentioned, issues with random initialization are *vanishing* and *exploding gradients*. In *vanishing gradients*, weight update is minor, which results in slower convergence, while in *exploding gradients*, large gradients can result in oscillation around the optimum.

For deep networks, heuristics can be used to initialize the weights depending on the nonlinear activation function. Heuristics set the normal distribution variance to k/n, where k is a constant value that depends on the activation function, and n is the number of input nodes to the weight tensor or both input and output nodes of the weight tensor. This is adjusted to a uniform distribution, which can be seen in the provided list of initializers from Keras library [5]. While these heuristics do not entirely solve the *exploding/vanishing gradients* issue, they help mitigate it to a great extent. Initializers with explained heuristics are LeCun, Glorot/Xavier, and He initializers.

Different weight initializers available [10] in Keras are listed below with *fan in* being the number of input units in the weight tensor and *fan_out* the number of output units in the weight tensor.

- *Zeros:* initializes weights to 0.
- *Ones:* initializes weights to 1.
- *Constant:* initializes weights to given constant, default is 0.
- *RandomNormal:* initializes weights with normal distribution, $mean = 0$, $stddev = 0.05$.
- *RandomUniform:* initializes weights with uniform distribution, $minval = -0.05, maxval = 0.05$.
- *TruncatedNormal:* similar to *RandomNormal* except that values more than two standard deviations from the mean are discarded and redrawn.
- *VarianceScaling:* adapts scale to the shape of weights, default values are $scale = 1, mode =' fan\_in'$ and normal distribution.
- *Orthogonal:* random orthogonal matrix, default value of multiplicative factor to apply to the matrix is 1.
- *Identity:* identity matrix, multiplicative factor again 1.
- *lecun_uniform:* uniform distribution within [-limit, limit] where limit is $sqrt(3/fan\_in)$.
- *lecun_normal:* truncated normal distribution centered on 0 with $stddev = sqrt(1/fan\_in)$.
- *glorot_normal:* truncated normal distribution centered on 0 with $stddev = sqrt(2/(fan\_in + fan\_out))$.
- *glorot_uniform:* uniform distribution within [-limit, limit] where limit is $sqrt(6/(fan\_in + fan\_out))$.
- *he_normal:* truncated normal distribution centered on 0 with $stddev = sqrt(2/fan\_in)$.
- *he_uniform:* uniform distribution within [-limit, limit] where limit is $sqrt(6/fan\_in)$.

3   Experimental Setup

Algorithms used for these experiments are taken from [11] and [23], where CNN hyperparameters were fine-tuned specifically for each dataset the authors used. We vary available weight initializers in our experiments to investigate the performance difference according to each weight initializer. All of the other hyperparameters are taken directly from the mentioned works. We consider these two architectures as they represent top-performing architectures from related works. Additionally, they differ in size, which will enable us to evaluate the influence of weight initializers on architectures of different complexity.

We will refer to CNN architecture as the *Noise* architecture for [11], and the *Methodology* architecture for [23]. For each architecture, two leakage models are used: Identity (ID) model [11,23] and Hamming weight (HW) model [20], in which there are 256 classes and nine classes respectively corresponding to the output of neural networks. In both architectures, hyperparameters are tuned with the ID model (as the original works consider only ID model), but we use the same hyperparameters for the HW model.

Kim et al. [11] used *glorot_uniform* weight initializer, and Zaid et al. [23] used *he_uniform* weight initializer. In the last layer, [23] does not set weight initializer to *he_uniform*, but instead, the default weight initializer is utilized, which is *glorot_uniform*. We are not aware of this implementation's motivation, so in our experiments, we vary weight initializers in all layers, including the last layer with a Softmax activation function. This change causes a difference between our results with *Methodology* architecture and ID leakage model compared to results presented in the work of Zaid et al. [23], as shown later in Sect. 4.

We are not running experiments with *Constant, VarianceScaling, Identity*, and *Orthogonal* initializers from all available Keras weight initializers. *Identity* and *Orthogonal* initializers are not actively used, and *Constant* and *VarianceScaling* correspond to *Zeros* and *lecun_normal*, respectively, when using default values. We simulate ten times with each initializer and average the results for comparison with other weight initializers.

We use the public source code provided on GitHub by Zaid et al. [23] in Keras with Tensorflow backend [5]. We consider three publicly available datasets that consist of side-channel measurements for the AES cipher for our experiments. Following, we shortly describe these datasets and then discuss the results for each dataset in detail.

DPA contest v4 (DPAv4) dataset[1] is obtained from a masked AES software implementation [2]. Knowing the masked values, this dataset is easily converted into an unprotected scenario. We attack the first round of S-box operation, and identify each trace with $Y^{(i)}(k^*) = Sbox[P_0^{(i)} \oplus k^*] \oplus M$ where $P_0^{(i)}$ is the first byte of the i-th plaintext and M is the known mask.

AES_RD dataset[2] is obtained from an implementation on an 8-bit AVR microcontroller with a random delay countermeasure [6]. This countermeasure shifts each trace following a random variable of 0 to $N^{[0]}$. The attack is on the first round S-box operation, as in DPAv4 dataset, where traces are labeled as $Y^{(i)}(k^*) = Sbox[P_0^{(i)} \oplus k^*]$.

---

[1] http://www.dpacontest.org/v4/42_traces.php.
[2] https://github.com/ikizhvatov/randomdelays-traces.

ASCAD dataset[3] is obtained from a masked AES-128 implementation on an 8-bit AVR microcontroller introduced in [21]. The leakage model is the first round S-box operation, such that $Y^{(i)}(k^*) = Sbox[P_3^{(i)} \oplus k^*]$. In contrast to the DPAv4 and AES_RD datasets, the third byte is exploited (as this is the first masked byte).

4   Experimental Results

This section shows the results for different weight initializers. We explore 1) how weight initializers impact the performance of the utilized CNN architectures, 2) which one is the best for a specific dataset and architecture, and 3) whether there is the best weight initializer for all datasets. As explained in Sect. 3, we use 11 weight initializers available in Keras and execute experiments on commonly used DPAv4, AES_RD, and ASCAD datasets. For each dataset, we run four experiments: *Methodology* architecture with ID and HW model, and *Noise* architecture with ID and HW model.

Recall, with *Zeros* and *Ones* initialization, the model is no better than a linear model. In our experiments, we still choose to show the results with *Zeros* and *Ones* weight initialization to show that a linear model is not sufficient for considered problems. There, all results show that guessing entropy is either staying at random guessing or increasing with *Zeros* and *Ones* weight initialization. Consequently, when discussing the performance of weight initializers, we usually ignore the performance of *Zeros* and *Ones*, as they never converge.

A good initializer is the one where GE decreases, preferably to zero, in the least number of traces, and is more stable, as observed from results from multiple independent experiments. As such, those weight initializers where GE behaves similarly in multiple experiments, we consider more stable than when this is not true. To get the best weight initializer, we consider two additional metrics: speed and stability. We sort the averaged GE value of all weight initializers to evaluate their "speed", and compare the consistency in multiple experiments to obtain the "stability". The key rank range shows the "best" GE from 10 experiments to present the range from multiple performed attacks. The "best" GE is the one that reaches the lowest value, and if multiple GE results reach the same minimum, then the one that reaches that value with fewer traces is considered better, and we plot key rank range for that experiment. The range is taken from the 100 attacks that are executed for calculating the GE. Weights' evolution figures show weights for each layer, and the layers in the legend are ordered from first input layer to the last output layer of the neural network. We provide a Table 1 as an overview of all experiments and best initializers in each setup.

4.1   Results for the DPAv4 Dataset

As in [23], we use 4 000 traces for the training set, 500 traces for the validation set, and 500 for attacking the device. Each trace has 4 000 features. The

---

[3] https://github.com/ANSSI-FR/ASCAD.

Table 1. An overview of all experiments and best initializers in each setup.

Dataset	Architecture	Best initializer (ID/HW)
DPAv4	*Methodology*	*RandomUniform*
	Noise	*RandomUniform/RandomNormal*
AES_RD	*Methodology*	*he_normal/lecun_normal*
	Noise	*RandomUniform*
ASCAD	*Methodology*	*he_normal*
	Noise	*lecun_normal*

GE rankings of the four experiments are shown in Fig. 1. In the two experiments with the *Methodology* architecture (Figs. 1a and 1b), most weight initializers perform similarly when weight initializer is varied, but *RandomUniform* is slightly faster in convergence and more stable with both leakage models. With the *Noise* architecture and ID leakage model (Fig. 1c), the best weight initializer is *RandomUniform*, and with the HW model (Fig. 1d), most weight initializers perform quite well, but we choose *RandomNormal* as the best one.

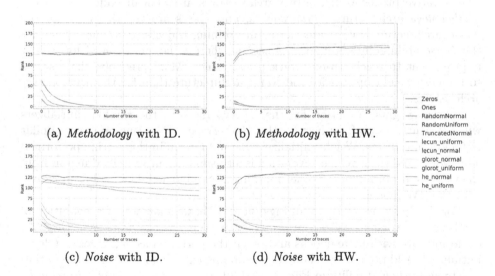

(a) *Methodology* with ID.

(b) *Methodology* with HW.

(c) *Noise* with ID.

(d) *Noise* with HW.

Fig. 1. Averaged GEs for all weight initializers with the DPAv4 dataset.

Figure 2 shows the key rank range for the best (Fig. 2a) and the worst initializer (Fig. 2b) with the *Noise* architecture and ID model for the DPAv4 dataset when ignoring the *Zeros* and *Ones*. While the GE is slowly converging with he_uniform initializer, in Fig. 2b, we can see significant differences in the key rank results from multiple performed attacks within one guessing entropy experiment.

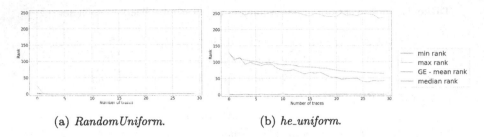

(a) *RandomUniform.*   (b) *he_uniform.*

Fig. 2. The key rank range of *Noise* architecture with ID model for decreasing GE in DPAv4 dataset.

When looking at the weights' evolution, we observe the change of weights and biases in every neural network layer in every epoch and find that weights and biases change in Convolutional layers and Batch Normalization layers, and other layers such as dense layers do not exhibit much change. In the *Methodology* architecture, both weights, and biases change significantly, while in the *Noise* architecture, only biases change, and weights stay almost constant. According to the result, we can peek into the training processes of the two architectures. The iterative processes of the two architectures are radically different: in the *Methodology* architecture, both weights, and biases are trained, while in the *Noise* architecture, biases are the main training objects. This indicates that the *Noise* architecture is more "robust" as there is not much need for weight improvement to reach strong attack performance. More precisely, there seems to be more weight optima for the *Noise* architecture than for the *Methodology* architecture.

In the weights' evolution for the DPAv4 dataset, the random initializers without heuristics perform best for the *Methodology* ID setting and very similar to Glorot initializers. Weight initializers He and LeCun in this setting performed a bit worse, and their weights' evolution is also similar, but visually different from the weights' evolution of the other initializers. Similar weights' evolution is seen with the HW model.

For the *Noise* architecture, in Figs. 3a and 3b, we show weights' evolution of the best and worst initializer, respectively. It seems as the *he_normal* (Fig. 3b) could improve with more epochs and reach the performance of, at least, Glorot initializers. Additionally, we show corresponding experiments of the same initializer to show their stability in Figs. 3c and 3d. Here, both are stable: *RandomUniform* is performing well, and *he_normal* consistently has a slow convergence. This is again visible through weights' evolution because the weights and biases' variance is not large. The performance of different weight initializers with both architectures and models on the DPAv4 dataset is quite similar, and most of the initializers reach GE of zero.

Lastly, we simulate experiments with the *Methodology* architecture and both leakage models to explore the influence of the weight initializer in the last fully-connected layer, similar to [23]. More precisely, we keep all hyperparameters

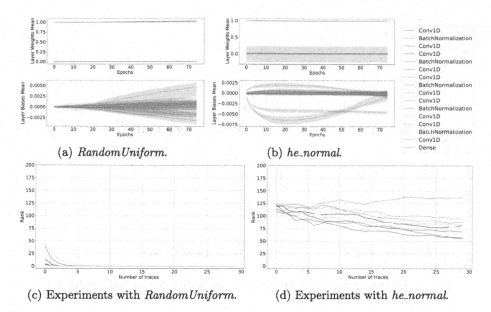

(a) *RandomUniform.*

(b) *he_normal.*

(c) Experiments with *RandomUniform.*

(d) Experiments with *he_normal.*

Fig. 3. Weights' evolution and experiments with *Noise* ID setting on the DPAv4 dataset.

of the two experiments except that the setting of the last layer in the neural network is the same as paper [23]. The results for the two experiments show that it has no impact on the outcome, and the performances of all the weight initializers in the ID and HW model are almost the same.

4.2 Results for the AES_RD Dataset

AES_RD dataset is a protected implementation, where adding random delays to the normal operation of AES makes it more difficult to conduct attack as features are misaligned. The dataset consists of 50 000 traces of 3 500 features each, where 20 000 traces are used for the training set, 5 000 for the validation, and 25 000 for the attack set. The GE rankings for the AES_RD dataset are illustrated in Fig. 4. By observing all weight initializers' speed and stability, we get the best weight initializers in all scenarios: *he_normal, lecun_normal, RandomUniform,* and *RandomUniform,* respectively.

Like the DPAv4 dataset, weights and biases change mostly in Convolutional layers and Batch Normalization layers, but not in other layers. We can also see that in the *Methodology* architecture, both weight and bias change significantly, while in the *Noise* architecture, only biases change, and weights remain almost constant.

Figures 5a and 5b display the best and the worst initializer respectively in weights' evolution for the *Methodology* architecture on the AES_RD dataset. The difference in the initializers' performance stems from their stability because all

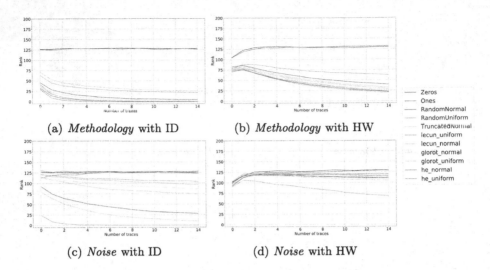

(a) *Methodology* with ID

(b) *Methodology* with HW

(c) *Noise* with ID

(d) *Noise* with HW

Fig. 4. Averaged GEs for all weight initializers with the AES_RD dataset.

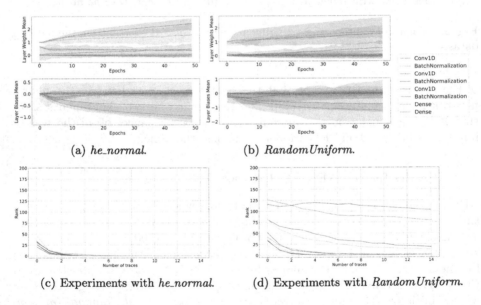

(a) *he_normal.*

(b) *RandomUniform.*

(c) Experiments with *he_normal.*

(d) Experiments with *RandomUniform.*

Fig. 5. Weights' evolution and experiments with *Methodology* ID setting on the AES_RD dataset.

reach GE equal to zero in several of ten simulations, which can be seen in Figs. 5c and 5d. The stability of the weight initializer is also seen in weights' evolution. Since we show the mean of the weights and the range for the ten simulations: the more the weights' evolution varies, the more GE is also likely to vary.

Finally, we investigate the weight initializer's influence in the last dense layer for the *Methodology* architecture. All hyperparameters are the same, except for the weight initializer in the last layer, which is set as default, according to the settings in paper [23]. The new results show that the change in the last layer also does not have a big effect on the initializer's stability, but it impacts the speed. With the HW model, the convergence for all weight initializers is slower. The best weight initializers for ID and HW model are *he_normal* and *lecun_normal*, respectively.

4.3   Results for the ASCAD Dataset

Next, we compare the performance of different weight initializers for the ASCAD dataset. We use the ASCAD dataset with 60 000 traces of 700 features without desynchronization. The dataset is divided into 45 000 training traces, 5 000 validation traces, and 10 000 attack traces. In Fig. 6, we show the GE rankings. In the experiment with the *Methodology* ID setting (Fig. 6a), increasing the number of attack traces leads to an increase of the GE for the correct key byte, even with *he_uniform*, which was used in paper [23] in all layers except for the last layer. By comparing the stability, we get that *he_normal* is the best one. We observe that the GE value of weight initializers with heuristics converges to zero with the HW model (Fig. 6b). *he_normal* is the fastest one. In the setting with the *Noise* architecture (Figs. 6c and 6d), the best weight initializers, *lecun_normal*, can be easily chosen by observing the speed.

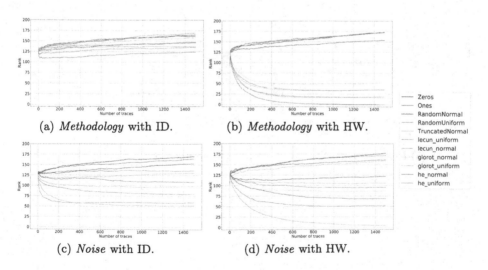

(a) *Methodology* with ID.   (b) *Methodology* with HW.

(c) *Noise* with ID.   (d) *Noise* with HW.

Fig. 6. Averaged GEs for all weight initializers with the ASCAD dataset.

Figure 7 shows the key rank range for *he_normal* initializer where GE reached zero (Fig. 7a), and *RandomUniform* where GE increases with an increased number of traces (Fig. 7b). Again, we see that even when the GE is increasing, some key rank results are showing perfect attacks.

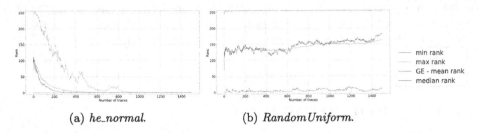

(a) *he_normal.*   (b) *Random Uniform.*

Fig. 7. The key rank range of *Methodology* architecture with HW model for decreasing and increasing GE in ASCAD dataset.

Next, we observe the weights and biases change of every layer throughout the epochs. Like the previous two datasets, weight and bias change mostly in Convolutional layers and Batch Normalization layers, but not in other layers. Once again, it can be seen that in the *Methodology* architecture, both weights and biases change significantly, while for the *Noise* architecture, only biases change and weights are almost constant.

In Fig. 8, we show the weights' evolution of the best initializer (Fig. 8a) and average performing one (Fig. 8b). The corresponding experiments are shown in

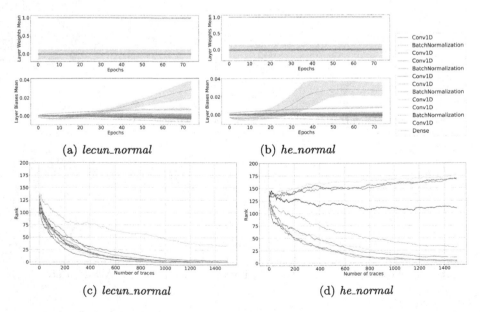

(a) *lecun_normal*   (b) *he_normal*

(c) *lecun_normal*   (d) *he_normal*

Fig. 8. Weights' evolution and experiments with *Noise* HW setting on the ASCAD dataset.

Figs. 8c and 8d for the *Noise* architecture and the HW model. In these experiments, the worst initializer, *RandomUniform* (see Fig. 6d), performed similarly to *Zeros* and *Ones*, as in every experiment, GE was increasing.

Finally, to explore the influence of weight initializers in the last layer, we run experiments with the *Methodology* architecture, using all the hyperparameters of the two experiments except the setting of the last layer in the neural network. Like [23], the weight initializer of the last layer is a default one. The new results show that weight initializer has a significant influence on the outcomes. In the experiments with the *Methodology* ID setting, the average GE values of all weight initializers (except *Zeros* and *Ones*) decrease, but there is a difference in the stability of the initializers. The best weight initializer is *he_normal*. With the *Noise* architecture, the average GE values of all weight initializers increase. The best weight initializer is *lecun_uniform*, since, for two out of ten simulations, GE converged to zero.

5   Weight Initializer Influence on Other Hyperparameters

Based on the best weight initializers that we find to provide better performance for specific neural network architectures and datasets, we now analyze whether a weight initializer's performance depends on its combination with other hyperparameters or if a weight initializer method is connected to the dataset itself. In other words, we wish to understand if the selection of a weight initializers is optimal for a restricted group of hyperparameters or if it is more dependent on the nature of the side-channel traces, meaning that any small variations on hyperparameters would still lead to a successful attack in the majority of tests.

We select the *Methodology* convolutional neural network architecture used in the previous sections and make small variations in their hyperparameters to investigate the influence on the best found weight initializer. To do this analysis, we select ASCAD dataset. For this dataset and the *Methodology* CNN architecture, we find that *he_normal* weight initializer provide better results. Table 2 shows the ranges of hyperparameters that we vary in different CNN training phases. In total, we train 400 CNNs, and we use the HW leakage model.

Table 2. Hyperparameter variations in the *Methodology* architecture.

Hyperparameters	Original	Minimum	Maximum	Step
Filters	4	4	8	1
Kernel Size	1	1	4	1
Neurons	10	5	15	1
Layers	2	2	3	1
Learning Rate	5e−3	1e−3	1e−2	1e−4
Mini-Batch	100	100	400	100
Activation function (all layers)	SELU	ReLU, Tanh, ELU, or SELU		

Figure 9 shows that *Tanh* is the only activation function that does not provide successful key recovery in any of the experiments. For the *ReLU*, *ELU* and *SELU* activation functions, the different trained CNNs architectures can return low GE.

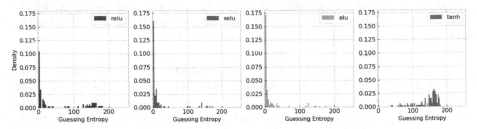

Fig. 9. Activation functions and guessing entropy.

Concerning the number of filters in the single convolution layer of this architecture, the usage of four filters tends to maximize the attack's success, as demonstrated in Fig. 10. Increasing the filter size decreases the probability of the attack to be successful. Regarding kernel sizes, we observe that small variations on this hyperparameter do not significantly affect the results. In Fig. 11, for kernel sizes varying from 1 to 4, the density of low GE values is similar in all the cases.

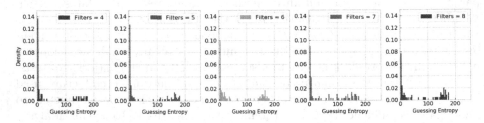

Fig. 10. Filters and guessing entropy.

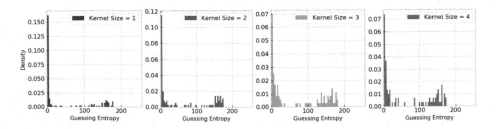

Fig. 11. Kernel sizes and guessing entropy.

Finally, we also observe that making small variations in the number of layers and neurons also does not provide too much effect on the final GE. As shown in Figs. 12a and 12b, more layers, and more neurons tend to provide a subtle increase in the concentration of low GE values. These variations are insufficient

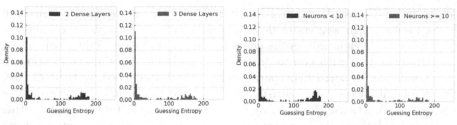

(a) Layers and guessing entropy.   (b) Neurons and guessing entropy.

Fig. 12. Different layers and neurons variations and their relation to final GE results.

to assume that the combination of architecture hyperparameters and weight initializer strictly depends on a specific number of layers and neurons.

We also do not observe a significant effect on the final GE results for different mini-batch sizes (from 100 to 400) and different learning rates (from 0.001 to 0.01). Therefore, this analysis's main conclusion is that the choice of a weight initializer for the *Methodology* CNN architecture (when using the ASCAD dataset with the Hamming weight model), depends mostly on the activation function rather than the rest of hyperparameters. However, for this scenario, a more precise conclusion would be to assume that for a specific dataset (and leakage model), there is an optimal combination of activation function and weight initializer. Weight initializers with heuristics are derived based on certain assumptions on the activation functions. For example, the *Glorot* initializer assumes that the activations are linear. This assumption is not valid for *ReLU* activation functions, so He et al. [8] derived a new initialization method, and it allowed their deep models to converge as opposed to the *Glorot* initialization method. Therefore, we see that weight initializers are closely related to activation functions, which supports our conclusion.

6   Conclusions and Future Work

In this paper, we evaluate the influence of the weight initializer choice on the performance of CNNs in the profiled side-channel analysis. We consider 11 weight initializers, three datasets, two leakage models, and two CNN architectures. We evaluate the weight initializer performance by observing guessing entropy, the stability of results, and the evolution of weights through the training process.

Our results show that when the dataset is easy to attack, it is not important what weight initializer to use. Going toward more difficult datasets, we observe more influence stemming from this selection. Interestingly, we see that specific key rank experiments can behave extremely well or extremely badly from the guessing entropy results. What is more, we see significant differences in individual training processes, which means that weight initializers play a significant role in the training process, and it is necessary to run multiple training phases (and not only attacks to obtain guessing entropy). Next, most of the changes in weights happen in the Convolutional and Batch Normalization layer, while we observe almost no change in weights in dense layers. Finally, we analyze the interconnection between weight initializers and other hyperparameters. Our results show a strong connection with activation functions and only marginal connection to other commonly explored hyperparameters. This is supported by the fact that the weight initializers with heuristics are designed based on certain properties of activation functions. However, more experiments could further support this observation. Mathematical explanations of weight initialization strategies were out of scope for this work, but this is an interesting and broad research topic that contributes to a deeper understanding of the deep learning models.

For future work, we see two particularly interesting directions. The first one is to explore the influence of weight initializers and activations functions. Indeed, our results indicate that changes in activation functions influence the results from different weight initializers significantly. The second direction is to explore the unsupervised pre-training setup. Results are showing that autoencoders can be used to assign weights to each layer in an unsupervised manner, which helps to guide the learning towards basins of attraction of minima that support better generalization from the training dataset [7].

References

1. Benadjila, R., Prouff, E., Strullu, R., Cagli, E., Dumas, C.: Deep learning for side-channel analysis and introduction to ASCAD database. J. Cryptographic Eng. **10**(2), 163–188 (2020). https://doi.org/10.1007/s13389-019-00220-8
2. Bhasin, S., Bruneau, N., Danger, J.-L., Guilley, S., Najm, Z.: Analysis and improvements of the DPA contest v4 implementation. In: Chakraborty, R.S., Matyas, V., Schaumont, P. (eds.) SPACE 2014. LNCS, vol. 8804, pp. 201–218. Springer, Cham (2014). https://doi.org/10.1007/978-3-319-12060-7_14
3. Cagli, E., Dumas, C., Prouff, E.: Convolutional neural networks with data augmentation against jitter-based countermeasures. In: Fischer, W., Homma, N. (eds.) CHES 2017. LNCS, vol. 10529, pp. 45–68. Springer, Cham (2017). https://doi.org/10.1007/978-3-319-66787-4_3
4. Chari, S., Rao, J.R., Rohatgi, P.: Template attacks. In: Kaliski, B.S., Koç, K., Paar, C. (eds.) CHES 2002. LNCS, vol. 2523, pp. 13–28. Springer, Heidelberg (2003). https://doi.org/10.1007/3-540-36400-5_3
5. Chollet, F., et al.: Keras (2015). https://keras.io
6. Coron, J.S., Kizhvatov, I.: An efficient method for random delay generation in embedded software. Cryptology ePrint Archive, Report 2009/419 (2009). https://eprint.iacr.org/2009/419
7. Erhan, D., Bengio, Y., Courville, A., Manzagol, P.A., Vincent, P., Bengio, S.: Why does unsupervised pre-training help deep learning? J. Mach. Learn. Res. **11**, 625–660 (2010)
8. He, K., Zhang, X., Ren, S., Sun, J.: Delving deep into rectifiers: surpassing human-level performance on imagenet classification. In: IEEE International Conference on Computer Vision (ICCV 2015) 1502, February 2015. https://doi.org/10.1109/ICCV.2015.123
9. Heuser, A., Zohner, M.: Intelligent machine homicide - breaking cryptographic devices using support vector machines. In: COSADE, pp. 249–264 (2012)

10. Keras: Layer weight initializers. https://keras.io/api/layers/initializers/
11. Kim, J., Picek, S., Heuser, A., Bhasin, S., Hanjalic, A.: Make some noise: Unleashing the power of convolutional neural networks for profiled side-channel analysis. Cryptology ePrint Archive, Report 2018/1023 (2018). https://eprint.iacr.org/2018/1023
12. Kingma, D., Ba, J.: Adam: a method for stochastic optimization. In: International Conference on Learning Representations, December 2014
13. Koturwar, S., Merchant, S.: Weight initialization of deep neural networks (DNNS) using data statistics. CoRR abs/1710.10570 (2017). http://arxiv.org/abs/1710.10570
14. Lerman, L., Bontempi, G., Markowitch, O.: Power analysis attack: An approach based on machine learning. Int. J. Appl. Cryptol. **3**(2), 97–115 (2014). https://doi.org/10.1504/IJACT.2014.062722
15. Lerman, L., Poussier, R., Bontempi, G., Markowitch, O., Standaert, F.-X.: Template attacks vs. machine learning revisited (and the curse of dimensionality in side-channel analysis). In: Mangard, S., Poschmann, A.Y. (eds.) COSADE 2014. LNCS, vol. 9064, pp. 20–33. Springer, Cham (2015). https://doi.org/10.1007/978-3-319-21476-4_2
16. Maghrebi, H., Portigliatti, T., Prouff, E.: Breaking cryptographic implementations using deep learning techniques. In: Carlet, C., Hasan, M.A., Saraswat, V. (eds.) SPACE 2016. LNCS, vol. 10076, pp. 3–26. Springer, Cham (2016). https://doi.org/10.1007/978-3-319-49445-6_1
17. Mangard, S., Oswald, E., Popp, T.: Power Analysis Attacks: Revealing the Secrets of Smart Cards. Advances in Information Security. Springer, Boston (2007). https://doi.org/10.1007/978-0-387-38162-6
18. Peng, A.Y., Sing Koh, Y., Riddle, P., Pfahringer, B.: Using supervised pretraining to improve generalization of neural networks on binary classification problems. In: Berlingerio, M., Bonchi, F., Gärtner, T., Hurley, N., Ifrim, G. (eds.) ECML PKDD 2018. LNCS (LNAI), vol. 11051, pp. 410–425. Springer, Cham (2019). https://doi.org/10.1007/978-3-030-10925-7_25
19. Picek, S., Heuser, A., Jovic, A., Bhasin, S., Regazzoni, F.: The curse of class imbalance and conflicting metrics with machine learning for side-channel evaluations. IACR Trans. Cryptographic Hardware Embed. Syst. **2019**(1), 209–237 (2018). https://doi.org/10.13154/tches.v2019.i1.209-237, https://tches.iacr.org/index.php/TCHES/article/view/7339
20. Picek, S., Samiotis, I.P., Kim, J., Heuser, A., Bhasin, S., Legay, A.: On the performance of convolutional neural networks for side-channel analysis. In: Chattopadhyay, A., Rebeiro, C., Yarom, Y. (eds.) SPACE 2018. LNCS, vol. 11348, pp. 157–176. Springer, Cham (2018). https://doi.org/10.1007/978-3-030-05072-6_10
21. Prouff, E., Strullu, R., Benadjila, R., Cagli, E., Dumas, C.: Study of deep learning techniques for side-channel analysis and introduction to ascad database. Cryptology ePrint Archive, Report 2018/053 (2018). https://eprint.iacr.org/2018/053
22. Xavier Glorot, Y.B.: Understanding the difficulty of training deep feedforward neural networks. J. Mach. Learn. Res. **9**, 249–256 (2010)
23. Zaid, G., Bossuet, L., Habrard, A., Venelli, A.: Methodology for efficient CNN architectures in profiling attacks. IACR Trans. Cryptographic Hardware Embed. Syst. **2020**(1), 1–36 (2019). https://doi.org/10.13154/tches.v2020.i1.1-36, https://tches.iacr.org/index.php/TCHES/article/view/8391

Leakage Assessment Through Neural Estimation of the Mutual Information

Valence Cristiani[1(✉)], Maxime Lecomte[1], and Philippe Maurine[2]

[1] Univ. Grenoble Alpes, CEA, LETI, Grenoble, France
valencecristiani@gmail.com
[2] LIRMM, Montpellier, France

Abstract. A large variety of side-channel attacks have been developed to extract secrets from electronic devices through their physical leakages. Whatever the utilized strategy, the amount of information one could gain from a side-channel trace is always bounded by the Mutual Information (MI) between the secret and the trace. This makes it, all punning aside, a key quantity for leakage evaluation. Unfortunately, traces are usually of too high dimension for existing statistical estimators to stay sound when computing the MI over full traces. However, recent works from the machine learning community have shown that it is possible to evaluate the MI in high dimensional space thanks to newest deep learning techniques. This paper explores how this new estimator could impact the side channel domain. It presents an analysis which aim is to derive the best way of using this estimator in practice. Then, it shows how such a tool can be used to assess the leakage of any device.

Keywords: Side channel analysis · Mutual information · Deep learning

1 Introduction

Side Channel Analysis (SCA) could be defined as the process of gaining information on a device holding a secret through its physical leakage such as power consumption [11] or Electromagnetic (EM) emanations [16]. The secret is usually a cryptographic key but could be as well basic block execution, assembly instructions, or even the value of an arbitrary register. The basic assumption is that the secret and the side-channel data are statistically dependent. Many techniques have been developed to extract part of these dependencies such as DPA [11], CPA [3], MIA [15], and profiling attacks [6]. This diversity makes it hard for designers and evaluators to draw an objective metric in order to assess leakage. Testing all the existing attacks is a possible strategy but the incentives to develop a leakage assessment protocol can be found in a couple of works [4,13,18].

From an information theory point of view, the maximum amount of information one could extract from a side-channel trace is bounded by the mutual

© Springer Nature Switzerland AG 2020
J. Zhou et al. (Eds.): ACNS 2020 Workshops, LNCS 12418, pp. 144–162, 2020.
https://doi.org/10.1007/978-3-030-61638-0_9

information, $\mathcal{I}(S, X)$ between the secret S and the trace X, seen as random variables. This quantity is, indeed, central in the side-channel domain. The goals of the different actors could be summarized as follows:

- **Designers** aim at implementing countermeasures to decrease as far as possible $\mathcal{I}(S, X)$, with computational, spatial and efficiency constraints.
- **Evaluators** aim at estimating $\mathcal{I}(S, X)$ as closely as possible to assess leakages in a worst-case scenario.
- **Attackers** aim at developing strategies to partially or fully exploit $\mathcal{I}(S, X)$ in order to recover a secret.

The main problem for designers and evaluators is that $\mathcal{I}(S, X)$ is known to be hard to estimate from drawn samples when the variables live in a high dimensional space, which is generally the case of X. Indeed, computing $\mathcal{I}(S, X)$ usually requires an estimation of the conditional density $\Pr(S|X)$ which is hard because of the well-known curse of dimensionality. This explains why conventional leakage assessment tools [18] (Signal to Noise Ratio (SNR), T-tests) and classical attack strategies such as CPA and MIA typically focus on one (or a few) samples at a time in the trace. As a result, the amount of information effectively used may be significantly lower than $\mathcal{I}(S, X)$.

Latest deep learning attacks have proved that neural networks are a very interesting tool able to combine information from many samples of the traces without any prior knowledge on the leakage model. For instance, [14] recently proposed a way to derive an estimation of $\mathcal{I}(S, X)$ from the success rate of their attacks and showed that in a supervised context, neural networks are close to optimal at extracting information from traces.

In a completely unrelated context, Belghazi *et al.* [1] lately introduced a Mutual Information Neural Estimator (MINE) which uses the power of deep learning to compute mutual information in high dimension. They have proposed applications in a pure machine learning context but we argue that this tool might be of great interest in the side-channel domain. Indeed, being able to efficiently compute $\mathcal{I}(S, X)$ in an unsupervised way (no profiling of the target needed), no matter the target, the implementation, or the countermeasures used, would be highly relevant for all the different parties.

Paper Organization. For this paper to be self-contained, the general method and the mathematical ideas behind MINE are recalled in Sect. 2. Section 3 proposes an in-depth analysis of MINE in a side-channel context supported with synthetic traces, and suggests ways of dealing with the overfitting problem. Section 4 provides some real case applications. It shows how this estimator constitutes a reliable leakage assessment tool that can be used to compare leakage from different implementations and devices. This section also shows that such an estimator can be used as a guide for an evaluator/attacker to maximize the MI captured from different hardware side-channel setups.

2   Background and Theory Behind MINE

Notations. Random variables are represented as upper case letters such as X. They take their values in the corresponding set $\mathcal{X}$ depicted with a calligraphic letter. Lower case letters such as x stand for elements of $\mathcal{X}$. Probability density function associated to the variable X is denoted by p_X.

Background. The entropy $H(X)$ [19] of a random variable is a fundamental quantity in information theory which typically tells how much information one would get in average by learning a particular realization x of X. It is defined as the expectation of the self-information $log_2(1/p_X)$. In a discrete context:

$$H(X) = \sum_{x \in \mathcal{X}} p_X(x) \cdot log_2\left(\frac{1}{p_X(x)}\right) \tag{1}$$

In a side-channel environment where X represents the acquired data, one is not interested in the absolute information provided by X but rather in the amount of information revealed about a second variable such as a secret S. This is exactly what is measured by the mutual information $\mathcal{I}(S, X)$. It is defined as: $\mathcal{I}(S, X) = H(S) - H(S|X)$ where $H(S|X)$ stands for the conditional entropy of S knowing X:

$$H(S|X) = \sum_{x \in \mathcal{X}} p_X(x) \cdot H(S|X = x) \tag{2}$$

The most common ways to estimate MI are the histogram method and the kernel density estimation both described in [15]. There also exists a non parametric estimation based on k-nearest neighbors [12]. This paper is interested in MINE [1], a new estimator based on deep learning techniques, which claims to scale well with high dimensions. Technical details about MINE are given hereafter.

MINE. A well known property of $\mathcal{I}(S, X)$ is its equivalence with the Kullback-Leibler (KL) divergence between the joint probability $p_{S,X} = \Pr(S, X)$ and the product of the marginals $p_S \otimes p_X = \Pr(S) \cdot \Pr(X)$:

$$\mathcal{I}(S, X) = D_{KL}(p_{S,X} \,\|\, p_S \otimes p_X) \tag{3}$$

where $D_{KL}(p, q)$ is defined as follow:

$$D_{KL}(p \,\|\, q) = \mathbb{E}_p[log\left(\frac{p}{q}\right)] \tag{4}$$

whenever p is absolutely continuous with respect to q. This property guarantees that when q is equal to 0, p is also equal to 0 and there is no division by 0 in the logarithm. By definition, $p_{S,X}$ is absolutely continuous with respect to $p_S \otimes p_X$.

The key technical ingredient of MINE is to express the KL-divergence with variational representations, especially the Donsker-Varadhan representation that is given hereafter. Let p and q be two densities over a compact set $\Omega \in \mathbb{R}^d$.

Theorem 1. *(Donsker-Varadhan, 1983) The KL-divergence admits the following dual representation:*

$$D_{KL}(p \,\|\, q) = \sup_{T:\, \Omega \to \mathbb{R}} \mathbb{E}_p[T] - log(\mathbb{E}_q[e^T]) \tag{5}$$

where the supremum is taken over all functions T such that the two expectations are finite.

A straightforward consequence of this theorem is that for any set $\mathcal{F}$ of functions $T : \Omega \to \mathbb{R}$ satisfying the integrability constraint of the theorem we have the following lower bound:

$$D_{KL}(p \,\|\, q) \geq \sup_{T \in \mathcal{F}} \mathbb{E}_p[T] - log(\mathbb{E}_q[e^T]) \tag{6}$$

Thus, using (3), one have the following lower bound for $\mathcal{I}(S, X)$:

$$\mathcal{I}(S, X) \geq \sup_{T \in \mathcal{F}} \mathbb{E}_{p_{S,X}}[T] - log(\mathbb{E}_{p_S \otimes p_X}[e^T]) \tag{7}$$

How to Compute $\mathcal{I}(S, X)$. To put it short, the idea is to define $\mathcal{F}$ as the set of all functions T_θ parametrized by a neural network with parameters $\theta \in \Theta$ and to look for the parameters maximizing the loss function $\mathcal{L} : \Theta \to \mathbb{R}$:

$$\mathcal{L}(\theta) = \mathbb{E}_{p_{S,X}}[T_\theta] - log(\mathbb{E}_{p_S \otimes p_X})[e^{T_\theta}]) \tag{8}$$

This loss function is itself bounded by $\mathcal{I}(S, X)$. The universal approximation theorem for neural networks guarantees that this bound can be made arbitrarily tight for some well-chosen parameters θ. The goal is then to find the best θ, potentially using all the deep learning techniques and, more generally, all the tools for optimization problem-solving. The expectations in (8) can be estimated using empirical samples from $p_{S,X}$ and $p_S \otimes p_X$ and the maximization can be done with the classical gradient ascent. A noticeable difference with a classical deep learning setup is that the trained network is not used for any kind of prediction. Instead, the evaluation of the loss function at the end of the training gives an estimation of $\mathcal{I}(S, X)$. We give hereafter the formal definition of the estimator as stated in the original paper [1].

Definition 1. *(MINE) Let $\mathcal{A} = \{(s_1, x_1), \dots, (s_n, x_n)\}$ and $\mathcal{B} = \{(\tilde{s}_1, \tilde{x}_1), \dots, (\tilde{s}_n, \tilde{x}_n)\}$ be two sets of n empirical samples respectively from $p_{S,X}$ and $p_S \otimes p_X$. Let $\mathcal{F} = \{T_\theta\}_{\theta \in \Theta}$ be the set of functions parametrized by a neural network. MINE is defined as follows:*

$$\widehat{\mathcal{I}(S, X)}_n = \sup_{T \in \mathcal{F}} \overline{\mathbb{E}_{\mathcal{A}}[T]} - log(\overline{\mathbb{E}_{\mathcal{B}}[e^T]}) \tag{9}$$

where $\overline{\mathbb{E}_S[\cdot]}$ stands for the expectation empirically estimated over the set S.

The main theoretical result proved in [1] is that MINE is strongly consistent.

Theorem 2. *(Strong consistency) For all $\epsilon > 0$ there exist a positive integer N such that:*

$$\forall n > N, \quad |\mathcal{I}(S,X) - \widehat{\mathcal{I}(S,X)}_n| < \epsilon \tag{10}$$

In practice one often only have samples from the joint distribution: $\mathcal{A} = \{(s_1, x_1), \ldots (s_n, x_n)\}$. Samples from the product of the marginals can be artificially generated by shuffling the variable X using a random permutation σ: $\mathcal{B} = \{(s_1, x_{\sigma(1)}), \ldots, (s_n, x_{\sigma(n)})\}$. We provide hereafter an implementation of MINE that uses minibatch gradient ascent. Note that $\mathcal{B}$ is regenerated after each epoch. Thus, this algorithm is not strictly implementing MINE as defined in (9) because $\mathcal{B}$ is fixed in this definition. Theoretical arguments are provided in Sect. 3.4 to explain why this regeneration limit overfitting in practice and is therefore mandatory.

Algorithm 1: Mine implementation

Input: $\mathcal{A} = \{(s_1, x_1), \ldots (s_n, x_n)\}$
$\theta \leftarrow$ Initialize network parameters
Choose b a batch size such that $b \mid n$
repeat
    Generate $\mathcal{B} = \{(s_1, x_{\sigma(1)}), \ldots, (s_n, x_{\sigma(n)})\}$ with a random permutation σ
    Divide $\mathcal{A}$ and $\mathcal{B}$ into $\frac{n}{b}$ packs of b elements: $A_1, \ldots, A_{\frac{n}{b}}$ and $B_1, \ldots, B_{\frac{n}{b}}$
    for $i = 1; i = \frac{n}{b}$ **do**
        $\mathcal{L}(\theta) \leftarrow \overline{\mathbb{E}_{A_i}[T_\theta]} - log(\overline{\mathbb{E}_{B_i}[e^{T_\theta}]})$, *Evaluate the loss function*
        $G(\theta) \leftarrow \nabla_\theta \mathcal{L}(\theta)$, *Compute the gradient*
        $\theta \leftarrow \theta + \mu G(\theta)$, *Update the network parameters (μ is the learning rate)*
    end
until *convergence of $\mathcal{L}(\theta)$*

---

3   Analysis of MINE in a Side-Channel Context

MI has found applications in a wide range of disciplines and it is not surprising that it is also of great interest for side-channel analysis. Unlike Pearson coefficient, it detects non-linear dependencies and thus does not require any assumptions on the leakage model. Another key property of the MI is that it is invariant to bijective transformations of the variables. This is of interest for side-channel as S usually represents the state of an internal variable (ex: $S = K \oplus P$ for an AES) and is therefore unknown but bijectively related to a known variable such as the plaintext P. In that case, there exists a bijective function f such that $S = f(P)$ and:

$$\mathcal{I}(S,X) = \mathcal{I}(f^{-1}(S), X) = \mathcal{I}(P, X) \tag{11}$$

Thus, one may estimate $\mathcal{I}(S, X)$ with only the knowledge of P and X and therefore quickly get the amount of leakage an attacker could potentially exploit.

In what follows, we consider that we are granted n samples $(s_1, x_1), \ldots, (s_n, x_n)$ of traces associated to the sensitive variable being processed in the device (or as stated above, to any bijection of this variable). These samples will be either generated on simulation or measured from real case experiments. The goal is to derive the best way to use MINE in a side-channel context in order to compute a reliable estimation of $\mathcal{I}(P, X)$.

3.1   Simulated Traces Environment

In order to assess the capabilities of MINE experiments on synthetic traces were first conducted. These traces have been generated using a leakage model which may seem awkward since the whole point of conducting MI analysis is to avoid any assumption on the leakage model. But we argue that as a first step, it brings a valuable advantage: the environment is perfectly controlled, thus the true MI is known and can be used to evaluate the results and compare different settings.

Trace Generation. To generate traces, featuring $n_l + n_r$ independent samples, a sensitive byte $0 \leq s \leq 255$ was first drawn uniformly. The leakage was spread over the n_l samples drawn from a normal distribution centered in the Hamming Weight (HW) of s and with noise $\sigma \sim \mathcal{N}(HW(s), \sigma)$. The n_r remaining samples are random points added to the trace to artificially increase the dimension and be closer from a real scenario. Each of the n_r samples is drawn from a normal distribution centered in c and with noise $\sigma \sim \mathcal{N}(c, \sigma)$, where c is an integer itself drawn uniformly between 0 and 8. A very simple yet informative case is to set $n_l = 1, n_r = 0$ and $\sigma = 1$. In that case, the true mutual information $\mathcal{I}(S, X)$ is equal to:

$$\mathcal{I}(S, X) = H(S) - H(S|X)$$

$$= 8 - \sum_{s=0}^{255} \int_{-\infty}^{\infty} \Pr(s, x) \cdot log_2 \left(\frac{1}{\Pr(s|x)} \right) dx$$

$$= 8 - \sum_{s=0}^{255} \int_{-\infty}^{\infty} \frac{1}{2^8} \frac{1}{\sqrt{2\pi}} e^{-\frac{1}{2}(x - HW(s))^2} \cdot log_2 \left(\frac{\sum_{s'=0}^{255} e^{-\frac{1}{2}(x - HW(s'))^2}}{e^{-\frac{1}{2}(x - HW(s))^2}} \right) dx$$

$$\approx 0.8 \text{ bits}$$

$$(12)$$

As a first step, we applied MINE to a set of 10k synthetic traces generated with these parameters. The network was set to be a simple Multi Layer Perceptron (MLP) with two hidden layers of size 20. The Exponential Linear Unit (ELU) was used as the activation function. The input layer was composed of two neurons, representing the value of the sensitive variable S and the one-dimensional trace X. The output was a single neuron giving the value of the function T_θ. The batch size was set to 500. The value of the loss function $\mathcal{L}(\theta)$ over time is plotted in Fig. 1. An epoch represents the processing of all the data so the parameters are updated 20 times per epoch.

As shown, the results are mixed. On one hand, the loss function is always under the true MI and it seems that the limit superior of MINE is converging over time towards 0.8, *i.e.* the true MI. On the other hand, the loss function experiences a lot of drops and the convergence is very slow (above 200k epochs). Drops may be due to the optimizer used (ADAM [10]) and happens when the gradient is very close to 0. Increasing the size/number of hidden layers did not produce any significantly better results. In that state MINE is clearly not of any use for side-channel: the convergence is not clear and a classical histogram method would compute the MI faster and better for one-dimensional traces.

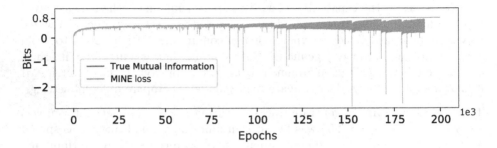

Fig. 1. Evolution of MINE's loss function over time

3.2   Input Decompression

Trying to gain intuition about the reasons causing the network to perform poorly in this situation, we hypothesized that the information in the first layer, especially the value of s, could be too condensed in the sense that only one neuron is used to describe it. Intuitively, the information provided by s about the corresponding trace x is not continuous in s. The meaning of this statement is that there is no reason that two close values of s induce two close values of x. For example, in a noise-free Hamming weight leakage model, the traces corresponding to a sensitive value of 127 and 128 would be very different since $HW(127) = 7$ and $HW(128) = 1$. Since neural networks are built using a succession of linear and activation functions which are all continuous, approximating functions with quick and high variations may be harder for them. Indeed, building a neural classifier that extracts the Hamming weight of an integer is not an easy task. However, if the value of this integer is split into multiple neurons holdings its binary representation, the problem becomes trivial as it ends up being a simple sum.

   This observation led us to increase the input size to represent the value of s in its binary form, thus using 8 neurons. However, computing $\mathcal{I}(S, X)$ in that case gives an unfair advantage to the arbitrarily chosen Hamming weight model. Indeed, the value of X would be closely related to the sum of the input bits. So we decided to compute $\mathcal{I}(S \oplus k, X)$ instead of $\mathcal{I}(S, X)$, with a fixed k. As stated above this bijective transformation does not change the MI anyway and removes a possible confusion factor in the analysis. Results with the same parameters as before ($n_l = 1, n_r = 0, \sigma = 1$) are presented in Fig. 2. They bear no comparison with the previous ones. With this simple trick, MINE quickly converges toward the true MI. The estimation seems robust as restarting the training from different initializations of the network always produces the same results. The order of magnitude of the computational time for the 500 epochs is around two minutes.

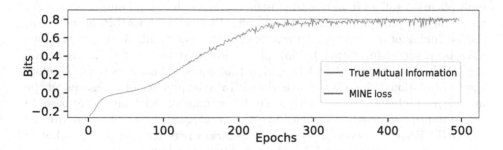

Fig. 2. MINE with input decompression

Remark 1. Note that any constant function T_θ would produce a loss function of 0. We argue that this could explain the knee point around 0 bit in the learning curve: it is indeed, easy for the network to quickly reach 0 tuning the parameters towards a constant function, before learning anything interesting.

Before testing this method for higher dimension traces, we propose to analyze more in-depth this Input Decompression (ID). The goal is to understand if this result was related in any way to our simulation setup or if ID could be applied to more generic cases. As a first step, we tried to decompress X instead of S, binning the value of X to the closest integers, then using its binary representation as input neurons. As expected, it did not work: results looked like Fig. 1, as X is by essence a continuous variable. If there is no interest in splitting into multiple neurons an intrinsically continuous variable, our hypothesis is that, for categorical variables, the greater the decompression, the faster the training.

Learning Random Permutations. In order to test this hypothesis in a more generic case, this section proposes to build a neural network P_θ which goal is to learn a random permutation P of $\{0, \ldots, n-1\}$ and to analyze its performance in terms of ID. Permutations have been chosen because they are arbitrary functions with no relation between close inputs. For an integer $m < n$ the network returns a float $P_\theta(m)$ which has to be as close as possible to $P(m)$. The loss function was defined as error: $\mathcal{L}(\theta) = |P_\theta(m) - P(m)|$. Network architecture was again a simple MLP but with 3 hidden layers of size 100. To study the effect of ID the input layer was defined to be the representation of m in different bases, with one neuron per digit. For example, with n = 256, all bases in $256, 16, 7, 4, 3, 2, 1$ were considered resulting in a first layer of respectively $\{1, 2, 3, 4, 6, 8, 256\}$ neurons (base 1 is actually the One Hot Encoding (OHE)). The training dataset was a list of 10k integers uniformly drawn from $\{0, \ldots, n-1\}$. Loss functions in terms of ID are depicted in Fig. 3. At the end of the training, plots are exactly ordered in the expected way: greater decompression leads to faster and better training.

In a recent analysis, Bronchain *et al.* [5] have shown that it was hard for a MLP to learn the Galois multiplication in $GF(2^n)$ when $n \geq 8$. As Galois multiplication suffers from the same non-continuity than random permutations, we argue that blue plots confirm this result. With no ID our MLP did not show the beginning of a convergence towards 0. But we do think their network may have been successful with ID. Pink plots show that the best choice is to use the OHE. The problem with OHE is that the number of neurons (and therefore the computational time) scales linearly with n (the number of categories of the underlying problem), where it only scales logarithmically with any other base. In side-channel, one mostly deals with bytes (256 categories) and will therefore use the OHE. However, Sect. 4.3 presents a scenario where using base 2 is a better choice, when computing the MI with assembly instructions.

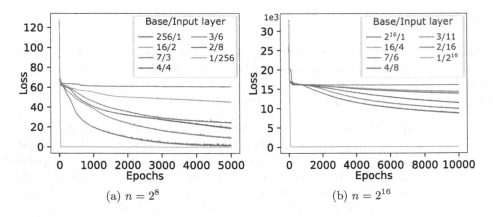

Fig. 3. Impact of input decompression on learning random permutations

Remark 2. Note that the constant function $P_\theta = \frac{n}{2}$ would result in an average loss function of $\frac{n}{4}$, which explains the knee point around $\frac{n}{4}$ observable in most of the curves: quickly converging towards this function is an efficient strategy for the network to minimize its loss at the beginning of the learning phase. We verified this statement by looking at the predictions of the network which were all close from $\frac{n}{2}$ in the early stage of the training.

3.3 MINE in Higher Dimension

This section presents results of simulations in higher dimension and compare MINE estimation to that provided by the classical histogram and KNN methods. The histogram estimator has been implemented following the description from [15] and Steeg's implementation [21] has been utilized for KNN. Network architecture described in Sect. 3.1 has been used with OHE to encode the S variable. We have kept $n_l = \sigma = 1$ so the true MI is still around 0.8 bits but n_r was no longer set to 0 in order to increase the traces dimension. Figure 4 shows the results for $n_r = 1$ and $n_r = 9$. In both case MINE correctly converges toward the true MI. The histogram method tends to overestimate the MI (as explained in [23]) while KNN method underestimates it. With dimension greater than 10 these methods are not reliable anymore. One could argue that any dimension reduction technique applied in the above experiments would allow to compute the MI with classical estimators. While this is true in this case it may result in a loss of information in a real case scenario where the information could be split into multiple samples of the traces. We have conducted many experiments with different parameters and MINE always returned reliable estimations even in very high dimension (ex: Fig. 5b with $n_l = 5$ and $n_r = 1000$).

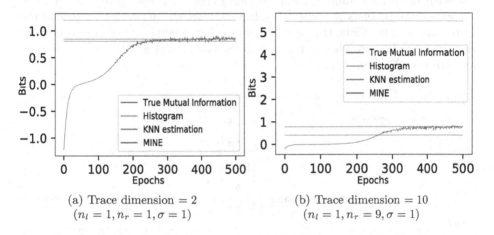

(a) Trace dimension = 2
$(n_l = 1, n_r = 1, \sigma = 1)$

(b) Trace dimension = 10
$(n_l = 1, n_r = 9, \sigma = 1)$

Fig. 4. Comparison of MINE with classical estimators in higher dimension

3.4 Analysis of the Overfitting Problem

Results of simulations are encouraging as they seem accurate with a lot of different parameters but one problem still has to be solved before testing MINE on real traces: when to stop the training? Until now, training has been manually stopped when the loss had converged towards the true MI. No such threshold value will be granted in real cases. One could argue that since the loss function is theoretically bounded by the true MI, a good strategy would be to let the training happen during a sufficiently long time and to retain the supremum of the loss function as the MI estimation. We argue that this strategy is not viable: in practice the bound does not hold as expectations in the loss are not the true expectations but are only estimated through empirical data. Thus, MINE can still produce output above the true MI. Figure 5 shows this phenomenon: training has been intentionally let running for a longer time in these experiments and MINE overestimates the MI at the end of the training. In other terms, MINE is no exception to the rule when it comes to the overfitting problem: the network can learn ways to exploit specificities of the data it is using to train, in order to maximize its loss function. We propose hereafter a detailed analysis of this problem and answer to the following question: is it possible to control (for example to bound with a certain probability) the error made by the network?

Let us return to the definition of MINE estimator:

$$\widehat{\mathcal{I}(S, X)}_n = \sup_{\theta \in \Theta} \overline{\mathbb{E}_{\mathcal{A}}[T_\theta]} - log(\overline{\mathbb{E}_{\mathcal{B}}[e^{T_\theta}]}) \tag{13}$$

The problem comes from the fact that the two expectations are estimated over the set of empirical data $\mathcal{A}$ and $\mathcal{B}$. The error can not be controlled in the classical way with the central limit theorem because there is a notion of order that is important: the two sets $\mathcal{A}$ and $\mathcal{B}$ are selected *before* the network tries to find the supremum over Θ. Thus, the network can exploit specificities of $\mathcal{A}$ and $\mathcal{B}$ in its research. We show in Theorem 3 that given two sets $\mathcal{A}$ and $\mathcal{B}$, the supremum may not even be bounded.

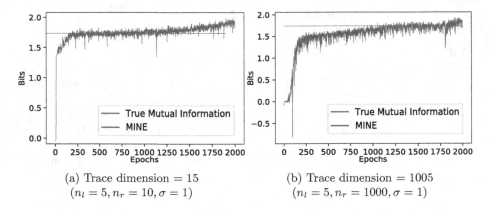

(a) Trace dimension = 15
$(n_l = 5, n_r = 10, \sigma = 1)$

(b) Trace dimension = 1005
$(n_l = 5, n_r = 1000, \sigma = 1)$

Fig. 5. Over estimation of MINE at the end the training (overfitting)

Theorem 3. *Let X, Y be two random variables over Ω. Let $\boldsymbol{x} = (x_1, \ldots, x_n) \in \Omega^n$ and $\boldsymbol{y} = (y_1, \ldots, y_n) \in \Omega^n$ be two samples of n realizations of respectively X and Y. Then,*

$$\sup_{T: \Omega \to \mathbb{R}} \overline{\mathbb{E}_{\boldsymbol{x}}[T(X)]} - log(\overline{\mathbb{E}_{\boldsymbol{y}}[e^{T(Y)}]}) < \infty \Leftrightarrow \forall i, \exists j \text{ such that } x_i = y_j$$

Proof. Let us introduce two new random variables, X' and Y' defined as follows:

$$\forall \omega \in \Omega, \; \mathbb{P}(X' = \omega) = \frac{1}{n} \cdot |\{x_i = \omega\}| \quad \text{and} \quad \mathbb{P}(Y' = \omega) = \frac{1}{m} \cdot |\{y_i = \omega\}|$$

The samples x and y are perfect samples of X' and Y' (by definition of X' and Y'), thus, the estimated expectations are equal to the true expectations computed over this new variables:

$$\sup_{T:\,\Omega\to\mathbb{R}} \overline{\mathbb{E}_x[T(X)]} - log(\overline{\mathbb{E}_y[e^{T(Y)}]}) = \sup_{T:\,\Omega\to\mathbb{R}} \mathbb{E}_{X'}[T(X')] - log(\mathbb{E}_{Y'}[e^{T(Y')}])$$

Now let us assume the right part of the equivalence. This condition means that there is no isolated x_i, or in other words: $\forall\omega, \Pr(Y'=\omega)=0 \Rightarrow \Pr(X'=\omega)=0$. This guarantees the absolute continuity of $p_{X'}$ with respect to $p_{Y'}$ and thus, that $D_{KL}(p_{X'}\|p_{Y'})$ exists. Therefore, using Theorem 1:

$$\sup_{T:\,\Omega\to\mathbb{R}} \overline{\mathbb{E}_x[T(X)]} - log(\overline{\mathbb{E}_y[e^{T(Y)}]}) = D_{KL}(p_{X'}\|p_{Y'}) < \infty$$

If, on the other hand, this condition is false: $\exists i$ such that $\forall j$, $x_i \neq y_j$. For any given function T one can exploit this isolated x_i modifying $T(x_i)$ without influencing the second expectation. In particular, if $T(x_i)$ tends towards infinity:

$$\lim_{T(x_i)\to\infty} \left[\overline{\mathbb{E}_x[T(X)]} - log(\overline{\mathbb{E}_y[e^{T(Y)}]}) \right] = \lim_{T(x_i)\to\infty} \left[\frac{1}{n}\sum_{k=1}^{n} x_k T(x_k) - log(\frac{1}{n}\sum_{k=1}^{n} y_k e^{T(y_k)}) \right]$$

$$= \lim_{T(x_i)\to\infty} \left[\frac{1}{n}\sum_{k=1}^{n} x_k T(x_k) \right] - log(\frac{1}{n}\sum_{k=1}^{n} y_k e^{T(y_k)})$$

$$= \infty$$

So in that case:

$$\sup_{T:\,\Omega\to\mathbb{R}} \overline{\mathbb{E}_x[T(X)]} - log(\overline{\mathbb{E}_y[e^{T(Y)}]}) = \infty$$

$\square$

This theorem means that most of the time (and especially for high dimensional variables) the supremum is infinite and MINE is not even well defined. The natural question that comes now is: why does MINE seem to work in practice?

We claim that this is due to the implementation and especially to the randomization of the set $\mathcal{B}$ evoked in Sect. 2: after each epoch a new permutation σ is drawn to generate samples from $p_S \otimes p_X$: $\mathcal{B} = \{(s_1, x_{\sigma(1)}), \ldots, (s_n, x_{\sigma(n)})\}$. Thus, the isolated samples from $\mathcal{A}$ are not always the same at each epoch which does not leave time for the network to exploit them. To verify that this was a key element, MINE was run without this randomization process. The loss function diverged towards infinity, as predicted by Theorem 3.

In the long run, the network can still learn statistical specificities of the dataset such as samples from $\mathcal{A}$ that has a greater probability of being isolated, and exploit them. This explains why MINE may overfit when it has a long time to train. That is why we suggest to add a validation loss function.

Validation Loss Function. A validation loss function is a common tool when it comes to detect overfitting and stop the training at the right time. The idea is to split the dataset $\mathcal{A}$ into a training dataset $\mathcal{A}_t$ and a validation one $\mathcal{A}_v$ and to only use $\mathcal{A}_t$ for the training. At the end of each epoch, the loss function is computed both on $\mathcal{A}_t$ and $\mathcal{A}_v$. As the data from $\mathcal{A}_v$ are never used during training, MINE can not overfit on them. Thus, it is safe to take the supremum of the loss computed over $\mathcal{A}_v$ as our MI estimation. It also provides a useful condition to stop the training as the decrease of the validation loss function is usually a sign of overfitting. Figure 6a shows an example where the true loss function and the validation one (computed on 80% and 20% of the data) respectively increase and decrease after a while. Training could have been stopped after the 500th epoch.

Fill the Holes. Theorem 3 states that there is still a case where the supremum is bounded: when $\forall a \in \mathcal{A}$, $\exists b \in \mathcal{B}$ such that $a = b$, or in other words, when there is no isolated value in $\mathcal{A}$. An alternative solution to prevent overfitting is thus to force this condition to be true instead of regenerating $\mathcal{B}$ after each epoch. Naively filling the holes by adding to $\mathcal{B}$ all the isolated values is not a good idea because the resulting set would be biased, not containing *stricto sensu* samples drawn from $p_S \otimes p_X$. However, with $\mathcal{A} = \{(s_1, x_1), \dots (s_n, x_n)\}$, $\mathcal{A}_s = \{s_1, \dots, s_n\}$ and $\mathcal{A}_x = \{x_1, \dots, x_n\}$ one can define $\mathcal{B}'$ as the Cartesian product[1] $\mathcal{B}' = \mathcal{A}_s \times \mathcal{A}_x$ which is by definition a non-biased dataset that covers all the elements of $\mathcal{A}$. The problem is that its size is no longer n but n^2 which drastically impacts the computational time of MINE as the network has to compute $T_\theta(b)$ for all $b \in \mathcal{B}'$ at each epoch. However, the number of network evaluations can be reduced to $c \cdot n$ where c is the cardinality of the set $\mathcal{S}$ made up of all the possible values taken by the sensitive variable S. For example, if S is a byte, $c = 256$. The idea is to evaluate T_θ on the $c \cdot n$ elements of the set $\mathcal{S} \times \mathcal{A}_x$ which is sufficient to cover all the couples from $\mathcal{B}'$ as elements from $\mathcal{A}_s \times \mathcal{A}_x$ can all be found in $\mathcal{S} \times \mathcal{A}_x$.

With this implementation MINE is fundamentally bounded by a quantity denoted $Maxmi$ equal to the KL-divergence between the empirical distributions associated to $\mathcal{A}$ and $\mathcal{B}$ as stated in the proof of Theorem 3. Figure 6b shows an example of MINE with this implementation applied to the already considered case ($n_l = 1, n_r = 0, \sigma = 1$). One may observe that the loss function is a lot smoother and is effectively bounded by $Maxmi$ (we tried to let the network train for more than 100k epochs) which is another empirical confirmation of Theorem 3.

However, when the dimension of the variables increases samples tend to be more and more unique. At the limit, they hold the full information about the corresponding secret s which means that $Maxmi$ will tends towards $H(S)$. Knowing if the network will always converge towards his supremum or will stabilize to a value close to the true MI is an open question. We do think that the randomization proposed in the precedent strategy may help to that aim and that is why we

---

[1] These sets are actually multisets as they may contains repetitions of a single elements but the Cartesian product can be canonicaly extended to multisets.

will stick to the validation method for our real-life experiments, which is faster anyway.

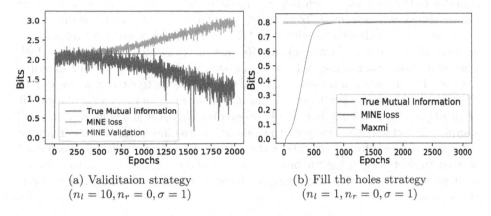

(a) Validitaion strategy
$(n_l = 10, n_r = 0, \sigma = 1)$

(b) Fill the holes strategy
$(n_l = 1, n_r = 0, \sigma = 1)$

Fig. 6. Two possible strategies against overfitting

4   Application of MINE in an Evaluation Context

This section provides real case examples where MINE could be useful especially in an evaluation context. Its most straightforward utilization is probably to assess the quantity of information leaking from a device when it computes a cryptographic algorithm. It can be seen as a first security metric, easy to compute whatever the target and the implementation, with low expertise required. However, MINE only returns an upper bound on the amount of leakage potentially usable. In practice, an attacker may not be able to fully exploit this information, depending on his strategy, and that is why classical evaluation methods still have to be performed.

That being said, MINE is also a great comparison tool. Indeed, its output is an interpretable number that allows to objectively rank different devices or implementations in terms of their leakage. It can be used to analyze the effect of a countermeasure or even to compare different hardware setup in order to maximize the MI for future attacks or evaluations.

4.1   Leakage Evaluation of an Unprotected AES

As a first real case experiment, our target was an unprotected AES implemented on a cortex M4 device. 20k EM traces centered on the first round of the AES have been acquired through a Langer probe (RF-B 0, 3-3) linked to an LNA and a Tektronix oscilloscope (MSO64, 2.5 GHz) with a sample rate of 1 GS/s. Resulting traces had a length of 50k samples. They have been labeled with the first byte of the corresponding plaintext which was drawn randomly for each computation of the AES.

The main goal of this first experiment was to demonstrate how adding more samples to the analysis, which is the purpose of MINE, increases the amount of information one can recover. To this end, only the n samples with the maximum SNR were kept in the traces, with n in $\{1, 5, 500\}$. Network architecture was the same as in the simulated experiments. Results are presented in Fig. 7. The thick blue plot shows that if one only uses one sample in his analysis (for example with a CPA or histogram-based MIA) he would be able to extract at most 1.15 bits about the secret, per trace. While it is a huge amount of information (it is an unprotected AES) it is possible to extract almost 4 times more using 500 samples. For clarity reasons, only the validation loss has been plotted. Training has been stopped after epoch 500 as these validations (especially the green one) started to decrease. Going further with $n \geq 500$ did not produce better results as it seems that the remaining samples were absolutely not informative about the secret.

ADC Comparison. The oscilloscope used in the former experiment offers the possibility to set the ADC precision to either 8 or 15 bits. This is a good opportunity to show MINE comparative interest and its ability to answer questions such as "Is it really worth it to buy the newest scope with the enhanced ADC precision?" in a quantitative and objective way. 10k traces instead of 20k (so that the occupied memory stayed constant) were thus acquired with the 15 bits precision. Results are represented by the thin plots on Fig. 7. In this case, the answer is that there is a slight improvement (around 10%) working with the 15 bits precision rather than the 8 bits one.

4.2 Leakage Evaluation of a Masked AES from the ASCAD Database

One of the main difficulties of side-channel analysis is to extract information even when the target algorithm has been masked. Indeed, masking removes all the first-order leakage and thus, obliges one to combine samples together to detect a dependency with the secret. This is usually very long as all the couples of samples (or n-tuple) have to be tested.

It is thus a great challenge for MINE to see if it is able to automatically perform this recombination, and detect higher-order leakages. For that purpose, the public dataset ASCAD [2] (with no jitter) has been used. It provides a database of 50k EM traces of 700 samples each, of an AES protected with a Boolean masking. A MI estimation, derived from deep learning attack results, has already been done on this dataset [14]. They reported a MI of 0.065 bit between the traces and the third key byte (the first two were not masked) which provides a reference point.

At first, MINE was not successful: the loss function increased but the validation started to decrease very early which is a direct sign of overfitting. Intuitively, when the underlying problem is more complex, it may be easier for the network to learn properties of the empirical data before the true structure of these data. Then, classical solutions against overfitting have been applied to MINE. These include Batch Normalization (BN) layers, dropout, and regularization techniques. While the last, did not impact performances significantly, the combination of BN and dropout greatly improved the results. A BN layer has been applied to the inputs in order to normalize them. This is known to make the loss function smoother and thus the optimization easier [17]. Dropout was activated with $p = 0.2$ so that each neuron has a probability p of being set to 0 when an output of the network is computed (except when the validation is computed). This is also known to reduce overfitting and make the training more robust [20].

Results are presented in Fig. 8: validation loss reached a value of 0.2 bits which is about three times bigger than the MI reported in [14]. Due to how validation is computed this value can not be an overestimation of the MI. Our MLP structure may be a little more adapted than the CNN used in [14] as there is no jitter in that case. We also suggest that the input decompression technique, only usable with MINE, could help the network to learn, especially for complex problems such as when the algorithm is masked. This may explain why MINE was able to extract more information in that case. One can observe that it took 100 epochs for the network to start to learn something. It may seem random but this period of 100 epochs was surprisingly repeatable across experiments.

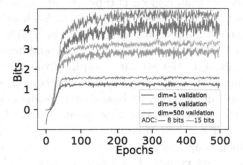

Fig. 7. Leakage evaluation of an unprotected AES

4.3   Instructions Leakage

Another advantage of MINE is that it cannot only compute MI for high dimensional traces but also for secrets with a high number of classes. This is the case if one is interested in recovering information about the raw assembly instructions that are being executed. This branch of SCA is called Side Channel Based Disassembling (SCBD) [7–9,22] and the main difficulty in this domain is the size of the attacked variable, generally the couple (opcode, operands) which is no longer a simple byte. For example the target device in [7,8,22] is a PIC16F from

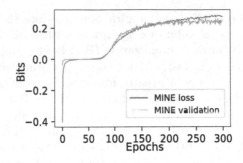

Fig. 8. Leakage evaluation of a masked AES (ASCAD)

Microchip which encodes its instruction on 14 bits. Even though some opcodes are not valid, the number of possible couples (opcode, operands) is around 2^{12}. It is even worse for more complex processors encoding their instruction on 16 or 32 bits. MINE treats the attacked variable as an input and the number of neurons used to encode it can be adjusted with ID as stated in Sect. 3.2. Using base 2, one only need 14 neurons to encode an instruction in the PIC example.

In order to test MINE in this context, we have generated a program with 12k randoms instructions for the PIC. Using the same experimental setup described in Sect. 4.2 of [7], an EM trace of the whole execution has been acquired (it was averaged on 500 traces as the program is repeatable). This trace has then been separated into 12k sub-traces of 2000 samples each. Each sub-trace was labeled with the executed instruction. As it has been shown in [7] that the probe position may be very important, MINE has been applied at 100 different positions (using a (10×10) grid) resulting in the MI cartography given in Fig. 9. The value at each position is the mean of the network's validation computed over the 100 last epochs of the training (all the training lasted 500 epochs and a Gaussian filter has been applied to the figure). Up to 8 bits of information have been found for the best positions which is a high amount if one compares to the full entropy of an instruction which is approximately 12 bits. This shows that MINE stays sound even when the target variable has a high number of classes.

Coil Comparison. Similar to what has been done regarding the selection of the oscilloscope precision, another hardware comparative experiment was conducted. Two probes with two different coil orientations (Langer ICR HH and HV 100-27) have been used. While the "hot" zones are globally the same, one may observe that the coil orientation may have a significant impact on the captured information for some specific positions. This experiment suggests that MINE could be used to guide the positioning of EM probes during evaluations.

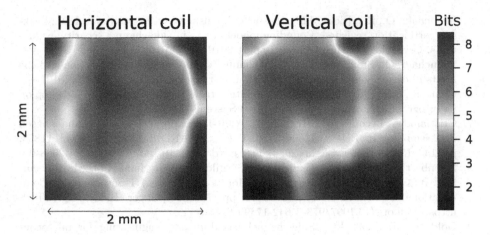

Fig. 9. Cartography of the MI between instructions and traces estimated by MINE on a PIC16F

5 Conclusion

This paper suggests ways MINE, a new deep learning technique to estimate mutual information, could constitute a new tool for side-channel analysis. The main advantage is its ability to estimate MI between high dimensional variables. Indeed, being able to consider full (or large part of) traces as a variable, allows to exploit all potential leakage sources with no *a priori* on the leakage model neither on the implementation. It seems that MINE could be used as a very simple tool to obtain an objective leakage evaluation from traces. Thus, it may be employed for massive and quick evaluations for designers in their development process as well as for evaluators as a first leakage metric.

These suggestions result from a theoretical and practical analysis of MINE in a side-channel context. MINE's overfitting problem has been deeply investigated as well as the way input representation may have a huge impact on performances. Our upcoming works will aim at investigating possible usages of MINE for extracting secrets in an unsupervised way *i.e.* in an attack context.

References

1. Belghazi, M.I., et al.: Mine: mutual information neural estimation (2018)
2. Benadjila, R., Prouff, E., Strullu, R., Cagli, E., Dumas, C.: Study of deep learning techniques for side-channel analysis and introduction to ascad database. ANSSI, France & CEA, LETI, MINATEC Campus, France (2018)
3. Joye, M., Quisquater, J.-J. (eds.): CHES 2004. LNCS, vol. 3156. Springer, Heidelberg (2004). https://doi.org/10.1007/b99451

4. Bronchain, O., Hendrickx, J.M., Massart, C., Olshevsky, A., Standaert, F.X.: Leakage certification revisited: Bounding model errors in side-channel security evaluations. Cryptology ePrint Archive, Report 2019/132 (2019)
5. Bronchain, O., Standaert, F.X.: Side-channel countermeasures' dissection and the limits of closed source security evaluations. Cryptology ePrint Archive (2019)
6. Chari, S., Rao, J.R., Rohatgi, P.: Template attacks. In: International Workshop on Cryptographic Hardware and Embedded Systems (2002)
7. Cristiani, V., Lecomte, M., Hiscock, T.: A bit-level approach to side channel based disassembling. In: Belaïd, S., Güneysu, T. (eds.) CARDIS 2019. LNCS, vol. 11833, pp. 143–158. Springer, Cham (2020). https://doi.org/10.1007/978-3-030-42068-0_9
8. Eisenbarth, T., Paar, C., Weghenkel, B.: Building a side channel based disassembler. In: Gavrilova, M.L., Tan, C.J.K., Moreno, E.D. (eds.) Transactions on Computational Science X. LNCS, vol. 6340, pp. 78–99. Springer, Heidelberg (2010). https://doi.org/10.1007/978-3-642-17499-5_4
9. Goldack, M., Paar, I.C.: Side-channel based reverse engineering for microcontrollers. Master's thesis, Ruhr-Universität Bochum, Germany (2008)
10. Kingma, D.P., Ba, J.: Adam: a method for stochastic optimization (2014)
11. Kocher, P., Jaffe, J., Jun, B.: Differential power analysis. In: Annual International Cryptology Conference (1999)
12. Kraskov, A., Stögbauer, H., Grassberger, P.: Estimating mutual information. Phys. Rev. **69**, 066138 (2004)
13. Macé, F., Standaert, F.X., Quisquater, J.J.: Information theoretic evaluation of side-channel resistant logic styles, vol. 2008, p. 5, January 2008
14. Masure, L., Dumas, C., Prouff, E.: A comprehensive study of deep learning for side-channel analysis. IACR Trans. Cryptographic Hardware Embed. Syst. **2020**, 348–375 (2019)
15. Prouff, E., Rivain, M.: Theoretical and practical aspects of mutual information based side channel analysis, pp. 499–518, January 2009
16. Quisquater, J.J., Samyde, D.: Electromagnetic analysis: measures and countermeasures for smart cards (2001)
17. Santurkar, S., Tsipras, D., Ilyas, A., Madry, A.: How does batch normalization help optimization? (2018)
18. Schneider, T., Moradi, A.: Leakage assessment methodology. In: International Workshop on Cryptographic Hardware and Embedded Systems (2015)
19. Shannon, C.E.: A mathematical theory of communication. Bell Syst. Tech. J. **27**(3), 379–423 (1948)
20. Srivastava, N., Hinton, G., Krizhevsky, A., Sutskever, I., Salakhutdinov, R.: Dropout: a simple way to prevent neural networks from overfitting. J. Mach. Learn. Res. **15**(56), 1929–1958 (2014)
21. Steeg, G.V.: Non-parametric entropy estimation toolbox (2014). https://github.com/gregversteeg/NPEET
22. Strobel, D., Bache, F., Oswald, D., Schellenberg, F., Paar, C.: Scandalee: a side-channel-based disassembler using local electromagnetic emanations. In: Proceedings of the Design, Automation & Test in Europe Conference & Exhibition (2015)
23. Vinh, N.X., Epps, J., Bailey, J.: Information theoretic measures for clusterings comparison: variants, properties, normalization and correction for chance. J. Mach. Learn. Res. **11**(95), 2837–2854 (2010)

Evolvable Hardware Architectures on FPGA for Side-Channel Security

Mansoureh Labafniya[1], Shahram Etemadi Borujeni[1(✉)], and Nele Mentens[2,3]

[1] University of Isfahan, Isfahan, Iran
{mlabaf,etemadi}@eng.ui.ac.ir
[2] Leiden University, LIACS, Leiden, The Netherlands
n.mentens@liacs.leidenuniv.nl
[3] KU Leuven, ESAT, ES&S and imec-COSIC, Leuven, Belgium
nele.mentens@kuleuven.be

Abstract. This paper proposes the use of Evolvable Hardware (EH) architectures as a countermeasure against power analysis attacks. It is inspired by the work of Sasdrich et al., in which the block cipher PRESENT is protected against power analysis attacks through the use of dynamic logic FPGA reconfiguration. The countermeasure consists of splitting the substitution boxes (S-boxes) into two parts with a register in between; the way the S-boxes are split is random and is altered before each new execution of the block cipher. This makes it very difficult (or even impossible) for an attacker to perform a Differential Power Analysis (DPA) attack by collecting many power traces of the same implementation.

Whereas the approach of Sasdrich et al. requires the external computation and communication of new configurations, our approach computes new configurations on the fly with an on-chip configuration generator based on evolutionary algorithms. This reduces the risk of an adversary tampering with the configuration data and takes away the communication delay. Our work is the first to propose the use of EH and Genetic Programming (GP) for this type of countermeasure. More precisely, we explore two methods, Genetic Programming (GP) and Cartesian Genetic Programming (CGP) and we evaluate the feasibility of these methods by measuring the overhead in terms of delay and resource occupation for the block ciphers PRESENT and PRINTcipher.

Keywords: Evolvable Hardware · Virtual reconfigurable circuit · Differential Power Analysis (DPA) · Field-Programmable Gate Array (FPGA)

1 Introduction

Side-channel attacks (SCAs) are a realistic security threat for devices populating the Internet of Things (IoT). When an attacker has access to side-channels, such as the power consumption [19], the electromagnetic radiation [1] or the timing behavior [20] of an electronic device, he/she can possibly extract secret

© Springer Nature Switzerland AG 2020
J. Zhou et al. (Eds.): ACNS 2020 Workshops, LNCS 12418, pp. 163–180, 2020.
https://doi.org/10.1007/978-3-030-61638-0_10

information related to the internal signals in the device. This way, the theoretical security provided by cryptographic primitives can easily be defeated if the device is not equipped with any SCA countermeasures.

Two common categories of countermeasures against SCA are hiding and masking [23]. The main concept behind masking is to randomize the processed values by applying masks, such that it becomes more difficult for an attacker to gain information on the internal signals. Hiding countermeasures, on the other hand, aim at breaking the correlation between the internally processed values and the observed side-channels. Examples of hiding countermeasures are given by Güneysu et al. in [11]. They propose generic countermeasures against power analysis attacks on FPGAs by reducing the signal-to-noise ratio, introducing timing disarrangement, and scrambling. Another example of an FPGA-specific countermeasure against power analysis attacks is presented by Sasdrich et al. in [29]. In that work, configurable lookup tables (CFGLUTs) are used in Xilinx FPGAs to randomly split the implementation of the substitution boxes (S-boxes) into two parts at runtime with a register in between the two parts. Since most power analysis attacks on block ciphers target the retrieval of the value stored in the register at the output of the nonlinear substitution layer, moving this register in between two randomly decomposed S-box parts increases the effort required for a successful attack. In addition to the use of CFGLUTs for random S-box decomposition, the authors of [29] propose to integrate two other counter-measures, namely, Boolean masking and register pre-charging. They evaluate the efficiency and effectiveness of their approach on the block cipher PRESENT [29].

The main drawback of the approach proposed in [29], is that the configurations needed for the random decomposition of the S-boxes are generated externally, which means that the FPGA should always be connected to another processing device. In this paper, we overcome this shortcoming by using the Evolvable Hardware (EH) paradigm for the implementation of the S-boxes. Whereas the approach in [29] mainly concentrates on the efficient implementation of the split S-box, our work also takes into account the time and resource overhead that is necessary to find new S-box configurations. Our FPGA architecture consists of a Virtual Reconfigurable Circuit (VRC) in combination with an on-chip configuration generator. We present two alternatives, one based on regular FPGA LUTs and one based on CFGLUTs. Our contributions are the following:

- We propose an FPGA architecture based on EH to allow the on-chip generation of randomly decomposed S-boxes. It is the first work that uses EH for SCA countermeasures.
- We implement two block ciphers following this approach: PRESENT and PRINTcipher.
- We evaluate the overhead in FPGA resources, power consumption, and computational delay of these ciphers.
- We compare architectures based on regular LUTs with architectures based on CFGLUTs.
- We compare the use of tree-based structures in Genetic Programming (GP) vs. graph-based structures in Cartesian Genetic Programming (CGP) for the implementation of the S-boxes.

– We discuss the limitations of our solution and point out to follow-up work.

The paper is organized as follows. In Sect. 2, we give background information on EH using VRCs, the evaluated ciphers, and related work. Section 3 and 4 describe our hardware architecture based on LUTs and CFGLUTs. The implementation results are presented in Sect. 5. Section 6 concludes the paper.

2 Preliminaries

2.1 Evolvable Hardware Using Virtual Reconfigurable Circuits

Evolutionary Algorithms (EAs) have been used for more than 50 years to solve various real-world problems in design automation using reconfigurable hardware. Combining EAs with hardware circuits leads to Evolvable Hardware (EH) architectures that target novel design solutions and circuit optimization. In EH architectures, the EA interacts with the environment and alters the system automatically without manual intervention. In most cases, the goal is to improve the performance of the hardware architecture, given the environmental constraints. While the EH architecture is in hardware, the EA can be implemented externally in software or internally in hardware. The software implementation of EAs is relatively easy but introduces large delays that are not desirable for most applications. On the other hand, implementing EAs in hardware, especially on parallel computing platforms like FPGAs, is more efficient. When the EAs are computed internally on the FPGA, the most straightforward way of reconfiguring the FPGA is to use dynamic partial reconfiguration (DPR) [35]. However, DPR leads to large reconfiguration delays. Therefore, virtual reconfigurable circuits (VRCs) consists of an array of programmable elements (PEs) with programmable interconnect that can be reconfigured through a reconfiguration layer. A genetic unit computes new configurations, which can be applied rapidly on the VRC [27,30]. Figure 1 shows an example of a VRC structure consisting of 25 PEs.

2.2 PRESENT and PRINTcipher

In this paper, we consider PRESENT [6] and PRINTcipher [18]. Both ciphers are proposed as lightweight ciphers.

PRINTcipher is a block cipher of which the block size can be chosen to be 48 or 96. If the block size is chosen to be 96, it has 96 rounds and a 160-bit key. In this paper, we select the block size to be 48. This means that both the plaintext and the ciphertext are 48 bits long. PRINTcipher-48 has a key size of 80 bits and performs encryption based on 48 rounds. Each round consists of five layers: (1) the XOR Layer, in which the cipher state is combined with a round key using a bitwise exclusive-or (XOR) operation, (2) the Diffusion Layer, in which the cipher state is shuffled using a fixed linear diffusion layer, (3) the

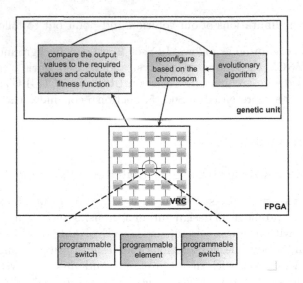

Fig. 1. Example of a VRC structure with 25 PEs and a genetic unit generating new configurations.

RC Layer, in which the cipher state is combined with a round constant using bitwise XOR, (4) the P Layer, in which the 48-bit state is divided into 16 parts of 3 bits that are each permuted with a key-independent permutation, (5) the S Layer, in which each 3-bit value is substituted by another 3-bit value based on a substitution box (S-box), which performs the table lookup shown in Table 1 (left).

Table 1. S-box table lookup in PRINTcipher (left) and PRESENT (right).

x	0	1	2	3	4	5	6	7		x	0	1	2	3	4	5	6	7	8	9	a	b	c	d	e	f
S[x]	0	1	3	6	7	4	5	2		S[x]	c	5	6	b	9	0	a	d	3	e	f	8	4	7	1	2

PRESENT. PRESENT is a block cipher with a block size of 64 bits. The key length can be 80 or 128 bits. The encryption is performed in 31 rounds. Each round consists of three layers: (1) the XOR Layer, which is similar to the PRINTcipher XOR Layer, (2) the S Layer, which divides the 64-bit state into sixteen 4-bit values, that are replaced using the S-box shown in Table 1 (right), (3) the P Layer, which performs a bit permutation according to a given table P in [6] and moves a bit in position i to bit position P(i).

2.3 Related Work

One way to design digital circuits automatically without human manipulation is to use bio-inspired algorithms. Evolutionary Algorithms (EAs), such as Genetic

Algorithms (GAs), Genetic Programming (GP), and Cartesian Genetic Programming (CGP) are methods to deal with the complexity of today's circuits.

Genetic Algorithms. Genetic Algorithms (GAs) were introduced in 1960 by John Holland. In [14], GAs were explained based on the concept of Darwin's theory of evolution. GA-based techniques are known to optimize multiple objectives, and automate the process of digital circuit design [4,13,17]. GAs mimic evolutionary principles by maintaining multiple candidate solutions in the form of a population. The GA performs the operations of crossover and mutation on individuals according to user-specified probabilities, with the intent to increase the fitness of individuals. After the application of these operators, the population for the next generation is selected based on a specific selection scheme [4]. In [8], the design of digital circuits for FPGA-based architectures using parallel GAs is introduced. The GA employed involves the use of a linear representation which can be readily employed for intrinsic evolution systems, e.g., through the direct manipulation of the FPGA configuration bitstream. In [4], the logic circuit is organized in a two-dimensional array consisting of $n_r * n_c$ cells in order to optimize the power consumption and the circuit delay.

Genetic Programming. Genetic Programming (GP) is a related technique popularized by John Koza [21]. GP often uses tree-based internal data structures to represent the computer programs for adaptation instead of the list structures that are typical for GAs. GP and GAs are both used to evolve the answer to a problem, by comparing the fitness of each candidate in a population of potential candidates over many generations with a difference in representation. GAs are commonly represented by a fixed length of numerical strings, whereas GP is represented by variable-length structures containing whatever elements are needed to solve the problem. The work of Hadjam et al. [12] discusses GP and a number of variants for designing digital circuits. There are some other applications that use GP for optimizing the efficiency of circuits like efficient edge detector circuits [10,32].

Cartesian Genetic Programming. Another approach consists of designing digital circuits using Cartesian Genetic Programming (CGP) [2,3,13,15,33]. CGP is a variation of GP which was proposed by Miller and Thomson [24]. In CGP, circuits are not encoded as trees like in GAs, but as graphs that usually have the form of $n_r * n_c$ Cartesian grids in which n_r is the number of rows and n_c is the number of columns [31]. This graph can have different levels of feedback, where the maximum is equal to n_c. The work of Brajer and Jakobović [7] shows that, if the selected parameters for CGP are close to human-made solutions, CGP-based evolutionary systems produce better results. In [16], the authors try to minimize the digital circuit size using CGP. The paper concludes that a larger CGP dimension results in a higher success rate to get to a working solution while sacrificing space and time for searching the larger chromosome space. Using CGP to self-reconfigure digital circuits is mentioned in [34], which designs a full adder that uses 32 percent of the resources of the selected FPGA.

VRC. There are many articles that use EAs with a VRC structure in different applications. Examples are filter optimizations in image processing algorithms [28], fault-tolerant systems [35], face recognition [9], systems with power consumption minimization [22], and arithmetic circuit optimization [36]. In the domain of hardware security, the work of Picek et al. [26] proposes to use VRCs for the design and optimization of lightweight Pseudo-Random Number Generators (PRNGs). The designed PRNGs are suitable for generating masks in high-throughput side-channel protected circuits. Picek et al. use CGP to evolve deterministic random number generators [25].

In the next section, we will use and compare tree and graph structures to implement the S-boxes of PRESENT and PRINTcipher in a more secure way. We use EAs to produce a runtime solution for protecting the ciphers against SCA attacks. This is the first application to designs secure against SCA using EAs.

3   First FPGA Architecture Using Regular LUTs

In many symmetric ciphers, S-boxes are used to present a nonlinear component in the encryption method and are usually implemented as simple lookup tables. Power analysis attacks typically focus on retrieving the output values of the S-boxes. An efficient countermeasure proposed by Sasdrich et al. [29] is to use dynamic logic reconfiguration of FPGAs to randomly split the S-box computation into two parts with a register in between. Although the S-box structure in [29] is very efficient in terms of occupation of FPGA resources, the computation of new configurations needs to be done offline, which causes a large overhead both in communication and computation space which is not reported in the paper. In our paper, we propose the use of a VRC for the S-box computation. Just like in [29], we split the S-box computation into two parts with a register in between. We generate random configurations using an internal genetic unit. Figure 2a shows an S-box with three inputs and three outputs (like the PRINTcipher S-box) that is implemented by the VRC structure without an intermediate register. Each output of the S-box is produced by reconfiguring three PEs and their interconnection. The first two PEs need two configuration bits for the interconnect of each input. The PE that generates the output bit needs one configuration bit for the interconnect of each input. The functionality of each PE is configured through three configuration bits, leading to the following functionalities: buffer (output equal to the input, like a wire), NOT, AND, OR, XOR, XNOR, NAND, NOR. Figure 2b shows the new structure of the S-box in which an intermediate register is added in between the two layers of PEs. Changing the functionality of the PEs causes a change in the value that is stored in the intermediate register, making it more difficult for an attacker to extract secret internal information by targeting the value in the intermediate register. Note that the overall S-box computation (i.e., the input-output behavior as a result of the computation of all the PEs together) always corresponds to Table 1 (left). The changes generated by the genetic unit can be imposed periodically in the spare time of the system before each new encryption or at random instances in time. Besides the VRC structure for the 3-bit PRINTcipher S-box, we implemented a similar architecture for the 4-bit PRESENT S-box.

The added value of our approach over the dynamic logic reconfiguration method proposed by Sasdrich et al. in [29] is that the configurations are generated internally. This reduces the external communication delay and the risk of eavesdropping. The security of the external module that creates the configurations is important in [29], which is not mentioned in the paper. Note that the security of the system can be improved by replacing the LFSR used to produce the chromosomes by a True Random Number Generator (TRNG), which we omit in our experiments. In order for the proposed countermeasures to be effective, the distribution of the generated configurations should be uniform, and repetitive generation of the same configuration should be avoided. We assume that, by generating configurations based on random seeds, this requirement is satisfied.

We use a fixed random seed for all calculations. The structure of our LFSR is based on a chain of gates with random feedback between them. The complexity of calculations and the time needed to produce new configurations in [29] is not mentioned, while it is very important, because finding a configuration that works properly is time-consuming. The resulting PRINTcipher architecture is shown in Fig. 3.

We compare CGP and GP for implementing the SCA-protected cipher architectures. Figure 4 shows the graphical scheme of our used method in CGP, which consists of one Linear Feedback Shift Register (LFSR) to produce the initial population in each run. In this figure, after producing four children by mutation from the primary chromosome, we perform an evaluation. In this phase, five chromosomes are evaluated according to the related truth table in Table 1 (left). For each input combination, the outputs of the candidate individuals are evaluated and compared with the originally required outputs, as described in the truth table of the digital function to be implemented. Bitwise comparison is made in this case, incrementing the fitness value with each output line match. This is accumulated over all possible input combinations. In our case, the PRINTcipher S-box has three input bits (8 input values), so the maximum fitness is equal to 8. The PRESENT S-box has four input bits (16 input values), and the maximum fitness is equal to 16.

In the last module in Fig. 4, we select the chromosome with the highest fitness value. All the other individuals are withdrawn. If a fitness value of 8 is acquired by the best chromosome, the algorithm is finished, and we reach a new structure for the cipher. If not, the algorithm will continue executing the mutation mechanism to produce four new children from the selected parent. Table 2 contains fixed parameters for implementing the PRINTcipher S-box. Our selection mechanism for GP is 3-tournament selection. There, after selecting three

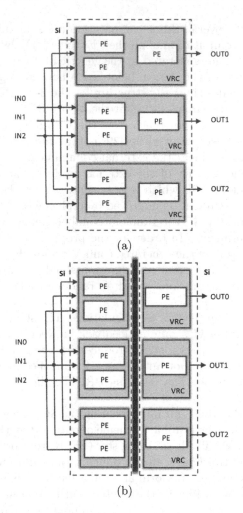

Fig. 2. VRC for the PRINTcipher S-box (a) without and (b) with an intermediate register.

random chromosomes from the population pool, the two best ones are kept. After crossover and node replacement mutation, as represented in Table 3, they will be used to create the next individual. We use node replacement mutation and subtree crossover. The computation model and selection mechanism for CGP is based on a $(1+4)$ evolution strategy, where the different mutation rate (for point crossover) for each strategy is shown in Table 6. For reducing the hardware overhead, the number of chromosomes in the population must be small. The big size of the population consumes FPGA resources for storing and processing the chromosomes. In the application that we consider, reducing the resource overhead is more important than reducing the calculation time to find the optimal chromosome. There are 4 offspring and 1 parent for CGP and 5 individuals for GP. So

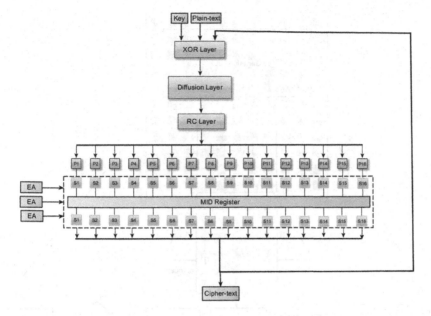

Fig. 3. PRINTcipher architecture using VRCs for the S-boxes.

in total the population size is five. In Fig. 4, the 4 individuals are offspring created from the parent (denoted as chromosome generation by LFSR). The maximum number of generations for each population is 2 000. These numbers are selected through experimental simulation, which shows that the optimal chromosome is calculated before the 2 000th generation. If after 2 000 generations from the initial population, the optimal individual is not found, the new population is produced randomly, and again 2 000 generations will be derived by mutation. The termination condition is finding an optimal individual or reaching the 500th run for producing a new population. Each PE in the VRC structure has two inputs and one output. Our function set is AND, OR, NAND, NOR, NOT, BUFFER (output is equal to the input, like a wire), XOR, XNOR. For synthesis, we neglect the overhead of the random number generator. The structure and length of each chromosome depend on the number of PEs in the VRC.

We simulate the tree and graph structures in different dimensions for implementing the S-box with fixed parameters given Table 2. Our simulation is done using the Vivado 2018.2 EDA tool of Xilinx. We use a Xilinx xc7vx485tffg1157-1 FPGA. Tables 3 and 4 show our simulation results for PRINT S-box implementation based on tree structure in GP. Tables 5 and 6 show our simulation results based on the graph structure in CGP. The different strategies introduced in Table 3, 4, 5 and 6, present various sizes of the VRC for implementing the PRINTcipher S-box in the form of GP and CGP structures. The output parameters of these implementations are reported. All strategies have the same number of inputs $n_i = 3$ and outputs $n_0 = 3$. The depth of the tree structure in GP is varied between $\#levels = 2$ to 5 in Table 3. Although the logic circuit is assumed

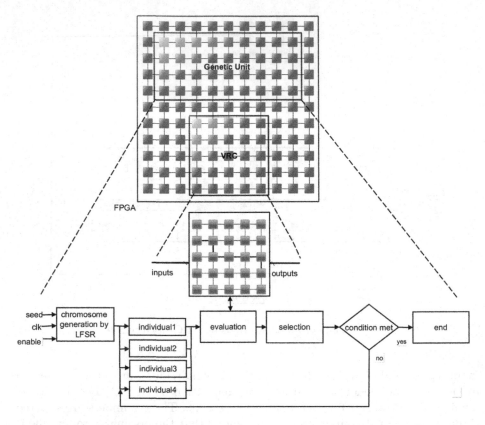

Fig. 4. Implemented algorithm for the splitting of the S-box.

Table 2. Fixed parameters for the PRINTcipher S-box.

Parameters	for CGP	for GP
Selection	$(1 + \lambda)$	3-Tournament
Population size	$1 + 4$	5
Max generation	2000	2000
Termination condition	500	500

to be organized on a two-dimensional array of cells, at least some of them are not used based on the random behavior of GP to shape the tree structure [5]. The dimension of the array is equal to $\#levels = n_r = n_c$ for each GP strategy in Table 3. We run three GP modules in parallel, such that each one has three inputs and one output.

The CGP with graph structure has a varied number of feedback levels from $\#fb = 1$ to 4, and the dimension is varied between $n_r * n_c = 3 * 3$ and $4 * 4$. It is indicated when the first optimal chromosome is found among all 500 popula-

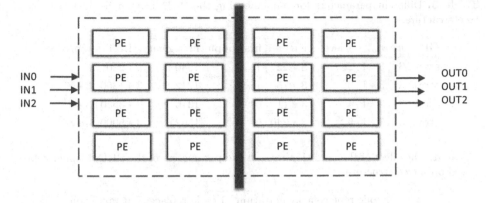

Fig. 5. Overview of the PRINTcipher S-box implementation by 4×4 CGP.

tions and 2 000 generations. The mutation rate (*mutrate*) shows the percentage of mutated bits in each strategy. Another parameter in the tables is the average fitness value (*avgfit*), which is below eight and is equal to the sum of all produced chromosome's fitness values at the end of each run, divided by 500. The success rate (*sucrate*) indicates the percentage of all optimal chromosome with fitness = 8 among 500 runs. The FPGA resource consumption is indicated as well in both tables. The Prediction level parameter (*#pred*) indicates the total number of configuration options that are possible through the applied strategy by considering eight different functionalities for each PEs. The bigger number for this parameter shows more security for the design. It is harder for an attacker to analyze the power consumption of the S-box by more variation in design.

In the tables, 'first popu' is the number of population and 'first gene' is the number of generations in the last population in which the first fit chromosome is found.

In Strategy 0, 1, 2, and 3, the final outputs can just be connected to the last PEs. Each PE can get its inputs from each PE in the first left column. Strategy 0 is indicated in Fig. 2b. In all GP strategies, three EA modules are running simultaneously to produce a proper circuit for three output pins, which is shown in Fig. 3. The simulation results in Table 3 and Table 4 show that, with an increase in the dimension of GP, the success rate and average fitness are increased, but hardware overhead is not satisfied. Because of the simple structure of GP, the first optimal chromosome with fitness value eight is achieved soon in the first run, and we can reach the optimum chromosome at the end of all runs in the majority structure of GP. A comparison of different mutation rates in the GP structure for each strategy shows that with an increased mutation rate, the number of optimal chromosomes equal to 8 increases as well as their average fitness. Strategies 4, 5, 6, and 7 have a graph structure, which means that the final outputs can be connected to each of the PEs in different levels. Increasing the mutation rate in Table 6 shows that the average of the fitness values and the percentage of optimal chromosome increases for each strategy. With a 2-node

Table 3. Different parameters for implementing the PRINTcipher S-box based on a tree structure.

GP	n_i	n_o	#levels	len	first popu	first gene	#LUT	#pred
stra0	3	$3*1$	2	$3*22$	1	1540	$3*250$	$3*8^4$
stra1	3	$3*1$	3	$3*75$	1	1242	$3*1200$	$3*8^9$
stra2	3	$3*1$	4	$3*118$	0	1316	$3*3540$	$3*8^{16}$
stra3	3	$3*1$	5	$3*240$	0	1562	$3*5000$	$3*8^{25}$

Table 4. The effect of the mutation rate on the parameters of the PRINTcipher S-box based on a tree structure.

GP	2-node replacement mutation			3-node replacement mutation		
	mutrate	avgfit	sucrate	mutrate	avgfit	sucrate
stra0	9	7.5	71	13.6	7.6	71.6
stra1	2	7.8	95.2	4	7.9	99.8
stra2	1.6	7.7	98	2.5	7.9	99.5
stra3	0.8	7.7	95.4	1.25	7.8	95.8

Table 5. Different parameters for implementing the PRINTcipher S-box based on a graph structure.

CGP	n_i	n_o	n_r*n_c	#fb	len	first popu	first gene	#LUT	#pred
stra4	3	3	$3*3$	3	111	-	-	-	8^9
stra5	3	3	$4*4$	1	156	91	1477	4429	8^{16}
stra6	3	3	$4*4$	2	183	21	1744	5956	8^{16}
stra7	3	3	$4*4$	4	183	2	1912	6376	8^{16}

Table 6. The effect of the mutation rate on the parameters of the PRINTcipher S-box based on a graph structure.

CGP	3-node replacement mutation			4-node replacement mutation		
	Mutrate	avgfit	sucrate	mutrate	avgfit	sucrate
stra4	2.7	3	–	3.6	4	–
stra5	1.9	5	2.4	2.5	5.4	3.2
stra6	1.6	5	2	2.1	5.4	2.6
stra7	1.6	5	1.6	2.1	5.1	1.7

replacement mutation rate, we did not get any optimum chromosome from the graph structure. The high-level view of the architectures generated by Strategy 5, 6, and 7 is shown in Fig. 5. In Strategy 4 and 7, because they have a graph structure and full feedback, each PE can get its input from the output of all PEs in the previous level or all PEs on the left side. Also, it is possible to get their inputs from the primary inputs, IN0 to IN2.

Because Strategy 5 has one feedback level, the PEs can get their inputs from the first left-side column or from the primary inputs. In Strategy 6 with 2 feedback levels, each PE can get its inputs from the PEs one or two levels to the left or from the primary inputs.

Strategy 4 did not find an optimal individual. The simulation results in Table 5 show that an increased CGP dimension leads to an increased average chromosome fitness, although the number of chromosomes with fitness = 8 decreases and the resource consumption gets worse.

According to the achieved results, Strategy 0 is the best solution with respect to resource consumption, although the security level is inferior to the security level of the other strategies. This is due to the low prediction level. Strategy 5 is the best solution with respect to the security level. It has a higher prediction level and features a moderate resource consumption. Simulation results show that with increasing the dimension and feedback of CGP for implementing the S-box, the time to find the first optimal individual is decreased. In addition, the number of optimal chromosomes decreases because the search space and the chromosome length are increased.

In addition to GP and CGP, we tested a random search for both tree and graph structures. Because the tree structure is simple and the outputs are independent of each other, random search could find an optimal structure. The optimal structure was found after generating the 2 028th random number on average for the 4 * 4 structure, which is equal to 2 028 clock cycles. For the GP structure, this iteration decreased to 1 316 clock cycles. For the graph structure, a random search did not find any optimal structure after evaluating 30 000 random numbers. The final result is that for securing circuits with two or three inputs and one output, a random search can be used to find optimal chromosomes, but for more complicated digital circuits with multiple inputs and multiple outputs, random search is not recommended as it takes a long time to find an optimal structure. In this case, the GP and CGP are recommended.

In Sect. 5, we implement PRINTcipher based on Strategy 0, because of the low hardware overhead of this structure. The PRESENT S-box has four inputs, which means its fitness function is equal to 16. According to the simulation results in this section for PRINTcipher, the tree-based structure has less hardware overhead. For PRESENT, we use the tree structure for each output, like Strategy 0, but with more PEs. The smallest possible tree structure for the PRESENT S-box contains 9 PEs in which each PEs has three inputs and one output. As the PRESENT S-box has four outputs, its total number of PEs is 4*9. Its PE function set consists of the same eight different functions as PRINTcipher.

4   Second FPGA Architecture Using CFGLUTs

Another alternative for the EH architecture is to use CFGLUTs instead of the VRC structure. In this architecture, each PE in Fig. 3 is replaced by a CFGLUT. Using CFGLUTs instead of a regular VRC structure will decrease the resource consumption but increase the time for reconfiguring the hardware. CFGLUTs are elements that were introduced first in Xilinx Virtex-5 FPGAs. CFGLUTs are LUTs that can be configured from within the FPGA at runtime. Figure 6 shows the structure of the CFGLUT5 in a Virtex-5, which consists of a 5-input and 1-output LUT or alternatively 4-input and 2-output LUT in addition to a configuration input (CDI) and a configuration output (CDO). This module can be used for partial reconfiguration of FPGAs at runtime instead of manipulating the bitstream for reconfiguration. The internal structure of the CFGLUT consists of a 16-bit shift configurable memory followed by a multiplexer stage. The configuration memory size is 16 bits in order to deal with 4-bit inputs. Each CFGLUT is loaded with an INIT value that presents the truth table of the LUT. The functionality of the LUT can be changed at runtime by changing this INIT value, which gives the user the power of partial reconfiguration of the FPGAs internally. Reconfiguration is done by activating the CE pin and simultaneously putting 1-bit reconfiguration data on the CDI pin, one bit is written in the INIT register in each clock cycle. Sixteen clock cycles are needed to reconfigure the CFGLUT entirely. In our solution based on CFGLUTs, only one CFGLUT is needed for each PE, while in the first method, described in Sect. 3, each PE consists of many LUTs. Using CFGLUTs decreases the number of LUTs such that, instead of using 9 LUTs for each S-box, 3 CFGLUTs and 4 LUTs are used. Another point is that the VRC structure in the first method is virtual, while the CFGLUT-based method is not virtual and thus better adapted to the underlying hardware. The routing between CFGLUTs is configured by the selected chromosome. Each chromosome, in addition to specifying the functionality of PEs, establishes the way the PEs connect to each other. For both PRINTcipher and PRESENT, the way of using CFGLUTs is similar.

5   Implementation Results

Table 7 shows that the proposed architectures lead to a drastic increase in the occupied FPGA resources, power consumption, and the critical path compared to unprotected architectures. The timing constraint used for all the examples is a clock period of 10 ns. The operating frequency for producing random chromosomes is 500 MHz and is determined by the critical path of the EA module, which is a combinational circuit. The number of clock cycles needed for the computation of the ciphertext is not changed and is equal to 16 cycles, but in the proposed structure, we need additional cycles for changing the implementation of the S-box. If we assume a system with significant idle time in between the encryptions, the reconfiguration time can be ignored. The critical path also increased significantly, but this is mainly caused by the genetic unit. If we use a different clock domain for the genetic unit and the cipher architecture, the effect on the encryption delay will be decreased. Table 7 shows that the use of CFGLUTs instead of VRC architecture leads to a reduction in the number of LUTs. The number of FFs is increased due to the additional clock cycles that are needed for reconfiguring the CFGLUTs. The dynamic power is increased

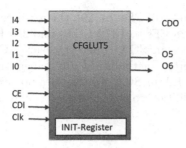

Fig. 6. Block diagram of a CFGLUT5.

Table 7. Implementation results of the cipher architectures.

Used structure	#LUTs	#FFs	Dynamic Power	#Clk Cycles	Clk Period
PRINTcipher	115	54	0.003 J	16	1 ns
prot PRINTcipher (par)	865	54	0.003 J	16 + time (EA)	7.5 ns
prot PRINTcipher (seq)	365	54	0.003 J	16 + time (EA)	7.5 ns
prot PRINTcipher with CFGLUTs	733	60	0.009 J	16 +16+ time(EA+CFGLUT)	7.5 ns
PRESENT	148	149	0.018 J	31	1 ns
prot PRESENT (par)	6998	149	0.056 J	31 + time (EA)	7.5 ns
prot PRESENT (seq)	2201	149	0.031 J	31 + time (EA)	7.5 ns

because of the higher number of clock cycles needed for reconfiguring the CFG-LUTs, but the static power consumption is always fixed and equal to 0.243 J. For decreasing the overhead of using EAs, we can use just one EA module in Fig. 3 and call it three times sequentially instead of using a parallel structure. This way, the overhead of using our solution is decreased according to Table 7. In this table, both the sequential (seq) and the parallel (par) architectures are presented, as well as the protected (prot) and the unprotected versions. Compared to the method proposed in [29], our work presents the following differences:

- The configurations needed for the random decomposition of the S-boxes are generated internally in our method but externally in [29].
- The time overhead of our method is the time for the EA to produce the final fit chromosomes. The simulation results in Table 3 and Table 5 show that the first successful chromosome is produced at least in the first population or at maximum in the 91th population, which means it takes from 1 to 91 clock cycles as the EA is implemented as a combinational circuit. In [29], the time overhead is 16 clock cycles.
- The hardware overhead of our method depends on the strategy and the structure. E.g., in Table 7, the resource utilization increases from 115 LUTs to 365

LUTs with a fixed number of FFs. In [29], the resource utilization is increased from 224 LUTs and 128 FFs to 1 172 LUTs and 260 FFs.
– We use one method as an SCA countermeasure SCA in contrast to [29], which uses three different methods. In our paper, the goal is to introduce a new application for EA in SCA, which does not exclude the use of other countermeasures in addition to the EA-based countermeasure.

6 Conclusion

In this work, we propose to use Evolvable Hardware in the form of a virtual reconfigurable circuit to implement the dynamic logic reconfiguration countermeasure presented by Sasdrich et al. in 2015. Our approach has the advantage of computing new configurations inside the FPGA instead of relying on an external device. This decreases the communication overhead and reduces the risk of eavesdropping. We evaluate the efficiency of our approach based on two lightweight cipher algorithms, namely PRINTcipher and PRESENT, with two different implementations using evolutionary algorithms based on tree and graph structures. Although our approach introduces a significant overhead in terms of FPGA resource occupation, power consumption, and delay, we stress that this is the first attempt to apply the dynamic logic reconfiguration countermeasure with internal configuration generation as an SCA countermeasure. Further optimizations of the genetic unit that generates the configurations and the virtual reconfigurable circuit will lead to more competitive implementation results.

References

1. Agrawal, D., Archambeault, B., Rao, J.R., Rohatgi, P.: The EM side—channel(s). In: Kaliski, B.S., Koç, K., Paar, C. (eds.) CHES 2002. LNCS, vol. 2523, pp. 29–45. Springer, Heidelberg (2003). https://doi.org/10.1007/3-540-36400-5_4
2. Asha, S., Hemamalini, R.R.: Synthesis of adder circuit using cartesian genetic programming. Middle-East J. Sci. Res. 23(6), 1181–1186 (2015)
3. Babu, K.S., Balaji, N.: Approximation of digital circuits using cartesian genetic programming. In: 2016 International Conference on Communication and Electronics Systems (ICCES), pp. 1–6. IEEE (2016)
4. Bao, Z., Watanabe, T.: A new approach for circuit design optimization using genetic algorithm. In: 2008 International SoC Design Conference, vol. 1, pp. I-383. IEEE (2008)
5. Benkhelifa, E., Pipe, A., Dragffy, G., Nibouche, M.: Towards evolving fault tolerant biologically inspired hardware using evolutionary algorithms. In: 2007 IEEE Congress on Evolutionary Computation, pp. 1548–1554. IEEE (2007)
6. Bogdanov, A., et al.: PRESENT: an ultra-lightweight block cipher. In: Paillier, P., Verbauwhede, I. (eds.) CHES 2007. LNCS, vol. 4727, pp. 450–466. Springer, Heidelberg (2007). https://doi.org/10.1007/978-3-540-74735-2_31
7. Brajer, I., Jakobović, D.: Automated design of combinatorial logic circuits. In: 2012 Proceedings of the 35th International Convention MIPRO, pp. 823–828. IEEE (2012)

8. Dechev, D., Ashraf, R., Luna, F., DeMara, R.: Designing digital circuits for FPGAS using parallel genetic algorithms. Technical report, Sandia National Lab. (SNL-NM), Albuquerque, NM (United States) (2012)
9. Glette, K.: Design and implementation of scalable online evolvable hardware pattern recognition systems (2008)
10. Golonek, T., Grzechca, D., Rutkowski, J.: Application of genetic programming to edge detector design. In: 2006 IEEE International Symposium on Circuits and Systems, 4 p. IEEE (2006)
11. Güneysu, T., Moradi, A.: Generic side-channel countermeasures for reconfigurable devices. In: Preneel, B., Takagi, T. (eds.) CHES 2011. LNCS, vol. 6917, pp. 33–48. Springer, Heidelberg (2011). https://doi.org/10.1007/978-3-642-23951-9_3
12. Hadjam, F.Z., Moraga, C., Benmohamed, M.: Cluster-based evolutionary design of digital circuits using all improved multi-expression programming. In: Proceedings of the 9th Annual Conference companion on Genetic and Evolutionary Computation, pp. 2475–2482. ACM (2007)
13. Hadjam, F.Z., Moraga, C., Rahmouni, M.K.: Evolutionary design of digital circuits using improved multi expression programming (IMEP). Mathware Soft Comput. 14(2), 103–123 (2007)
14. Holland, J.H., et al.: Adaptation in natural and artificial systems: an introductory analysis with applications to biology, control, and artificial intelligence. MIT Press (1992)
15. Irfan, M., Habib, Q., Hassan, G.M., Yahya, K.M., Hayat, S.: Combinational digital circuit synthesis using cartesian genetic programming from a nand gate template. In: 2010 6th International Conference on Emerging Technologies (ICET), pp. 343–347. IEEE (2010)
16. Kazarlis, S., Kalomiros, J., Kalaitzis, V.: A cartesian genetic programming approach for evolving optimal digital circuits. J. Eng. Sci. Technol. Rev. 9(5), 88–92 (2016)
17. Keller, R.E., Banzhaf, W.: The evolution of genetic code in genetic programming. In: Proceedings of the 1st Annual Conference on Genetic and Evolutionary Computation-Volume 2, pp. 1077–1082. Morgan Kaufmann Publishers Inc. (1999)
18. Knudsen, L., Leander, G., Poschmann, A., Robshaw, M.J.B.: PRINTCIPHER: a block cipher for IC-printing. In: Mangard, S., Standaert, F.-X. (eds.) CHES 2010. LNCS, vol. 6225, pp. 16–32. Springer, Heidelberg (2010). https://doi.org/10.1007/978-3-642-15031-9_2
19. Kocher, P., Jaffe, J., Jun, B.: Differential power analysis. In: Wiener, M. (ed.) CRYPTO 1999. LNCS, vol. 1666, pp. 388–397. Springer, Heidelberg (1999). https://doi.org/10.1007/3-540-48405-1_25
20. Kocher, P.C.: Timing attacks on implementations of diffie-Hellman, RSA, DSS, and other systems. In: Koblitz, N. (ed.) CRYPTO 1996. LNCS, vol. 1109, pp. 104–113. Springer, Heidelberg (1996). https://doi.org/10.1007/3-540-68697-5_9
21. Koza, J.R.: Genetic programming (1994)
22. López, B., Valverde, J., de la Torre, E., Riesgo, T.: Power-aware multi-objective evolvable hardware system on an FPGA. In: 2014 NASA/ESA Conference on Adaptive Hardware and Systems (AHS), pp. 61–68. IEEE (2014)
23. Mangard, S., Oswald, E., Popp, T.: Power Analysis Attacks: Revealing the Secrets of Smart Cards (Advances in Information Security). Springer-Verlag, New York Inc, Secaucus, NJ, USA (2007)
24. Miller, J.F., Harding, S.L.: Cartesian genetic programming. In: Proceedings of the 10th Annual Conference Companion on Genetic and Evolutionary Computation, pp. 2701–2726. ACM (2008)

25. Picek, S., Sisejkovic, D., Rozic, V., Yang, B., Jakobovic, D., Mentens, N.: Evolving cryptographic pseudorandom number generators. In: Handl, J., Hart, E., Lewis, P.R., López-Ibáñez, M., Ochoa, G., Paechter, B. (eds.) PPSN 2016. LNCS, vol. 9921, pp. 613–622. Springer, Cham (2016). https://doi.org/10.1007/978-3-319-45823-6_57

26. Picek, S., et al.: Prngs masking applications and their mapping to evolvable hardware. In: International Conference on Smart Card Research and Advanced Applications, pp. 209–227. Springer (2016)

27. Salvador, R., Otero, A., Mora, J., de la Torre, E., Riesgo, T., Sekanina, L.: Implementation techniques for evolvable HW systems: Virtual vs. dynamic reconfiguration. In: 2012 22nd International Conference on Field Programmable Logic and Applications (FPL), pp. 547–550. IEEE (2012)

28. Salvador, R., Otero, A., Mora, J., de la Torre, E., Riesgo, T., Sekanina, L.: Self-reconfigurable evolvable hardware system for adaptive image processing. IEEE Trans. Comput. **62**(8), 1481–1493 (2013)

29. Sasdrich, P., Moradi, A., Mischke, O., Guneysu, T.: Achieving side-channel protection with dynamic logic reconfiguration on modern FPGAS. In: 2015 IEEE International Symposium on Hardware Oriented Security and Trust (HOST), pp. 130–136. IEEE (2015)

30. Sekanina, L., Friedl, Š.: An evolvable combinational unit for fpgas. Comput. Inform. **23**(5–6), 461–486 (2012)

31. Sekanina, L., Vasicek, Z., Mrazek, V.: Automated search-based functional approximation for digital circuits. In: Reda, S., Shafique, M. (eds.) Approximate Circuits, pp. 175–203. Springer, Cham (2019). https://doi.org/10.1007/978-3-319-99322-5_9

32. Sharma, P., Sasamal, T.N.: Minimization of digital combinational circuit using genetic programming with modified fitness function. In: 2016 2nd International Conference on Applied and Theoretical Computing and Communication Technology (iCATccT), pp. 406–410. IEEE (2016)

33. da Silva, J.E., Bernardino, H.: Cartesian genetic programming with crossover for designing combinational logic circuits. In: 2018 7th Brazilian Conference on Intelligent Systems (BRACIS), pp. 145–150. IEEE (2018)

34. Srivastava, A.K., Gupta, A., Chaturvedi, S., Rastogi, V.: Design and simulation of virtual reconfigurable circuit for a fault tolerant system. In: International Conference on Recent Advances and Innovations in Engineering (ICRAIE-2014), pp. 1–4. IEEE (2014)

35. Swarnalatha, A., Shanthi, A.: Complete hardware evolution based sopc for evolvable hardware. Appl. Soft Comput. **18**, 314–322 (2014)

36. Wang, J., Piao, C.H., Lee, C.H.: Implementing Multi-VRC cores to evolve combinational logic circuits in parallel. In: Kang, L., Liu, Y., Zeng, S. (eds.) ICES 2007. LNCS, vol. 4684, pp. 23–34. Springer, Heidelberg (2007). https://doi.org/10.1007/978-3-540-74626-3_3

Simple Electromagnetic Analysis Against Activation Functions of Deep Neural Networks

Go Takatoi[✉], Takeshi Sugawara, Kazuo Sakiyama, and Yang Li[✉]

Graduate School of Informatics and Engineering, Department of Informatics,
The University of Electro-Communications,
1-5-1 Chofugaoka, Chofu, Tokyo 182-8585, Japan
{g.takatoi,liyang}@uec.ac.jp

Abstract. From cloud computing to edge computing, the deployment of artificial intelligence (AI) has been evolving to fit a wide range of applications. However, the security over edge AI is not sufficient. Edge AI is computed close to the device and user, therefore allowing physical attacks such as side-channel attack (SCA). Reverse engineering the neural network architecture using SCA is an active area of research. In this work, we investigate how to retrieve an activation function in a neural network implemented to an edge device by using side-channel information. To this end, we consider multilayer perceptron as the machine learning architecture of choice. We assume an attacker capable of measuring side channel leakages, in this case electromagnetic (EM) emanations. The results are shown on an Arduino Uno microcontroller to achieve high quality measurements. Our experiments show that the activation functions used in the architecture can be obtained by a side-channel attacker using one or a few EM measurements independent of inputs. We replicate the timing attack in previous research by Batina et al., and analyzed it to explain how the timing behavior acts on different implementations of the activation function operations. We also prove that our attack method has the potential to overcome constant time mitigations.

Keywords: Machine learning · Deep learning · Side-channel · Activation function · SEMA

1 Introduction

Machine learning has been researched in many areas due to its practicality and effectiveness. Deep learning especially is rapidly becoming a popular machine learning method. Image recognition [9,15], robotics [13], natural language processing [24], security [1,16,28], and medical science [6,7] are all areas in which deep learning are being used.

Neural networks are trained with high costs, and has a possibility of including confidential information from the training phase. Machine learning models are

J. Zhou et al. (Eds.): ACNS 2020 Workshops, LNCS 12418, pp. 181–197, 2020.
https://doi.org/10.1007/978-3-030-61638-0_11

stored with valuable intellectual property, which are quickly becoming a target. Therefore, security over artificial intelligence (AI) is a growing concern. There are already a variety of attacks against AI [2,12,20]. For example, model extraction attacks [26], membership inference attacks [22], and model inversion attacks [5] are all attacks that target valuable information from AI. Model extraction attack presented by Tramer et al. can reverse engineer a machine learning model with high efficiency, as it only requires less than 10,000 online queries to the target machine learning model to replicate their attack. [26]. Shokri et al. proved that by using membership inference attack, prediction application programming interface (API) leaks information if an input was used as the training data [22]. Fredrikson et al. discussed that the model inversion attack could reverse engineer the training data just from the label and access to the prediction API [5].

In recent years, communication, privacy, and latency issues have caused deep neural networks to be calculated on the edge instead of the cloud servers. Edge devices are existent close by, therefore allowing physical attacks such as side-channel attacks. There are side-channel attacks to recover the architectures and parameters of neural networks. Leaked side-channel information include information from the operation. Recovering neural network architectures with cache side-channel attack is one way to attack edge AI [11,29]. Fault attacks are also used to recover neural network parameters [4]. There are side-channel attacks against specific neural network accelerators [27,30].

One recent work by Batina et al. has shown that a black box multilayer perceptron (MLP) and convolutional neural network (CNN) implemented on a 8bit and 32bit CPU can be reverse engineered using merely side-channel information [3]. They had separated the recovery of the network architecture into 4 key parameters: the activation function, pre-trained weights, the number of hidden layers, and the number of neurons in each layer. The activation function was discerned by timing attack from its distinctive computation time. Timing patterns or average timing can be compared with the profile of each function to determine the activation function. They recovered weight parameters with correlation electromagnetic analysis (CEMA), looking at the leakage in the Hamming weight of the input and weight multiplications. The layer boundaries and the number of nodes can be distinguished from the electromagnetic (EM) trace using the leakage signatures.

In this work, we have focused on the problem in the recovery of the activation function. The previously proposed recovery on the activation function has a limitation that it depends on non-constant timing behavior. By implementing constant time activation function, their attack can be easily mitigated. In this work, we have the following contributions.

– We propose a new type of attack to identify activation functions based on simple electromagnetic analysis (SEMA) [14]. Our proposed attack is implemented and demonstrated on a Arduino Uno, we were able to identify the activation functions used in the network.
– We have replicated the timing attack on the activation functions by Batina et al., and analyzed their attack and how the timing behavior acts on different

implementations of the activation function operations. This has shown the significance of our proposed method as it is versatile to different activation function implementations and independent of inputs to the network.

– We have compared our new attack to the attack proposed in previous work, and we have discussed the potential of our attack to overcome constant time mitigation.

The rest of this paper is organized as follows. In Sect. 2, we briefly review the background. Section 3 outlines the methodology and the benefits of the SEMA attack. Subsequently, our experiment setup is shown in 4.1, and the proposed signal processing method is described in Sect. 4.2. The proposed signal processing is applied in Sect. 4.3. The analysis of the experiment results are shown in Sect. 5. Section 5.3 also discusses the analysis of previous work and constant time activation function implementations. Finally, the conclusions are presented in Sect. 6.

2   Background

In this section, we describe the details and architectures of the artificial neural network (ANN) used in this work.

2.1   Multilayer Perceptron

A MLP is a very simple type of neural network, and is made of fully connected layers. Fully connected layers means that all of the nodes in a layer is connected to all of the nodes in the next layer. A model of a node is depicted in Fig. 1. The circle surrounding a and y is called a node (or neuron). The output y of a node is calculated in Eq. (1) as follows.

$$y = h\left(\sum_{i=1}^{n} x_i \times w_i + b\right) \tag{1}$$

Here, $(x_1, x_2, \ldots, x_n)$ represents the inputs, $(w_1, w_2, \ldots, w_n)$ represents the weights, b represents the bias, and $h(a)$ represents the activation function. The bias is often programmed as the weight of an input value 1.

The model of a 4 layer MLP that is used in this work is depicted in Fig. 2. A MLP must have at least 3 layers, composed of at least one input layer, hidden layer, and output layer. The MLP in Fig. 2 consists of an input layer, two hidden layers, and an output layer.

2.2   Activation Functions

Here we describe the activation functions used in this works, which are sigmoid function, tanh function, softmax function, and Rectified Linear Unit (ReLU) function.

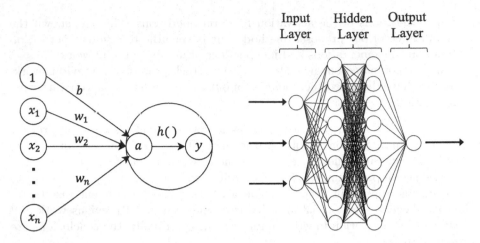

Fig. 1. A model of a node   **Fig. 2.** A model of a multilayer perceptron

The sigmoid (logistic) function is a nonlinear function as shown in Eq. (2). This function will be most effective when used in a neural network trained with back propagation. The sigmoid function plots inputs ranged $(-\infty, \infty)$ to outputs ranged $(0, 1)$.

$$h(a) = \frac{1}{1 + e^{-a}} \tag{2}$$

The tanh function is a rescaling of the sigmoid function, and the main difference is that it is symmetric by the origin. The tanh function maps inputs ranged $(-\infty, \infty)$ to outputs ranged $(-1, 1)$ as shown in Eq. (3).

$$h(a) = \frac{e^a - e^{-a}}{e^a + e^{-a}} = \frac{2}{1 + e^{-2a}} - 1 \tag{3}$$

The softmax function is able to map values into several outputs (or classes) which sum becomes 1. The output range is $(0, 1)$. It is able to be seen as probability, and is used for classification problems. Equation (4) below is the softmax function where the vector is shown in bold.

$$h(\mathbf{a})_j = \frac{e^{a_j}}{\sum_{k=1}^{K} e^{a_k}}, \text{ for } j = 1, \ldots, K \text{ and } \mathbf{a} = (a_1, \ldots, a_K) \in \mathbb{R}^K \tag{4}$$

As shown in Eq. (5), the ReLU function is an extremely simple function, therefore mainly used as an activation function for ANNs. For networks with many nodes, this type of simple function can reduce the time of training and computing.

$$h(a) = \begin{cases} 0, & \text{for } a \leq 0 \\ a, & \text{for } a > 0 \end{cases} \tag{5}$$

3 Problem and Methodology

3.1 Identification of Activation Functions

Activation functions are used in many neural networks, and they play a very important role in the network. Non-linear functions are used as activation functions to output a result from the sum of the inputs and to solve non-linear problems. Designing and choosing activation functions that enable fast training of accurate deep neural networks is an active area of research. From this, it can be said that it is important to conceal the information of activation functions used in a neural network architecture.

3.2 Previous Work: Identification Based on Timing Behavior

In the previous work by Batina et al., they have used timing attacks to identify activation functions. The activation function was discerned by timing attack from its distinctive computation time. They showed that the timing behavior of the activation function can be directly observed on the EM trace. They collected EM traces and measured the timing of the activation function computation. The measurements were taken when the network were processing random inputs in the range they had chosen beforehand. A total of 2000 EM measurements were captured for each activation function. By plotting the processing time of each activation function by inputs, distinct signatures can be seen from each timing behavior. By making a profile, timing patterns or averaged timing can be compared with the profile of each function to determine the activation function.

The method proposed by Batina et al. has a few limitations as listed as follows.

1. Multiple measurements are required to use the distribution of the calculation time to identify the activation function.
2. Multiple inputs following a uniform distribution are required.
3. The distinct signatures of each activation function from the timing behavior has a possibility to differ depending on the implementation or processor.
4. The timing difference could be mitigated with constant time implementation of the activation functions.

3.3 New Method: Identification Using SEMA

The timing attack proposed by Batina et al. had several limitations. Therefore we took a different approach. While they collected EM traces and measured the timing of the activation function computation, we observe the leakage patterns of the EM trace directly and try to discern what operation is being computed in the trace from the different leakage signatures. We call this SEMA attack. SEMA attack requires only one or a few EM traces, compared to the timing attack which required multiple EM traces. We were successful in recovering the activation function by applying signal processing to the measurement. By reducing the noise in the EM trace, we were able to extract peak patterns from the measurement. We have found out that there are unique peak patterns for each operation in the activation function. Our attack is also independent of the inputs, as the patterns generally are invariant for any input. We observe the activation function operations from the peaks of the EM trace, thus this method has potential to overcome constant time mitigation.

4   Experiments

4.1   Experimental Setup

Here we describe the experimental setup to measure the EM emanations from an MLP trained for 3-input XOR.

Target Device. The MLP is implemented on the microcontroller Atmel ATmega328P. The reasons for using Atmel ATmega328P as a target platform is motivated as follows.

- CPU and GPU are frequently used platforms for DNN computation, and use optimized libraries for its operations [23]. By using Atmel ATmega328P, we can implement the operations in a similar way.

Software Setup. There are several ways to implement activation functions into a neural network. In our work, we have used activation functions that operates mathematically as shown in Eqs. (2)–(5). The exponential function and tanh function are implemented using standard library functions in C++ language. The MLP used in this work has the same architecture as Fig. 2, and has 2 hidden layers with 9 nodes in both layers. However for the MLP with the softmax function, the dimensions for the 2 hidden layers are 3 nodes for the first hidden layer, and 9 nodes for the second hidden layer.

Hardware Setup. Tektronix MS064 oscilloscope was used to capture EM measurements, and used an RF-U 5-2 near-field EM probe from Langer to collect EM measurements. All measurements were $500M$Samples/s. We also used a low-pass filter BLP-50+ from Mini-Circuits with cutoff frequency of 48MHz to get a clear signal. To improve the quality of measurement of the microcontroller, we scraped the outer package, and decapsulated the microcontroller [21] as shown in Fig. 3. The EM probe is placed above the decapsulated chip and is chosen by hand. The full measurement setup is depicted in Fig. 4.

4.2   Attack Scenario

The goal of this work is to show an alternative method to recover the activation function instead of observing the pattern in the process time distribution that was presented in previous work. The proposed method has a few advantages over the previous method.

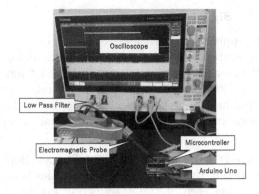

Fig. 3. Target microcontroller decapsulated

Fig. 4. Measurement setup

- No information and access to the inputs required.
- Less executions required.
- Less implementation dependency, as we can show that the timing behavior used to identify sigmoid function and tanh function in previous work is implementation dependent.

Here we specify the considered attack scenario. Several pre-trained networks are implemented in C++ language and then compiled on to the edge device. Pre-trained networks are intellectual property, and accordingly the activation functions in those networks are confidential. The attacker's motive is to identify the activation functions used in the network. The attacker's capability is as follows.

- The attacker does not know the architecture of the network, but can access the network predictions.
- The attacker knows what set of activation functions could be implemented on the architecture, in this work, the sigmoid function, tanh function, softmax function, and ReLU function.
- The attacker is capable of measuring electromagnetic emanations from the target device.

Batina et al. has used the MLP to validate their attack methodology [3]. In this work, we also use the MLP as the DNN of choice. The motives are as follows.

- MLP is a widely used neural network architecture [8,10,19,25].
- Every node from a MLP is fully connected. Fully connected layer is a feature that can be seen in convolutional neural networks, recurrent neural networks, and other neural network architectures.
- All layers are identical, making side-channel analysis difficult than other neural network architectures.

Thereby, a generic attack is possible in developing our methodology. In other words, our methodology can be applied to many other DNN models.

4.3 Signal Processing

We apply several methods to retrieve distinctive patterns from the EM trace. In this section, we propose a 4-step methodology to obtain the desired EM trace. First, a measurement (or trace) is taken from the target device. Next, averaging is applied to the measured trace. Then, to extract the peaks, we compute the upper half of the EM trace's envelope. For the last step, by smoothing the trace, the desired trace is acquired. The detailed actions of each step are as follows.

Step 1: Measuring the EM Trace. Here, an EM measurement of a MLP predicting the output class probabilities is taken from a microcontroller. MLPs including each of the 4 activation functions discussed in Sect. 2.2 are being computed. Then a EM trace is collected by an electromagnetic probe from the predicting MLP.

In our experiment, the measurements were taken from the device processing the input to the outputs of the first hidden layer's first node. In other words, the measurement is from the device computing Eq. (1). 4 measurements are obtained, each with 4 different activation functions mentioned in Sect. 2.2.

Step 2: Averaging the EM Trace. For this step, averaging is applied to the trace collected in step 1. By averaging the trace, it can improve the signal-to-noise ration (SNR). We used the oscilloscope in-built feature for averaging.

Each measurement from step 1 was averaged with 400 traces. However even with noise reduction, it is difficult to separate the boundaries of the nodes, multiplication operations and activation functions. The peaks are still very hard to distinguish, therefore signal processing is applied.

Step 3: Extracting the Upper Half of the EM Trace's Envelope. To make the peak stand out from the averaged trace, we apply signal processing using Matlab. The upper half of the EM trace's envelope is calculated to check the peak of the trace. However, if only the envelope is calculated, the pulse component still remains.

The averaged traces in step 2 were processed using Matlab. The peaks of the traces were extracted by calculating the upper half of the envelope. The peaks can be seen, however there is still noise in the trace, making it hard to characterize each pattern.

Step 4: Smoothing the EM Trace. Last step is signal smoothing, to extract the noise from the envelope. In this work, we used the Gaussian-weighted moving average filter, calculated using Matlab. The smaller the window size, the higher frequency components stand out, and larger the window size, the lower frequency components are extracted. We want to extract the high frequency noise, therefore we use a large window size.

For the last step by using the Gaussian-weighted moving average filter, smoothing was applied to the noisy traces keeping important patterns in our measurements while leaving out noise. Table 1 presents the window size used for smoothing each of the measurements. The smoothed trace is shown in Fig. 5. The patterns can be compared easier with smoothing. The multiplication and activation function can be easily distinguished with their different patterns. The red lines in Fig. 5 represents the boundary of the multiplication and activation function. By observing the patterns of the multiplication operation, the weight multiplication, the addition of the outputs, and addition of the bias can be distinguished from the trace.

Table 1. Window size (in sample points) for different activation functions

Activation function	Window size
Sigmoid	4000
Tanh	4000
Softmax	1000
ReLU	2000

5   Analysis of the Results

5.1   Analysis of the Activation Function Operations

Here we analyze the processed measurements to discern activation functions. First, we start by examining the computation time of the activation functions. The computation time can be observed from Fig. 5. Table 2 presents the computation time of the activation functions.

Table 2. Computation time (in μs) for different activation functions

Activation function	Computation time
Sigmoid	190.79
Tanh	204.35
Softmax	695.52
ReLU	13.76

As the activation functions differ in operations, so does the computation time. It can be observed from Table 2 that the ReLU function has the least computation time at $13.76\,\mu s$, and that the softmax function has the most computation time at $695.52\,\mu s$. Due to the simplicity of the ReLU function, it can be computed in a short time. The ReLU function does not have an exponentiation operation, unlike the other 3 activation functions. The softmax function

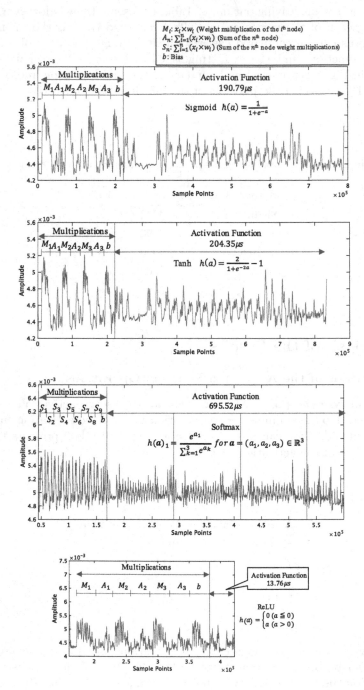

Fig. 5. Extracted pattern measurements of activation functions as Sigmoid, Tanh, Softmax and Relu.

computes the exponentiation operation several times, depending on the number of nodes in the output layer as shown in Eq. (4). Due to the complexity of the function, it takes the longest time to process. These two activation functions can be easily distinguished. However the sigmoid function and tanh function have similar computation times, sigmoid at $190.79\,\mu s$ and tanh at $204.35\,\mu s$.

Next, we observe the processed leakage patterns through SEMA. The softmax function computes the exponentiation operation several times, therefore the pattern of the exponentiation operation will repeat itself for the number of nodes in the output layer. The number of nodes in the output layer is 3 in this work, thus the multiplication pattern will repeat 9 times, and the exponentiation pattern 3 times. The vertical red lines separate the exponentiation operations and the division operation in the activation function.

The ReLU function does not include the exponentiation operation, therefore cannot observe the same patterns in the other activation functions.

Figure 6 compares the leakage patterns of sigmoid and tanh function. It can be observed that although there is no obvious gap in the processing time, the peak patterns differ. Extra peaks can be seen in 2 sections from the tanh function when comparing with the sigmoid function. The extra peaks observed are surrounded in a red box. The first peak can be seen right after the multiplication. The second peak can be seen in the latter half of the activation function. The differences in peaks comes from the difference in the functions. Tanh function has an additional multiplication and subtraction compared with the sigmoid function. We have observed that these operations causes the difference in peak patterns. The sigmoid function and tanh function can be distinguished with the different peak patterns, with tanh function having more peaks patterns.

5.2   Distinctive Features of Activation Functions from SEMA

Table 3 presents the features of each activation function when we used SEMA. To conclude, softmax function and ReLU function can be distinguished out of the 4 activation functions with their computation time. Also, by examining at the processed measurement patterns, all 4 activation functions can be discerned. Our experiments has shown that the EM trace leaks information on the operations in the activation function. Our method can be applied to an attack to identify the activation functions by making a template and pre-characterizing the operations in the EM trace.

Table 3. Features of activation functions from SEMA

Activation function	Computation Time	Trace pattern
Sigmoid	–	2 less peaks than tanh
Tanh	–	2 more peaks than sigmoid
Softmax	Long	Repeated exponentiation pattern
ReLU	Short	Not have exponentiation pattern

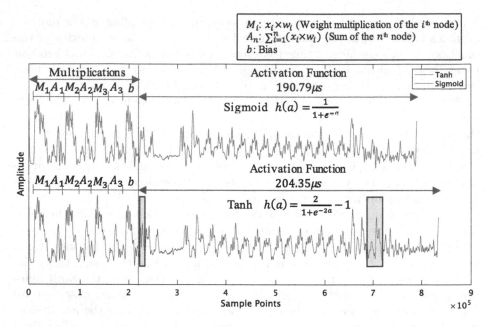

Fig. 6. Comparison of the patterns of sigmoid and tanh function

5.3   Discussions

We were able to extract features from the EM trace, and identify each activation function, sigmoid function, tanh function, softmax function, and ReLU function. The results could be expected as the information of the operation leaks itself from EM emanations. Our hypothesis was that since the operations leaks information into the measurements, we could recover the operations from the measurements itself if we can reduce the noise in the trace. The signal processing allowed the peaks to have distinctive features for each operation. We were able to match the features to the activation functions for identification. We believe this attack could be applied to different neural network models as long as the activation functions operate directly. We have used Arduino Uno as the target platform. We believe our approach and methodology could be applied to different platforms such as a similar microcontroller platform, a GPU platform or a FPGA platform. This is because side-channel analysis are demonstrated on these platforms on several previous works [3,17,27].

Analyzing Previous Work. We have also analyzed the work by Batina et al. and their timing attack against activation functions. They plot the processing time of each activation function by inputs, and stated that distinct signatures could be seen from each timing behavior. However, the problem lies on why the timing behavior acts in such a way, which they have not explained in their work.

We were able to recreate the timing behavior of sigmoid function and the tanh function as shown in Fig. 7. The timing delay is displayed in μs. The experiments were done on an Arduino Uno simulator Tinkercad. The timing delay were measured with micros function, which returns the number of microseconds since the Arduino board began running the program. The processing time were averaged 10 times per input.

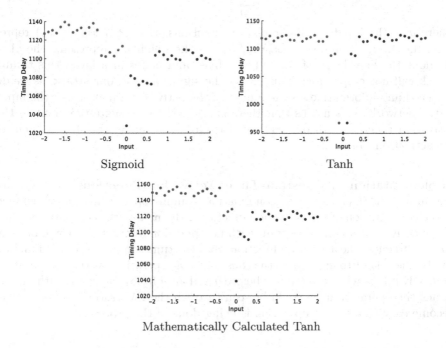

Sigmoid   Tanh

Mathematically Calculated Tanh

Fig. 7. Timing behavior for different activation functions

Batina et al. have stated that tanh is more symmetric in pattern compared to sigmoid, for both positive and negative inputs which has been completely replicated in Figs. 7a and 7b. Based on our analysis of the results, we believe that the standard library functions in C++ language cause the distinct signatures. The exponentiation function causes the symmetric pattern in timing delay, with positive inputs having slightly longer computation time. The tanh function is an optimized operation, having symmetric patterns for both positive and negative inputs. However, if we did not use the standard library tanh function, and used the exponentiation function to mathematically calculate the tanh function, the timing behavior acts the same way as the sigmoid function as depicted in Fig. 7c. The patterns are both symmetric with positive inputs having slightly shorter computation time for Figs. 7a and 7c. The minimum, maximum, and mean values of the timing delay do not differ as significantly as Figs. 7a and 7b. The similarity in pattern and timing behavior makes the two activation functions very difficult to distinguish depending on the implementation method.

They have also stated that they take measurements when the network is processing random inputs in the range, i.e., $x \in \{-2, 2\}$. This input refers to the inputs to the activation function. To plot the timing behavior for different activation functions based on the inputs, there would be a need to calculate Eq. (6) below.

$$a = \left(\sum_{i=1}^{n} x_i \times w_i + b \right) \qquad (6)$$

where a is the input to the activation functions. Here, $(x_1, x_2, \ldots, x_n)$ represents the inputs, $(w_1, w_2, \ldots, w_n)$ represents the weights, b represents the bias. Without the knowledge of the weights, bias, and nodes in a layer, this timing attack will not be possible. This proves the significance of our attack, as we do not need any information on the inputs to the activation function nor the input to the network. This means that there is no need to calculate the input to the activation function with our method, therefore shortening the step to identify the activation function.

Implementation of Constant-Time Activation Functions. To mitigate the timing attack on the activation function, dummy operations can be included to the computation of the activation functions. By making the computation time of the activation function constant with no operation instruction, it will become difficult to guess the activation function from the time computed. ReLU function will be the easiest to implement the constant-time operation, as the computation time only differs when the input is before 0 and after 0 [18]. However, with SEMA attack the operation itself could be seen through the EM trace, therefore it will become easy to see what operation is being done in the processor.

6   Conclusion

The need for implementations of neural networks on to the edge device is increasing. These edge devices, however, tend to be vulnerable to side-channel attacks. In this paper, we introduce an attack methodology that can recover activation functions from a black box network using side-channel information. We conducted the experiment on a MLP processing 3-input XOR implemented on a Arduino Uno microcontroller. Using SEMA and signal processing, the activation functions were successfully identified. Compared with previous work by that identify the activation functions using timing behavior, the SEMA attack proposed in this work does not rely on the inputs, requires fewer measurement and is less dependant on non-constant timing behavior of the activation function. Our experiment showed the vulnerabilities of edge AI to side-channel attacks. Neural networks on edge devices need to implement effective countermeasures against side-channel attacks to strengthen their security.

In future works, we will further research how SEMA could potentially break the constant-time implementation. We have also left out relatively new activation functions such as Exponential Linear Unit (ELU) function, Leaky Rectified Linear Unit (Leaky ReLU) function, and Scaled Exponential Linear Unit (SELU) function. We will further look into these activation functions and see how to distinguish them from ReLU function as they all have the same outputs for positive inputs, making them hard to identify with our current method.

Acknowledgements. This work was supported by JST AIP Acceleration Research Grant Number JPMJCR20U2, Japan.

References

1. Riscure. https://www.riscure.com/blog/automatedneural-network-construction-genetic-algorithm/. Accessed 10 June 2020
2. Ateniese, G., Mancini, L.V., Spognardi, A., Villani, A., Vitali, D., Felici, G.: Hacking smart machines with smarter ones: How to extract meaningful data from machine learning classifiers. Int. J. Secur. Networks **10**(3), 137–150 (2015)
3. Batina, L., Bhasin, S., Jap, D., Picek, S.: CSI NN: reverse engineering of neural network architectures through electromagnetic side channel. In: Heninger, N., Traynor, P. (eds.) 28th USENIX Security Symposium, USENIX Security 2019, Santa Clara, CA, USA, 14–16 August 2019, pp. 515–532. USENIX Association (2019)
4. Breier, J., Jap, D., Hou, X., Bhasin, S., Liu, Y.: SNIFF: reverse engineering of neural networks with fault attacks. CoRR abs/2002.11021 (2020)
5. Fredrikson, M., Jha, S., Ristenpart, T.: Model inversion attacks that exploit confidence information and basic countermeasures. In: Ray, I., Li, N., Kruegel, C. (eds.) Proceedings of the 22nd ACM SIGSAC Conference on Computer and Communications Security, Denver, CO, USA, 12–16 October 2015, pp. 1322–1333. ACM (2015)
6. Fredrikson, M., Lantz, E., Jha, S., Lin, S.M., Page, D., Ristenpart, T.: Privacy in pharmacogenetics: an end-to-end case study of personalized warfarin dosing. In: Fu, K., Jung, J. (eds.) Proceedings of the 23rd USENIX Security Symposium, San Diego, CA, USA, 20–22 August 2014, pp. 17–32. USENIX Association (2014)
7. Gilad-Bachrach, R., Dowlin, N., Laine, K., Lauter, K.E., Naehrig, M., Wernsing, J.: Cryptonets: applying neural networks to encrypted data with high throughput and accuracy. In: Balcan, M., Weinberger, K.Q. (eds.) Proceedings of the 33nd International Conference on Machine Learning, ICML 2016, New York City, NY, USA, 19–24 June 2016. JMLR Workshop and Conference Proceedings, vol. 48, pp. 201–210 (2016). JMLR.org
8. Gilmore, R., Hanley, N., O'Neill, M.: Neural network based attack on a masked implementation of AES. In: IEEE International Symposium on Hardware Oriented Security and Trust, HOST 2015, Washington, DC, USA, 5–7 May 2015, pp. 106–111. IEEE Computer Society (2015)
9. He, K., Zhang, X., Ren, S., Sun, J.: Deep residual learning for image recognition. In: 2016 IEEE Conference on Computer Vision and Pattern Recognition, CVPR 2016, Las Vegas, NV, USA, June 27–30, 2016. pp. 770–778. IEEE Computer Society (2016)
10. Heuser, A., Picek, S., Guilley, S., Mentens, N.: Lightweight ciphers and their side-channel resilience. IEEE Trans. Comput. (2017)
11. Hong, S., Davinroy, M., Kaya, Y., Dachman-Soled, D., Dumitras, T.: How to 0wn the NAS in your spare time. In: 8th International Conference on Learning Representations, ICLR 2020, Addis Ababa, Ethiopia, 26–30 April 2020 (2020). OpenReview.net

12. Ilyas, A., Engstrom, L., Athalye, A., Lin, J.: Black-box adversarial attacks with limited queries and information. In: Dy, J.G., Krause, A. (eds.) Proceedings of the 35th International Conference on Machine Learning, ICML 2018, Stockholmsmässan, Stockholm, Sweden, 10–15 July 2018, Proceedings of Machine Learning Research, vol. 80, pp. 2142–2151. PMLR (2018)
13. Kober, J., Bagnell, J.A., Peters, J.: Reinforcement learning in robotics: a survey. I. J. Robotics Res. **32**(11), 1238–1274 (2013)
14. Kocher, P., Jaffe, J., Jun, B.: Differential power analysis. In: Wiener, M. (ed.) CRYPTO 1999. LNCS, vol. 1666, pp. 388–397. Springer, Heidelberg (1999). https://doi.org/10.1007/3-540-48405-1_25
15. Krizhevsky, A., Sutskever, I., Hinton, G.E.: ImageNet classification with deep convolutional neural networks. In: Bartlett, P.L., Pereira, F.C.N., Burges, C.J.C., Bottou, L., Weinberger, K.Q. (eds.) Advances in Neural Information Processing Systems 25: 26th Annual Conference on Neural Information Processing Systems 2012. Proceedings of a meeting held 3–6 December 2012, Lake Tahoe, Nevada, United States, pp. 1106–1114 (2012)
16. Kucera, M., Tsankov, P., Gehr, T., Guarnieri, M., Vechev, M.T.: Synthesis of probabilistic privacy enforcement. In: Thuraisingham, B.M., Evans, D., Malkin, T., Xu, D. (eds.) Proceedings of the 2017 ACM SIGSAC Conference on Computer and Communications Security, CCS 2017, Dallas, TX, USA, 30 October–03 November 2017, pp. 391–408. ACM (2017)
17. Luo, C., Fei, Y., Luo, P., Mukherjee, S., Kaeli, D.R.: Side-channel power analysis of a GPU AES implementation. In: 33rd IEEE International Conference on Computer Design, ICCD 2015, New York City, NY, USA, 18–21 October 2015, pp. 281–288. IEEE Computer Society (2015)
18. Nakai, T., Suzuki, D., Omatsu, F., Fujino, T.: Evaluation of timing attacks against deep learning on a microcontroller and countermeasures. In: 2020 Symposium on Cryptography and Information Security - SCIS 2020, Kochi, Japan, 28–31 January 2020, vol. 3E4-4. The Institute of Electronics, Information and Communication Engineers (2020)
19. Naraei, P., Abhari, A., Sadeghian, A.: Application of multilayer perceptron neural networks and support vector machines in classification of healthcare data. In: 2016 Future Technologies Conference (FTC), pp. 848–852. IEEE (2016)
20. Papernot, N., McDaniel, P.D., Goodfellow, I.J., Jha, S., Celik, Z.B., Swami, A.: Practical black-box attacks against machine learning. In: Karri, R., Sinanoglu, O., Sadeghi, A., Yi, X. (eds.) Proceedings of the 2017 ACM on Asia Conference on Computer and Communications Security, AsiaCCS 2017, Abu Dhabi, United Arab Emirates, 2–6 April 2017, pp. 506–519. ACM (2017)
21. Patranabis, S., Mukhopadhyay, D. (eds.): Fault Tolerant Architectures for Cryptography and Hardware Security. CADM. Springer, Singapore (2018). https://doi.org/10.1007/978-981-10-1387-4
22. Shokri, R., Stronati, M., Song, C., Shmatikov, V.: Membership inference attacks against machine learning models. In: 2017 IEEE Symposium on Security and Privacy, SP 2017, San Jose, CA, USA, 22–26 May 2017, pp. 3–18. IEEE Computer Society (2017)
23. Sze, V., Chen, Y., Yang, T., Emer, J.S.: Efficient processing of deep neural networks: a tutorial and survey. Proc. IEEE **105**(12), 2295–2329 (2017)
24. Teufl, P., Payer, U., Lackner, G.: From NLP (natural language processing) to MLP (machine language processing). In: Kotenko, I., Skormin, V. (eds.) MMM-ACNS 2010. LNCS, vol. 6258, pp. 256–269. Springer, Heidelberg (2010). https://doi.org/10.1007/978-3-642-14706-7_20

25. Thomas, P., Suhner, M.: A new multilayer perceptron pruning algorithm for classification and regression applications. Neural Process. Lett. **42**(2), 437–458 (2015)
26. Tramèr, F., Zhang, F., Juels, A., Reiter, M.K., Ristenpart, T.: Stealing machine learning models via prediction APIS. In: Holz, T., Savage, S. (eds.) 25th USENIX Security Symposium, USENIX Security 16, Austin, TX, USA, 10–12 August 2016, pp. 601–618. USENIX Association (2016)
27. Wei, L., Luo, B., Li, Y., Liu, Y., Xu, Q.: I know what you see: Power side-channel attack on convolutional neural network accelerators. In: Proceedings of the 34th Annual Computer Security Applications Conference, ACSAC 2018, San Juan, PR, USA, 03–07 December 2018, pp. 393–406. ACM (2018)
28. Xu, X., Liu, C., Feng, Q., Yin, H., Song, L., Song, D.: Neural network-based graph embedding for cross-platform binary code similarity detection. In: Thuraisingham, B.M., Evans, D., Malkin, T., Xu, D. (eds.) Proceedings of the 2017 ACM SIGSAC Conference on Computer and Communications Security, CCS 2017, Dallas, TX, USA, 30 October– 03 November 2017, pp. 363–376. ACM (2017)
29. Yan, M., Fletcher, C.W., Torrellas, J.: Cache telepathy: Leveraging shared resource attacks to learn DNN architectures. CoRR abs/1808.04761 (2018)
30. Yu, H., Ma, H., Yang, K., Zhao, Y., Jin, Y.: DeepEM: deep neural networks model recovery through EM side-channel information leakage (2020)

Performance Analysis of Multilayer Perceptron in Profiling Side-Channel Analysis

Léo Weissbart[1,2(✉)]

[1] Delft University of Technology, Delft, The Netherlands
weissbart@cs.ru.nl
[2] Digital Security Group, Radboud University, Nijmegen, The Netherlands

Abstract. In profiling side-channel analysis, machine learning-based analysis nowadays offers the most powerful performance. This holds especially for techniques stemming from the neural network family: multilayer perceptron and convolutional neural networks. Convolutional neural networks are often favored as results suggest better performance, especially in scenarios where targets are protected with countermeasures. Multilayer perceptron receives significantly less attention, and researchers seem less interested in this method, narrowing the results in the literature to comparisons with convolutional neural networks. On the other hand, a multilayer perceptron has a much simpler structure, enabling easier hyperparameter tuning and, hopefully, contributing to the explainability of this neural network inner working.

We investigate the behavior of a multilayer perceptron in the context of the side-channel analysis of AES. By exploring the sensitivity of multilayer perceptron hyperparameters over the attack's performance, we aim to provide a better understanding of successful hyperparameters tuning and, ultimately, this algorithm's performance. Our results show that MLP (with a proper hyperparameter tuning) can easily break implementations with a random delay or masking countermeasures. This work aims to reiterate the power of simpler neural network techniques in the profiled SCA.

1 Introduction

Side-channel analysis (SCA) exploits weaknesses in cryptographic algorithms' physical implementations rather than the algorithms' mathematical properties [16]. There, SCA correlates secret information with unintentional leakages like timing [13], power dissipation [14], and electromagnetic (EM) radiation [25]. One standard division of SCA is into non-profiling (direct) attacks and profiling (two-stage) attacks. Profiling SCA is the worst-case security analysis as it considers the most powerful side-channel attacker with access to a clone device (where keys can be chosen and known by the attacker). During the past few

© Springer Nature Switzerland AG 2020
J. Zhou et al. (Eds.): ACNS 2020 Workshops, LNCS 12418, pp. 198–216, 2020.
https://doi.org/10.1007/978-3-030-61638-0_12

years, numerous works showed the potential and strength of machine learning in profiling side-channel analysis. Across various targets and scenarios, researchers were able to show that machine learning can outperform other techniques considered state-of-the-art in the SCA community [2,15]. More interestingly, some machine learning techniques are successful, even on implementations protected with countermeasures [2,12]. There, in the spotlight are techniques from the neural network family, most notably, multilayer perceptron (MLP) and convolutional neural networks (CNNs).

When considering the attack success, we commonly take into account only the performance as measured by the number of traces needed to obtain the key. While this is an important criterion, it should not be the only one. For instance, attack complexity (complexity of tuning and training a model) and interpretability of the attack are also essential but much less researched. For instance, CNNs are often showed to perform better than MLPs in SCA's context [2,15,22], as they make the training of a model more versatile and alleviate the feature engineering process. On the other hand, MLP has a more straightforward structure and is probably easier to understand than CNNs, but still, the performance of MLP for SCA raises less attention. Consequently, this raises an interesting dilemma: do we consider profiling SCA as a single-objective problem where the attack performance is the only criterion or should it be a multi-objective problem where one considers several aspects of "success"? We believe the proper approach is the second one as, without a better understanding of attacks, we cannot make better countermeasures, which is an integral part of the profiling SCA research.

In this paper, we experimentally investigate the performance of MLP when applied to real-world implementations protected with countermeasures and explore the sensitivity of the hyperparameter tuning of a successful MLP architecture. We emphasize that this work does not aim to compare the performance of different techniques, but rather to explore the multilayer perceptron's capabilities. To achieve this, we use two datasets containing different AES implementations protected with random delay countermeasure and masking countermeasure. Our results show that we require larger architectures only if we have enough high-quality data. Hence, one can (to a certain degree) overcome the limitation in the number of hidden layers by providing more perceptrons per layer or vice versa. Finally, while our experiments clearly show the difference in the performance concerning the choice of hyperparameters, we do not notice that MLP is overly sensitive to that choice. This MLP "stability" means it is possible to conduct a relatively short tuning phase and still expect not to miss a hyperparameter combination yielding high performance.

2   Background

2.1   Profiling Side-Channel Analysis

Profiling side-channel analysis is an efficient set of methods where one works under the assumption that the attacker is in full control of an exact copy of the targeted device. By estimating leakage profiles for each target value during the profiling step (also known as the training phase), the adversary can classify new traces obtained from the targeted device by computing the probabilities of each target value to match the profile. There are multiple approaches to compute these probabilities, such as template attack [3], stochastic attack [26], multivariate regression model [28], and machine learning models [12,15]. When profiling the leakage, one must choose the appropriate leakage model, which will result in a certain number of classes (i.e., possible outputs). The first common model is the intermediate value leakage model, which results in 256 classes if we consider the AES cipher with an 8-bit S-box:

$$Y(k) = \text{Sbox}[P_i \oplus k].$$

The second common leakage model is the Hamming weight (HW) leakage model:

$$Y(k) = \text{HW}(\text{Sbox}[P_i \oplus k]).$$

The Hamming weight leakage model results in nine classes for AES. Note that the distribution of classes is imbalanced, which can lead to problems in the classification process [22].

2.2   Multilayer Perceptron

The multilayer perceptron (MLP) is a feed-forward neural network that maps sets of inputs onto sets of appropriate outputs. MLP has multiple layers of nodes in a directed graph, where each layer is fully connected to the next layer. The output of a neuron is a weighted sum of m inputs x_i evaluated through a (nonlinear) activation function A:

$$Output = A(\sum_{i=0}^{m} w_i \cdot x_i). \tag{1}$$

An MLP consists of three types of layers: an input layer, an output layer, and one or more hidden layers [5]. If there is more than one hidden layer, the architecture can be already considered as deep. A common approach when training a neural network is to use the backpropagation algorithm, which is a generalization of the least mean squares algorithm in the linear perceptron [9].

The multilayer perceptron has many hyperparameters one can tune, but we concentrate on the following ones:

1. The number of hidden layers. The number of hidden layers will define the depth of the algorithm and, consequently, the complexity of relations the MLP model can process.
2. The number of neurons (perceptrons) per layer. The number of neurons per layer tells us the width of the network and what is the latent space. Interestingly, there exists a well-known result in the machine learning community called the Universal Approximation Theorem that states (very informally) that a feed-forward neural network with a single hidden layer, under

some assumptions, can approximate a wide set of continuous functions to any desired non-zero level of error [7]. Naturally, for this to hold, there need to be many neurons in that single hidden layer, and knowing how many neurons are needed is not straightforward.

3. Activation functions. Activation functions are used to convert an input signal to an output signal. If complex functional mappings are needed, one needs to use nonlinear activation functions.

When discussing machine learning algorithms, it is common to differentiate between parameters and hyperparameters. Hyperparameters are all those configuration variables that are external to the model, e.g., the number of hidden layers in a neural network. The parameters are the configuration variables internal to the model and whose values can be estimated from data. One example of parameters is the weights in a neural network. Consequently, when we talk about tuning a machine learning algorithm, we mean tuning its hyperparameters.

2.3 Datasets

We consider two datasets presented in previous researches and that we denote as ASCAD and AES_RD. Both datasets are protected with countermeasures: the first one with masking and the second one with the random delay interrupts.

The ASCAD dataset, introduced in the work of Prouff et al. [24], consists of electromagnetic emanations (EM) measurements from a software implementation of AES-128 protected with first-order Boolean masking running on an 8-bit AVR microcontroller (ATMega8515). This dataset counts 60 000 traces of 700 samples each and targets the third byte of the key. The SNR for this dataset is around 0.8 if the mask is known and 0 if it is unknown. The trace set is publicly available at https://github.com/ANSSI-FR/ASCAD/tree/master/ATMEGA_AES_v1/ATM_AES_v1_fixed_key.

The AES_RD dataset, introduced in the work of Coron and Kizhvatov [6], consists of power traces from a software implementation of AES-128 protected with random delayed interruptions running on an 8-bit AVR microcontroller (ATmega16). This dataset has 50 000 traces with 3 500 samples each, and targets the first byte of the key. The SNR has a maximum value of 0.0556. The trace set is publicly available at https://github.com/ikizhvatov/randomdelays-traces.

3 Related Work

The corpus of works on machine learning and SCA so far is substantial, so we concentrate only on works considering multilayer perceptron. Yang et al. considered neural networks and backpropagation as a setting for profiling SCA [32]. They indicated that "...neural network based power leakage characterization attack can largely improve the effectiveness of the attacks, regardless of the impact of noise and the limited number of power traces". Zeman and Martinasek investigated MLP for profiling SCA where they mentioned the machine learning algorithm simply as "neural network" [17]. They considered an architecture with only a single hidden layer and experimented with several possible numbers of neurons in that layer. Finally, they only considered a sigmoid for the activation function. After those, there have been several papers using MLP with good results, but usually comparable with other machine learning techniques [8,11,18]. Still, the hyperparameter tuning was often not sufficiently explored. Despite our attempts, we could not confirm the first paper using MLP in a deep learning paradigm, i.e., with more than a single hidden layer. Interestingly, first papers with MLP were often not clear on the number of layers, as the tuning phase played an even smaller role than today.

In 2016, Maghrebi et al. conducted the first experiments with convolutional neural networks for SCA, and they compared their performance with several other techniques (including MLP) [15]. Their results indicated that, while MLP is powerful, CNNs can perform significantly better. From that moment on, we observe a number of papers where various deep learning techniques have been considered in comparison with MLP, see, e.g., [10,20,22,23].

Pfeifer and Haddad considered how to make additional types of layers for MLP to improve the performance of profiling SCA [19]. B. Timon investigated the "non-profiled" deep learning paradigm, where he first obtained the measurements in a non-profiled way, which are then fed into MLP or CNN [30]. Interestingly, the author reported better results with MLP than CNNs. Finally, Picek et al. connected the Universal Approximation Theorem and performance of the side-channel attack, where they stated that if the attacker has unlimited power (as it is usually considered), most of the MLP-based attacks could (in theory) succeed in breaking implementation with only a single measurement in the attack phase [21].

4   Experimental Setup

In this section, we present our strategy to evaluate and compare the performance of the different MLP attacks on different datasets. We want to observe the influence of the choice of leakage model, information reduction, and major hyperparameters defining an MLP (i.e., number of layers, number of perceptrons per layers, and activation function).

We provide results with power leakage models of both the S-box output (intermediate value model) and the Hamming Weight (HW) representation of the S-box output.

Besides considering the raw traces (i.e., no pre-processing and feature engineering), we apply the Difference-of-Means (DoM) feature selection method [16]. DoM method selects the samples of a dataset that have the highest variance for a given leakage model. Even though selecting features with high variance is likely to preserve the information about the leakage, it is better to select a number of features with different variance since the features containing the leakage are not always the features with the highest or the lowest variance.

To compare the hyperparameters' influence, we conduct a grid search for hyperparameter optimization and consider each resulting model as a profiling model for an attack. Considering the MLP hyperparameters, we fix some parameters (i.e., number of training epochs and learning rate) and explore the influence of the three following hyperparameters:

- The number of perceptrons, with a fixed number of layers.
- The number of layers, with a fixed number of perceptrons.
- The activation function used for the perceptrons in the hidden layers.

In Table 1, we list all the explored hyperparameters. The total number of models trained per experiment is of $n_{act} * n_l * n_p = 2 * 6 * 10 = 120$, where n_{act}, n_l, n_p, represent the number of activation functions, layers and perceptrons per layers explored respectively. We run our experiments with Keras [4], and we use 200 epochs for the training phase, with a learning rate of 0.001. To assess the performance of a profiling model for an attack, we use the guessing entropy (GE) metric [27]. GE defines the average rank position of the correct key candidate in the guessing vector. In other words, when considering N attack traces, each of which results in a guessing vector $\mathbf{g} = [g_0, g_1, \ldots, g_{|K-1|}]$ containing the probabilities of each key candidates in the keyspace K, ordered by decreasing probability. For all experiments, when computing GE, we use the generalized guessing entropy introduced in [31]. GE equal to 0 means that the first key guess is correct, while GE of 128 indicates a random behavior. GE can also show stability or consistent increase above 200 for the correct key candidate when the computation method for GE don't consider averaging several attacks on different traces. Such behavior indicates that the trained model failed to learn how to classify data.

The metric used during a neural network training phase is training accuracy. Note, this metric can be deceiving for assessing the quality of a side-channel attack because it evaluates the attack one trace at a time, while SCA metrics take several traces into account, giving a more accurate estimation for a real attack scenario [22].

Table 1. List of evaluated hyperparameters.

Hyperparameter	Range
Activation function	$ReLU, Tanh$
Number of layers	$1, 2, 3, 4, 5, 6$
Number of perceptrons per layer	$10, 20, 30, 40, 50, 100, 150, 200, 250, 300$

5 Experimental Results

The results for all experiments on both datasets (ASCAD, AES_RD) and leakage models are given in four figures: the final key ranking from the guessing entropy of each model is represented for the activation functions explored in the first two figures. Next, we depict guessing entropy of the attack for all trained

MLP architectures. The last figure presents the integrated gradient of the best-obtained model and the median model with the corresponding color value of its final guessing entropy. By doing so, we depict the differences in important features when comparing the best attack model and average model. The integrated gradient is a method introduced in [29], which attributes the prediction of a deep neural network to its inputs. The integrated gradient can be used in the side-channel analysis to visualize the part of the traces that influence the most a network prediction and understand what trace samples the network evaluates as the leakage.

5.1   ASCAD Results

Intermediate Leakage Model: In Fig. 1, we depict the influence of all combinations of hyperparameter choices for the *ReLU* and *Tanh* activation functions when considering the intermediate value leakage model. For both choices of activation functions, some models reach guessing entropy of 0 within 1 000 attack traces. More models achieve a low guessing entropy with the *ReLU* activation function than with *Tanh*. On the other hand, *Tanh* seems to behave more stable as the resulting GE is more uniform across many explored hyperparameters settings. Several models with *ReLU* activation function and a low number of perceptrons (down to 50) can reach GE near zero.

The authors of the ASCAD dataset report the best performance using an MLP with six layers containing 200 units and *ReLU* activation function trained over 200 epochs. The same hyperparameters are also evaluated and show similarly good results. However, This hyperparameters choice is not unique, and other models show equivalent performances with fewer layers and perceptrons per layers. As represented in Fig. 1a, for settings with 200 perceptrons per layer, all MLPs with more than two hidden layers converge approximately equally fast to GE of 0. In Figu. 1c, we see that many settings reach GE of 0 and that some have poor performance even after 2 500 attack traces with GE around 200. We interpret this as expected sensitivity to the hyperparameter tuning. Models with too few layers and perceptron per layers failed to properly fit the data because of their poor learnability. Finally, Fig. 1d shows that the model that reaches the smaller GE in the attack (in blue) is more sensitive to the various samples of the input than other models that fail to learn the leakage. The leakage seems entirely spread over all samples, which indicates reducing the number of features will reduce the attack performance. The model that reaches a median GE considering all experiments (in orange) has smaller integrated gradients on every data sample, which explains why this model shows poor performance for the attack.

Reduced Number of Features: We now reduce the number of features to 50 with the Difference-of-Mean method. We train different MLPs with the traces that have a reduced number of features. We apply the same reduction for the attack dataset and compute guessing entropy, and we show the results in Fig. 2.

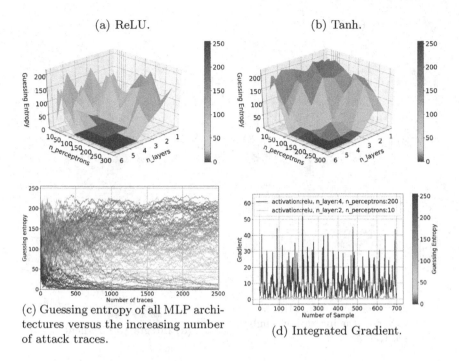

(a) ReLU.

(b) Tanh.

(c) Guessing entropy of all MLP architectures versus the increasing number of attack traces.

(d) Integrated Gradient.

Fig. 1. ASCAD guessing entropy for the intermediate leakage model. (Color figure online)

The area where GE converges toward zero is now smaller. For the *ReLU* activation function, this area is located around three and four layers with 250 and 300 perceptrons per layer. For the *Tanh* activation function, it is located above five layers and 250 perceptrons per layer. Interestingly, the highest score in Fig. 2a is not obtained for the highest number of layers. For both activation functions, the hyperparameters leading to a good attack performance are shifted toward larger hyperparameter values. This indicates that when considering features selected with the DoM method (i.e., using less information), we require deeper MLP to reach the same performance level, as the information is still present but more difficult to fit for the model. Fig. 2c shows sensitivity to hyperparameter tuning similar to the case with no feature selection. From Fig. 2d, the best fitting model has higher gradient values than the median model. Consequently, for the best model, we use most of the available features, while the average models do not manage to combine available features in any way that would indicate influence in the classification process.

HW Leakage Model: Next, we consider the Hamming Weight (HW) leakage model. From Fig. 3, we see similar results when compared to the intermediate value leakage model. Still, in Fig. 3b, the number of perceptrons per layer has a more substantial influence on the guessing entropy than the number of layers. We can notice a better behavior for MLP with a small number of layers compared

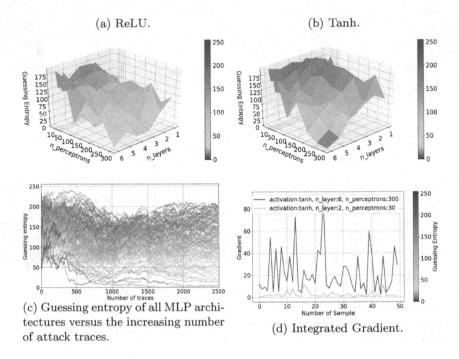

(a) ReLU.

(b) Tanh.

(c) Guessing entropy of all MLP architectures versus the increasing number of attack traces.

(d) Integrated Gradient.

Fig. 2. ASCAD guessing entropy with a reduced number of features and the intermediate leakage model.

to the intermediate value leakage model scenario. We believe this happens as more perceptrons per layer give more options on how to combine features, while deeper networks would contribute to more complex mappings between input and output, which is not needed for the HW leakage model as the classification task is simpler than when using the intermediate value leakage model. We can also see a stable area for several models with a number of perceptrons above 150 and a number of layers above three. In this area, the hyperparameters choice does not influence the performance of the MLP anymore. Like the intermediate value leakage model, the sensitivity to the hyperparameter tuning (Fig. 3c) is as expected, with many settings reaching top performance, but also many performing poorly. Interestingly, again we observe a more stable behavior from *Tanh* than the *ReLU* activation function. From Fig. 3d, the best fitting model and the median model have similar integrated gradient values. However, the highest peaks are different, showing that the leakage learned by the two models is different, which also accounts for the differences in GE results.

HW Leakage Model and Reduced Number of Features: We use the reduced number of feature representation of the dataset and apply the Hamming weight leakage model. We can see in Fig. 4c that many MLP architectures differ significantly with a GE spread between 0 and 175. In Fig. 4b, no MLP with the *Tanh* activation function succeeds in the attack. Finally, in Fig. 4a, MLP with

(a) ReLU.   (b) Tanh.

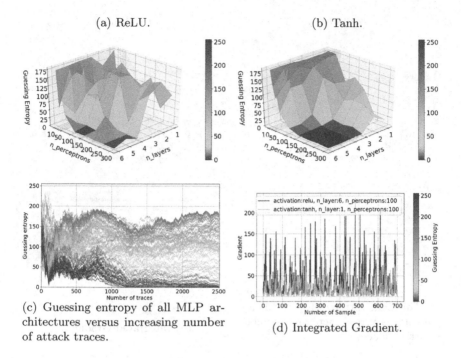

(c) Guessing entropy of all MLP architectures versus increasing number of attack traces.

(d) Integrated Gradient.

Fig. 3. ASCAD guessing entropy in the Hamming weight leakage model.

ReLU reaching GE of 0 has only one hidden layer, and when the number of layers increases, the performance decreases. Based on the ruggedness of the landscape for *ReLU*, it is clear that the choice of the number of layers/perceptrons plays a significant role. In Fig. 4c, slightly differing from previous cases (cf. Fig. 3c), we see more groupings in the GE performance. This indicates that a reduced number of features in the HW leakage model is less expressive, so more architectures reach the same performance. From Fig. 4d, the median model presents a higher integrated gradient than the best fitting model. This behavior differs from the previous experiments and shows that a wrong fitting model has high sensitivity on samples that do not correlate with the correct leakage. This also explains the spread of GE results, as there are many subsets of features combinations that result in high GE.

5.2 AES_RD Results

Intermediate Leakage Model: Given the intermediate value leakage model (Fig. 5), all MLP architectures, including the smallest ones (one hidden layer with ten perceptrons), are capable of reaching GE below 30 within 2 500 attack traces. Increasing the number of layers does not have an impact on the *ReLu* activation function. For the *Tanh* activation function, it even seems to increase GE (thus, decreasing the attack performance). For both activation functions,

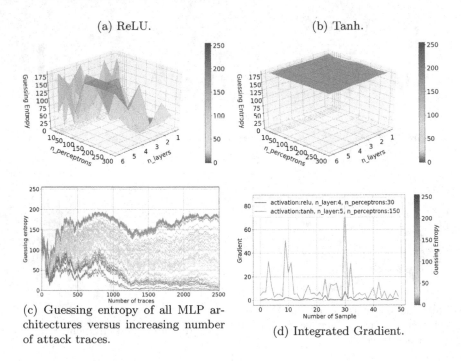

(a) ReLU.   (b) Tanh.

(c) Guessing entropy of all MLP architectures versus increasing number of attack traces.

(d) Integrated Gradient.

Fig. 4. ASCAD guessing entropy with a reduced number of features and the Hamming weight leakage model.

increasing the number of perceptrons per layer decreases GE. Still, from Fig. 5c, regardless of the architecture chosen, all MLP settings converge within the same amount of attack traces. This indicates that there is not enough useful information that larger networks can use, and as such, using them brings no performance gain (consequently, there is not much benefit from detailed hyperparameter tuning). The best-fitting model and the median model are both models that fit the dataset correctly. However, from Fig. 5d, the integrated gradient method reveals that the two models have very different sensitivity on the input. Such a result could have been expected as the AES_RD dataset deals with randomly delayed traces, meaning that the leakage is not located in a precise area of the input.

Reduced Number of Features: In Fig. 6, we observe a similar performance when training MLPs with a reduced number of features for the AES_RD dataset and the intermediate leakage model (containing only 50 selected features). Again, this implies there is no useful information in additional features, and that is why MLP cannot perform better even if we use larger/deeper architectures. This is following the expected behavior for the random delay countermeasure as the features are not aligned. Finally, the landscape is smoother for *Tanh* than for *ReLU* (similar to ASCAD but also different from AES_RD with all features). The outcome from Fig. 6d is quite similar to the integrated gradient obtained on the raw traces. While the gradient values for the two models have the same

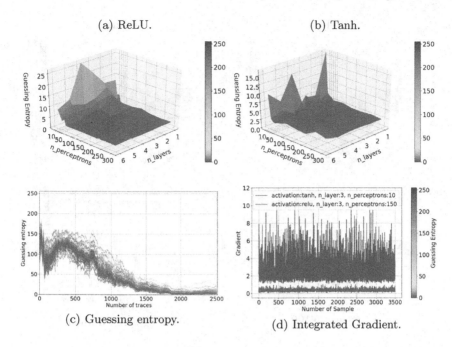

(a) ReLU.   (b) Tanh.

(c) Guessing entropy.   (d) Integrated Gradient.

Fig. 5. AES_RD guessing entropy for the intermediate leakage model.

levels, no maximum or minimum values are the same, meaning that no samples contribute significantly to network prediction.

Hamming Weight Leakage Model: When considering the HW leakage model for the AES_RD dataset, even after 2 500 traces, the attack is still unsuccessful. More precisely, in Fig. 7, no hyperparameter setting results in a model that can reach a GE below 60, which is not even close to a successful attack. Note we do not depict results for the reduced number of features as the attack was not successful even with the full number of features. With the intermediate value leakage model, we required around 1 500 traces to succeed in the attack. Now, we use a leakage model with a simpler classification problem and fail with more measurements. This result shows that the HW leakage is either not present or that the trained models are too simple to fit the leakage. Interestingly, all architectures behave relatively similarly, as visible in Fig. 7c. The integrated gradient on Fig. 7d shows similar results as obtained for the intermediate value leakage model, but in this case, both models do not fit the dataset correctly, which means it is difficult to talk about features that contribute more to the classification result. No trace samples show a higher sensitivity for the network prediction because of the random delay nature of the dataset.

As no MLP architecture can succeed in the HW leakage model's attack on the AES_RD dataset, we cannot conclude whether more layers or perceptrons would improve the attack performance. The phenomenon preventing MLPs from obtaining good attack performance might be linked to the class imbalance,

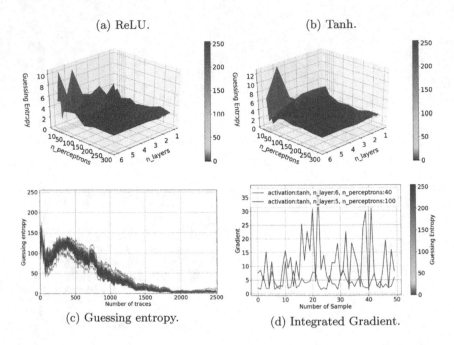

(a) ReLU.   (b) Tanh.

(c) Guessing entropy.   (d) Integrated Gradient.

Fig. 6. AES_RD guessing entropy with a reduced number of features and the intermediate leakage model.

pointed out by Picek et al. [22], where they obtain similar results for different architectures of MLP using the HW leakage model. Additionally, they observe increasing performance when balancing the training data among the classes.

6   Discussion

MLP can break the masking countermeasure of the ASCAD dataset and the random delay countermeasure of the AES_RD implementation even when training a rather small model. For AES_RD, the smallest models (one layer, 200 perceptrons, and six layers, ten perceptrons) share the best outcome of all the models in the comparison. The same results are observed when using only the most important features. An important leakage of the secret could explain these results if the countermeasure were turned off. Although the random delays shift the first round S-box operation from the start of the encryption execution, a strong leakage of the operation handling the secret information is still present. Consequently, using an MLP is enough to overcome this countermeasure. This result indicates that the current consensus in the SCA community on MLP performance should change. Indeed, CNNs are considered especially good for random delay countermeasure and MLP for masking countermeasure [15,22]. Our results indicate there is no reason not to consider MLP successful against the random delay countermeasure given the satisfying results obtained on AES_RD with

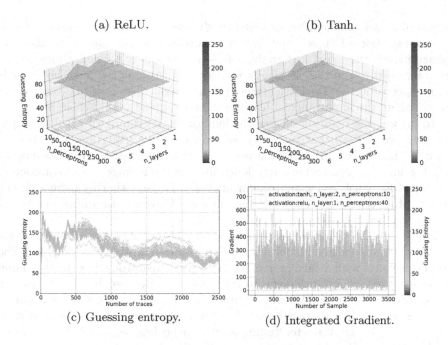

(a) ReLU.

(b) Tanh.

(c) Guessing entropy.

(d) Integrated Gradient.

Fig. 7. AES_RD guessing entropy for the Hamming weight leakage model.

intermediate value. When selecting 50 POIs with a Difference-of-Mean method, the selected points represent only $50/3\,500 \simeq 1\%$ of the original traces in the dataset, and the information about the leakage is reduced. Still, the attack succeeds in the same way, which can be explained because the leakage only comes from the selected POIs. Finally, the integrated gradient is more difficult to interpret as the dataset has randomness in the time domain, which means it becomes difficult to pinpoint a few features with a significant contribution toward the classification result.

For the ASCAD dataset, we observe that the best score obtained for MLP has the following hyperparameters: six layers and 200 perceptrons. Still, we see in Figs. 1a and 1b that MLP with similar hyperparameters can perform equally good (where the red point represents the result obtain with the architecture of the best MLP MLP_{best} from the ASCAD paper). When selecting POIs with the Difference-of-Mean method, we can observe that the performance decreases, meaning that the useful information is decreased. This, in turn, results in attacks not able to recover the full secret key. Still, some MLPs can obtain the secret key in the given number of traces, and we observe that both the number of layers and the number of perceptrons influence their performance. Finally, the performance of MLPs with the Hamming weight leakage model gives better performance than for the intermediate value. The range of hyperparameters that can achieve the best results is smaller than for the intermediate value leakage model. From the integrated gradient perspective, we see that many features contribute to a successful attack, but MLP makes slightly different feature selection than DoM, as obviously not all 50 selected features contribute significantly. For the HW leakage model, the integrated gradient is somewhat more aligned, which means that more features in this leakage model contribute similarly. Such behavior is again expected as the HW leakage model forms larger clusters with S-box output values, where the importance of features is more spread within clusters.

To answer the question of how challenging is the tuning of MLP hyperparameters, we observe that there is nearly no influence using a (relatively) big or small MLP for the AES_RD dataset. When considering the ASCAD dataset with the masking countermeasure, depending on the leakage model considered, the size of the MLP can play a significant role. There, either by increasing the number of perceptrons per layer or the number of layers with a fixed number of perceptrons, we can decrease the guessing entropy.

From the activation function perspective, *ReLU* behaves somewhat better for the intermediate leakage model when compared to *Tanh*, i.e., it can reach the top performance with a smaller number of layers/perceptrons. For the Hamming weight leakage model, *Tanh* seems to work better on average, but *ReLU* reaches top performance with smaller architectures than *Tanh*. Finally, *Tanh* gives more stable behavior when averaged over all settings, i.e., with the *Tanh* activation function, the hyperparameter tuning seems to be less sensitive. To conclude, *ReLU* appears to be the preferred option if going for top performance or using smaller architectures. In contrast, *Tanh* should be preferred if stability over a more scenarios is required.

MLP is (or, at least, can be) a deep learning algorithm that has a simple architecture and a few hyperparameters but can show good performance in the side-channel analysis. What is more, our results show it can break implementations protected with both masking or hiding countermeasures. If there is no sufficient useful input information (as one would expect when dealing with the random delay countermeasure), a reasonable choice is to go with a relatively small architecture. For masked datasets, the number of perceptrons or the number of layers must be large, but the activation function's choice also plays an important role. Finally, we observe that in all considered scenarios, the MLP architectures are not overly sensitive to the hyperparameter choice, i.e., there does not seem to be a strong motivation to run very fine-grained hyperparameter tuning.

Based on those observations, we list general recommendations for MLP in the profiled SCA context[1]:

1. Many hyperparameter settings can lead to good performance, which makes the benefit of an exhaustive search very limited.

---

[1] The recommendations are based on the tested configurations. There is no guarantee that different results could not be achieved with significantly different settings, e.g., having a different number of perceptrons per layer. Still, following our recommendations should provide good performance in most of the scenarios commonly encountered in profiling SCA.

2. *ReLU* is better for top performance, while *Tanh* is more stable over different hyperparameter combinations.
3. Smaller depth of an MLP can be compensated with wider layers.
4. Integrated gradient is an efficient method for evaluating the influence of features if MLP manages to reach good performance.
5. Simpler leakage models require fewer layers.

7   Conclusions and Future Work

In this paper, we considered the behavior of a multilayer perceptron for profiling side-channel analysis. We investigated two datasets protected with countermeasures and a number of different MLP architectures concerning three hyperparameters. Our results clearly show that the input information to the MLP plays a crucial role, and if such information is limited, larger/deeper architectures are not needed. On the other hand, if we can provide high-quality input information to the MLP, we should also use larger architectures. At the same time, our experiments revealed no need for very fine-grained hyperparameter tuning. While the results for MLP maybe cannot compare with state-of-the-art results for CNNs, we note that they are not far apart in many cases. If we additionally factor in that MLP is simpler and faster to train, the choice between those two techniques becomes even more difficult to make and should depend on additional goals and constraints. For example, reaching the top performance is the argument for the usage of CNNs, but if one requires small yet powerful architecture, a more natural choice seems to be MLP.

In this work, we concentrated on scenarios where each hidden layer has the same number of perceptrons. It would be interesting to investigate the performance of MLP when each layer could have a different number of perceptrons. Naturally, this opens a question of what combinations of neurons/layers to consider as one could quickly come to thousands of possible settings to explore. Similarly, for activation functions, we consider only the two most popular ones where all hidden layers use the same function. It would be interesting to allow different layers to have different activation functions. Recent experiments showed that MLP could outperform CNNs when considering different devices for training and testing (i.e., the portability case) [1]. We plan to explore the influence of the hyperparameter choice in those scenarios. Finally, as we already mentioned, MLP architectures are usually simpler than CNNs, which should mean they are easier to understand. We aim to explore whether we can design stronger countermeasures against machine learning based-attacks based on MLP inner working.

References

1. Bhasin, S., Chattopadhyay, A., Heuser, A., Jap, D., Picek, S., Shrivastwa, R.R.: Mind the portability: a warriors guide through realistic profiled side-channel analysis. Cryptology ePrint Archive, Report 2019/661 (2019). https://eprint.iacr.org/2019/661

2. Cagli, E., Dumas, C., Prouff, E.: Convolutional neural networks with data augmentation against jitter-based countermeasures. In: Fischer, W., Homma, N. (eds.) CHES 2017. LNCS, vol. 10529, pp. 45–68. Springer, Cham (2017). https://doi.org/10.1007/978-3-319-66787-4_3

3. Chari, S., Rao, J.R., Rohatgi, P.: Template attacks. In: Kaliski, B.S., Koç, K., Paar, C. (eds.) CHES 2002. LNCS, vol. 2523, pp. 13–28. Springer, Heidelberg (2003). https://doi.org/10.1007/3-540-36400-5_3

4. Chollet, F., et al.: Keras (2015). https://github.com/fchollet/keras

5. Collobert, R., Bengio, S.: Links between perceptrons, MLPs and SVMs. In: Proceedings of the Twenty-First International Conference on Machine Learning, ICML 2004, p. 23. ACM, New York (2004). https://doi.org/10.1145/1015330.1015415

6. Coron, J.-S., Kizhvatov, I.: An efficient method for random delay generation in embedded software. In: Clavier, C., Gaj, K. (eds.) CHES 2009. LNCS, vol. 5747, pp. 156–170. Springer, Heidelberg (2009). https://doi.org/10.1007/978-3-642-04138-9_12

7. Cybenko, G.: Approximation by superpositions of a sigmoidal function. Math. Control Sig. Syst. **2**(4), 303–314 (1989). https://doi.org/10.1007/BF02551274

8. Gilmore, R., Hanley, N., O'Neill, M.: Neural network based attack on a masked implementation of AES. In: 2015 IEEE International Symposium on Hardware Oriented Security and Trust (HOST), pp. 106–111, May 2015. https://doi.org/10.1109/HST.2015.7140247

9. Goodfellow, I., Bengio, Y., Courville, A.: Deep Learning. MIT Press (2016). http://www.deeplearningbook.org

10. Hettwer, B., Gehrer, S., Güneysu, T.: Profiled power analysis attacks using convolutional neural networks with domain knowledge. In: Cid, C., Jacobson Jr., M. (eds.) Selected Areas in Cryptography - SAC 2018–25th International Conference, Calgary, AB, Canada, 15–17 August 2018, Revised Selected Papers. Lecture Notes in Computer Science, vol. 11349, pp. 479–498. Springer, Cham (2018). https://doi.org/10.1007/978-3-030-10970-7_22

11. Heuser, A., Picek, S., Guilley, S., Mentens, N.: Side-channel analysis of lightweight ciphers: does lightweight equal easy? In: Hancke, G.P., Markantonakis, K. (eds.) RFIDSec 2016. LNCS, vol. 10155, pp. 91–104. Springer, Cham (2017). https://doi.org/10.1007/978-3-319-62024-4_7

12. Kim, J., Picek, S., Heuser, A., Bhasin, S., Hanjalic, A.: Make some noise. Unleashing the power of convolutional neural networks for profiled side-channel analysis. IACR Trans. Cryptographic Hardware Embed. Syst. **2019**(3), 148–179 (2019). https://doi.org/10.13154/tches.v2019.i3.148-179. https://tches.iacr.org/index.php/TCHES/article/view/8292

13. Kocher, P.C.: Timing attacks on implementations of Diffie-Hellman, RSA, DSS, and other systems. In: Koblitz, N. (ed.) CRYPTO 1996. LNCS, vol. 1109, pp. 104–113. Springer, Heidelberg (1996). https://doi.org/10.1007/3-540-68697-5_9

14. Kocher, P., Jaffe, J., Jun, B.: Differential power analysis. In: Wiener, M. (ed.) CRYPTO 1999. LNCS, vol. 1666, pp. 388–397. Springer, Heidelberg (1999). https://doi.org/10.1007/3-540-48405-1_25. http://dl.acm.org/citation.cfm?id=646764.7-03989

15. Maghrebi, H., Portigliatti, T., Prouff, E.: Breaking cryptographic implementations using deep learning techniques. In: Carlet, C., Hasan, M.A., Saraswat, V. (eds.) SPACE 2016. LNCS, vol. 10076, pp. 3–26. Springer, Cham (2016). https://doi.org/10.1007/978-3-319-49445-6_1

16. Mangard, S., Oswald, E., Popp, T.: Power Analysis Attacks: Revealing the Secrets of Smart Cards. Springer, Boston (2006). http://www.springer.com/. ISBN 0-387-30857-1. http://www.dpabook.org/
17. Martinasek, Z., Zeman, V.: Innovative method of the power analysis. Radioengineering **22**(2) (2013)
18. Martinasek, Z., Hajny, J., Malina, L.: Optimization of power analysis using neural network. In: Francillon, A., Rohatgi, P. (eds.) Smart Card Research and Advanced Applications, pp. 94–107. Springer, Cham (2014). https://doi.org/10.1007/978-3-319-08302-5_7
19. Pfeifer, C., Haddad, P.: Spread: a new layer for profiled deep-learning side-channel attacks. Cryptology ePrint Archive, Report 2018/880 (2018). https://eprint.iacr.org/2018/880
20. Picek, S., Heuser, A., Alippi, C., Regazzoni, F.: When theory meets practice: A framework for robust profiled side-channel analysis. Cryptology ePrint Archive, Report 2018/1123 (2018). https://eprint.iacr.org/2018/1123
21. Picek, S., Heuser, A., Guilley, S.: Profiling side-channel analysis in the restricted attacker framework. Cryptology ePrint Archive, Report 2019/168 (2019). https://eprint.iacr.org/2019/168
22. Picek, S., Heuser, A., Jovic, A., Bhasin, S., Regazzoni, F.: The curse of class imbalance and conflicting metrics with machine learning for side-channel evaluations. IACR Trans. Cryptogr. Hardw. Embed. Syst. **2019**(1), 209–237 (2019). https://doi.org/10.13154/tches.v2019.i1.209-237
23. Picek, S., Samiotis, I.P., Kim, J., Heuser, A., Bhasin, S., Legay, A.: On the performance of convolutional neural networks for side-channel analysis. In: Chattopadhyay, A., Rebeiro, C., Yarom, Y. (eds.) Security, Privacy, and Applied Cryptography Engineering, pp. 157–176. Springer International Publishing, Cham (2018). https://doi.org/10.1007/978-3-030-05072-6_10
24. Prouff, E., Strullu, R., Benadjila, R., Cagli, E., Dumas, C.: Study of deep learning techniques for side-channel analysis and introduction to ASCAD database. Cryptology ePrint Archive, Report 2018/053 (2018). https://eprint.iacr.org/2018/053
25. Quisquater, J.-J., Samyde, D.: ElectroMagnetic analysis (EMA): measures and counter-measures for smart cards. In: Attali, I., Jensen, T. (eds.) E-smart 2001. LNCS, vol. 2140, pp. 200–210. Springer, Heidelberg (2001). https://doi.org/10.1007/3-540-45418-7_17
26. Schindler, W., Lemke, K., Paar, C.: A stochastic model for differential side channel cryptanalysis. In: Rao, J.R., Sunar, B. (eds.) CHES 2005. LNCS, vol. 3659, pp. 30–46. Springer, Heidelberg (2005). https://doi.org/10.1007/11545262_3
27. Standaert, F.-X., Malkin, T.G., Yung, M.: A unified framework for the analysis of side-channel key recovery attacks. In: Joux, A. (ed.) EUROCRYPT 2009. LNCS, vol. 5479, pp. 443–461. Springer, Heidelberg (2009). https://doi.org/10.1007/978-3-642-01001-9_26
28. Sugawara, T., Homma, N., Aoki, T., Satoh, A.: Profiling attack using multivariate regression analysis. IEICE Electron. Express **7**(15), 1139–1144 (2010)
29. Sundararajan, M., Taly, A., Yan, Q.: Axiomatic attribution for deep networks. arXiv preprint arXiv:1703.01365 (2017)
30. Timon, B.: Non-profiled deep learning-based side-channel attacks with sensitivity analysis. IACR Trans. Cryptographic Hardware Embed. Syst. **2019**(2), 107–131 (2019). https://doi.org/10.13154/tches.v2019.i2.107-131. https://tches.iacr.org/index.php/TCHES/article/view/7387

31. Wu, L., et al.: Everything is connected: From model learnability to guessing entropy. Cryptology ePrint Archive, Report 2020/899 (2020). https://eprint.iacr.org/2020/899
32. Yang, S., Zhou, Y., Liu, J., Chen, D.: Back propagation neural network based leakage characterization for practical security analysis of cryptographic implementations. In: Kim, H. (ed.) ICISC 2011. LNCS, vol. 7259, pp. 169–185. Springer, Heidelberg (2012). https://doi.org/10.1007/978-3-642-31912-9_12

The Forgotten Hyperparameter:
Introducing Dilated Convolution for Boosting CNN-Based Side-Channel Attacks

Servio Paguada[1,2](✉)[iD] and Igor Armendariz[2](✉)[iD]

[1] Digital Security Group, Radboud University, Nijmegen, The Netherlands
servio.paguadaisaula@ru.nl
[2] Ikerlan Technology Research Centre, Arrasate-Mondragón, Gipuzkoa, Spain
{slpaguada,iarmendariz}@ikerlan.es

Abstract. In the evaluation of side-channel resilience, convolutional neural network-based techniques have been proved to be very effective, even in the presence of countermeasures. This work is introducing the use of dilated convolution in the context of profiling side-channel attacks. We show that the convolutional neural network that uses dilated convolution increases its performance by taking advantage of the leakage distributed through scattered points in leakage traces. We have validated the feasibility of the proposal by comparing it with the state-of-the-art approach. We have conducted experiments using ASCAD (with random key), and as a result the guessing entropy of the attack converges to zero for around 550 synchronized traces and for 3 000 desynchronised traces. In both groups of experiments, we have used the same architecture to train the model, changing just dilatation rate and kernel length, which indicates a reduction of the complexity in the deep learning model.

Keywords: Profiled attacks · Side-channel analysis · Dilated convolutions · CNNs · Dilatation rate

1 Introduction

The profiled attack is considered to be one of the most powerful attacks in Side-Channel Analysis (SCA). The overall idea is to build a model (profile) by using a clone of the target device and then use this model to attack the non-controlled target device. Template Attack is the first example of these types of attacks [6], and some related works followed introducing new attack scenario and improving the execution phase [10,14,33]. Profiled attacks became even more powerful with the usage of deep learning techniques. Since profiled attacks can be seen as a classification problem, existing deep learning architectures like VGG [34] were taken as a baseline for applications in SCA [20,32]. Several publications presented different types of deep learning models such as Multi-Layer Perceptron (MLP) [23,24], and Convolutional Neural Network (CNN) [4] that were able to compromise the secure implementation of cryptographic algorithms. They both showed the potential to outperform previous results of template attacks.

© Springer Nature Switzerland AG 2020
J. Zhou et al. (Eds.): ACNS 2020 Workshops, LNCS 12418, pp. 217–236, 2020.
https://doi.org/10.1007/978-3-030-61638-0_13

Many efforts are made to improve our understanding of how these deep learning-based attacks work. One direction is to find the best combinations of hyperparameter values of the learning algorithm, e.g. those that improve the attack. Results of those efforts are the different methodologies that explain how evaluators and researchers should build CNN models. Thanks to that, tests over commercial devices for assessing their resilience are becoming more feasible and reliable.

Recently, the methodology presented in [40] has shown that, by reducing the use of relevant features in the convolutional blocks, not only the efficiency but also the effectiveness of the attack increases. Additionally, the experiments made in [21] suggest that an important improvement in CNN-based attacks could be achieved, if features where the intermediate values leak and where the mask leaks are combined in its convolution operation. CNN almost always are built with two main parts, the convolutional part, and the classification part. The former is composed of convolutional blocks, and it is the part where that convolution operation is performed.

We take the arguments from the two papers mentioned above as our starting point. Then, we conducted preliminary experiments using dilated convolutions. Dilated convolution is a type of convolutional block where its kernel is modified (dilated) in a way such that it covers wider areas than the normal convolution, and at the same time does not overuse relevant points. Dilated convolution is used to face the problem of scattered dependencies, meaning that the leak is scattered through sample points in the leakage traces [16, 21, 22]. Some works in high-order side-channel also explain the phenomenon from the perspective of this analysis [2, 11, 36, 38]. The dilatation of the kernel is controlled by a hyperparameter known as *dilatation rate*. It turned out that by using dilated convolution, we increased the performance of the CNN model. The preliminary experiments were conducted using ASCAD fixed key dataset [32], with the CNN model suggested in the latest work [40]. The results have shown that dilated convolution is feasible and might represent a useful hyperparameter when building CNN models for SCA. Then, ASCAD random key dataset [32] was used in experiments where the guessing entropy [35] converges to zero for around 550 traces, whilst the baseline value produced by a model from [21] converges to zero for around 4 500 traces. The results of these latter experiments were achieved by a CNN model that uses dilated convolutions.

Contribution

By taking dilated convolution into account, we are aiming to understand better how the architecture of CNNs should be designed for evaluations. To be more specific, we introduce the use of dilated convolution by explaining and demonstrating how this type of kernels is feasible to evaluate implementations of cryptographic algorithms. As it turns out, it brings a new possibility to reduce the complexity of the deep learning models. To prove what we claim, we conducted the following:

1. The first experiment compares state-of-the-art results from [40], showing the feasibility of the dilated convolution. Gradient visualization [25], *Signal-to-Noise Ratio* (SNR) [22], and Weight visualisation [40] techniques are used to evaluate the classification and feature selection of both approaches. Further experiments involve a CNN model that outperforms the state-of-the-art approach. These latter experiments aim to compare CNN's effectiveness by using different values of kernel length, and dilatation rate. They demonstrate the effect of reducing redundant points in the first convolutional block, but also the importance of combining enough relevant ones.
2. Experiments for mimicking the behaviour of the dilated convolution using small values of kernel lengths and stride are also performed. Proving that in fact, dilated convolution takes advantage of the long-range dependencies leakage when combining the involved sample points in the same convolution operation.
3. Experiments that show how dilated kernels reduce the impact of the desynchronisation. This latter experiment aims at reducing the complexity of the convolutional part. As we show, the deep learning model used for bypassing desynchronisation is almost the same as the experiment without this effect. Changes were only made in the kernel length and the dilatation rate of the first convolutional block.
4. We also propose considerations that serve as a guide when using dilated convolutions.

Paper Organisation

The remainder of this paper is organised as follows. Section 2 includes a background in CNN, theoretical aspect of normal and dilated convolutions, the datasets we used, and the metric to assess the performance as well as the visualisation techniques. Section 3 summarises previous works regarding CNN for SCA. Section 4 presents the consideration when building dilated convolution-based CNN. Section 5 and Sect. 6 contain the result of experiments and the conclusion, respectively.

2   Background

In this section, we start by giving an overview of convolutional neural networks. We also include some theory on how the dilatation rate affects the convolutional operation. To show the arithmetic relation, we have used the mathematical expression of the most general case of convolution operation [13], which involves all the possible variables, i.e. padding, kernel and input map lengths, and stride.

2.1   Convolutional Neural Networks

Convolutional neural networks (CNNs) are a type of neural network; they were initially designed to address classification problems in images. Some recent works have also shown their performance for time series analysis [8,28]. As depicted in Fig. 1(a), CNNs are composed of two main parts; the convolutional part and the fully-connected part. The convolutional part is where the convolutions take place, and as the name suggests they are the convolution layers of a CNN. In such a layer, a kernel is required to perform the operation using the input map; being the first convolution layer the input signal. The elements of the kernel are also known as weights. The back-propagation operation updates these weights after a loss function determines the error in the classification. Back-propagation is a powerful characteristic of the neural network learning algorithms [15].

The input map contains features that characterise itself; not all features are relevant; in fact, irrelevant features lead to an ineffective neural network [27]. When the input map is convolved with a kernel of length l_k, the sparse combination of features produces a feature map, whose elements represent more abstract features than the ones in the input. Such a resultant feature map serves as input for the next convolutional block. The number of kernels used represents the number of feature maps that will be created; all of them will characterise in an abstract way the input signal. Feature map could also be seen as a reduction of the space volume of information. The length l_k determines how many points are involved in computing such reduction. Both, the kernel length, and the number of kernels in the convolutional block are hyperparameters for the neural network architecture.

As those feature maps progress through the hidden convolution layers, even more abstract feature maps are created. A 1D convolution operation can be expressed as in Eq. 1, where f is the input map and k is the kernel; a graphic example is depicted in Fig. 1(b). Feature map might pass to a pooling layer; this layer acts as a downsampler which takes the output of a convolution layer and creates a spatial feature map. This spatial feature map is an invariant representation of the original sparse features in the input map; we named this pooling feature map in Fig. 1(b). In the convolutional part, the operation must catch relevant features that aim for the proper classification. Which also implies that the goal is not to have a long kernel that mixes many features in the operation; indeed, such a practice could lead to poor results. At the end of the convolutional part, the feature maps are reduced to a vector (i.e. flattened) to feed it into the fully connected part where the classification is conducted.

$$f[x] \circledast k[x] = \sum_{n=-\infty}^{\infty} f[n] \cdot k[x-n] \tag{1}$$

Normal Convolutions

Different hyperparameters setup the convolution operation, and they affect the output dimension l_o of the resultant feature map. To explain this relation, in Eq. 2 it is assumed a convolution layer with kernel of length l_k, a padding parameter p whose value determines the dimension with zero values used to contour input map; this latter would have an original length denoted by l_i. Finally, the

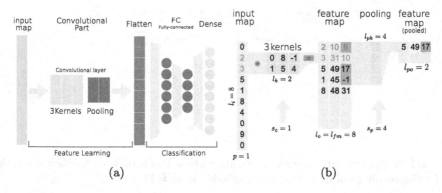

Fig. 1. (a) Convolution neural network common architecture (N = 0); (b) Convolution operation example

stride parameter s_c represents the distance between two consecutive applications of the kernel over the input map.

$$l_o = l_{fm} = \left\lfloor \frac{l_i + 2p - l_k}{s_c} \right\rfloor + 1 \tag{2}$$

As we mentioned, the output of the convolution layer could pass through a pooling operation. Commonly, this is the case because such operation grants invariant property to a CNN against small translations of the input maps. Pooling layer uses a window that we called it pooling kernel, its length l_{pk} represents the number of features taken from the feature map to conduct the pooling operation. A stride value s_p (named pooling stride) controls the displacement of the pooling kernel through the feature map. This operation also affects the output dimension l_o that in such a case becomes l_{po}, Eq. 3 shows the relation. Although there are different kinds of pooling operation Eq. 3 applies for all of them. Figure 1(b) also show example of these parameters.

$$l_{po} = \left\lfloor \frac{l_{fm} - l_{pk}}{s_p} \right\rfloor + 1 \tag{3}$$

Dilated Convolutions

A dilated convolution takes place when the effective size of the kernel is increased by a factor, known as dilatation rate dr. Normally, this factor is bigger than 1, (where $dr = 1$ is a normal convolution layer) which allows the convolution operation to cover a wider area, without heavily affecting the original convolution operation performance. The effect could be seen as if we take a kernel and inflate it by inserting zeros between kernel elements; some features are nullified from the operation because of those zero value elements; i.e. there are terms of zero value in the right side of Eq. 1. Therefore, only the non-zero kernel elements contribute to compose the feature maps; using features that are even more sparse. The rest

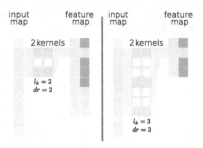

Fig. 2. Dilated convolutions explanatory illustration, two kernels with different lengths and different values of dilatation rate (considering $s_c = 1$)

of the operations remain as they were normal convolutions. Each time kernel moves according to the stride value, the resultant feature map includes less redundant features and at the same time keeps enough relevant ones. Equation 4 shows how the length of a kernel l_k is affected by the dilatation rate dr. Figure 2 illustrates a dilated convolution with two examples.

$$\hat{l_k} = l_k + (l_k - 1)(dr - 1) \tag{4}$$

It is clear that, dilated convolution also changes the output dimension of the feature maps. Equation 5 is a modification of Eq. 2, and shows the relation of the output dimension, when dilatation rate (dr) already changed the kernel length $\hat{l_k}$. It is also clear that when $l_k = 1$ Eq. 5 becomes exactly as Eq. 2; this is something to be considered for choosing the criteria to build the deep learning architecture (Sect. 4).

$$l_o = l_{fm} = \left\lfloor \frac{l_i + 2p - \hat{l_k}}{s_c} \right\rfloor + 1 \tag{5}$$

2.2 ASCAD Dataset

ASCAD dataset was introduced in [32] with the purpose of being a common dataset, to conduct benchmarking related to side-channel profiled attacks using machine learning techniques. The ATMega8515 was the device from which the traces were collected. The EM radiation was recorded while the device executed an AES-128 [12] software implementation. A masking countermeasure was used to protect the cryptographic operation [3]. In the acquisition campaign, an oscilloscope with the EM sensor sampled the signal at 2 GS/s.

The structure of this dataset allocates traces into two groups; *profiling_traces* which contains traces to perform the profiling stage and *attack_traces*, which contains traces to perform the attack stage. The dataset has two versions, collected traces with fixed key encryption and collected traces with random key encryption. In the work [40], they used ASCAD fixed key; to establish a comparison we have used this dataset in the first experiment. The *profiling_traces* group contains 50 000 traces and the *attack_traces* group contains 10 000. The traces in both of the groups have 700 sample points, and they are the points of interest of the crypto operation (the masked S-box for the sensitive value).

For the rest of the experiments, we have used ASCAD random key version since it represents a challenging way to conduct a profiling attack. For this version, *profiling_traces* contains 200 000 traces and *attack_traces* contains 100 000 traces. In the experimental section (Sect. 5), Tables 2 and 3 show the amount of traces of each group used to perform training. Each trace has a length of 1 400 sample points. As in the fixed version, these are the points of interest of the crypto operation.

Traces can be desynchronised by applying a threshold (N) that moves traces around x-axis. The common values to perform the benchmarking are $N = 0$, $N = 50$, and $N = 100$. In the experiment, we have only used $N = 0$ and $N = 100$; the latter value lets enough evidence that the proposed method is feasible as well for $N = 50$.

Sensitive value of traces has the model represented by the Eq. 6 where the value of Z represents the class that labelled the traces associated with the same index. The byte that is intended to exploit is the third value ($i = 3$). The p represents the plain text, and k is the possible key hypothesis.

$$Z[i] = \text{Sbox}[p[i] \oplus k[i]] \tag{6}$$

All the samples were standardised and normalised between 0 and 1 to accelerate the learning process [15]. For the first experiment, we have used the same training hyperparameters as in [40] as well as the same setup for the attack phase. For the experiments using ASCAD random key, the attack traces are randomly shuffled and a battery of 100 attacks are performed to obtain the average value.

2.3 Guessing Entropy

The guessing entropy (GE) [35] is commonly used as a metric to assess the performance of a side-channel attack. It represents the average number of the key candidates required to obtain the secret key k after conducting a side-channel analysis. To give a specific example, let consider the 5000 randomly chosen traces, an attack using these traces results in a GE vector $\vec{g} = [g_1, g_2, \ldots, g_{|K|}]$ where K represents the keyspace. Each component g_i is ordered from the maximum to the minimum value of probability. Then, the GE is the average position of k in the vector $\vec{g}$ over many experiments. By using a battery of 100 experiments, we obtain an *averaged guessing entropy* for adequately estimating the performance of the attack.

2.4 Visualisation of Feature Selection

The ability of a neural network to extract relevant feature can be visualised using the following techniques. *Gradient visualisation* [25] computes the value of the derivatives regarding the input trace, the resultant value is used to point out what feature needs to be modified the least, to affect the loss function the most. This technique gives information about what time samples influence the most in the classification; when those time samples are compared with other visualisation techniques, one can evaluate how well the neural network extracts the important features. *Signal-to-Noise Ratio* (SNR) [22] points out the time samples in leakage traces that contain exploitable information. We used it to compare with gradient visualisation and see how the time points match in each result. *Weight Visualisation* [40] helps to understand how the convolutional part of a CNN performs the feature selection. By comparing the shape of this latter technique with gradient visualisation, one can evaluate how well the feature learning part did to help the classification part.

3   Works in CNN for Side-Channel Analysis

In this section, we briefly mention related works in the context of using CNN for SCA.

The first works in using CNN architecture for SCA were [20,32] concluding that VGG [34] was the best architecture in addressing side-channel analysis. After these papers, others became available showing results against countermeasures such as those jitter-based and masking [4,5]. Other publications focused on understanding theoretically, and visually how deep learning models are capable of bypassing the countermeasure and compromising the security such as [25,29,40]. CNN has also been used for non-profiled attacks [37]. Additionally, in the same contribution, the ability of deep neural networks to fit high-order side-channel leakages was shown.

Recent works have looked into modifications of the architecture of the CNN, not just on changing the hyperparameters, but trying to feed the neural network with more inputs (with additional data) to improve the performance [18]. Feature selection has also been covered in SCA, Picek et al. show the relevance of applying techniques for choosing features to increase the performance of the learning algorithm [30]. In [21], the authors present several experiments for building the first convolutional block related to scattered leaks[1].

One of the most recent works in showing a methodology to build a CNN for side-channel analysis is [40]. In that paper, the conducted analysis shows how to setup kernels in the first convolutional block; for avoiding composing feature maps that include many irrelevant as well as redundant features. As we already mentioned in the previous section, such mis practice impacts negatively on the performance. The work assesses other aspects concerning pooling operation, and they claim that a *pooling stride* should also be set in a way that the pooling kernel does not take repetitive features.

All these works have integrated reliable conclusions that are still used in the state-of-the-art. To the best of our knowledge, dilated convolutions have not been presented into SCA context yet. Some references on using them in image classification applications exist [7,17,28,39].

---

[1] i.e. intermediate value and mask leaks.

4   Dilated Convolutions Design Considerations

Here we discuss the design considerations for CNN architectures with dilated convolutions for SCA, as well as the potential pitfall of using them.

We offer a takeaway when one opts for the presented approach. As the reader can see, they are substantially similar to the state-of-the-art. This is because dilated convolution follows the basis of avoiding collecting irrelevant features. What follows are the criteria and their explanation for building deep learning architecture. At the same time, they justify the usage of the dilated convolution. It must be understood that dilatation rate is also a hyperparameter so that the process to find the best value for it relies on a trade-off between it and the others.

- **Reduce overusing of relevant features:** It has been shown that a kernel which covers long areas of the signal, tends to build feature maps that contain a lot of redundant features. When that happens, the elements in the feature map do not represent the actual relevance of the essential points [19]. Their values are close or equivalent to each other. Dilated convolution reduces the overuses of relevant points because zeros between kernel weights nullify a portion of them.
- **Kernel length and dilatation rate:** Having evidenced that the leak could be scattered through sample points [2,11,38], and a kernel length should cover the leak of the intermediate values as well as the leak of the mask [21,36]. It is not enough to avoid the overuse of relevant points by setting the first convolutional block with small kernel length. The kernel must be able to take these scattered leaks and conducts the operation; dilated convolution covers this issue.
- **Pooling stride:** Keeping the pooling stride S_p value big enough is also mandatory to have in mind. This resolution was already addressed in [40]; a pooling operation should not compromise relevant features already refined by the convolution layer.
- **Desynchronisation:** The conclusions in [40] also stresses the fact that avoiding deep architecture could have a positive impact on the presence of desynchronisation. This is an aspect that we cover by using dilated convolutions, recall that having gathered better feature maps in earlier convolutional blocks reduce the need for adding more of them. We depict this fact in the last experiment, we have used the same architecture for both ASCAD sync and ASCAD desync with $N = 100$, achieving good results. We have only changed values for each training stage and values for the kernel length as well as the dilatation rate for the first convolutional block.
- **Do not dilate too much:** Regarding the fact that we can lose too much information. It is clear that there isn't total control about how relevant the points are being nullified when using dilated convolution, so it's also possible to lose too many of them; this is a potential pitfall of using dilated convolution.

Takeaway Message:

1. For the two first points, we suggest evaluating with a small kernel length and dilatation rate values, e.g. $l_k = 7$ and $dr = 2$. Then, one should increase them iteratively finding a good trade-off. Recall, those values are related to the way the leaks are scattered in the leakage signal. A leakage analysis might help to identify the leaky points [19].
2. A recommended value for the *pooling stride* is at least the length of the pooling kernel i.e. $l_{pk} = S_p$ (as is exemplified in Fig. 1(b)).
3. In the presence of desynchronization, it is feasible to go for longer kernels, since the leakage is even more scattered. As in the first point the values to begin with heavily depend on the length of the input map, set these values having in mind that a low dilatation rate, dilates the kernel in a multiplicative way.
4. To avoid the pitfall, we recommend finding a trade-off in the number of kernels specified for the convolution layer that uses dilated convolutions. By doing so, one composes enough feature maps and preserves as many relevant features as possible. Another recommendation is to try with different kernel lengths to see the impact of changing the value. We provide one experiment to exemplify this.

Taking these considerations, the suggested architecture is summarised in Table 1 in Sect. 5.2. Note that the proposed architecture follows the rule of thumbs about the number of kernels. We use this single architecture to perform different experiments. Some values in Table 1 are fixed according to experiments, and they are set to the respective ones. To build deep learning models for the experiment we have used Python *Keras* library [9], and TensorFlow as back-end [1]. As a classification problem that has more than one class, we have use *Softmax* as the activation function for the output layer, and categorical cross-entropy [26] as the loss function. The optimiser was set to *Adam* [15] using *batch size* of 256 and a *learning rate* of 10^{-3}. Recall that these training hyperparameters and this CNN architecture are only used in the experiment with ASCAD random key version.

5   Experimental Results and Discussions

In this section, we report on the results that were achieved by using dilated convolution using synchronised and desynchronised ASCAD traces.

5.1   ASCAD Fixed Key (N = 0)

To compare with state-of-the-art results[2], we conducted experiments using different values of l_k and dr to train the CNN suggested in the latest work in [40].

---

[2] https://github.com/gabzai/Methodology-for-efficient-CNN-architectures-in-SCA.

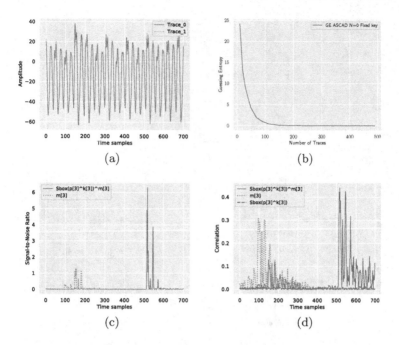

Fig. 3. (a) Two traces from ASCAD fixed key (N = 0); (b) GE baseline using CNN from [40]; (c) SNR of unmasked sensitive value and mask; (d) Correlation analysis

We have keep all the training hyperparameters as in that work[3]. Then, the experiments are conducted with the following hyperparamenters of the first convolutional block: $A1 : [l_k = 1]$, $A2 : [l_k = 16, dr = 4]$, $A3 : [l_k = 16, dr = 6]$, $A4 : [l_k = 32, dr = 3]$, $A5 : [l_k = 64, dr = 2]$.

We have in Fig. 3(b) the value of GE obtained from the CNN model in [40]. Thanks to the fact that the information of the masks and the sensitive values are available in ASCAD dataset [37], we can compute the SNR of the unmasked sensitive value and the mask Fig. 3(c) and Fig. 3(d) shows the correlation analysis, both with regard to the third byte. As we said, SNR gives us information about the points of the leakage signal that are exploitable. In ASCAD fixed key two intervals are remarkable $I_1 = [90, 300]$ and $I_2 = [450, 600]$. Although I_1 regard to unmasked sensitive value is barely visible in the SNR plot, the correlation analysis emphasises that in this area, there is some exploitable information [37]. In fact, I_1 is the interval where the two signals overlap, which represents a convenient situation because both leaks are matched.

Figure 4(a) depicts all the five attacks. Looking at these results, we argue that by having achieved the same outcome with most of the cases, the dilated convolution approach is feasible. Recall that the CNN model presented in [40] is

---

[3] Including *One Cycle Policy* to deal with the learning rate.

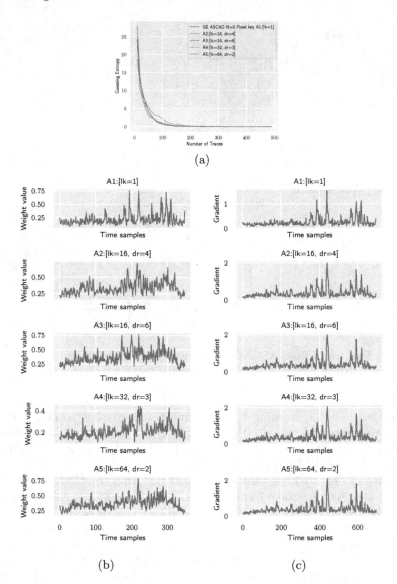

Fig. 4. (a) GE from different values of l_k and dr; (b) Weight visualisation; (c) Gradient visualisation

one of the minimal models regard to the complexity ever presented. The model relies on the analysis and performance of having a $l_k = 1$. It indicates that the dilatation rate is a useful hyperparameter for building CNN for SCA.

Figure 4(b) and (c) depict the weight visualisation and gradient visualisation of the five models trained respectively. In general, all the models detect points of interest in similar intervals of time samples, some of those points match with the SNR and correlation analysis in Fig. 3(c) and (d). The gradient visualisation gives us a sign that no feature information was lost from the feature learning process (convolutional part) to the classification part [40].

It's worth mentioning that the configuration of $A4$ appears to be an outlier. Its GE converges to zero in $[200, 300]$ and not in $[100, 200]$ like the others. The reader can interpret it as an example of finding a trade-off of the kernel length and dilatation rate.

5.2 Attack over Synchronised ASCAD Random Key (N = 0)

In the following experiments, we show a CNN with dilated convolution that performs better than previous approaches. To set a baseline to compare with Fig. 5(a) depicts the shape of two *synchronised* traces from ASCAD dataset random key (profiling_traces) and Fig. 5(b) shows a guessing entropy achieved by the model presented in [21]. As we did in the previous experiment, we have computed the SNR (and the correlation) to visualise the intervals in the leakage traces which are exploitable; the results are depicted in Fig. 5(c) and (d).

Table 1. Architecture of the CNN for experiments using ASCAD random key

Hyperparameter	Value	Additional info of values
Input shape	(1400, 1)	
Conv layers	(32, 64, 128)	SeLU, He uniform, l_{k1} and dr varies according to experiments, $l_{k2} = 25$, $l_{k3} = 3$
Regulatization	Batch normalisation	
Pooling type	Average	$(l_{pk1} = s_{p1} = 2, l_{pk2} = s_{p2} = 25,$ $l_{pk3} = s_{p3} = 4)$
FC	3 FC layers of 15 units each	SeLU, He uniform
Dense	256 units	Softmax

Comparing Lengths and Dilatation Rate

We consider the length of the kernel that could be the best choice, to achieve an efficient and effective attack (in terms of number of traces), and at the same time to show that is not only about covering all the time samples where the leak happens. To show this in practice, we performed 4 experiments under the next combinations of values; $l_k = 1$, $l_k = 32$, $l_k = 64$, $l_k = 32, dr = 2$ with the deep learning architecture as presented in Table 1. In Table 2, a summary of the values used in the training stage is presented.

During training, 75 *epochs* were used in all the experiments. However, when we had found out the presence of overfitting or underfitting, we adjusted these values, until we notice almost the same tendency in the loss and validation loss for all of them. Besides, as those two metrics have been shown to be not

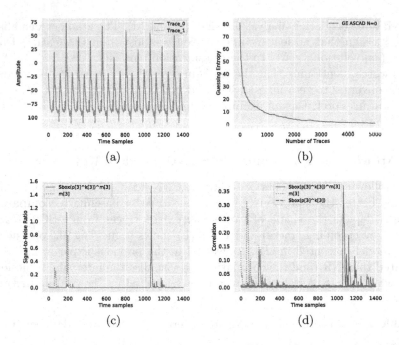

Fig. 5. (a) Two traces from ASCAD random key (N = 0); (b) GE baseline using CNN from [21]; (c) SNR of unmasked sensitive value and mask; (d) Correlation analysis

reliable as a side-channel metric [31], also a cross-validation setup was used. All four results are depicted in Fig. 6(a). Our goal is to show how a dilated convolution outperforms the attack effectiveness. So, the comparison was using the same architecture with values of kernel lengths suggested in the state of the art publications.

Note how the GE result of $l_k = 32$ and $l_k = 64$ are worse in approximating to the baseline. It might be caused for the accumulation of irrelevant features. In contrast, observe how the result with $l_k = 32, dr = 2$ outperform the GE. Note, the length of the kernel is practically the same as in the third one, but

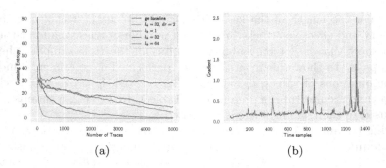

Fig. 6. (a) Guessing entropy of the four experiments; (b) Gradient visualisation result of $l_k = 32, dr = 2$

here we include less irrelevant and redundant features because of the dilatation. Figure 6(b) shows the gradient visualisation of the latter result; the relevant time samples match with the SNR in Fig. 5(c).

Table 2. Values of the training stage for synchronised traces

Parameter	Value
Number of profiling traces	45000
Number of validation traces	5000
Epochs	75

Mimic Dilated Convolution with Stride Values

In this experiment, we show the achieved performance when the behaviour of the dilated convolution is imitated with small kernel sizes, and stride values that allow skipping some features. The GE of this experiment is depicted in Fig. 7(a).

The result tells us, that although the efficiency achieved by doing this imitation is less than using dilated convolutions, kernel length of 1 with a stride value of 3 tends towards a successful attack[4], demonstrating the effect of taking many times the same features. By comparing with dilated convolution, we demonstrate that reducing redundant and irrelevant features is not the total answer. In some cases, the efficiency could improve if the evaluator considers the fact that features in the input map might present long-range dependencies, i.e. the scattered leakage of the mask and intermediate values, so a dilated convolution comes to outperform the results of the evaluation. By comparing the gradient results in Fig. 6(b), and Fig. 7(c)–(d) one can see how efficiently each model performs the feature selection. Each one of them matches respectively with its GE.

Different Lengths with Same Dilatation Rate

Dilatation rate is also under the heuristic nature of deep learning, and it must be included in the tuning process of the deep learning architecture. Although dilated convolution discards features being or not irrelevant, there is no way (at least at the moment) to say that it is performing feature engineering, the feature selection is still not under the control of the evaluator or designer. The experiment, whose result is depicted in Fig. 7(b), was conducted to show that by using the approach of dilated convolution, one could also damage the performance. The kernel is taking not enough relevant features, or a lot of relevant features are being nullified in the interval covers by the kernel.

As we mentioned in Sect. 4, it is recommended to apply a longer kernel or increase the number of kernels, a trade-off should be found over these two hyperparameters. Keep in mind that by increasing the number of kernels in a

---

[4] As well as kernel length of 3 with stride value of 6.

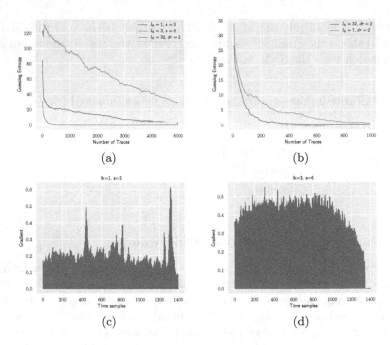

Fig. 7. (a) GE of examples that mimic dilated convolution; (b) Effect over GE with same dilatation rate and different lengths; (c) Gradient visualisation result of $l_k = 1, s = 3$; (d) Gradient visualisation result of $l_k = 3, s = 6$

convolutional block, the next one should follow the rule of thumb, i.e. increase the number of kernels by the power of 2. In Fig. 7(b) we have the result of having two dilated kernel whose lengths are considerably different in terms of dilatation rate, i.e. using a dilatation rate of 2 with a kernel size of 7, its effective size becomes 14, whilst the effective size of a kernel of 32 becomes 64. As the reader can see, different performances are achieved.

5.3   Attack over Desynchronised ASCAD Random Key (N = 100)

The last experiment considers the impact of having desynchronised traces. For this, we have used the same architecture as in the previous experiments. Figure 8 shows four combinations of values, a kernel length of 64 with a dilatation rate of 3 being the best where these were the only changes in the architecture. It is demonstrated that dilated convolution can bypass desynchronisation, reaching a considerable good performance. Mention that by having used the same architecture as in the experiment without it, we have evidenced that dilated convolution also reduces the complexity of the deep learning model. Over certain circumstances, a convolutional block that uses dilated convolution composes better feature maps. Those lead to a better characterisation of the leakage traces. So, there is no need to add more layers to the architecture.

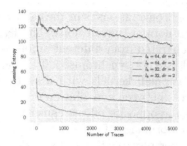

Fig. 8. Guessing entropy over desynchronised ASCAD traces (N = 100)

Table 3. Values of the training stage for desynchronised traces (N = 100)

Parameter	Value
Number of profiling traces	55000
Number of validation traces	7000
Epochs	100

Recall that to attack desynchronised signals successfully is trickier. Even though the same architecture was used, we did a few changes in the kernel length and dilatation rate, as well as changes in the training values. Table 3 summarises the latter. As we said, to deal with the effect of the desynchronisation, a trade-off of kernel length and dilatation rate must be found. Being advantageous is the fact that one can find an architecture that is useful for different scenarios.

These values make sense; longer kernel is required to combine the leaks cause relevant points between traces are more scattered when they are desynchronised, the same reason why the kernel needs to be more dilated. One could argue that if this is the case, an even simpler architecture could be found for the previous experiments. While we do not question that statement, being in a scenario where the evaluator must address synchronised and desynchronised tests, he could rely on the fact that the same architecture could achieve suitable results in both.

6 Conclusions and Perspectives

In this paper, we have used dilated convolution to build up a CNN. The results show that by using this type of convolutions, a boosting effect over the performance of a deep learning-based side-channel attack is achieved. The arguments that support our theory are taken from the already addressed aspect about decreasing the redundancy of relevant points of the input signal. These points are used for composing feature maps in the convolutional blocks of a CNN. Having a useful feature map that characterises well enough the input signal, leads to a reduction of the number of convolutional blocks in the architecture, which directly represents a reduction of the deep learning model complexity.

The potential of dilated convolutions is in the capability to inflate the kernel, covering wider areas than normal convolutions. The leakage in the trace could imply samples that are separated from different amounts of samples in between, more if the leakage signals are not synchronised. This capability is not presented in large kernels as well as small kernels with a stride value big enough, that allows them to avoid points between convolution operations. The lack of this in normal convolutions has the opposite effect, causing a negative impact on not being able to reach the performance of the dilated convolution.

From the evaluator's perspective, it has been shown that a single dilated convolutional-based model could reach enough performance boost to address the requirement of a test in both synchronised and desynchronised scenarios. However, one should bear in mind that small changes in the hyperparameter are still required. Dilated convolutions have demonstrated to be a hyperparameter that could lead to new CNN architectures which increase the threat of profiled attacks. In future works, we will systematically exploit the effect of using this approach for building deep learning models. Also, we will study other architectures that may present different behaviour when this alteration is applied, as well as study more complex data, i.e. 32-bits platforms, covering scenarios where the noise becomes an important factor when evaluating implementations of cryptographic algorithms.

Concerning the way, we could protect the latter; we are aiming for evaluating a combination of countermeasures, i.e. higher level of masking and hiding. Since hiding countermeasures try to stabilise the power consumption, the learning algorithm will detect fewer variations; this is going to impact its classification score, which could be a way to affect the performance of the attack.

References

1. Abadi, M., et al.: TensorFlow: large-scale machine learning on heterogeneous systems, software available from tensorflow.org (2015). https://www.tensorflow.org/
2. Belgarric, P., et al.: Time-frequency analysis for second-order attacks. In: Francillon, A., Rohatgi, P. (eds.) CARDIS 2013. LNCS, vol. 8419, pp. 108–122. Springer, Cham (2014). https://doi.org/10.1007/978-3-319-08302-5_8
3. Blömer, J., Guajardo, J., Krummel, V.: Provably secure masking of AES. In: Handschuh, H., Hasan, M.A. (eds.) SAC 2004. LNCS, vol. 3357, pp. 69–83. Springer, Heidelberg (2004). https://doi.org/10.1007/978-3-540-30564-4_5
4. Cagli, E., Dumas, C., Prouff, E.: Convolutional neural networks with data augmentation against jitter-based countermeasures. In: Fischer, W., Homma, N. (eds.) CHES 2017. LNCS, vol. 10529, pp. 45–68. Springer, Cham (2017). https://doi.org/10.1007/978-3-319-66787-4_3
5. Cagli, E., Dumas, C., Prouff, E.: Kernel discriminant analysis for information extraction in the presence of masking. In: Lemke-Rust, K., Tunstall, M. (eds.) CARDIS 2016. LNCS, vol. 10146, pp. 1–22. Springer, Cham (2017). https://doi.org/10.1007/978-3-319-54669-8_1
6. Chari, S., Rao, J.R., Rohatgi, P.: Template attacks. In: Kaliski, B.S., Koç, K., Paar, C. (eds.) CHES 2002. LNCS, vol. 2523, pp. 13–28. Springer, Heidelberg (2003). https://doi.org/10.1007/3-540-36400-5_3

7. Chen, L., Papandreou, G., Kokkinos, I., Murphy, K., Yuille, A.L.: DeepLab: semantic image segmentation with deep convolutional nets, atrous convolution, and fully connected CRFs. IEEE Trans. Pattern Anal. Mach. Intell. **40**(4), 834–848 (2018)
8. Choi, K., Fazekas, G., Sandler, M., Cho, K.: Convolutional recurrent neural networks for music classification. In: 2017 IEEE International Conference on Acoustics, Speech and Signal Processing (ICASSP), pp. 2392–2396. IEEE (2017)
9. Chollet, F., et al.: Keras (2015). https://keras.io
10. Choudary, M.O., Kuhn, M.G.: Efficient, portable template attacks. IEEE Trans. Inf. Forensics Secur. **13**(2), 490–501 (2018)
11. Coron, J.S., Prouff, E., Rivain, M., Roche, T.: Higher-order side channel security and mask refreshing. In: Moriai, S. (ed.) Fast Software Encryption, pp. 410–424. Springer, Heidelberg (2014). https://doi.org/10.1007/978-3-662-43933-3_21
12. Daemen, J., Rijmen, V.: The Design of Rijndael. Springer, Heidelberg (2002). https://doi.org/10.1007/978-3-662-04722-4
13. Dumoulin, V., Visin, F.: A guide to convolution arithmetic for deep learning. arXiv preprint arXiv:1603.07285 (2016)
14. Fan, G., Zhou, Y., Zhang, H., Feng, D.: How to choose interesting points for template attacks more effectively? In: Yung, M., Zhu, L., Yang, Y. (eds.) INTRUST 2014. LNCS, vol. 9473, pp. 168–183. Springer, Cham (2015). https://doi.org/10.1007/978-3-319-27998-5_11
15. Goodfellow, I., Bengio, Y., Courville, A.: Deep Learning. MIT press (2016)
16. Hajra, S., Mukhopadhyay, D.: Multivariate leakage model for improving non-profiling DPA on noisy power traces. In: Lin, D., Xu, S., Yung, M. (eds.) Inscrypt 2013. LNCS, vol. 8567, pp. 325–342. Springer, Cham (2014). https://doi.org/10.1007/978-3-319-12087-4_21
17. Hamaguchi, R., Fujita, A., Nemoto, K., Imaizumi, T., Hikosaka, S.: Effective use of dilated convolutions for segmenting small object instances in remote sensing imagery. In: 2018 IEEE Winter Conference on Applications of Computer Vision (WACV), pp. 1442–1450 (2018)
18. Hettwer, B., Gehrer, S., Güneysu, T.: Profiled power analysis attacks using convolutional neural networks with domain knowledge. In: Selected Areas in Cryptography - SAC 2018–25th International Conference, Calgary, AB, Canada, 15–17 August 2018, Revised Selected Papers, pp. 479–498 (2018)
19. Hettwer, B., Gehrer, S., Güneysu, T.: Deep neural network attribution methods for leakage analysis and symmetric key recovery. In: Paterson, K.G., Stebila, D. (eds.) SAC 2019. LNCS, vol. 11959, pp. 645–666. Springer, Cham (2020). https://doi.org/10.1007/978-3-030-38471-5_26
20. Kim, J., Picek, S., Heuser, A., Bhasin, S., Hanjalic, A.: Make some noise: unleashing the power of convolutional neural networks for profiled side-channel analysis. IACR Cryptology ePrint Archive **2018**, 1023 (2018)
21. Maghrebi, H.: Deep learning based side channel attacks in practice. IACR Cryptology ePrint Archive **2019**, 578 (2019)
22. Mangard, S., Oswald, E., Popp, T.: Power Analysis Attacks: Revealing the Secrets of Smart Cards, vol. 31. Springer, Boston (2008). https://doi.org/10.1007/978-0-387-38162-6
23. Martinasek, Z., Dzurenda, P., Malina, L.: Profiling power analysis attack based on MLP in DPA contest V4.2. In: 2016 39th International Conference on Telecommunications and Signal Processing (TSP), pp. 223–226 (2016)
24. Martinasek, Z., Zapletal, O., Vrba, K., Trasy, K.: Power analysis attack based on the MLP in DPA contest v4 (07 2015)

25. Masure, L., Dumas, C., Prouff, E.: Gradient visualization for general characterization in profiling attacks. In: Polian, I., Stöttinger, M. (eds.) International Workshop on Constructive Side-Channel Analysis and Secure Design, pp. 145–167. Springer (2019). https://doi.org/10.1007/978-3-030-16350-1_9

26. Masure, L., Dumas, C., Prouff, E.: A comprehensive study of deep learning for side-channel analysis. IACR Trans. Cryptographic Hardware Embed. Syst. **2020**, 348–375 (2020)

27. Ng, A.Y.: Feature selection, L1 vs. L2 regularization, and rotational invariance. In: Proceedings of the Twenty-First International Conference on Machine Learning, ICML 2004, p. 78. Association for Computing Machinery, New York (2004)

28. van den Oord, A., et al.: WaveNet: a generative model for raw audio. In: SSW (2016)

29. Perin, G., Ege, B., Chmielewski, L.: Neural Network Model Assessment for Side-Channel Analysis. IACR Cryptology ePrint Archive **2019**, 722 (2019)

30. Picek, S., Heuser, A., Jovic, A., Batina, L., Legay, A.: The secrets of profiling for side-channel analysis: feature selection matters. IACR Cryptology ePrint Archive **2017**, 1110 (2017)

31. Picek, S., Heuser, A., Jovic, A., Bhasin, S., Regazzoni, F.: The curse of class imbalance and conflicting metrics with machine learning for side-channel evaluations. IACR Trans. Cryptogr. Hardw. Embed. Syst. **2019**, 209–237 (2018)

32. Prouff, E., Strullu, R., Benadjila, R., Cagli, E., Canovas, C.: Study of deep learning techniques for side-channel analysis and introduction to ASCAD database. IACR Cryptology ePrint Archive **2018**, 53 (2018)

33. Rechberger, C., Oswald, E.: Practical template attacks. In: Lim, C.H., Yung, M. (eds.) WISA 2004. LNCS, vol. 3325, pp. 440–456. Springer, Heidelberg (2005). https://doi.org/10.1007/978-3-540-31815-6_35

34. Simonyan, K., Zisserman, A.: Very deep convolutional networks for large-scale image recognition. CoRR abs/1409.1556 (2014)

35. Standaert, F.-X., Malkin, T.G., Yung, M.: A unified framework for the analysis of side-channel key recovery attacks. In: Joux, A. (ed.) EUROCRYPT 2009. LNCS, vol. 5479, pp. 443–461. Springer, Heidelberg (2009). https://doi.org/10.1007/978-3-642-01001-9_26

36. Thiebeauld, H., Vasselle, A., Wurcker, A.: Second-order scatter attack. IACR Cryptology ePrint Archive **2019**, 345 (2019)

37. Timon, B.: Non-profiled deep learning-based side-channel attacks with sensitivity analysis. IACR Trans. Cryptogr. Hardw. Embed. Syst. **2019**(2), 107–131 (2019)

38. Waddle, J., Wagner, D.: Towards efficient second-order power analysis. In: Joye, M., Quisquater, J.-J. (eds.) CHES 2004. LNCS, vol. 3156, pp. 1–15. Springer, Heidelberg (2004). https://doi.org/10.1007/978-3-540-28632-5_1

39. Yu, F., Koltun, V.: Multi-scale context aggregation by dilated convolutions. CoRR abs/1511.07122 (2016)

40. Zaid, G., Bossuet, L., Habrard, A., Venelli, A.: Methodology for efficient CNN architectures in profiling attacks. IACR Trans. Cryptographic Hardware Embed. Syst. **2020**(1), 1–36 (2019)

AIoTS – Artificial Intelligence and Industrial IoT Security

ARM-AFL: Coverage-Guided Fuzzing Framework for ARM-Based IoT Devices

Rong Fan$^{(\boxtimes)}$ (iD), Jianfeng Pan, and Shaomang Huang

Security Engineering Institute, Qihoo 360, Beijing, China
fanrong1@360.cn, panjianfeng@360.cn, huangshaomang@360.cn

Abstract. With the proliferation of IoT devices, an increasing number of attack surfaces are exposed to malicious hackers. Discovering vulnerabilities in IoT devices and patching them is imperative. However, there is a lack of effective tools to help IoT developers discover vulnerabilities in their code. Fuzzing is an effective and widely used technique to discover software vulnerabilities in general-purpose computers. In this paper, we present ARM-AFL, an effective, coverage-guided fuzzing framework for ARM-based IoT devices. ARM-AFL instruments software during compilation and runs fuzzing directly on IoT devices. This addresses compatibility issues in user-mode emulation and provides higher throughput than full-system emulation. We also design a light-weight heap memory corruption detector (lwHMCD), which is able to detect three kinds of silent heap memory corruptions. By combining ARM-AFL and lwHMCD, IoT developers can discover vulnerabilities before an attacker does.

Keywords: IoT · Fuzzing · Vulnerability · Compatibility · Throughput

1 Introduction

The growth of people's desire for convenient life makes the intellectualization of embedded devices an irresistible trend. And with the evolution of IoT Technology, more and more embedded devices are being connected to the internet. At the end of 2019, the total number of IoT devices that are in use worldwide has reached 9.5 billion, excluding mobile phones, tablets and laptops. And the number of IoT devices is expected to increase to 28 billion by 2025 [1]. But the lack of effective IoT vulnerability detection tools could make IoT devices vulnerable to attack and leave almost everyone at danger. Therefore, it is an urgent matter to help IoT developers secure their code.

Fuzzing is proved to be an effective technique to discover vulnerabilities in real-world programs. In early time, fuzzers only feed a program with random inputs and monitor its running status. Modern fuzzers, like AFL, use code coverage to guide the fuzzing process. This makes Modern fuzzers much more effective than traditional fuzzers. Unfortunately, modern fuzzers are mainly focused on i386 or x86_64 architectures, but most of the IoT devices are based on ARM. As

© Springer Nature Switzerland AG 2020
J. Zhou et al. (Eds.): ACNS 2020 Workshops, LNCS 12418, pp. 239–254, 2020.
https://doi.org/10.1007/978-3-030-61638-0_14

a consequence, IoT developers are unable to utilize modern fuzzing technique to secure their code.

There are three fundamental problems in IoT fuzzing. The first is compatibility. IoT programs strongly depend on particular hardware components of their devices. Without proper hardware support, testing IoT programs with fuzzers would encounter unexpected failures. For instance, using AFL's user-mode emulation to fuzz IoT programs would not work in most cases. The second is throughput. Throughput is one of the most important benchmark of fuzzing. For IoT fuzzing, full-system emulation may solve some compatibility issues, but throughput is quite low. The third is code coverage. The higher the code coverage, the more likely it is to trigger a vulnerability. Despite the high compatibility and throughput of directly performing blackbox fuzzing on real IoT devices, code coverage is far from satisfied.

Recent research on the vulnerability detection of IoT programs has tried to solve these problems from different perspectives. Avatar [10] combines emulator and real device to enable dynamic analysis for embedded firmware. FIRMA-DYNE [6] takes advantage of full-system emulation to achieve high compatibility. IoTFuzzer [4] utilizes the information embedded in the companion apps to perform blackbox fuzzing on real devices. FIRM-AFL combines full-system emulation and user-mode emulation to overcome the limitations of using only one of them.

All of these techniques can apply fuzzing on IoT programs, but they only solve some of the problems and have limitations. The compatibility and throughput of the techniques which utilize emulation cannot be obtained at the same time. Zheng et al. [3] points out, although full-system emulation could provide a high compatibility, it sacrifices 10 times more throughput than user-mode emulation. Despite the information collected, the code coverage of blackbox fuzzing is much lower than that of coverage-guided fuzzing.

Our Approach. In this work, we present ARM-AFL, a high throughput greybox fuzzer, which is able to run coverage-guided fuzzing on ARM-based IoT devices. Unlike existing techniques which mainly rely on emulation for IoT fuzzing, ARM-AFL performs greybox fuzzing directly on real devices. To achieve this, we add an instrument function for ARM jump instructions to ARM-AFL, so that it could properly instrument with ARM assembly files. We also implement *trampoline* and *payload* for ARM architecture, which can enable code coverage calculation for ARM-AFL.

Contributions. In summary, we make following contributions in this paper:

- We summary the state-of-the-art IoT vulnerability detection techniques. Both static and dynamic techniques are discussed and their limitations are analyzed.
- We implement ARM-AFL which is able to run coverage-guided fuzzing on ARM-based IoT devices.
- We design a light-weight heap memory corruption detector (lwHMCD) for ARM-AFL.

- We evaluate our approach with open source software to show its efficiency and effectiveness. The result shows that our approach has both high compatibility and high throughput, and it is able to find the known vulnerabilities.

The rest of this paper is organized as follow: In Sect. 2, we discuss fuzzing, AFL and AddressSanitizer. While in Sect. 3, the workflow of AFL and the implementation details of ARM-AFL are explained. Experimental evaluations and analysis are given in Sect. 4. In addition, a review of related work is described in Sect. 5. Finally, the conclusion and potential for future work are presented in Sect. 6.

2 Background

2.1 Fuzzing

Fuzzing is one of the most effective techniques to discover vulnerabilities in program by repeatedly executing it with random inputs. State-of-the-art fuzzers according to how much information is collected and used for the execution, can be categorized into whitebox, blackbox and greybox. Whitebox fuzzers usually utilize program analysis techniques like symbolic execution and taint analysis which introduce extremely high performance overhead to generate the inputs. Blackbox fuzzers don't have any information about the target program, they treat the program as blackbox and execute it without feedback. Greybox fuzzers utilize feedback from the target program execution to guide the generation of inputs.

The most popular fuzzing technique is coverage-guided greybox fuzzing. Greybox fuzzers instrument the target program with extra code, and these code help to collect code coverage information when executing random inputs. Then greybox fuzzers choose input with higher code coverage as seed to generate new inputs. Obviously, continuing to implement this strategy will trigger more and more code paths of the target program. The lightweight instrumentation of greybox fuzzer does not have much impact on target program execution speed. Overall, graybox fuzzers have much higher throughput than whitebox fuzzers and much higher code coverage than blackbox fuzzers.

2.2 AFL

AFL [5] is one of the most popular greybox fuzzer. It has already found numerous vulnerabilities in real-world targets. Compared to other coverage-guided fuzzers, AFL is designed to be practical. It has moderate performance overhead, uses a series of highly effective fuzzing strategies (bitflip, arithmetic, interest, dictionary, havoc, etc) and deduplication of crash tricks. When the source code is available, AFL employs a compile-time instrumentation and genetic algorithms to figure out test cases which are able to trigger new execution path in the target program. These test cases will be added to the seed queue for further fuzzing. And when the source code is not available, AFL utilizes user-mode emulation provided by a patched version of QEMU to instrument the target binary dynamically. QEMU's user-mode emulation uses basic blocks as translation units, and the dynamic instrumentation is implemented on top of this. As a result, AFL is able to perform coverage-guided fuzzing on binary-only targets. The techniques adopted by AFL can help to improve the code coverage for the target program.

2.3 AddressSanitizer

AddressSanitizer (ASAN) [14] is a fast memory corruption detector developed by Google. It detects buffer overflows, use after frees, memory leaks, etc, by instrumenting the memory access instructions and replacing the `malloc()`, `free()` and related functions with a run-time library. If a corruption is detected, the program will print an error message to `stderr` and exit with a non-zero exit code. On average, ASAN's slowdown is just 73% and it has already found hundreds of bugs in web browsers and other software. It is a part of LLVM starting with version 3.1 and a part of GCC starting with version 4.8.

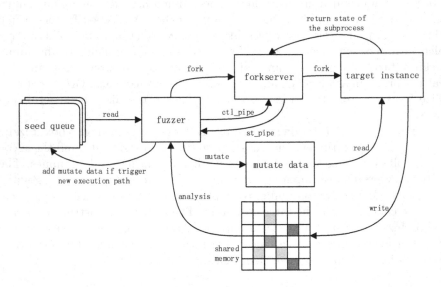

Fig. 1. Workflow of ARM-AFL

3   Implementation

In this section, we will give the implementation details of ARM-AFL.

3.1 Workflow of ARM-AFL

The main components of ARM-AFL are described below:

– **afl-gcc** is a wrapper for *gcc*. It adds several compilation options, like *-g*, *-O*, *-B*, etc. Among them, *-B* is the most critical option, it adds *afl-as*'s path to the assembler's search paths, which leads *afl-as* to perform the actual assembly works.
– **afl-as** performs the instrumentation and converts the assembly code into executable machine code. Instrument function of *afl-as* adds *trampoline* assembly to basic blocks of the target program. And if there is any *trampoline* assembly added, instrument function will add *payload* assembly to target program.
– **afl-fuzz** does the main business of fuzzing the instrumented target program.

We implement the workflow of ARM-AFL basically the same as that of AFL (shown in Fig. 1). At the beginning of fuzzing, *afl-fuzz* forks a child process and this child process uses `execve()` to run the target program up to entry point of the main function. This target program process acts as *forkserver* and repeatedly fork child process which will be fed with mutated inputs. With the help of *forkserver* mechanism, *afl-fuzz* can avoid overhead of `execve()` calls. The parent process of *forkserver* is called *fuzzer*. It communicates with *forkserver* through two pipes. One is *ctl_pipe*, which is used to send commands to *forkserver*. The other is *st_pipe*, which is used to receive `pid` and return state of child process of *forkserver*.

When *forkserver* completes the initialization, it sends a four-byte hello message to *fuzzer*. And if there are any new test cases, *forkserver* will receive a command from *fuzzer*, fork a target program process and send its `pid` back. During the running of the forked process, the instrumented code records executed branches to shared memory created by *fuzzer*. When the forked process finishes executing, *fuzzer* will analysis the record in shared memory and append the test case to seed queue if it triggers new execution path. Finally, *fuzzer* displays on the status screen if the forked process crashes.

3.2   ARM-AFL

In order to allow ARM-AFL to run fuzzing on ARM-based IoT devices, we implement an instrument function, *trampoline* and *payload* for ARM architecture.

Instrument Function. The instrument function in *afl-as* adds *trampoline* to target program basic blocks mainly according to jump instructions. Jump instructions of ARM architecture are different from that of i386 or x86_64 architectures, so we implement a new instrument function for ARM architecture. In the instrument function, a while loop reads assembly files of the target program line by line and write instrumented assembly to a new file. Specifically, instrumentation begins with `.cfi_startproc` and ends with `.cfi_endproc`, which indicate the beginning and ending of a function. *trampoline* is added when the read line contains `.L[digit]` which indicate a jump destination, or jump instructions except `bic`, `b`, `bl` and `blx`. And ARM-AFL also use an environment variable `AFL_INST_RATIO` (a value between 0 and 100) to reduce the odds of instrumenting every discovered branch. The instrument function would generate a random number between 0 and 100, and compare it with AFL_INST_RATIO before instrumenting a branch, the branch is instrumented only if the random number less than AFL_INST_RATIO. After the while loop, if any *trampoline* is added, instrument function will also add *payload* to the new file.

Trampoline. *Trampoline* of ARM architecture is shown in Listing 1.1. The main task of *trampoline* is jumping to __afl_maybe_log (label of *payload*) with a random number as parameter. And this parameter will be used to indicate the current basic block later.

Listing 1.1. assembly of trampoline

```
 1 static const u8 *trampoline_fmt_arm =
 2 "\n"
 3 "/* --- AFL TRAMPOLINE --- */\n"
 4 "\tpush {r0, lr}\n"
 5 "\tldr r0, =#%u\n"
 6 "\tbl __afl_maybe_log\n"
 7 "\tb 1f\n"
 8 "\t.ltorg\n"
 9 "\t1:\n"
10 "\tpop {r0, lr}\n"
11 "/* --- END --- */\n"
12 "\n";
```

Payload. *Payload* has two major modules, *forkserver* and *branch recorder*. *forkserver* module runs only once during whole fuzzing process. As shown in Listing 1.2, it utilizes environment variable (whose name is stored in .AFL_SHM_ENV) created by *fuzzer* to get the shared memory ID (shm_id), then attaches the shared memory segment to the process' address space, finally writes a four-byte message (__afl_temp, an uninitialized variable in the bss section) to *fuzzer* through FORKSRV_FD+1 (which is a copy of *st_pipe*). If *fuzzer* successfully reads four bytes form *forkserver*, it is all set.

Listing 1.2. setup of fork server

```
 1    ldr r0, =.AFL_SHM_ENV
 2    bl getenv
 3
 4    cmp r0, #0
 5    beq __afl_setup_abort
 6
 7    bl atoi
 8
 9    mov r5, r0
10    mov r1,#0
11    mov r2,#0
12    bl shmat
13
14 ...
15
16 __afl_forkserver:
17    ldr r1, =__afl_area_ptr
```

```
18   str r0, [r1]
19   ldr r5, =__afl_temp
20   mov r0, #FORKSRV_FD+1
21   mov r1, r5
22   mov r2, #4
23   bl write
```

After that, *forkserver* enters __afl_fork_wait_loop (shown in Listing 1.3). It waits for fork-command by reading from *fuzzer* (via FORKSRV_FD which is a copy of *ctl_pipe*), then forks a child process when reading successfully. The child process enters __afl_fork_resume which closes pipes, records current branch to shared memory and resumes execution of the target program. Concurrently the parent process writes child_pid to *fuzzer* and waits until the child process ends, then writes the child process end state to *fuzzer*, finally goes to the beginning of __afl_fork_wait_loop and loops again.

Listing 1.3. wait loop of fork server

```
1 __afl_fork_wait_loop:
2    mov r0, #FORKSRV_FD
3    mov r1, r5
4    mov r2, #4
5    bl read
6
7    cmp r0, #4
8    bne __afl_die
9
10   bl fork
11
12   cmp r0, #0
13   blt __afl_die
14
15   beq __afl_fork_resume
16
17   ldr r1, =__afl_fork_pid
18   str r0, [r1]
19   mov r6, r0
20   mov r0, #FORKSRV_FD+1
21   mov r2, #4
22   bl write
23
24   cmp r0, #4
25   bne __afl_die
26
27   mov r0, r6
28   mov r1, r5
29   mov r2, #0
30   bl waitpid
31
32   cmp r0, #0
33   blt __afl_die
34   mov r0, #FORKSRV_FD+1
35   mov r1, r5
36   mov r2, #4
37   bl write
38
39   cmp r0, #4
40   beq __afl_fork_wait_loop
```

Branch recorder runs every time the instrumented branch is triggered. Its pseudo code is shown in Listing 1.4.

Listing 1.4. pseudo code of branch recorder

```
1 cur_location = <COMPILE_TIME_RANDOM>;
2 shared_mem[cur_location^prev_location]++;
3 prev_location = cur_location >> 1;
```

The locations of basic blocks are represented by random values generated during compilation. The *branch recorder* module uses the value of previous location XOR current location as index of the current branch in shared memory and records the number of executions of the current branch there. Assembly of *branch recoder* is shown in Listing 1.5.

Listing 1.5. assembly of branch recorder

```
1 __afl_store:
2   ldr r0, =__afl_area_ptr
3   ldr r0, [r0]
4   ldr r1, =__afl_prev_loc
5   ldr r2, [r1]
6   eor r2, r2, r4
7   ldrb r3, [r0, r2]
8   add r3, r3, #1
9   strb r3, [r0, r2]
10  mov r0, r4, asr#1
11  str r0, [r1]
12 __afl_return:
13  msr APSR_nzcvq, r7
14  pop {r1-r7, pc}
```

3.3   Light-Weight Heap Memory Corruption Detector

According to Muench et al. [24], the vast majority of fuzzing techniques find bugs by detecting crashes which terminate the program immediately or cause some recovery procedures. However, many common security mechanisms (e.g. heap consistency check) which trigger crashes are rarely present on IoT devices. As a result, our fuzzer can encounter unobservable memory corruptions under particular conditions. So we draw on the experience of ASAN and design a light-weight heap memory corruption detector (lwHMCD).

lwHMCD aims to detect *use after free*, *double free* and *heap buffer overflow*. They are unobservable memory corruptions under particular conditions and cannot be detected using ARM-AFL alone. A brief introduction of these three kinds of heap memory corruptions are as follow:

- **Use after free** (uaf) refers to the reuse of a freed pointer which is not set to NULL (also called dangling pointer) [26], and if the memory pointed by the pointer has not been modified, the program is likely to work properly.
- **Double free** [27] occurs when free() is called twice or more with the same pointer as an argument. The program is able to work properly with *double free* under certain circumstances.

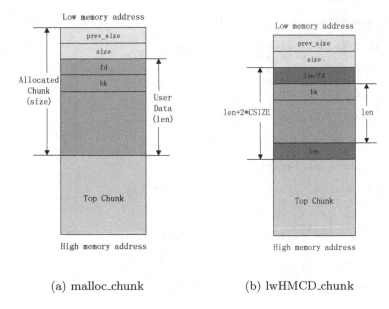

(a) malloc_chunk   (b) lwHMCD_chunk

Fig. 2. Schematic diagram of lwHMCD

- **Heap buffer overflow** [25] is caused by writing more data to a fixed-length buffer located on the heap than what is actually allocated for that buffer. In most cases, *heap buffer overflow* does not crash the program.

Figure 2(a) shows the basic structure of heap buffer implemented in glibc. To achieve heap memory corruption detection, we add the parameter of malloc() at the beginning and end of malloc_chunk's user data (as shown in Fig. 2(b)). The lwHMCD_chunk is implemented by replacing the glibc's dynamic memory functions (free(), malloc(), realloc(), calloc()) with our custom functions (__wrap_free(), __wrap_malloc(), __wrap_realloc(), __wrap_calloc()).

Listing 1.6 depicts the core logic of lwHMCD's functions (__wrap_free() and __wrap_malloc()). They are actually wrappers for glibc's free() and malloc(). When lwHMCD_chunk is freed for the first time, its added field at the beginning (len/fd) would be set to 0 or address of another free chunk by glibc. So if len/fd is equal to 0 or not equal to the added field at the end (at line 9–12), there may be a double free vulnerability. When a heap buffer overflow happens, the added field at the end of lwHMCD_chunk is overwritten, so the checking conditions in __wrap_free() (at line 10–12) would trigger crash.

Listing 1.6. Light weight heap memory corruption detector

```
1 #define CSIZE sizeof(size_t)
2
3 void __wrap_free(void *addr)
4 {
5   if (addr) {
6     // prevent uaf
```

```
 7      memset(addr,0,*(size_t*)((size_t)addr-CSIZE));
 8      // check double free and overflow
 9      if (*(size_t*)((size_t)addr-CSIZE) == 0 ||
10          *(size_t*)((size_t)addr-CSIZE) !=
11          *(size_t*)((size_t)addr +
12          *(size_t*)((size_t)addr-CSIZE))) {
13        raise(SIGSEGV);
14      }
15      __real_free((void*)((size_t)addr-CSIZE));
16    }
17 }
18
19 void* __wrap_malloc(size_t len)
20 {
21   void *addr = __real_malloc(len+2*CSIZE);
22   if (addr) {
23     // add parameter at the beginning and end
24     *(size_t*)addr = len;
25     *(size_t*)((size_t)addr+len+CSIZE) = len;
26   } else {
27     return NULL;
28   }
29   return (void*)((size_t)addr+CSIZE);
30 }
```

Listing 1.7 shows a uaf vulnerability example, it runs properly with glibc's free() and malloc(). After replacing them with lwHMCD's functions, the heap buffer would be cleared by __wrap_free(), resulting in a null pointer dereference in the printf()'s parameter (at line 19).

Listing 1.7. Uaf vulnerability example

```
 1 struct stu {
 2   char *name;
 3 };
 4
 5 struct mentor {
 6   char *name;
 7   struct stu *s;
 8 };
 9
10 int main()
11 {
12   struct stu *stu1 = (struct stu *)malloc(sizeof(struct stu));
13   stu1->name = "stu1";
14   struct mentor *men1 =
15     (struct mentor *)malloc(sizeof(struct mentor));
16   men1->name = "mentor1";
17   men1->s = stu1;
18   free(men1);
19   printf("%s", men1->s->name); // uaf here
20   return 0;
21 }
```

4   Evaluation

In this section, we evaluate our fuzzer ARM-AFL on Raspberry Pi Model 3 B with programs including openssl-1.0.1f, c-ares, libpng-1.2.56, etc, which contain four already known vulnerabilities (CVE-2014-0160, CVE-2016-5180, two artificial vulnerabilities). We use these programs selected by Google [11] to imitate software which can only run on ARM-based IoT devices and test whether our approach is effective in IoT vulnerability detection.

4.1 Experimental Setup

We run ARM-AFL on Raspberry Pi Model 3 B, with 4 cores and 1 GB memory [12]. The OS is Raspbian 2019-07-12 32bit [13]. The programs used in our experiment is briefly described as below:

- **OpenSSL** is an open source toolkit for the Transport Layer Security (TLS) and Secure Sockets Layer (SSL) protocols. It is also a general-purpose cryptography library. It is widely used on servers on the Internet [15].
- **c-ares** is a C library for asynchronous DNS requests. It is intended for applications which need to perform DNS queries without blocking, or need to perform multiple DNS queries in parallel [16].
- **libpng** is an open source library for use in applications that read, create and manipulate PNG (Portable Network Graphics) raster image files [17].
- **Little CMS** is an open source color management engine, with special focus on accuracy and performance. It uses the International Color Consortium standard (ICC), which is the modern standard when regarding to color management [18].
- The **PCRE** library is a set of functions that implement regular expression pattern matching using the same syntax and semantics as Perl 5 [19].
- **Wakaama** (formerly liblwm2m) is an implementation of the Open Mobile Alliance's LightWeight M2M protocol (LWM2M). It is not a library but files to be built with an application [20].
- **LwIP** is a small independent implementation of the TCP/IP protocol suite that is intended to reduce resource usage. It is suitable for use in embedded systems with tens of kilobytes of free RAM and room for around 40 kbytes of code ROM [21].

4.2 Efficiency

We compile each program into three versions with ARM-AFL, the first one with ASAN (ASAN version), the second one with lwHMCD (lwHMCD version) and the last one with neither of them (original version). ARM-AFL use environment variable AFL_USE_ASAN to enable ASAN. When AFL_USE_ASAN is set, AFL_INST_RATIO is set to 33 to probabilistically skip ASAN-specific branches. And when compiling without ASAN, AFL_INST_RATIO is initialized to 100 by default. Figure 3 shows the throughput of these three versions. The lwHMCD version's average slowdown is just 2.5%, so it is much faster than the ASAN version.

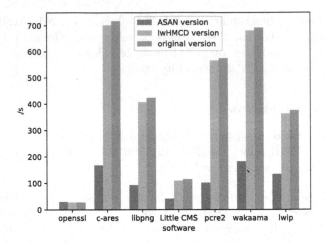

Fig. 3. Throughput of ARM-AFL

4.3   Effectiveness

There are four already known vulnerabilities in these programs we chosen from Google's test suite. And they are described as below:

- **CVE-2014-0160.** This vulnerability is caused by an unchecked user input flaw in the TLS/DTLS heartbeat functionality of OpenSSL versions 1.0.1 through 1.0.1f. Specifically, the `memcpy()` in `dtls1_porcess_heartbeat()` takes unchecked user input as size parameter, and this allows an attacker to retrieve private memory of an application that uses the vulnerable OpenSSL library in chunks of 64k at a time. As a result, the secret key, usernames and passwords, emails and communication on the servers protected by the vulnerable OpenSSL library can be stolen by anyone on the Internet [22].
- **CVE-2016-5180.** This vulnerability is caused by an incorrect size calculation in `ares_create_query()` function of c-ares 1.x before 1.12.0. In detail, the size of a hostname with an escaped trailing dot (such as `"BB\."`) would be calculated incorrectly in `ares_create_query()` function, this leads to a single byte out-of-bounds written on a heap-based buffer. A remote attacker is able to cause a denial of service or possibly execute arbitrary code via such a hostname.
- **Two artificial vulnerabilities.** Our approach of bug insertion was inspired by LAVA [28]. We manually added a uaf bug to libpng and a double free bug to Wakaama. As Listing 1.8 shows, the uaf bug is at the end of libpng's `main()` function and the double free bug is in the middle of Wakaama's `free_multi_option`.

Listing 1.8. Two artificial vulnerabilities

```
 1 int main(int argc, char *argv[]) {
 2   ...
 3   if (height == width*2) {
 4     free(0);
 5     0->buf_state->data = NULL; // uaf here
 6   }
 7   return 0;
 8 }
 9
10 void free_multi_option(multi_option_t *dst)
11 {
12   if (dst) {
13     multi_option_t *n = dst->next;
14     dst->next = NULL;
15     if (dst->is_static == 0) {
16       free(dst);
17       free(dst->data);
18     }
19     free(dst);   // double free here
20     free_multi_option(n);
21   }
22 }
```

Table 1. Result of ARM-AFL

Version	CVE-2014-0160	CVE-2016-5180	uaf	Double free
ASAN version	15 min 27 s	2 min 15 s	10 min 40 s	56 min 36
lwHMCD version	N/A	56 s	3 min 11 s	18 min 46 s
Original version	N/A	N/A	N/A	N/A

As Table 1 shows, without the help of ASAN or lwHMCD, ARM-AFL is not able to find the particular vulnerabilities. The lwHMCD version can find the heap buffer overflow, uaf and double free vulnerabilities, but cannot find the memory leak vulnerability. The ASAN version can find all the vulnerabilities, but 2.4 to 3.4 times slower than the lwHMCD version. IoT developers can make a trade-off between efficiency and effectiveness. If device resources are limited (common feature of IoT devices) or using a gcc version lower than 4.8 (does not support ASAN), lwHMCD is a good choice.

5 Related Work

As the number of IoT devices increases and their security needs grow, researchers have already made many related security studies including several vulnerability detection techniques. These techniques include static analysis and dynamic detection.

5.1 Static Analysis

Costin et al. [2] collected a large number of firmware images from the Internet and implemented a distributed system to unpack and run static analysis tasks on these firmware images. Their approach compares and finds similarities between all the files unpacked to detect known vulnerabilities.

Shoshitaishvili et al. [9] also proposed a static analysis-based IoT vulnerability detection technique. Firmalice takes security policies to identify a set of privileged program points of firmware, then use the Static-Program-Analysis module to create an authentication slice from an entry point to the privileged program point. After that, Firmalice utilizes a symbolic execution engine to find paths that can reach a privileged program point. Finally, Firmalice's Authentication-Bypass-Check module determines whether the found paths actually cause authentication bypass vulnerabilities.

Feng et al. [7] has implemented an IoT vulnerability search engine called Genius which was inspired by image retrieval techniques. Firstly, Genius extracts the attributed control flow graph (ACFG) from a binary function. Then it utilizes unsupervised learning methods to learn categorizations from ACFGs. Next it maps ACFG of a function into a high-level numeric vector. Finally, given a function, Genius finds its most similar functions to search cross-platform vulnerability for firmware images. Xu et al. [8] present a novel binary code similarity detection approach which was based on neural network. This approach is able to detect similar functions directly in binaries across multiple platforms, e.g., x86, ARM or MIPS. So it can help to detect known vulnerabilities in released IoT firmware.

Static analysis techniques for IoT may have high false-positive deficiencies and are rarely able to find new vulnerabilities.

5.2 Dynamic Detection

In contrast, dynamic detection techniques have higher efficiency and accuracy. Avatar enables dynamic analysis for firmware by combining emulator and real device. It utilizes the emulator to do the execution and analysis of the firmware, and redirect the I/O operations to the real device to address compatibility issues. In addition, the author applies a whitebox fuzzing to find vulnerabilities as a demonstration. Due to the data transmission and whitebox fuzzing, the throughput of Avatar is quite low.

FIRMADYNE [6] downloads firmware images from vendor websites with its web crawler component, then automatically extract kernel and root filesystem from the firmware. It starts up a QEMU full-system emulator with the extracted filesystem and a pre-build linux kernel to do the dynamic analysis. FIRM-AFL [3] is built on top of AFL and FIRMADYNE. And its main idea is to augment user-mode emulation with full-system emulation. The target program is fuzzed in user-mode emulation to achieve higher efficiency and switches to full-system emulation to ensure correct program execution.

From another perspective, Chen et al. [4] observes that most IoT devices are controlled through their official mobile apps, and such an app often carries rich information about the device. Examples of such information include protocol messages and encryption/decryption strategies in the app. Based on such information, IoTFuzzer can generate better test cases for blackbox fuzzing on the real device. Even so, it has a low code coverage and throughput.

6   Conclusion and Future Work

Coverage-guided fuzzing is proved to be an effective technique to discover vulnerabilities in program. However, it has not been applied to IoT devices. Therefore, we present ARM-AFL in this paper, a coverage-guided vulnerability detection framework which can run on ARM-based IoT devices. To achieve this, we implement a new instrument function, *trampoline* and *payload* assembly for ARM architecture. Heavy-weight memory error detectors like ASAN, Valgrind [29] (10–50 times slower than natively), etc, can detect more types of vulnerabilities, but the large amount of memory consumed and the resulting slowdown are not suitable for embedded devices [30]. We implement a light-weight heap memory corruption detector, which can turn three kinds of silent heap corruptions into observable crashes with little impact on performance. With the help of ARM-AFL, IoT developers can secure their code before being attacked by malicious hackers.

Our fuzzing framework can only detect vulnerabilities on ARM with Linux operating system, although it accounts for the majority of the IoT, there are still some essential devices that are other architectures with different operating systems. For future work, we would add support for other mainstream architectures and operating systems of IoT devices.

References

1. IoT 2019 in Review: The 10 Most Relevant IoT Developments of the Year. https:// iot-analytics.com/iot-2019-in-review/, 7 January 2020
2. Costin, A., Zaddach, J., Francillon, A., Balzarotti, D.: A large-scale analysis of the security of embedded firmwares. In: 23rd USENIX Security Symposium (USENIX Security 14) 2014, pp. 95–110 (2014)
3. Zheng, Y., Davanian, A., Yin, H., Song, C., Zhu, H., Sun, L.: FIRM-AFL: high-throughput greybox fuzzing of IoT firmware via augmented process emulation. In: 28th USENIX Security Symposium (USENIX Security 19), pp. 1099–1114 (2019)
4. Chen, J., et al.: IoTFuzzer: discovering memory corruptions in IoT through app-based fuzzing. In: NDSS 2018, February 2018
5. American fuzzy lop. http://lcamtuf.coredump.cx/afl/
6. Chen, D.D., Woo, M., Brumley, D., Egele, M.: Towards automated dynamic analysis for linux-based embedded firmware. In: NDSS 2016, 21 February, pp. 1–16 (2016)

7. Feng, Q., Zhou, R., Xu, C., Cheng, Y., Testa, B., Yin, H.: Scalable graph-based bug search for firmware images. In: Proceedings of the 2016 ACM SIGSAC Conference on Computer and Communications Security 2016, 24 October, pp. 480–491. ACM (2016)

8. Xu, X., Liu, C., Feng, Q., Yin, H., Song, L., Song, D.: Neural network-based graph embedding for cross-platform binary code similarity detection. In: Proceedings of the 2017 ACM SIGSAC Conference on Computer and Communications Security 2017, 30 October, pp. 363–376. ACM (2017)

9. Shoshitaishvili, Y., Wang, R., Hauser, C., Kruegel, C., Vigna, G.: Firmalice-automatic detection of authentication bypass vulnerabilities in binary firmware. In: NDSS 2015, 8 February (2015)

10. Zaddach, J., Bruno, L., Francillon, A., Balzarotti, D.: AVATAR: a framework to support dynamic security analysis of embedded systems' firmwares. In: NDSS 2014, 23 February, pp. 1–16 (2014)

11. Set of tests for fuzzing engines. https://github.com/google/fuzzer-test-suite/

12. Raspberry. https://www.raspberrypi.org/downloads/raspbian/

13. Raspberry Pi 3 Model B. https://www.raspberrypi.org/products/raspberry-pi-3-model-b/

14. Serebryany, K., Bruening, D., Potapenko, A., Vyukov. D.: AddressSanitizer: a fast address sanity checker. In: Presented as part of the 2012 USENIX Annual Technical Conference (USENIXATC 12) 2012, pp. 309–318

15. OpenSSL. https://www.openssl.org/

16. c-ares. https://c-ares.haxx.se/

17. libpng. http://www.libpng.org/

18. Little CMS. http://www.littlecms.com/

19. PCRE - Perl Compatible Regular Expressions. https://www.pcre.org/

20. Wakaama. https://www.eclipse.org/wakaama/

21. lwIP - A Lightweight TCP/IP stack. https://savannah.nongnu.org/projects/lwip/

22. The Heartbleed Bug. http://heartbleed.com/

23. CVE-2016-5180. https://www.cvedetails.com/cve/CVE-2016-5180/

24. Muench, M., Stijohann, J., Kargl, F., Francillon, A., Balzarotti, D.: What you corrupt is not what you crash: challenges in fuzzing embedded devices. In: NDSS 2018, February 2018

25. Wikipedia. Heap overflow (2019). https://en.wikipedia.org/wiki/Heap_overflow

26. Wikipedia. Dangling pointer (2019). https://en.wikipedia.org/wiki/Dangling_pointer

27. Wikipedia. C dynamic memory allocation (2019). https://en.wikipedia.org/wiki/C_dynamic_memory_allocation

28. Dolan-Gavitt, B., et al.: Large-scale automated vulnerability addition. In: 2016 IEEE Symposium on Security and Privacy (SP) 2016, 22 May, pp. 110–121. IEEE (2016)

29. Valgrind. https://valgrind.org/

30. Zhang, C., Zhu, L., Xu, C., et al.: Reliable and privacy-preserving truth discovery for mobile crowdsensing systems. IEEE Trans. Dependable Secure Comput. (2019). https://doi.org/10.1109/TDSC.2019.2919517

Post-exploitation and Persistence Techniques Against Programmable Logic Controller

Andrei Bytes[(✉)] and Jianying Zhou

Singapore University of Technology and Design, Singapore, Singapore
andrei_bytes@mymail.sutd.edu.sg, jianying_zhou@sutd.edu.sg

Abstract. The rising appearance of system security threats against real-world Critical Infrastructure (CI) sites over the past years brought significant research attention into the security of Industrial Control Systems (ICS). Academic institutions and major industrial appliance vendors have since increased efforts on effective vulnerability discovery in these systems. However, from the investigation of the major recent ICS incidents, it is evident that a targeted post-exploitation chain plays a crucial role for an attack to succeed. After the initial access to the system is gained, typically through a previously unknown (zero-day) or unpatched vulnerability, weak credentials or insider assistance, a specific knowledge on the system architecture is applied to achieve stealthy and persistent presence in the system before the physical process is disrupted. In this work, we propose a set of post-exploitation and persistence techniques against WAGO PFC200 Series Programmable Logic Controller (PLC). It will help to raise the awareness of stealthy and persistent threats to PLCs built on top of the variations of CODESYS runtime.

Keywords: Programmable Logic Controller · Vulnerability discovery · Industrial control system security

1 Introduction

Industrial Control Systems (ICS) are widely deployed to control and supervise the safe operation of nation-wide critical infrastructure: electric power grid, water treatment and distribution, transportation. Numerous domains of modern life and economy rely on real-time stability, safety and security of ICS. Programmable Logic Controllers (PLC), as well as sensors and actuators, play a key role in ICS as field devices.

The importance of security research in ICS domain has become especially evident after a series of major security incidents which relied on the exploitation of PLCs and other industrial appliance to corrupt the control logic and therefore affect the physical process [7,22,63]. The IEC61131 standard [15] defines the programming languages and system operation requirements to be followed by PLCs, to fulfill highest safety and security standards in the physical process

© Springer Nature Switzerland AG 2020
J. Zhou et al. (Eds.): ACNS 2020 Workshops, LNCS 12418, pp. 255–273, 2020.
https://doi.org/10.1007/978-3-030-61638-0_15

implementation. A key difference of PLCs from traditional embedded systems is their real-time operation design, extended fault tolerance and redundancy capabilities [27]. A single corruption of physical process control logic or availability shortage, even on the software level, can have serious consequences, ranging from immediate financial loss to man-made environmental disaster.

In this work, we analyze the software internals of widely used WAGO PFC200 Series PLCs and provide a set of potentially applicable techniques which allow for post-exploitation and persistence in these devices. While the methodology is provided in relation to WAGO PLCs, a similar approach is potentially helpful for the vulnerability discovery research in other ICS products, which are built on top of the variations of CODESYS runtime. This includes more than 360 devices from Hitachi, Advantech, Schneider Automation, ABB, Bosch Rexroth and other vendors [19,42].

Contributions: We perform a study of the popular WAGO PFC200 Series (750-8202/025-001) controller and identify a set of targeted post-exploitation techniques which can be applied on the firmware components to support the attack payload persistence. We also discuss the options of detection and defence, which take into account the internal components of the above-mentioned system.

Organization: The remainder of this paper is organized as follows. Section 2 introduces the typical ICS architecture and PLC components. Section 3 formulates the threat model of the system being studied. Section 4 provides an overview of recent exploits which assist in unauthorized access to the controller, and propose a set of techniques for post-exploitation and persistence. Section 5 gives two examples of attack scenarios that leverage the post-exploitation and persistence techniques, and Sect. 6 discusses the options of detection and defence. Section 7 reviews the related work, and Sect. 8 concludes the paper.

2   Background

2.1   WAGO PFC200 Series PLC

The PFC200 Controller, produced by WAGO Kontakttechnik is built on relatively powerful hardware (ARM Cortex CPU, 256 Mbytes RAM) and a modern software stack (real-time operating system (RTOS) with a modified Linux kernel). The controller implements a variety of well-known and vendor-proprietary network protocols for remote management, I/O connectivity and general networking.

This hardware and software design allows for rich connectivity (two embedded webservers, on-board Java HMI, extensions, integration with "cloud" back-ends, interconnection with mobile applications over TCP) and relatively high security standards (SSL, SSH, OpenVPN, firewall) offered out-of-the-box.

Software: A key advantage of WAGO PFC200 Series controller for security research is the access to the privileged user and unrestricted access to the kernel space. A typical identification string of WAGO PFC200 is as follows: Linux PFC200-450B5E 4.9.115-rt93-w02.03.00_02+2 #2 PREEMPT RT armv7l GNU/Linux.

The target architecture is ARMv7. The key modifications to the Linux 4.9 kernel are provided by the real-time kernel patchset [51] (Preempt RT). In particular, it extends the mainline kernel with additional preemption models, changes the task scheduling and priority policies. This turns the PFC200 system into a real-time OS (RTOS).

2.2 Firmware Availability

A significant advantage of WAGO controllers from a research perspective is the public availability of the Board Support Package (BSP) for its firmware [43]. In embedded systems, BSP is a common way to provide the developers with essential tools to cross-compile the firmware for a given hardware platform [28,31].

While there are many closed-source components (such as, system daemons and runtime software), the BSP contains a root file system, a compiler toolchain for ARM instruction set, hardware-specific drivers, kernel modules, configuration utilities and documentation. A native customization utility also allows to include the components and routines which facilitate the dynamic analysis of the firmware, such as tracing and debugging tools. The build process consists of the following chain:

- PTXdist, a build system for creating Embedded Linux distributions
- Pengutronix build environment, optimized for PFC controllers
- OSELAS toolchain for ARM cross-compilation
- Other utilities and components to build the firmware image
- WAGO rule-sets and configuration scenarios for CODESYS runtime

As compared to firmware analysis routine for ICS products from other major vendors, such as Rockwell Automation Allen-Bradley [16] or Siemens SIMATIC [17,18], the availability of BSP for WAGO PFC200 significantly extends the opportunity for the analysis of exploitation context.

Generic Runtime System: CODESYS (Controller Development System) [35] is widely adopted by ICS device vendors as a generic, portable third-party runtime software component responsible for control program execution [42]. In addition to the actual execution environment on field devices, CODESYS includes its own IDE (Integrated Development Environment) to construct IEC61131 compatible control logic applications. Control programs use proprietary binary format produced by a built-in compiler. CODESYS also ships with multiple emulation tools and supports a broad set of extensions which can be called from the control project as external libraries [23,35].

Numerous variations of CODESYS runtime are reportedly being used in at least 20% of PLCs worldwide [19]. The device directory list includes more than 360 devices from Hitachi, Advantech, Schneider Automation, ABB, Bosch Rexroth, Owen, Berghof Automation [19,42]. Typically, ICS vendors use it as a white-label platform for their own-branded IDE and device firmware. This implies an extensive amount of customization with additional software components to be introduced in the end products.

Adoption in WAGO PLC: The WAGO PFC200 firmware embeds the CODESYS runtime for control program deployment and execution on top of its real-time operating system (RTOS) and a customized Linux kernel [44].

The newest generation of CODESYS-based runtime, named WAGO e!RUNTIME, supports the latest generation of WAGO PFC200 Series controllers. The documentation clearly specifies that this runtime system is based on the original CODESYS v3, with the extended functionality introduced to it by WAGO [37]. In addition to the conventional CODESYS IDE, PFC100 and PFC200 controllers can be programmed and configured with WAGO e!COCKPIT - the desktop software also provided by WAGO, which is CODESYS v3 compatible and potentially can be used to work with non-WAGO controllers which have the non-customized revision of v3 runtime system in their firmware.

Compatibility Mode: The above mentioned PFC100 and PFC200 series of WAGO controllers can be switched to using a previous generation of the WAGO runtime, WAGO-I/O-SYSTEM 750. The documentation states that this system is based on CODESYS v2.3 and is incompatible with the newer IDE [37]. For WAGO-I/O-SYSTEM 750 runtime, an older development from WAGO should be used, named WAGO-IO-PRO. The latter has significantly lower memory and computational power requirements and is also used with low-end, non-ARM controller series [37,39].

2.3   Vendor-Specific Components

To support and tweak the runtime WAGO system includes a set of additional configuration interfaces and remote controller management tools. These also allow for physical process visualization, native integration of remote back-ends, and recently introduced "cloud" IoT connectivity [41,45,46].

One of the key toolsets, "WAGO CBM", provides a Command-Line Interface (CLI) which is capable for essential hardware and network configuration on the controller.

An embedded Human Machine Interface (HMI) system, "WebVisu", can execute Java applets, downloaded to the controller by the IDE to allow the developers to build dynamic HMI screens straight from the control application programming environment and expose them as web services on the PLC.

A separate embedded web server on the PLC runs WAGO Web-Based Management System (WBM) - a configuration and remote control wrapper built on top of the CBM toolset mentioned earlier.

Such a wide variety of custom pre-installed components motivate us to perform research on how to find opportunities for post-exploitation of the PLC and how the persistent payload can be hidden among these services to evade detection.

3   Threat Model

For the exploitation cycle analysis, we consider a threat model which is described below.

A remote attacker has a generic exploit in possession which utilises a previously unknown or unpatched vulnerability of the controller. However, preliminary knowledge about the particular deployed system and the physical process is limited. The threat actor obtains access to the system through one of the remotely exposed interfaces and seeks for long-term stealthy persistence in the system which would allow gathering a sufficient set of operational information to proceed with a targeted attack against the physical process.

4   Methodology

Objectives: A threat actor who has established the one-time unauthorized access to the system is motivated to ensure the long-term stealthy presence of the malicious payload on the PLC. This allows for passive observation on the system and its state changes, fingerprinting of the deployed configuration and ensuring the remote access in future.

Techniques: A common way to support these attack objectives at the PLC in the operational state is to place a persistent backdoor into one of its software components. In this section, we provide an overview of the attack cycle and system components which can perform invocation of the malicious payload and are suitable for placement of the backdoor executable.

4.1   Obtaining the Remote Access

At the time of writing, the most recent firmware release for PFC200 revision is FW16. This version introduced several of patches for critical security vulnerabilities. Supporting each other in a chain, these vulnerabilities facilitate a remote attacker to gain remote unauthorized access to the controller. We analyze multiple vulnerability chains below to provide an overview of unauthorized access scenarios.

Vulnerabilities in Management Interfaces: In [47], an exposed Web-Based Management (WBM) component demonstrates a serious authentication flaw which can be exploited to reduce the password trial entropy and obtain access to the configuration interface. A related authentication bypass [40] was also demonstrated in the older revision of the firmware (FW10) through the CODESYS remote control component exposed via TCP port.

Authentication Flaws: Similarly, in [52], a vulnerable encryption mechanism caused user credentials leakage in packets sent between the WAGO e!Cockpit IDE and the PLC runtime. Due to the hard-coded encryption key, it was possible to derive login credentials for any user and perform the unauthorised access to the controller. Another attack vector against the PFC200 update mechanism from the operator workstation [53], allows burning the incorrect version of WAGO update package (WUP) with false metadata in order to downgrade the firmware revision, which has known unpatched vulnerabilities for further access bypass. Previous, older implementations of the WBM component and its companion visualisation application, WebVisu, have also been proven to have authentication bypass flaws [29,38] in older firmware revisions.

Code Execution via File Uploads: The above can be chained with [54] for arbitrary code execution through package upload to the controller. The packaging system of the PFC200 through `ipk` archives provides no integrity checks on its content and is passed to opkg activation utility which executes the injected payload with superuser privileges.

Vulnerable Extension Packages: The newly added extension for Cloud Connectivity functionality of WAGO PFC200 was exploited in [48,56,57]. A manipulated remote firmware update command string is interpreted on the controller site and passed to the CBM utility without validation. As the former runs with superuser privileges, this results in a high-privileged remote code execution.

Exploitation of Network Services: A direct exploitation of the privileged services is one of the most dangerous attack vectors for the remote attacker. In [58–62], the "I/O-Check" service which implements the WAGO service protocol and is reachable through TCP port 6626 of the PFC200 controller allowed for a heap buffer overflow with a potential code execution. The above-mentioned service protocol provides the capability to read and write data to the EEPROM of the controller, which can lead to the controlled memory corruption. Notably, this vulnerable behaviour does not require any authentication and can be invoked by an anonymous client.

In an unpatched system, a vulnerability chain similar to the scenarios described above can provide an attacker with an unauthorised access to the affected PFC200 system. Once the one-time access is established, a more specific knowledge of the system is required to perform post-exploitation operations and prepare the attack against the physical process.

4.2 Privilege Escalation Techniques

Access Control System: The access control in WAGO PFC200 implements customized, vendor-built procedures which apply in multiple contexts of the controller configuration invoked by CBM and WBM utilities. As mentioned in the documentation, user management in the custom access control system is isolated from system user groups for security reasons [36]. In practice, this means that the services which run CLI and Web configuration applications run themselves with root privileges and perform the access control validation on the application layer. This design bypasses more robust access control mechanisms which are provided by the Linux kernel, replacing it with vendor-added validation logic. Since the impact of potential vulnerabilities in CBM and WBM is no longer mitigated by system user isolation, this builds up a major privilege escalation vector.

Vulnerabilities in Privileged Services: The controller also runs a set of high-privileged system services which are not always reachable through the network. However, there are known scenarios in which such services process input files which can be tampered with by unprivileged user. Successful exploitation of file processing vulnerability in one of the privileged services bypasses the vendor-built access control gives an extensive opportunity for privilege escalation into a superuser. Thus, in [49,50], a vulnerable "WAGO IO-Check" privileged service can be exploited through a low privilege user-writable cache file in the controller filesystem. The cache file parser does not fully sanitize the retrieved arguments and allows for command injection with root privileges. Similarly, in [50], it demonstrated that the privileged process could also deliver the payload from fields in the tampered cache into `sprintf()` call without validation, resulting in a stack buffer overflow and command execution in superuser context. This introduces another vector for code execution and privilege escalation on the controller.

4.3   Gathering System Information

Logging: By default, the PFC200 controller is configured with multiple logging services. A wide range of debug information in PFC200 is populated into log files in different locations. The data retrieved from log files can be used in a post-exploitation stage to determine the controller runtime state, network events, date and time patterns of operator assistance and firmware updates. Types of information and log file locations are summarized in Table 1.

Runtime Configuration: The CODESYS runtime on the controller writes its state information into multiple configuration files on the controller filesystem. From the [SysFileMap] of the eRUNTIME.cfg configuration file located under the home path of the codesys_root user, a list of useful state file mappings can be determined. From Project.xml, it is possible to identify the state of configured modules of the control program project, initialized names and values of local and global variables. The timestamps contained in ProjectCfg.txt allow to identify when the latest configuration update for the control program was performed.

Thus, the PlcLogic path under codesys_root u hosts multiple status files related to the currently uploaded control program.

Current mapping of the hardware indicators on the front panel of the controller is written to /tmp/led.xml and /var/www/wbm/led.xml.

More information about the exposed management interfaces of the controller, mode of authentication, MODBUS and serial port initialization can be obtained at /etc/rts3s.cfg.

The configuration of the embedded webserver, embedded into the controller runtime, can be found at CODESYSControl.cfg,CmpWSServer.cfg,/etc/webserver_conf.xml.

In [55], the abuse of the concurrent process pool limitation set by these configuration files was demonstrated, leading to a denial of service attack against the controller management interface.

Table 1. Logged information of PFC200

Useful information	Location
booted runtime mode	/var/run/runtime
runtime init log	/tmp/runtime_state.log
hardware port mapping	/var/run/ifstate
Per-thread trace log: OPC UA, MODBUS events	/var/log/runtime
WAGO events and diagnostic information	/var/log/wago/wagolog.log
Booted firmware revision	/etc/REVISIONS
Firmware update log	/log/fwupdate.log
latest executed privileged commands	/var/log/sudo.log
WAGO CBM calls, firewall rules and state transitions	/var/log/messages
PLC boot events	/home/check-system/events.log

Analysis of the Control Program: The control logic, compiled by the WAGO e!Cockpit IDE can be retrieved from PlcLogic/Application/Application.app binary in the codesys_root user home path in the controller. Alternatively, in the older firmware, the binary is deployed as DEFAULT.PRG to the home path of codesys_root on the controller. If such option is enabled, the IDE can include the full source code of the control program which can be retrieved from source.dat binary file in the same path.

If the source file is lacking due to the project deployment configuration, an analysis of the compiled program binary can be done based on the techniques and file layout described in [19]. Re-construction of the control flow allows for context-aware post-exploitation payload generation.

Visualisation Applet Extraction: The PFC200 supports embedded rendering of visualisation applets, assembled and deployed to the controller by a CODESYS-based IDE. Extraction of `webvisu.jar` is possible from the home path of `codesys` user. Further decompilation and analysis of this applet give additional information about the control components and prioritized metrics, performed on the physical process.

4.4   Persistence

One of the primary objectives for the malicious code, deployed into the PLC is persistence - an ability to re-execute the payload in the affected system regardless of possible reboots, control switches to and from other PLCs by the fault-tolerance logic, planned and unexpected power cycles.

To support this operation, the malicious payload performs a set of modifications to the selected components system. A number of system components in PFC200 provide an opportunity to establish execution persistence.

Aiming to the long-term, passive presence of a deployed payload, modification of default but vendor-specific components of the PLC firmware places lower detection risk as compared to generic Linux persistence techniques.

Injection to CBM Modules: WAGO CBM is a vendor-added set of command-line interface (CLI) utilities which play a key role in the controller setup, monitoring, management of its hardware and the state of CODESYS runtime. These contain a set of scripts which obey the custom access permission system [44]. Many of these utilities are not only meant to be manually invoked by the operator but provide a call interface for other software on the controller.

Table 2 lists some of the frequently invoked CBM scripts with the location path related to `/etc/config-tools/`. The systematic invocation of high-privileged CBM scripts makes them a reliable target for payload injection and system persistence.

Table 2. Frequently invoked WAGO CBM scripts

Utility name	Trigger condition
`cbm-script-modules/*`	Multiple: configuration protocol
`events/*`	Multiple: power cycle and interface up/down
`start_reboot`	Power cycle
`firmware_restore`	PLC boot and firmware update

Web Components: The PFC200 controller runs two groups of web applications via separate embedded web servers. Running as root, the `/usr/sbin/webserver` is responsible for serving web components of the pure CODESYS distribution (including WebVisu visualisation applets). The `/usr/sbin/lighttpd` web-server with `/usr/bin/php-cgi` interpreter is running as www user and serves the WAGO WBM remote management utility. The deployed configuration of lighttpd also turns it into a reverse proxy, which redirects its certain routes to the CODESYS server.

This can be observed by inspecting `/etc/webserver_conf.xml`, `redirect_wbm.conf`, and host configurations under `/etc/lighttpd/`.

The important property which makes these web components attractive for persistence hook execution is extensive non-traditional privileges of the www user. With a sudoers record, a list of additional commands is granted to it. These include powerful actions like hardware devices access, firmware replacement and service configuration.

To achieve the payload persistence though the ability of its remote invocation from WBM, `/var/www/wbm/page_elements`, `/var/www/wbm/fs_utils` are suitable injection points for a malicious payload hook. To ensure that a given component can be accessed from WBM with an authenticated request, a reference can be checked against a permission rules file `wbm/paperm.inc.php`.

Process Migration Candidates: Once the superuser privileges are gained, an efficient option would be to host the persistent payload stealthily among the running processes.

A reason behind this method is an additional detection countermeasure effect. While these processes will be likely common for every PFC200 series controller which runs in a given mode of operation (CODESYS 2.5 and 3 have significant difference and are supported by PFC200 as separate modes), a generic Linux rootkit detection tool would likely not be able to attest the integrity of these binaries.

A good candidate for this is the `codesys3` process itself. In a typical configuration, it spawns 36 named threads for different jobs of its execution cycle. In particular, this includes I\O operations, MODBUS and networking, visualization thread, cycle scheduling, webserver threads, load monitoring and other systematic tasks. Many of these threads happen to be dormant, judging by consumed CPU time as their functionality or target network interface is always enabled. However, even in this case, the same number of named threads is still spawned by the runtime.

For a stealthy backdoor on the controller, this makes the `codesys3` process a right candidate for process migration.

Another potential target could be the custom vendor-built `oms.d` service which is responsible for handling the hardware button events in the controller and triggers call-backs for power on, soft and factory reset actions with root privileges.

The downside of this method is the unavailability of debugging and function hooking tools in the typical firmware build configuration. However, the board support package [43] provides rules to include these utilities to the firmware distribution for debugging purposes.

Generic Techniques: In addition to the targeted techniques which leverage vendor-specific components in PFC200, the persistence opportunities are extended by a number of generic assets present in the firmware. These techniques are widely used by Linux malware [9] to obtain persistence in desktop platforms. Despite being very limited in available kernel modules and user-space utilities, the real-time operating system (RTOS) of WAGO PFC200 embeds a Linux kernel and multiple generic system services. This makes such techniques applicable for persistence purposes on the PLC.

Crontab Records: PFC200 actively uses Cron daemon for purposes of auxiliary system operations. If Cron daemon is available in the system, it is often possible to achieve persistence by adding a record to a given user's crontab [9] with access privileges of this user.

To reduce the risk of detection, an attacker can append the malicious payload to one of known script invocation records or forge the process name with one of the default cron jobs, preserving same invocation frequency to reflect in system logs. A suitable candidate for this in WAGO PFC200 can be the default crontab record for `logrotate` service, which is systematically called to perform the management of multiple system and event logs on the controller filesystem.

Terminal Sessions: One of the conventional persistence techniques in Linux systems is backdooring the terminal session initialization file to invoke additional commands when the user initiates the session [9].

For the purposes of local and remote in-network configuration, CLI capabilities are provided by PFC200 out-of-the-box. By default, pre-configured users of the system are also enabled to initiate Bash terminal sessions. When such session is opened, typically through the built-in Dropbear SSH server or serial interface, multiple configuration files are invoked. In particular, the following scripts are part of the terminal session invocation chain:

- /etc/wago-screen-prompt.sh
- /etc/profile.passwd
- /etc/config-tools/get_user_info

Altering these scripts give an additional opportunity to invoke the backdoor when a session is opened for a given user.

5   Attack Scenarios

In this section, we provide two examples of attack chains which leverage the post-exploitation and persistent techniques proposed in Sect. 4.

Example 1. A WAGO PFC200 controller runs firmware revision 03.01.07(13) which contains unpatched vulnerabilities known to the attacker. A remote attacker accesses the WBM service through the exposed TCP port and uses the authentication flaw [47] to derive login credentials (Fig. 1). The attacker crafts a malicious `ipk` package and achieves its execution in the system using the remote code execution flaw [54], resulting in privilege escalation to the superuser. Using the same vulnerability, the attacker uploads a crafted backdoor, compiled for ARMv7 instruction set [5] to the persistent partition on the PLC (Fig. 2). During the post-exploitation, the attacker analyses the logfiles located at `var/log/wago/wagolog.log`, and `/var/log/messages`. She observes that systematic maintenance is done on the controller, through command-line sessions over the serial interface. To achieve the persistence of the malicious backdoor, the attacker adds an additional record to `/etc/wago-screen-prompt.sh` to invoke the previously uploaded binary every time the operator logins (Fig. 3). The payload potentially preserves its dormant state until the second stage of the attack is activated, affecting the physical process of the plant. In the system logs and historian server data, the actions placed by the malicious implant will conform timestamps of legitimate operator actions.

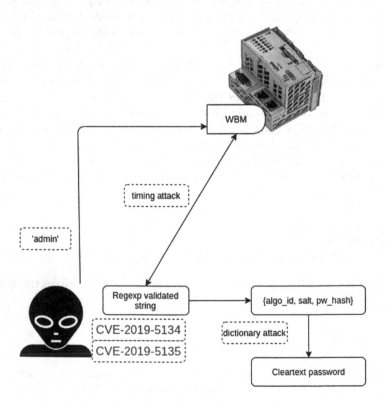

Fig. 1. E1 Stage I: Authentication bypass

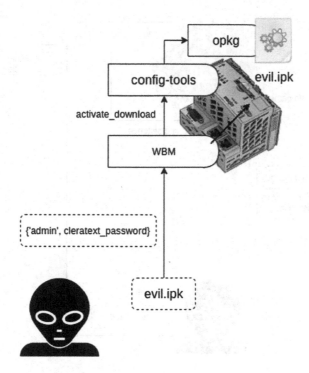

Fig. 2. E1 Stage II: Code execution

Example 2. A WAGO PFC200 controller runs firmware revision 03.01.07(13) which contains unpatched vulnerabilities known to the attacker. The attacker exploits a buffer overflow flaw [59] in WAGO service protocol reachable through TCP port 6626 on the controller. This results in arbitrary code execution with superuser privileges. The attacker crafts a malicious executable and writes it into the persistent partition on the controller. To secure the re-execution of the payload, an attacker appends the malicious executable invocation hook to the `/etc/config-tools/events/networking/update_config` event rule. This results in persistence on the system after power cycle of the PLC or its network interfaces re-configuration.

6 Discussion

We have to note that the research is significantly facilitated in the case of CODESYS runtime by having direct access to the device filesystem through a number of control interfaces and protocols. The ability to have shell access to the PLC and process monitoring utilities in the embedded OS plays an important role to understand the architecture.

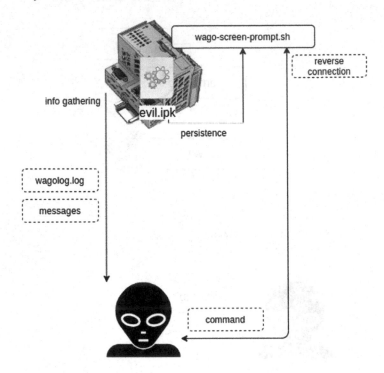

Fig. 3. E1 Stage III: Post-exploitation

Defence and Detection: The objective of a persistent backdoor placed on the affected PLC is to minimize detection risk in a long-term perspective. The assumed detection mechanisms can be categorised in the following categories:

- Generic Linux rootkit detection utilities
- Network activity anomaly detection
- System behaviour analysis
- Manual in-system investigation

In relation to the techniques described in Sect. 4, the customization to specific PLC firmware components is assumed as an advantage against detection by generic detection algorithms. Use of a generic Linux rootkit detection software would likely not be able to verify the integrity of modified vendor-specific utilities.

Assumed that the attack payload is in a dormant state but persists in the PLC system long-term, the in-network behaviour analysis mechanisms similar to [13] and [2] will not apply as there is no immediate deviation from the historical data or change of physical process state.

Applicability: In this work, we have studied the methodology in relation to RTLinux-based WAGO PLCs, which introduces vendor-specific system services to manage the CODESYS runtime. A similar approach is potentially helpful for attack cycle research in other ICS products, which are built on top of the variations of CODESYS runtime. This includes more than 360 devices from Hitachi, Advantech, Schneider Automation, ABB, Bosch Rexroth and other vendors [19,42].

7 Related Work

From analysis of the major security ICS incidents [7,22,63], a key difference from traditional IT systems can be observed in the crucial importance of a post-exploitation chain for a successful attack. This motivates us to specifically focus on the post-exploitation stage in this work, to research its practical implication against PLCs.

Similarly, multiple works on the security of PLCs and ICS field devices [3, 10,14,20,33,34] focus on the attacks which could enable remote unauthorised access. In [27], authors survey the hardware components used in most common field devices. This provides a view on the share of ARM platforms among other hardware platforms in ICS at the time of writing. Since then, the growth of WAGO PFC200 on the market further altered this proportion.

A wider view on the internals of the CODESYS runtime used in WAGO PFC200 is given in [23]. In [1], WAGO 750-8202 controllers are used as a test target for the proposed I/O-aware rootkit to facilitate a stealthy attack against the physical process.

Extensive research is done with a focus on the security of the control code, executed by PLCs [6,8,11,24–26,30,32,64]. The security design challenges for PLC and other field devices were studied in [4,21].

To achieve the persistence of a malicious payload, Govil et al. demonstrate the PLC "Logic Bombs" [12]. Written in Ladder Logic or other PLC programming language, compiled and deployed, e.g. to CODESYS runtime, such code is hard to be detected in the controller operation. The trigger condition of such an implant can be constructed as a pre-defined set of physical process events, which pass the control to the malicious payload. In [9], a study is done on the effective persistence techniques used by real-world Linux malware samples.

From the defence perspective, Hsio et al. [13] have proposed an ICS security monitoring solution to reveal anomalies which can be applied to the detection of malicious rootkit activity on the PLC. In [2], authors propose to detect the attacks against the physical process using noise analysis of the field devices.

A significant contribution was made recently in the domain of reverse engineering of WAGO PFC200 CODESYS-compiled binaries. In [19], authors propose a structured way of reverse-engineering the CODESYS-compiled binaries. The proposed open-source framework is aware of the proprietary binary format and canto reconstruct the Control Flow Graph from the given binaries automatically. In the post-exploitation context, a fully automated, targeted attack generation was demonstrated against WAGO PLCs.

8   Conclusion

In this work, we proposed a set of post-exploitation and persistence techniques for WAGO PFC200 Series PLC and crafted two examples of attack scenarios. We further analyzed detection and defence options, taking into account the internal system components utilized by the persistence chain.

We highlighted that in the ICS domain, in addition to the initial vulnerabilities which provide a way to penetrate the system, the targeted post-exploitation techniques play a crucial role in the attack to succeed. Apart from attacks against PLCs, this is also relevant to a wide range of other ICS devices.

Acknowledgement. This work was partly supported by the SUTD start-up research grant SRG-ISTD-2017-124.

References

1. Abbasi, A., Hashemi, M.: Ghost in the PLC: designing an undetectable programmable logic controller rootkit via pin control attack, pp. 1–35. Black Hat, November 2016. https://research.utwente.nl/en/publications/ghost-in-the-plc-designing-an-undetectable-programmable-logic-con

2. Ahmed, C.M., et al.: Noiseprint: attack detection using sensor and process noise fingerprint in cyber physical systems. In: Proceedings of the 2018 on Asia Conference on Computer and Communications Security. ASIACCS 2018, pp. 483–497. Association for Computing Machinery, New York (2018). https://doi.org/10.1145/3196494.3196532

3. Bytes, A., Adepu, S., Zhou, J.: Towards semantic sensitive feature profiling of IoT devices. IEEE Internet Things J., (2019). https://doi.org/10.1109/JIOT.2019.2903739

4. Cardenas, A., Amin, S., Sastry, S.: Secure control: towards survivable cyber-physical systems. In: 2008 28th International Conference on Distributed Computing Systems Workshops. ICDCS 2008, pp. 495–500, June 2008

5. Casey, P., Topor, M., Hennessy, E., Alrabaee, S., Aloqaily, M., Boukerche, A.: Applied comparative evaluation of the metasploit evasion module. In: 2019 IEEE Symposium on Computers and Communications (ISCC), pp. 1–6 (2019)

6. Castellanos, J.H., Ochoa, M., Zhou, J.: Finding dependencies between cyber-physical domains for security testing of industrial control systems. ACM, December 2018. https://doi.org/10.1145/3274694.3274745

7. Cobb, P.: German steel mill meltdown: rising stakes in the internet of things (2015). https://securityintelligence.com/german-steel-mill-meltdown-rising-stakes-in-the-internet-of-things/

8. Costin, A., Zaddach, J.: Embedded Devices Security and Firmware Reverse Engineering. ResearchGate, July 2013. https://www.researchgate.net/publication/259642928_Embedded_Devices_Security_and_Firmware_Reverse_Engineering

9. Cozzi, E., Graziano, M., Fratantonio, Y., Balzarotti, D.: Understanding Linux malware. In: 2018 IEEE Symposium on Security and Privacy (SP), pp. 161–175 (2018)

10. Dragos: CRASHOVERRIDE: Analyzing the Malware that Attacks Power Grids—Dragos, April 2019. https://dragos.com/resource/crashoverride-analyzing-the-malware-that-attacks-power-grids. Accessed 14 Apr 2019

11. Garcia, L.A., Brasser, F., Cintuglu, M.H., Sadeghi, A.R., Zonouz, S.A.: Hey, my malware knows physics! Attacking PLCs with physical model aware rootkit. ResearchGate, January 2017. https://doi.org/10.14722/ndss.2017.23313
12. Govil, N., Agrawal, A., Tippenhauer, N.O.: On ladder logic bombs in industrial control systems. In: Katsikas, S.K., et al. (eds.) CyberICPS/SECPRE -2017. LNCS, vol. 10683, pp. 110–126. Springer, Cham (2018). https://doi.org/10.1007/978-3-319-72817-9_8
13. Hsiao, S.W., Sun, Y.S., Chen, M.C., Zhang, H.: Cross-level behavioral analysis for robust early intrusion detection. In: 2010 IEEE International Conference on Intelligence and Security Informatics (ISI), pp. 95–100. IEEE (2010)
14. Huang, T., Zhou, J., Bytes, A.: ATG: an attack traffic generation tool for security testing of in-vehicle CAN bus. ResearchGate, pp. 1–6, August 2018. https://doi.org/10.1145/3230833.3230843
15. IEC 61131-3 industrial control programming standard. https://www.isa.org/standards-publications/isa-publications/intech-magazine/2012/october
16. Firmware from Rockwell Automation - Software Download, April 2019. https://www.rockwellautomation.com/rockwellsoftware/support/firmware.page. Accessed 15 Apr 2019
17. Operating System Update for SIMATIC S7-1200 CPU Firmware V3 - ID: 64789124 - Industry Support Siemens, April 2019. https://support.industry.siemens.com/cs/document/64789124/operating-system-update-for-simatic-s7-1200-cpu-firmware-v3?dti=0&pnid=13615&lc=en-WW. Accessed 15 Apr 2019
18. Support Packages for the hardware catalog in the TIA Portal (HSP) - ID: 72341852 - Industry Support Siemens, April 2019. https://support.industry.siemens.com/cs/document/72341852/support-packages-for-the-hardware-catalog-in-the-tia-portal-(hsp)?dti=0&pnid=13615&lc=en-US. Accessed 15 Apr 2019
19. Keliris, A., Maniatakos, M.: ICSREF: a framework for automated reverse engineering of industrial control systems binaries. In: The Network and Distributed System Security Symposium (NDSS) (2019)
20. Krotofil, M., Gollmann, D.: Industrial control systems security: what is happening?, pp. 664–669. ResearchGate, July 2013. https://doi.org/10.1109/INDIN.2013.6622963
21. Lee, E.A.: cyber-physical systems: design challenges. Technical report UCB/EECS-2008-8, EECS Department, University of California, Berkeley, January 2008. http://www.eecs.berkeley.edu/Pubs/TechRpts/2008/EECS-2008-8.html
22. Lipovsky, R.: New wave of cyber attacks against Ukrainian power industry, January 2016. http://www.welivesecurity.com/2016/01/11
23. Lufkin, D.: Programmable Logic Controllers: A Practical Approach to IEC 61131-3 using CoDeSys (12 2015)
24. McLaughlin, S.: On dynamic malware payloads aimed at programmable logic controllers, p. 10. ResearchGate, August 2011. https://www.researchgate.net/publication/262355936_On_dynamic_malware_payloads_aimed_at_programmable_logic_controllers
25. McLaughlin, S., McDaniel, P.: SABOT: specification-based payload generation for Programmable Logic Controllers, pp. 439–449. ResearchGate, October 2012. https://doi.org/10.1145/2382196.2382244
26. McLaughlin, S., Zonouz, S., Pohly, D., McDaniel, P.: A trusted safety verifier for process controller code. ResearchGate, January 2014. https://doi.org/10.14722/ndss.2014.23043

27. Mulder, J., Schwartz, M., Berg, M., Van Houten, J., Urrea, J.M., Pease, A.: Analysis of field devices used in industrial control systems. In: Butts, J., Shenoi, S. (eds.) ICCIP 2012. IAICT, vol. 390, pp. 45–57. Springer, Heidelberg (2012). https://doi.org/10.1007/978-3-642-35764-0_4

28. Noergaard, T.: Embedded Systems Architecture: A Comprehensive Guide for Engineers and Programmers. Newnes (2013). https://books.google.com.sg/books/about/Embedded_Systems_Architecture.html?id=piGhuAAACAAJ&source=kp_book_description&redir_esc=y

29. Online: Wago-i/o-system codesys 2.3 webvisu password extraction (2019). https://packetstormsecurity.com/files/127438/WAGO-I-O-SYSTEM-CODESYS-2.3-WebVisu-Password-Extraction.html

30. Siddiqi, A., Tippenhauer, N.O., Mashima, D., Chen, B.: On practical threat scenario testing in an electric power ICS testbed. In: Proceedings of the Cyber-Physical System Security Workshop (CPSS), co-located with ASIACCS, June 2018. https://doi.org/10.1145/3198458.3198461

31. Toolchains - eLinux.org, April 2019. https://elinux.org/Toolchains. Accessed 15 Apr 2019

32. Giraldo, J., Urbina, D., Cardenas, A.A., Tippenhauer, N.O.: Hide and seek: an architecture for improving attack-visibility in industrial control systems. In: Deng, R.H., Gauthier-Umaña, V., Ochoa, M., Yung, M. (eds.) ACNS 2019. LNCS, vol. 11464, pp. 175–195. Springer, Cham (2019). https://doi.org/10.1007/978-3-030-21568-2_9

33. Urias, V., Van Leeuwen, B., Richardson, B.: Supervisory Command and Data Acquisition (SCADA) system cyber security analysis using a live, virtual, and constructive (LVC) testbed. In: 2012 Military Communications Conference - MILCOM 2012, pp. 1–8 (2012)

34. Valentine, S., Farkas, C.: Software security: application-level vulnerabilities in SCADA systems, pp. 498–499. ResearchGate, August 2011. https://doi.org/10.1109/IRI.2011.6009603

35. Codesys. The system. https://www.codesys.com/the-system.html

36. Security for controller pfc100/pfc200 v 1.1.0, 5 December 2018. https://www.wago.com/medias/mxxxxxxxx-CyberSecurity-0en.pdf

37. Wago controllers brochure. https://www.wago.com/infomaterial/pdf/60386168.pdf

38. Wago ethernet web-based management authentication bypass vulnerability. https://ics-cert.us-cert.gov/advisories/ICSA-16-357-02

39. (May 2014). https://www.wago.com/infomaterial/pdf/51236524.pdf. Accessed 15 Apr 2019

40. Vulnerabilities in WAGO PFC 200 Series (2017). https://sec-consult.com/en/blog/advisories/wago-pfc-200-series-critical-codesys-vulnerabilities/index.html

41. (Apr 2019). https://www.wago.com/sg/download/public/IoT-Brosch%25C3%25BCre/AU-NA-DE-DE-FP-180827_001%2BIoT-Box%2BBrochure_web.pdf. Accessed 15 Apr 2019

42. Codesys device directory, April 2019. https://devices.codesys.com/device-directory.html. Accessed 15 Apr 2019

43. WAGO Global—swreg_linux_c, April 2019. https://www.wago.com/global/d/swreg_linux_c. Accessed 15 Apr 2019

44. WAGO—Controllers with Embedded Linux, April 2019. https://www.wago.com/sg/embedded-linux. Accessed 15 Apr 2019

45. WAGO—IoT PLC Controllers with MQTT Protocol for Industry 4.0, April 2019. https://www.wago.com/sg/automation-technology/plc-mqtt-iot. Accessed 15 Apr 2019
46. WAGO—WebVisu, April 2019. https://www.wago.com/global/automation-technology/discover-software/webvisu. Accessed 15 Apr 2019
47. Talos Vulnerability Report 2019–0923 (2020). https://talosintelligence.com/vulnerability_reports/TALOS-2019-0923
48. Talos Vulnerability Report 2019–0950 (2020). https://talosintelligence.com/vulnerability_reports/TALOS-2019-0950
49. Talos Vulnerability Report 2019–0961 (2020). https://talosintelligence.com/vulnerability_reports/TALOS-2019-0961
50. Talos Vulnerability Report 2019–0962 (2020). https://talosintelligence.com/vulnerability_reports/TALOS-2019-0962
51. Technical basics: Preempt RT (2020). https://wiki.linuxfoundation.org/realtime/documentation/technical_basics/start
52. WAGO e!Cockpit authentication hard-coded encryption key vulnerability (2020). https://talosintelligence.com/vulnerability_reports/TALOS-2019-0898
53. WAGO e!COCKPIT Firmware Downgrade Vulnerability (2020). https://talosintelligence.com/vulnerability_reports/TALOS-2019-0951
54. WAGO PFC 200 Web-Based Management (WBM) Code Execution Vulnerability (2020). https://talosintelligence.com/vulnerability_reports/TALOS-2020-1010
55. WAGO PFC100/200 Web-Based Management (WBM) FastCGI configuration insufficient resource pool denial of service (2020). https://talosintelligence.com/vulnerability_reports/TALOS-2019-0939
56. WAGO PFC200 Cloud Connectivity Multiple Command Injection Vulnerabilities (2020). https://talosintelligence.com/vulnerability_reports/TALOS-2019-0948
57. WAGO PFC200 Cloud Connectivity Remote Code Execution Vulnerability (2020). https://talosintelligence.com/vulnerability_reports/TALOS-2019-0954
58. WAGO PFC200 iocheckd service "I/O-Check" getcouplerdetails remote code execution vulnerability (2020). https://talosintelligence.com/vulnerability_reports/TALOS-2019-0864
59. WAGO PFC200 iocheckd service "I/O-Check" ReadPCBManuNum remote code execution vulnerability (2020). https://talosintelligence.com/vulnerability_reports/TALOS-2019-0873
60. WAGO PFC200 iocheckd service "I/O-Check" ReadPCBManuNum remote code execution vulnerability (2020). https://talosintelligence.com/vulnerability_reports/TALOS-2019-0874
61. WAGO PFC200 iocheckd service "I/O-Check" ReadPCBManuNum remote code execution vulnerability (2020). https://talosintelligence.com/vulnerability_reports/TALOS-2019-0863
62. WAGO PFC200 iocheckd service "I/O-Check" ReadPSN remote code execution vulnerability (2020). https://talosintelligence.com/vulnerability_reports/TALOS-2019-0871
63. Weinberger, S.: Computer security: is this the start of cyberwarfare? Nature **174**, 142–145 (2011)
64. Zonouz, S., Rrushi, J., McLaughlin, S.: Detecting industrial control malware using automated PLC code analytics. IEEE Secur. Priv. Mag. **12**(6), 40–47 (2014). https://doi.org/10.1109/MSP.2014.113

Investigation of Cyber Attacks on a Water Distribution System

Sridhar Adepu[1]([envelope]), Venkata Reddy Palleti[2], Gyanendra Mishra[1], and Aditya Mathur[1]

[1] iTrust Centre for Research in Cyber Security,
Singapore University of Technology and Design, Singapore, Singapore
adepu_sridhar@mymail.sutd.edu.sg, aditya_mathur@sutd.edu.sg
[2] Indian Institute of Petroleum and Energy-Visakhapatnam, Sabbavaram, India
venkat_palleti.che@iipe.ac.in

Abstract. A Cyber Physical System (CPS) consists of cyber components for computation and communication, and physical components such as sensors and actuators for process control. These components are networked and interact in a feedback loop. CPS are found in critical infrastructure such as water distribution, power grid, and mass transportation. Often these systems are vulnerable to attacks as the cyber components are potential targets for attackers. In this work, we report a study to investigate the impact of cyber attacks on a water distribution (WADI) system. Attacks were designed to meet attacker objectives and launched on WADI using a specially designed tool. This tool enables the launch of single and multi-point attacks where the latter are designed to specifically hide one or more attacks. The outcome of the experiments led to a better understanding of attack propagation and behavior of WADI in response to the attacks as well as to the design of an attack detection mechanism for water distribution system.

Keywords: Critical infrastructure protection · Industrial control system security · Cyber attacks · SCADA security · Water distribution systems · Cyber physical systems

1 Introduction

Cyber Physical Systems (CPSs) are found in critical infrastructure such as water distribution, energy and transportation. CPS consists of a physical process controlled by an Industrial Control System (ICS). In a CPS, a set of sensors measure process variables such as temperature, flow rate, level etc., from the physical process and send these values to the controllers through communication channels. Based on these values the controller makes decisions and initiates actions on the physical process.

The increase in successful cyber attacks on ICS [15], and many unsuccessful attempts [15], points to the importance of research in the design of ICS

© Springer Nature Switzerland AG 2020
J. Zhou et al. (Eds.): ACNS 2020 Workshops, LNCS 12418, pp. 274–291, 2020.
https://doi.org/10.1007/978-3-030-61638-0_16

that is resilient to cyber attacks. Attacks are a result of exploitation of one or more vulnerabilities in an ICS. Such vulnerabilities might be due to the lack of access control in the system [6], software vulnerabilities in the Programmable Logic Controllers (PLCs), Supervisory Control and Data Acquisition (SCADA) software systems, and weaknesses in the communication channels.

Motivation: Several attacks on water distribution systems have been reported in recent years such as the Kemuri Water Company (KWC)[1] attack, in 2016. The attack resulted in the exposure of personal information of the utility's 2.5 million customers. Reports from ICS-CERT [15] indicate that an understanding of these attacks against critical infrastructure is important for rapid investigation and evaluation of detection methods. The work presented in this paper is a step towards realizing a safe and secure water distribution infrastructure. The following questions are addressed through experimentation on WADI: **RQ1:** *How do cyber attacks impact a water distribution system?* **RQ2:** *How does knowledge of the response of a water distribution system to one or more cyber attacks help in designing an attack detection mechanism?*

Contributions: In the context of a specific water distribution plant: (a) A tool to launch attacks and (b) design and implementation of attacks on a water distribution system.

Organization: The remainder of this paper is structured as follows. Background on vulnerability assessment in ICS is explained in Sect. 2. Section 3 presents the context of this work and includes architecture of WADI, vulnerability assessment, and how attacks can be launched on WADI. Section 4 describes the attack design and investigation on WADI. Response to the research questions and lessons learned are discussed in Sect. 5. Related work is presented in Sect. 6. Section 7 offers a summary of this work and future work.

2 Vulnerability Assessment in ICS

Vulnerability assessment on ICSs follows four main steps[2]: 1) identify list of assets and resources in the system, 2) assign importance to the resources, 3) identify security vulnerabilities in each asset and resource, 4) propose mitigation for the most serious vulnerabilities. In order to know all the vulnerabilities in ICS, one must know the associated paths within ICS communications. In [19] authors explained different paths through which an attacker can enter into the system using various devices, communications paths, and methods that can be used for communicating with process system components. An attacker who wishes to attack ICS has to go through the following steps: 1) gain access to the ICS network 2) perform reconnaissance and understanding of the process 3) gain control of ICSs.

---

[1] http://www.securityweek.com/attackers-alter-water-treatment-systems-utility-hack-report.

[2] https://www.secureworks.com/blog/vulnerability-assessments-versus-penetration-tests.

Some of the industries conducted the vulnerability assessments in industrial systems and published the results. Following are the summary of reports from Kasper-sky and Honywell. *Kasper-sky* [22] summarized the findings of it's research on ICS vulnerabilities as follows: Over the years, 19 vulnerabilities in 2010 increased to 189 vulnerabilities in 2015. Even though the vulnerabilities are fixed by the product manufactures, the ICS management not upgrading soon. At least 5% of the vulnerabilities published by ICS-CERT were not fully fixed. Sometimes the vulnerable component was removed from the market and vendor support may not be available anymore. *Honeywell XL Web II Controller Vulnerabilities* [31] are found by an independent researcher. An attacker may use these to expose a password by accessing a specific URL. The XL Web II becomes an entry point into the network.

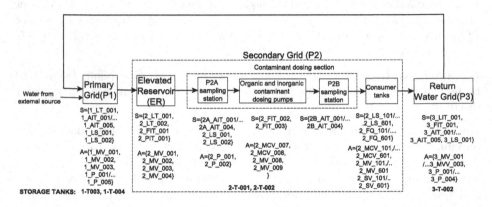

Fig. 1. Three stages in WADI are shown. Solid arrows indicate flow of water and sequence of processes. S: set of sensors; A: set of actuators. LT-Level Transmitter, AIT-Analyzer Indication Transmitter, FIT-Flow Indication Transmitter, PIT-Pressure Indication Transmitter, LS-Level Switch. Actuators: P-Pump, MV-Motorized valve, MCV-Modulating Control Valve, SV-Solenoid Valve. Tag name of the instrument is indicated as XXX_YYY_ZZZ, where XXX, YYY and ZZZ represent stage number, instrument type and instrument index, respectively.

3   Context: WADI Testbed

This study centers around a Water Distribution (WADI) testbed[3]. This section covers the testbed architecture and the communication channels.

3.1   Architecture of the WADI

Water distribution (WADI) plant [7] is an operational testbed supplying 10 US gallons/min of filtered water. It represents a scaled-down version of a large water

---

[3] https://itrust.sutd.edu.sg/research/testbeds/water-distribution-wadi/.

distribution network in a city. WADI consists of three stages (Fig. 1), namely primary grid (P1), secondary grid (P2), and return water grid (P3). Primary grid consists of two raw water (RW) tanks of 2500 liters each. These tanks are fed by three incoming sources including Public Utility Board (PUB), return water grid, and from a water treatment plant. A level sensor (1_LT_001) is installed in the primary grid to monitor the levels in the RW tanks. Water quality analyzers are installed to measure pH, turbidity, conductivity and residual chlorine. Secondary grid consists of two Elevated Reservoir (ER) tanks, consumer tanks, and contamination sampling stations. RW tanks supply water to the ER tanks using raw water pump (1_P_003) which is installed in the primary grid. Two level sensors, 2_LT_001 and 2_LT_002 are installed in ER tanks to measure water levels. Further, water from ER tanks flows into the consumer tank based on the preset demand pattern.

Two water quality monitoring stations are installed at consumer tanks. One station is at the immediate downstream of reservoir and another is before the consumer tanks (P2A and P2B stations in Fig. 1). These stations ensure water quality before it is sent to the consumer tanks. Once a consumer tank is filled, a level switch installed raises an alarm and water from the tank drains into the return water grid. To recycle water, return water grid pumps water to the primary grid. Water quality analyzers are installed in return water grid to check water quality before pumping it into the primary grid.

Three PLCs are installed to control each stage of WADI. These PLCs use CompactRIO as RIO (Remote Input Output) from National Instruments. In addition to the PLC in the secondary grid, two Schneider Electric Remote Terminal Units (RTUs), which use SCADAPack, are installed to measure water quality. There is a total of 103 sensors and actuators operating to measure water levels, water quality, flow rates, pressure, and status of motorized valves and pumps. There are three levels of networks in WADI. Level 0 corresponds to the communication between PLC's and sensors over Modbus RS485. Level 1

Table 1. Assets Table

Asset	Version/Model used	Location
SCADA System	SCADA System from Labview is used for the application	SCADA System computer running on Windows 7
PLCs	NI PLC is used in WADI to control various operations	Control and network panel and works based on the firmware and control logic program. Communicates with NI-PSP and Modbus TCP/IP communication in few cases
Network Switches	Moxa ES5 301	Network Control panel
Access points	Wifi access points	Network Control panel

corresponds to communications using the National Instrument's publish subscribe protocol (NI-PSP) while the SCADAPack RTUs communicate through Modbus TCP. PLCs at Stage-1 and Stage-3 are connected to analyzers capable of communicating through Modbus Serial. Level 2 consists of communication between the HMI and the plant control network. The interconnection of HMI, workstations and PLCs allows remote monitoring.

List of Assets and Resources in the System: The list of assets are mentioned in the Table 1. As mentioned in Sect. 2, this list of assets in Table 1 are useful for vulnerability assessment in WADI.

WADI supports various different communication channels like Modbus between RTUs and SCADA, NI-PSP between various controllers and RTUs. To develop an attack tool all communication channels were studied and investigated to identify any vulnerabilities. It is observed that a lot of them were lacked any form of access control.

3.2   Attacking WADI

As mentioned in Sect. 3.1, WADI uses a multi layered network comprising of different protocols at different levels and between different devices. For this paper the focus is on the National Instruments Publish Subscribe Protocol (NI-PSP). NI-PSP is the most used protocol in the entire WADI network and provides access to all data on the network. We developed an attack tool named NiSploit[4] that uses custom LabVIEW Virtual Instruments (VIs) that communicate with shared variables present on different PLCs across the plant using NI-PSP. Earlier exploration into various other mechanisms gave limited access to the variables [6].

Shared variables are used by a controller and SCADA to expose data over the network via a shared variable engine. These variables reside in controllers and the SCADA, have publish-subscribe architecture, and are shared using the NI-PSP. Network shared variables publish data through the shared variable engine. The shared variable engine resides on a SCADA and manages variables using the NI-PSP protocol. In the publish subscribe model the publishers do not publish to clients; instead they send data to the shared variable engine after every update and the subscribers subscribe to the shared variable engine for changes.

LabVIEW programs, or VIs, are drag and drop programs. We have written custom VIs for the purpose of attacking the National Instruments Publish Subscribe Protocol Variables. Several different custom VIs have been created, each one for attacking different types of cluster variables used in WADI. The Python module is the front end of the tool and an attacker needs to be concerned only with the use of this module. The module uses ActiveX [25] to control the LabVIEW application from python code. It connects to ActiveX controls using the Pywin32 library. ActiveX allows the user to run programs and specific functions that the program has exposed via it's ActiveX server. LabVIEW exposes a lot

---

[4] https://gitlab.com/gyani/NiSploit.

of different functionality including the ability to run VIs, set values for different controls and to fetch values of interest. The custom VIs along with the python module allow for creating powerful and complex controlled attacks. The attacks designed and executed in the following Section (Sect. 4) are realized through the NI-PSP attack tool called NiSploit.

4   Attack Investigation on WADI

This section presents a detailed case study which includes attack design, execution of attacks and results. We assumed an attacker [30] has an ability to enter into the system through vulnerabilities and social engineering. Further, we considered an insider attacker profile in which attacker has the process, communication knowledge, and access to the communication channels.

4.1   Attack Design

Attacks considered in this paper are launched on primary grid (P1) and secondary grid (P2) of WADI (Sect. 3.1). Stage-1 contains a tank whose level is measured by 1_LT_001. The stage-2 tank is responsible for water received by the consumer and its level is measured by 2_LT_002. Valve 1_MV_001 is responsible for the flow of water from RW tanks to the drain. Valve 1_MV_002 is responsible for the inflow of water to the RW tank. Valve 2_MV_003 is responsible for inflow of water to the ER tank. Water flows from the RW tank to the ER tank. In this study, an attacker is an insider, who has an access to the system: process, communication knowledge, and access to the communication channels.

Cyber attacks on WADI were derived from a CPS-specific generalized attacker model [4]. This model contains the attacker's intents (set I), and the attack domain (D). For example, in a water distribution system attacker's intent could be water pump damage or overflow the water from a tank. An attack model for a CPS is represented as a six-tuple (M, G, D, P, S_o, S_e). An attack procedure M is designed by the attacker to realize an attack on a finite set of attack points P in a CPS when this CPS is in state S_o, and possibly removed when the CPS is in state S_e. This attacker model is useful in generating a variety of attacks. Attack procedure M contains the attack vectors which include how an attacker enters into the system and manipulate different communication channels. The procedure M essentially the use of the NiSploit tool as described in Sect. 3.2. Goal G is equal to Intent I. Domain D is derived from the CPS domain [4]. For each CPS, domain is different based on the kind of physical process and components involved. Here, P is a set of sensors, actuators or any other potential attack points. S_o is the starting state of the system at the time of attack launch starting and S_e is the end state of the system when the attacker ends an attack. When S_e and I is identical then it shows that attacker reached his intent or attacker made an impact on the system.

Impact of attacks can be viewed along three [4] dimensions: (C_m, P_r, P_e), where C_m represents the impact on components of the system, P_r is the impact on properties such as water pH, ORP (Oxidation Reduction Potential), conductivity and hardness, P_e is performance of the overall plant - e.g.. if a water distribution system supplies 10 million gallons per day, attacker intent may be to reduce it to 5-million gallons per day. The attacks are on 1_LT_001, 2_LT_002, 1_MV_002, 2_MV_003, and 1_MV_001 which form the C_m dimension of the attack domain. For the dimensions considered in this paper, refer to Table 2. The attacks also affect the flow of water that falls along the P_e dimension. P_r is an empty set as the attacks do not affect the property dimension. Based on the above description, six attacks were designed and launched one at a time (refer to the Table 2 for summary of all attacks).

As we discussed in the attacker model, we derived the attacks from an intent of the attack. Based on the existing realistic attacks and incidents reported in the literature on water distribution systems, we considered the following intents in our experiments: 1) stop water supply to consumers, 2) damage water pumps in water distribution system, 3) overflow the water tanks, 4) wastage of water by

Table 2. Summary of attacks launched on WADI

Attack No	Attack Sensor/Actuator	Intent	Start state(S_o)	End state(S_e)
Single point attacks				
1	LIT - 1_LT_001	Block flow of water to ER tank	48%	40%
2	LIT - 2_LT_002	Stop flow of water to consumers and damage pump		80%
3	MV - 1_MV_002	No flow of water to the consumers	Open	Close
4	MV - 1_MV_001	Block flow of water to raw water tank	Open	Close
Multi point attacks				
5	1_AIT_002, 2_MV_003	Supply contaminated water to the elevator tank	1_AIT_002 is 0.5 and 2_MV003 is Close	1_AIT_002 is 6 and 2_MV003 is Open
6	2_MCV_101, 2_MCV_201	Intermittent supply to consumer tank	Both Close	Open both valves at 50%

leaking the pipe, 5) burst the water pipes, 6) manipulate the dosing mechanisms in a water distribution systems.

One might attempt to realize only one or more than one intent (mentioned in Table 2) at a time. There are a couple of steps in going through to realize an intent: 1) understand the physical process, 2) based on the intent, identify the set of sensors or actuators to manipulate, and 3) control process to reach the intent. Initially, we understand the WADI process behavior and identify the set of sensors and actuators to be attacked in order to reach the intent. We divided the attacks into two categories based on the number of sensors and actuators attacked. A single-point attack is when only one sensor or actuator is attacked. When the attack occurs on more than one sensor or actuator, it is classified as a multi-point attack. In Table 2, four single point and two multi point attacks are listed.

4.2   Execution of Attacks

We used the NiSploit (see Sect. 3.2) to launch the attacks listed in Table 2. The remaining subsection offers details of each attack.

Attack 1: Attack on 1_LT_001. This is an attack on level indicator 1_LT_001. This level indicator measures the level in the raw water tank (stage 1). The related shared variable is stored at the path *P1-CompactRIO/HMI_HOST/HMI_1_LT_001* and contains measurements for the water level in raw water tank 1. The shared variable cluster can be broken further into the following variables.

- PV - Process value measures water level.
- SIM PV - Process value used in simulation Mode.
- SIMULATION - This variable is a boolean, sets whether the PV is to be used in the simulation PV or the actual PV.
- SAHH - Set point Alarm High High, the HH alarm default is 90.
- SAH - Set point Alarm High, the High (H) alarm set point default is 70.
- SAL - Set point Alarm Low, the Low (L) alarm set point default is 60.
- SALL - Set point Alarm Low Lo (LL), the Low Low alarm set point default is 40.
- S EMPTY - Set point for the state in which the tank is considered empty, default is 35.
- A EMPTY - Alarm indicating S EMPTY is reached.
- AHH - Alarm indicating SAHH is reached
- AH - Alarm indicating SAH has been reached.
- AL - Alarm indicating SAL is reached.
- ALL - Alarm indicating SALL is reached.

In this attack the attacker sets SIMULATION to True and also sets Simulation PV to 40 while setting S_EMPTY to 40 using a script written using the NiSploit library. Thus, the state of WADI moves from S_o={SIMULATION=False, S EMPTY=35, 2_MV_004=Open} to S_e={SIMULATION=True, S EMPTY=40, 2_MV_004=Close}.

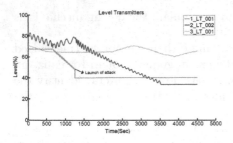

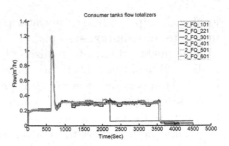

Fig. 2. Attack1: Water level readings of three stages. Attacker brings the level of 1_LT_001 to 40%.

Fig. 3. Attack 1: Flow to the consumer tanks and consumers are cut-off from water supply from little over 3500 s onwards.

Attack 2: Attack on 2_LT_002. This is an attack on level indicator 2_LT_002. This level indicator measures ER tank-2 level in process 2. The related shared variable is stored at the path P2-CompactRIO/HMI_HOST/HMI_2_LT_002 and contains measurements for the water level in ER tank-2. The shared variable cluster can be broken further into smaller variables as described in Sect. 4.2. In this attack the attacker sets PV to 80 by running a continuous loop. The state of valves and pumps remains unchanged, i.e. open and running, but the level of water falls in both the Raw Water Tank and the ER.

Attack 3: Attack on Motorized Valve 1_MV_002. This attack is on motorized valve 1_MV_002. This motorized valve is an actuator in process 1, the related shared variable is stored at the path P1-CompactRIO/HMI_HOST/HMI_1_MV_002 and contains the current status of the respective motorized valve governing the flow of water to the drain.

The shared variable cluster can be broken further into smaller variables. The state of the system moves from $S_o=\{1\_MV\_002=Close, 2\_MV\_004=Open\}$ to $S_e=\{1\_MV\_002=Open, 2\_MV\_004=Close\}$.

- Auto - If set to True, the motorized valve works according to the programmed logic.
- Open Command - open the valve
- Close Command - close the valve
- Reset - reset valve state to default state
- Available - Check if the Valve is available for control.
- Fully Open - Boolean indicating whether the Valve is fully open.
- Fully Close - Boolean indicating whether the valve is fully closed.
- Failed to Open - When the open command is sent but the valve could not be opened.
- Failed to Close - When the close command is sent and the valve could not be closed.
- Status - The current status of the valve.
- State - The current state of the valve, i.e. open or closed.

The attacker sets Auto to False and force opens the drain valve.

Attack 4: Attack on Motorized Valve 1_MV_001. This attack is on motorized valve 1_MV_001. This motorized valve is an actuator in process 1. The related shared variable is stored at the path P1-CompactRIO/HMI_HOST/ HMI_1_MV_001 and contains the current status of the motorized valve governing the inflow of water to raw water tanks. The attacker sets Auto to False and sends the Close command. The state of WADI moves from S_o={1_MV_001=Open, 2_MV_004=Open} to S_e={1_MV_001=Close, 2_MV_004=Close}.

In the previous sections, we described the single point of attacks. It is also possible an attacker can target multi points at a time, within the single stage and/or across multiple stages. However, in this study we investigated attacks on maximum two points. As shown in the Table 2, two multi-point attacks are launched on the system.

In attack 5, the attacker intention is to supply contaminated water to the elevator tank. In order to realize this intent attacker targets multistage multi point attack across the processes P1 and P2. In this attack, attacker targets 1_AIT_002 in process1 and 2_MV002 in process2. In attack 6, the attacker intention is to cause intermittent supply to consumer tank. This is an single stage multi point attack, where attacker targeted two actuators (2_MCV_101, 2_MCV_201) in process P2. Initial and final states of the system during attack 5 and attack 6 are mentioned in Table 2.

4.3 Results

The results show how an attacker is able to reach his intent. This kind of study is helpful to perform the impact analysis of the system. The remaining subsection presents the results for the attacks designed in the Table 2.

Attack 1: Attack on 1_LT_001. From Fig. 2 it can be seen that the attack begins slightly after 1000 s when the 1_LT_001 is set to simulation mode with SIM PV at 40. Figure 2 shows the attack on 1_LT_001 in which the attacker alters the reading from 48% to 40% of the RW tank level which corresponds to a LowLow (LL) state. Since the raw water tank is in LL state the controller sends a command to open the PUB inlet valve, or the return water grid pump, to fill the tank. Further, due to LL state of the RW tank there is no flow of water from primary to the secondary grid. It is to be noted that at the time of attack launch on RW tank, the secondary grid is at 50% of the maximum tank level. Therefore, the secondary grid supplies water to the consumer tanks until it reaches to 35% of the maximum tank level which is considered an "Empty" state. The secondary grid tank level (2_LT_002) behavior is shown in Fig. 2. Figure 3 indicates that no water flows to the consumers when the secondary grid tank is in Empty state. Further, the RW tank overflows as there is no flow from the primary grid to the secondary grid though there is continuous supply of water to RW tank through the PUB valve.

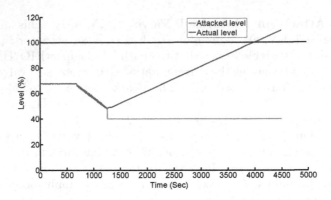

Fig. 4. Attack 1: Actual level of the RW tank as it overflows.

It is possible to estimate from first principles the water level in a tank. Mass balance equations, in continuous and discrete forms, for the change in water level h for a given input Q_{in} and output Q_{out}, flow rate, as follows,

$$A\frac{dh}{dt} = Q_{in} - Q_{out}, \tag{1}$$

$$h(t+1) = h(t) + \frac{\Delta t(Q_{in}(t) - Q_{out}(t))}{A}, \tag{2}$$

where A is the cross sectional area of the tank. Assuming linear dynamics, Q_{in} and Q_{out} are either 0 (when valve closes) or constant (when valve opens). We use Eq. 2 to estimate the tank level when a sensor is under attack. In this attack, the attacker sets the value of 1_LT_001 to 40% which corresponds to LL state. Consequently the outlet flow rate Q_{out} is zero. Hence, Eq. 2 reduces to the following

$$h(t+1) = h(t) + \frac{\Delta t(Q_{in}(t))}{A}. \tag{3}$$

Using Eq. 3 we estimate the actual level of the tank. As shown in Fig. 4 the tank overflows when the attacker sets a constant value to 40%.

Attack 2: Attack on 2_LT_002. In Fig. 5 it can be seen that the attack begins after 1000 s when 2_LT_002 is set to 80% of the tank level which corresponds to High (H) state. This leads to no flow of water from the RW tank to ER tank. However, the ER tank continuously supplies water to the consumers. After sufficient time has elapsed, the actual ER tank level moves to Empty state as seen in Fig. 6. It can be observed that in this situation the booster pump will be running continuously assuming that ER level is at H. Consequently the booster pump will run dry and may be damaged unless a physical protection, e.g.., a temperature cut off, are installed. Further, supply to the consumers stops completely.

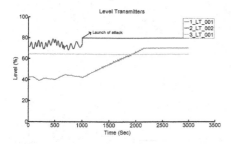
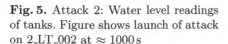
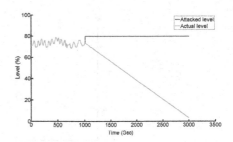

Fig. 5. Attack 2: Water level readings of tanks. Figure shows launch of attack on 2_LT_002 at ≈ 1000 s

Fig. 6. Attack 2: Actual water level of ER tank (2_LT_002) goes into Empty state.

Attack 3: Attack on Motorized Valve 1_MV_002. In Fig. 7 it can be seen that the attack begins after 1000 s when valves 1_MV_002 and 1_MV_003 (also called drain valves) are forced open. When these valves are open, water starts draining from the RW tank. Also, water is supplied to the ER tank when its level reaches the L state. After some time water level in the RW tank reaches to LL state and consequently PUB inlet valve, or return water grid pump, turns on to fill the tank. Note that water filling (through the PUB valve or return water grid) and draining (through 1_MV_002 and 1_MV_003) happens simultaneously. This leads to the water level in the tank at 40% or below depending on the inlet and drain water flow rate. Figure 8 shows that water level falls below 40% gradually leading to no water supply from RW tank to the ER tank. Consequently water supply will be stopped to the consumer tanks (shown in Fig. 9) when the level in the ER tank falls to 35% of the maximum tank level.

Attack 4: Attack on Motorized Valve 1_MV_001. As in Fig. 10 the attack begins after 1000 s when 1_MV_001 valve is forced shut. This leads to no water flow into the RW tank. Figure 11 shows that RW tank level is kept at 40% as a result of the attack. Hence, there is no flow from the RW to the ER tank. However, the ER tank continuously supplies water to the consumers. It can be observed from Fig. 11 that ER tank level reaches Empty state after sometime and there is no water flowing to the consumers.

4.4 Multi Point Attacks

Attack 5. In this attack, attacker launches multi point attack on 1_AIT_001 and 2_MV_003 as shown in Fig. 12 and 13 respectively. Initially, the attacker manipulates 1_AIT_002 value from 0.5 to 6 which is above threshold at around 400 s. And, at around 500 s the attacker intentionally tries to open the inlet valve (2_MV_003) of elevated reservoir tank. As a result water from the raw

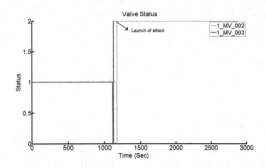

Fig. 7. Attack 3: Attack on valves 1_MV_002 and 1_MV_003.

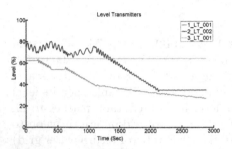

Fig. 8. Attack 3: Water tank levels of 1_LT_001 reduces gradually. At ≈ 2250 s 2_LT_002 reaches to Empty state (35% of tank level).

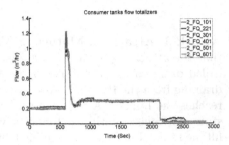

Fig. 9. Attack 3: Water flow to the consumers.

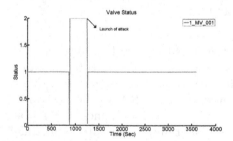

Fig. 10. Attack 4: Attack on valve 1_MV_001 at ≈ 1250 s

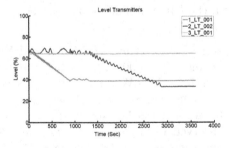

Fig. 11. Attack 4: Water tank levels when 1_MV_001 is attacked.

water tank will be pumped to the elevated reservoir tank. Therefore, the attacker successfully achieves his goal by launching attack on 1_AIT_002 and 2_MV_003. Similarly, attack 6 is launched on the system to achieve his goals based on the attacker intentions.

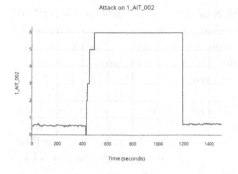

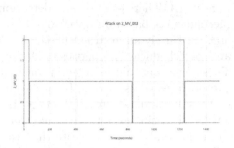

Fig. 12. Attack 5: Attack on 1_AIT_001   **Fig. 13.** Attack 5: Attack on 2_MV_003

5 Discussion

Next we summarize what we learned during this investigation and provide answers to research questions stated earlier.

Value of a Testbed: Researchers have studied [8,32] the attacks on water distribution systems. However, these studies have concentrated on small systems with a few sensors and actuators, and thus are not adequate to investigate cyber attacks on larger systems. Characterization of cyber attacks on water distribution systems [32] launched in a simulated environment may not be realistic though they do offer hints on the design of experiments reported here. The study reported here overcomes the limitations of past studies by using a realistic water distribution system as the testbed, namely WADI.

RQ1: *How do cyber attacks impact a water distribution system?*:

Section 4.3 describes how six attacks affect the water distribution process in WADI. In summary, an attack may lead to any one or more of the following undesirable consequences: (a) tank overflow, (b) pressure drop at the consumer end, (c) no water at consumer end, and (d) equipment damage. In addition to the six attacks mentioned in Sect. 4.3, several other attacks can be launched on WADI. For example organic and inorganic contaminants may be added to water and the chemical sensors compromised [27] so that the attack is not detected. WADI also has a leakage simulator that can be used to launch leakage or water theft attacks. Such attacks and their impact on WADI will be study in the future.

RQ2: *How does knowing the response of a CPS to one or more cyber attacks, help in designing an attack detection mechanism?*:

Traditional attack detection is often based on network traffic monitoring. [11] Proposed water marking schemes are based on control theory. [23] It is well understood that cyber attacks or faults on the system affect specific sensor readings.

Future research will focus on the detection of attacks such as those described in Sect. 4.1. There exist several detection mechanisms in the literature. One such mechanism is based on invariants derived from plant design. A "process invariant," or simply an invariant [3] is a mathematical relationship among "physical" and/or "chemical" properties of the process controlled by the PLCs in a CPS. These invariants aid in detecting such attacks. For example, attack 1 in Sect. 4.1 can be detected as follows. In this attack, attacker sets the raw water tank level to LL state and as a result 1_MV_001 opens to fill the tank. Further, the tank level is not rising even though the inlet valve is open and also there is no outflow from this tank. One can write the invariant for the valve and the tank level as follows. If the tank level is in LL and the inlet valve opens, then after sufficient time the tank level should rise to L or H state. However, in this case the tank level neither reaches L nor the H state. Clearly, in this case the invariant is violated and hence the attack is detected. Therefore, these kinds of invariants are useful in attack detection. Note that violation of an invariant does not necessarily imply that there is a cyber attack; it could also be due to communication or component failure.

6   Related Work

Attack Modeling and Analysis: The attacks designed in this work are based on a cyber-physical attacker model [4]. Jajodia et al. [20] proposed a detailed procedure for modeling cyber systems using attack graphs. Such graphs model practical vulnerabilities in distributed networked systems. Chen et al. [13] have proposed argument graphs as a means to capture the workflow in a CPS. The graphs are intended to assess a system in the presence of an attacker. The graphs are formed based on information in the workflow such as use case or state, physical system topology such as network type, and an attacker model such as an order to interrupt, power supply, physical tampering, network connection, denial of service, etc. Typed graphs [12] are other important contributions to the modeling of cyber attacks.

Attacks on Water Systems: The first well known attack on water supply was Maroochy Shire [1] in 2000 in Australia. Industrial Control Systems Cyber Response Team [15] has reported several attacks on water systems and remedial actions to protect against these. Amin et al. [8,9] studied attacks on water canal systems and presented attack detection methods based on control, hydrodynamic models. However, this paper focuses on an ICS system consisting of a few sensors and actuators. The formal approach [21,29] is used to analyse the security of a water treatment system. We aim at investigating the impact of attacks on a larger system such as WADI, which has more than 100 sensors and actuators. Riccardo et al. [32] presented a modeling framework to characterize the cyber physical attacks on water distribution systems. This framework consists of a few categories of attacks and EPANET simulation models. The analysis is applied to C-Town network to show the usage of the framework. This work is mostly performed in a simulation environment while the study reported here was performed on an operational water distribution system [7]. This research is helpful to understand the differences between simulation based attack investigation in water distribution systems, real time water distribution attacks.

Attack Detection in Water Systems: Mitchel and Chen surveyed [26] intrusion detection techniques for CPS. They presented existing works based on a classification tree. They also presented the advantages and limitations of the techniques. The use of invariants for detecting attacks on CPS has been proposed and evaluated by several researchers such as in [3,17,28]. In this work it is claimed that the use of controlled invariant sets in detecting cyber attacks uses little information about the controller and hence is useful for a large range of control laws. Yuqi et al. [14] proposed an approach for learning physical invariants that combine machine learning with ideas from mutation testing. Data driven [18,24] approaches for attack detection is studied on a water treatment system.

Security of cyber physical systems are also studied as decision games [16]. The BATADAL [33] is a battle of the attack detection algorithms competition in water distribution symposium. The goal of the battle was to compare the different detection methods to detect cyber physical attacks. The BATADAL was conducted on a C-Town network, a real-world, medium-sized water distribution system operated through PLCs and a SCADA. Total seven different teams participated in the BATADAL and their effectiveness of was evaluated in terms of time-to-detection and classification accuracy. This emphasis of dealing with real-life infrastructure and equipment for training and research is also seen in the development of Capture the Flag style gamification of an ICS testbed platform [5,10].

7   Conclusions and Future Work

This paper reports an investigation into the response of an operational water distribution plant to cyber attacks. The outcome of the investigation points to the importance of testbeds in understanding stealthy and a varied set of attacks and practical issues in operational water distribution plants. The case study also indicates that an attacker will likely be able realize an intent when adequate resources are available and the required accessibility exists. The work presented in this paper is a step towards realizing a safe and secure critical infrastructure. Future work includes understanding more stealthy attacks and the implementation of a prototype defence mechanism in WADI. We plan to implement some of the attack detection mechanism mentioned in the related work section and assess in a real time water distribution system. We are also planning to extend similar work on power systems [2].

Acknowledgment. This work was supported in part by the National Research Foundation (NRF), Prime Minister's Office, Singapore, under its National Cybersecurity R&D Programme (Award No. NRF2014NCR-NCR001-40, NRF2015NCR-NCR003-001) and administered by the National Cybersecurity R&D Directorate. The WADI testbed is built with the support from Ministry of Defense, Singapore and SUTD-MIT International Design Centre (IDC).

References

1. Abrams, M., Weiss, J.: Malicious control system cyber security attack case study-Maroochy Water Services. The MITRE Corporation, Australia (2008)
2. Adepu, S., Kandasamy, N.K., Mathur, A.: EPIC: an electric power testbed for research and training in cyber physical systems security. In: Katsikas, S.K., et al. (eds.) SECPRE/CyberICPS -2018. LNCS, vol. 11387, pp. 37–52. Springer, Cham (2019). https://doi.org/10.1007/978-3-030-12786-2_3
3. Adepu, S., Mathur, A.: Distributed detection of single-stage multipoint cyber attacks in a water treatment plant. In: Proceedings of the 11th ASIACCS, pp. 449–460 (2016)
4. Adepu, S., Mathur, A.: Generalized attacker and attack models for cyber physical systems. In: 2016 IEEE 40th Annual COMPSAC, vol. 1, pp. 283–292 (2016)
5. Adepu, S., Mathur, A.: Assessing the effectiveness of attack detection at a hackfest on industrial control systems. IEEE Trans. Sustain. Comput. (2018)
6. Adepu, S., Mishra, G., Mathur, A.: Access control in water distribution networks: a case study. In: QRS (2017)
7. Ahmed, C.M., Palleti, V.R., Mathur, A.: WADI: a water distribution testbed for research in the design of secure cyber physical systems. In: 3rd CysWater (2017)
8. Amin, S., Litrico, X., Sastry, S., Bayen, A.: Cyber security of water SCADA systems; Part I: analysis and experimentation of stealthy deception attacks. IEEE Trans. Control Syst. Technol. (2013)
9. Amin, S., Litrico, X., Sastry, S., Bayen, A.: Cyber security of water SCADA systems; Part II: attack detection using enhanced hydrodynamic models. IEEE Trans. Control Syst. Technol. (2013)
10. Antonioli, D., Ghaeini, H.R., Adepu, S., Ochoa, M., Tippenhauer, N.O.: Gamifying ICS security training and research: design, implementation, and results of S3. In: Proceedings of the 2017 Workshop on Cyber-Physical Systems Security and PrivaCy, pp. 93–102. ACM (2017)
11. Baig, Z., Ahmad, S., Sait, S.: Detecting intrusive activity in the smart grid communications infrastructure using self-organizing maps. In: 12th IEEE TrustCom, pp. 1594–1599, July 2013
12. Bhave, A., Krogh, B., Garlan, D., Schmerl, B.: View consistency in architectures for cyber-physical systems. In: Proceedings of the 2nd ACM/IEEE International Conference on Cyber-Physical Systems (2011)
13. Chen, B., et al.: Go with the flow: toward workflow-oriented security assessment. In: Proceedings of the 2013 Workshop on New Security Paradigms Workshop. NSPW 2013, pp. 65–76 (2013)
14. Chen, Y., Poskitt, C.M., Sun, J.: Learning from mutants: using code mutation to learn and monitor invariants of a cyber-physical system. In: Proceedings of the IEEE Symposium on Security and Privacy (S&P 2018) (2018)
15. ICS-CERT Advisories. https://ics-cert.us-cert.gov/advisories
16. Frey, S., Rashid, A., Anthonysamy, P., Pinto-Albuquerque, M., Naqvi, S.A.: The good, the bad and the ugly: a study of security decisions in a cyber-physical systems game. IEEE Trans. Softw. Eng. (2018)

17. Gamage, T., McMillin, B., Roth, T.: Enforcing information flow security properties in cyber-physical systems: a generalized framework based on compensation. In: IEEE 34th Annual COMPSACW, pp. 158–163 (2010)
18. Goh, J., Adepu, S., Tan, M., Lee, Z.S.: Anomaly detection in cyber physical systems using recurrent neural networks. In: 2017 IEEE 18th International Symposium on High Assurance Systems Engineering (HASE), pp. 140–145. IEEE (2017)
19. Homeland Security: DHS common cybersecurity vulnerabilities in ICS. https://ics-cert.us-cert.gov/sites/default/files/recommended_practices/DHS_Common_Cybersecurity_Vulnerabilities_ICS_2010.pdf
20. Jajodia, S., Noel, S.: Advanced cyber attack modeling, analysis, and visualization. Technical report AFRL-RI-RS-TR-2010-078. Final Technical Report, George Mason University, March 2010
21. Kang, E., Adepu, S., Jackson, D., Mathur, A.P.: Model-based security analysis of a water treatment system. In: In Proceedings of 2nd International Workshop on Software Engineering for Smart Cyber-Physical Systems, May 2016
22. Kasper Sky: Industrial control systems vulnerabilities statistics. https://kasperskycontenthub.com/securelist/files/2016/07/KL_REPORT_ICS_Statistic_vulnerabilities.pdf
23. Kwon, C., Liu, W., Hwang, I.: Security analysis for cyber-physical systems against stealthy deception attacks. In: ACC, pp. 3344–3349 (2013)
24. Lin, Q., Adepu, S., Verwer, S., Mathur, A.: Tabor: a graphical model-based approach for anomaly detection in industrial control systems. In: Proceedings of the 2018 on Asia Conference on Computer and Communications Security, pp. 525–536. ACM (2018)
25. Microsoft: Activex controls. https://msdn.microsoft.com/en-us/library/aa751968(v=vs.85).aspx
26. Mitchell, R., Chen, I.R.: A survey of intrusion detection techniques for cyber-physical systems. ACM Comput. Surv. (CSUR) 46(4), 55 (2014)
27. Palleti, V.R., Narasimhan, S., Rengaswamy, R., Teja, R., Bhallamudi, S.M.: Sensor network design for contaminant detection and identification in water distribution networks. Comput. Chem. Eng. 87, 246–256 (2016)
28. Palleti, V.R., Tan, Y.C., Samavedham, L.: A mechanistic fault detection and isolation approach using Kalman filter to improve the security of cyber physical systems. J. Process Control 68, 160–170 (2018)
29. Patlolla, S.S., McMillin, B., Adepu, S., Mathur, A.: An approach for formal analysis of the security of a water treatment testbed. In: 2018 IEEE 23rd Pacific Rim International Symposium on Dependable Computing (PRDC), pp. 115–124. IEEE (2018)
30. Rocchetto, M., Tippenhauer, N.O.: On attacker models and profiles for cyber-physical systems. In: Askoxylakis, I., Ioannidis, S., Katsikas, S., Meadows, C. (eds.) ESORICS 2016. LNCS, vol. 9879, pp. 427–449. Springer, Cham (2016). https://doi.org/10.1007/978-3-319-45741-3_22
31. Rupp, M.: Honeywell XL web II controller vulnerabilities. https://ics-cert.us-cert.gov/advisories/ICSA-17-033-01
32. Taormina, R., Galelli, S., Tippenhauer, N.O., Salomons, E., Ostfeld, A.: Characterizing cyber-physical attacks on water distribution systems. J. Water Resour. Plann. Manag. 143(5), 04017009 (2017)
33. Taormina, R., et al.: Battle of the attack detection algorithms: disclosing cyber attacks on water distribution networks. J. Water Resour. Plann. Manag. 144(8), 04018048 (2018)

Cloud S&P – Cloud Security and Privacy

Cloud IaaS – Cloud Security and
Trust

Computing Neural Networks with Homomorphic Encryption and Verifiable Computing

Abbass Madi, Renaud Sirdey[✉], and Oana Stan

CEA, LIST, Point Courrier 172, 91191 Gif-sur-Yvette Cedex, France
{abbass.madi,renaud.sirdey,oana.stan}@cea.fr

Abstract. The widespread use of machine learning and in particular of Artificial Neural Networks (ANN) raises multiple security and data privacy issues. Recent works propose to preserve data confidentiality during the inference process, available as an outsourced service, using Homomorphic Encryption techniques. However, their setting is based on an honest-but-curious service provider and none of them addresses the problem of result integrity. In this paper, we propose a practical framework for privacy-preserving predictions with Homomorphic Encryption (HE) and Verifiable Computing (VC). We propose here a partially encrypted Neural Network in which the first layer consists of a quadratic function and its homomorphic evaluation is checked for integrity using a VC scheme which is slight adaption of the one of Fiore et al. [13]. Inspired by the neural network model proposed by Ryffel et al. [26] which combines adversarial training and functional encryption for partially encrypted machine learning, our solution can be deployed in different application contexts and provides additional security guarantees.

We validate our work on the MNIST handwritten recognition dataset for which we achieve high accuracy (97.54%) and decent latency for a practical deployment (on average 3.8 s for both homomorphic evaluation and integrity proof preparation and 0.021 s for the verification).

Keywords: Neural Networks · Homomorphic Encryption · Verifiable Computing

1 Introduction

Despite limitations due to high communication overheads, computing costs or expressivity, techniques for computing over encrypted data such as Fully Homomorphic (FHE), Functional Encryption (FE) or Multi Party Computation (MPC), to name a few, are becoming practical for a number of applications. At the same time, Artificial Intelligence (AI) techniques and, especially, Neural Networks ones are becoming omnipresent in our connected society and have already lead to countless practical applications impacting, for better or worse,

© Springer Nature Switzerland AG 2020
J. Zhou et al. (Eds.): ACNS 2020 Workshops, LNCS 12418, pp. 295–317, 2020.
https://doi.org/10.1007/978-3-030-61638-0_17

our daily lives. Yet, the AI applications ecosystem has so far developed with a limited concern for user privacy.

In this context, this paper contributes to the study of how the aforementioned emerging cryptographic techniques can contribute to address AI privacy challenges. More specifically, we address the issue of ensuring the end-to-end confidentiality of some *user* data when they pass through a neural network operated on some cloud *server* with the aim of providing classification results to an *operator*. We do so by means of Homomorphic Encryption, which is used to execute the neural network on the server, associated to Verifiable Computing techniques in order to guarantee both the *confidentiality* of the user data as well as the *integrity* of the execution of the network with respect to threats coming from the server. Still, this is easier said than done, and in order to cope with the various constraints coming when using these techniques we also have to open the machine learning box and to propose a specific solution in which both the neural net structure and the crypto techniques are co-designed in order to achieve the desired overall system security properties.

1.1   Problem Statement and Contribution

We propose an approach to build privacy preserving neural networks, combining a FHE cryptosystem (here the BFV scheme [12]) with the Verifiable Computation protocol from Fiore et al. [13], adapted for BFV encrypted data.

More specifically, we show how to evaluate the first layer of a neural network on homomorphically encrypted data on a server and how the operator, which decrypts them, can check the result validity. The operator then pursue, in the clear domain, the network evaluation to reach a final classification.

We present here a global architecture made of these three entities: the client, owner of some private data, the server performing the computation over the encrypted layers of the neural network and the operator computing the remaining layers of the neural network. This architecture allows to deploy our semi-private evaluation of a neural network in order to ensure data privacy for clients and also provide integrity proofs with respect to the server computations. A complete description of the proposed architecture and an analysis of the associated security threats are given in Sect. 3.

To achieve this we reuse the neural network model proposed in [26] in which the first layer of the network acts as a whitener, ensuring, by means of adversarial training, that the knowledge of the outputs of the first layer does not allow to recover selected (sensitive) features of the input data while still preserving an ability to perform good quality classification. However, as shown in Sect. 3, the implementation of our approach targets different use cases and deployment scenarios as the ones from [26]. Although based on different reference problems, since the underlying cryptographic primitives we use are different (i.e. HE and VC), our work has similar security guarantees. This work thus complements [26] approach by providing more versatility to their network partitioning approach. Also note that that the neural network design, partitioning and training approaches underlying [26] is widely applicable to virtually any classification problem.

We also provide an efficient implementation and demonstrate practical results on the MNIST dataset [21], for the recognition of handwritten digits. Within our approach we perform the classification of the encrypted image in less than 3.8 s and the integrity check for the evaluation of the first layer in approx. 0.015 sec, with an overall accuracy of 97.54% for 128 bits of security.

2 Related Work

FHE for Encrypted Machine Learning. Research on the application of techniques for computing over encrypted data, FHE or others "competing" techniques, to neural networks-related privacy issues is only at its beginning. The first attempts at applying homomorphic encryption techniques to neural networks have almost all focused on the inference phase and more specifically, as the present work does, on the problem of evaluating a public (from the point of view of the computer doing the evaluation) network over an encrypted input (hence producing an encrypted output). The first work of this kind is CryptoNets [16] where the authors successfully evaluate an approximation of a simple 6-layer Convolutional NN able to achieve 99% success recognition on the well-known MNIST hand-written digits database. That network was composed only of simple Convolution, Square Activation and Mean Pool Scaling layers with only one application of the "FHE-unfriendly" Sigmoid function at the last layer which, in that specific case, could be dropped without affecting prediction quality (hence the final network only had 2 nonlinear Square Activation layers leading to a small multiplicative depth). Their implementation uses the BFV FHE scheme [12] and achieves network evaluation timings of around 4 min on a high-end PC. Yet, thanks to the SIMD/batching property of FV-like schemes, one network evaluation can in fact lead to 4096 evaluations of the network done in parallel on independent inputs (i.e. the network is evaluated once on ciphertexts which have many "slots" and thus contain different cleartexts). So, although the latency remains of 4 min, the authors rightfully claim their system to be able to sustain a throughput of around 60000 digit recognitions per hour. In subsequent papers, Chabanne et al. [7,9] are building approximations with small multiplicative depth of networks with up to 6 nonlinear layers by combining batch normalization layers with degree 2 approximations of the ReLU function (the former allowing to stabilize the inputs of the latter in order to decrease the sensitivity of the network to approximation errors). Through significant hand-tuning of the learning step of their networks, they show that these can achieve state-of-the-art prediction quality on both hand-digit (MNIST) and face recognition. However their work lacks an implementation and, hence, they did not provide FHE evaluation timings. More recently, Bourse et al. [5], have fine-tuned the TFHE cryptosystem towards a slight generalization of BNNs (Binary Neural Networks) called DiNNs in which the nonlinear activation function is the sign function which they intricate with the TFHE bootstrapping procedure for more efficiency. Overall, they are able to evaluate small DiNN networks (100 neurons and only one hidden layer) in around 1.5 s resulting in a (just decent) 96% prediction accuracy on the MNIST database. This line of research has also been pursued in [19] where the authors have fine-tuned the TFHE cryptosystems for efficient evaluation of Hopfield networks and tested their approach on a face recognition application achieving the evaluation of an encrypted network (with 256 neurons) over an encrypted input in 0.6 secs, however for a recognition accuracy of only 86%. This latter work is the first to attempt at both hiding the network and its input (and, by construction, its output). Also, in [32], the authors focus on applying FHE to hide the model of a neural network-based system in the case of a plain input for the special case of embedding-based networks.

Other notable works on the application of homomorphic encryption techniques to the private inference step of ANN include, in a non-exhaustive way, nGraph-HE [4], nGraph-HE2 [3], LOLA [6], TAPAS [28], NED [18], Faster CryptoNets [11]. As already emphasized, all the previously mentioned papers focus only on the inference phase under the hypothesis of an honest-but-curious evaluation server. It should also be mentioned that the applications to ANN of other "competing" techniques for computing over encrypted data, the main one being Secure Multiparty Computations (MPC) also start to be investigated in their associated communities (e.g., [2,25]).

VC for Machine Learning. As for applying the verifiable computing protocols for the computation of Neural Networks, there are only a few recent works on this subject.

The SafetyNets [15] is an interactive proof protocol to execute a deep neural network on a cloud, using Interactive Proof Systems [30] to prove the correctness of the calculated result returned by the cloud server. As such, it requires multiple interactions and calculations with the server to complete the verification step and it replaces the ReLu function by the function $x \rightarrow x^2$, which reduces the neural network accuracy. Since it is impossible for the prover to prove a non-deterministic computation (i.e. to prove the correctness of a computation while hiding some inputs) then the verifier and the prover need to share the model. Zaho et al. [31] propose VeriML to verify a neural network using QAP-based zk-SNARK. The VeriML ensures both security statement (privacy and integrity) but, it has a fairly large proof complexity $O(|\vec{a}| \cdot |\vec{x}| + |\vec{y})$ where $\vec{a}$ denotes the kernel, $\vec{x}$ the input and $\vec{y}$ the output. The combination of the GKR protocol and QAP (Quadratic Arithmetic Programs) scheme has been proposed by Chabanne et al. [8]. To do this the verifying process of GKR is verified in the QAP circuit. However; this still leads to a large computation complexity of $O(|\vec{a}| \cdot |\vec{x}| + |\vec{y}|)$ (according to [22]).

In the same line of research, Keuffer et al. build [20] a Verifiable Computing scheme, by combining other two VC schemes: a general-purpose VC (GVC) like [17,24] and a specialized one (EVC), namely Sum-Check protocol [23]. As such, they achieve efficient verification of complex operations as for example for large matrix-multiplication. In order to verify a function, they perform the complex

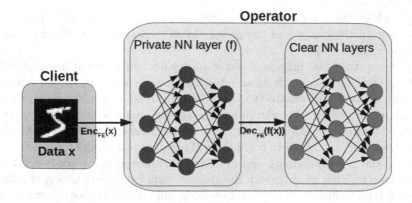

Fig. 1. Semi-encrypted Neural Network with Functional encryption

operation with the EVC protocol where the GVC is least efficient, the remaining functions being handled by the GVC. They apply this VC scheme to prove the correctness of a neural network evaluation.

As seen in this section and to the best of our knowledge, so far there are no approaches for an outsourced machine learning method which support the integrity of its execution while guaranteeing the data privacy by means of verifiable computation and homomorphic encryption.

2.1   Encrypted Machine Learning Using Functional Encryption

As already emphasized, our model for the neural network builds on the one from [26] in which it is used for a partial encrypted-domain network evaluation using Functional Encryption. Let us describe it here more in details.

To evaluate the first layer of the neural network, they use the Functional Encryption (FE) scheme, from [27], designed for quadratic multi-variate polynomials, based on bilinear pairings and with adaptive security under chosen-plaintext attacks (IND-CPA security). As illustrated in Fig. 1, the method they propose achieves user data privacy when performing classification in a classical user-operator model. It is based on a neural network composed of a private (running in the encrypted domain) and a public (running in the clear domain) part, with the private part consisting of a quadratic evaluation function. In their approach, the user encrypts his/her data x using a FE public key pk and sends the encryption $Enc_{FE}(x)$ to the operator.

To classify, the operator applies the first layer of the neural network over the data it received. More formally, the operator runs the quadratic activation function f over encrypted data by means of the FE scheme and uses the decryption key dk_f to decrypt the result of this layer as plaintext. This decrypted results are injected in the remaining of the neural network which is then evaluated on clear data with the argmax function applied at the end to obtain the cleartext output. They run the overall neural network on top of a modified version of

MNIST where there are two types of classes to predict: the public label which is the digit on the image and the private label associated with the font used to draw the image.

Moreover, they also propose a counter-measure to the threat associated from collateral learning, coming from an adversary having access to the output of the quadratic network and wanting to learn the private label (e.g. the font). As such, in order to reduce the information leakage on the operator hosting the partially encrypted neural network, they employ a semi-adversarial training method.

In this paper, we choose to build upon their quadratic model for the first layer as well as the same remaining neural network. However, our work is different in several aspects. First at all, even if the architectural framework is very similar our approach target different deployment scenarios and use cases (see below). Second, we ensure the data privacy and security using BFV homomorphic encryption scheme as well as a VC protocol, adapted from [13] so we use different underlying cryptographic primitives. Finally, as shown in the experimental part, in terms of performances, we obtain similar and sometimes even better execution times for the different steps of the private classification.

In essence, the two approaches are complementary: in the Functional Encryption approach, there is also a server playing the role of a trusted authority for the generation and distribution of the keys but which does not perform any calculations. Therefore, it has only an offline key management role i.e., it only has to provide (once) the master public key to the user as well as the secret functional decryption key associated to the first network layer to the operator and plays no role in the processing of a client request. In our setting, the server has an online active role in the sense that it is the entity receiving the encrypted client data and evaluating the first network layer (in the encrypted domain). Thanks to the use of VC in our approach which provides the server with the execution integrity which FHE alone does not provide, both approaches are equivalent in terms of security model. They differ on where the main computing burden (primarily due to the encrypted data processing) occurs: on the operator in the Functional Encryption approach or on the server in our FHE/VC approach. It is difficult to state which of the two is more relevant in practice as it clearly depends on the use-case at hand and where some computational power is most naturally available (e.g., if the operator is a mobile device such as a tablet then our approach is more relevant whereas in other cases it may not be so).

3   Scenario and Threat Model

This section provides a general scenario of deployment for our method, the different threats we address as well as the possible use cases.

We start by describing the general architecture in which we apply a neural network for a semi-private evaluation of an user data. There are mainly three entities involved: the user, owner of some confidential data x, the server performing the privacy-preserving part of the neural network and an operator having access to the evaluation of this preliminary classification and performing the remaining of the neural network in the clear domain.

As such, the server evaluates in the homomorphic domain the first layer of the neural network over the private data of one or many users. In our approach, this private step is equivalent to the homomorphic evaluation of a quadratic function (which is totally feasible and moreover with really good performances by existing FHE means).

Unlike other works using homomorphic encryption for private inference, we set up our study in the case of a *malicious* server, which can possible alter the results of the evaluation (e.g. by not running the specified algorithm). To counter this, within our setting, the server has to generate an integrity proof aside of the homomorphic results without any interaction with the user or the operator. To do so, we make use of the VC protocol of Fiore et al. [13] which allows to efficiently check that a computation over encrypted data as been properly performed. To the best of our knowledge, this scheme is presently the most practical to address the validity of computation over encrypted data with the evaluation of multi-variate polynomials of degree at most 2. As VC schemes for degree beyond 2 are not practical, this is one of the reasons we restrain the homomorphic evaluation to a first quadratic layer (practical Functional Encryption scheme also have the same limitations[1]).

Then, the homomorphic evaluation of the private neural network along with the associated integrity proof is sent to the operator. The last one decides (based on the proof) if the server output is correct and, when it is so, can decide to decrypt the homomorphic results of this first layer and to continue with the prediction on clear data. As a counter-measure in the case of an operator which could take advantage of the decrypted results of this intermediate layer operated by the server to recover the user sensitive data, the quadratic first layer is trained based on the adversarial learning technique from [26]. Let us also note that, since it is performed on plaintext data, this remaining part of the network can involve more complex machinery and obviously more than one additional layers (including non linear activation functions).

In summary, under the hypothesis of non collusion between these the entities involved, the architecture we propose has the following security properties:

- The user has access (obviously) to its own data x and, in function of the use case, can have access to the overall classification result or the evaluation of the intermediate first layer (if the operator shares it).
- The server, evaluating the first private layer of the neural network, has no access to the inputs x nor to the output of the function $f(x)$. While the homomorphic encryption addresses the confidentiality threats on the user inputs, the verifiable computation addresses the integrity threats to the homomorphic evaluation, in the case of a malicious server.
- The operator, performing the remaining layers of the neural network, has access to the decryption result of the first layer and can check the validity of the server computation. It can then exploit the overall result of the evaluation of the neural network to its own advantage or return it to the user. The

---

[1] This is due to the need to go beyond bilinear maps to achieve higher degrees in the underlying cryptographics primitives involved in both VC and FE.

adversarial training model for the first layer addresses the case of an honest-but-curious operator which may try to learn sensitive information about the user inputs based on the intermediate results.

Table 1 illustrates the threat analysis in terms of the access to the sensitive data x and to the result of the evaluation of the function f over x for all three entities involved in our architecture.

Table 1. Threat analysis in our architecture (Y: Yes, he has access; N: Non, he has no access)

	User	*Server*	*Operator*
x	Y	N	N
$Enc(x)$	Y	Y	N
$f(x)$	N	N	Y
$Enc(f(x))$	N	Y	Y

Let us know illustrate some applications in which our architecture could be useful.

Mail Filter. In this application, we consider the scenario were an employer (operator) wishes to perform statistics on its employees (users) emails. For example, she wishes to know when an email is received whether it is professional or personal, a phishing attempt, some advertisement or some spam. The employer needs to do so without having access to the employees mail contents. In this context, a cloud provider can play the role of the server. First, the employees encrypts their emails under the employer's public key and forward them to the cloud provider. The cloud provider then runs the first neural net layer in the encrypted domain and sends the results to the employer (along with the proof that the first layer was applied correctly) which then turns them into a concrete classification to compute her statistics. In this setup, employees have to trust only that the cloud server will not collude with their employer (e.g. by forwarding its encrypted emails). In particular, the confidentiality of their emails is safe from server threats thanks to the FHE layer. Thanks to VC protocol, the employer is guaranteed that the cloud provider evaluates properly the first layer of her network. Also, because it reveals only the first layer of its networks, the employer does not have to disclose the exact statistics she in fine computes to the cloud provider.

Medical Use-Case. Suppose that a pharmaceutical firm wishes to conduct an epidemiologic study over a group of people. To do so, they need to evaluate for example a specific neural network on some health-related data over a large set of patients while respecting the following properties: (1) the evaluation of the NN should not be done by the patients (i.e. for either or both cost and intellectual property issues) and (2) it needs to access only the outputs of the neural net and it is not allowed to access the inputs of this network. For this goal, consider a trusted health authority (server) in the center between these patients (clients) and the firm (operator). The firm is the owner of all keys in our architecture (FHE and VC keys). To apply its network, the firm (the operator in our architecture) discloses its first network layer to the health authority. It is the authority responsibility to guarantee that the first layer is acceptable in terms of privacy of the input data (one nice thing is that the firm discloses only the first layer of its network to the authority) i.e. that knowledge of the outputs of the first layer does not allow to recover specific features of the associated inputs (after decryption of these outputs by the operator). If the authority validates the first layer, it distributes the firm's public key to the patients, which they use to encrypt their data which are then sent to the authority. The authority then evaluates the first layer of the neural network in the FHE domain and then sends its (encrypted) results along with short proof of correctness to the firm. Finally, the firm uses its secret key with the short proof it received, to verify the calculation of the server. Then if the verification is successful, the firm decrypts the result and evaluates the remainder of its network performed on clear data. The security properties are specified as above.

4   Technical Preliminaries

4.1   FHE

Fully Homomorphic Encryption (FHE) schemes allow to perform arbitrary computations directly over encrypted data. That is, with a fully homomorphic encryption scheme E, we can compute $E(m_1 + m_2)$ and $E(m_1 \times m_2)$ from encrypted messages $E(m_1)$ and $E(m_2)$.

In this section we recall the general principles of the **BFV** homomorphic cryptosystem [12], which we use in combination with a $\mathcal{VC}$ scheme. Since we know in advance the function to be evaluated homomorphically, we can restrain to the somewhat homomorphic version described below. Moreover, we skip the description of the relinearisation step no needed in our approach which evaluates only multi-variate quadratic polynomials.

Let $R = \mathbb{Z}[x]/\Phi_m(x)$ denote the polynomial ring modulo the m-cyclotomic polynomial with $n' = \varphi(m)$. The ciphertexts in the scheme are elements of polynomial ring R_q, where R_q is the set of polynomials in R with coefficients in $\mathbb{Z}_q$. The plaintexts are polynomials belonging to the ring $R_t = R/tR$.

As such, **BFV** scheme is defined by the following probabilistic polynomial-time algorithms:

BFV.ParamGen(λ): $\rightarrow (n', q, t, \chi_{key}, \chi_{err}, w)$.
It uses the security parameter λ to fix several other parameters such as n', the degree of the polynomials, the ciphertext modulus q, the plaintext modulus t, the error distributions, etc.

BFV.KeyGen($n', q, t, \chi_{key}, \chi_{err}, w$): $\rightarrow (pk, sk, evk)$.
Taking as input the parameters generated in **BFV.ParamGen**, it calculates the private, public and evaluation key. Besides the public and the private keys,

an evaluation key is generated to be used during computation on ciphertexts in order to reduce the noise.

$\mathbf{BFV.Enc}_{pk}(m) \rightarrow c = (c_0, c_1, c_2 = 0)$

It produces a ciphertext c according to BFV-cryptosystem for a plaintext m using the public key pk.

$\mathbf{BFV.Dec}_{sk}(c) :\rightarrow m$

It computes the plaintext m from the ciphertext c, using private key sk.

$\mathbf{BFV.Eval}_{pk,evk}(f, c_1, \ldots, c_n):\rightarrow c$, with $c = \mathbf{BFV.Enc}_{pk}(f(m_1, \ldots, m_n))$, where $c_i = \mathbf{BFV.Enc}_{pk}(m_i)$, and f has n inputs and has degree at most two. It allows the homomorphic evaluation of f, gate-by-gate over c_i using the following functions: $\mathbf{BFV.Add}(c_1, c_2)$ and $\mathbf{BFV.Mul}_{evk}(c_1, c_2)$.

For further details on this scheme, we refer the reader to the paper [12].

Let us just note that a BFV ciphertext c can be seen as an element in $R_q[y] = \mathbb{Z}/q\mathbb{Z}[X, Y]/\Phi_m(x)$ with a degree at most 2 (i.e., $c = c_0 + c_1 y + c_2 y^2$).

4.2 $\mathcal{VC}$

Verifiable computation $\mathcal{VC}$ techniques allow to prove and verify the integrity of computations on authenticated data. A Verifiable Computation scheme is defined as a protocol in which a client (usually weak) has a function f and some data denoted x and delegates to another client (in most cases a server) the computation of $y = f(x)$. Then the same client or another one can receive the result y plus a short proof of its correctness. More in details, a user generates an authentication tag σ_x associated with his/her data x with his/her secret key and the server computes an authentication tag $\sigma_{f,y}$ that certifies the value $y = f(x)$ as an output of the function f. Now, anyone using the verification key (public or secret) can verify y to check that y is indeed the result of $f(x)$.

A $\mathcal{VC}$ scheme includes the following algorithms:

1. (PK,SK)←$\mathbf{KeyGen}(f, \lambda)$: Taking as input the security parameter λ and a function f, this randomized key generation algorithm generates a public key (that encodes the target function f) used by the server to compute f. It also computes a matching secret key, kept private by the client.
2. (σ_x, τ_x)←$\mathbf{ProbGen}_{SK}(x)$: The problem generation algorithm uses the secret key SK to encode the input x as a public value σ_x, given to the server to compute with, and a secret value τ_x which is kept private by the client.
3. σ_y ←$\mathbf{Compute}_{PK}(\sigma_x)$: Using the client's public key and the encoded input, the server computes an encoded version for the function output $y = f(x)$.
4. (acc, y) ←$\mathbf{Verify}_{SK}(\tau_x, \sigma_y)$: Using the secret key SK and the secret τ_x, this algorithm converts the server output into a bit acc and a string y. If $acc = 1$ we say that the client accepts $y = f(x)$, meaning that the proof is correct, else (i.e. $acc = 0$) we say the client rejects it.

In the extended version, we recall in Appendix A the three main properties of VC protocols (correctness, security, privacy) as defined in [14] and some other properties (function privacy, outsourceability, adaptive security) as described in [13].

4.3   Pseudo Random Function with Amortized Closed-Form Efficient

We present here the notion of Pseudo Random Function(**PRF**) with Amortized Closed-Form Efficiency [1]. In the extended version (Appendix B) we also present the definition of security for a PRF and we will present a realization of a PRF satisfying the amortized closed-form efficiency.

A **PRF** consists of two algorithms (**F.KG, F**). The key generation method **F.KG** takes as input the security parameter λ to generate a secret key K and some public parameters pp that specify the domain χ and the range $\mathcal{R}$ of the function F. The function F_K takes as input the data $x \in \chi$ and uses the key K to generate a value $R \in \mathcal{R}$ satisfying the following pseudorandom property:

Definition 1. *[1] Consider a computation* **Comp** *that takes as input n random values* $R_1, \ldots, R_n \in \mathcal{R}$, *and a vector of m arbitrary values* $z = (z_1, \ldots, z_m)$, *and assume that the computation of* **Comp**$(R_1, \ldots, R_n, z_1, \ldots, z_m)$ *requires time* $t(n, m)$. *Let* $L = (L_1, \ldots, L_n)$ *be arbitrary values in the domain* χ *of* **F** *such that each one can be interpreted as* $L_i = (\Delta, \tau_i)$. *We say that a PRF (KG, F) satisfies amortized closed-form efficiency for* $(Comp, L)$ *if there exist two algorithms* **CFEval**$_{Comp,\tau}^{off}$ *and* **CFEval**$_{Comp,\Delta}^{on}$ *such that:*

1. *Given* $w \leftarrow CFEval_{Comp,\tau}^{off}(K, z)$ *we have that:*
   $CFEval_{Comp,\Delta}^{on}(K, w) = Comp(F_K(\Delta, \tau_1), \ldots, F_K(\Delta, \tau_p), z_1, \ldots, z_m)$
2. *the running time of* $CFEval_{Comp,\Delta}^{on}(K, w)$ *is* $o(t)$.

4.4   Homomorphic Hash Function

Informally, a family of key homomorphic hash functions **H** with domain $\mathcal{X}$ and range $\mathcal{R}$ consists of three algorithms (**H.KeyGen, H, H.Eval**). The first one, the key generation hash **H.KeyGen**, generates the description of the hash function H_K, where K is the key, the function **H** computes the hash and, finally, **H.Eval** allows the computation over $\mathcal{R}$ satisfying the following homomorphic property: $H.Eval(f, (H(x_1), \ldots, H(x_n))) = H(f(x_1, \ldots, x_n))$ where $x_i \in \mathcal{X}$ (**H** is a ring homomorphism).

In the $\mathcal{VC}$ scheme for quadratic multi-variate polynomial over BFV encrypted data, we are interested in the calculation of **H.Eval** for one level of multiplication (with two inputs) and any numbers of additions over $\mathcal{D}$.

In the extended version (Appendix C) we present a realization of homomorphic hash $\tilde{\mathbf{H}}$, based on bilinear groups. It allows to reduce a **BFV** ciphertext $\mu \in R_q[y]$ into a $v \in \mathbb{Z}/q\mathbb{Z}$ depending on the degree of μ denoted $deg_y(\mu)$ with preservation of the homomorphic properties. Hence $H.Eval(f, (H(\mu_1), \ldots, H(\mu_n))) = H(f(m_1, \ldots, m_n))$ where $\mu_i = \mathbf{BFV.Enc}_{PK}(m_i)$ with m_i a BFV plaintext.

5 $\mathcal{VC}$ for Quadratic Polynomials over BFV Encrypted Data

In this section, we present an application of the VC scheme of Fiore et al. [13] for the case of multi-variate polynomials of degree 2, over **BFV** encrypted data instead over **BGV** encrypted data as in the original paper. First the client encrypts his/her data $x = (x_1, \ldots, x_n)$ as a **BFV** ciphertext, where the plaintext modulus q is chosen to be prime. In parallel with the encryption of x_i, he/she also generates a tag σ_i for his/her data, using the combination of the PRF output and the hash collision-resistant functions (that compresses a **BFV** ciphertext into a double of group elements). Once the server receives the BFV ciphertexts $[x_i]_{BFV}$ and the tags σ_i from the user, it computes f over $[x_i]_{BFV}$ and over σ_i and it obtains $y = f([x_i]_{BFV})$ and respectively a tag $\sigma = f(\sigma_i)$. The server sends y with the associated tag to the user owning the verification keys, which then checks the output in constant time (because he has already done a pre-computation phase).

In this scheme, we require to authenticate with our scheme:

1. Each of the $2n' - \mathbb{F}_q$ components of a BFV ciphertext;
2. The BFV evaluation circuit $\hat{f} : \mathbb{F}_q^{2nn'} \to \mathbb{F}_q^{3n'}$ instead of $f : \mathbb{F}_q^n \to \mathbb{F}_q$.

More formally, our $\mathcal{VC}$ scheme is specified by the following algorithms:

1. **KeyGen**$(f, \lambda) \to (PK, SK)$, with the following steps:
   - First generate $bgpp = (q, g, h, e)$ some bilinear group parameters, where $\mathbb{G}_1 =< g >$, $\mathbb{G}_2 =< h >$, $q = order(\mathbb{G}_i)$ for $i = \{1, 2\}$ and $e : \mathbb{G}_1 \times \mathbb{G}_2 \to \mathbb{G}_T$ a non-degenerate bilinear map ($\mathbb{G}_T =< e(g, h) >$).
   - Run **BFV.ParamGen**$(\lambda) \to (n', q, t, \chi_{err}, \chi_{key}, w)$ to generate the parameters for the **BFV** encryption scheme. Run **BFV.KeyGen**$() \to (pk, sk, evk)$.
   - Run $\tilde{H}.KeyGen \to (\kappa, \tilde{K})$ to choose a random member of the hash function family $\tilde{H} : \mathcal{D} = \{\mu \in \mathbb{Z}_q[x][y] : deg_x(\mu) \leq 2(n' - 1), deg_y(\mu) \leq 2\} \subset R_q[y] \to \mathbb{G}_1 \times \mathbb{G}_2$. In our scheme, we do not use the public key of $\tilde{H}$, so it is not necessary to calculate it. (For details see Appendix C) in the extended version.
   - Sample a random value $r \leftarrow \mathbb{F}_q$.
   - Run **PRF.KeyGen**$(\lambda) \to (K, pp)$ to build $F_K : \{0, 1\}^* \to \mathbb{G}_1 \times \mathbb{G}_2$. In this adaptation, we need F_K to be computationally indistinguishable from a function that outputs $(R, S) \in \mathbb{G}_1 \times \mathbb{G}_2$ such that $Dlog_g(R) = Dlog_h(S)$ is uniform over $\mathbb{F}_q$ (i.e. $e(R, h) = e(g, S)$).
   - Run $CFEval_r^{off}(K, f) \to w_f$, called concise information for f. (For details on PRF and CFEval see Sect. 4.3).
   - Set $SK = (pk, sk, \kappa, r, K, w_f)$ and $PK = (pk, pp, f)$.
2. **ProbGen**$_{SK}(\vec{x} = (x_1, \ldots, x_n)) \to \sigma_x, \tau_x$, requiring the operations below:
   - Choose an arbitrary string $\Delta \in \{0, 1\}^\lambda$ (identifier for $\vec{x}$).
   - For i=1 to n:
     (a) Run BFV.Enc$(x_i) = \mu_i \in R_q^2$ and compute its hash value $(T_i, U_i) = \tilde{H}_\kappa(\mu) \in \mathbb{G}_1 \times \mathbb{G}_2$. Next run $F_K(\Delta, i) = (R_i, S_i) \in \mathbb{G}_1 \times \mathbb{G}_2$.
     (b) Compute $X_i = (R_i \cdot T_i^{-1})^{1/r}$ and $Y_i = (S_i \cdot U_i^{-1})^{1/r} \in \mathbb{G}_1, \mathbb{G}_2$ respectively.
     (c) Set $\sigma_i = (T_i, U_i, X_i, Y_i, \Lambda_i = \mathbb{1}_{\mathbb{G}_T}) \in (\mathbb{G}_1 \times \mathbb{G}_2)^2 \times \mathbb{G}_T$. We denote the level of tag as $lev(\sigma_i)$ and we set $lev(\sigma_i) = 1$.

– Set $\sigma_x = (\Delta, \mu_1, \sigma_1, \ldots, \mu_n, \sigma_n)$ and $\tau_x = \perp$.

3. **Compute**$_{PK}(\sigma_x) \to \sigma_y$ consisting of the following steps:
   – Let f be an admissible circuit.
   – Run the evaluation circuit f over the **BFV** encrypted data and obtain $\mu = \mathbf{BFV.Eval}(f, \mu_1, \ldots, \mu_n)$. Let us note that, for preserving the homomorphic properties of the hash, the difference with the normal evaluation of the BFV scheme is that here the multiplication of polynomials is performed over R_q without the $mod\ \Phi_m(x)$-reduction and without the rounding step, and we assume thus that this modulus reduction and this rounding operations are performed at the end by the verifier receiving the result of the evaluation of f.
   – Apply (gate-by-gate) f over the authentication tags $(\sigma_1, \ldots, \sigma_n)$, using the following gate functions **GateEval()**. **GateEval**:$(f_g, \sigma_1, \sigma_2) \to \sigma$
   Parse $(T_i, U_i, X_i, Y_i, \Lambda_i) \in (\mathbb{G}_1 \times \mathbb{G}_2)^2 \times \mathbb{G}_T$ for $i = 1, 2$, where f_g stands for tag addition ("+") or tag multiplication ("×"). We try to compute $\sigma = (T, U, X, Y, \Lambda)$.
     - **Add two tags together.** If $f_g =$ "+", the addition takes different forms depending on the levels of the input tags.
       If $lev(\sigma_1) = lev(\sigma_2)$, then $\sigma = (T_1 \cdot T_1, U_1 \cdot U_2, X_1 \cdot X_2, Y_1 \cdot Y_2, \Lambda_1 \cdot \Lambda_2)$ with $lev(\sigma) = 1$.
       Else, without loss of generality, let suppose that $lev(\sigma_1) = 1$ and $lev(\sigma_2) = 2$(i.e. there is a multiplication gate before this gate). The idea is to create a level-2 tag (σ_1') from σ_1 as follows: $\sigma_1' = (e(T_1, h), e(g, U_1), e(X_1, h), e(g, Y_1), \Lambda_1)$. Then compute $\sigma = \sigma_1' + \sigma_2$ as in the first case but set $lev(\sigma) = 2$.
     - **Add a constant to a tag** $(c + \sigma_1)$. This method depends on the level of the tag as follows:
       If $lev(\sigma_1) = 1$, then the result tag $\sigma = (T_1 \cdot (g^c), U_1 \cdot (h^c), X_1, Y_1, , \Lambda_1)$.
       If $lev(\sigma_1) = 2$, then we obtain: $\sigma = (T_1 \cdot (e(g, h)^c), U_1 \cdot (e(g, h)^c), X_1, Y_1, Z_1, \Lambda_1)$.
       In both cases $lev(\sigma) = lev(\sigma_1)$.
     - **Multiplication by a constant** $(c \cdot \sigma_1)$. The result tag is $\sigma = (T_1^c, U_1^c, X_1^c, Y_1^c, \Lambda_1^c)$ and $lev(\sigma) = lev(\sigma_1)$.
     - **Multiplication.** For $f_g =$ "×" on two tags $(\sigma_1 \times \sigma_2)$
       If $lev_y(\sigma_1) > 1$ or $lev_y(\sigma_2) > 1$ then reject. **Else** calculate $T = e(T_1, U_2)$, $U = e(T_2, U_1)$, $X = e(X_1, U_2) \cdot e(X_2, U_1)$, $Y = e(T_2, Y_1) \cdot e(T_1, Y_2)$, $\Lambda = e(X_1, Y_2)$. Also set $lev(\sigma) = 2$.
       It is not necessary to keep U and Y after a multiplication because $T = U$ and $X = Y$. We keep them only for the sake of clarity. As noted in [13], one can see the function f as the composition of two functions $f_g(f_1, f_2)$ in the last gate f_g of f.
     - Set $\sigma_y = (\Delta, \mu, \sigma)$, where σ is the tag obtained after evaluating the last tag of f.

4. **Verify**$_{SK}(\sigma_y, \tau_x) \to (acc, y)$, for $\sigma_y = (\Delta, \mu, \sigma)$, using the following operations:

- Compute $\tilde{\mathbf{H}}_\kappa(\mu) \to \tilde{\nu}$.
- Run $\mathbf{CFEval}_\Lambda^{on}(K, w_f) \to W$ (see Sect. 4.3 for details on the online closed-form method).
- Check, depending on the of degree of f, as follows:
  (a) If $\deg(f) = 1$, check the following equations:

$$(T, U) = \tilde{\nu}(= (g^{((\mu(\alpha))(\beta))}, h^{((\mu(\alpha))(\beta))}))$$
$$e(X, h) = e(g, Y)$$
$$W = e(T \cdot X^a, h).$$

  (b) Else, check over $\mathbb{G}_T$ the following equations:

$$T = U = \tilde{\nu}(\text{ i.e. } = e(g, h)^{((\mu(\alpha))(\beta))}) \tag{1}$$
$$X = Y \tag{2}$$
$$W = T \cdot (X)^r \cdot (\Lambda)^2 \tag{3}$$

- If all equations are satisfied set the check bit **acc** to 1 (accept), otherwise set it to 0 (reject).
- Finally, if **acc**=1, $\mu' = \mu \bmod \Phi_m(x) = (c_0, c_1, c_2)$ and set $\mu' = (\lceil t \cdot c_0/q \rfloor, \lceil t \cdot c_1/q \rfloor, \lceil t \cdot c_2/q \rfloor)$ $y = BFV.Dec_{dk}(\mu')$, otherwise set $y = \perp$.

Theorem 1. *If **BFV** is a semantically secure homomorphic encryption scheme, $\tilde{H}$ is a collision-resistant homomorphic hash function and **F** is a pseudorandom function, then $\mathcal{VC}$ described above is correct, adaptive secure and input private.*

Proof. Same proof as for the scheme $\mathcal{VC}_{quad}$ from [13].

6   VC and FHE for First Layer

In this section, we present more in details our architecture for partially encrypted machine learning using Verifiable Computing for BFV homomorphic encrypted data.

As illustrated in Fig. 2, the client sends the homomorphic data encrypted at the server along with a authentication tag. The server computes the first layer (f) of a neural network on the homomorphic encrypted data, generates a short proof-calculation for verifying the homomorphic results and sends them to an operator. He later on checks using the short proof that the calculation of the first layer is correct and, if so, he decrypts the result of this first layer and completes the neural network on clear data. More precisely, the user runs the **ProbGen** algorithm (described below) to encrypt and to generate a tag corresponding to his/her data. We note that a preliminary step consists in the generation of the keys by the operator (**Setup** algorithm). The server runs the **Compute** function (described below) over the received data to apply f, the first layer of the neural network and to compute the tag associated with the result. It returns thus the ciphertext $Enc(f(x))_{BFV}$ and the result tag $\sigma = f(\sigma_i)$ to the operator which verifies the results it receives with the **Verify** function. If the calculation is correct, he decrypts the result using the homomorphic secret key and he completes the evaluation of the remaining of the neural network over the clear data for obtaining the prediction result.

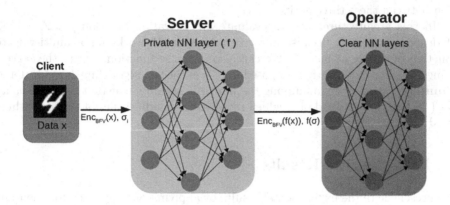

Fig. 2. Semi-encrypted neural network using FHE and VC.

Let us now go into more details. The data represented as $x = (x_0, \ldots, x_n)$ is encrypted with a BFV cryptosystem. For authentication the client uses the secret key to generate a series of tags $(\sigma_1, \ldots, \sigma_n)$, that will help the server to produce (without any secret key) the authentication tag σ corresponding to the result of the first private layer of the neural network, i.e. the quadratic activation function f (**Compute** algorithm). This tag $\sigma = f(\sigma_1, \ldots, \sigma_n)$ authenticates the ciphertext $\mu = f(\mu_0, \ldots, \mu_n)$ using the properties of homomorphic BFV ciphertexts obtained. The one receiving $f(\mu_0, \ldots, \mu_n)$ can verify effectively that the server performed the computation correctly (using the secret key of $\mathcal{VC}$) and can decrypt it to obtain $f(m_0, \ldots, m_n)$ (using the homomorphic secret key). This decrypted result is the input of the remaining of the neural network performed on clear data (Clear-NN algorithm).

Our steps are specified as follows:

Setup(NN, λ): Takes as input the neural network and generates the public (PK) and secret key (SK) to the VC scheme for BFV data.

ProbGen$_{PK}(\overrightarrow{x} = (x_1, \ldots, x_n))$: Takes as input the data $\overrightarrow{x}$. For all $i \in [1, n]$, it generates in parallel the encrypted $\mu_i \leftarrow BFV.Enc_{pk}(x_i)$ and the tags σ_i corresponding to the μ_i as shown in the above section.

Finally, it outputs $\sigma_x = (\mu_1, \sigma_1, \ldots, \mu_n, \sigma_n)$ and $\tau_x = \perp$.

Compute$_{PK}(\sigma_x)$: Taking as input the encrypted data and the corresponding tags, it runs the evaluation circuit BFV f over the BFV encrypted data μ_i, and, in the same time, it generates the tag corresponding to the evaluation of the circuit f over the tags σ_i gate-by-gate as mentioned above in the GateEval algorithm. Finally, it returns $\sigma_y = (\Delta, \mu, \sigma)$.

Complete$_{SK}(\sigma_y, \mu)$: Taking as inputs the tag and the encrypted result, it verifies the calculation using $\mathcal{VC}.Verify_{SK}(\sigma_y, \tau_x)$ and if it is true, it decrypts the result and completes the remaining of neural network Clear-NN over $f(x_1, \ldots, x_n)$, else it refuses the result .

The security of this architecture such as defined in Sect. 3 is based on the security of VC over BFV encrypted data and under the hypothesis of non collusion between these three entities.

In this architecture, we can evaluate an activation function $f : \mathbb{F}_q^n \to \mathbb{F}_q$ of degree at most 2, because our adaptation of $\mathcal{VC}$ works for a multi-variate function of degree at most 2. We can also hide the function f from the server, using the same modification proposed in [13] in the two algorithms **KeyGen** and **Compute** (namely, by modifying the multiplication-by-constant method, using $\tilde{H}_K(Enc_{BFV}(c))$ instead of c, which requires the modification in the algorithms cited above).

7   Experimental Results

We present here the experimental results of applying our approach for the digit recognition on the standard MNIST dataset.

In this section we work more to characterize the computational performances of our architecture than really building an operational machine learning system. In other words, despite that we use a small dataset size, this allows us to obtain a representative view for our architecture in terms of execution times and performances.

Hardware and Software. Let us precise that all tests were performed on an 2016 DELL PC(Genuine-Intel Core $i7 - 6600U$, 4 cores at 2.60 GHz with 16 GB RAM at 2.13 GHz), on Ubuntu (linux kernel 4.15.0-91-generic, with the architecture x86 − 64) as operating system.

Choosing a Model. For the training, we apply the adversarial training approach from [27]. They learned $P \in \mathbb{Z}^{d \times n}$ and $(D_i)_{i \in [\ell]} \in (\mathbb{Z}^{d \times d})^\ell$, with the model defined as $f_i(x) = (Px)^T D_i(Px), \forall i \in [\ell]$. Then, they generalized this model by adding a bias term: $f_i(x) = (Px + b)^T D_i(Px + b)$ for $b \in \mathbb{Z}_p^d$, and, for simplicity, they used an equivalent of this model by systematically adding a 1 at the beginning of x when encrypting it $x' = (1, x_1, \ldots, x_n)^T$. The prediction for the class of $x \in [0, 255]^{785}$ is $argmax_i(f_i(x))$ for $i \in [\ell]$. This modelling is important for FE efficiency [27], because it reduces the number of pairing computations. In our implementation, we used an equivalent model g defined as $g(x) = Q^t(Px)^2$, where $Q \in \mathbb{Z}^{d \times \ell}$ and $Q[i, j] = D_j[i, i]$ (i.e. $f_i(x) = g_i(x) = Q_i^T(Px)^2$ with Q_i the i-th row of Q). The prediction for the class of $x \in [0, 255]^{785}$ is $argmax(g(x))$. As such, instead of using a matrix per label, we use a new matrix Q for all labels. Therefore, the resulting model is a polynomial network of degree 2 with one hidden layer of d neurons and a square for the activation function.

Implementation Tools.

Homomorphic Encryption. We use the SEAL library [29], a homomorphic encryption library developed by Microsoft and written in modern standard C++. In terms of security, we choose parameters for providing 128 bits of security. We run SEAL with the following parameters: $n' = 4096$, $log_2(q) = 109$ and $t = 1032193$. These parameters are chosen using the Homomorphic Encryption Standardization report [10].

The table 2 illustrates the evolution of the noise budget for the prediction, and, as expected, the noise growth caused by the homomorphic multiplications increases rapidly (in our case $h_i \times h_i$ grows the noise by 38 bits).

Table 2. Noise budget where Q_i and P_i are the $i - th$ row of Q and $i - th$ row of P respectively.

	$[x_i]_{BFV}$	$h_i = P_i \cdot [x]_{BFV}$	h_i^2	$Q_i^2 \cdot h$
Noise budget	45 bits	40 bits	8 bits	5 bits

Verifiable Computing. We use the HAL library [33], a library for Homomorphic Authentication over encrypted BGV data, written in C and providing 128 bits of security, by using the Barreto-Naehrig curve for pairings.

In our experiments, we encrypt and decrypt homomorphically the data with SEAL library and we use the HAL library for authentication but for BFV encrypted data.

7.1   Results

Our tests consist in classifying a MNIST image data, a greyscale RGB image with 784 pixels, represented as a vector $x \in [0, 255]^{784}$. As illustrated in Fig. 3, we add 1 at the beginning of x when encrypting it (encrypting pixel by pixel) by the user. The server evaluates the model g over encrypted data (Hidden layer). Now the operator runs the Clear-NN algorithm for verifying the results and decrypting it to obtain $g(x)$ and calculate the argmax($g(x)$). Our model achieves $97,54\%$ accuracy on a test set of 10000 labeled images. We note that in our test we obtain the same confusion matrix as for the FE-model (see Fig. 4 in [27]).

Table 3. Costs (in seconds) for our architecture, where $x = (x_1, \ldots, x_{785})$

	User-side		Server-side		Operator-side	
Operation	*Enc*	*GenTag*	$g(Enc(x))$	$g(\sigma_1, \ldots, \sigma_n)$	*Verify*	*Dec*
Times	1.760	2.525	3.8	3.35	0.015	0.006

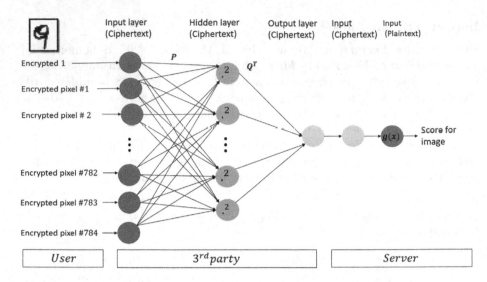

Fig. 3. Overview of our architecture with model g.

Table 4. Size (in KB) for MNIST test, where $x = (x_1, \ldots, x_i, \ldots, x_n)$, with $i = \{1, \ldots, 785\}$.

	User-side		Server-side	
	$Enc(x_i)$	$tag(\sigma_i)$	$Enc(f(x))$	$f(\sigma_i)$
$Size$	194	0.408	291	1.2

Performance. In Table 3, we describe the time evaluation for our approach. We remark that the user can execute the encryption function and the tags generation in parallel, so the user runs this step in average in less than 2.5 s. (Let us note that this time is inferior to the time of user for encryption using the $FE-$mode, of 8s.) Similarly, the server calculates the quadratic function g over encryption and over the authentication tag in parallel. Then, the server execution time is less than 3.8 s. We note that for computing the function g for all labels, we run in parallel the $g_i(\sigma_1, \ldots, \sigma_{785})$ for $i \in [10]$. Finally using our architecture, the time on the operator side is negligible. Namely, the operator time is 0.021s (decryption and verification together), while the time for $argmax$ on the decrypted results is negligible, as expected. In terms of memory requirements, Table 4 describes the size in KiloBytes of the data used our architecture. More precisely, we report the size of the homomorphic ciphertexts and of the authentication tags on both user and server sides.

8   Conclusion

In this paper, we presented a solution for private classification of sensitive data based on Homomorphic Encryption combined with a Verifiable Computing (VC) protocol to ensure the result integrity. We built on a semi-encrypted neural-network trained using a semi-adversarial model [26] and then preserve the confidentiality of sensitive data and the integrity for treatments using an application of VC over BFV encrypted data. Our experimental results for the MNIST image dataset are encouraging giving good classification accuracy (nearly 97.54%) with decent execution performances (less than 6s for the overall protocol). However, due to the limitations on the classes of functions supported in today practical VC techniques for encrypted data, our work was to some extend restricted to a private evaluation only for a first quadratic layer and we had to finalize (on another entity) the rest of the classification process on clear data from the decrypted intermediate values.

As such, one open research problem worth investigating consists in developing efficient verifiable delegation protocols with support for the computation of a broader class of functions, in particular any multi-variate polynomials. This will allow us to provide more complete privacy and integrity solutions for the evaluation of neural networks. Another more concrete research line we plan to follow is to improve the performances of the proposed approach by exploring the use of batching and other optimization techniques dedicated to HE computation. Finally, we hope that this work is a first step and will inspires further contributions around the application of Verifiable Computation and Homomorphic Encryption techniques for the design of secure AI methods.

A   Properties of VC

Let us now present a summary for some general properties of $\mathcal{VC}$ schemes, for more details see [13, 14]:

Correctness: The $\mathcal{VC}$ is correct if the client running the verification algorithm accepts, with a high probability, the output send by the server only when this one is correct.

Security: A $\mathcal{VC}$ scheme is secure if a malicious server cannot persuade the verification algorithm to accept an incorrect output.

Privacy: A $\mathcal{VC}$ scheme is private when the public outputs of the problem generation algorithm **ProbGen** over two different inputs are indistinguishable.

Function Privacy: This requirement guarantees that the public key PK, sampled via $(PK, SK) \leftarrow$ **KeyGen**(f, λ), does not leak information on the encoded function f, even after a polynomial amount of runs of **ProbGen**$_{SK}$ on adversarially chosen inputs.

Outsourceability: A $\mathcal{VC}$ can be outsourced if it allows efficient generation and efficient verification. (i.e. the time of (**ProbrGen**$_{SK}(x)$ + **Verify**(σ_y)) is in $O(T)$, where T is the time required to compute $f(x)$).

Adaptive Security: The adaptive security for a $\mathcal{VC}$ scheme is defined by the security when the adversary chooses f after having seen many "encodings" of σ_x for adaptively-chosen values x.

This type of schemes allows to compute σ_x independently of f so we can calculate σ_x before choosing f.

B   Realization of PRF with Amortized Closed-Form Efficiency

Definition 2. *A **PRF** (F.KG, F) is secure if, for every PPT adversary $\mathcal{A}$, we have that:*
$$\left| Pr[\mathcal{A}^{F_K(\cdot)}(\lambda, pp) = 1] - Pr[\mathcal{A}^{\Phi(\cdot)}(\lambda, pp) = 1] \right| \leq neg(\lambda) \ \text{where:} \ (K, pp) \leftarrow$$
$KG(\lambda)$ and $\Phi : \chi \rightarrow \mathcal{R}$ is a random function (i.e. it is not possible to distinguish between F and Φ).

Let $f : \mathbb{F}_q^n \rightarrow \mathbb{F}_q$ be an arithmetic circuit of degree 2, and, without loss of generality, parse $f(x_1, \ldots, x_n) = \sum_{i,j}^n \zeta_{i,j} \cdot x_i \cdot x_j + \sum_{k=1}^n \zeta_k \cdot x_k$

for some $\zeta_{i,j}, \zeta_k \in \mathbb{F}_q$. we $\hat{f} : (\mathbb{G}_1 \times \mathbb{G}_2)^n \rightarrow \mathbb{G}_T$ as the compilation of f on group elements such as: $\hat{f}(A_1, B_1 \ldots, A_n, B_n) = \prod_{i,j}^n \zeta_{i,j} \cdot e(A_i, B_j) \cdot \sum_{k=1}^n \zeta_k \cdot e(A_k, h)$

We will show the realization for the PRF with amortized closed-form efficiency For $\textbf{Comp}(R_1, S_1, V_1 \ldots, R_n, S_n, V_n, f) = \hat{f}(R_1, S_1, V_1 \ldots, R_n, S_n, V_n)$. That is the adaptation of the scheme of Bakes et al. in [1] to work with the asymmetric bilinear group.

- **F.KG**$(\lambda) \rightarrow K = (K_1, K_2)$:
  First generate $bgpp = (q, g, h, e)$ some bilinear group parameter, where $\mathbb{G}_1 = <g>, \mathbb{G}_2 = <h>$ *and* $q = order(\mathbb{G}_i)$ *for* $i = 1, 2$ and $e : \mathbb{G}_1 \times \mathbb{G}_2 \rightarrow \mathbb{G}_T$ non$-$degenerate$(\mathbb{G}_T = < e(g, h) >)$ bilinear map.
  Choose two seeds K_1, K_2 for a family of $PRFs$ $F'_{K_{1,2}} : \{0, 1\}^* \rightarrow \mathbb{F}_q^2$.
  Output K_1, K_2. The parameters define $F : \chi = \{0, 1\}^* \times \{0, 1\}^* \rightarrow \mathcal{R}^3$.
- **F**$_K(\Delta, \tau) \rightarrow (R, S, V)$:
  It generates $(u, v) \leftarrow F'_{K_1}(\tau)$ and $(a, b) \leftarrow F'_{K_2}(\Delta)$
  Finally it calculates $(R, S) = (g^{ua+vb}, h^{ua+vb})$.
- **CFEval**$_\tau^{off}(K, f) \rightarrow w_f = \rho$:
  For $i = 1$ *to* t : calculate $(u_i, v_i) = F'_{K_1}(\tau_i)$ and construct a linear map ρ_i using (u_i, v_i) as $\rho_i(x_1, x_2) = u_i \cdot x_1 + v_i \cdot x_2$
  Run $\rho \leftarrow f(\rho_1, \ldots, \rho_t)$, i.e., $\forall z_1, z_2 \in \mathbb{F}_q$: $\rho(z_1, z_2) = f(\rho_1(z_1, z_2), \ldots, \rho_t(z_1, z_2))$.
- **CFEval**$_\Delta^{on}(K, w_f) \rightarrow W$:
  It generates $(a, b) \leftarrow F'_{k_2}(\Delta)$ and computes $W = e(g, h)^{w_f(a,b)}$.
  for the proof of this scheme follow theorem 4 of [13].

C   Realizations of Homomorphic Hash [13]

In the construction of $\tilde{\textbf{H}}$, we use the $bgpp = (q, g, h, e)$ where q be a prime of λ bit and let $\mathbb{F}_q = \mathbb{Z}/q\mathbb{Z}$. Let us define a function $H_{\alpha,\beta}(\mu)$ as follow: for

$\mu \in \mathcal{D} = \{\mu \in \mathbb{Z}_q[x][y] : deg_x(\mu) = N, deg_y(\mu) = c\} \subset R_q[y]$, $H_{\alpha,\beta}(\mu)$ first evaluates μ at $y = \alpha$ and then evaluates $\mu(\alpha)$ at β i.e. $H_{\alpha,\beta}(\mu) = ev_\beta \circ ev_\alpha(\mu)$.

The family of hash functions $(\tilde{H}.KeyGen, \tilde{H}, \tilde{H}.Eval)$ with domain $\mathcal{D}$ and range $\mathbb{G}_1 \times \mathbb{G}_2$ is defined as below:

- $\tilde{\mathbf{H}}.\mathbf{KeyGen} \to (K, \kappa = (\alpha, \beta))$:
  First at all, generate $bgpp = (g, h, q)$
  Next, sample a random $(\alpha, \beta) \leftarrow (\mathbb{F}_q)^2$ Afterwords, for $i = 0, \ldots, c$ and, $j = 1, \ldots, N$ and we calculate $g^{\alpha^i \beta^j}$, and $h^{\alpha_i \alpha_j}$ and include them to K.
  Output K and $\kappa = (\alpha, \beta)$.
- $\tilde{\mathbf{H}}$: For $\mu \in \mathcal{D}$, in function of its degree $deg_y(\mu)$, $\tilde{H}_\kappa(\mu)$ is computed differently. If $deg_y(\mu) \leq 1$ then $\tilde{H}_\kappa(\mu) = (T, U) = (g^{H_\kappa(\mu)}, h^{H_\kappa(\mu)}) \in \mathbb{G}_1 \times \mathbb{G}_2$. If $deg_y(\mu) = 2$, then $e(g, h)^{H_\kappa(\mu)}$
- $\tilde{\mathbf{H}}.\mathbf{Eval}(f_g, \nu_1, \nu_2)$: It computes in a homomorphic way a function of degree 2 on the outputs of $\tilde{H}$.
  For $\nu_1 = (T_1, U_1)$, $\nu_2 = (T_2, U_2)$ and (respectively, $\tilde{T}_1, \tilde{T}_2 \in \mathbb{G}_T$).

$$\begin{cases} \nu_1 + \nu_2 = (T_1 \cdot T_2, U_1 \cdot U_2) \text{ (resp } \tilde{T} \leftarrow \tilde{T}_1 \cdot \tilde{T}_2) \\ c \cdot \nu = (T^c, U^c) \text{ (resp } \tilde{T}^c) \text{ for } c \in \mathbb{F}_q \\ \nu_1 \cdot \nu_2 = e(T_1, U_2) \in \mathbb{G}_T \end{cases}$$

References

1. Backes, M., Fiore, D., et al.: Verifiable delegation of computation on outsourced data. In: Proceedings of the 2013 ACM SIGSAC Conference on Computer & Communications Security, pp. 863–874 (2013)
2. Ball, M., Carmer, B., et al.: Garbled neural networks are practical. Cryptology ePrint Archive, Report 2019/338 (2019)
3. Boemer, F., Costache, A., et al.: Ngraph-HE2: a high-throughput framework for neural network inference on encrypted data. In: Proceedings of the 7th ACM Workshop on Encrypted Computing & Applied Homomorphic Cryptography. WAHC 2019, pp. 45–56 (2019)
4. Boemer, F., Lao, Y., et al.: nGraph-HE: a graph compiler for deep learning on homomorphically encrypted data. CoRR (2018)
5. Bourse, F., Minelli, M., Minihold, M., Paillier, P.: Fast homomorphic evaluation of deep discretized neural networks. In: Shacham, H., Boldyreva, A. (eds.) CRYPTO 2018. LNCS, vol. 10993, pp. 483–512. Springer, Cham (2018). https://doi.org/10.1007/978-3-319-96878-0_17
6. Brutzkus, A., Oren Elisha, O., et al.: Low latency privacy preserving inference. In: Proceedings of the 36th International Conference on Machine Learning, Long Beach, California, PMLR 97 (2019)
7. Chabanne, H., de Wargny, A., et al.: Privacy-preserving classification on deep neural network. Cryptology ePrint Archive, Report 2017/035 (2017)
8. Chabanne, H., Keuffer, J., et al.: Embedded proofs for verifiable neural networks. IACR Cryptology ePrint Archive, 2017:1038 (2017)
9. Chabanne, H., Lescuyer, R., Milgram, J., Morel, C., Prouff, E.: Recognition over encrypted faces. In: Renault, É., Boumerdassi, S., Bouzefrane, S. (eds.) MSPN 2018. LNCS, vol. 11005. Springer, Cham (2019). https://doi.org/10.1007/978-3-030-03101-5_16

10. Chase, M., Chen, H., et al.: Security of homomorphic encryption. Technical report, HomomorphicEncryption.org, Redmond WA, USA, July 2017
11. Chou, E., Beal, J., et al.: Faster CryptoNets: leveraging sparsity for real-world encrypted inference. CoRR (2018)
12. Fan, J., Vercauteren, F.: Somewhat practical fully homomorphic encryption. IACR Cryptology ePrint Archive 2012:144 (2012)
13. Fiore, D., Gennaro, R., et al.: Efficiently verifiable computation on encrypted data. In: Proceedings of the 2014 ACM SIGSAC Conference on Computer and Communications Security, pp. 844–855 (2014)
14. Gennaro, R., Gentry, C., Parno, B.: Non-interactive verifiable computing: outsourcing computation to untrusted workers. In: Rabin, T. (ed.) CRYPTO 2010. LNCS, vol. 6223, pp. 465–482. Springer, Heidelberg (2010). https://doi.org/10.1007/978-3-642-14623-7_25
15. Ghodsi, Z., Gu, T., et al.: SafetyNets: verifiable execution of deep neural networks on an untrusted cloud. In: Advances in Neural Information Processing Systems, pp. 4672–4681 (2017)
16. Gilad-Bachrach, R., Dowlin, N., et al.: CryptoNets: applying neural networks to encrypted data with high throughput and accuracy. In: International Conference on Machine Learning, pp. 201–210 (2016)
17. Groth, J.: On the size of pairing-based non-interactive arguments. In: Fischlin, M., Coron, J.-S. (eds.) EUROCRYPT 2016. LNCS, vol. 9666, pp. 305–326. Springer, Heidelberg (2016). https://doi.org/10.1007/978-3-662-49896-5_11
18. Hesamifard, E., Takabi, H., et al.: Deep neural networks classification over encrypted data. In: Proceedings of the Ninth ACM Conference on Data and Application Security and Privacy. CODASPY 2019, pp. 97–108 (2019)
19. Izabachène, M., Sirdey, R., Zuber, M.: Practical fully homomorphic encryption for fully masked neural networks. In: Mu, Y., Deng, R.H., Huang, X. (eds.) CANS 2019. LNCS, vol. 11829, pp. 24–36. Springer, Cham (2019). https://doi.org/10.1007/978-3-030-31578-8_2
20. Keuffer, J., Molva, R., Chabanne, H.: Efficient proof composition for verifiable computation. In: Lopez, J., Zhou, J., Soriano, M. (eds.) ESORICS 2018. LNCS, vol. 11098, pp. 152–171. Springer, Cham (2018). https://doi.org/10.1007/978-3-319-99073-6_8
21. LeCun, Y., Cortes, C., et al.: Mnist handwritten digit database 7:23, 2010 (2010). http://yann.lecun.com/exdb/mnist
22. Lee, S., Ko, H., et al.: VCNN: Verifiable convolutional neural network. IACR Cryptology ePrint Archive, 2020:584 (2020)
23. Lund, C., Fortnow, L., et al.: Algebraic methods for interactive proof systems. J. ACM (JACM) **39**(4), 859–868 (1992)
24. Parno, B., Howell, J., et al.: Pinocchio: nearly practical verifiable computation. In: 2013 IEEE Symposium on Security and Privacy, pp. 238–252. IEEE (2013)
25. Rouhani, B.D., Riazi, M.S., et al.: DeepSecure: scalable provably-secure deep learning. CoRR (2017)
26. Ryffel, T., Sans, E.D., et al.: Partially encrypted machine learning using functional encryption. arXiv preprint arXiv:1905.10214 (2019)
27. Sans, E.D., Gay, R., et al.: Reading in the dark: Classifying encrypted digits with functional encryption. IACR Cryptology ePrint Archive 2018:206 (2018)
28. Sanyal, A., Kusner, M., et al.: ICML, June 2018
29. Microsoft SEAL (release 3.0). http://sealcrypto.org, October 2018

30. Thaler, J.: Time-optimal interactive proofs for circuit evaluation. In: Canetti, R., Garay, J.A. (eds.) CRYPTO 2013. LNCS, vol. 8043, pp. 71–89. Springer, Heidelberg (2013). https://doi.org/10.1007/978-3-642-40084-1_5
31. Zhao, L., Wang, Q., et al.: VeriML: enabling integrity assurances and fair payments for machine learning as a service. arXiv preprint arXiv:1909.06961 (2019)
32. Zuber, M., Carpov, S., et al.: Towards real-time hidden speaker recognition by means of fully homomorphic encryption. Cryptology ePrint Archive, Report 2019/976 (2019)
33. Zuber, M., Fiore, D.: Hal: A library for homomorphic authentication (2016–2017). http://www.myurl.com

Attribute-Based Symmetric Searchable Encryption

Hai-Van Dang[1], Amjad Ullah[1], Alexandros Bakas[2(✉)], and Antonis Michalas[2]

[1] University of Westminster, London, UK
{H.Dang,A.Ullah}@westminster.ac.uk
[2] Tampere University, Tampere, Finland
{alexandros.bakas,antonios.michalas}@tuni.fi

Abstract. Symmetric Searchable Encryption (SSE) is an encryption technique that allows users to search directly on their outsourced encrypted data while preserving the privacy of both the files and the queries. Unfortunately, majority of the SSE schemes allows users to either decrypt the whole ciphertext or nothing at all. In this paper, we propose a novel scheme based on traditional symmetric primitives, that allows data owners to bind parts of their ciphertexts with specific policies. Inspired by the concept of Attribute-Based Encryption (ABE) in the public setting, we design a scheme through which users can recover only certain parts of an encrypted document if and only if they retain a set of attributes that satisfy a policy. Our construction satisfies the important notion of forward privacy while at the same time supports the multi-client model by leveraging SGX functionality for the synchronization of users. To prove the correctness of our approach, we provide a detailed simulation-based security analysis coupled with an extensive experimental evaluation that shows the effectiveness of our scheme.

Keywords: Cloud security · Database security · Forward privacy · Symmetric searchable encryption

1 Introduction

Symmetric Searchable Encryption (SSE) [15,16,19] is a promising encryption technique that squarely fits the cloud paradigm and can pave the way for the development of cloud services that will respect users' privacy even in the case of a compromised Cloud Service Provider (CSP). SSE schemes can be seen as a first, fundamental step for protecting users' data from both external and *internal* attacks (e.g. a malicious administrator). This is due to the fact that in an SSE scheme, users generate all the secret information (encryption key) locally and encrypt all of their data on client side (i.e. the encryption key is *never* revealed to the CSP). The service offered by the CSP is only used for storing and retrieving

This work was funded by the ASCLEPIOS EU research project (Project No. 826093).

© Springer Nature Switzerland AG 2020
J. Zhou et al. (Eds.): ACNS 2020 Workshops, LNCS 12418, pp. 318–336, 2020.
https://doi.org/10.1007/978-3-030-61638-0_18

the generated ciphertexts. In contrast to traditional encryption schemes, SSE offers a remarkable functionality – it allows users to search for specific keywords directly through the stored ciphertexts. However fascinating, SSE schemes [16] "suffer" from several disadvantages with most prominent ones being their efficiency and security. Despite the importance of these issues, in this paper we mostly focus on a new problem that, to the best of our knowledge, has not be addressed in the literature. By studying the implementation and application of SSE in important sectors such as the healthcare industry, we realized that the traditional problem of encryption that cannot enforce granular access control is becoming really important. Consider, a patient who has encrypted with an SSE scheme all of her medical information in a single file. Then, assume she wishes to give access to her medical data to a dermatologist. The problem that arises here is that the patient has no way of giving out only the related to a dermatologist examination information from her medical records (i.e. keep the rest of the information private). While this is a well-known limitation of traditional encryption schemes, in SSE is of paramount importance since such schemes are built for the cloud – an environment that supports data sharing between multiple users. We believe that it is time to adopt a new broad vision of cryptosystems that will take advantage of the cloud features without compromising users' privacy. To this end, we explore the concept of granular access control in SSE schemes with the use of trusted hardware.

Apart from focusing on the aforementioned problem, we also try to enhance our scheme with the best security guarantees. Leaked information in SSE schemes has become a problem of paramount importance since it is the main factor in defining the overall level of security. In works such as [13] and [25] it is pointed out that even a small leakage can lead to several privacy attacks. These works were further extended in [33] where the authors assumed that an active adversary can perform file-injection attacks and record the output. This "new" ability allowed the adversary to recover information about past queries only after ten file insertions. This result led researchers to design *forward private* SSE schemes [7,10,17]. Forward privacy is a notion introduced in [32] and guarantees that that newly added files cannot be related to past search queries. While forward privacy is a very important property, unfortunately it has been shown to also be vulnerable to certain file-injection attacks [33]. While forward privacy secures the contents of a past query, its binary property, *backward privacy*, ensures the privacy of future queries. Backward privacy was formalized in [11]. Informally, an SSE scheme is said to be backward private if whenever a (w, id) is deleted from the database, subsequent search queries for w do not reveal id. More information on backward privacy can be found in [11]. In our case, our construction does not support a delete function and as a result, there is no need to worry about deleted entries.

Our Contributions: The contribution of this paper is manifold: *(1)* We introduce the first SSE scheme that provides granular access control and does not fall under the *All-or-Nothing* category[1]. Using our scheme, a user can only decrypt parts of the ciphertexts based on a policy and a list of attributes. *(2)* Our construction is among the first SSE schemes that preserve the notion of *forward privacy in the multi-client setting* – a very challenging problem since we need to ensure that at any given time, all users are synchronized. *(3)* Our scheme is asymptotically optimal. The update cost is $O(m)$ and the search time is $O(\ell)$, where m is the number of unique keywords in a file and ℓ is the number of the resulted files. *(4)* Our construction is parallelizable. *(5)* We test the overall performance of the scheme in an experimental test-bed, that realistically imitates a client-server approach. We built an in-house OpenStack private cloud and a client that communicates with the cloud over the Internet. Additionally, for the storage of data we used PostgreSQL – a proper database in contrast to other similar works, that rely on the use of data structures such as arrays, maps, etc.

2   Background

Notation: Let s be a string. The length of s is denoted by $|s|$, its prefix of length ℓ by $\overline{s}(\ell)$, and its suffix of length ℓ by $\underline{s}(\ell)$, where $\ell \leq |s|$. The i–th position of s is denoted by $s[i]$. A function $negl(\cdot)$ is called negligible if $\forall c \in \mathbb{N}, \exists n_0 \in \mathbb{N} : \forall n \geq n_0, negl(n) < n^{-c}$. A file collection $\mathcal{F}$ is denoted by $\mathcal{F} = \{f_1, \ldots, f_n\}$. The unique identifier of a file $f_i \in \mathcal{F}$ is denoted by $id(f_i)$ and its corresponding ciphertext is $c_{id(f_i)}$. The universe of keywords is denoted by $\mathcal{W} = \{w_1, \ldots, w_m\}$ and the ciphertext of a keyword $w_j \in \mathcal{W}$ is c_{w_j}. A *probabilistic polynomial time* (PPT) adversary $\mathcal{ADV}$ is a randomized algorithm for which there exists a polynomial $p(\cdot)$ such that for all input x, the running time of $\mathcal{ADV}(x)$ is bounded by $p(|x|)$. Finally, a truth table is a mathematical table used to determine if a statement is true (T) or false (F). In this work, each statement is represented by a binary string and hence, T = 1 and F = 0. The logical conjunction ($\wedge$) of two strings s_1 and s_2 outputs 1 (True) iff $\exists i : s_1[i] = s_2[i] = 1$. For example (Table 1):

Table 1. Truth table for the conjunction of binary strings

s_1	s_2	$s_1 \wedge s_2$
001	011	1 (T)
010	101	0 (F)
100	010	0 (F)
111	001	1 (T)

Definition 1 (Symmetric Searchable Encryption). *A Symmetric Searchable Encryption scheme consists of the following PPT algorithms:*

---

[1] *All-or-Nothing* refers to the restriction of existing SSE to offer granular access control on encrypted data (i.e. once you decrypt a file you get access to all of its information).

- KeyGen(1^λ) : *A probabilistic algorithm that takes as input a security parameter λ and outputs a symmetric key* K.
- Add(f_i) : *A user runs this algorithm whenever she wants to upload a new file f_i to the CSP.*
- Search(w_j) : *A user runs this algorithm to search on the encrypted data collection for those files that contain a keyword w_j.*

Security Definitions: To formalize the leakage of our scheme, we make use of a leakage function $\mathcal{L}$ such that $\mathcal{L} = (\mathcal{L}_{add}, \mathcal{L}_{search})$ where the components $\mathcal{L}_{add}$ and $\mathcal{L}_{search}$ correspond to the leakage associated with addition and search operations. The adversary $\mathcal{ADV}$ has full control of the client and thus, can trigger add and search operations at will. $\mathcal{ADV}$ issues a polynomial number of queries and for each query she records the output. The scheme is $\mathcal{L}$−adaptively secure if there exists a simulator $\mathcal{S}$ that, given the leakage function $\mathcal{L}$, can simulate add and search tokens.

Definition 2 ($\mathcal{L}$−Adaptive Security). *Let* SSE = (KeyGen, Add, Search) *be a symmetric searchable encryption scheme. Moreover, let $\mathcal{L} = (\mathcal{L}_{add}.\mathcal{L}_{search})$ be the leakage function of the SSE scheme. We consider the following experiments between an adversary $\mathcal{ADV}$ and a simulator $\mathcal{S}$.*

Real$_{\mathcal{ADV}}(1^\lambda)$

> $\mathcal{ADV}$ *makes a polynomial time of adaptive queries $q = \{w, f_1\}$ such that f_1 has not been uploaded to the CSP and for each q she receives back either a search token for w, $\tau_s(w)$ or an add token $\tau_\alpha(f_1)$ for f_1 and a sequence of ciphertexts $\{c_{w_1}, \ldots, c_{w_n}\}, \forall w_i \in f_1$. $\mathcal{ADV}$ outputs a bit b.*

Ideal$_{\mathcal{ADV},\mathcal{S}}(1^\lambda)$

> $\mathcal{ADV}$ *makes a polynomial time of adaptive queries $q = \{w, f_1\}$ and for each q, $\mathcal{S}$ is given $\mathcal{L} = (\mathcal{L}_{add}, \mathcal{L}_{search})$. $\mathcal{S}$ then returns a token and, in the case of addition, a sequence of ciphertexts c_i. $\mathcal{ADV}$ outputs a bit b.*

We say that the DSSE scheme is $\mathcal{L}$-i secure if for all probabilistic polynomial adversaries $\mathcal{ADV}$, there exists a probabilistic simulator $\mathcal{S}$ such that:

$$|Pr[(Real) = 1] - Pr[(Ideal) = 1]| \leq negl(\lambda)$$

Definition 3 (Search Pattern). *The Search Pattern is a vector sp that shows which query each keyword corresponds to. For example, $sp[t] = w_j$ means that w_j was queried at time t.*

Definition 4 (Access Pattern). *The Access Pattern for a keyword w_i is the set of all files containing w_i at a given time t. The set is denoted by $\mathcal{F}_{w_i,t}$.*

Definition 5. (Leakage Function $\mathcal{L}$). *Let $\mathcal{L} = (\mathcal{L}_{add}, \mathcal{L}_{search})$.*

- $\mathcal{L}_{add} = (id(f_i), \#w_i \in f_i)$. *This function leaks the unique identifier of each file as well as the number of keywords contained in it.*
- $\mathcal{L}_{search} = (sp[t], \mathcal{F}_{w_i,t})$. *This function leaks the search and access patterns.*

Definition 6 (Forward Privacy). *An SSE scheme is said to be forward pri-vate, if for all additions $\mathcal{L}_{add}$ can be written as $\mathcal{L}_{add} = (id(f_i), \#w_i \in f_i)^2$.*

3   Architecture

In this section, we introduce the system model by describing the entities par-ticipating in our construction. Figure 1 depicts the high-level architecture of the system, where the core entities and their interaction can be seen.

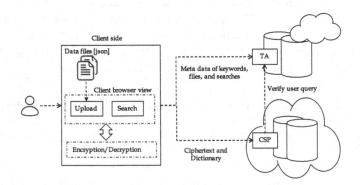

Fig. 1. High-level architecture

Access Control: We design an access control mechanism based on a truth table. In particular, each user has a specific role and each attribute is associated with a rule. These roles and rules are represented as binary strings and thus, if the conjunction of these strings outputs 1, then the underlying role can access the specified attribute. The Roles and Rules tables are defined later in Table 2.

Registration Authority (RA): We assume the existence of a registration authority RA that generate the SSE key K and share it with registered users[3]. Additionally, RA generates Roles – a dictionary that contains mappings between roles and their access rights (represented in binary). For example, as can be seen in Table 2a, the access rights for the role of a doctor is 001, or $R(Doctor) = 001$. Upon its generation, Roles is sent to the CSP.

Users: We denote by $\mathcal{U} = \{u_1, \ldots, u_n\}$ the set of users that have been regis-tered to a cloud service that supports our scheme. Users are classified into two categories: data owners and users that have not yet uploaded any encrypted data to the CSP. The latter category simply queries the CSP for files containing a specific keyword. The role of the data owner however, is the most important since it is the one that creates and outsources all the necessary indexes that will allow the rest of the users to generate consistent search tokens and search over the stored ciphertexts. A data owner creates the following indexes:

---

[2] More details about forward privacy can be found in [11].

[3] RA and its key sharing protocol are out of the scope of this paper.

1. No.Files[**w**, att]: Contains a hash of each keyword/attribute pair $\{w.att\}$, along with the number of files that each pair can be found at.
2. No.Search[**w**, att]: Contains a hash of each keyword/attribute pair $\{w.att\}$, along with the number of files that each pair has been queried for.
3. Rules: A dictionary mapping attributes to specific rules (represented in binary values). As an example, in Table 2b, the rule for the attribute "Disease" is 010, or $A(Disease) = 010$. A user u_i can access an attribute att$_j$ bound by a specific rule, iff $(R(u_i)) \wedge ((A(att_j)) \neq 0$.
4. Dict: A dictionary containing mappings between hash values of keywords and file identifiers.
5. EDB: A dictionary containing mappings between file identifiers and encrypted keywords.

Cloud Service Provider (CSP): We consider a cloud computing environment similar to the one described in [30]. The CSP storage will consist of two tables Dict and EDB. Dict contains a mapping between keywords and file identifiers while EDB contains the inverse mapping (i.e between file identifiers and keywords). Additionally, the CSP stores the Roles and Rules tables, that enable access control on each search query. The CSP verifies each query of the users to make sure that the user is authorised and has access to the TA.

Trusted Authority (TA): TA is an index storage that stores the No.Files[w, att] and No.Search[w, att] values for a keyword w. These values are needed to create the search tokens that will allow users to search directly on the encrypted data. The TA must run inside the trusted execution enviornment in order to guarantee the integrity and confidentiality of its security-sensitive computation. Intel SGX provides such a protected execution environment. Hence, the proposed SSE scheme expects, the TA must support SGX. The TA must remotely attest itself to the Client application and to the CSP service, prior to its use, to prove that it runs in a trusted execution enviornment. A detailed description on SGX functionalities can be found in [18].

Structured Data: It is worth noting that the proposed scheme works only with structured data. In particular, we require all files to be presented as lists of attribute/keyword pairs (e.g. "Age = 42", "Surname = Adams", etc). This requirement makes our construction suitable for practical use-cases that normally rely on structured data (e.g. healthcare records).

4 Our Construction

This section constitutes the core contribution of our paper as we present a detailed description of the construction. We assume the existence of an IND-CPA secure symmetric key cryptosystem SKE = (Gen, Enc, Dec) and that of a cryptographic hash function $h : \{0,1\}^* \rightarrow \{0,1\}^\lambda$. It is important to mention here that for most SSE schemes, retrieving the actual files from the CSP is considered to be a trivial process and as such is not taken into consideration. In our construction, this is essential as the user does not retrieve the entire files but encrypted parts of it. Before we proceed with the formal construction we provide a high-level description in the form of a toy example, with three files, f_1, f_2 and f_3. Each file contains structured data with multiple keyword/attribute pairs.

Toy Example: We assume a scenario with three different roles, Doctor, Nurse and Researcher and three files (f_1, f_2, f_3) as shown in Table 2 . The Role table maps each role to a binary value; whereas, the Rule table maps each attribute to a specific rule which is also presented in binary format. An attribute att_j is accessible to a user u_i iff $R(u_i) \wedge A(att_j) \neq 0$. For instance, if u_i is a nurse and $att_j = surname$, then $R(nurse) \wedge A(surname) = 010 \wedge 011 = 010 \neq 0$. Hence, a nurse can access surnames. Similarly, a nurse can access disease, but not age since $R(nurse) \wedge A(age) = 010 \wedge 101 = 0$. We now assume that a nurse u_i wishes to search for the keyword w_1 that refers to surname. After u_i requests the No.Files$[w_1, surname]$ and No.Search$[w_1, surname]$ values from the TA, she can create the search token $\tau_s(w_1)$ that will be sent to the CSP. Upon reception, the CSP verifies that u_i, as a nurse, is allowed to access surname and disease. As a next step, the CSP locates the files f_i such that $w_1 \in f_i$ (in this case, f_1). Finally, based on f_i, the CSP retrieves EDB, and sends back to u_i the ciphertexts c_{w_1} and c_{w_3} (since c_{w_2} corresponds to an attribute that u_i is unauthorized to access, it will not be sent back to her).

Table 2. CSP tables

Role	Value	Attr	Rule
Doctor	001	Surname	011
Nurse	010	Age	101
Researcher	100	Disease	010
(a) Roles		(b) Rules	

Kw	File
$h(w_4)$	f_2
$h(w_5)$	f_2
$h(w_6)$	f_2
$h(w_3)$	f_1
$h(w_2)$	f_1
$h(w_1)$	f_1
$h(w_8)$	f_3
$h(w_7)$	f_3
$h(w_9)$	f_3
(c) Dict.	

File	Attr	Ciphertext
f_1	Surname	c_{w_1}
f_1	Age	c_{w_2}
f_1	Disease	c_{w_3}
f_2	Surname	c_{w_4}
f_2	Age	c_{w_5}
f_2	Disease	c_{w_6}
f_3	Surname	c_{w_7}
f_3	Age	c_{w_8}
f_3	Disease	c_{w_9}
(d) EDB		

4.1   Formal Construction

Key Generation. RA runs the KeyGen algorithm to generate the secret key $K = (K_1, K_2)$ where $K_1, K_2 \leftarrow$ SKE.Gen. K will be shared with all users upon their registration to the service, whereas K_1 is used to encrypt/decrypt data (line 9 of Algorithm 1) and K_2 will be sent to TA to generate a proof for search query verification (lines 11–14 of Algorithm 2).

File Addition. To add a new file f_i, a user u_i first extracts all the keywords and attributes from f_i. For each pair of (attribute, keyword), requests the No.Files and No.Search values from the TA. These will allow u_i to compute the unique keyword key K_w and the address $addr_w$ (hash value of the keyword as in lines 5–6 of Algorithm 1). Next, u_i encrypts the keywords locally and sends them to the CSP who stores them in the EDB dictionary. Additionally, u_i sends a list Map $= \{addr_w, id(f_i)\}$ to the CSP that will be inserted in Dict. Finally, an acknowledgement is sent to the TA to update the No.Files and No.Search indexes accordingly.

Algorithm 1. File Addition

1: Map $= \{\}$
2: $C_w = \{\}, Att_w = \{\}$
3: **for** all $w_j \in f_i$ **do**
4:     No.Files$[w_j, att_j]++$
5:     $K_{w_j} = \mathsf{SKE.Enc}(K_2, h(w_j)||att_j||\mathsf{No.Search}[w_j, att_j])$
6:     $addr_{w_j} = h(K_{w_j}, \mathsf{No.Files}[w_j, att_j]||0)$
7:     $val_{w_j} = id(f_i)$
8:     Map $=$ Map $\cup \{addr_{w_j}, id(f_i)\}$
9:     $c_{w_j} = \mathsf{SKE.Enc}(K_1, w_j)$
10:    $C_w = C_w \cup c_{w_j}, Att_w = Att_w \cup att_j$
11: Send $\{\mathsf{No.Files}[w_j, att_j]\}$ values to be updated at TA
12: Send $(\mathsf{Map}, id(f_i), \{C_w\}, \{Att_w\})$ to the CSP
13: CSP adds Map into Dict and $id(f_i), \{C_w\}, \{Att_w\}$ to EDB

Search. Assume a user u_k wishes to perform a search operation for a given keyword/attribute pair (e.g. age $= 42$). To do so, she first contacts the TA to request No.Files$[w_j, att_j]$ and No.Search$[w_j, att_j]$ values, where att_j and w_j is the keyword/attribute pair she wishes to search for. Based on No.Search$[w_j, att_j]$, u_k can compute the unique keyword key K_{w_j}. Additionally, u_k also computes the updated addresses for Dict by incrementing the value of No.Search$[w_j, att_j]$ by one (lines 3–8 of Algorithm 2). Finally, u_k computes and sends to the CSP the search token that consists of the keyword key K_{w_j}, No.Files$[w_j, att_j]$ and the updated addresses. Upon reception, the CSP forwards K_{w_j} to the TA who decrypts it using K_2 and calculates the updated addresses. The updated addresses will be sent back to the CSP who can verify their correctness[4]. Then the CSP locates all the Dict entries (file identifiers $id(f_i)$), associated with w_j. Based on the list of $id(f_i)$ and u_k 's role, the CSP retrieves all encrypted keywords (c_w) associated with each f_i that u_k is eligible to access. The result is finally sent to u_k in a result list R.

---

[4] At a first glance, this extra round of communication between the CSP and the TA seems unnecessary. However, it is essential for preventing an attack in which a malicious user would send to the CSP a list of wrong addresses.

Algorithm 2. Search

User u_k:

1: Request No.Files$[w_j, att_j]$ and No.Search$[w_j, att_j]$ values from TA
2: $\mathsf{K}_{\mathsf{w_j}} = \mathsf{SKE.Enc}(\mathsf{K_2}, h(w_j) \| att_j \| \mathsf{No.Search}[\mathsf{w_j}, \mathsf{att_j}])$
3: No.Search$[w_j, att_j]++$
4: $\mathsf{K}_{\mathsf{w_j}}' = \mathsf{SKE.Enc}(\mathsf{K_2}, h(w_j) \| att_j \| \mathsf{No.Search}[\mathsf{w_j}, \mathsf{att_j}])$
5: $L_u = \{\}$
6: **for** $i = 1$ to No.Files$[w_j, att_j]$ **do**
7:     $\mathrm{addr}_{\mathsf{w_i}} = h(\mathsf{K}_{\mathsf{w_i}}', i \| 0)$
8:     $L_u = L_u \cup \{\mathrm{addr}_{\mathsf{w_i}}\}$
9: Send $\tau_s(w_j) = (\mathsf{K}_{\mathsf{w_j}}, \mathsf{No.Files}[w_j, att_j], L_u, att_j)$ to CSP.

CSP:

10: Forward K_{w_j} to TA

TA:

11: Decrypt $\mathsf{K}_{\mathsf{w_j}}$, and repeat steps 3-8 with locally stored values of No.Files, No.Search to produce a list $L_{TA} = \{\mathrm{addr}_{\mathsf{w_i}}\}$

CSP:

12: Send L_{TA} to the CSP
13: **if** $L_u \neq L_{TA}$ **then**
14:     Output $\perp$
15: **else**
16:     $\mathbf{F}_{\mathbf{w_j}} = \{\}$
17:     **for** $i = 1$ to No.Files$[w_i, att_i]$ **do**
18:         $id(f_i) = \mathrm{Dict}[h(\mathsf{K}_{\mathsf{w_j}}, i \| 0)]$
19:         $F_{w_j} = F_{w_j} \cup \{id(f_i)\}$
20:         Remove $\mathrm{Dict}[h(\mathsf{K}_{\mathsf{w_j}}, i \| 0)]$
21:     Add the new addresses as specified in L_u
22:     $R = \{\}$
23:     **for all** $id(f_i) \in F_{w_j}$ **do**
24:         **for all** $c_{w_\ell} \in f_i$ **do**
25:             **if** $R(u_k) \wedge A(att_\ell) \neq 0$ **then**
26:                 $R = R \cup \{att_\ell, c_{w_l}\}$
27:     Send R to u_k
28:     Send acknowledgement to TA to update No.Search

5   Security Analysis

In this section, we prove the security of our construction according to Definition 2. We will prove that we can construct a simulator $\mathcal{S}$ that can simulate addition and search tokens in a way that no PPT adversary $\mathcal{ADV}$ will be able to distinguish between the real and ideal experiments as they were defined in Sect. 2. Note that, similarly to all SSE schemes, our goal is to prove that addition and search tokens can be simulated given only the leakage function $\mathcal{L}$.

Theorem 1. *Let* SKE $= (\mathsf{Gen}, \mathsf{Enc}, \mathsf{Dec})$ *be a CPA-secure symmetric key cryptosystem. Moreover, let* $h : \{0,1\}^* \rightarrow \{0,1\}^\lambda$ *be a secure cryptographic hash function. Then our construction is secure according to Definition 2.*

Proof. To prove the security of our construction, we use a hybrid argument where the simulator S is given as input the leakage function $\mathcal{L} = (\mathcal{L}_{add}, \mathcal{L}_{search})$ and simulates the SSE functionalities. In a pre-processing phase S generates a key $K_{EXP} \leftarrow$ SKE.Gen(1^λ) that is given to $\mathcal{ADV}$. Moreover, S creates a dictionary KeyStore to store the last K_w of each keyword and one dictionary FOracle to reply to random oracle queries.

Hybrid 0: Everything runs as specified in the protocol.

Hybrid 1: Like Hybrid 0 but instead of the addition algorithm, S is given $\mathcal{L}_{add}$ and proceeds as shown in Algorithm 3.

Algorithm 3. Add Token Simulation

1: $L = \{\}$
2: $C = \{\}$
3: **for** $i = 1$ to $i = \#w_i \in f$ **do**
4:     Simulate addresses a_i such that $|a_i| = \lambda$
5:     Add $(id(f), a_i)$ in Dict
6:     $L = L \cup \{a_i\}$
7:     $c_{w_i} \leftarrow$ SKE.Enc($K_{EXP}, 0^\lambda$)
8:     $C = C \cup c_{w_i}$
9: $\tau_\alpha(f) = (c_{id(f)}, C, L)$

In particular, S simulates random strings of the correct length as the addresses and stores them in a list L. Apart from that, S encrypts sequences of zeros and stores them in a list C. Since the simulated addresses have the same length as the real ones, $\mathcal{ADV}$ cannot distinguish between the list L and Map from Algorithm 1. Moreover, the CPA-security of SKE ensures us that $\mathcal{ADV}$ cannot distinguish between the encryption of zeros and that of real data. Hence, Hybrid 1 is indistinguishable from Hybrid 0. As a result,

$$Pr[(Hybrid\ 0) = 1] - Pr[(Hybrid\ 1) = 1] | \leq negl(\lambda) \qquad (1)$$

Note that since S successfully simulates $\tau_\alpha(f)$ given only $\mathcal{L}_{add}$, our scheme preserves the notion of forward privacy.

Hybrid 2: Like Hybrid 1 but now S is given $\mathcal{L}_{search}$ and proceeds as presented in Algorithm 4. More Specifically, the KeyStore[w] dictionary is used to keep track of the last key K_w used for each keyword w. The FOracle[K_w][j][i] dictionary is used to reply to ADV's queries. For example, FOracle[K_w][0][i] represents the address of a Dict entry assigned to the $i - th$ file in the collection. Similarly, FOracle[K_w][1][i] represents $id(f)$. The simulated search token has exactly the same size and format as the real one, and as a result no PPT adversary can distinguish between them. Moreover, $\mathcal{ADV}$ cannot tamper with the quotes generated by the enclaves during the execution of the remote attestation protocols. The reason for this, is that these quotes are signed with secret key provided by Intel. As a result, tampering with the quotes implies producing a valid signature without owning the corresponding key, which can only happen with negligible probability. Thus, Hybrid 2 is indistinguishable from Hybrid 1. Hence:

$$Pr[(Hybrid\ 1) = 1] - Pr[(Hybrid\ 2) = 1]| \leq negl(\lambda) \tag{2}$$

By combining Eqs. 1 and 2 we get:

$$Pr[(Hybrid\ 0) - 1] - Pr[(Hybrid\ 2) = 1]| \leq negl(\lambda) \tag{3}$$

Which implies:

$$Pr[(Real) = 1] - Pr[(Ideal) = 1]| \leq negl(\lambda)\square \tag{4}$$

Side-Channel Attacks. Recent works have shown that SGX is vulnerable to software attacks. However, according to [18] leakage can be avoided if the programs running in the enclaves do not have memory access patterns or control flow branches that depend on the values of sensitive data. In our case, no sensitive computations occur in the SGX enclave and thus, there is no possibility of leaking encryption keys. Hence, by assuming a constant time implementation our construction is secure against timing attacks.

Does the Removal of TEE Affects the Security of the Scheme? While the use of a TEE can be seen as a subterfuge to improve the security of a scheme this is not true in our case. In contrast to other SGX-based approaches [2, 24], where the SGX enclave hosts sensitive information such as encryption and decryption keys and hence, removing the SGX would lead to a downgrade in the security of the schemes, in our case the only information stored in the Enclaves are metadata (No.Search and No.Files) about the files. It is clear that in our approach the use of SGX only facilitates the multi-client model and thus, while removing the TEE does not affect the security of the scheme, it results to a single-client model.

6   Experimental Results

This section provides an overview of the experimental setup used for the evaluation and reports the obtained computational results. As already stated, our construction works with structured data of a certain form. To this end, and for reasons of simplicity, all of our experiments are conducted with json files.

Experimental Setup. We have setup an experimental testbed, that realistically imitates the system model described in Sect. 3. For this purpose, an in-house OpenStack based private cloud environment has been utilized. Three different virtual machines (VMs) are created, where each VM is used to run service for one of the three entities (i.e. *Client*, TA and CSP) respectively. The resource configurations of all the three VMs are identical and as follows: [4 virtual CPUs, 8 GB RAM, 80 GB disk, Ubuntu 18.04 LTS as operating system].

Algorithm 4. Search Token Simulation

1: d : Number of file identifiers to be returned
2: $R = \{\}$
3: **if** KeyStore$[w] = Null$ **then**
4:    KeyStore$[w] \leftarrow \{0,1\}^{\lambda}$
5: **for** $i = 1$ to $i = d$ **do**
6:    **if** FOracle$[0][i] = Null$ **then**
7:       Pick a $id(f), a_i)$ pair
8:    **else**
9:       $a_i = $ FOracle$[K_w][0][i]$
10:    Remove a_i from the dictionary
11:    $R = R \cup \{id(f)\}$
12: $UpdatedVal = \{\}$
13: $K_w' \leftarrow \{0,1\}^{\lambda}$
14: KeyStore$[w] = K_w'$
15: **for** $i = 1$ to $i = d$ **do**
16:    Generate a new a_i such that $|a_i| = \lambda$
17:    Add $id(f), a_i)$ to the dictionary
18:    $UpdatedVal = UpdatedVal \cup \{id(f), a_i\}$
19:    FOracle$[K_w][0][i] = a_i$
20:    FOracle$[K_w][1][i] = id(f)$
21: $\tau_s(w) = (K_w, d, UpdatedVal)$

The implementation of all three applications was done in Python with the use of Django framework and Tastypie API. For data storage on the TA and the CSP, we used a PostgreSQL database; therefore, these components also rely on Psycopg PostgreSQL database adapter. The Client is a web application that provides an interface to end-users for uploading and searching data by utilising the TA and the CSP. Since the client encrypts/decrypts data locally, its implementation heavily relies on JavaScript. For this purpose, the Stanford JavaScript Crypto Library (SJCL) [31], has been utilized for hashing and encryption. SHA256 has been used for hashing, while the encryption is performed using AES with key size of 128 bits and CCM mode (Counter with CBC-MAC mode of operation, which provides both authentication and confidentiality).

Similar to the Client, the TA also requires hashing, encryption and decryption functions, however different to the Client, it is implemented on the server side. For this purpose, the python package sjcl 0.2.12 of the same library [8] has been used. This package allows the TA to encrypt/decrypt messages compatible with the message format of the SJCL library used by the client.

Each application is wrapped in containers and then deployed on the respective VMs. This was mainly done to easily setup and reproduce the experiments. The hosting of each application is handled through the Gunicorn WSGI http server. In the case of CSP and TA, the corresponding PostgreSQL database instances ran in separate containers on same VMs (i.e. on each VM, there are two containers – the service and the database container).

Open Science and Reproducible Research: To support open science and reproducible research and give the opportunity to use, test and extend our scheme, we release all code on GitLab [5] and research artifacts on Zenodo [4]. Additionally, we dockerize the implementation and publish the images on Docker Hub [3].

*Datasets.*To evaluate the computational complexity of the various functions of our scheme, synthetic structural data of different size were generated. As a benchmark, we considered a system consisting of data belonging to 300 individuals, where each individual data is provided through a json file. Hence, the data of 300 individuals means 300 json files, where every json file contains a fixed number of attributes and their values. The value of each attribute is also synthetically generated and consists of randomly selected number of characters, (i.e. between 5 to 30). Using these settings, we then considered sub-scenarios, where the number of files remains fixed (i.e 300), but, the number of attributes varies from 50 to 400. Our datasets can be seen in Table 3.

Choosing the Parameters for the Experiments: We used json files, as inputs, due to its simplistic nature and wide adoption. To choose appropriate parameters for the experiments (300 instances with attributes varying from 50 to 400), we relied on popular medical datasets, such as Breast Cancer Wisconsin (Diagnostic) (569 instances, 32 attributes) and Heart Disease Data Set (303 instances, 75 attributes), from the UC Irvine Machine Learning Repository [1]. The aim of experiments was to evaluate the performance of the scheme. Hence, the actual contents of the data was not important. Therefore, the data were synthetically generated to avoid any data compatibility and/or transformation issues. To get more accurate results, each experiment was run 30 times.

Table 3. Datasets

No of attributes	Size in database
50	4.82 MB
100	9.6 MB
150	14 MB
200	19 MB
250	23 MB
300	28 MB
350	33 MB
400	37 MB

Computational Time and Overhead. We have used Apache Jmeter, a load testing tool, combined with Selenium WebDriver, a web automation testing framework, and Chrome driver, to automate and measure the execution of web application in Chrome version 78.0.3904.108. The performance tests were conducted on a computer with 8GB RAM, Intel Core i5-6500 CPU 3.20GHz 4 cores, 250GB disk size and Ubuntu 16.04 LTS 64-bit operating system. The reported measurements are the average result of 30 simulation runs.

Search: To measure the performance of *Search* we focused on *(1)* Evaluating the impact of the number of attributes per file to the search time. Our measurements included files with a variable number of attributes ranging from 50 to 400 and *(2)* Evaluating the impact of the size of result list R (as defined in Algorithm 2) to the search processing time for files containing different number of attributes (ranging from 50 to 400). Figures 2a and 2b present the aggregated results. From Fig. 2a, we conclude that the processing time increases as the number of matching keywords in a search query increases. For example, for files containing 50 attributes, the completion time for a search query that returned 0 matches was approximately 4 s, whereas nearly 7 seconds were required when 20 matches were found. A similar pattern was observed in all the remaining scenarios (i.e. when the number of attributes increases from 100 to 400 per file). Figure 2b, illustrates the impact of the result list R to the processing time. We observe that the processing time grows almost linearly with the size of R. Note that the times presented in Figs. 2a and 2b, include the generation of the search token, the communication between the CSP and TA, the time required for the CSP to find all matching files and finally, the decryption of the matching files.

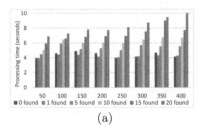 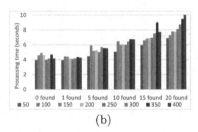

(a)   (b)

Fig. 2. Search function processing time for (a) Variable data sizes against number of found occurrences, (b) Number of found occurrences against variable data sizes

Insert: In this part of the experiments, we measured the time required to insert new data in a non-empty database. For the purpose of our experiments, we first ran our tests with a database containing 50 files and then increased the number of files to 300. In each case, different measurements were recorded based on the number of attributes (ranging from 50 to 400). Figures 3a and 3b present the obtained results. Each measurement, in both plots, represents the average processing time of 30 runs, where the line bar represents the minimum and maximum measurement amongst those runs. The key points from the above-mentioned results is that the measurements in both cases are almost identical. However, as the number of attributes per file increases, the processing time increases significantly.

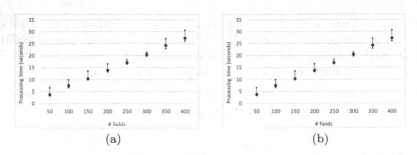

(a)   (b)

Fig. 3. Processing time of new file insertion whilst (a) 300 files present in database, (b) 50 files present in database

Data Storage Overhead: In the last phase of our experiments, we measured the data storage overhead. We recorded the size of the databases for the CSP and the TA. When final measurements were taken, the databases contained data of 300 files with different number of attributes (ranging from 50 to 400). Figure 4 presents the summarized results where data(blue line) refers to the ciphertexts stored in the CSP, the overhead of CSP is the size of the dictionary stored in the CSP, the overhead of the TA is the size of metadata stored in the *TA* and the total overhead is the sum of the two.

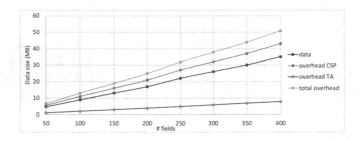

Fig. 4. Data table sizes containing data of 300 files

7   Related Work and Comparison

Recently, there have been multiple systems that suggest moving beyond the traditional boundaries of encryption and allowing users of a cloud service to search over encrypted data [6, 28, 29]. Our construction is based on the scheme presented in [17] where authors designed a *single-client* forward private SSE scheme that achieves optimal search and update costs. Another single-client forward private SSE scheme is proposed in [10], where authors designed *Sophos*. Even though Sophos achieves optimal search ($O(\ell)$) and update costs ($O(m)$), a file addition requires $O(m)$ asymmetric operations on the user's side. In [12], authors leverage the functionality offered by Intel's SGX to minimize the leakage. Their construction achieves logarithmic search costs. However, it is *static* and does *not* support file insertions after the initial creation of the indexes. Despite their strong points, all the aforementioned schemes provide an *"All-or-Nothing"* functionality in the sense that the decryptor will either decrypt the whole ciphertext and get access to all the information that is enclosed or will not get access at all. SSE schemes can also be constructed by Oblivious RAM [22] as for example in [20]. However, as mentioned in [10], such constructions induce large bandwidth overhead, large client storage and multiple roundtrips and as a result, the use of ORAM-based approaches seems unrealistic. However, despite these inefficiencies, ORAM-based techniques can be leveraged to design even more secure SSE schemes as in the case of [11] where there authors presented, among others, *Moneta*. Moneta is an SSE scheme based on the TWORAM construction presented in [20] and satisfies both forward and backward privacy [11]. However, as argued in [21], the use of TWORAM renders Moneta impractical for realistic scenarios and the scheme can serve mostly as a theoretical result for the feasibility of more secure SSE schemes. More recently, in [21] authors present *Orion*, another ORAM-based SSE scheme with similar security guarantees as Moneta. While Orion outperforms Moneta, the number of interactions between the user and the CSP depends on the size of the encrypted database. In [2], authors propose an SGX-assisted ORAM-based construction called *Bunker-B*. While this approach achieves both forward and backward privacy with optimal search and update costs, it does not offer any kind of access control. Finally, in [14], authors present three more forward and backward private schemes that offer small client storage. However, their schemes require multiple rounds of interaction, does not offer access control and only support the single-client model. The idea of enabling access control in keyword search is not novel. However, existing approaches [23,26,27] are based on Public key Encryption with Keyword Search (PEKS), a notion first introduced and formalized in [9], and thus, are not efficient when dealing with large amounts of data. Moreover, in [24], authors propose an access control mechanism based on the use of SGX alongside oblivious data structures such as Circuit-ORAM and Path-ORAM. However, their scheme requires the client to share a key with the SGX enclave that will be used to perform sensitive operations such as encryptions and decryptions. However, as mentioned in Sect. 5, performing sensitive operations inside an SGX enclave, can lead to the leakage of the encryption key. Given the inadequacy of current searchable encryption schemes to offer granular access on encrypted data, we propose a construction that enables data owners to specify exactly which parts of their encrypted data may be decrypted and by whom. As can be seen in Table 4, our construction not only clearly outperforms ORAM-based approaches but also improves the search time by a factor of $1/p$ in comparison to asymptotical optimal constructions. This is due to the fact that our construction is parallelizable. In particular, each search operation in our scheme is reduced to the problem of locating to $O(\ell)$ independent hashes on Dict, where ℓ is the result size and p the numbers of the processors. Hence, if the load is distributed to p processors, we achieve optimal search cost $O(\ell/p)$. Similarly, the update cost is $O(m/p)$, where m is the number of keywords. Most importantly, our construction is the only one that supports forward privacy in the multi-client model, and the only one providing an access control mechanism.

Table 4. N: number of (w, id) pairs, n: total number of files, m: total number of keywords, p: number of processors, k: number of keys, a_w: number of updates matching w, MC: Multi-Client, FP: Forward Privacy, BP: Backward Privacy.

Comparison							
Scheme	MC	FP	BP	Search time	Update time	Client storage	Access control
Etemad et al. [17]	✗	✓	✗	$O(\ell/p)$	$O(m/p)$	$O(m+n)$	✗
HardIDX	✗	✗	✗	$O(\log k)$	–	None	✗
Sophos	✗	✓	✗	$O(\ell)$	$O(m)$	$O(m)$	✗
Moneta	✗	✓	✓	$\widetilde{O}(a_w \log N + \log^3 N)$	$\widetilde{O}(\log^2 N)$	$O(1)$	✗
Orion	✗	✓	✓	$O(\ell \log N^2)$	$O(log N^2)$	$O(1)$	✗
Bunker-B	✗	✓	✓	$O(\ell)$	$O(1)^{\text{a}}$	$O(m \log n)$	✗
Ours	✓	✓	✗	$O(\ell/p)$	$O(m/p)$	None	✓

[a]The authors only consider deleting a single (w, id) pair.

8   Conclusion

In this paper we proposed the first dynamic SSE scheme that provides granular access control on encrypted data and does *not* fall under the *All-or-Nothing* category. Our construction, works with structured data in the form of (`Attribute: Value`) and allows users to encrypt their data and provide a policy defining who can access each part of the encrypted data. Our scheme preserves essential properties of traditional SSE schemes such as *forward privacy* and *constant rounds of interactions*. We see this work as a first step towards an Attribute-Based Symmetric Searchable Encryption scheme and we hope that it will inspire researchers to further explore and develop this fascinating and promising field.

References

1. Uc irvine machine learning repository. https://archive.ics.uci.edu/ml/index.php, Accessed 25 Feb 2020
2. Amjad, G., Kamara, S., Moataz, T.: Forward and backward private searchable encryption with SGX. In: Proceedings of the 12th European Workshop on Systems Security, pp. 1–6 (2019)
3. Asclepios: Docker images of symmetric searchable encryption (2020). https://hub.docker.com/r/uowcpc/asclepios-client, https://hub.docker.com/r/uowcpc/asclepios-server, https://hub.docker.com/r/uowcpc/asclepios-ta
4. Asclepios: Research artifacts of symmetric searchable encryption (2020). https://zenodo.org/record/3986839#.Xzj7tJNKiqA
5. Asclepios: Symmetric searchable encryption source code (2020) https://gitlab.com/asclepios-project/sseta, https://gitlab.com/asclepios-project/symmetric-searchable-encryption-server, https://gitlab.com/asclepios-project/sseclient, https://gitlab.com/asclepios-project/ssemanual

6. Bakas, A., Michalas, A.: Modern Family: a revocable hybrid encryption scheme based on attribute-based encryption, symmetric searchable encryption and SGX. In: Chen, S., Choo, K.-K.R., Fu, X., Lou, W., Mohaisen, A. (eds.) SecureComm 2019. LNICST, vol. 305, pp. 472–486. Springer, Cham (2019). https://doi.org/10.1007/978-3-030-37231-6_28

7. Bakas, A., Michalas, A.: Multi-client symmetric searchable encryption with forward privacy. Cryptology ePrint Archive, Report 2019/813 (2019). https://eprint.iacr.org/2019/813

8. Bartel, U.: Python-SJCL (2020). https://pypi.org/project/sjcl/

9. Boneh, D., Di Crescenzo, G., Ostrovsky, R., Persiano, G.: Public key encryption with keyword search. In: Cachin, C., Camenisch, J.L. (eds.) EUROCRYPT 2004. LNCS, vol. 3027, pp. 506–522. Springer, Heidelberg (2004). https://doi.org/10.1007/978-3-540-24676-3_30

10. Bost, R.: $\sum o\varphi o\varsigma$: Forward secure searchable encryption. In: Proceedings of the 2016 ACM SIGSAC Conference on Computer and Communications Security, Vienna, Austria, 24–28 October 2016 (2016)

11. Bost, R., Minaud, B., Ohrimenko, O.: Forward and backward private searchable encryption from constrained cryptographic primitives. In: Proceedings of the 2017 ACM SIGSAC Conference on Computer and Communications Security (2017)

12. Brasser, F., Hahn, F., Kerschbaum, F., Sadeghi, A.R., Fuhry, B., Bahmani, R.: Hardidx: Practical and secure index with SGX (2017)

13. Cash, D., Grubbs, P., Perry, J., Ristenpart, T.: Leakage-abuse attacks against searchable encryption. In: Proceedings of the 22nd ACM SIGSAC Conference on Computer and Communications Security. ACM (2015)

14. Demertzis, I., Ghareh Chamani, J., Papadopoulos, D., Papamanthou, C.: Dynamic searchable encryption with small client storage. In: NDSS, 2020 (2020)

15. Dowsley, R., Michalas, A., Nagel, M.: A report on design and implementation of protected searchable data in iaas. Technical report, Swedish Institute of Computer Science (SICS) (2016)

16. Dowsley, R., Michalas, A., Nagel, M., Paladi, N.: A survey on design and implementation of protected searchable data in the cloud. Computer Science Review (2017). http://www.sciencedirect.com/science/article/pii/S1574013716302167

17. Etemad, M., Küpçü, A., Papamanthou, C., Evans, D.: Efficient dynamic searchable encryption with forward privacy. Popets **2018**(1), 5–20 (2018)

18. Fisch, B., Vinayagamurthy, D., Boneh, D., Gorbunov, S.: Iron: functional encryption using intel sgx. In: Proceedings of the 2017 ACM SIGSAC Conference on Computer and Communications Security, pp. 765–782. ACM (2017)

19. Frimpong., E., Bakas., A., Dang., H., Michalas., A.: Do not tell me what i cannot do! (the constrained device shouted under the cover of the fog): implementing symmetric searchable encryption on constrained devices. In: Proceedings of the 5th International Conference on Internet of Things, Big Data and Security, IoTBDS, vol. 1, pp. 119–129. INSTICC, SciTePress (2020). DOI: https://doi.org/10.5220/0009413801190129

20. Garg, S., Mohassel, P., Papamanthou, C.: TWORAM: efficient oblivious RAM in two rounds with applications to searchable encryption. In: Robshaw, M., Katz, J. (eds.) CRYPTO 2016. LNCS, vol. 9816, pp. 563–592. Springer, Heidelberg (2016). https://doi.org/10.1007/978-3-662-53015-3_20

21. Ghareh Chamani, J., Papadopoulos, D., Papamanthou, C., Jalili, R.: New constructions for forward and backward private symmetric searchable encryption. In: Proceedings of the 2018 ACM SIGSAC Conference on Computer and Communications Security, CCS '18. Association for Computing Machinery (2018)

22. Goldreich, O., Ostrovsky, R.: Software protection and simulation on oblivious rams. J. ACM **43**(3), 431–473 (1996)
23. Han, J., Yang, Y., Liu, J.K., Li, J., Liang, K., Shen, J.: Expressive attribute-based keyword search with constant-size ciphertext. Soft Comput. **22**(15), 5163–5177 (2017). https://doi.org/10.1007/s00500-017-2701-9
24. Hoang, T., Ozmen, M.O., Jang, Y., Yavuz, A.A.: Hardware-supported oram in effect: practical oblivious search and update on very large dataset. Proc. Priv. Enhancing Technol. **2019**(1), 172–191 (2019)
25. Islam, M.S., Kuzu, M., Kantarcioglu, M.: Access pattern disclosure on searchable encryption: ramification, attack and mitigation. In: NDSS. Citeseer (2012)
26. Li, J., Zhang, L.: Attribute-based keyword search and data access control in cloud. In: Proceedings - 2014 10th International Conference on Computational Intelligence and Security, CIS 2014, pp. 382–386 (2015)
27. Miao, Y., et al.: Privacy-preserving attribute-based keyword search in shared multi-owner setting. IEEE Trans. Dependable Secure Comput. (2019)
28. Michalas, A., Bakas, A., Dang, H.V., Zalitko, A.: Abstract: access control in searchable encryption with the use of attribute-based encryption and sgx. In: Proceedings of the 2019 ACM SIGSAC Conference on Cloud Computing Security Workshop, CCSW'19, p. 183. ACM (2019)
29. Michalas, A., Bakas, A., Dang, H.-V., Zaltiko, A.: MicroSCOPE: enabling access control in searchable encryption with the use of attribute-based encryption and SGX. In: Askarov, A., Hansen, R.R., Rafnsson, W. (eds.) NordSec 2019. LNCS, vol. 11875, pp. 254–270. Springer, Cham (2019). https://doi.org/10.1007/978-3-030-35055-0_16
30. Paladi, N., Gehrmann, C., Michalas, A.: Providing user security guarantees in public infrastructure clouds. IEEE Trans. Cloud Comput. **5**(3), 405–419 (2017). https://doi.org/10.1109/TCC.2016.2525991
31. Stanford: Stanford javascript crypto library (2020). https://github.com/bitwiseshiftleft/sjcl
32. Stefanov, E., Papamanthou, C., Shi, E.: Practical dynamic searchable encryption with small leakage. In: NDSS, vol. 71, pp. 72–75 (2014)
33. Zhang, Y., Katz, J., Papamanthou, C.: All your queries are belong to us: the power of file-injection attacks on searchable encryption. In: 25th USENIX Security Symposium, pp. 707–720 (2016)

Towards Inclusive Privacy Protections
in the Cloud

Tanusree Sharma, Tian Wang, Carlo Di Giulio, and Masooda Bashir[✉]

University of Illinois at Urbana-Champaign, Champaign, IL 61820, USA
{tsharma6,tianw7,mnb}@illinois.edu, carlo.digiulio85@gmail.com

Abstract. The adoption of cloud computing has created tremendous prospects and cost savings for a variety of organizations. Although increasing resources and effort have been devoted to fighting cyber-threats in cloud environments, cloud computing continues to be associated with a range of severe and complex security and privacy issues that may challenge the overall benefits that CSPs offer. While security protections in cloud computing has been widely discussed and comprehensive guidelines have been established, privacy protections in the cloud does not have the same level of focus or set of guideline or framework that has been established. In this paper, we present a systematic review of previous literature related to privacy issues in cloud computing, analyze multiple general privacy frameworks, policies, and principles to highlight the critical need for creating privacy protection criteria's for cloud computing. Our research and review illustrates that privacy protections focused on cloud computing is deficient and it can serve as an initial guide towards building and improving privacy protections in order to meet cloud privacy requirements and ensure data protection.

Keywords: Privacy protection · Cloud computing · Privacy risks

1 Introduction

Cloud computing represents a major evolution of computer technology and has become a dominant model for delivering information technology (IT) infrastructure, components, and applications [2]. It is a model for enabling ubiquitous, convenient, on-demand network access to a shared pool of configurable computing resources that can be rapidly provisioned and released with minimal management effort or service provider interaction [3]. The main way cloud computing can be offered to consumers is through cloud service providers (CSPs). Since cloud computing offers mobility, cost effectiveness, and availability, large and small enterprises as well as government are reorienting their overall information technology (IT) infrastructure and strategies to include cloud computing for high-level collaboration possibilities [4]. Whereas industry, government, and everyday online users widely rely on the cloud for access to and processing of their data, concerns with information assurance and information security and privacy in cloud computing have captured much attention in particular. The adoption of cloud technology has created new threats to security and privacy. Although increasing resources and

© Springer Nature Switzerland AG 2020
J. Zhou et al. (Eds.): ACNS 2020 Workshops, LNCS 12418, pp. 337–359, 2020.
https://doi.org/10.1007/978-3-030-61638-0_19

effort have been devoted to fighting cyber-threats and privacy concerns in cloud environments [5], cloud computing continues to be associated with a range of severe and complex security and privacy issues that may challenge the overall benefits that CSPs offer [7]. In particular, any of the three main cloud computing model (IaaS, PaaS, and SaaS) can be vulnerable to serious threats related to data integrity, confidentiality, and privacy principles.

Consideration of information privacy has become an essential element of all computing and online services. Not only does information privacy refer to confidentiality of personal information, but also to protection of personal information and safeguard of collection, access, use, dissemination, and storage of personally identifiable information (PII) [11]. Cloud computing continues to be a prime target for cyber-attacks because the cloud holds much of our most personal and sensitive data. Data in the cloud are easier to manipulate, but also easier to lose control of. Storage of personal data on a server somewhere in cyberspace can pose a major threat to individual privacy [6]. Solutions to information privacy issues in the cloud are increasingly needed to promote trust and boost a safe and data-secure economic development.

Currently, there are already many straightforward, comprehensive set of measures on cloud computing security, but the focus on privacy is still behind and ambiguous. Although there are many overlaps between security and privacy in cloud computing, it is important to distinguish privacy from security. Instead of focusing on preventing or solving technical issues like security, privacy in cloud computing might be more difficult to define since the concept of privacy itself can vary under different circumstances. In cloud environment, privacy issues include, but are not limited to what data should be collected, with whom the data will be shared, how the data is stored and transmitted, and who has access to it. Those questions should be considered and addressed carefully in cloud computing, not only by creating technical measures to prevent privacy threats, but also keeping in mind that the concept of privacy and all its possible implications related to data processing in the cloud need to be established and clarified in the first place.

While privacy considerations need to be addressed and emphasized in cloud computing, to the best of our knowledge, there has been no current or published research with a well-established comprehensive guideline or framework specifically related to information privacy in cloud computing. The National Institute of Standards and Technology (NIST) has published the Privacy Framework 1.0 on January 2020, but it is intended to generally help organizations build better privacy foundations by bringing privacy risk into parity with their broader enterprise risk portfolio, instead of focusing on the cloud computing environment. Meanwhile, although there has been some preliminary examination of CSPs and their security controls [1, 8–10] with respect to different certifications, there is still no established set of controls or criteria for information privacy in cloud computing. For example, there is still much debate and confusion about the terms and words that are used in discussing security or privacy. Even the term data protection is used for both security and privacy, so it is not always clear which domain is being protected. As the first step, a scientific, systematic review of previous studies on information privacy under cloud environment is essential and necessary to better understand the current situation on cloud computing privacy before any measures or steps can be taken to develop a comprehensive protection framework to be used as a benchmark for privacy in cloud computing.

In this paper, we systematically review previous published studies related to information privacy protection in cloud computing. The research goals are to 1) summarize and analyze scholarly papers that discuss privacy in cloud computing and 2) discuss the need of a comprehensive guideline or framework of privacy protection in cloud computing. Our systematic review will provide an important step in identifying a current gap in cloud computing privacy.

2 Background

The concept of privacy has been widely discussed in the past decades, and it is still difficult to define given the fact that its definition may vary under different circumstances. Not only is privacy one of the most important concepts, but also one of the most elusive, since the amount of available information keeps increasing as technology changes rapidly, which makes scholars and policymakers struggle to define it [57]. As a result, researchers have been putting significant effort in building a comprehensive and systematic framework or taxonomy to explain privacy in modern life. One of the most commonly referred privacy frameworks is the taxonomy developed by Solove in 2005. In his book, A Taxonomy of Privacy, Solove provides a framework to better understand privacy by focusing on the activities that invade it [58]. The taxonomy includes four groups: 1) information collection, 2) information processing, 3) information dissemination, and 4) invasion, and has been widely applied as guidelines in further studies of privacy, especially in cloud computing.

Meanwhile, governments and organizations all over the world have created various privacy laws and frameworks for regulation of individual's personal information collected by governments, organizations, or other individuals. Below are some of the main privacy frameworks that have been developed and applied.

NIST Privacy Framework. A tool for improving privacy through enterprise risk management and helping with optimizing beneficial uses of data while protecting individual privacy, developed by NIST with version 1.0 published on January 16, 2020. The framework provides a useful set of privacy protection strategies for organizations to have better approaches to use and protect personal data. It also provides "clarification about privacy risk management concepts", as well as the relationship between the Privacy Framework and NIST's Cybersecurity Framework [53].

Fair Information Practice Principles (FIPPs). A set of eight principles that are rooted in the tenets of the Privacy Act of 1974 [59]. FIPPs are the basis for analyzing privacy risks and determining appropriate mitigation strategies. The principles are "used as the framework for privacy policy and implementation at the Department of Homeland (DHS)", as well as being mentioned in many state laws, foreign nations, and international organizations. FIPPs include: Transparency, Individual Participation, Purpose Specification, Data Minimization, Use Limitation, Data Quality and Integrity, Security, and Accountability and Auditing [54].

General Data Protection Regulation (GDPR). The European Union Regulation on data protection and privacy. It is "on the protection of natural persons with regard to the processing of personal data and on the free movement of such data," and is currently the common regulatory privacy framework for all 27 Member States of the European Union. The GDPR was published on April 27, 2016 [55].

Cloud Security Alliance Cloud Controls Matrix (CSA CCM). Updated to its latest version on August 3, 2019, the CCM is defined by the Cloud Security Alliance (CSA) as "the only meta-framework of cloud-specific security controls." It provides structure, detail, and clarity related to information security tailored to cloud computing. The CCM includes fundamental security principles for cloud vendors as guidelines and for cloud users to assess the security risk of a cloud provider [56]. The new version released in 2019 included minor update that incorporates specific mappings like AICPA TSC 2017 or NIST 800-53. In this paper, the version being analyzed is the original base version published in 2017, and the updated document in 2019 is also considered if there is any new change in that version.

3 Methodology

To conduct our literature review and analysis of privacy protections focused on cloud computing, we proceeded in three sequential steps: first is the selection of relevant scholarly papers, then the analysis of those papers to indicate particular privacy and security guidelines, followed by highlighting privacy terminologies.

Purpose of **the first stage** of literature review is to find elements in existing research on privacy-specific frameworks. We initially searched and collected the most relevant ones from publicly available scholarly papers through our selected search based on terms of privacy that would help pinning down privacy-relevant work. The terms used are "Privacy in Cloud", "Privacy certification in cloud", "Privacy and security certification", "Privacy and security certifications in cloud". It is important to note that we selected and limited our search terms to make sure that we concentrated our search on cloud-relevant publications that included explicit content referring to privacy and therefore reducing the noise generated by less relevant work.

After our extensive search in our database of scholarly papers, we have initially recorded the main elements of each papers, classified by 1) paper title with author names, 2) methodology of those papers (if original/adopted from other guidelines), 3) privacy-related terms used in the paper, 4) summary, and 5) references. This initial classification helps us organize the papers in groups and understand how they relate to privacy studies. In particular, from this classification we are able to highlight three main aspects of the papers: concentration of the paper, guidelines followed by that paper, and potential privacy terminologies which we considered as our final variables for scholarly paper analysis in our preliminary section.

In the second stage, from the literature review of selected paper, we obtained different variables as our database columns (method followed by those papers; originality/adaptation of methods from different guidelines; summary of paper; privacy-related terms). This information leads us to initially evaluate guidelines and standards as well as to measure their relevancy towards building a list of comprehensive criteria for cloud privacy protection. From the analysis of the academic papers, we have collected several recurring guidelines/standards, on the base of being frequently mentioned in the papers. From this list, and based on the frequency criteria, we have selected the most relevant guidelines, standards, principles. The guidelines we have selected at this stage are the General Data Protection Regulation (GDPR), California Customers Privacy Acts (CCPA), the recent "NIST Privacy Framework" and special publication 800-53 (Rev 5) by NIST, FIPPs (Fair Information Practices) Principles (by OECD, CSA CCM).

In the third stage, we initially started analyzing most frequently mentioned guidelines and standards from the scholarly paper analysis to understand the current standing of those principles' privacy viewpoint. The selected guidelines and standards are: NIST guidelines, the GDPR, FIPPs, the CCPA, CSA CCM and FIPPs) to understand the current standing of those principles' privacy viewpoint.

4 Preliminary Results

In contrast to security, privacy has not been studied and examined substantially in a comprehensive way. Taking this challenge into consideration, we designed our initial study in our method section to review scholarly papers and available guidelines (NIST2020, GDPR, CCPA, FIPPs, NIST 800-53) and certifications available for privacy and security (ISO/IEC, FedRAMP, C5, SOC2) frequently introduced in those papers to identify privacy requirements for cloud.

4.1 Scholarly Paper Analysis

The initial search has produced a total of 55 papers, which we further refined by lowering the number down to 42. The initial selection and refinement are based on a direct review of the papers, using criteria of relevance and reference to substantial privacy requirements, terminology related to data protection, privacy in cloud environments and general privacy protection for users. We have assessed the landscapes of privacy literature from 2001 to 2020.

In our assessment, **the first variable** we call "Area of concentration" refers to the field or area to which the paper is contributing: security with a general view on privacy; solely privacy focused; framework-based privacy risk assessment; privacy's legal point of view; privacy paper review. For example, if any paper is aligned towards information security and includes generalized elucidation of privacy, we categorized it as security-focused, while if any papers is focused on building a framework for privacy-aware systems or risk assessment, we categorized it as framework-based. A paper can be in more than one category if it has more than one concentration. **The second variable** is guidelines/standards, those scholarly papers followed to develop their methodology. For example, in Table 1, if we refer to paper [28], it followed NIST guidelines for articulating their methods. Finally, **the third variable** is related privacy terminology which helped us to understand potential possible privacy criteria for our future research goal of building a list of criteria to protect cloud privacy.

We have found 4 of those papers' methodology are solely based on FIPPS (Fair Information practices) [17, 20, 27, 34] and their area of concentration is on privacy measures and social and legal aspects. Some of the other papers [35] also mentioned FIPPs principles loosely as their choice of requirements to explain regulatory terms. For example, they state their compliance with laws and users' preferences as a form of feedback to improve data practices in cloud computing by following guidelines of FIPPs. Mainly they try to describe privacy risks and challenges for public cloud computing and how the considerations of guidelines mainly FIPPs and other Acts (USA-PATRIOT Act, the European Directive 95/46/EC, HIPPA, USA Gramm-Leach-Bliley Act) are utilized for the evaluation of existing solutions and can make progress in preserving privacy cloud computing.

From Table 1 of the Scholarly paper analysis result, we can easily map that 4 of the papers and posters are based on Solove's taxonomy of privacy [18, 19, 42] and Nissenbaum's contextual integrity [33]. In Privacy and information security, these two names are consistently significant while we are trying to construct design and application involving rules of privacy by design or formalize the data life cycle and building blocks of data handling for big and small organizations. Solove's taxonomy is designed to consider aspects related to privacy of information that are of interest of the larger community, such as the desire of individuals on their information being collected, processed, disseminate and prevent their invasion [58]. Our reviewed papers based on Solove's taxonomy of privacy further explain their point of view on different subcategories of main four attributes. For example, in the category of Information Dissemination, Distortion is a sub-component which is about false or misleading information about an individual where "a creditor reporting a paid bill as unpaid to a credit bureau" considered as distortion [18]. In one paper, the attributes from Solove's taxonomy for classifying Privacy Policies of Social Networks Sites and possible mechanisms to preserve privacy are used as the exclusive guideline, [19] while one other paper only uses Solove's taxonomy with the integration of certification (ISO/IEC) to conduct its literature review and point out the main features and challenges in particular application of cloud identity management [42].

From our list of selected papers, 3 of the papers follow GDPR data protection and EU Directive (95/46/EC) guidelines solely [29, 46, 59] while 3 more still use GDPR and EU Directive, but among other guidelines and Acts [35, 39, 47] to present privacy from both legal and social aspects. While 5papers adopt GDPR EU Directives guidelines to design privacy framework to support users in their adoption decisions, establishing reliance between users and legal compliance published by cloud services and proposing international privacy requirements with the concentration with direct privacy, social/legal and framework based approach [29], some other papers have relied on GDPR from directly legal aspects of privacy in developing regulatory instruments and bridge the gap between technology and law [35, 46, 47, 49] and sometimes only explaining privacy from the aspects of user empowerment and privacy preservation of cloud functionalities broadly [39].

From our selected papers of review, 9 papers are solely concentrated on security and they mention very little about privacy directly. Three of these papers have their

Table 1. Scholarly Paper Analysis

Paper list	Concentration of paper				Review paper	Guideline followed	Possibly related to privacy
	Security focused	Privacy focused	Framework based	Social/legal focused			
[14]	√	×	×	×	×	N/A	Availability, integrity and confidentiality
[12, 15]	√	×	×	×	×	Original	Data Privacy and Security including access control and storage
[16]	√	×	×	×	×	Original	Data analytic and cryptographic terms data centric security, privacy-preserving data mining
[18, 19]	×	√	√	×	×	Solove's taxonomy	Info-Processing, collection, dissemination, invasion
[21]	×	√	×	×	×	Original	Data privacy with quality, security, and integrity.

(continued)

Table 1. (*continued*)

Paper list	Concentration of paper					Review paper	Guideline followed	Possibly related to privacy
	Security focused	Privacy focused	Framework based	Social/legal focused				
[22, 60]	×	×	×	×		√	N/A	Control over data, accountability, choice, and responsibility.
[23]	×	√	×	×		×	Acts and ISO/IEC 15408	Access right management, customer identification and authentication, certification of user
[24]	×	×	×	×		√	HIPPA	Health data privacy preserving requirements, anonymity, accountability

(*continued*)

Table 1. (*continued*)

Paper list	Concentration of paper					Guideline followed	Possibly related to privacy
	Security focused	Privacy focused	Framework based	Social/legal focused	Review paper		
[25, 44]	×	√	×	√	×	CSA, EuroCloud	User's trust by continuous dynamic certification, reliability concerns, legal-compliance, transparent
[26]	×	√	×	×	×	Original	Trust assurance service, privacy as criteria
[28]	√	√	×	×	×	NIST Security Standards	Encryption, authentication, access control, client-side protection, data isolation, standards and certification, data storage location

(*continued*)

Table 1. (*continued*)

Paper list	Concentration of paper				Review paper	Guideline followed	Possibly related to privacy
	Security focused	Privacy focused	Framework based	Social/legal focused			
[29]	×	√	√	√	×	EU Directive 95/46/EC	Privacy policy, legal compliance, and privacy, privacy framework, international privacy requirements
[30]	×	√	√	√	×	IT Act 2000, Swiss Federal DPA, Data Security Council of India, CCPA	Users' requirement and expectation to design privacy, privacy controls, cloud storage privacy
[31]	×	√	×	×	×	Original	Availability and confidentiality for specific application

(*continued*)

Table 1. (continued)

Paper list	Concentration of paper					Guideline followed	Possibly related to privacy
	Security focused	Privacy focused	Framework based	Social/legal focused	Review paper		
[32]	×	√	×	√	×	HIPPA, EnCoRe	Privacy controls: purpose limitation, users centric design, user feedback, transparency
[33]	×	√	√	√	×	Nissenbaum's Contextual Integrity	Accessibility of data, privacy of individuals, privacy for cloud-storage systems
[17, 20, 27, 34]	×	√	×	√	×	FIPPs	FIPPs principles: collection, limitation, compliance rights, obligations, and change of status on disclosure

(continued)

Table 1. (*continued*)

Paper list	Concentration of paper					Review paper	Guideline followed	Possibly related to privacy
	Security focused	Privacy focused	Framework based	Social/legal focused				
[35]	×	√	×	√		×	FIPPs, USA PATRIOT Act, EU Directive 95/46/EC, HIPPA, USA Gramm-Leach-Bliley Act	Compliance with laws and user's preferences, accountability, privacy issues in cloud
[36]	√	√	×	×		√	CSA	Security and privacy issues in CC, solution for client-based privacy manager
[37]	√	√	×	×		×	NIST, CICA	Privacy in the data life cycle (generation, transfer, use, share, storage, archival, and destruction)
[38]	√	×	√	×		×	N/A	Three-layer storage framework for cloud data privacy

(*continued*)

Table 1. (*continued*)

Paper list	Concentration of paper					Guideline followed	Possibly related to privacy
	Security focused	Privacy focused	Framework based	Social/legal focused	Review paper		
[39]	×	√	×	×	×	GDPR, CSA	User empowerment, low overhead, transparency, preservation of cloud functionalities, interoperability
[40]	√	×	×	×	√	N/A	Physical isolation, cryptography, confidentiality
[41]	√	√	×	×	√	NIST, CSA	Trust, data protection, governance, security as a key to privacy

(*continued*)

Table 1. (*continued*)

Paper list	Concentration of paper					Guideline followed	Possibly related to privacy
	Security focused	Privacy focused	Framework based	Social/legal focused	Review paper		
[42]	√	√	×	×	√	Solove's Taxonomy, ISO/IEC	Transparency, controllability, minimization, accountability, data quality, use limitation, user-friendly, trust, obfuscation
[43]	√	√	×	√	√	Sarbanes-Oxley-Act, HIPPA	Agreement and regulations for privacy, accountability for both cloud providers and customers
[61]	×	√	√	×	×	N/A	Data control, transparency, multi-tenancy, virtualization

(*continued*)

Table 1. (*continued*)

Paper list	Concentration of paper					Guideline followed	Possibly related to privacy
	Security focused	Privacy focused	Framework based	Social/legal focused	Review paper		
[45]	×	√	×	×	×	N/A	Privacy policy certification notification screen (application)
[46, 49]	×	√	×	√	×	GDPR	Regulatory instrument in data protection
[47]	×	√	×	√	×	DPA, GDPR	Interplay between the law and technological design
[8–10]	√	×	×	×	×	ISO, SOC2, C5, FedRAMP, CSA	Comparing security controls
[48]	√	×	×	×	×	EuroCloud, FedRAMP, CSA	Authorization-based privacy storage confidentiality

(*continued*)

Table 1. (*continued*)

Paper list	Concentration of paper					Guideline followed	Possibly related to privacy
	Security focused	Privacy focused	Framework based	Social/legal focused	Review paper		
[50]	√	×	×	×	×	TOE Framework, DOI Theory	Continuously technical, security, and privacy requirements, continuous certification

own articulated methodology for reviewing cloud computing security components [14–16] and achieving security in Cloud Computing by data classification; six uses existing standards or guidelines of security; three of them use their own methodology which includes data mining, analytics, cryptographic data-centric security, employing granular access control as privacy aware computing [15, 16]. Although strongly focused on security rather than privacy, we reviewed and recorded data from these 9 papers. Some privacy measures are still loosely mentioned as part of the security recommendations they suggest, and we believe these measures could serve as some of the initial criteria's towards building baseline privacy protection in cloud computing. Other 4 papers present mixed analysis from different certifications (ISO, FedRAMP, C5, SOC2) for their method of comparing existing certifications' comprehensiveness. In those research papers [1, 8–10], there is an analysis of four highly regarded IT security standards that are used to assess, improve, and demonstrate information systems' assurance and cloud security: ISO/IEC 27001, SOC 2, C5, and FedRAMP. They further use Cloud Security Alliances' Cloud Control Matrix to examine their adequacy in addressing current threats to cloud security and provided an overview of the evolution over the years of their ability to cope with threats and vulnerabilities. By comparing the standards to each other, they investigate their complementarity, their redundancies, and the levels of protection they offer to information stored in cloud environments [1, 8–10]. In addition, they unveil vulnerabilities left unaddressed in the four frameworks and suggested necessary improvements to meet the security requirements of the current threat landscape. Lastly, two of the papers are based on certifications such as FedRAMP, CSA, Eurocloud (non-profit and vendor-neutral organization delivering legal orientation, quality guidance and best practice policies globally), Technology-Organization-Environment (TOE) framework and the Diffusion of Innovations (DOI) theory for proposing trustworthy certification process (authorized-based and confidential). Those are mainly for industrial eHealth application and designing a service from companies that consumers can participate in a continuous certification process [48, 50].

From the paper review, we have found significant importance of NIST frameworks for privacy and security. NIST standards are among the most well-known guidelines and frameworks for major companies and even for the US Government on aspects related to information technology, including but not limited to cyber and physical security, and privacy. One of the best implemented and effective example of NIST guidelines is the Security assessment Framework based on NIST Special Publication 800-53 [51]. Three of the analyzed papers [28, 37, 41] are focused on NIST standards and guidelines. Although those standards are concentrated on security and privacy at the same time, the papers only stress security-related aspects, with central security features of encryption, authentication, access control, client-side protection, backup, data isolation [28]. Other papers also mention privacy in the data life cycle (generation, transfer, use, share, storage, archival, and destruction) for ensuring three main security triad confidentiality, integrity, and authorization to maintain privacy [37]. One survey paper briefly analyzes cloud security problems, different existing approaches and highlighted challenges in data processing over the cloud [41] but fails in developing the research into a complete privacy framework.

In our review, we have noticed how different regulatory frameworks are also used (HIPPA, IT Act 2000, Swiss Federal Data Protection Acts, Data Security Council of India, CCPA, USA-PATRIOT Act, USA Gramm Leach Bliley Act, CICA, Sarbanes Oxley Act) as well as less frequent guidelines (EuroCloud, EnCoRe). The approach of using those guidelines and Acts is to ensure privacy for particular application (HIPPA for Health applications), establishing users' trust towards cloud provider by ensuring transparency and fixing reliability concerns (EuroCloud), taking users' requirements, expectation and feedback into consideration in designing privacy controls, ensuring cloud storage private and making both providers and consumers responsible and accountable for the usage of data with specific regulation. From our literature review, we have found directions for further analysis of particular guidelines and standards to start build ways of enlisting all the necessary criteria for privacy protection in cloud computing.

4.2 Available Standards Analysis

From our literature review, we found GDPR, CCPA, "NIST Privacy Framework" and special publication 800-53 (Rev 5) by NIST, FIPPs (by OECD), CSA CCM to be the most frequently included. We chose to initially conduct our review on these guidelines in quest for the potential of developing our privacy protection criteria.

Most of the GDPR is concentrated in data protection law enforcement and other rules concerning the protection of personal data [55]. The EU Commission mainly designed the Regulation for data protection, privacy, and fair business practices in EU and European Economic Area. The GDPR, that is structured in articles (Art.) and recitals (R), aims at creating rules for transparent information, communication, free choice of data subject, while attributing clear responsibility and accountability to data controllers [55]. Few main objectives, listed in Article 1, that are maintained as a rule of thumb in the GDPR are:

- To lay "down rules relating to the protection of natural persons with regard to the processing of personal data and rules relating to the free movement of personal data."
- To protect "fundamental rights and freedoms of natural persons and in particular their right to the protection of personal data."
- "The free movement of personal data within the Union shall be neither restricted nor prohibited for reasons connected with the protection of natural persons with regard to the processing of personal data" [52].

GDPR's principles are leaning towards data subject which best infer "Privacy and "Data Protection" and therefore, a potential source for creating the criteria list for privacy protection in cloud computing [55]. Among recent NIST publications, one of the most relevant could be considered the NIST special publication 800-53 (Rev 5), which was last reviewed on March 2020 adding security and privacy controls for information systems and organizations [13]. With its latest review, NIST has added controls and measures that can be all considered worth of being part of the baseline on privacy protection for cloud computing. In addition to the SP 8000-53, NIST has published its NIST Privacy Framework in January 16, 2020, which is an all-privacy framework, based on NIST's other security and cybersecurity guidelines [53]. These publications of NIST has the basis in FIPPs, FISMA, and Privacy Act of 1974 [54]. We found a significant number of reviewed papers' method are based on FIPPs Principles which is internationally recognized for information privacy policies and both from government and private sectors [54]. Furthermore, we have come across the reference towards California customers privacy Acts which is the most recent Acts to enhance privacy rights and consumers protection for residents in California which can be a potential source for our further criteria list for cloud computing privacy protection.

5 Conclusion

From our literature review and preliminary results, we notice that privacy issues in cloud computing have been emphasized and extensively discussed in the past decades. Still, there is no existing standard or principle specifically applicable to privacy in cloud computing and therefor the urgent need for the development of baseline protections that includes a comprehensive list of criteria focused on privacy protection in cloud computing.

While most of previous papers point out privacy risks and challenges in cloud computing, those risks and challenges are mostly tackled from a security perspective. For example, how data should be stored and processed in cloud environment, and what kind of techniques should be applied for software engineers to protect data. The literature shows that when it comes down to identifying security issues and proposing potential solutions, the answer is straight-forward since there are already well-established controls and criteria for security in the cloud. Professionals and researchers can easily use these controls and criteria as guidelines to assess security issues in cloud environment with no need to come up with new solutions.

Unlike security, the concept of privacy is more ambiguous since there is no concrete definition of the term "privacy" as related to the cloud. Previous research papers tend to combine privacy and security, with the result that there is no clear borderline between the two concepts in cloud computing. For example, when referring to Availability, Integrity, and Confidentiality in the context of cloud computing, it might be difficult to interpret the criteria as related to privacy, security, or both.

A separate standard that only focuses on privacy needs to be built to distinguish privacy from security. Also, because of the development of technology, PII could be shared globally, making the creation of a global privacy protection standard even more important. Each region in the world has so far developed its own privacy framework, making it necessary to create a comprehensive and systematic approach for privacy protection in cloud computing to ensure that PII is consistently collected, processed, and stored regardless of the geography.

6 Future Work

From our analysis of scholarly papers and most appeared guidelines/standards presented in this paper, we have initiated and established our strategies to build a comprehensive listing of privacy requirements that we would like to coin as the "Comprehensive Criteria of Privacy Protection (C2P2)" which will be presented in subsequent publications for the privacy and security scholars and practitioners' consideration and evaluation. Based on the findings of this review and existing standards, we have decided to choose FIPPs, CSA, NIST2020, NIST 800-53, GDPR, CCPA for building our comprehensive list of criteria for privacy protection in cloud computing. We will be interactively considering more guidelines as our sources for retrieving privacy protection criteria for our comprehensive list. Currently, we are not including certifications (ISO, FedRAMP, SOC2, C5) in this initial list to avoid biasness towards particular certifications. After finalizing the comprehensive criteria list for privacy protection in cloud computing, we will compare the criteria in the list with the cloud certifications, in order to evaluate the performance of each certification in addressing privacy considerations in cloud computing.

Acknowledgement. This work has been supported by Cisco. This study is a part of the project on *Privacy Standards Evaluation for the cloud: A proposal for Cisco,* University of Illinois at Urbana-Champaign. We want to acknowledge and thank all of those who have contributed to this work.

References

1. Bashir, M., Di Giulio, C., Kamhoua, C.A.: Certifications past and future: a future model for assigning certifications that incorporate lessons learned from past practices. In: Campbell, R.H., Kamhoua, C.A., Kwiat, K.A. (eds.) Assured Cloud Computing, pp. 277–311. Wiley-IEEE Computer Society Press (2018)
2. Benlian, A., Kettinger, W.J., Sunyaev, A., Winkler, T.J., Guest Editors: The transformative value of cloud computing: a decoupling, platformization, and recombination theoretical framework. J. Manag. Inf. Syst. **35**(3), 719–739 (2018)
3. Mell, P., Grance, T.: The NIST Definition of Cloud Computing (Draft): Recommendations of the National Institute of Standards and Technology. Special Publication 800–145 (draft), Gaithersburg, MD (2018). Published 28 September 2011, Updated 10 November 2018
4. Ellis, R., Mohan, V. (eds.): Rewired: Cybersecurity Governance. Wiley, Hoboken (2019)
5. Lamps, J., Palmer, I., Sprabery, R.: WinWizard: expanding Xen with a LibVMI intrusion detection tool. In: Proceedings of the 2014 IEEE 7th International Conference on Cloud Computing, pp. 849–856 (2014)
6. Guilloteau, S., Venkatesen, M.: Privacy in Cloud Computing. ITU-T Technology Watch Report March 2012 (2013)
7. Svantesson, D., Clarke, R.: Privacy and consumer risks in cloud computing. Comput. Law Secur. Rev. **26**(4), 391–397 (2010)
8. Di Giulio, C., Sprabery, R., Kamhoua, C., Kwiat, K., Campbell, R.H., Bashir, M.N.: Cloud standards in comparison: are new security frameworks improving cloud security? In: Proceedings of the 2017 IEEE 10th International Conference on Cloud Computing (CLOUD), Honolulu, CA, pp. 50–57 (2017)
9. Di Giulio, C., Kamhoua, C., Campbell, R.H., Sprabery, R., Kwiat, K., Bashir, M.N.: IT security and privacy standards in comparison: improving FedRAMP authorization for cloud service providers. In: Proceedings of the 17th IEEE/ACM International Symposium on Cluster, Cloud and Grid Computing (CCGrid 2017), pp. 1090–1099. IEEE Press, Piscataway, May 2017
10. Di Giulio, C., Sprabery, R., Kamhoua, C., Kwiat, K., Campbell, R.H., Bashir, M.N.: Cloud security certifications: a comparison to improve cloud service provider security. In: Proceedings of the 2nd International Conference on Internet of Things and Cloud Computing (ICC 2017). ACM, New York (2017). Article 120, 12 pages

11. McCallister, E., Grance, T., Scarfone, K.: Guide to Protecting the Confidentiality of Personally Identifiable Information (PII). NIST Special Publication SP 800-122, National Institute of Standards and Technology, U.S. Department of Commerce (2010). https://nvlpubs.nist.gov/nistpubs/Legacy/SP/nistspecialpublication800-122.pdf

12. Sharma, T., Bambenek, J.C., Bashir, M.: Preserving Privacy in Cyber-physical-social Systems: An Anonymity and Access Control Approach (2020)

13. Force, J.T.: Security and Privacy Controls for Information Systems and Organizations (No. NIST Special Publication (SP) 800-53 Rev. 5 (Draft)). National Institute of Standards and Technology (2017)

14. Idrissi, H.K., Kartit, A., El Marram, M.: A taxonomy and survey of cloud computing. In: 2013 National Security Days (JNS3), pp. 1–5. IEEE, April 2013

15. Shaikh, R., Sasikumar, M.: Data classification for achieving security in cloud computing. Procedia Comput. Sci. **45**(1C), 493–498 (2015)

16. Big Data Taxonomy. https://downloads.cloudsecurityalliance.org/. Accessed 16 Mar 2020

17. Cavoukian, A.: Privacy by design: The 7 foundational principles. Information and privacy commissioner of Ontario, Canada, May 2009

18. IAPP - A Taxonomy of Privacy (Poster). https://iapp.org/. Accessed 16 Mar 2020

19. Zorzo, S.D., Botelho, R.P., de'Avila, P.M.: Taxonomy for privacy policies of social networks sites. Soc. Netw. (2013)

20. Antón, A.I., Earp, J.B.: A taxonomy for web site privacy requirements. North Carolina State University at Raleigh, Raleigh, NC (2001)

21. Miller, H.E.: Big-data in cloud computing: a taxonomy of risks (2013)

22. Sun, Y., Zhang, J., Xiong, Y., Zhu, G.: Data security and privacy in cloud computing. Int. J. Distrib. Sens. Netw. **10**(7), 190903 (2014)

23. Kang, M., Kwon, H.Y.: A study on the needs for enhancement of personal information protection in cloud computing security certification system. In: 2019 International Conference on Platform Technology and Service (PlatCon), pp. 1–5. IEEE, January 2019

24. Abbas, A., Khan, S.U.: A review on the state-of-the-art privacy-preserving approaches in the e-health clouds. IEEE J. Biomed. Health Inform. **18**(4), 1431–1441 (2014)

25. Lins, S., Grochol, P., Schneider, S., Sunyaev, A.: Dynamic certification of cloud services: trust, but verify! IEEE Secur. Priv. **14**(2), 66–71 (2016)

26. Lansing, J., Schneider, S., Sunyaev, A.: Cloud service certifications: measuring consumers' preferences for assurances. In: ECIS, p. 181, June 2013

27. Katzan Jr, H.: On the privacy of cloud computing. Int. J. Manag. Inf. Syst. (IJMIS) **14**(2) (2010)

28. Abuhussein, A., Bedi, H., Shiva, S.: Evaluating security and privacy in cloud computing services: a stakeholder's perspective. In: 2012 International Conference for Internet Technology and Secured Transactions, pp. 388–395. IEEE, December 2012

29. Sunyaev, A., Schneider, S.: Cloud services certification. Commun. ACM **56**(2), 33–36 (2013)

30. Ion, I., Sachdeva, N., Kumaraguru, P., Čapkun, S.: Home is safer than the cloud! Privacy concerns for consumer cloud storage. In: Proceedings of the Seventh Symposium on Usable Privacy and Security, pp. 1–20, July 2011

31. Karkouda, K., Nabli, A., Gargouri, F.: Privacy and availability in cloud data warehouse. In: Proceedings of the 10th International Conference on Education Technology and Computers, pp. 388–391, October 2018

32. Mowbray, M., Pearson, S.: A client-based privacy manager for cloud computing. In: Proceedings of the Fourth International ICST Conference on COMmunication System softWAre and MiddlewaRE, pp. 1–8, June 2009

33. Grodzinsky, F.S., Tavani, H.T.: Privacy in "the cloud" applying Nissenbaum's theory of contextual integrity. ACM SIGCAS Comput. Soc. **41**(1), 38–47 (2011)

34. Pearson, S.: Taking account of privacy when designing cloud computing services. In: 2009 ICSE Workshop on Software Engineering Challenges of Cloud Computing, pp. 44–52. IEEE, May 2009
35. Ghorbel, A., Ghorbel, M., Jmaiel, M.: Privacy in cloud computing environments: a survey and research challenges. J. Supercomput. **73**(6), 2763–2800 (2017). https://doi.org/10.1007/s11227-016-1953-y
36. Zhou, M., Zhang, R., Xie, W., Qian, W., Zhou, A.: Security and privacy in cloud computing: a survey. In: 2010 Sixth International Conference on Semantics, Knowledge and Grids, pp. 105–112. IEEE, November 2010
37. Chen, D., Zhao, H.: Data security and privacy protection issues in cloud computing. In: 2012 International Conference on Computer Science and Electronics Engineering, vol. 1, pp. 647–651. IEEE, March 2012
38. Wang, T., Zhou, J., Chen, X., Wang, G., Liu, A., Liu, Y.: A three-layer privacy preserving cloud storage scheme based on computational intelligence in fog computing. IEEE Trans. Emerg. Top. Comput. Intell. **2**(1), 3–12 (2018)
39. Domingo-Ferrer, J., Farras, O., Ribes-González, J., Sánchez, D.: Privacy- preserving cloud computing on sensitive data: a survey of methods, products and challenges. Comput. Commun. **140**, 38–60 (2019)
40. Aloraini, A., Hammoudeh, M.: A survey on data confidentiality and privacy in cloud computing. In: Proceedings of the International Conference on Future Networks and Distributed Systems, pp. 1–7, July 2017
41. Kumar, S.N., Vajpayee, A.: A survey on secure cloud: security and privacy in cloud computing. Am. J. Syst. Softw. **4**(1), 14–26 (2016)
42. Werner, J., Westphall, C.M., Westphall, C.B.: Cloud identity management: a survey on privacy strategies. Comput. Netw. **122**, 29–42 (2017)
43. Lar, S.U., Liao, X., Abbas, S.A.: Cloud computing privacy security global issues, challenges, mechanisms. In: 2011 6th International ICST Conference on Communications and Networking in China (CHINACOM), pp. 1240–1245. IEEE, August 2011
44. Sharma, T., Bashir, M.: Privacy apps for smartphones: an assessment of users' preferences and limitations. In: Moallem, A. (ed.) HCII 2020. LNCS, vol. 12210, pp. 533–546. Springer, Cham (2020). https://doi.org/10.1007/978-3-030-50309-3_35
45. Tsai, J.: U.S. Patent Application No. 14/984,830 (2017)
46. Lachaud, E.: The general data protection regulation and the rise of certification as a regulatory instrument. Comput. Law Secur. Rev. **34**(2), 244–256 (2018)
47. Easton, C.R.: Information systems for crisis response and management: The EU data protection regulation, privacy by design and certification (2016)
48. Anisetti, M., Ardagna, C.A., Damiani, E., El Ioini, N., Gaudenzi, F.: Modeling time, probability, and configuration constraints for continuous cloud service certification. Comput. Secur. **72**, 234–254 (2018)
49. Ardagna, C.A., Asal, R., Damiani, E., Dimitrakos, T., El Ioini, N., Pahl, C.: Certification-based cloud adaptation. IEEE Trans. Serv. Comput. (2018)
50. Teigeler, H., Lins, S., Sunyaev, A.: Drivers vs. inhibitors-what clinches continuous service certification adoption by cloud service providers? In: Proceedings of the 51st Hawaii International Conference on System Sciences, January 2018
51. FedRAMP Security Assessment Framework. https://www.fedramp.gov/assets/resources/. Accessed 17 Mar 2020
52. GDPR, General Provision. https://gdpr-info.eu/chapter-1/. Accessed 17 Mar 2020
53. NIST Privacy Framework: A Tool for Improving Privacy Through Enterprise Risk Management, 16 January 2020. https://www.nist.gov/privacy-framework

54. Privacy Policy Guidance Memorandum 2008-01, The Fair Information Practice Principles, 29 December 2008. https://www.dhs.gov/publication/privacy-policy-guidance-memorandum-2008-01-fair-information-practice-principles
55. General Data Protection Regulation (GDPR): Off. J. Eur. Union (2016). https://eur-lex.europa.eu/legal-content/EN/TXT/PDF/?uri=CELEX:32016R0679
56. Cloud Controls Matrix v3.0.1: Cloud Security Alliance, 3 August 2019. https://cloudsecurityalliance.org/artifacts/cloud-controls-matrix-v3-0-1/
57. Solove, D.J.: Understanding Privacy. Harvard University Press, Cambridge (2008)
58. Solove, D.J.: A taxonomy of privacy. Univ. Pa. Law. Rev. **154**, 477 (2005)
59. Privacy Act of 1974. The United States Department of Justice, 15 January 2020. https://www.justice.gov/opcl/privacy-act-1974
60. Sharma, T., Bashir, M.: Use of apps in the COVID-19 responses and the loss of privacy protection. Nat. Med. **26**, 1165–1167 (2020)
61. Almtrf, A., Alagrash, Y., Zohdy, M.: Framework modeling for user privacy in cloud computing. In: 2019 IEEE 9th Annual Computing and Communication Workshop and Conference (CCWC), pp. 0819–0826. IEEE, January 2019

A Study on Microarchitectural Covert Channel Vulnerabilities in Infrastructure-as-a-Service

Benjamin Semal[✉], Konstantinos Markantonakis, Raja Naeem Akram, and Jan Kalbantner

Royal Holloway University of London, Egham, UK
`benjamin.semal.2018@live.rhul.ac.uk`

Abstract. Microarchitectural cross-VM covert channels are software-launched attacks which exploit multi-tenant environments' shared hardware. They enable transmitting information from a compromised system when the information flow policy does not allow to do so. These attacks represent a threat to the confidentiality and integrity of data processed and stored on cloud platforms. Although potentially severe, covert channels tend to be overlooked due to an allegedly strong adversary model. The literature focuses on mechanisms for encoding information through timing variations, without addressing practical considerations. Furthermore, the field lacks a realistic evaluation framework. Covert channels are usually compared to each other using the channel capacity. While a valuable performance metric, the capacity is inadequate to assess the severity of an attack. In this paper, we conduct a comprehensive study on the severity of microarchitectural covert channels in public clouds. State-of-the-art attacks are evaluated against the Common Vulnerability Scoring System in its most recent version (CVSS v3.1). The study shows that a medium severity score of 5.0 is achieved. In comparison, the SSLv3 POODLE (CVE-2014-3566) and OpenSSL Heartbleed (CVE-2014-0160) vulnerabilities achieved respective scores of 3.1 and 7.5. As such, the paper successfully demonstrates that covert channels are not theoretical threats, and that they require the immediate attention of the community. Furthermore, we devise a new and independent scoring system, the Covert Channel Scoring System (CCSS). The scoring of related works under the CCSS shows that cache-based covert channels, although more and more popular, are the least practical ones to deploy. We encourage authors of future cross-VM covert channel attacks to include a CCSS metric in their study, in order to account for deployment constraints and provide a fair point of comparison for the adversary model.

Keywords: Covert channel · Microarchitectural attack · Cloud privacy · Vulnerability study

© Springer Nature Switzerland AG 2020
J. Zhou et al. (Eds.): ACNS 2020 Workshops, LNCS 12418, pp. 360–377, 2020.
https://doi.org/10.1007/978-3-030-61638-0_20

1   Introduction

The multi-tenant nature of cloud platforms prompts concerns over the confidentiality and integrity of data [31]. When multiple virtual machines (VMs) are scheduled on the same hardware platform, they compete with each other for processor resources. Such conflicts can delay the execution of certain instructions, resulting in timing variations to occur during the execution of an application. These timing variations can in turn be exploited by two colluding entities in order to encode and decode binary information. *Microarchitectural covert channel attacks* allow tunneling information out of a compromised system when the security policy does not allow doing so. A sending-end is embedded into the victim's environment, and transmits information to the receiving-end located in the attacker's environment. Furthermore, covert channel attacks are relevant when there is no other mean of leaking information in a non-conspicuous manner, e.g. as part of an advanced persistent threat malware. We note that side channel attacks, which rely on an accidental leakage of information from the victim, are beyond the scope of this study.

Microarchitectural covert channels allegedly rely on a strong adversary model. First, the attacker must infect the victim's instance with a malicious sending-end. Second, the attacker requires co-locating her instance on the same hardware platform as the victim's instance. Researchers devising these attacks tend to focus on new mechanisms for generating timing variations, rather than addressing deployment constraints. Indeed, the trend is to propose covert channels that are always faster and more robust, while assuming an ideal scenario for the attacker. Meanwhile, experts responsible for implementing security policies are free to re-brand microarchitectural covert channels as non-practical exploits, due to the above-mentioned challenges.

This paper investigates the operational constraints of launching a covert channel attack across Infrastructure-as-a-Service (IaaS) instances. To do so, a measurement study on the practicality and severity of these attacks is conducted. The Common Vulnerability Scoring System (CVSS) is used as a support for our analysis. Criteria are discussed in the context of microarchitectural attacks and potentially re-interpreted. Our study shows that microarchitectural covert channels achieve a medium severity score of up to 5.0, discarding the assumption that covert channels aren't practical. In comparison, the MySQL Stored SQL Injection vulnerability [2] achieved a medium severity scrore of 6.4 (CVSS v3.1), and was patched shortly after its disclosure. To this day, there are still no practical countermeasures against severe covert channels released several years ago [21,30]. Secondly, we propose a new evaluation framework dedicated to microarchitectural covert channels, the Covert Channel Scoring System (CCSS). This framework evaluates state-of-the-art attacks, and outlines the effect of operational constraints on the severity score. Among other findings, this evaluation shows that cache-based covert channels achieve the lowest severity scores, despite being increasingly popular. Overall, the paper reveals the existence of a growing gap between academic efforts and the commercial ecosystem.

The contributions of this paper are summarised as follows:

- We propose the first comprehensive study on the practicality and severity of microarchitectural covert channels in IaaS, resulting in CVSS scores ranging from 4.2 to 5.0.
- We devise a new and independent Covert Channel Scoring System, so as to provide a fair and realistic evaluation framework for future research.

The paper is organised as follows. Section 2 provides a background on cloud services, processor architecture, and defines covert channel attacks. In Sect. 3, the criteria discussed in this paper are defined. Section 4 rates criteria which can be evaluated generically. Section 5 discusses state-of-the-art covert channels, and provides an individual rating for the remaining criteria. Section 6 details the resulting scores. Finally, we conclude in Sect. 7.

2   Background

2.1   Infrastructure-as-a-Service

Infrastructure-as-a-Service (IaaS) delivers internet-accessible storage, processing, and network resources. The end-user controls every component inside the virtual machine, while the service provider manages servers and orchestrators (or containers). Customers remain in control of the (sensitive) data being processed within the VM, including data from any other service built upon it, i.e. platform or software. Also, the user can interact with the instance as with any other machine (e.g. root access, hardware selection APIs, etc). IaaS minimises the trust that needs to be extended to the cloud provider, and emphasises responsibilities mostly on the customer.

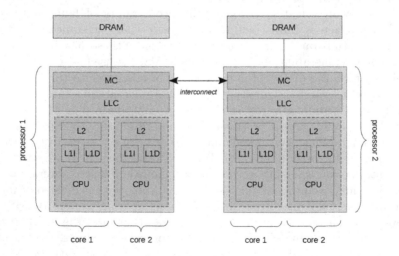

Fig. 1. Processor overview (NUMA configuration).

2.2   Processor Organisation

We use the term processor to refer to the processor die, which includes the cores and the last-level cache (LLC). The core contains the CPU along with the level-2 (L2), level-1 instruction (L1-I) and data (L1-D) caches. The memory bus refers to the front side bus present on older microarchitectures. Since the Nehalem microarchitecture, Intel processors mainly rely on a non-uniform memory access (NUMA) configuration. As a result, the memory bus has been removed, and memory controllers (MC) have been integrated into the processor die. The interconnect allows a processor accessing a region of DRAM that is managed by another processor. Figure 1 provides a representation of a multi-processor multi-core system in the NUMA configuration.

2.3   Scope of the Evaluation

Microarchitectural covert channels exploit vulnerabilities in the implementation of a processor's architecture. In contrast, network covert channels abuse network protocols. This study focuses on the former case. Also, not all covert channels have malicious intents. Nevertheless, we use the terms covert channel and covert channel attack interchangeably, for the sake of simplicity. We assume that a covert channel has a malicious nature. Microarchitectural covert channels differ from microarchitectural side channels in the attack scenario. Although they share the same underlying mechanisms, side channels rely on an accidental leakage of information from the victim, and they do not require compromising the victim's environment a priori. Side channel attacks are beyond the scope of our work. Finally, a covert channel does not necessarily allow communication across VMs. Because this paper focuses on the threat against IaaS, only cross-VM covert channels are considered. In parallel, this study could be applied to environments similar to IaaS, e.g. private clouds. This evaluation is specific to IaaS, and does not account for variations in similar environments. Table 1 surveys relevant covert channel attacks. We note that the respective channel capacities have been calculated here under the binary symmetric model [23].

3   Criteria of Evaluation

This section lists the criteria used to assess the impact of malicious covert channels in IaaS environments. We use the Common Vulnerability Scoring System in its most recent version (CVSS v3.1) [3] as a base for our evaluation metrics. The CVSS is an open industry standard that is widely used in the security community in order to assist responses to threats. While other evaluation frameworks exist, these have been adapting the traditional calculation of the CVSS to specific industrial environments. Certain criteria can be directly applied to all covert channels (**C1** to **C8**), while others are specific to the covert channel considered (**C9** to **C12**). We note that the criteria **C11** and **C12** are not part of the CVSS framework. These have been selected in order to provide an optimal representation of cross-VM covert channels' adversary model.

Table 1. Cross-VM covert channel attacks.

Attack	Exploited resource	Bitrate	Error	Capacity
[22]	Last-level cache	0.2 bps	–	–
[32]	Last-level cache	3.2 bps	9.28%	1.77 bps
[30]	Memory bus	343 bps	0.39%	330 bps
[14]	Last-level cache	1.2 Mbps	22%	287 kbps
[16]	Last-level cache	751 bps	5.7%	514 bps
[21]	DRAM row-buffer	596 kbps	0.4%	573 kbps
[17]	Last-level cache	45.25 kbps	0%	45.25 kbps
[24]	Memory order buffer	1.49 Mbps	∼5%	1.06 Mbps
[23]	Memory controller	150 bps	7.8%	90.7 bps

C1 Attack vector evaluates the proximity between the attacker and its target. This criterion can be rated as "network" for remote interaction, "adjacent" when the attacker needs physical or logical proximity with the target (e.g. Bluetooth), "local" if it relies on user interaction (e.g. social engineering), or "physical" when physical manipulation is required.

C2 Attack complexity assesses the difficulty of exploiting a vulnerability once access to the targeted platform is gained, ranked either as "low" when no specialised access condition exists, or "high" when the attack requires a significant amount of preparation such that it cannot be performed at will. We discuss under this criterion the VM co-location problem.

C3 User interaction indicates whether human interaction other than the adversary is required. As such, this criteria can be rated as either "none" or "required". We discuss under this criterion the trojan insertion problem.

C4 Scope assesses the impact that a vulnerability might have on components other than the one affected by the vulnerability. This metric accounts for the overall system damage caused by the exploitation of the reported vulnerability. Scope can be rated as "changed" when a scope change occurs, or "unchanged" otherwise.

C5 Confidentiality impact assesses the severity of a disclosure of information, as well as the quantity of information that can be leaked. This criterion can be rated as "none", "low" when the attacker can only access a small amount of data and loss of this data does not result in serious consequences, or "high" otherwise.

C6 Integrity impact measures the attacker's capability to tamper with the victim's data. It can be rated as "none", "low" when the amount of data that can be modified is limited and modification of this data does not result in serious consequences, or "high" otherwise.

C7 Exploit code maturity evaluates the state of an attack, from a conceptual exploit to a fully autonomous malware. Exploitability can be rated as "unproven", "proof-of-concept" when the attack has been demonstrated but is not practical, "functional" when the exploit works in most systems where the vulnerability is present but is still not widely accessible, or "high" otherwise.

C8 Report confidence assesses the credibility of the source which reported the vulnerability. This criterion is rated as "confirmed" when originating from a publication, "reasonable" when multiple non-official sources reported the vulnerability, or "unknown" when a single non-official source is involved.

C9 Privileges required evaluates the level of privileges that the adversary must acquire before launching the attack. This criterion can be rated as "none", "low" if privileges that allow performing basic user operations are required (e.g. changing settings), or "high" for administrative privileges. We note that this criterion is relative to the covert channel's sending-end, concealed in the victim's environment.

C10 Remediation level accounts for potential countermeasures. This criterion can be rated as "unavailable", "workaround" for non-official mitigation, "temporary fix" for official but not permanent countermeasures, or "official fix" otherwise.

C11 Hardware configuration specifies the attacker's proximity with regard to the victim's VM. Covert channels can require both VMs to be scheduled on the same core, on the same processor, or on the same system. Accordingly, hardware configuration can be rated as "core", "processor", or "system". A "system" rating makes for a higher severity score.

C12 Initialisation evaluates whether a covert channel attack requires the sender and receiver to perform an initialisation phase before leaking the victim's data. This criterion can be rated as "mandatory" or "optional". In the latter case, the covert channel remains functional in the absence of an initialisation phase, which increases the severity score. The absence of initialisation eases the deployment of the attack and decreases visible side-effects (e.g. large memory footprint).

The confidentiality, integrity, and availability requirements (CR, IR, AR) allow tuning the CVSS evaluation depending on the targeted asset. In the case of a cloud platform, the three requirements are equally important. Therefore, we set these to "medium", i.e. their default value. Furthermore, the availability impact is rated to "none". Covert channel attacks do not aim to compromise the availability of a computing environment.

4   Evaluation of Generic Criteria (C1–C8)

This section discusses the criteria for which the rating can be applied generically to the cross-VM covert channel attacks surveyed in Table 1.

C1. The attack vector is "local". The sending-end is a malicious program running inside the instance of the victim. This trojan must be inserted either using social engineering, or by corrupting the machine image. Independently of the chosen attack vector, user interaction is required. The attack vector is further discussed under requirement **C3**.

C2. Attack complexity is rated as "high". Prior to launching the attack, the adversary must achieve VM co-location, independently of the covert channel considered. Cloud services' application programming interfaces do not allow an attacker to place an instance at will on a chosen physical machine. VM co-location consists in moving the attacker's VM until it is executing on the same hardware platform as the victim's. Several proposals suggested using networking utilities to map the internal network topology of the data center, allowing an attacker to place two instances on the same platform [10,22,25,33]. Microarchitectural covert channels can later be used to find out whether co-residency is achieved at core-level, package-level, or system-level. While these approaches require some knowledge of the network topology, an adversary can choose instead to directly apply microarchitectural covert channels to detect co-residency. In a purely microarchitectural co-residency attack, the sending-end can broadcast messages on the covert channel, until a receiving-end picks up. Thus targeted co-residency is still possible without access to a reliable network topology of the data centre. Recently, Atya et al. [7] successfully demonstrated this approach on AWS EC2, using the memory bus and the cache as communication mediums.

C3. User interaction is rated as "required". The Amazon Web Service Elastic Compute Cloud (AWS EC2) service is a practical example of means to compromise a victim's instance before its deployment. Amazon Machine Images (AMIs) are the basic unit of the EC2 service. An AMI contains the OS along with libraries, applications, and other components which personalise the instance. Before deploying a VM, a user must choose an AMI, and set permissions for its AWS account(s). AMI selection presents a unique vulnerability: anyone with an AWS account can customise and share an AMI. As a result, an attacker can conceal and distribute a trojan across a large pool of users. While Amazon warns its customers against such practise, it doesn't forbid it. Also, because the AMI contains a tremendous amount of code, it is extremely difficult (if not impossible) to uncover malicious code once it is embedded into the image. Whether trojan insertion is performed using social-engineering, or via machine image corruption, specific actions must be performed by the victim.

C4. The scope metric is rated as "unchanged". The mechanism responsible for enforcing access control over the vulnerable component, also known as the *security authority*, depends on the form of the trojan. For example, if the sending-end is part of a user application (e.g. plugin), the vulnerable component is the affected application (e.g. web-browser) and the security authority is the guest operating system, responsible for enforcing isolation between user applications. However, the covert channel attack does not allow accessing the data of other applications running in the same guest operating system. The same reasoning holds if the sending-end takes the form of a malicious kernel module. The affected component becomes the guest operating system, and the security authority becomes the hypervisor. The sending-end would be able to leak all the information of the guest operating system, but it would not allow accessing the data of other guests under the same hypervisor. Therefore, the fact that data is exfiltrated across virtual machines does not constitute a change of scope.

The sole purpose of a covert channel attack is to exfiltrate information, or carry out modifications as instructed by the other communicating entity. Any exploit built on top of the covert channel attack (e.g. privilege escalation) is beyond the scope of this study.

C5. Confidentiality impact is rated as "high". Covert channels intend to leak a selected amount of information rather than the entire set of system files. However, a successful attack against a public cloud instance can have a significant impact on a victim, such as theft of proprietary information, leakage of personal data, or theft of cryptographic keys. We note that covert channels are only relevant when there is no alternative mean of leaking information in a non-conspicuous manner, e.g. to avoid generating network traffic and associated logs [5]. As such, covert channels constitute an ideal basis for advanced persistent threats, where the attacker employs state-of-the-art techniques in order to maintain long-term intrusion and data exfiltration capabilities. Such an attacker has other incentives than simple financial gain [12].

C6. Integrity impact is rated as "low". The attacker can issue modifications to be applied to the victim's environment, although this requires bi-directional communication, as well as the ability to instruct data tampering operations. Such a covert channel was demonstrated by Maurice et al. [17], who managed to establish a rogue SSH connection between two AWS EC2 instances. Data modification is therefore possible, however it remains a specific case, the primarily objective being data extraction.

C7. Exploit code maturity is rated as "proof-of-concept". The state-of-the-art covert channels surveyed in this paper all demonstrate a functional attack in a virtualised environment. However, researchers rarely disclose their full source-code. Therefore, current microarchitectural covert channels are not directly applicable without a skilled attacker.

C8. As per the CVSS specification [3], disclosure of an exploit in external events such as publications automatically rates the report confidence as "confirmed". A research publication is considered an official source which is corroborated by multiple experts.

To the best of our knowledge, there hasn't been any reported exploit related to cross-VM microarchitectural covert channels. Therefore, a universal approach is adopted in this study. We note that the CVSS v3.1 also provides a set of modified base metrics, allowing the analyst to override base metrics so as to fit the victim's environment specifically. For instance, if the data that was leaked was not considered sensitive, the confidentiality impact can be overwritten to "low". Similarly, if the covert channel allowed modifying data used in critical decision making processes, the integrity impact can be overwritten to "high".

5   Evaluation of Covert Channel-Specific Criteria (C9–C12)

In this section, covert channel attacks surveyed in Table 1 are analysed individually in order to proceed with the criteria evaluation. Results are reported in Table 3, along with the CVSS and CCSS scores for each attack. We note that the two scores are independent from each other. Additional details on scoring are provided in Sect. 6.

5.1   Memory Order Buffer

The memory order buffer (MOB) attack [24] exploits a side-effect of write-after-read hazards, called 4k-aliasing. This effect occurs whenever the lower twelve bits of the addresses contained in the load and store registers match, i.e. there is a data dependency between the load and the out-of-order store. This causes the load operation to be re-issued, resulting in the load/store bandwidth to drop. Authors leverage 4k-aliasing to create a covert communication between two hyperthreads. The sender either fills the store buffer with page-aligned addresses to transmit a one, or empties the store buffer to transmit a zero. Concurrently, the receiver probes load operations on every page-aligned addresses. When the load/store bandwidth drops, the receiver will observe a higher latency.

This effect is exploitable only at the thread-level, as it is linked to the load and store buffers located within the CPU. Neither the sender nor the receiver processes require root privileges, and the covert channel works across processes. Therefore, the sending-end can be embedded into a different program than the receiving-end. Both entities need to be scheduled on the same physical core.

With regard to countermeasures, authors acknowledge that disabling SMT is a straightforward way of mitigating the vulnerability. However, they also argue that "hyperthreading is expected to become more popular on IaaS platforms in the near future in order to keep them affordable". Indeed, SMT remains available on dedicated instances or for general-purpose workloads.

5.2   Last-Level Cache

LLC-based covert channels [14,16,17,22,32] derive from the PRIME+PROBE technique [18]. The receiver initialises the cache by filling it with its own cache lines, waits for the sender to execute, and probes its accesses to the same cache lines. If the sender chooses to modify the cache sets of the receiver, the latter will experience a slower access to its cache lines. PRIME+PROBE relies on the existence of congruent addresses between the sender and receiver, i.e. virtual addresses that map to the same cache set.

Identifying congruent addresses requires translating virtual pointers into physical addresses, which is performed by accessing the privileged page tables. Alternatively, entities can use the page offset of *huge pages* (e.g. 2 MB) as it is not translated, and it is long enough to include index bits. The communicating entities need to agree on a set of congruent addresses, which cannot be performed in the absence of an existing communication channel. In order to cope with this issue, Maurice et al. [17] suggested using a jamming agreement. Independently of the chosen strategy, LLC-based attacks are not functional without an initialisation phase. LLC-based covert channels are limited to cross-core communication.

Several cloud-oriented mitigation techniques were proposed to tackle LLC-based timing channels, such as cache partitioning or noise injection [9,11,13,26]. Intel Xeon processors support a similar mechanism, i.e. Intel's Cache Allocation Technology [4], which allows locking down portions of the LLC during execution, and ultimately defeat PRIME+PROBE attacks [13]. With a different approach, an auditing technique is suggested by Zhang et al. [34] which consists of using the performance monitoring unit to detect abnormal behaviour.

5.3 DRAM Row-Buffer

The DRAM addressing covert channel [21] exploits the DRAM bank row-buffer to create timing variations on uncached memory accesses. The sending-end allocates memory, and performs memory accesses either in the cache or in the DRAM. When the sender accesses the DRAM, it causes the row-buffer to be updated with the sender's row. Concurrently, the receiver accesses the same DRAM bank as the sender. If the sender evicted the receiver's row from the row-buffer, a row-miss occurs resulting in a higher latency.

Pessl et al. [21] relied on a privileged adversary model in order to access the pagemap file. We note that it is trivial to extend the original author's threat model to remote and unprivileged adversaries. One entity can simply write zeroes and ones on a random memory location, and the other entity scans its memory address space to detect the bit pattern, i.e. consecutive row-hits and row-misses. This approach also enables implementing a covert channel without knowledge of the DRAM addressing function, at the cost of an initialisation phase. This covert channel has the advantage that the communicating entities do not necessarily need to be scheduled on the same processor, as the DRAM memory is shared at a system-level via the interconnect.

Auditing can be used as a mitigation strategy. Indeed, the constant probing to DRAM results in a significant amount of cache-misses, observable by cache-miss counters. Alternatively, these authors proposed restricting access to the `clflush` instruction, which would render the covert channel harder to implement. Semal et al. [23] also suggest enforcing a close-page policy in order to inhibit the effect of the row-buffer.

5.4 Memory Controller

Semal et al. [23] proposed modulating the load on the channel scheduler in order to induce timing variations in the receiver's memory accesses to DRAM. The sender allocates three memory pages, and then reads one byte either in each of the three pages, or in a single page. The receiver observes a higher latency when the sender is increasing the load on the channel scheduler.

Authors demonstrated the attack both with and without privileges. The communicating-entities need to agree on a memory channel. As in the row-buffer attack, this can be achieved by having the sender broadcasting his position. Because the memory controller is accessible at a system level, this attack could be extended to multi-processor configurations. Further research is required to evaluate the impact of accessing memory regions in external NUMA nodes on the latency variations induced by the sender.

The memory controller covert channel can be addressed with the same countermeasures as the row-buffer one, at the exception of the page policy. Alternatively, the controller can be redesigned in order to enforce temporal [27] or spatial isolation.

5.5   Memory Bus

Wu et al. [30] devised a covert channel based on the memory bus. Authors suggested using atomic operations on exotic memory operations, i.e. operations on cache line-crossing memory regions, in order to trigger a bus lock emulation. The sender either performs an exotic access, or remains idle. Meanwhile the receiver probes its uncached memory accesses. A high latency is observed whenever the sender accesses exotic memory regions.

This attack allows cross-core communication on NUMA architectures, cross-processor communication on front side bus architectures, and it does not require privileges. Furthermore, it is functional without an initialisation phase.

Wu et al. suggest monitoring the cache-miss memory bus lock counters in order to detect performance anomalies at runtime with minimal overhead. Another suggestion consists of enforcing a policy where each tenant can only be neighbour with one other tenant [30]. This approach renders covert channel attacks almost impractical, however the operational cost remains an open-question.

5.6   Summary of Findings

C9. The CVSS v3.1 [3] specifies that exploits which rely on social engineering can be rated as "none". However, the works of Ristenpart et al. [22] and Xu et al. [32] require accessing page tables in order to find congruent addresses, and are thus rated as "high". All remaining covert channels are feasible from a user-level program. These are rated as "none".

C10. The remediation level varies depending on the party that is enforcing countermeasures. Table 2 shows that among the countermeasures proposed in the literature, several rely on an alternative hardware design. This approach has the benefit of being the most efficient, however it is also the hardest to deploy. Furthermore, security by design tends to have a significant performance cost which is not always justified. For instance, Wang et al. [27] suggested a new design of the memory controller which enforces temporal isolation among different security domains. While effective, this technique results in performance cost of up to 150%. As a result, remediation strategies consisting of alternative designs are evaluated as "unavailable".

Other countermeasures have been proposed which can be taken directly by the cloud customer. For example, Zhang et al. [35] devised the *HomeAlone* technique which allows cloud users detecting the presence of a LLC-based timing channel. The victim continuously probes memory accesses to detect anomalies, and takes reactive measures accordingly. Yet, this approach can result in a high number of false positives depending on the workload. This type of strategy is not official and cannot be generalised to all IaaS users. Therefore, remediation level is rated as "workaround" at the cloud customer level.

The most practical means of deploying countermeasures is if they are enforced by the cloud provider. The AWS EC2 and GCE services propose a type of instance where the user runs on a platform that is isolated from other users [1,6]. Note that these have a significant cost, e.g. an on-demand EC2 a1.2xlarge instance costs 0.204 USD per hour while a dedicated EC2 a1.2xlarge instance costs 2.2162 USD per hour. This approach is valid for running a selected workload only. Cloud providers have reportedly encouraged the disabling of SMT in order to prevent core-level timing channels [15]. We rate these strategies as "temporary fix", as they are recommended by vendors but are only applicable to a set of instances. Researchers also advanced mitigation strategies which can be implemented via the hypervisor. For example, Liu et al. [13] leverage Intel's Cache Allocation Technology to thwart PRIME+PROBE cache attacks. To the best of our knowledge, this strategy is not applied by cloud providers. As a result, this type of remediation is rated as "workaround".

Table 2. Remediation level (**C10**) criterion analysis.

C10	Hardware manufacturer	Cloud provider	Cloud customer
Workaround	–	Software partitioning [8,9,11]; Noise injection [26,29]; Auditing hardware counters [34]	Probing memory accesses [35]; Auditing hardware counters [30]
Unavailable	Temporal isolation [27]; Spatial isolation [13,19,20,29]; Restricting `clflush` [21]; Close-page policy [23]	VM clusters [30]	–
Temporary fix	-	Disabling SMT [15]; Dedicated instances [1]	–

Table 3. Summary of cross-VM covert channel attacks' criteria evaluation and scoring.

Attack	C9	C10	C11	C12	CVSS/CCSS
[22]*	*Privileged*	*Workaround*	*Core*	*Mandatory*	4.2/1.6
[32]*	*Privileged*	*Workaround*	*Core*	*Mandatory*	4.2/1.6
[30]†	*Unprivileged*	*Unavailable*	*Processor*	*Optional*	5.0/6.7
[14]*	*Unprivileged*	*Workaround*	*Processor*	*Mandatory*	4.9/4.3
[16]*	*Unprivileged*	*Workaround*	*Processor*	*Mandatory*	4.9/3.7
[21]¶	*Unprivileged*	*Unavailable*	*System*	*Mandatory*	5.0/6.8
[17]*	*Unprivileged*	*Workaround*	*Processor*	*Mandatory*	4.9/3.8
[24]‡	*Unprivileged*	*Temporary fix*	*Core*	*Optional*	4.8/5.7
[23]§	*Unprivileged*	*Workaround*	*Processor*	*Mandatory*	4.9/4.7

*LLC, †Memory bus, ¶Row-buffer, ‡Memory order buffer, §Memory controller.
C1 = *Local*, **C2** = *High*, **C3** = *Required*, **C4** = *Unchanged*, **C5** = *High*, **C6** = *Low*, **C7** = *Proof-of-concept*, **C8** = *Confirmed*.

C11. Ristenpart et al. [22] and Xu et al. [32] use a busy-loop mechanism to synchronise receiver and sender, implying that both VMs share CPU resources. Therefore, these attacks do not meet the requirements for cross-core covert channels. Similarly, the memory order buffer attack [24] requires both entities to share CPU resources. These attacks are set to "core". Remaining LLC-based covert channels are bound to the "processor" rating as the LLC cannot be shared across processors. Note that, as defined in Sect. 2.2, we use the term processor to refer to the entire processor die. Furthermore, while the memory controller attack [23] exploits a system-level component, the authors didn't demonstrate the attack on a multi-processor system. Similarly, Wu et al [30] assigned different virtual CPUs to each entity without specifying whether these were pinned to distinct hardware processors. These covert channels are also rated as "processor". Finally, the DRAM row-buffer [21] attack can transmit data across processors as DRAM memory is shared at system-level. As such, it is rated as "system".

C12. Only the memory bus [30] and the memory order buffer [24] covert channels can be rated as "optional". Every other covert channel requires an initialisation phase, and are thus rated as "mandatory" for this criterion.

6   Severity Scores

6.1   Design of the CCSS Equations

In order to provide a classification of covert channels, we create a new scheme which accounts for criteria **C9, C10, C11, C12,** and the channel capacity. These criteria are specific to the covert channel considered, and provide a point of comparison for the adversary model. The CCSS is by no means a representation of the severity of the attack. Instead, it should be taken as a complement to the CVSS which cannot solely be used to classify cross-VM covert channels.

Criteria scores have been selected such that the scoring equation is as uniform as possible. That is, the five criteria all have the same weight. The motivation behind this decision is that the importance of one factor over another is subjective. For example, one could give a higher weight to the channel capacity, arguing that communication speed and robustness is the most important. From one perspective, this is true. A set of log, data, and application files of a password manager ($\sim$1 GB) would take 99 days 10 h and 5 min at a bitrate of 1 Kb/s to be transmitted, and 2 h and 23 min at a bitrate of 1 Mb/s. Cloud instances are rescheduled onto different platforms depending on resource availability and demand. Therefore, the communication speed is critical. However, from another perspective, this is false. Faster communication rates are usually achieved by covert channels that exploit microarchitectural components closer from the execution units, which can easily be addressed by existing countermeasures (i.e. disabling SMT), or that have been extensively studied and resulted in multiple countermeasure proposals [8,9,11,13,26,28,29,36]. Thus faster covert channels will not necessarily be practical.

Furthermore, improving an evaluation scheme is usually performed over time by comparing the scores with the reality. For instance, the HeartBleed vulnerability was given a medium severity score of 5.0 in CVSS v2. Yet, it could easily be exploited and had significant consequences. It now has a high severity score of 7.5 in the CVSS v3.1 To the best of our knowledge, no covert channel exploit has been reported so far. Therefore, we consider that starting with an impartial scoring equation for the CCSS is the best approach. The scoring equation is,

$$Score = 2 \times (C9 + C10 + C11 + C12 + CapScore) \qquad (1)$$

Each CCSS criteria is given a value between 0 and 1: criterion **C9** is scored 0 for "Privileged" and 1 for "Unprivileged"; criterion **C10** is scored 0 for "Temporary fix", 0.5 for "Workaround", and 1 for "Unavailable"; criterion **C11** is given a score of 0 for "Core", 0.5 for "Processor", and 1 for "System"; **C12** is scored 0 for "Mandatory" and 1 for 'Optional"; the capacity score *CapScore* is modelled as an affine function between the highest and lowest channel capacity observed in this study, such that it outputs a score between 0 and 1,

$$CapScore = 1/(1.06e06 - 1.77) \times Capacity \qquad (2)$$

The final CCSS score varies between 0 and 10. Again, the CCSS score is only used for comparing covert channel attacks, and is complementary to the CVSS.

6.2   Results

Figure 2 represents the score of each covert channel under the CCSS and the CVSS. Due to missing information, Ristenpart et al.'s attack [22] was assigned an error rate of 22%, i.e. the maximum error rate observed in this study. Highest scores are achieved by the memory bus [30] and DRAM row-buffer [21] covert channels. Although not the most recent, these were able to reach high-speed

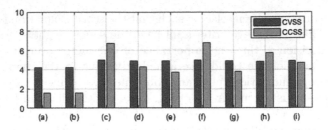

Fig. 2. Scoring of cross-VM covert channel attacks under the CVSS and CCSS: (**a**) = LLC [22], (**b**) = LLC [32], (**c**) = Memory bus [30], (**d**) = LLC [14], (**e**) = LLC [16], (**f**) = Row-buffer [21], (**g**) = LLC [17], (**h**) = Memory order buffer [24], (**i**) = Memory controller [23].

effective communication rates while minimising operational constraints. Meanwhile, LLC-based covert channels tend to achieve lower severity scores, due to the necessity of finding congruent addresses as well as the LLC locality. This shows that future works should emphasise on exploiting system-level resource, while working on making the communication more robust.

The CVSS scores were computed with the CVSS v3.1 equations [3]. According to our study, microarchitectural covert channels achieve a medium severity score ranging from 4.2 to 5.0. It shows that covert channels in IaaS are practical, that they should not be overlooked, and that suitable countermeasures should be devised in the short term in order to tackle timing channel vulnerabilities. More specifically, we suggest addressing the DRAM row-buffer and memory bus covert channels, as cache-based covert and side channel attacks have already been extensively studied.

When comparing the two evaluation frameworks, we observe that the CCSS outlines disparities among covert channel attacks which the CVSS does not. For example, the works proposed by Ristenpart el al. [22] and Wu et al. [30] would both be rated as medium severity vulnerabilities under the CVSS. Yet, the former attack has significant shortcomings including obtaining privileges (**C9**), achieving core-level co-location (**C11**), finding congruent addresses (**C12**), and a low communication speed. Thus the resulting CVSS scoring of the covert channel proposed by Ristenpart et al. [22] as a medium severity vulnerability is not adequate. In comparison, the proposed evaluation framework successfully highlights the benefit of one covert channel over another, with respective scores of 1.6 and 6.7. This shows that the evaluation of microarchitectural covert channels cannot be performed entirely based on the current industry standard, and that the criteria studied in the CCSS should be accounted for when devising new cross-VM covert channel attacks. Authors of future covert channels are encouraged to use the CCSS in order to provide a fair and realistic point of comparison with other works.

7   Conclusion

In this paper, we proposed the Covert Channel Scoring System (CCSS) as a new framework for evaluating microarchitectural covert channels. It allows comparing covert channel attacks based both on their performance (speed and robustness) and their practicality (operational constraints). The analysis revealed that the fastest covert channels are not necessarily the most eminent attacks, as they usually assume a close locality between sender and receiver, or a complex initialisation phase, resulting in lower severity scores. We advocate future works to use the CCSS in order to include a fair comparison metric in their proposal.

Furthermore, we systematically evaluated microarchitectural covert channels in the Infrastructure-as-a-Service ecosystem, using the Common Vulnerability Scoring System in its latest version (CVSS v3.1), and revealing medium severity scores ranging from 4.2 to 5.0. In comparison, the OpenSSL Heartbleed vulnerability achieved a severity score of 7.5 (CVSS v3.1). Although not as severe, the microarchitectural covert channel threat to IaaS is present and not negligible. In parallel, services built on cloud computing continue offering guarantees on the confidentiality and integrity of their customers' data. The loss of data, e.g. under GDPR requirement, could result in dramatic consequences for the cloud provider, the software provider, and their customers.

References

1. Amazon EC2 dedicated instances. https://aws.amazon.com/ec2/pricing/dedicated-instances/. Accessed 25 July 2020
2. CVE-2013-0375 detail. https://nvd.nist.gov/vuln/detail/CVE-2013-0375. Accessed 25 July 2020
3. CVSS v3 Equations. https://nvd.nist.gov/vuln-metrics/cvss/v3-calculator/equations. Accessed 25 July 2020
4. Improving real-time performance by utilizing cache allocation technology, Intel Corporation (2015)
5. Monitoring your instances using CloudWatch. https://docs.aws.amazon.com/AWSEC2/latest/UserGuide/using-cloudwatch.html. Accessed 25 July 2020
6. Sole-tenant nodes. https://cloud.google.com/compute/docs/nodes. Accessed 25 July 2020
7. Atya, A.O.F., Qian, Z., Krishnamurthy, S.V., La Porta, T., McDaniel, P., Marvel, L.M.: Catch me if you can: a closer look at malicious co-residency on the cloud. IEEE/ACM Trans. Netw. **27**(2), 560–576 (2019)
8. Cock, D., Ge, Q., Murray, T., Heiser, G.: The last mile: an empirical study of timing channels on sel4. In: ACM CCS, pp. 570–581 (2014)
9. Godfrey, M.M., Zulkernine, M.: Preventing cache-based side-channel attacks in a cloud environment. IEEE TCC **2**(4), 395–408 (2014)
10. Herzberg, A., Shulman, H., Ullrich, J., Weippl, E.: Cloudoscopy: services discovery and topology mapping. In: ACM CCSW, pp. 113–122. ACM (2013)
11. Kim, T., Peinado, M., Mainar-Ruiz, G.: STEALTHMEM: system-level protection against cache-based side channel attacks in the cloud. In: USENIX Security, pp. 189–204 (2012)

12. Langner, R.: Stuxnet: dissecting a cyberwarfare weapon. IEEE S&P **9**(3), 49–51 (2011)
13. Liu, F., et al.: Catalyst: defeating last-level cache side channel attacks in cloud computing. In: IEEE HPCA, pp. 406–418. IEEE (2016)
14. Liu, F., Yarom, Y., Ge, Q., Heiser, G., Lee, R.B.: Last-level cache side-channel attacks are practical. In: IEEE S&P, pp. 605–622. IEEE (2015)
15. Marshall, A., Howard, M., Bugher, G., Harden, B., Kaufman, C., Rues, M., Bertocci, V.: Security best practices for developing windows azure applications, p. 42. Microsoft Corp (2010)
16. Maurice, C., Neumann, C., Heen, O., Francillon, A.: C5: cross-cores cache covert channel. In: Almgren, M., Gulisano, V., Maggi, F. (eds.) DIMVA 2015. LNCS, vol. 9148, pp. 46–64. Springer, Cham (2015). https://doi.org/10.1007/978-3-319-20550-2_3
17. Maurice, C., et al.: Hello from the other side: SSH over robust cache covert channels in the cloud. In: NDSS, vol. 17, pp. 8–11 (2017)
18. Osvik, D.A., Shamir, A., Tromer, E.: Cache attacks and countermeasures: the case of AES. In: Pointcheval, D. (ed.) CT-RSA 2006. LNCS, vol. 3860, pp. 1–20. Springer, Heidelberg (2006). https://doi.org/10.1007/11605805_1
19. Page, D.: Partitioned cache architecture as a side-channel defence mechanism (2005)
20. Percival, C.: Cache missing for fun and profit (2005)
21. Pessl, P., Gruss, D., Maurice, C., Schwarz, M., Mangard, S.: DRAMA: Exploiting DRAM addressing for cross-CPU attacks. In: USENIX Security, pp. 565–581 (2016)
22. Ristenpart, T., Tromer, E., Shacham, H., Savage, S.: Hey, you, get off of my cloud: exploring information leakage in third-party compute clouds. In: ACM CCS, pp. 199–212. ACM (2009)
23. Semal, B., Markantonakis, K., Akram, R.N., Kalbantner, J.: Leaky controller: cross-VM memory controller covert channel on multi-core systems. EasyChair Preprint no. 2941, EasyChair (2020)
24. Sullivan, D., Arias, O., Meade, T., Jin, Y.: Microarchitectural minefields: 4k-aliasing covert channel and multi-tenant detection in IaaS clouds. In: NDSS (2018)
25. Varadarajan, V., Zhang, Y., Ristenpart, T., Swift, M.: A placement vulnerability study in multi-tenant public clouds. In: USENIX Security, pp. 913–928 (2015)
26. Vattikonda, B.C., Das, S., Shacham, H.: Eliminating fine grained timers in Xen. In: ACM CCSW, pp. 41–46 (2011)
27. Wang, Y., Ferraiuolo, A., Suh, G.E.: Timing channel protection for a shared memory controller. In: IEEE HPCA, pp. 225–236. IEEE (2014)
28. Wang, Y., Ferraiuolo, A., Zhang, D., Myers, A.C., Suh, G.E.: SecDCP: secure dynamic cache partitioning for efficient timing channel protection. In: DAC, pp. 1–6 (2016)
29. Wang, Z., Lee, R.B.: New cache designs for thwarting software cache-based side channel attacks. In: ISCA, pp. 494–505 (2007)
30. Wu, Z., Xu, Z., Wang, H.: Whispers in the hyper-space: high-bandwidth and reliable covert channel attacks inside the cloud. IEEE/ACM Trans. Netw. **23**(2), 603–615 (2014)
31. Xiao, Z., Xiao, Y.: Security and privacy in cloud computing. IEEE Commun. Surv. Tutorials **15**(2), 843–859 (2012)
32. Xu, Y., Bailey, M., Jahanian, F., Joshi, K., Hiltunen, M., Schlichting, R.: An exploration of L2 cache covert channels in virtualized environments. In: ACM CCSW, pp. 29–40. ACM (2011)

33. Xu, Z., Wang, H., Wu, Z.: A measurement study on co-residence threat inside the cloud. In: USENIX Security, pp. 929–944 (2015)
34. Zhang, T., Zhang, Y., Lee, R.B.: CloudRadar: a real-time side-channel attack detection system in clouds. In: Monrose, F., Dacier, M., Blanc, G., Garcia-Alfaro, J. (eds.) RAID 2016. LNCS, vol. 9854, pp. 118–140. Springer, Cham (2016). https://doi.org/10.1007/978-3-319-45719-2_6
35. Zhang, Y., Juels, A., Oprea, A., Reiter, M.K.: HomeAlone: co-residency detection in the cloud via side-channel analysis. In: IEEE S&P, pp. 313–328. IEEE (2011)
36. Zhou, Z., Reiter, M.K., Zhang, Y.: A software approach to defeating side channels in last-level caches. In: ACM CCS, pp. 871–882 (2016)

SCI – Secure Cryptographic Implementation

On New Zero-Knowledge Proofs for Fully Anonymous Lattice-Based Group Signature Scheme with Verifier-Local Revocation

Yanhua Zhang[1(✉)], Ximeng Liu[2], Yifeng Yin[1], Qikun Zhang[1], and Huiwen Jia[3]

[1] Zhengzhou University of Light Industry, Zhengzhou 450001, China
{yhzhang,yinyifeng,kzhang}@zzuli.edu.cn
[2] Fuzhou University, Fuzhou 350108, China
snbnix@gmail.com
[3] Guangzhou University, Guangzhou 510006, China
hwjia@gzhu.edu.cn

Abstract. The first lattice-based verifier-local revocation group signature (GS-VLR) was introduced by Langlois et al. in 2014, and subsequently, a full and corrected version was proposed by Ling et al. in 2018. However, zero-knowledge proofs in both schemes are within a structure of *Bonsai Tree*, and thus have bit-sizes of the group public-key and member secret-key proportional to $\log N$, where N is the group size. On the other hand, the revocation tokens in both schemes are related to the member secret-key and only obtain a weaker security, *selfless-anonymity*. For the tracing algorithms in both schemes, they just run in the linear time of N. Therefore, for a large group, the zero-knowledge proofs in lattice-based GS-VLR schemes are not that secure and efficient.

In this work, we firstly utilize a compact and scalable identity-encoding technique which only needs a constant number of public matrices to encode the member's identity information and it saves a $\mathcal{O}(\log N)$ factor in both bit-sizes for the group public-key and member secret-key. Secondly, separating from the member secret-key, we generate revocation token within some public matrix and a short Gaussian vector, and thus obtain the strongest security, *full-anonymity*. Moreover, the explicit-traceability, to trace the signer's identity in a constant time, independent of N, for the tracing authority is also satisfied. In particular, a new Stern-type statistical zero-knowledge proof protocol for a fully anonymous lattice-based GS-VLR scheme enjoying the above three advantages is proposed.

Keywords: Lattice-based group signatures · Verifier-local revocation · Zero-knowledge proofs · Explicit-traceability · Full-anonymity

1 Introduction

Group signature (GS), introduced by Chaum and van Heyst [7] in 1991, is accepted as a central cryptographic primitive enjoying two key privacy-preserving

© Springer Nature Switzerland AG 2020
J. Zhou et al. (Eds.): ACNS 2020 Workshops, LNCS 12418, pp. 381–399, 2020.
https://doi.org/10.1007/978-3-030-61638-0_21

properties, *anonymity* and *traceability*. For the former, it means that any group member can sign a message on the behalf of the whole group, meanwhile, without divulging the signer's identity information; for the latter, it means that there exists a tracing authority owning some secret information to reveal the anonymity and track the signer's identity efficiently. With these two appealing properties, GS has found several applications in real-life, such as in the trusted computing, anonymous online communications, e-commerce systems, and much more.

At a theoretical level, to construct such an efficient GS scheme three critical and relatively independent cryptographic ingredients are required and within some sophisticated combinations, these key building blocks include: a digital signature scheme, a public-key encryption scheme, and an efficient non-interactive zero-knowledge proof protocol. Therefore to design a theoretical secure and efficient GS scheme is a challenging work for the research community and over the last three decades GS schemes with different security notions, different levels of efficiency and based on different hardness assumptions have been proposed (e.g., [1–4, 10] ⋯).

LATTICE-BASED GS-VLR. The conventional number-theoretic problems (such as integer factoring problem and discrete logarithm problem) and GS schemes based on these hardness assumptions are vulnerable to quantum computers, and it is urgent to design a secure and efficient GS scheme in post-quantum cryptography (PQC) era. Believed to be one of the promising candidates for PQC, lattice-based cryptography (LPC) enjoys several competive advantages over number-theoretic cryptography: security reduction in the *worst-case* hardness assumptions, simpler arithmetic operations and provision of rich cryptographic functionality and services. The first lattice-based GS scheme was introduced by Gordon et al. [10] in 2010, a series of lattice-based GS schemes with static or dynamic design techniques [5, 11, 13, 15–17, 20–23, 25] were then proposed.

As an orthogonal problem of group member enrollment, the support for membership revocation is another desirable functionality for GS scheme. As a flexible revocation approach for group-type cryptographic constructions, verifier-local revocation (VLR) mechanism [3] is quite practical since it only requires verifier to download the up-to-date revocation information for signature verification, and no signer is required. The first lattice-based GS-VLR scheme was introduced by Langlois et al. [14] in 2014, subsequently, a full and corrected version was proposed by Ling et al. [18] in 2018, furthermore, four schemes achieving different security notions (*almost-full anonymity v.s. dynamical-almost-full anonymity*) were constructed by Perera and Koshiba [26–28].

However, all mentioned lattice-based GS-VLR schemes are within a structure of *Bonsai Tree* [6], and thus features bit-sizes of the group public-key and member secret-key proportional to $\log N$, where N is the group size, the maximum number of group members. The only three exceptions are [8, 29, 30] which adopt an identity-encoding function introduced in [25] to encode the member's identity index and thus save a $\mathcal{O}(\log N)$ factor for both bit-sizes. However, the two schemes [8, 29] involve a series of sophisticated encryptions and zero-knowledge proofs (ZKP) protocols in the signing phase, on the other hand, revocation tokens in [8,14,18,29] are all related to some public matrix and a member secret-key (a modular multiplication of the public matrix and the first part of member secret-key), thus all schemes only obtain a weaker security, called *selfless-anonymity* as introduced in [3]. In [30], though the revocation token is generated within an independent short Gaussion vector, the scheme can only obtain a slightly stronger security, called *almost full-anonymity*, first defined in [28]. For the tracing algorithms in [8,14,18,29], they all just run in a linear time in N (i.e., one by one for group members until the signer is traced). Therefore for a large group, ZKP protocols in lattice-based GS-VLR are not that secure and efficient. These somewhat unsatisfactory state-of-affairs highlights a challenge to construct a more secure and efficient lattice-based GS-VLR scheme, in particular, to design an efficient statistical ZKP protocol corresponding to all these constructions.

OUR RESULTS AND TECHNIQUES. In this work, we reply positively to the problems discussed above. Specifically, we pay attention to the new design of Stern-type statistical ZKP protocol for a fully anonymous lattice-based GS-VLR scheme. Firstly, by adopting an efficient identity-encoding technique, the bit-sizes of the group public-key and the member secret-key save a $\mathcal{O}(\log N)$ factor in comparison with the existing lattice-based schemes. Secondly, separating from the member secret-key, the revocation token is generated within some public matrix and a short Gaussian vector, and thus obtaining *full-anonymity*, the strongest security. Thirdly, based on a lattice-based verifiable encryption protocol corresponding to the dual learning with errors (LWE) cryptosystem, the explicit-traceability (ET), to trace the signer's identity in constant time, independent of N, is also satisfied.

We declare that the new and efficient Stern-type statistical ZKP protocol for a fully anonymous lattice-based GS-VLR scheme with the shorter key-sizes, the strongest security and explicit-traceability can be obtained in a relatively simple manner, thanks to three main techniques discussed below.

Firstly, to realize the simpler and efficient Stern-type statistical ZKP protocol for lattice-based GS-VLR with the shorter key-sizes, some efficient mechanisms are required to encode the member's identity information. We utilize a compact identity-encoding technique as in [25] which needs a constant number of public matrices to encode the member's identity index. We consider the group of $N = 2^\ell$ members and each member is identified by a ℓ-bits string id $= (d_1, d_2, \cdots, d_\ell) \in \{0,1\}^\ell$ which is a binary representation of its index $i \in \{0, 1, \cdots, N-1\}$, i.e., id $=$ bin$(i) \in \{0,1\}^\ell$. In our new Stern-type ZKP protocol (without a structure of *Bonsai Tree*), the group public-key only consists of a random vector $\mathbf{u} \in \mathbb{Z}_q^n$ and five random matrices $\mathbf{A}, \mathbf{A}_0, \mathbf{A}_1 \in \mathbb{Z}_q^{n \times m}$ (used for identity-encoding), $\mathbf{A}_2 \in \mathbb{Z}_q^{n \times m}$ (used for explicit-traceability) and $\mathbf{A}_3 \in \mathbb{Z}_q^{n \times m}$ (used for revocation token). For member i, instead of generating a short trapdoor basis matrix for a hard random lattice as signing secret-key as in [25], we sample a $2m$-dimensional Gaussian vector $\mathbf{e}_i = (\mathbf{e}_{i,0}, \mathbf{e}_{i,1}) \in \mathbb{Z}^{2m}$ satisfying $0 < \|\mathbf{e}_i\|_\infty \leq \beta$, $\mathbf{B}_i \cdot \mathbf{e}_i = \mathbf{u} \bmod q$, where $\mathbf{B}_i = [\mathbf{A}|\mathbf{A}_0 + i\mathbf{A}_1] \in \mathbb{Z}_q^{n \times 2m}$. Furthermore, for the VLR feature to obtain *full-anonymity*, the revocation token of member i is constructed by $\mathbf{A}_3$

and a short Gaussian vector $\mathbf{f}_i \in \mathbb{Z}^m$ satisfying $\mathbf{A} \cdot \mathbf{f}_i = \mathbf{A} \cdot \mathbf{e}_{i,0} + \mathbf{A}_0 \cdot \mathbf{e}_{i,1} \bmod q$, i.e., $\mathrm{grt}_i = \mathbf{A}_3 \cdot \mathbf{f}_i \bmod q$.

Secondly, to realize the simper and efficient design of Stern-type statistical ZKP protocol for lattice-based GS-VLR with ET, we further need some mechanism to hide the member's index i (in our new design, just to hide $\mathrm{id} = \mathrm{bin}(i) \in \{0,1\}^\ell$) into a ciphertext $\mathbf{c}$ and a verifiable encryption protocol to prove that $\mathbf{c}$ is a correct encryption of id. Thus, besides the public matrices $\mathbf{A}$, $\mathbf{A}_0$ and $\mathbf{A}_1$ for identity-encoding, a fourth matrix $\mathbf{A}_2$ is required to encrypt $\mathrm{bin}(i)$ using the lattice-based dual LWE cryptosystem [9]. The relation then can be expressed as $\mathbf{c} = (\mathbf{c}_0 = \mathbf{A}_2^\top \mathbf{s} + \mathbf{e}_1 \bmod q, \mathbf{c}_1 = \mathbf{G}^\top \mathbf{s} + \mathbf{e}_2 + \lfloor q/2 \rfloor \mathrm{bin}(i) \bmod q)$ where $\mathbf{G} \in \mathbb{Z}_q^{n \times \ell}$ is a random matrix from certain oracle and $\mathbf{s}$, $\mathbf{e}_1$, $\mathbf{e}_2$ are random vectors having certain specific norm.

Thirdly, the major challenge for our new Stern-type ZKP protocol lies in how to prove the following relations: (a) $[\mathbf{A}|\mathbf{A}_0 + i\mathbf{A}_1] \cdot \mathbf{e}_i = \mathbf{u} \bmod q$; (b) $\mathrm{grt}_i = \mathbf{A}_3 \cdot \mathbf{f}_i \bmod q$; (c) $\mathbf{c} = (\mathbf{c}_0, \mathbf{c}_1) = (\mathbf{A}_2^\top \mathbf{s} + \mathbf{e}_1, \mathbf{G}^\top \mathbf{s} + \mathbf{e}_2 + \lfloor q/2 \rfloor \mathrm{bin}(i)) \bmod q$. For relation (b), we utilize a creative idea introduced by Ling et al. [18] by drawing a matrix $\mathbf{B} \in \mathbb{Z}_q^{n \times m}$ from some random oracle and a vector $\mathbf{e}_0 \in \mathbb{Z}^m$ from the LWE error distribution, define $\mathbf{b} = \mathbf{B}^\top \mathrm{grt}_i + \mathbf{e}_0 = (\mathbf{B}^\top \mathbf{A}_3) \cdot \mathbf{f}_i + \mathbf{e}_0 \bmod q$, thus the member i's token grt_i is now bound to a one-way and injective LWE function. For relation (c), we also utilize a creative idea introduced by Ling et al. [20] by constructing a matrix $\mathbf{P} \in \mathbb{Z}_q^{(m+\ell) \times (n+m+\ell)}$ (obtained from the public matrices $\mathbf{A}_2$ and $\mathbf{G}$, see Sect. 3 for details), and a vector $\mathbf{e} = (\mathbf{s}, \mathbf{e}_1, \mathbf{e}_2) \in \mathbb{Z}^{n+m+\ell}$, define $\mathbf{c} = (\mathbf{c}_0, \mathbf{c}_1) = \mathbf{Pe} + (\mathbf{0}^m, \lfloor q/2 \rfloor \mathrm{bin}(i)) \bmod q$, thus the index i is bound to this new form which is convenient to construct a Stern-type statistical ZKP protocol. For relation (a), since $\mathbf{e}_i \in \mathbb{Z}^{2m}$ is a valid solution to the inhomogeneous short integer solution (ISIS) instance $(\mathbf{B}_i, \mathbf{u})$, where $\mathbf{B}_i = [\mathbf{A}|\mathbf{A}_0 + i\mathbf{A}_1] \in \mathbb{Z}_q^{n \times 2m}$, a direct way for signer i to prove its validity as a certified group member without leaking $\mathbf{e}_i$ is to perform a Stern-type statistical zero-knowledge argument of knowledge (ZKAoK) as in [19]. However, in order to protect the anonymity of i, the structure of matrix $\mathbf{B}_i$ should not be given explicitly, thus how to realize a Stern-type statistical ZKP protocol without leaking $\mathbf{B}_i$ and $\mathbf{e}_i$ simultaneously? To solve this open problem, we firstly transform $\mathbf{B}_i$ to $\mathbf{B}'$ which enjoys some new form, independent of the index i, i.e., $\mathbf{B}' = [\mathbf{A}|\mathbf{A}_0|\mathbf{g}_\ell \otimes \mathbf{A}_1] \in \mathbb{Z}_q^{n \times (\ell+2)m}$, where $\mathbf{g}_\ell = (1, 2, 2^2, \cdots, 2^{\ell-1})$ is a power-of-two vector and notation $\otimes$ denotes a concatenation with vectors or matrices and the index i can be rewritten as $i = \mathbf{g}_\ell^\top \cdot \mathrm{bin}(i)$, the detailed definition will be given later (see Sect. 3). A corresponding change to signing secret-key of member i, $\mathbf{e}_i = (\mathbf{e}_{i,0}, \mathbf{e}_{i,1}) \in \mathbb{Z}^{2m}$ is now transformed to $\mathbf{e}_i' = (\mathbf{e}_{i,0}, \mathbf{e}_{i,1}, \mathrm{bin}(i) \otimes \mathbf{e}_{i,1}) \in \mathbb{Z}^{(\ell+2)m}$. Thus, to argue the relation $\mathbf{B}_i \cdot \mathbf{e}_i = \mathbf{u} \bmod q$, we instead show that $\mathbf{B}' \cdot \mathbf{e}_i' = \mathbf{u} \bmod q$.

Taking all the above transformations ideas and the versatility of Stern-type argument system introduced by Ling et al. [19] together, we design an efficient Stern-type interactive ZKP protocol for the relations (a), (b) and (c). Furthermore, this interactive protocol is repeated $\omega(\log n)$ times to reduce the soundness error to a negligible value, and then transformed to an efficient and secure non-interactive Stern-type statistical ZKP protocol by using the *Fiat-Shamir* heuristic in the random oracle model. To summarize, by incorporating a scalable and compact identity-encoding technique, a shorter Gaussian vector separating from the member secret-key and the lattice-based dual LWE cryptosystem to hide the index, a new Stern-type statistical ZKP protocol for an implicit fully anonymous lattice-based GS-VLR scheme is proposed, therefore, obtaining shorter key-sizes for the group public-key and member secret-key, *full-anonymity*, which is stronger than *selfless-anonymity* and *almost-full anonymity*, and supporting the explicit-traceability.

ORGANIZATION. In the forthcoming sections, we recall some background knowledge on lattice-based cryptography in Sect. 2. Section 3 turns to develop an improved identity-encoding technique, a new creation of group member revocation token and an explicit-traceability mechanism. Our new Stern-type statistical ZKP protocol for a fully anonymous lattice-based GS-VLR scheme is designed in Sect. 4, and analyzed in Sect. 5.

2 Preliminaries

NOTATIONS. Let $\mathcal{S}_k$ denote the set of permutations of k elements, and $\xleftarrow{\$}$ denotes that sampling elements from a distribution uniformly. Let $\|\cdot\|$ and $\|\cdot\|_\infty$ denote the Euclidean norm (ℓ_2) and infinity norm (ℓ_∞) of a vector, respectively. Given $\mathbf{e} = (e_1, e_2, \cdots, e_n) \in \mathbb{R}^n$, $\mathsf{Parse}(\mathbf{e}, k_1, k_2)$ denotes $(e_{k_1}, e_{k_1+1}, \cdots, e_{k_2}) \in \mathbb{R}^{k_2-k_1+1}$ for $1 \leq k_1 \leq k_2 \leq n$. The notation $\log a$ denotes the logarithm of a with base 2, and PPT stands for "probabilistic polynomial-time."

For integers n, m, $q \geq 2$, a random matrix $\mathbf{A} \in \mathbb{Z}_q^{n \times m}$, the m-dimensional q-ary lattice $\Lambda_q^\perp(\mathbf{A})$ is defined as

$$\Lambda_q^\perp(\mathbf{A}) = \{\mathbf{e} \in \mathbb{Z}^m \mid \mathbf{A} \cdot \mathbf{e} = \mathbf{0} \bmod q\}.$$

We recall two well-known *average-case* lattices problems, short integer solution (SIS) and learning with errors (LWE).

Definition 1. *The* $\mathsf{SIS}^\infty_{n,m,q,\beta}$ *problem is defined as follows: given a uniformly random* $\mathbf{A} \in \mathbb{Z}_q^{n \times m}$, *a real* $\beta > 0$, *to get* $\mathbf{e} \in \mathbb{Z}^m$ *such that* $\mathbf{A} \cdot \mathbf{e} = \mathbf{0} \bmod q$, *and* $0 < \|\mathbf{e}\|_\infty \leq \beta$.

The ISIS problem is an variant of SIS, additionally given a random syndrome vector $\mathbf{u} \in \mathbb{Z}_q^n$, the $\mathsf{ISIS}^\infty_{n,m,q,\beta}$ problem is asked to get a vector $\mathbf{e} \in \mathbb{Z}^m$ such that $\mathbf{A} \cdot \mathbf{e} = \mathbf{u} \bmod q$, $\|\mathbf{e}\|_\infty \leq \beta$. For both problems, they are as hard as certain worst-case lattice problems, such as shortest independent vectors problem (SIVP).

Lemma 1 ([9,24]). *For* m, $\beta = poly(n)$, $q \geq \beta \cdot \widetilde{\mathcal{O}}(\sqrt{n})$, *the average-case* $\mathsf{SIS}^\infty_{n,m,q,\beta}$ *and* $\mathsf{ISIS}^\infty_{n,m,q,\beta}$ *problems are at least as hard as the* $\mathsf{SIVP}_{\beta \cdot \widetilde{\mathcal{O}}(n)}$ *problem in the worst-case.*

Definition 2. *The* $\mathsf{LWE}_{n,q,\chi}$ *problem is defined as follows: given a random vector* $\mathbf{s} \in \mathbb{Z}_q^n$, *a probability distribution* χ *over* $\mathbb{Z}$, *let* $\mathcal{A}_{\mathbf{s},\chi}$ *be a distribution obtained* by sampling $\mathbf{A} \in \mathbb{Z}_q^{n \times m}$, $\mathbf{e} \xleftarrow{\$} \chi^m$, and output $(\mathbf{A}, \mathbf{A}^\top \mathbf{s} + \mathbf{e} \bmod q)$, and make distinguish between $\mathcal{A}_{\mathbf{s}, \chi}$ and a uniform distribution $\mathcal{U} \xleftarrow{\$} \mathbb{Z}_q^{n \times m} \times \mathbb{Z}_q^m$.

Let $\beta \geq \sqrt{n} \cdot \omega(\log n)$, for a prime power q, given a β-bounded distribution χ, the $\mathsf{LWE}_{n,q,\chi}$ problem is as least as hard as $\mathsf{SIVP}_{\widetilde{\mathcal{O}}(nq/\beta)}$.

3 Preparations

3.1 The Improved Identity-Encoding Technique

A public $\mathbf{u} \in \mathbb{Z}_q^n$ and $\mathbf{A}_3 \in \mathbb{Z}_q^{n \times m}$ are required, i.e., $\mathsf{Gpk} = (\mathbf{A}, \mathbf{A}_0, \mathbf{A}_1, \mathbf{A}_2, \mathbf{A}_3, \mathbf{u})$, furthermore, the secret-key of member i is not yet a trapdoor basis matrix for $\Lambda_q^\perp(\mathbf{B}_i)$, instead of a short $2m$-dimensional vector $\mathbf{e}_i = (\mathbf{e}_{i,0}, \mathbf{e}_{i,1}) \in \mathbb{Z}^{2m}$ in the coset of $\Lambda_q^\perp(\mathbf{B}_i)$, i.e., $\Lambda_q^{\mathbf{u}}(\mathbf{B}_i) = \{\mathbf{e}_i \in \mathbb{Z}^{2m} \mid \mathbf{B}_i \cdot \mathbf{e}_i = \mathbf{u} \bmod q\}$.

In order to design a new and efficient Stern-type statistical ZKP protocol corresponding to the above variant, we need to transform identity-encoding matrix $\mathbf{B}_i = [\mathbf{A} | \mathbf{A}_0 + i\mathbf{A}_1]$ of member i to a new form. Before that, we define:

1. $\mathbf{g}_\ell = (1, 2, 2^2 \cdots, 2^{\ell-1})$: a power-of-two vector, for $i \in \{0, 1, \cdots, N-1\}$, $i = \mathbf{g}_\ell^\top \cdot \mathrm{bin}(i)$ where $\mathrm{bin}(i) \in \{0, 1\}^\ell$ denotes a binary representation of i.
2. $\otimes$: a concatenation with vectors or matrices, given $\mathbf{e} = (e_1, e_2, \cdots, e_\ell) \in \mathbb{Z}_q^\ell$, $\mathbf{A} \in \mathbb{Z}_q^{n \times m}$ and $\mathbf{e}' \in \mathbb{Z}_q^m$, define: $\mathbf{e} \otimes \mathbf{e}' = (e_1 \mathbf{e}', e_2 \mathbf{e}', \cdots, e_\ell \mathbf{e}') \in \mathbb{Z}_q^{m\ell}$, $\mathbf{e} \otimes \mathbf{A} = [e_1 \mathbf{A} | e_2 \mathbf{A} | \cdots | e_\ell \mathbf{A}] \in \mathbb{Z}_q^{n \times m\ell}$.

We transform $\mathbf{B}_i$ to $\mathbf{B}'$ that is independent of the index of member i, where $\mathbf{B}' = [\mathbf{A} | \mathbf{A}_0 | \mathbf{A}_1 | \cdots | 2^{\ell-1}\mathbf{A}_1] = [\mathbf{A} | \mathbf{A}_0 | \mathbf{g}_\ell \otimes \mathbf{A}_1] \in \mathbb{Z}_q^{n \times (\ell+2)m}$. As a corresponding revision to the secret-key of i, $\mathbf{e}_i = (\mathbf{e}_{i,0}, \mathbf{e}_{i,1})$ is transformed to $\mathbf{e}'_i$, a vector with a special structure, $\mathbf{e}'_i = (\mathbf{e}_{i,0}, \mathbf{e}_{i,1}, \mathrm{bin}(i) \otimes \mathbf{e}_{i,1}) \in \mathbb{Z}^{(\ell+2)m}$.

Thus from the above transformations, the relation $\mathbf{B}_i \cdot \mathbf{e}_i = \mathbf{u} \bmod q$ is now transformed to the following new form,

$$\mathbf{B}_i \cdot \mathbf{e}_i = \mathbf{B}' \cdot \mathbf{e}'_i = \mathbf{u} \bmod q. \tag{1}$$

3.2 The New Creation of Revocation Token

The revocation token of member i is generated within the fifth public matrix $\mathbf{A}_3$ and a short Gaussian vector $\mathbf{f}_i \in \mathbb{Z}^m$, satisfying $\mathbf{A} \cdot \mathbf{f}_i = \mathbf{A} \cdot \mathbf{e}_{i,0} + \mathbf{A}_0 \cdot \mathbf{e}_{i,1} \bmod q$, i.e., $\mathrm{grt}_i = \mathbf{A}_3 \cdot \mathbf{f}_i \bmod q$, which is separating from member secret-key. In the proof of *full-anonymity* for the implicit lattice-based GS-VLR, the challenger is allowed to provide all members' secret-keys to adversary, therefore the underlying GS-VLR can obtain the strongest security, *full-anonymity*, as in [1].

For the revocation mechanism, as it was stated in [18], due to a flaw in the revocation mechanism of [14] which adopts the *inequality test* method to check whether the signer's revocation token belongs to a given revocation list or not, a corrected technique which realizes revocation by binding signer's revocation token grt_i to an LWE function was proposed,

$$\mathbf{b} = \mathbf{B}^\top \mathrm{grt}_i + \mathbf{e}_0 = (\mathbf{B}^\top \mathbf{A}_3) \cdot \mathbf{f}_i + \mathbf{e}_0 \bmod q. \tag{2}$$

3.3 The Explicit-Traceability Mechanism

For the ET mechanism to trace the signer's identity in constant time, independent of N, as it was shown in [20], the lattice-based dual LWE cryptosystem [9]
can be used to hide the index of signer i. In our new design, the binary string
$\mathsf{bin}(i) \in \{0,1\}^\ell$ is treated as plaintext, and the cipertext can be expressed as

$$\mathbf{c} = (\mathbf{c}_0, \mathbf{c}_1) = (\mathbf{A}_2^\top \mathbf{s} + \mathbf{e}_1, \mathbf{G}^\top \mathbf{s} + \mathbf{e}_2 + \lfloor q/2 \rfloor \mathsf{bin}(i)) \bmod q,$$

where $\mathbf{G} \in \mathbb{Z}_q^{n \times \ell}$ is a random matrix, and $\mathbf{s}, \mathbf{e}_1, \mathbf{e}_2$ are random vectors sampled
from the LWE error $\chi^n, \chi^m, \chi^\ell$, respectively.
   Thus, the above relation can be expressed as:

$$\mathbf{c} = (\mathbf{c}_0, \mathbf{c}_1) = \mathbf{Pe} + (\mathbf{0}^m, \lfloor q/2 \rfloor \mathsf{bin}(i)) \bmod q, \tag{3}$$

where $\mathbf{P} = \begin{pmatrix} \mathbf{A}_2^\top \\ \cdots\cdots \\ \mathbf{G}^\top \end{pmatrix} \mathbf{I}_{m+\ell} \end{pmatrix} \in \mathbb{Z}_q^{(m+\ell) \times (n+m+\ell)}$ and $\mathbf{e} = (\mathbf{s}, \mathbf{e}_1, \mathbf{e}_2) \in \mathbb{Z}^{n+m+\ell}$.

   Taking the above transformations ideas and the versatility of Stern-extension
argument system introduced by Ling et al. [19] together, in the next section, we
design a new and efficient Stern-type statistical ZKP protocol to prove the above
new relations (1), (2) and (3).

4 The New Underlying Stern-Type ZKP Protocol

A new underlying Stern-type statistical ZKP protocol that allows the signer $\mathcal{P}$
to convince any verifier $\mathcal{V}$ that $\mathcal{P}$ is indeed a member who honestly signed the
message $\mathsf{m} \in \{0,1\}^*$ will be introduced, i.e., $\mathcal{P}$ owns a valid member secret-key,
its revocation token is correctly embedded into an LWE instance, and its identity
information, a binary representation of its index is correctly hidden within the
lattice-based dual LWE cryptosystem.
   In our design of new Stern-type statistical ZKP protocol, the classical decomposition (Dec) technique, extension (Ext) technique, matrix-extension (Mat-Ext)
technique are adopted. Moreover, some specific sets, e.g., $\mathsf{B}_{2\ell}, \mathsf{B}_{3m}, \mathsf{Sec}_\beta(\mathsf{id})$,
$\mathsf{SecExt}(\mathsf{id}^*)$, permutations, e.g., $\pi, \varphi \in \mathcal{S}_{3m}, \tau \in \mathcal{S}_{2\ell}$, a composition $\mathcal{F}$ are
also used. Because of page limitation, we omit these duplicate concepts and the
detailed definitions can be referred to the full version or [8,13,14,18,29].
   The new Stern-type statistical ZKP protocol between $\mathcal{P}$ and $\mathcal{V}$ can be summarized as follows:

1. The public inputs are $\mathbf{B}' = [\mathbf{A}|\mathbf{A}_0|\mathbf{g}_\ell \otimes \mathbf{A}_1] \in \mathbb{Z}_q^{n \times (\ell+2)m}$, $\mathbf{b} \in \mathbb{Z}_q^m$, $\mathbf{u} \in \mathbb{Z}_q^n$,
   $$\mathbf{B} \in \mathbb{Z}_q^{n \times m}, \mathbf{P} = \begin{pmatrix} \mathbf{A}_2^\top \\ \cdots\cdots \\ \mathbf{G}^\top \end{pmatrix} \mathbf{I}_{m+\ell} \end{pmatrix} \in \mathbb{Z}_q^{(m+\ell) \times (n+m+\ell)} \text{ and } \mathbf{c} = (\mathbf{c}_0, \mathbf{c}_1).$$

2. $\mathcal{P}$'s valid witnesses are $\mathbf{e}' = (\mathbf{e}_0', \mathbf{e}_1', \mathsf{bin}(i) \otimes \mathbf{e}_1') \in \mathsf{Sec}_\beta(\mathsf{id})$ for a secret index
   $i \in \{0, 1, \cdots, N-1\}$, and three short vectors $\mathbf{f}, \mathbf{e}_0 \in \chi^m$ and $\mathbf{e} = (\mathbf{s}, \mathbf{e}_1, \mathbf{e}_2) \in \mathbb{Z}^{n+m+\ell}$, where $\mathbf{s} \in \chi^n, \mathbf{e}_1 \in \chi^m, \mathbf{e}_2 \in \chi^\ell$, the LWE errors.

3. $\mathcal{P}$'s goal is to convince $\mathcal{V}$ in zero-knowledge that:

   3.1. $\mathbf{B}' \cdot \mathbf{e}' = \mathbf{u} \bmod q$, where $\mathbf{e}' \in \mathrm{Sec}_\beta(\mathrm{id})$ and keeping $\mathrm{id} \in \{0,1\}^\ell$ secret.

   3.2. $\mathbf{b} = (\mathbf{B}^\top \mathbf{A}_3) \cdot \mathbf{f} + \mathbf{e}_0 \bmod q$, where $\mathbf{A} \cdot \mathbf{f} = \mathbf{A} \cdot \mathbf{e}'_0 + \mathbf{A}_0 \cdot \mathbf{e}'_1 \bmod q$, $\|\mathbf{f}\|_\infty, \|\mathbf{e}_0\|_\infty \le \beta$.

   3.3. $\mathbf{c} = \mathbf{P} \cdot \mathbf{e} + (\mathbf{0}^m, \lfloor q/2 \rfloor \mathrm{bin}(i)) \bmod q$, where $0 < \|\mathbf{e}\|_\infty \le \beta$ and keeping $\mathrm{bin}(i) \in \{0,1\}^\ell$ secret.

Firstly, we sketch the **Group Membership Mechanism**, that is, $\mathcal{P}$ is a certified group member and its goal is shown as in 3.1.

1. Parse $\mathbf{B}' = \left[\mathbf{A}|\mathbf{A}_0|\mathbf{A}_1|2\mathbf{A}_1|\cdots|2^{\ell-1}\mathbf{A}_1\right]$, use Mat-Ext technique to extend it to $\mathbf{B}^* = \left[\mathbf{A}|\mathbf{0}^{n \times 2m}|\mathbf{A}_0|\mathbf{0}^{n \times 2m}|\cdots|2^{\ell-1}\mathbf{A}_1|\mathbf{0}^{n \times 2m}|\mathbf{0}^{n \times 3m\ell}\right]$.
2. Parse $\mathrm{id} = (d_1, \cdots, d_\ell) \in \{0,1\}^\ell$, extend it to $\mathrm{id}^* = (d_1, \cdots, \cdots, d_{2\ell}) \in \mathsf{B}_{2\ell}$.
3. Parse $\mathbf{e}' = (\mathbf{e}'_0, \mathbf{e}'_1, d_1\mathbf{e}'_1, d_2\mathbf{e}'_1, \cdots, d_\ell\mathbf{e}'_1)$, use Dec, Ext techniques extending $\mathbf{e}'_0$ to k vectors $\mathbf{e}'_{0,1}, \mathbf{e}'_{0,2}, \cdots, \mathbf{e}'_{0,k} \in \mathsf{B}_{3m}$, $\mathbf{e}'_1$ to k vectors $\mathbf{e}'_{1,1}, \mathbf{e}'_{1,2}, \cdots, \mathbf{e}'_{1,k} \in \mathsf{B}_{3m}$, respectively. For each $j \in \{1, 2, \cdots, k\}$, we define a new vector $\mathbf{e}'_j = (\mathbf{e}'_{0,j}, \mathbf{e}'_{1,j}, d_1\mathbf{e}'_{1,j}, d_2\mathbf{e}'_{1,j}, \cdots, d_{2\ell}\mathbf{e}'_{1,j})$, it can be checked that $\mathbf{e}'_j \in \mathrm{SecExt}(\mathrm{id}^*)$.

Thus, $\mathcal{P}$'s goal in 3.1 is transformed to a new structure,

$$\mathbf{B}^* \cdot \left(\textstyle\sum_{j=1}^k \beta_j \mathbf{e}'_j\right) = \mathbf{u} \bmod q, \quad \mathbf{e}'_j \in \mathrm{SecExt}(\mathrm{id}^*). \tag{4}$$

To prove the new relation (4) in zero-knowledge, we take 2 steps as follows:

1. Pick k random vectors $\mathbf{r}'_1, \cdots, \mathbf{r}'_k \xleftarrow{\$} \mathbb{Z}_q^{(2\ell+2)3m}$ to mask $\mathbf{e}'_1, \cdots, \mathbf{e}'_k$, then it can be checked that $\mathbf{B}^* \cdot \left(\sum_{j=1}^k \beta_j(\mathbf{e}'_j + \mathbf{r}'_j)\right) - \mathbf{u} = \mathbf{B}^* \cdot \left(\sum_{j=1}^k \beta_j\mathbf{r}'_j\right) \bmod q$.
2. Pick two permutations $\pi, \varphi \in \mathcal{S}_{3m}$, one permutation $\tau \in \mathcal{S}_{2\ell}$, then it can be checked that $\forall j \in \{1, 2, \cdots, k\}$, $\mathcal{F}_{\pi,\varphi,\tau}(\mathbf{e}'_j) \in \mathrm{SecExt}(\tau(\mathrm{id}^*))$, where $\mathrm{id}^* \in \mathsf{B}_{2\ell}$ is an extension of $\mathrm{id} = \mathrm{bin}(i) \in \{0,1\}^\ell$.

Secondly, we sketch the **Revocation Mechanism**, that is, $\mathcal{P}$'s revocation token is correctly embedded in an **LWE** function and its goal is shown as in 3.2.

1. Let $\mathbf{C} = \mathbf{B}^\top \mathbf{A}_3 \bmod q \in \mathbb{Z}_q^{m \times m}$.
2. Parse $\mathbf{f} = (f_1, f_2, \cdots, f_m) \in \mathbb{Z}^m$, use Dec and Ext techniques to extend $\mathbf{f}$ to k vectors $\mathbf{f}^{(1)}, \mathbf{f}^{(2)}, \cdots, \mathbf{f}^{(k)} \in \mathsf{B}_{3m}$.
3. Parse $\mathbf{e}_0 = (e_1^0, e_2^0, \cdots, e_m^0) \in \mathbb{Z}^m$, use Dec and Ext techniques to extend $\mathbf{e}_0$ to k vectors $\mathbf{e}_1^0, \mathbf{e}_2^0, \cdots, \mathbf{e}_k^0 \in \mathsf{B}_{3m}$.
4. Let $\mathbf{C}^* = [\mathbf{C}|\mathbf{0}^{n \times 2m}|\mathbf{I}_m|\mathbf{0}^{n \times 2m}]$, where $\mathbf{I}_m$ is the identity matrix of order m.
5. Let $\mathbf{A}^* = [\mathbf{A}|\mathbf{0}^{n \times 2m}]$, $\mathbf{e}'_{j,0} = \mathrm{Parse}(\mathbf{e}'_j, 1, m)$, $\mathbf{e}'_{j,1} = \mathrm{Parse}(\mathbf{e}'_j, 3m+1, 4m)$.

Thus, $\mathcal{P}$'s goal in 3.2 is transformed to a new structure,

$$\mathbf{b} = \mathbf{C}^* \cdot \left(\textstyle\sum_{j=1}^k \beta_j(\mathbf{f}^{(j)}, \mathbf{e}_j^0)\right) \bmod q, \quad \mathbf{f}^{(j)}, \mathbf{e}_j^0 \in \mathsf{B}_{3m},$$
$$\mathbf{A}^* \cdot \left(\textstyle\sum_{j=1}^k \beta_j\mathbf{f}^{(j)}\right) = \mathbf{A} \cdot \left(\textstyle\sum_{j=1}^k \beta_j\mathbf{e}'_{j,0}\right) + \mathbf{A}_0 \cdot \left(\textstyle\sum_{j=1}^k \beta_j\mathbf{e}'_{j,1}\right) \bmod q. \tag{5}$$

To prove the new relation (5) in zero-knowledge, we take 5 steps as follows:

1. Let $\mathbf{r}'_{j,0} = \mathsf{Parse}(\mathbf{r}'_j, 1, m)$, $\mathbf{r}'_{j,1} = \mathsf{Parse}(\mathbf{r}'_j, 3m+1, 4m)$.

2. Pick k uniformly random vectors $\mathbf{f}_1, \cdots, \mathbf{f}_k \xleftarrow{\$} \mathbb{Z}_q^{3m}$ to mask $\mathbf{f}^{(1)}, \cdots, \mathbf{f}^{(k)}$.

3. Pick k random vectors $\mathbf{r}_1^0, \cdots, \mathbf{r}_k^0 \xleftarrow{\$} \mathbb{Z}_q^{3m}$ to mask $\mathbf{e}_1^0, \cdots, \mathbf{e}_k^0$, it can be checked that $\mathbf{C}^* \cdot (\sum_{j=1}^k \beta_j(\mathbf{f}^{(j)} + \mathbf{f}_j, \mathbf{e}_j^0 + \mathbf{r}_j^0)) - \mathbf{b} = \mathbf{C}^* \cdot (\sum_{j=1}^k \beta_j(\mathbf{f}_j, \mathbf{r}_j^0)) \bmod q$.

4. Use $\mathbf{r}'_{j,0}$, $\mathbf{r}'_{j,1}$ to mask $\mathbf{e}'_{j,0}$, $\mathbf{e}'_{j,1}$, respectively, it can be checked that $\mathbf{A}^* \cdot (\sum_{j=1}^k \beta_j(\mathbf{f}^{(j)} + \mathbf{f}_j)) - \mathbf{A} \cdot (\sum_{j=1}^k \beta_j(\mathbf{e}'_{j,0} + \mathbf{r}'_{j,0})) - \mathbf{A}_0 \cdot (\sum_{j=1}^k \beta_j(\mathbf{e}'_{j,1} + \mathbf{r}'_{j,1})) = \mathbf{A}^* \cdot (\sum_{j=1}^k \beta_j \mathbf{f}_j) - \mathbf{A} \cdot (\sum_{j=1}^k \beta_j \mathbf{r}'_{j,0}) - \mathbf{A}_0 \cdot (\sum_{j=1}^k \beta_j \mathbf{r}'_{j,1}) \bmod q$.

5. Pick two permutations ξ, $\phi \in \mathcal{S}_{3m}$, then it can be checked that,

$$\forall j \in \{1, 2, \cdots, k\}, \ \xi(\mathbf{f}^{(j)}), \ \phi(\mathbf{e}_j^0) \in \mathsf{B}_{3m}.$$

Thirdly, we sketch the Explicit-Traceability Mechanism, that is, $\mathcal{P}$'s identity index is correctly hidden in a lattice-based dual LWE cryptosystem and its goal is shown as in 3.3.

1. Let $\mathbf{P}^* = [\mathbf{P}|\mathbf{0}^{(m+\ell)\times 2(n+m+\ell)}]$.

2. Let $\mathbf{Q} = \begin{pmatrix} \mathbf{0}^{m\times\ell} & \mathbf{0}^{m\times\ell} \\ \cdots\cdots & \cdots\cdots \\ \lfloor q/2 \rfloor \mathbf{I}_\ell & \mathbf{0}^{\ell\times\ell} \end{pmatrix}$, where $\mathbf{I}_\ell$ is the identity matrix of order ℓ.

3. Parse $\mathbf{e} = (\mathbf{s}, \mathbf{e}_1, \mathbf{e}_2) \in \mathbb{Z}^{n+m+\ell}$, use Dec and Ext techniques to extend $\mathbf{e}$ to k vectors $\mathbf{e}^{(1)}, \mathbf{e}^{(2)}, \cdots, \mathbf{e}^{(k)} \in \mathsf{B}_{3(n+m+\ell)}$.

4. Let $\mathsf{id}^* = \mathsf{bin}(i)^* \in \mathsf{B}_{2\ell}$ be an extension of $\mathsf{id} = \mathsf{bin}(i)$.

Thus, $\mathcal{P}$'s goal in 3.3 is transformed to a new structure,

$$\mathbf{c} = \mathbf{P}^* \cdot (\textstyle\sum_{j=1}^k \beta_j \mathbf{e}^{(j)}) + \mathbf{Q} \cdot \mathsf{id}^* \bmod q, \ \mathbf{e}^{(j)} \in \mathsf{B}_{3(n+m+\ell)}, \ \mathsf{id}^* \in \mathsf{B}_{2\ell}. \quad (6)$$

To prove the new relation (6) in zero-knowledge, we take 3 steps as follows:

1. Pick a random vector $\mathbf{r}_{\mathsf{id}^*} \xleftarrow{\$} \mathbb{Z}_q^{2\ell}$ to mask id^*.

2. Pick k random vectors $\mathbf{r}_1'' \cdots, \mathbf{r}_k'' \xleftarrow{\$} \mathbb{Z}_q^{3(n+m+\ell)}$ to mask $\mathbf{e}^{(1)}, \cdots, \mathbf{e}^{(k)}$, it can be checked that,

$$\mathbf{P}^* \cdot (\textstyle\sum_{j=1}^k \beta_j(\mathbf{e}^{(j)} + \mathbf{r}_j'')) + \mathbf{Q} \cdot (\mathsf{id}^* + \mathbf{r}_{\mathsf{id}^*}) - \mathbf{c} = \mathbf{P}^* \cdot (\textstyle\sum_{j=1}^k \beta_j \mathbf{r}_j'') + \mathbf{Q} \cdot \mathbf{r}_{\mathsf{id}^*} \bmod q.$$

3. Pick one permutation $\rho \in \mathcal{S}_{3(n+m+\ell)}$, it can be checked that,

$$\forall j \in \{1, 2, \cdots, k\}, \ \rho(\mathbf{e}^{(j)}) \in \mathsf{B}_{3(n+m+\ell)}, \ \tau(\mathsf{id}^*) \in \mathsf{B}_{2\ell},$$

where τ has been picked in the proof of Group Membership Mechanism.

Putting all the above techniques together, we obtain a new underlying Stern-type interactive statistical ZKP protocol, and the details will be given below.

In our new design, we utilize a statistically hiding and computationally blinding commitment scheme (COM) as proposed in [12]. $\mathcal{P}$ and $\mathcal{V}$ interact as follows:

1. **Commitments:** $\mathcal{P}$ randomly samples the randomness of COM, i.e., $\theta_1, \theta_2, \theta_3$, and the following random objects:

$$\begin{cases} \mathbf{r}'_1, \cdots, \mathbf{r}'_k \xleftarrow{\$} \mathbb{Z}_q^{(2\ell+2)3m}; \mathbf{f}_1, \cdots, \mathbf{f}_k, \mathbf{r}_1^0, \cdots, \mathbf{r}_k^0 \xleftarrow{\$} \mathbb{Z}_q^{3m}; \mathbf{r}_{\mathsf{id}^*} \xleftarrow{\$} \mathbb{Z}_q^{2\ell}; \\ \mathbf{r}''_1, \cdots, \mathbf{r}''_k \xleftarrow{\$} \mathbb{Z}_q^{3(n+m+\ell)}; \pi_1, \cdots, \pi_k \xleftarrow{\$} \mathcal{S}_{3m}; \varphi_1, \cdots, \varphi_k \xleftarrow{\$} \mathcal{S}_{3m}; \\ \rho_1, \cdots, \rho_k \xleftarrow{\$} \mathcal{S}_{3(n+m+\ell)}; \xi_1, \cdots, \xi_k, \phi_1, \cdots, \phi_k \xleftarrow{\$} \mathcal{S}_{3m}; \tau \xleftarrow{\$} \mathcal{S}_{2\ell}. \end{cases}$$

For $\forall j \in \{1, 2, \cdots, k\}$, define $\mathbf{r}'_{j,0} = \mathsf{Parse}(\mathbf{r}'_j, 1, m)$, $\mathbf{r}'_{j,1} = \mathsf{Parse}(\mathbf{r}'_j, 3m + 1, 4m)$, then $\mathcal{P}$ sends the commitment CMT $= (\dot{\mathbf{c}}_1, \dot{\mathbf{c}}_2, \dot{\mathbf{c}}_3)$ to $\mathcal{V}$, where

$$\begin{cases} \dot{\mathbf{c}}_1 = \mathsf{COM}(\{\pi_j, \varphi_j, \xi_j, \phi_j, \rho_j\}_{j=1}^k, \tau, \mathbf{B}^* \cdot (\sum_{j=1}^k \beta_j \mathbf{r}'_j), \mathbf{A}^* \cdot (\sum_{j=1}^k \beta_j \mathbf{f}_j) - \\ \quad \mathbf{A} \cdot (\sum_{j=1}^k \beta_j \mathbf{r}'_{j,0}) - \mathbf{A}_0 \cdot (\sum_{j=1}^k \beta_j \mathbf{r}'_{j,1}), \mathbf{C}^* \cdot (\sum_{j=1}^k \beta_j (\mathbf{f}_j, \mathbf{r}_j^0)), \\ \quad \mathbf{P}^* \cdot (\sum_{j=1}^k \beta_j \mathbf{r}''_j) + \mathbf{Q} \cdot \mathbf{r}_{\mathsf{id}^*}; \theta_1), \\ \dot{\mathbf{c}}_2 = \mathsf{COM}(\{\mathcal{F}_{\pi_j,\varphi_j,\tau}(\mathbf{r}'_j), \xi_j(\mathbf{f}_j), \phi_j(\mathbf{r}_j^0), \rho_j(\mathbf{r}''_j)\}_{j=1}^k, \tau(\mathbf{r}_{\mathsf{id}^*}); \theta_2), \\ \dot{\mathbf{c}}_3 = \mathsf{COM}(\{\mathcal{F}_{\pi_j,\varphi_j,\tau}(\mathbf{e}'_j + \mathbf{r}'_j), \xi_j(\mathbf{f}^{(j)} + \mathbf{f}_j), \phi_j(\mathbf{e}_j^0 + \mathbf{r}_j^0), \rho_j(\mathbf{e}^{(j)} + \mathbf{r}''_j)\}_{j=1}^k, \\ \quad \tau(\mathsf{id}^* + \mathbf{r}_{\mathsf{id}^*}); \theta_3). \end{cases}$$

2. **Challenge:** $\mathcal{V}$ chooses a challenge CH $\xleftarrow{\$} \{1, 2, 3\}$ and sends it to $\mathcal{P}$.
3. **Response:** Depending on CH, $\mathcal{P}$ replies as follows:

   o If CH $= 1$. For $j \in \{1, 2, \cdots, k\}$, let $\mathbf{v}'_j = \mathcal{F}_{\pi_j,\varphi_j,\tau}(\mathbf{e}'_j)$, $\mathbf{w}'_j = \mathcal{F}_{\pi_j,\varphi_j,\tau}(\mathbf{r}'_j)$, $\mathbf{v}_j = \xi_j(\mathbf{f}^{(i)})$, $\mathbf{w}_j = \xi_j(\mathbf{f}_j)$, $\mathbf{v}_j^0 = \phi_j(\mathbf{e}_j^0)$, $\mathbf{w}_j^0 = \phi_j(\mathbf{r}_j^0)$, $\mathbf{v}^{(j)} = \rho_j(\mathbf{e}^{(j)})$, $\mathbf{w}''_j = \rho_j(\mathbf{r}''_j)$, $\mathbf{t}_{\mathsf{id}} = \tau(\mathsf{id}^*)$, $\mathbf{v}_{\mathsf{id}} = \tau(\mathbf{r}_{\mathsf{id}^*})$, define

   $$\mathsf{RSP} = (\{\mathbf{v}'_j, \mathbf{w}'_j, \mathbf{v}_j, \mathbf{w}_j, \mathbf{v}_j^0, \mathbf{w}_j^0, \mathbf{v}^{(j)}, \mathbf{w}''_j\}_{j=1}^k, \mathbf{t}_{\mathsf{id}}, \mathbf{v}_{\mathsf{id}}).$$

   o If CH $= 2$. For $j \in \{1, 2, \cdots, k\}$, let $\hat{\pi}_j = \pi_j$, $\hat{\varphi}_j = \varphi_j$, $\hat{\xi}_j = \xi_j$, $\hat{\phi}_j = \phi_j$, $\hat{\rho}_j = \rho_j$, $\hat{\tau} = \tau$, $\mathbf{x}'_j = \mathbf{e}'_j + \mathbf{r}'_j$, $\mathbf{x}_j = \mathbf{f}^{(j)} + \mathbf{f}_j$, $\mathbf{x}_j^0 = \mathbf{e}_j^0 + \mathbf{r}_j^0$, $\mathbf{x}''_j = \mathbf{e}^{(j)} + \mathbf{r}''_j$, $\mathbf{x}_{\mathsf{id}} = \mathsf{id}^* + \mathbf{r}_{\mathsf{id}^*}$, define

   $$\mathsf{RSP} = (\{\hat{\pi}_j, \hat{\varphi}_j, \hat{\xi}_j, \hat{\phi}_j, \hat{\rho}_j, \mathbf{x}'_j, \mathbf{x}_j, \mathbf{x}_j^0, \mathbf{x}''_j\}_{j=1}^k, \hat{\tau}, \mathbf{x}_{\mathsf{id}}).$$

   o If CH $= 3$. For $j \in \{1, 2, \cdots, k\}$, let $\tilde{\pi}_j = \pi_j$, $\tilde{\varphi}_j = \varphi_j$, $\tilde{\xi}_j = \xi_j$, $\tilde{\phi}_j = \phi_j$, $\tilde{\rho}_j = \rho_j$, $\tilde{\tau} = \tau$, $\mathbf{h}'_j = \mathbf{r}'_j$, $\mathbf{h}_j = \mathbf{f}_j$, $\mathbf{h}_j^0 = \mathbf{r}_j^0$, $\mathbf{h}''_j = \mathbf{r}''_j$, $\mathbf{h}_{\mathsf{id}} = \mathbf{r}_{\mathsf{id}^*}$, define

   $$\mathsf{RSP} = (\{\tilde{\pi}_j, \tilde{\varphi}_j, \tilde{\xi}_j, \tilde{\phi}_j, \tilde{\rho}_j, \mathbf{h}'_j, \mathbf{h}_j, \mathbf{h}_j^0, \mathbf{h}''_j\}_{j=1}^k, \tilde{\tau}, \mathbf{h}_{\mathsf{id}}).$$

4. **Verification:** Receiving RSP, $\mathcal{V}$ checks as follows:

   o If CH $= 1$. Check that $\mathbf{t}_{\mathsf{id}} \in \mathsf{B}_{2\ell}$, for $j \in \{1, 2, \cdots, k\}$, $\mathbf{v}'_j \in \mathsf{SecExt}(\mathbf{t}_{\mathsf{id}})$, $\mathbf{v}_j \in \mathsf{B}_{3m}$, $\mathbf{v}^{(j)} \in \mathsf{B}_{3(n+m+\ell)}$, $\mathbf{v}_j^0 \in \mathsf{B}_{3m}$ and that,

   $$\begin{cases} \dot{\mathbf{c}}_2 = \mathsf{COM}(\{\mathbf{w}'_j, \mathbf{w}_j, \mathbf{w}_j^0, \mathbf{w}''_j\}_{j=1}^k, \mathbf{v}_{\mathsf{id}}; \theta_2), \\ \dot{\mathbf{c}}_3 = \mathsf{COM}(\{\mathbf{v}'_j + \mathbf{w}'_j, \mathbf{v}_j + \mathbf{w}_j, \mathbf{v}_j^0 + \mathbf{w}_j^0, \mathbf{v}^{(j)} + \mathbf{w}''_j\}_{j=1}^k, \mathbf{t}_{\mathsf{id}} + \mathbf{v}_{\mathsf{id}}; \theta_3). \end{cases}$$

○ If $\mathsf{CH} = 2$. For $j \in \{1, 2, \cdots, k\}$, define $\mathbf{x}'_{j,0} = \mathsf{Parse}(\mathbf{x}'_j, 1, m)$ and $\mathbf{x}'_{j,1} = \mathsf{Parse}(\mathbf{x}'_j, 3m+1, 4m)$, and check that,

$$
\begin{cases}
\acute{\mathbf{c}}_1 = \mathsf{COM}(\{\hat{\pi}_j, \hat{\varphi}_j, \hat{\xi}_j, \hat{\phi}_j, \hat{\rho}_j\}_{j=1}^k, \hat{\tau}, \mathbf{B}^* \cdot (\sum_{j=1}^k \beta_j \mathbf{x}'_j) - \mathbf{u}, \mathbf{A}^* \cdot (\sum_{j=1}^k \beta_j \mathbf{x}_j) \\
\quad - \mathbf{A} \cdot (\sum_{j=1}^k \beta_j \mathbf{x}'_{j,0}) - \mathbf{A}_0 \cdot (\sum_{j=1}^k \beta_j \mathbf{x}'_{j,1}), \mathbf{C}^* \cdot (\sum_{j=1}^k \beta_j (\mathbf{x}_j, \mathbf{x}_j^0)) \\
\quad - \mathbf{b}, \mathbf{P}^* \cdot (\sum_{j=1}^k \beta_j \mathbf{x}''_j) + \mathbf{Q}^* \cdot \mathbf{x}_{\mathsf{id}} - \mathbf{c}; \theta_1), \\
\acute{\mathbf{c}}_3 = \mathsf{COM}(\{\mathcal{F}_{\hat{\pi}_j, \hat{\varphi}_j, \hat{\tau}}(\mathbf{x}'_j), \hat{\xi}_j(\mathbf{x}_j), \hat{\phi}_j(\mathbf{x}_j^0), \hat{\rho}_j(\mathbf{x}''_j)\}_{j=1}^k, \hat{\tau}(\mathbf{x}_{\mathsf{id}}); \theta_3).
\end{cases}
$$

○ If $\mathsf{CH} = 3$. For $j \in \{1, 2, \cdots, k\}$, define $\mathbf{h}'_{j,0} = \mathsf{Parse}(\mathbf{h}'_j, 1, m)$ and $\mathbf{h}'_{j,1} = \mathsf{Parse}(\mathbf{h}'_j, 3m+1, 4m)$, and check that,

$$
\begin{cases}
\acute{\mathbf{c}}_1 = \mathsf{COM}(\{\tilde{\pi}_j, \tilde{\varphi}_j, \tilde{\xi}_j, \tilde{\phi}_j, \tilde{\rho}_j\}_{j=1}^k, \tilde{\tau}, \mathbf{B}^* \cdot (\sum_{j=1}^k \beta_j \mathbf{h}'_j), \mathbf{A}^* \cdot (\sum_{j=1}^k \beta_j \mathbf{h}_j) \\
\quad - \mathbf{A} \cdot (\sum_{j=1}^k \beta_j \mathbf{h}'_{j,0}) - \mathbf{A}_0 \cdot (\sum_{j=1}^k \beta_j \mathbf{h}'_{j,1}), \mathbf{C}^* \cdot (\sum_{j=1}^k \beta_j (\mathbf{h}_j, \mathbf{h}_j^0)), \\
\quad \mathbf{P}^* \cdot (\sum_{j=1}^k \beta_j \mathbf{h}''_j) + \mathbf{Q}^* \cdot \mathbf{h}_{\mathsf{id}}; \theta_1), \\
\acute{\mathbf{c}}_2 = \mathsf{COM}(\{\mathcal{F}_{\tilde{\pi}_j, \tilde{\varphi}_j, \tilde{\tau}}(\mathbf{h}'_j), \tilde{\xi}_j(\mathbf{h}_j), \tilde{\phi}_j(\mathbf{h}_j^0), \tilde{\rho}_j(\mathbf{h}''_j)\}_{j=1}^k, \tilde{\tau}(\mathbf{h}_{\mathsf{id}}); \theta_2).
\end{cases}
$$

$\mathcal{V}$ outputs 1 if and only if all the above conditions hold, otherwise 0.

Thus, the associated relation $\mathcal{R}(n, k, \ell, q, m, \beta)$ in the above protocol can be defined as:

$$
\mathcal{R} = \left\{
\begin{array}{l}
\mathbf{A}, \mathbf{A}_{i \in \{0,1,2,3\}}, \mathbf{B} \in \mathbb{Z}_q^{n \times m}, \mathbf{P} \in \mathbb{Z}_q^{(m+\ell) \times (n+m+\ell)}, \mathbf{u}, \mathbf{b} \in \mathbb{Z}_q^m, \mathbf{c} \in \mathbb{Z}_q^{m+\ell}, \\
\mathsf{id} = \mathrm{bin}(i) \in \{0,1\}^\ell, \mathbf{e}' = (\mathbf{e}'_0, \mathbf{e}'_1, \mathrm{bin}(i) \otimes \mathbf{e}'_1) \in \mathsf{Sec}_\beta(\mathsf{id}), \mathbf{f}, \mathbf{e}_0 \in \mathbb{Z}^m, \\
\mathbf{e} = (\mathbf{s}, \mathbf{e}_1, \mathbf{e}_2) \in \mathbb{Z}^{n+m+\ell}; \ s.t. \ 0 < \|\mathbf{e}'\|_\infty, \|\mathbf{f}\|_\infty, \|\mathbf{e}_0\|_\infty, \|\mathbf{e}\|_\infty \le \beta, \\
[\mathbf{A}|\mathbf{A}_0|\mathbf{g}_\ell \otimes \mathbf{A}_1] \cdot \mathbf{e}' = \mathbf{u} \bmod q, \mathbf{b} = (\mathbf{B}^\top \mathbf{A}_3) \cdot \mathbf{f} + \mathbf{e}_0 \bmod q, \\
\mathbf{A} \cdot \mathbf{f} = \mathbf{A} \cdot \mathbf{e}'_0 + \mathbf{A}_0 \cdot \mathbf{e}'_1 \bmod q, \mathbf{c} = \mathbf{P} \cdot \mathbf{e} + (\mathbf{0}^m, \lfloor q/2 \rfloor \mathrm{bin}(i)) \bmod q.
\end{array}
\right\}
$$

5   Analysis of the Protocol

A detailed analysis of the underlying interactive protocol constructed in Sect. 4 including four aspects: communication cost, perfect completeness, statistical zero-knowledge and argument of knowledge.

Theorem 1. *Let* COM *be a statistically hiding and computationally binding commitment scheme, thus for a given* CMT, *three valid responses* RSP_1, RSP_2 *and* RSP_3 *with respect to three different challenges* CH_1, CH_2 *and* CH_3, *the proposed protocol is a statistical* ZKAoK *for* $\mathcal{R}(n, k, \ell, q, m, \beta)$, *where each round has perfect completeness, soundness error* $2/3$, *argument of knowledge property and communication cost* $\widetilde{\mathcal{O}}(\ell n)$.

Proof. The proof for Theorem 1 will employ standard proof techniques for Stern-type protocol as in [12–14], and it includes the following four aspects:

Communication Cost:

- The output of COM, a vector of $\mathbb{Z}_q^n$, has bit-sizes $n \log q$, thus $\mathcal{P}$ sends 3 commitments amounting to $3n \log q$ bits.
- The challenge $\mathsf{CH} \in \{1, 2, 3\}$ could be represented by 2 bits.
- The response RSP from $\mathcal{P}$ consist of the following items:
  1. one permutation in $\mathcal{S}_{2\ell}$, $4k$ permutations in $\mathcal{S}_{3m}$ and k permutations in $\mathcal{S}_{3(n+m+\ell)}$,
  2. $2k$ vectors in $\mathbb{Z}_q^{(2\ell+2)3m}$ and $2k$ vectors in $\mathbb{Z}_q^{3(n+m+\ell)}$,
  3. $4k$ vectors in $\mathbb{Z}_q^{3m}$, one vector in $\{0,1\}^{2\ell}$ and one vector in $\mathbb{Z}_q^{2\ell}$.

Thus, the bit-size of RSP is bound by $\mathcal{O}(\ell m k) \log q$. Recall that $k = \lfloor \log \beta \rfloor + 1 = \mathcal{O}(\log \beta) = \widetilde{\mathcal{O}}(1)$, the communication cost of proposed Stern-type statistical ZKP protocol is bounded by $\widetilde{\mathcal{O}}(\ell n)$.

Perfect Completeness:

To show that given a tuple $(\mathbf{A}, \mathbf{A}_0, \mathbf{A}_1, \mathbf{A}_2, \mathbf{A}_3, \mathbf{P}, \mathbf{u}, \mathbf{B}, \mathbf{b}, \mathbf{c})$, if an honest $\mathcal{P}$ owns witness $(\mathsf{id} = \mathsf{bin}(i) \in \{0,1\}^\ell, \mathbf{e}' \in \mathsf{Sec}_\beta(\mathsf{id}), \mathbf{f}, \mathbf{e}_0, \mathbf{e}_1 \in \mathbb{Z}^m, \mathbf{s} \in \mathbb{Z}^n, \mathbf{e}_2 \in \mathbb{Z}^\ell)$ and follows the proposed protocol (constructed in Sect. 4) correctly, then $\mathcal{P}$ can generate a valid Stern-type statistical ZKP protocol satisfying the verification processes, and gets accepted by $\mathcal{V}$ with a high probability.

Firstly, the public inputs and $\mathcal{P}$'s witness are transformed to $\mathbf{B}^*$, $\mathbf{C}^*$, $\mathbf{P}^*$, id^* and $\{\mathbf{e}'_j, \mathbf{f}^{(j)}, \mathbf{e}^0_j, \mathbf{e}^{(j)}\}_{j=1}^k$ using the Dec, Ext and Mat-Ext techniques, thus these new results satisfy the following new structures,

$$\mathbf{B}^* \cdot \left(\sum_{j=1}^k \beta_j \mathbf{e}'_j\right) = \mathbf{u} \bmod q, \ \mathbf{e}'_j \in \mathsf{SecExt}(\mathsf{id}^*),$$

$$\mathbf{C}^* \cdot \left(\sum_{j=1}^k \beta_j (\mathbf{f}^{(j)}, \mathbf{e}^0_j)\right) = \mathbf{b} \bmod q, \ \mathbf{f}^{(j)}, \mathbf{e}^0_j \in \mathsf{B}_{3m}.$$

$$\mathbf{A}^* \cdot \left(\sum_{j=1}^k \beta_j \mathbf{f}^{(j)}\right) = \mathbf{A} \cdot \left(\sum_{j=1}^k \beta_j \mathbf{e}'_{j,0}\right) + \mathbf{A}_0 \cdot \left(\sum_{j=1}^k \beta_j \mathbf{e}'_{j,1}\right) \bmod q,$$

$$\mathbf{e}'_{j,0} = \mathsf{Parse}(\mathbf{e}'_j, 1, m), \ \mathbf{e}'_{j,1} = \mathsf{Parse}(\mathbf{e}'_j, 3m+1, 4m),$$

$$\mathbf{c} = \mathbf{P}^* \cdot \left(\sum_{j=1}^k \beta_j \mathbf{e}^{(j)}\right) + \mathbf{Q} \cdot \mathsf{id}^* \bmod q, \ \mathbf{e}^{(j)} \in \mathsf{B}_{3(n+m+\ell)}, \ \mathsf{id}^* \in \mathsf{B}_{2\ell}.$$

Next, to show that $\mathcal{P}$ can correctly pass all the verification checks for each challenge $\mathsf{CH} \in \{1, 2, 3\}$ with a high probability. Furthermore, apart from considering the checks for correct computations, it only needs to note that:

○ If $\mathsf{CH} = 1$. $\mathsf{id} = \mathsf{bin}(i) \in \{0,1\}^\ell$, $\mathsf{id}^* \in \mathsf{B}_{2\ell}$ is an extension of id and $\mathsf{B}_{2\ell}$ is invariant under the permutation $\tau \in \mathcal{S}_{2\ell}$, thus we have that $\mathbf{t}_{\mathsf{id}} = \tau(\mathsf{id}^*) \in \mathsf{B}_{2\ell}$. Similarly, for each $j \in \{1, \cdots, k\}$, $\mathbf{f}^{(j)}$, $\mathbf{e}^0_j \in \mathsf{B}_{3m}$ and B_{3m} is invariant under $\xi_j, \phi_j \in \mathcal{S}_{3m}$, we have that $\mathbf{v}_j = \xi_j(\mathbf{f}^{(j)}) \in \mathsf{B}_{3m}$ and $\mathbf{v}^0_j = \phi_j(\mathbf{e}^0_j) \in \mathsf{B}_{3m}$; $\mathbf{e}^{(j)} \in \mathsf{B}_{3(n+m+\ell)}$, and $\mathsf{B}_{3(n+m+\ell)}$ is invariant under $\rho_j \in \mathcal{S}_{3(n+m+\ell)}$, thus we have that $\mathbf{v}^{(j)} = \rho_j(\mathbf{e}^{(j)}) \in \mathsf{B}_{3(n+m+\ell)}$. As for $\mathbf{e}'_j$, we have that

$$\mathbf{v}'_j = \mathcal{F}_{\pi_j, \varphi_j, \tau}(\mathbf{e}'_j) \in \mathsf{SecExt}(\tau(\mathsf{id}^*)) = \mathsf{SecExt}(\mathbf{t}_{\mathsf{id}}).$$

$\circ$ If CH $= 2$. The key point is to check $\dot{\mathbf{c}}_1$, for $j \in \{1, 2, \cdots, k\}$, $\mathcal{P}$ can pass this step by generating $\mathbf{x}_j'$, $\mathbf{r}_j'$, $\mathbf{x}_j$, $\mathbf{f}_j$, $\mathbf{x}_j^0$, $\mathbf{r}_j^0$, $\mathbf{x}_j''$, $\mathbf{r}_j''$, $\mathbf{x}_{\mathsf{id}}$, $\mathbf{r}_{j,0}' = \mathsf{Parse}(\mathbf{r}_j', 1, m)$, $\mathbf{r}_{j,1}' = \mathsf{Parse}(\mathbf{r}_j', 3m+1, 4m)$, such that the followings hold true:

$$
\begin{aligned}
\mathbf{B}^* \cdot \left(\textstyle\sum_{j=1}^k \beta_j \mathbf{x}_j'\right) - \mathbf{u} &= \mathbf{B}^* \cdot \left(\textstyle\sum_{j=1}^k \beta_j (\mathbf{e}_j' + \mathbf{r}_j')\right) - \mathbf{u} \\
&= \mathbf{B}^* \cdot \left(\textstyle\sum_{j=1}^k \beta_j \mathbf{r}_j'\right) \bmod q.
\end{aligned}
$$

$$
\begin{aligned}
\mathbf{C}^* \cdot \left(\textstyle\sum_{j=1}^k \beta_j (\mathbf{x}^{(j)}, \mathbf{x}_j^0)\right) - \mathbf{b} &= \mathbf{C}^* \cdot \left(\textstyle\sum_{j=1}^k \beta_j (\mathbf{f}^{(j)} + \mathbf{f}_j, \mathbf{e}_j^0 + \mathbf{r}_j^0)\right) - \mathbf{b} \\
&= \mathbf{C}^* \cdot \left(\textstyle\sum_{j=1}^k \beta_j (\mathbf{f}_j, \mathbf{r}_j^0)\right) \bmod q,
\end{aligned}
$$

$$
\begin{aligned}
\mathbf{A}^* \left(\textstyle\sum_{j=1}^k \beta_j \mathbf{x}_j\right) - \mathbf{A}\left(\textstyle\sum_{j=1}^k \beta_j \mathbf{x}_{j,0}'\right) - \mathbf{A}_0\left(\textstyle\sum_{j=1}^k \beta_j \mathbf{x}_{j,1}'\right) &= \mathbf{A}^*\left(\textstyle\sum_{j=1}^k \beta_j \mathbf{f}_j\right) \\
&\quad - \mathbf{A}\left(\textstyle\sum_{j=1}^k \beta_j \mathbf{r}_{j,0}'\right) - \mathbf{A}_0\left(\textstyle\sum_{j=1}^k \beta_j \mathbf{r}_{j,1}'\right) \bmod q
\end{aligned}
$$

$$
\begin{aligned}
\mathbf{P}^* \cdot \left(\textstyle\sum_{j=1}^k \beta_j \mathbf{x}_j''\right) + \mathbf{Q}^* \cdot \mathbf{x}_{\mathsf{id}} - \mathbf{c} &= \mathbf{P}^*\left(\textstyle\sum_{j=1}^k \beta_j (\mathbf{e}^{(j)} + \mathbf{r}_j'')\right) + \mathbf{Q}(\mathsf{id}^* + \mathbf{r}_{\mathsf{id}^*}) - \mathbf{c} \\
&= \mathbf{P}^* \cdot \left(\textstyle\sum_{j=1}^k \beta_j \mathbf{r}_j''\right) + \mathbf{Q} \cdot \mathbf{r}_{\mathsf{id}^*} \bmod q.
\end{aligned}
$$

$\circ$ If CH $= 3$. It only needs to consider the checks for correct computations, and obviously these are true.

Statistical Zero-Knowledge:

To design a PPT simulator $\mathcal{S}$ who interacts with a verifier $\mathcal{V}'$ (maybe dishonest) to output a simulated transcript that is statistically close to one generated by an honest $\mathcal{P}$ in the real interaction with probability negligibly close to $2/3$.

The construction is as follows: $\mathcal{S}$ picks a value $\widetilde{\mathsf{CH}} \xleftarrow{\$} \{1, 2, 3\}$ as a prediction that $\mathcal{V}'$ will not choose, and three randomness of COM, i.e., θ_1', θ_2', θ_3'.

$\circ$ If $\widetilde{\mathsf{CH}} = 1$. $\mathcal{S}$ does as follows:
1. Use linear algebra algorithm to compute k vectors $\mathbf{e}_1'', \cdots, \mathbf{e}_k'' \in \mathbb{Z}_q^{(2\ell+1)3m}$ such that $\mathbf{B}^* \cdot \left(\sum_{j=1}^k \beta_j \mathbf{e}_j''\right) = \mathbf{u} \bmod q$.
2. Use linear algebra algorithm to compute k vectors $\mathbf{f}^{(1')}, \cdots, \mathbf{f}^{(k')} \in \mathbb{Z}_q^{3m}$ and k vectors $\widehat{\mathbf{e}}_1, \cdots, \widehat{\mathbf{e}}_k \in \mathbb{Z}_q^{3m}$ such that $\mathbf{C}^* \cdot \left(\sum_{j=1}^k \beta_j (\mathbf{f}^{(j')}, \widehat{\mathbf{e}}_j)\right) = \mathbf{b} \bmod q$.
3. Use linear algebra algorithm to compute k vectors $\mathbf{e}_1''', \cdots, \mathbf{e}_k''' \in \mathbb{Z}_q^{3(n+m+\ell)}$ and $\mathsf{id}^* \in \mathbb{Z}_q^{2\ell}$ such that $\mathbf{P}^* \cdot \left(\sum_{j=1}^k \beta_j \mathbf{e}_j'''\right) + \mathbf{Q} \cdot \mathsf{id}^* = \mathbf{c} \bmod q$.
4. Sample several random vectors and permutations,

$$
\begin{cases}
\mathbf{r}_1', \cdots, \mathbf{r}_k' \xleftarrow{\$} \mathbb{Z}_q^{(2\ell+2)3m}; \mathbf{f}_1, \cdots, \mathbf{f}_k; \mathbf{r}_1^0, \cdots, \mathbf{r}_k^0 \xleftarrow{\$} \mathbb{Z}_q^{3m}; \mathbf{r}_{\mathsf{id}^*} \xleftarrow{\$} \mathbb{Z}_q^{2\ell}; \\
\mathbf{r}_1'', \cdots, \mathbf{r}_k'' \xleftarrow{\$} \mathbb{Z}_q^{3(n+m+\ell)}; \pi_1, \cdots, \pi_k \xleftarrow{\$} \mathcal{S}_{3m}; \varphi_1, \cdots, \varphi_k \xleftarrow{\$} \mathcal{S}_{3m}; \\
\rho_1, \cdots, \rho_k \xleftarrow{\$} \mathcal{S}_{3(n+m+\ell)}; \xi_1, \cdots, \xi_k; \phi_1, \cdots, \phi_k \xleftarrow{\$} \mathcal{S}_{3m}; \tau \xleftarrow{\$} \mathcal{S}_{2\ell}.
\end{cases}
$$

5. Compute CMT $= (\dot{\mathbf{c}}_1', \dot{\mathbf{c}}_2', \dot{\mathbf{c}}_3')$, where

$$\begin{cases} \dot{c_1}' = \mathsf{COM}(\{\pi_j, \varphi_j, \xi_j, \phi_j, \rho_j\}_{j=1}^k, \tau, \mathbf{B}^* \cdot (\sum_{j=1}^k \beta_j \mathbf{r}'_j), \mathbf{A}^* \cdot (\sum_{j=1}^k \beta_j \mathbf{f}_j) - \\ \qquad \mathbf{A} \cdot (\sum_{j=1}^k \beta_j \mathbf{r}'_{j,0}) - \mathbf{A}_0 \cdot (\sum_{j=1}^k \beta_j \mathbf{r}'_{j,1}), \mathbf{C}^* \cdot (\sum_{j=1}^k \beta_j (\mathbf{f}_j, \mathbf{r}_j^0)), \\ \qquad \mathbf{P}^* \cdot (\sum_{j=1}^k \beta_j \mathbf{r}''_j) + \mathbf{Q} \cdot \mathbf{r}_{\mathsf{id}^*}; \theta'_1), \\ \dot{c_2}' = \mathsf{COM}(\{\mathcal{F}_{\pi_j, \varphi_j, \tau}(\mathbf{r}'_j), \xi_j(\mathbf{f}_j), \phi_j(\mathbf{r}_j^0), \rho_j(\mathbf{r}''_j)\}_{j=1}^k, \tau(\mathbf{r}_{\mathsf{id}^*}); \theta'_2), \\ \dot{c_3}' = \mathsf{COM}(\{\mathcal{F}_{\pi_j, \varphi_j, \tau}(\mathbf{e}''_j + \mathbf{r}'_j), \xi_j(\mathbf{f}^{(j')} + \mathbf{f}_j), \phi_j(\widehat{\mathbf{e}}_j + \mathbf{r}_j^0), \rho_j(\mathbf{e}'''_j + \mathbf{r}''_j)\}_{j=1}^k, \\ \qquad \tau(\mathsf{id}^* + \mathbf{r}_{\mathsf{id}^*}); \theta'_3). \end{cases}$$

6. Send CMT to $\mathcal{V}'$.

Receiving a challenge $\mathsf{CH} \in \{1, 2, 3\}$, $\mathcal{S}$ replies as follows:

1. If $\mathsf{CH} = 1$, $\mathcal{S}$ outputs $\perp$ and aborts.
2. If $\mathsf{CH} = 2$, $\mathcal{S}$ sends

$$\mathsf{RSP} = (\{\pi_j, \varphi_j, \xi_j, \phi_j, \rho_j, \mathbf{e}''_j + \mathbf{r}'_j, \mathbf{r}^{(j')} + \mathbf{r}_j, \widehat{\mathbf{e}}_j + \mathbf{r}_j^0, \mathbf{e}'''_j + \mathbf{r}''_j\}_{j=1}^k, \tau, \mathsf{id}^* + \mathbf{r}_{\mathsf{id}^*}).$$

3. If $\mathsf{CH} = 3$, $\mathcal{S}$ sends $\mathsf{RSP} = (\{\pi_j, \varphi_j, \xi_j, \phi_j, \rho_j, \mathbf{r}'_j, \mathbf{f}_j, \mathbf{r}_j^0, \mathbf{r}''_j\}_{j=1}^k, \tau, \mathbf{r}_{\mathsf{id}^*}).$

○ If $\widetilde{\mathsf{CH}} = 2$. $\mathcal{S}$ does as follows:

1. Sample several random vectors and permutations,

$$\begin{cases} \mathbf{r}'_1, \cdots, \mathbf{r}'_k \xleftarrow{\$} \mathbb{Z}_q^{(2\ell+2)3m}; \mathbf{f}_1, \cdots, \mathbf{f}_k \xleftarrow{\$} \mathbb{Z}_q^{3m}; \mathbf{r}_1^0, \cdots, \mathbf{r}_k^0 \xleftarrow{\$} \mathbb{Z}_q^{3m}; \\ \mathbf{r}''_1, \cdots, \mathbf{r}''_k \xleftarrow{\$} \mathbb{Z}_q^{3(n+m+\ell)}; \pi_1, \cdots, \pi_k \xleftarrow{\$} \mathcal{S}_{3m}; \varphi_1, \cdots, \varphi_k \xleftarrow{\$} \mathcal{S}_{3m}; \\ \xi_1, \cdots, \xi_k \xleftarrow{\$} \mathcal{S}_{3m}; \rho_1, \cdots, \rho_k \xleftarrow{\$} \mathcal{S}_{3(n+m+\ell)}; \phi_1, \cdots, \phi_k \xleftarrow{\$} \mathcal{S}_{3m}; \\ \tau \xleftarrow{\$} \mathcal{S}_{2\ell}; \mathbf{r}_{\mathsf{id}^*} \xleftarrow{\$} \mathbb{Z}_q^{2\ell}; \mathsf{id}^* \xleftarrow{\$} \mathsf{B}_{2\ell}; \mathbf{e}'_1, \cdots, \mathbf{e}'_k \xleftarrow{\$} \mathsf{SecExt}(\mathsf{id}^*); \\ \widehat{\mathbf{e}}_1, \cdots, \widehat{\mathbf{e}}_k \xleftarrow{\$} \mathsf{B}_{3m}; \mathbf{r}^{(1')}, \cdots, \mathbf{r}^{(k')} \xleftarrow{\$} \mathsf{B}_{3m}; \mathbf{e}'''_1, \cdots, \mathbf{e}'''_k \xleftarrow{\$} \mathsf{B}_{3m}. \end{cases}$$

2. Compute $\mathsf{CMT} = (\dot{c_1}', \dot{c_2}', \dot{c_3}')$ as in $\widetilde{\mathsf{CH}} = 1$.
3. Send CMT to $\mathcal{V}'$.

Receiving a challenge $\mathsf{CH} \in \{1, 2, 3\}$, $\mathcal{S}$ replies as follows:

1. If $\mathsf{CH} = 1$, $\mathcal{S}$ sends

$$\mathsf{RSP} = (\{\mathcal{F}_{\pi_j, \varphi_j, \tau}(\mathbf{e}''_j), \mathcal{F}_{\pi_j, \varphi_j, \tau}(\mathbf{r}'_j), \xi_j(\mathbf{r}^{(j')}), \xi_j(\mathbf{f}_j), \phi_j(\widehat{\mathbf{e}}_j), \phi_j(\mathbf{r}_j^0), \\ \rho_j(\mathbf{e}'''_j), \rho_j(\mathbf{r}''_j))\}_{j=1}^k, \tau(\mathsf{id}^*), \tau(\mathbf{r}_{\mathsf{id}^*})).$$

2. If $\mathsf{CH} = 2$, $\mathcal{S}$ outputs $\perp$ and aborts.
3. If $\mathsf{CH} = 3$, $\mathcal{S}$ sends $\mathsf{RSP} = (\{\pi_j, \varphi_j, \xi_j, \phi_j, \rho_j, \mathbf{r}'_j, \mathbf{f}_j, \mathbf{r}_j^0, \mathbf{r}''_j\}_{j=1}^k, \tau, \mathbf{r}_{\mathsf{id}^*}).$

○ If $\widetilde{\mathsf{CH}} = 3$. $\mathcal{S}$ does as follows:

1. Sample several random vectors and permutations as in $\widetilde{\mathsf{CH}} = 2$.

2. Compute $\mathsf{CMT} = (\dot{\mathbf{c}}_1{}', \dot{\mathbf{c}}_2{}', \dot{\mathbf{c}}_3{}')$, where $\mathbf{r}'_{j,0} = \mathsf{Parse}(\mathbf{e}''_j + \mathbf{r}'_j, 1, m)$, $\mathbf{r}'_{j,1} = \mathsf{Parse}(\mathbf{e}''_j + \mathbf{r}'_j, 3m + 1, 4m)$,

$$
\begin{cases}
\dot{\mathbf{c}}_1{}' = \mathsf{COM}(\{\pi_j, \varphi_j, \xi_j, \phi_j, \rho_j\}_{j=1}^k, \tau, \mathbf{B}^* \cdot (\sum_{j=1}^k \beta_j(\mathbf{e}''_j + \mathbf{r}'_j)) - \mathbf{u}, \\
\qquad \mathbf{A}^* \cdot (\sum_{j=1}^k \beta_j(\mathbf{f}^{(j')} + \mathbf{f}_j)) - \mathbf{A} \cdot (\sum_{j=1}^k \beta_j \mathsf{Parse}(\mathbf{e}''_j + \mathbf{r}'_j, 1, m)) - \\
\qquad \mathbf{A}_0 \cdot (\sum_{j=1}^k \beta_j \mathsf{Parse}(\mathbf{e}''_j + \mathbf{r}'_j, 3m + 1, 4m)), \\
\qquad \mathbf{C}^* \cdot (\sum_{j=1}^k \beta_j(\mathbf{f}^{(j')} + \mathbf{f}_j, \widehat{\mathbf{e}}_j + \mathbf{r}^0_j)) - \mathbf{b}, \\
\qquad \mathbf{P}^* \cdot (\sum_{j=1}^k \beta_j(\mathbf{e}'''_j + \mathbf{r}''_j)) + \mathbf{Q} \cdot (\mathsf{id}^* + \mathbf{r}_{\mathsf{id}^*}) - \mathbf{c}; \theta'_1), \\
\dot{\mathbf{c}}_2{}' = \mathsf{COM}(\{\mathcal{F}_{\pi_j, \varphi_j, \tau}(\mathbf{r}'_j), \xi_j(\mathbf{f}_j), \phi_j(\mathbf{r}^0_j), \rho_j(\mathbf{r}''_j)\}_{j=1}^k, \tau(\mathbf{r}_{\mathsf{id}^*}); \theta'_2), \\
\dot{\mathbf{c}}_3{}' = \mathsf{COM}(\{\mathcal{F}_{\pi_j, \varphi_j, \tau}(\mathbf{e}''_j + \mathbf{r}'_j), \xi_j(\mathbf{r}^{(j')} + \mathbf{f}_j), \phi_j(\widehat{\mathbf{e}}_j + \mathbf{r}^0_j), \rho_j(\mathbf{e}'''_j + \mathbf{r}''_j)\}_{j=1}^k, \\
\qquad \tau(\mathsf{id}^* + \mathbf{r}_{\mathsf{id}^*}); \theta'_3).
\end{cases}
$$

3. Send CMT to $\mathcal{V}'$.

Receiving a challenge $\mathsf{CH} \in \{1, 2, 3\}$, $\mathcal{S}$ replies as follows:

1. If $\mathsf{CH} = 1$, $\mathcal{S}$ sends as in $(\widetilde{\mathsf{CH}} = 2, \mathsf{CH} = 1)$.
2. If $\mathsf{CH} = 2$, $\mathcal{S}$ sends as in $(\widetilde{\mathsf{CH}} = 1, \mathsf{CH} = 2)$.
3. If $\mathsf{CH} = 3$, $\mathcal{S}$ outputs $\perp$ and aborts.

Based on the statistically hiding property of the commitment scheme COM, the three distributions of $\mathsf{CMT}, \mathsf{CH}, \mathsf{RSP}$ are statistically close to those in the real interaction, $\mathcal{S}$ outputs $\perp$ and aborts with probability negligibly close to $1/3$. Furthermore, once $\mathcal{S}$ does not halt, then a valid transcript will be given and the distribution of the transcript is statistically close to that in the real interaction, therefore $\mathcal{S}$ can impersonate an honest prover $\mathcal{P}$ with probability negligibly close to $2/3$.

Argument of Knowledge:

To prove that our new protocol is an argument of knowledge for the relation $\mathcal{R}(n, k, \ell, q, m, \beta)$ (as shown in Sect. 4), thus to show the proposed protocol has the special soundness property. In the followings, we show that if there exists a prover $\mathcal{P}'$ (maybe cheating) who can correctly respond to three challenges $\mathsf{CH} \in \{1, 2, 3\}$ corresponding to the same commitment CMT with the public inputs $(\mathbf{A}, \mathbf{A}_0, \mathbf{A}_1, \mathbf{A}_2, \mathbf{A}_3, \mathbf{B}, \mathbf{P}, \mathbf{u}, \mathbf{b}, \mathbf{c})$, then there exists an extractor $\mathcal{K}$ who produces $(\mathsf{id} = \mathsf{bin}(i) \in \{0, 1\}^\ell$, $\mathbf{f}, \mathbf{e}_0, \mathbf{e}_1 \in \mathbb{Z}^m$, $\mathbf{e}' = (\mathbf{e}'_0, \mathbf{e}'_1, \mathsf{bin}(i) \otimes \mathbf{e}'_1) \in \mathsf{Sec}_\beta(\mathsf{id})$, $\mathbf{s} \in \mathbb{Z}^n, \mathbf{e}_2 \in \mathbb{Z}^\ell)$ such that

$$(\mathbf{A}, \mathbf{A}_0, \mathbf{A}_1, \mathbf{A}_2, \mathbf{A}_2, \mathbf{B}, \mathbf{P}, \mathbf{u}, \mathbf{b}, \mathbf{c}; \mathsf{id} = \mathsf{bin}(i), \mathbf{e}', \mathbf{f}, \mathbf{e}_0, \mathbf{s}, \mathbf{e}_1, \mathbf{e}_2) \in \mathcal{R}.$$

Indeed, based on three valid responses $\mathsf{RSP}_1, \mathsf{RSP}_2, \mathsf{RSP}_3$ given by $\mathcal{P}'$, the extractor $\mathcal{K}$ can extract the following information:

$$
\begin{cases}
\mathbf{t}_{\mathsf{id}} \in \mathsf{B}_{2\ell}, \forall j \in \{1, 2, \cdots, k\}, \mathbf{v}'_j \in \mathsf{SecExt}(\mathbf{t}_{\mathsf{id}}), \mathbf{v}_j \in \mathsf{B}_{3m}, \mathbf{x}'_{j,0} = \mathsf{Parse}(\mathbf{x}'_j, 1, m), \\
\mathbf{x}'_{j,1} = \mathsf{Parse}(\mathbf{x}'_j, 3m+1, 4m), \mathbf{h}'_{j,0} = \mathsf{Parse}(\mathbf{h}'_j, 1, m), \mathbf{h}'_{j,1} = \mathsf{Parse}(\mathbf{h}'_j, 3m+1, 4m), \\
\mathbf{c}'_1 = \mathsf{COM}(\{\hat{\pi}_j, \hat{\varphi}_j, \hat{\xi}_j, \hat{\phi}_j, \hat{\rho}_j\}_{j=1}^k, \hat{\tau}, \mathbf{B}^*(\sum_{j=1}^k \beta_j \mathbf{x}'_j) - \mathbf{u}, \mathbf{A}^*(\sum_{j=1}^k \beta_j \mathbf{x}_j) - \mathbf{A}(\sum_{j=1}^k \beta_j \mathbf{x}'_{j,0}) - \\
\qquad \mathbf{A}_0(\sum_{j=1}^k \beta_j \mathbf{x}'_{j,1}), \mathbf{C}^*(\sum_{j=1}^k \beta_j(\mathbf{x}_j, \mathbf{x}_j^0)) - \mathbf{b}, \mathbf{P}^*(\sum_{j=1}^k \beta_j \mathbf{x}''_j) + \mathbf{Q}\mathbf{x}_{\mathsf{id}} - \mathbf{c}; \theta_1), \\
\quad = \mathsf{COM}(\{\tilde{\pi}_j, \tilde{\varphi}_j, \tilde{\xi}_j, \tilde{\phi}_j, \tilde{\rho}_j\}_{j=1}^k, \tilde{\tau}, \mathbf{B}^*(\sum_{j=1}^k \beta_j \mathbf{h}'_j), \mathbf{A}^*(\sum_{j=1}^k \beta_j \mathbf{h}_j) - \mathbf{A}(\sum_{j=1}^k \beta_j \mathbf{h}'_{j,0}) - \\
\qquad \mathbf{A}_0(\sum_{j=1}^k \beta_j \mathbf{h}'_{j,1}), \mathbf{C}^*(\sum_{j=1}^k \beta_j(\mathbf{h}_j, \mathbf{h}_j^0)), \mathbf{P}^*(\sum_{j=1}^k \beta_j \mathbf{h}''_j) + \mathbf{Q}\mathbf{h}_{\mathsf{id}}; \theta_1), \\
\mathbf{c}'_2 = \mathsf{COM}(\{\mathbf{w}'_j, \mathbf{w}_j, \mathbf{w}_j^0, \mathbf{w}''_j\}_{j=1}^k, \mathbf{v}_{\mathsf{id}}; \theta_2) \\
\quad = \mathsf{COM}(\{\mathcal{F}_{\hat{\pi}_j, \hat{\varphi}_j, \hat{\tau}}(\mathbf{h}'_j), \tilde{\xi}_j(\mathbf{h}_j), \tilde{\phi}_j(\mathbf{h}_j^0), \tilde{\rho}_j(\mathbf{h}''_j)\}_{j=1}^k, \tilde{\tau}(\mathbf{h}_{\mathsf{id}}); \theta_2), \\
\mathbf{c}'_3 = \mathsf{COM}(\{\mathbf{v}'_j + \mathbf{w}'_j, \mathbf{v}_j + \mathbf{w}_j, \mathbf{v}_j^0 + \mathbf{w}_j^0, \mathbf{v}^{(j)} + \mathbf{w}''_j\}_{j=1}^k, \mathbf{t}_{\mathsf{id}} + \mathbf{v}_{\mathsf{id}}; \theta_3), \\
\quad = \mathsf{COM}(\{\mathcal{F}_{\hat{\pi}_j, \hat{\varphi}_j, \hat{\tau}}(\mathbf{x}'_j), \hat{\xi}_j(\mathbf{x}_j), \hat{\phi}_j(\mathbf{x}_j^0), \hat{\rho}_j(\mathbf{x}''_j)\}_{j=1}^k, \hat{\tau}(\mathbf{x}_{\mathsf{id}}); \theta_3).
\end{cases}
$$

Based on the computationally binding property of COM, $\mathcal{K}$ deduces that:

$$
\begin{cases}
\mathbf{t}_{\mathsf{id}} \in \mathsf{B}_{2\ell}, \hat{\tau} = \tilde{\tau}, \forall j \in \{1, \cdots, k\}, \hat{\xi}_j = \tilde{\xi}_j, \hat{\phi}_j = \tilde{\phi}_j, \hat{\pi}_j = \tilde{\pi}_j, \\
\hat{\varphi}_j = \tilde{\varphi}_j, \hat{\rho}_j = \tilde{\rho}_j; \mathbf{t}_{\mathsf{id}} = \tilde{\tau}(\mathbf{h}_{\mathsf{id}}), \mathbf{t}_{\mathsf{id}} + \mathbf{v}_{\mathsf{id}} = \hat{\tau}(\mathbf{x}_{\mathsf{id}}); \\
\mathbf{A}^* \cdot (\sum_{j=1}^k \beta_j \mathbf{x}_j) - \mathbf{A} \cdot (\sum_{j=1}^k \beta_j \mathbf{x}'_{j,0}) - \mathbf{A}_0 \cdot (\sum_{j=1}^k \beta_j \mathbf{x}'_{j,1}) = \\
\mathbf{A}^* \cdot (\sum_{j=1}^k \beta_j \mathbf{h}_j) - \mathbf{A} \cdot (\sum_{j=1}^k \beta_j \mathbf{h}'_{j,0}) - \mathbf{A}_0 \cdot (\sum_{j=1}^k \beta_j \mathbf{h}'_{j,1}); \\
\mathbf{B}^* \cdot (\sum_{j=1}^k \beta_j \mathbf{x}'_j) - \mathbf{u} = \mathbf{B}^* \cdot (\sum_{j=1}^k \beta_j \mathbf{h}'_j); \\
\mathbf{C}^* \cdot (\sum_{j=1}^k \beta_j(\mathbf{x}_j, \mathbf{x}_j^0)) - \mathbf{b} = \mathbf{C}^* \cdot (\sum_{j=1}^k \beta_j(\mathbf{h}_j, \mathbf{h}_j^0)); \\
\mathbf{P}^* \cdot (\sum_{j=1}^k \beta_j \mathbf{x}''_j) + \mathbf{Q} \cdot \mathbf{x}_{\mathsf{id}} - \mathbf{c} = \mathbf{P}^* \cdot (\sum_{j=1}^k \beta_j \mathbf{h}''_j) + \mathbf{Q} \cdot \mathbf{h}_{\mathsf{id}}; \\
\mathbf{w}'_j = \mathcal{F}_{\tilde{\pi}_j, \tilde{\varphi}_j, \tilde{\tau}}(\mathbf{h}'_j), \mathbf{v}'_j + \mathbf{w}'_j = \mathcal{F}_{\hat{\pi}_j, \hat{\varphi}_j, \hat{\tau}}(\mathbf{x}'_j), \mathbf{v}'_j \in \mathsf{SecExt}(\mathbf{t}_{\mathsf{id}}); \\
\mathbf{w}_j = \tilde{\xi}_j(\mathbf{h}_j), \mathbf{v}_j + \mathbf{w}_j = \hat{\xi}_j(\mathbf{x}_j), \mathbf{v}_j \in \mathsf{B}_{3m}, \mathbf{w}_j^0 = \tilde{\phi}_j(\mathbf{h}_j^0), \mathbf{v}_j^0 \in \mathsf{B}_{3m}. \\
\mathbf{v}_j^0 + \mathbf{w}_j^0 = \hat{\phi}_j(\mathbf{x}_j^0), \mathbf{w}''_j = \tilde{\rho}_j(\mathbf{h}_j), \mathbf{v}^{(j)} + \mathbf{w}''_j = \hat{\rho}_j(\mathbf{x}''_j), \mathbf{v}^{(j)} \in \mathsf{B}_{3(n+m+\ell)}.
\end{cases}
$$

For $j \in \{1, \cdots, k\}$, let $\mathbf{e}'_j = \mathbf{x}'_j - \mathbf{h}'_j = \mathcal{F}^{-1}_{\tilde{\pi}_j, \tilde{\varphi}_j, \tilde{\tau}}(\mathbf{v}'_j), \mathbf{f}^{(j)} = \mathbf{x}_j - \mathbf{h}_j = \tilde{\xi}_j^{-1}(\mathbf{v}_j), \mathbf{e}_j^0 = \mathbf{x}_j^0 - \mathbf{h}_j^0 = \tilde{\phi}_j^{-1}(\mathbf{v}_j^0), \mathbf{e}^{(j)} = \mathbf{x}''_j - \mathbf{h}''_j = \tilde{\rho}_j^{-1}(\mathbf{v}^{(j)}), \mathsf{id}^* = \mathbf{x}_{\mathsf{id}} - \mathbf{h}_{\mathsf{id}} = \tilde{\tau}^{-1}(\mathbf{t}_{\mathsf{id}})$, we have that $\mathbf{e}'_j \in \mathsf{SecExt}(\tilde{\tau}^{-1}(\mathbf{t}_{\mathsf{id}})) = \mathsf{SecExt}(\mathsf{id}^*), \mathbf{f}^{(j)}, \mathbf{e}_j^0 \in \mathsf{B}_{3m}, \mathbf{e}^{(j)} \in \mathsf{B}_{3(n+m+\ell)}$. Furthermore, $\mathbf{B}^* \cdot (\sum_{j=1}^k \beta_j \mathbf{e}'_j) = \mathbf{u} \bmod q$, $\mathbf{C}^* \cdot (\sum_{j=1}^k \beta_j(\mathbf{f}^{(j)}, \mathbf{e}_j^0)) = \mathbf{b} \bmod q$, and $\mathbf{P}^* \cdot (\sum_{j=1}^k \beta_j \mathbf{e}^{(j)}) + \mathbf{Q} \cdot \mathsf{id}^* = \mathbf{c} \bmod q$.

The knowledge extractor $\mathcal{K}$ produces $\mathsf{id} = \mathsf{bin}(i) \in \{0,1\}^\ell, \mathbf{e}' \in \mathsf{Sec}_\beta(\mathsf{id}), \mathbf{f}, \mathbf{e}_0, \mathbf{e}_1 \in \mathbb{Z}^m, \mathbf{s} \in \mathbb{Z}^n$ and $\mathbf{e}_2 \in \mathbb{Z}^\ell$ as follows:

1. Let $\mathsf{id}^* = (d_1, d_2, \cdots, d_\ell, d_{\ell+1}, \cdots, d_{2\ell}) = \tilde{\tau}^{-1}(\mathbf{t}_{\mathsf{id}})$, we obtain $\mathsf{bin}(i) = \mathsf{id} = (d_1, d_2, \cdots, d_\ell)$ and the index $i = \mathbf{g}_\ell^\top \cdot \mathsf{bin}(i)$ where $\mathbf{g}_\ell = (1, 2, \cdots, 2^{\ell-1})$.

2. Let $\mathbf{e}^* = \sum_{j=1}^k \beta_j \mathbf{e}'_j \in \mathbb{Z}_q^{(2\ell+2)3m}$, thus $0 < \|\mathbf{e}^*\|_\infty \leq \sum_{j=1}^k \beta_j \|\mathbf{e}'_j\|_\infty \leq \beta$. Since $\mathbf{e}'_j \in \mathsf{SecExt}(\mathsf{id}^*)$, there exist $\mathbf{e}_0^*, \mathbf{e}_1^* \in \mathbb{Z}^{3m}$ such that $\|\mathbf{e}_0^*\|_\infty, \|\mathbf{e}_1^*\|_\infty \leq \beta$ and $\mathbf{e}^* = (\mathbf{e}_0^*, \mathbf{e}_1^*, d_1\mathbf{e}_1^*, d_2\mathbf{e}_1^*, \cdots, d_{2\ell}\mathbf{e}_1^*)$. Let $\mathbf{e}' = (\mathbf{e}'_0, \mathbf{e}'_1, d_1\mathbf{e}'_1, \cdots, d_\ell\mathbf{e}'_1) = (\mathbf{e}'_0, \mathbf{e}'_1, \mathsf{bin}(i) \otimes \mathbf{e}'_1)$, where $\mathbf{e}'_0, \mathbf{e}'_1$ are obtained from $\mathbf{e}_0^*, \mathbf{e}_1^*$ by removing the last $2m$ coordinates. Thus $\mathbf{e}' \in \mathsf{Sec}_\beta(\mathsf{id})$, and

$$[\mathbf{A}|\mathbf{A}_0|\mathbf{g}_\ell \otimes \mathbf{A}_1] \cdot (\mathbf{e}'_0, \mathbf{e}'_1, \mathsf{bin}(i) \otimes \mathbf{e}'_2) = \mathbf{u} \bmod q.$$

3. Let $\hat{\mathbf{f}} = \sum_{j=1}^{k} \beta_j \mathbf{f}^{(j)} \in \mathbb{Z}^{3m}$, $\widehat{\mathbf{e_0}} = \sum_{j=1}^{k} \beta_j \mathbf{e}_j^0 \in \mathbb{Z}^{3m}$, thus,

$$0 < \|\hat{\mathbf{f}}\|_\infty \le \sum_{j=1}^{k} \beta_j \|\mathbf{f}^{(j)}\|_\infty \le \beta, \ 0 < \|\widehat{\mathbf{e_0}}\|_\infty \le \sum_{j=1}^{k} \beta_j \|\mathbf{e}_j^0\|_\infty \le \beta.$$

Let $\mathbf{f} \in \mathbb{Z}^m$ be a vector obtained from $\hat{\mathbf{f}}$ by removing the last $2m$ coordinates, $\mathbf{e}_0 \in \mathbb{Z}^m$ obtained from $\widehat{\mathbf{e_0}}$ by removing the last $2m$ coordinates. So $\mathbf{f} \in \mathbb{Z}^m$, $0 < \|\mathbf{f}\|_\infty \le \beta$, $\mathbf{e}_0 \in \mathbb{Z}^m$, $0 < \|\mathbf{e}_0\|_\infty \le \beta$ and $\mathbf{b} = (\mathbf{B}^\top \mathbf{A}_3) \cdot \mathbf{f} + \mathbf{e}_0 \bmod q$.

4. Let $\hat{\mathbf{e}} = \sum_{j=1}^{k} \beta_j \mathbf{e}^{(j)} \in \mathbb{Z}^{3(n+m+\ell)}$, so $0 < \|\hat{\mathbf{e}}\|_\infty \le \sum_{j=1}^{k} \beta_j \|\mathbf{e}^{(j)}\|_\infty \le \beta$, let $\mathbf{e} \in \mathbb{Z}^{n+m+\ell}$ be a vector obtained from $\hat{\mathbf{e}}$ by removing the last $2(n+m+\ell)$ coordinates. Parse $\mathbf{e} = (\mathbf{s}, \mathbf{e}_1, \mathbf{e}_2)$ where $\mathbf{s} \in \mathbb{Z}^n$, $\mathbf{e}_1 \in \mathbb{Z}^m$, $\mathbf{e}_2 \in \mathbb{Z}^\ell$, so $\|\mathbf{e}\|_\infty \le \beta$, and $\mathbf{c} = (\mathbf{c}_0, \mathbf{c}_1) = \mathbf{P} \cdot \mathbf{e} + (\mathbf{0}^m, \lfloor q/2 \rfloor \mathsf{bin}(i)) \bmod q$.

Finally, the knowledge extractor $\mathcal{K}$ outputs a tuple

$$(\mathsf{id} = \mathsf{bin}(i) \in \{0,1\}^\ell, \mathbf{e}' \in \mathsf{Sec}_\beta(\mathsf{id}), \mathbf{f}, \mathbf{e}_0, \mathbf{e}_1 \in \mathbb{Z}^m, \mathbf{s} \in \mathbb{Z}^n, \mathbf{e}_2 \in \mathbb{Z}^\ell),$$

which is a valid witness for $\mathcal{R} = (n, k, \ell, q, m, \beta)$. This concludes the proof.

Acknowledgments. The authors would like to thank the anonymous reviewers of ACNS-SCI 2020 for their helpful comments, and this research is supported by the National Natural Science Foundation of China (No. 61772477) and Science and Technology Development of Henan Province (No. 20210222210356).

References

1. Bellare, M., Micciancio, D., Warinschi, B.: Foundations of group signatures: formal definitions, simplified requirements, and a construction based on general assumptions. In: Biham, E. (ed.) EUROCRYPT 2003. LNCS, vol. 2656, pp. 614–629. Springer, Heidelberg (2003). https://doi.org/10.1007/3-540-39200-9_38

2. Bellare, M., Shi, H., Zhang, C.: Foundations of group signatures: the case of dynamic groups. In: Menezes, A. (ed.) CT-RSA 2005. LNCS, vol. 3376, pp. 136–153. Springer, Heidelberg (2005). https://doi.org/10.1007/978-3-540-30574-3_11

3. Boneh, D., Shacham, H.: Group signatures with verifier-local revocation. In: CCS, pp. 168–177. ACM (2004). https://doi.org/10.1145/1030083.1030106

4. Bootle, J., Cerulli, A., Chaidos, P., Ghadafi, E., Groth, J.: Foundations of fully dynamic group signatures. In: Manulis, M., Sadeghi, A.-R., Schneider, S. (eds.) ACNS 2016. LNCS, vol. 9696, pp. 117–136. Springer, Cham (2016). https://doi.org/10.1007/978-3-319-39555-5_7

5. Camenisch, J., Neven, G., Rückert, M.: Fully anonymous attribute tokens from lattices. In: Visconti, I., De Prisco, R. (eds.) SCN 2012. LNCS, vol. 7485, pp. 57–75. Springer, Heidelberg (2012). https://doi.org/10.1007/978-3-642-32928-9_4

6. Cash, D., Hofheinz, D., Kiltz, E., Peikert, C.: Bonsai trees, or how to delegate a lattice basis. In: Gilbert, H. (ed.) EUROCRYPT 2010. LNCS, vol. 6110, pp. 523–552. Springer, Heidelberg (2010). https://doi.org/10.1007/978-3-642-13190-5_27

7. Chaum, D., van Heyst, E.: Group signatures. In: Davies, D.W. (ed.) EUROCRYPT 1991. LNCS, vol. 547, pp. 257–265. Springer, Heidelberg (1991). https://doi.org/10.1007/3-540-46416-6_22

8. Gao, W., Hu, Y., Zhang, Y., Wang, B.: Lattice-based group signature with verifier-local revocation. J. Shanghai JiaoTong Univ. (Sci.) **22**(3), 313–321 (2017). https://doi.org/10.1007/s12204-017-1837-1

9. Gentry, C., Peikert, C., Vaikuntanathan, V.: Trapdoor for hard lattices and new cryptographic constructions. In: STOC, pp. 197–206. ACM (2008). https://doi.org/10.1145/1374376.1374407

10. Gordon, S.D., Katz, J., Vaikuntanathan, V.: A group signature scheme from lattice assumptions. In: Abe, M. (ed.) ASIACRYPT 2010. LNCS, vol. 6477, pp. 395–412. Springer, Heidelberg (2010). https://doi.org/10.1007/978-3-642-17373-8_23

11. Katsumata, S., Yamada, S.: Group signatures without NIZK: from lattices in the standard model. In: Ishai, Y., Rijmen, V. (eds.) EUROCRYPT 2019. LNCS, vol. 11478, pp. 312–344. Springer, Cham (2019). https://doi.org/10.1007/978-3-030-17659-4_11

12. Kawachi, A., Tanaka, K., Xagawa, K.: Concurrently secure identification schemes based on the worst-case hardness of lattice problems. In: Pieprzyk, J. (ed.) ASIACRYPT 2008. LNCS, vol. 5350, pp. 372–389. Springer, Heidelberg (2008). https://doi.org/10.1007/978-3-540-89255-7_23

13. Laguillaumie, F., Langlois, A., Libert, B., Stehlé, D.: Lattice-based group signatures with logarithmic signature size. In: Sako, K., Sarkar, P. (eds.) ASIACRYPT 2013. LNCS, vol. 8270, pp. 41–61. Springer, Heidelberg (2013). https://doi.org/10.1007/978-3-642-42045-0_3

14. Langlois, A., Ling, S., Nguyen, K., Wang, H.: Lattice-based group signature scheme with verifier-local revocation. In: Krawczyk, H. (ed.) PKC 2014. LNCS, vol. 8383, pp. 345–361. Springer, Heidelberg (2014). https://doi.org/10.1007/978-3-642-54631-0_20

15. Libert, B., Ling, S., Mouhartem, F., Nguyen, K., Wang, H.: Signature schemes with efficient protocols and dynamic group signatures from lattice assumptions. In: Cheon, J.H., Takagi, T. (eds.) ASIACRYPT 2016. LNCS, vol. 10032, pp. 373–403. Springer, Heidelberg (2016). https://doi.org/10.1007/978-3-662-53890-6_13

16. Libert, B., Ling, S., Nguyen, K., Wang, H.: Zero-knowledge arguments for lattice-based accumulators: logarithmic-size ring signatures and group signatures without trapdoors. In: Fischlin, M., Coron, J.-S. (eds.) EUROCRYPT 2016. LNCS, vol. 9666, pp. 1–31. Springer, Heidelberg (2016). https://doi.org/10.1007/978-3-662-49896-5_1

17. Libert, B., Mouhartem, F., Nguyen, K.: A lattice-based group signature scheme with message-dependent opening. In: Manulis, M., Sadeghi, A.-R., Schneider, S. (eds.) ACNS 2016. LNCS, vol. 9696, pp. 137–155. Springer, Cham (2016). https://doi.org/10.1007/978-3-319-39555-5_8

18. Ling, S., Nguyen, K., Roux-Langlois, A., Wang, H.: A lattice-based group signature scheme with verifier-local revocation. Theor. Comput. Sci. **730**, 1–20 (2018). https://doi.org/10.1016/j.tcs.2018.03.027

19. Ling, S., Nguyen, K., Stehlé, D., Wang, H.: Improved zero-knowledge proofs of knowledge for the isis problem, and applications. In: Kurosawa, K., Hanaoka, G. (eds.) PKC 2013. LNCS, vol. 7778, pp. 107–124. Springer, Heidelberg (2013). https://doi.org/10.1007/978-3-642-36362-7_8

20. Ling, S., Nguyen, K., Wang, H.: Group signatures from lattices: simpler, tighter, shorter, ring-based. In: Katz, J. (ed.) PKC 2015. LNCS, vol. 9020, pp. 427–449. Springer, Heidelberg (2015). https://doi.org/10.1007/978-3-662-46447-2_19

21. Ling, S., Nguyen, K., Wang, H., Xu, Y.: Lattice-based group signatures: achieving full dynamicity with ease. In: Gollmann, D., Miyaji, A., Kikuchi, H. (eds.) ACNS 2017. LNCS, vol. 10355, pp. 293–312. Springer, Cham (2017). https://doi.org/10.1007/978-3-319-61204-1_15

22. Ling, S., Nguyen, K., Wang, H., Xu, Y.: Forward-secure group signatures from lattices. In: Ding, J., Steinwandt, R. (eds.) PQCrypto 2019. LNCS, vol. 11505, pp. 44–64. Springer, Cham (2019). https://doi.org/10.1007/978-3-030-25510-7_3

23. Ling, S., Nguyen, K., Wang, H., Xu, Y.: Constant-size group signatures from lattices. In: Abdalla, M., Dahab, R. (eds.) PKC 2018. LNCS, vol. 10770, pp. 58–88. Springer, Cham (2018). https://doi.org/10.1007/978-3-319-76581-5_3

24. Micciancio, D., Peikert, C.: Hardness of SIS and LWE with small parameters. In: Canetti, R., Garay, J.A. (eds.) CRYPTO 2013. LNCS, vol. 8042, pp. 21–39. Springer, Heidelberg (2013). https://doi.org/10.1007/978-3-642-40041-4_2

25. Nguyen, P.Q., Zhang, J., Zhang, Z.: Simpler efficient group signatures from lattices. In: Katz, J. (ed.) PKC 2015. LNCS, vol. 9020, pp. 401–426. Springer, Heidelberg (2015). https://doi.org/10.1007/978-3-662-46447-2_18

26. Perera, M.N.S., Koshiba, T.: Fully dynamic group signature scheme with member registration and verifier-local revocation. In: Ghosh, D., Giri, D., Mohapatra, R.N., Sakurai, K., Savas, E., Som, T. (eds.) ICMC 2018. SPMS, vol. 253, pp. 399–415. Springer, Singapore (2018). https://doi.org/10.1007/978-981-13-2095-8_31

27. Perera, M.N.S., Koshiba, T.: Zero-knowledge proof for lattice-based group signature schemes with verifier-local revocation. In: Barolli, L., Kryvinska, N., Enokido, T., Takizawa, M. (eds.) NBiS 2018. LNDECT, vol. 22, pp. 772–782. Springer, Cham (2019). https://doi.org/10.1007/978-3-319-98530-5_68

28. Perera, M.N.S., Koshiba, T.: Achieving strong security and verifier-local revocation for dynamic group signatures from lattice assumptions. In: Katsikas, S.K., Alcaraz, C. (eds.) STM 2018. LNCS, vol. 11091, pp. 3–19. Springer, Cham (2018). https://doi.org/10.1007/978-3-030-01141-3_1

29. Zhang, Y., Hu, Y., Gao, W., Jiang, M.: Simpler efficient group signature scheme with verifier-local revocation from lattices. KSII Trans. Internet Inf. Syst. **10**(1), 414–430 (2016). https://doi.org/10.3837/tiis.2016.01.024

30. Zhang, Y., Yin, Y., Liu, X., Zhang, Q., Jia, H.: Zero-knowledge proofs for improved lattice-based group signature scheme with verifier-local revocation. In: Shen, B., Wang, B., Han, J., Yu, Y. (eds.) FCS 2019. CCIS, vol. 1105, pp. 107–127. Springer, Singapore (2019). https://doi.org/10.1007/978-981-15-0818-9_8

Proofs of Ownership on Encrypted Cloud Data via Intel SGX

Weijing You[1] and Bo Chen[2](✉)

[1] Department of Computer Science and Technology, University of Chinese Academy of Sciences (UCAS), Beijing, China
youweijing16@mails.ucas.ac.cn
[2] Department of Computer Science, Michigan Technological University, Michigan, USA
bchen@mtu.edu

Abstract. To deal with surging volume of outsourced data, cloud storage providers (CSPs) today prefer to use deduplication, in which if multiple copies of a file across cloud users are found, only one unique copy will be stored. A broadly used deduplication technique is client-side deduplication, in which the client will first check with the cloud server whether a file has been stored or not by sending a short checksum and, if the file was stored, the client will not upload the file again, and the cloud server simply adds the client to the owner list of the file. This can significantly save both storage and bandwidth, but introduces a new attack vector that, if a malicious client obtains a checksum of a victim file, it can simply claim ownership of the file. Proofs of ownership (PoWs) were thus investigated to allow the cloud server to check whether a client really possesses the file. Traditional PoWs rely on an assumption that the cloud server is fully trusted and has access to the original file content. In practice, however, the cloud server is not fully trusted and, data owners may store their encrypted data in the cloud, hindering execution of the traditional PoWs.

In this work, we make it possible to execute PoWs over encrypted cloud data by leveraging Intel SGX, a security feature which has been broadly equipped in processors of today's cloud servers. By using Intel SGX, we can create a trusted execution environment in a cloud server, and the critical component of the PoW verification process will be executed in this secure environment (with confidentiality and integrity assurance). Security analysis and experimental evaluation show that our design can allow PoWs over encrypted data with modest additional overhead.

Keywords: Client-side deduplication · Cloud storage · Proofs of ownership · Intel SGX

1 Introduction

Cloud outsourcing can significantly reduce cost as well as burden of data storage and management. Therefore, more and more data owners choose to outsource

© Springer Nature Switzerland AG 2020
J. Zhou et al. (Eds.): ACNS 2020 Workshops, LNCS 12418, pp. 400–416, 2020.
https://doi.org/10.1007/978-3-030-61638-0_22

their data to cloud storage providers (CSPs), e.g., Amazon AWS [1], Microsoft Azure [2]. Since an ever-surging amount of data is now stored in clouds, an urgent need for the CSPs is how to host those data with reduced cost. Deduplication [3] can immediately help, in which only a unique copy of data will be stored when multiple duplicate copies across different data owners are found. Based on where deduplication is performed, we can have *server-side* and *client-side* deduplication. In the server-side deduplication, deduplication will happen purely in the cloud server, transparently to the client. In the *client-side deduplication*, the client will collaborate with the cloud server to perform deduplication. Specifically, the client will first check with the cloud server (i.e., by sending a checksum of the file) and, if a file has been stored, the client will not upload it again; instead, the client will simply claim ownership of this file. The client-side deduplication can save both storage and bandwidth, and hence has been used broadly by popular file hosting services including Dropbox [4], Box [5], Google Drive [6].

The client-side deduplication, however, suffers from various attacks. For example, a malicious user can claim ownership of a file by only possessing the checksum rather than the actual file; or an attacker can easily create and send some arbitrary checksums and become owners of the corresponding files. Proofs of Ownership (PoWs) [7] were thus investigated to combat those attacks. In a PoW protocol, the cloud server will require the client to prove the ownership of the claimed file, so that without actually possessing the original file, the client will not be able to pass the PoW check.

Conventional PoW protocols will work correctly if the cloud server itself has access to the original file. This, however, may not be realistic in practice. Due to their openness nature, the CSPs should not be fully trusted, and a lot of data owners today will choose to encrypt their valuable data before data outsourcing. For deduplication purpose, secure message-locked encryption (MLE) [8,9] ensures that different data owners can securely derive the same encryption key for duplicate data possessed individually. But, the encrypted data will create a significant obstacle for correctly executing PoWs. This is because, by possessing an encrypted file, the server cannot verify a PoW proof, which was computed by a potential data owner over the original file. An immediate remediation is to ask the potential data owner to first encrypt the original file, and then compute the PoW proof over the encrypted file [10]. This however will be problematic since now the PoW protocol can only ensure that the client possesses an encrypted version of the original file, rather than the original file itself[1]. How to adapt the PoW protocol so that it can work correctly on encrypted cloud data is still an open problem.

You et al. proposed DEW, a PoW protocol for outsourced multimedia data embedded with watermarks [11]. The idea is to create some sort of "miniatures" over the original file, and send the "miniatures" to the cloud server to assist the PoW verification. This idea can be used in adapting PoWs for encrypted data,

---

[1] Note that for ownership proving, we need to ensure that the prover really "owns" the original file.

but it has some limitations: First, the additional storage overhead will be $O(n)$, where n is the size of the file; Second, it neglects the fact that the cloud server still possesses an encrypted version of the file (which may still be utilized), and thus the resulting design is general and not optimized for our unique application scenario.

Having observed that today's cloud servers are broadly equipped with Intel Software Guard Extensions (SGX) [12], we design a new PoW protocol for encrypted cloud data by leveraging this new hardware feature. SGX can allow creating an isolated memory region (i.e., an enclave) with both confidentiality and integrity assurance at the hardware level, i.e., security of this isolated memory region can be assured even when the operating system is compromised. In the PoW protocol, only the PoW verification process requires accessing the original file, and therefore, it is possible to separate this process and move it into an SGX enclave, within which the encrypted data will be decrypted for PoW verification but the decrypted data will not be leaked to the untrusted cloud server. The resulting design, PoWIS, is the first secure Proof of Ownership protocol on encrypted cloud data via Intel SGX. Our key insights are: 1) The PoW verification process is separated and delegated to the SGX enclave; 2) The decryption key for decryptng the encrypted cloud data and the PoW proof will be transmitted via a secure channel established between the secure enclave and the client, which will remain confidential to the untrusted cloud server. 3) The secure enclave and the untrusted cloud server collaborate to validate the received PoW proof based on the stored encrypted cloud data (which will be decrypted in the secure enclave via the decryption key sent by the client).

Contributions. Our contributions are summarized as follows:

- To the best of our knowledge, we are the first to identify the gap of existing PoWs over encrypted data, and the resulting design, PoWIS, is the first secure PoW protocol designed for encrypted cloud data.
- PoWIS ensures security by combining both cryptography and secure hardware equipped broadly in cloud servers.
- We implement and evaluate PoWIS in terms of security and performance.

2   Background

2.1   Deduplication and Proofs of Ownership (PoWs)

Deduplication has been broadly used in the cloud environment, focusing on eliminating unnecessary storage space by removing duplicate data outsourced to clouds by different data owners. Since deduplication only removes unnecessary duplicates across owners, it does not contradict with another known data security feature, namely, durability [13–16], in which duplicates are created for the *same* data owner to be resilient against potential future failures. For different data owners, duplicates among them will be unknown to each other, and hence are useless. Based on deduplication granularity, we have file-based (i.e., the deduplication granularity is a file) and block-based (i.e., the deduplication granularity is a block) deduplication; while based on deduplication location, we have server-side (i.e., deduplication happens in the server, unknown to the client) and client-side (i.e., the server and the client collaborate for deduplication, not transparent to the client) deduplication. In this paper, we focus on the more beneficial client-side deduplication; additionally, we mainly focus on the file-based deduplication, which is extensible to the block-based deduplication.

The client-side deduplication faces some new attacks. One of the known attacks is that, a malicious data owner can claim ownership of a file by only possessing its checksum, rather than the file itself. Proofs of Ownership (PoWs) [7] were thus explored to mitigate such an attack. A PoW protocol gets the cloud server and the client involved, in which the cloud server (i.e., the verifier) checks whether or not the client (i.e., the prover) really possesses the file. Halevi et al. [7] instantiated the PoW as: a Merkle tree is first constructed over a file, and the resulting Merkle root will be stored by the verifier; upon receiving a claim of ownership on a file, the verifier will issue a challenge, requiring the prover to prove possession of the file; based on the challenge, the prover will construct correct Merkle-tree paths, and the verifier then checks: 1) whether the leaf node of each Merkle-tree path matches the hash value computed on each chosen file block, and 2) whether the root computed along each Merkle-tree path is identical to the stored root; only when the two conditions are both satisfied, the prover can pass the PoW check and become a valid data owner. Note that, to reduce the computation during each challenge, the verifier usually uses spot checking [17] for large files, i.e., checking a random subset of file blocks, rather than the entire file. It shows that if a certain faction of the file is corrupted, by randomly checking a constant number (e.g., 460 [17]) of the file blocks (rather than the entire file), the verifier is able to detect the corruption with a high probability; in addition, the cloud server is assumed to be trusted and can have access to the original file.

2.2   Message-Locked Encryption (MLE)

Various encryption schemes, in which the encryption key is derived from the message being encrypted is so called Message-Locked Encryption (MLE) [8,9,18]. By using MLE in deduplication, different clients owning identical message are able to derive the same encryption key, and hence could obtain the same ciphertext, such that deduplication will not be disturbed by client-side encryption.

2.3   Trusted Execution Environment and Intel SGX

Hardware-enforced trusted execution environment (TEE) can be used to isolate sensitive code and data from other software running on the same platform, e.g., the operation system (OS), or the hypervisor. The TEE which has been broadly used today includes Intel Software Guard Extensions (SGX) [12] and ARM TrustZone [19]. SGX is equipped in an Intel processor, which has been used by a majority of servers around the world. SGX is a set of x86-64 instruction extensions that makes it possible to create a trusted execution environment (called *enclave*), which can be used to protect sensitive code and data. The Intel processor strictly controls access to the enclave memory so that any unauthorized instruction outside the enclave will fail to read/ write the memory of a running enclave. The confidentiality and integrity of cache lines of enclave are ensured by the Intel processor with SGX enabled. The processor is the only hardware-driven trusted computing base (TCB), which eliminates various advanced attacks. The software TCB is the code that the client wants to run inside the enclave. The code inside the enclave can be called from outside through a customized entry point, which is defined as "ECALL" in SGX. The processor will save the register context to the enclave memory, allocate a buffer from the protected memory for data transfer, and copy data from outside to the secure buffer. The secure buffer and the register context will be scrub before resuming execution outside the enclave. Other components, like the network interface, will be shared by all applications, including both SGX and non-SGX applications running on the same server.

In cloud outsourcing, both the code and the data supposed to be executed securely will be outsourced to the untrusted cloud. In this case, it is necessary for the client to establish trust on the remote cloud server. In SGX, this can be achieved via Remote Attestation (RA) [20], in which a specific enclave can prove to the client that it is successfully launched by and running on a genuine SGX processor. Specifically, the SGX processor will measure the enclave in terms of its layout, memory content, and other customized information which must be included and has been hardcoded by developers of the SGX applications. During the enclave initialization, any interference from untrusted software, e.g., the OS, will result in a different measurement. The measurement of the enclave and a signed digest of it form a public verifiable trust commitment, called *Quote*. The *Quote* will be signed by a special enclave, called Quoting Enclave (QE), and the enclave signing is an asymmetric anonymous group signing scheme, in which the private key used to sign the digest is derived from the platform-unique secret, which is only accessible to the platform-unique Architectural Enclaves (AE). The signature on the *Quote* can be verified through the SGX Attestation API [21]. Via the RA, the client can ensure that the enclave is running on the remote cloud server and executions inside the enclave are trustworthy. A secure channel can be established between the client and the enclave at the same time, which allows the client to communicate with the enclave directly. To support the RA, the platform being attested must support the SGX and must enable the SGX in BIOS, but the verifier of the RA does not require SGX to be supported and enabled.

3   System Model and Adversarial Model

System Model. We consider a cloud storage system which is consists of two entities, namely, the cloud server (S) and the data owner (O). The cloud server is equipped with Intel processors with SGX enabled in BIOS. Using SGX, the cloud server can be logically viewed as two components: a trusted execution environment created by the SGX processor (i.e., *enclave*), and an untrusted environment outside the enclave (still denoted as S). S provides storage services and enables client-side deduplication. O outsources data to S but encrypts them before uploading. Since S deploys client-side deduplication, each time when O wants to outsource a file, it will first check with S to find out whether the file has been stored in S (i.e., was uploaded before by another data owner). If not, O will upload the file, otherwise, S will perform a PoW check on O and add O to the owner list of the file if the check can be passed.

Adversarial Model. The cloud server S is honest-but-curious [22,23]. S will honestly store the outsourced file, correctly execute required protocols (e.g., the PoW protocol), and timely respond to data owners as contracted by the Service Level Agreements (SLA). However, it is curious and tries to learn sensitive information from the encrypted file. There is a malicious data owner which wants to pass the PoW check on a file without actually possessing this file. We assume that the cloud server will not collude with the malicious data owner; otherwise, the cloud server can simply add the malicious data owner to owner list of the file, and PoW becomes meaningless. This is a reasonable assumption, since collusion is not an honest behavior, and additionally, the cloud server will not gain additional advantage of learning sensitive information from the file by colluding with a malicious data owner. In addition, we assume that the data owner which initially uploads the file is honest. This assumption is also reasonable, since by uploading an arbitrary file initially, the data owner will gain nothing from this outsourcing but will lose money due to paying the storage service. The communication channel between S and O is assumed to be secure, e.g., protected by SSL/TLS.

4   PoWIS

In this section, we present the design details of PoWIS, a Proof of Ownership scheme on encrypted cloud data via Intel SGX for secure client-side deduplication. Note that PoWIS is instantiated for the file-based deduplication, which is extensible to the block-based deduplication.

4.1   The Overall Design of PoWIS

A secure client-side deduplication for plaintext data works as follows: The file F is initially uploaded by a data owner O (i.e., the first uploader) during the *Initial Upload* phase. During the *Client-side Deduplication* phase, a client[2] which possesses the same file F will check with the cloud server whether F was stored previously, and the cloud server will issue a PoW check and the client will be

---

[2] For simplicity, we use the term "client" to refer to peers interacting with the cloud server, including both the honest and the malicious data owner.

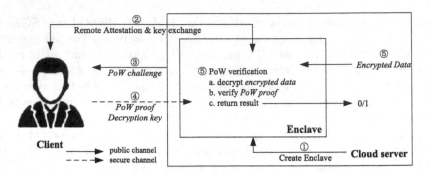

Fig. 1. The workflow of PoWIS in the Client-side Deduplication phase

added to the owner list of the file F if and only if it can successfully pass the PoW check (Sect. 2.1). PoWIS enables the client-side deduplication for encrypted cloud data, by modifying both the Initial Upload and the Client-side Deduplication phase as follows:

The Initial Upload Phase. Upon uploading a file F for the first time, the data owner O will construct a Merkle-tree over it, and encrypt it using an MLE key (denoted as K_{mle}, which is derived using a secure MLE instantiation introduced in Sect. 2.2). O will also encrypt the Merkle-tree root using K_{mle}, and then send both the encrypted F and the encrypted Merkle-tree root to the cloud server.

The Client-Side Deduplication Phase. Before uploading a file, the client will first check with the cloud server whether the file has been uploaded before. The client will derive the K_{mle} based on the file, encrypt the file using the K_{mle}, and compute a checksum over the encrypted file, and send the checksum to the cloud server [10]. If the cloud server finds out that the checksum matches a stored encrypted file, it will check whether the client really owns the file by running the PoW protocol. The traditional PoW protocol designed for the plaintext data can be directly used here but can only prove that the client possesses the encrypted file since the cloud server only has access to the encrypted file. We adapt the traditional PoW protocol to support encrypted cloud data by leveraging Intel SGX, a security feature built into the processor of the cloud server (which is honest but curious as described in Sect. 3). A complete workflow of the new PoW protocol is as follows (Fig. 1):

1. The cloud server creates an SGX enclave.
2. The client attests and negotiates a session key (K) with the enclave.
3. The cloud server sends a PoW challenge to the client. Note that, the cloud server can use spot checking (Sect. 2.1) if the file has more than 460 4KB file blocks, i.e., a random subset of file blocks will be checked if the file is large; otherwise, the server simply checks the entire file.
4. The client first derives K_{mle} from the possessed file F. The client then computes the PoW proof based on the received challenges. Specifically, it constructs the Merkle-tree based on F, and for each file block being challenged,

it computes the hash value of the file block, which is a leaf in the Merkle-tree, and extracts the path from this leaf to the Merkle-tree root (i.e., consisting of all the hash values of "siblings" along the path). The final PoW proof includes: 1) a set of leaves corresponding to the file blocks being checked; 2) the corresponding sibling-paths. Lastly, the client encrypts both the K_{mle} and the PoW proof using the session key K. Note that, due to the use of spot checking, both the computation and communication overhead will remain constant for large files [17]. The encrypted K_{mle} and PoW proof will be sent back to the server.

5. The cloud server will rely on the enclave to check correctness of the PoW proof. Both the encrypted K_{mle} and the PoW proof will be passed to the enclave. In addition, the cloud server will send to the enclave: 1) the encrypted Merkle-tree root (initially uploaded by the first uploader); and 2) the subset of encrypted file blocks which is corresponding to the subset of file blocks being checked. The enclave will then perform the following sensitive operations transparently to the cloud server: 1) Using the session key K, the enclave will perform decryption, obtain K_{mle} and the PoW proof; 2) Using K_{mle}, the enclave will decrypt the encrypted Merkle-tree root as well as the subset of encrypted file blocks; 3) Using the Merkle-tree root and the subset of file blocks in plaintext, the enclave can check whether the PoW proof is correct or not and the final verification result will be returned to the cloud server. The verification is performed as:

For each file block being challenged:

- the enclave computes the hash value of the file block and compares it with the corresponding leaf sent back by the client;
- if it does not match, the verification fails and exits;
- if it matches, the enclave will compute a sibling-path corresponding to this file block, and check whether the resulting root matches the Merkle-tree root sent from the cloud server;
- if it does not match, the verification fails and exits;
- if it matches, this sibling-path is valid.

4.2   Remote Attestation and Establishing a Secure Communication Channel

The enclave is a vital component in PoWIS that enables the PoW verification without disclosing the original file to the untrusted cloud server. Therefore, ensuring that the enclave is really initialized in a genuine Intel SGX processor and the verification process of PoWIS is actually running inside the enclave, is necessary for security of PoWIS. This is achieved by Remote Attestation [20] (RA) in SGX, which allows the client to attest the enclave and to negotiate a session key to protect communication between the client and the enclave.

To ensure the session key is not modified by a man-in-the-middle attacker during the RA process such that the client communicates with the intended

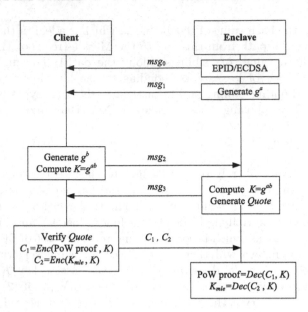

Fig. 2. The sequence of interactions between the client and the enclave during the RA process

enclave, an EC signing based on elliptic curve (satisfying the NIST P-256 standard) and an enclave signing will be used. Specifically, the EC public key will be hardcoded in the SGX application which will be running in the cloud server side, and the EC private key will be hardcoded in the application which will be running in the client side. The private key for the enclave signing is derived from the unique secret embedded on each SGX processor, which is only accessible to the special Architectural Enclaves (AE), e.g., the Quoting Enclave (QE), and the Platform Service Enclave (PSE). The public key for the enclave signing is possessed by the Intel. The interactions between the client and the enclave during the RA process is shown in Fig. 2, which is an elaborated SIGMA key exchange protocol based on the discrete logarithm Diffie-Hellman key agreement (DHKE) protocol:

– Initiate RA context: The enclave accepts a handle of a trusted session created by PSE, and accepts the EC public key as an argument, and returns an opaque context for the key exchange that will be invoked during RA.
– Enclave $\xrightarrow{msg_0}$ client: The enclave selects the attestation mode, one of which is based on the Enhanced Private ID (EPID), and the other is based on the Elliptic Curve Digital Signature Algorithm (ECDSA). The attestation mode is the main content of msg_0.
– Enclave $\xrightarrow{msg_1}$ client: The enclave generates its public session key share g^a, where g is a global generator of a secure DH group G in order n, and a is a random big integer generated inside the enclave. The enclave retrieves the

extended Group ID $(GID)^3$. g^a and the extended GID form msg_1. Note that msg_0 and msg_1 can be sent together (up to system setting).

- Client $\xrightarrow{msg_2}$ enclave: The client synchronizes RA context based on msg_0 and extracts the public key share g^a from msg_1. Then the client generates its public key share g^b, where b is a random big integer picked by the client, and computes the session key $K = g^{ab}$. Further, $(g^a||g^b)$ will be processed to a digest and signed using the client's EC private key, where "——" denotes concatenation. g^b and the signed $(g^a||g^b)$ will be included in msg_2, which will be sent back to the enclave.

- Enclave $\xrightarrow{msg_3}$ client: The enclave verifies the integrity of $(g^a||g^b)$ using the EC public key, and computes the session key $K = g^{ab}$. The most critical payload of msg_3 is a special cross-platform commitment, i.e., *Quote*, which is generated by the SGX processor. Specifically, the statement of enclave is strictly measured by the SGX processor during the RA, including the data generated inside the enclave, e.g. g^a, the data received during the RA, e.g., g^b, and the code running inside the enclave. The resulting measurement, called *Report*, will be further processed to *Quote* by the QE. QE will compute a digest of *Report* and sign it using the private key for enclave signing. Note that the private key for enclave signing is derived from a platform-specific secret, the accessibility of which is strictly controlled by the SGX processor.

- Client $\xrightarrow{C_1,C_2}$ enclave: The client validates the *Quote* through the online Intel Attestation Service [21] to ensure that the intended enclave is created and run in the cloud server, and the key shares are not modified. At this point, the client can be convinced that the *Quote* is signed by a valid SGX processor, and hence the integrity of the code running in the cloud server side as well as the data exchanged during the RA is ensured. Therefore, the key exchange process is trustworthy and the communication channel is well protected. The PoW proof and K_{mle} will be encrypted using the session K to C_1 and C_2, respectively, and then will be sent back to the enclave.

5   Analysis and Discussion

5.1   Security Analysis

In the following, we show that PoWIS is a secure proof of ownership protocol and, the server will not be able to learn sensitive information about the original file.

A Malicious Client Which Does Not Possess the Original File Cannot Pass the PoW Check. In PoWIS, the client is required to provide both the MLE key and the PoW proof to pass the PoW check. We first show that a malicious client which does not possess the original file will not be able to learn it. The only known approach for the malicious client to learn the original file

---

[3] Currently, the Intel Attestation Service only supports the value of zero for the extended GID.

in the client-side deduplication is to perform the side-channel attacks [24]. This is infeasible in PoWIS because: at the beginning of the client-side deduplication phase, the client is required to send a hash value over the encrypted file, rather than the original file; in other words, by performing the side-channel attack, the malicious client can at most learn the encrypted file rather than the original file. Then, without being able to have access to the original file, a malicious client will not be able to obtain the correct MLE key, considering a secure MLE protocol is used. In addition, the PoW proof in PoWIS is constructed based on the traditional PoW protocol using Merkle tree [7] and, the client is guaranteed to be unable to pass the PoW check without having access to the original file considering the traditional PoW protocol is secure. Note that for performance consideration, this guarantee would be probabilistic if spot checking is used [17] during the checking; especially, if a certain percentage of the original file is missing in the client side (e.g., 1%), by randomly checking a certain number of file blocks (e.g., 460), the cloud server can detect this misbehavior with a high probability (e.g., 99%).

The Cloud Server Cannot Learn Anything About the Original File in PoWIS. What the cloud server can have access to is the encrypted file and the encrypted Merkle-tree root, which are both protected by the MLE key derived through a secure MLE instantiation. It is infeasible for the cloud server to find out the MLE key considering a secure MLE protocol is used. In addition, each PoW proof is encrypted using a session key, which is established through the secure key exchange protocol between the client and the enclave. Without having access to the session key, the cloud server cannot gain any additional advantage of learning the original file by accumulating the PoW proofs. Last, considering the SGX enclave is secure[4], the cloud server is not able to learn anything about the file blocks being processed inside the enclave.

5.2 Discussion

Side channel attacks against Intel SGX. The Intel SGX has been shown to be vulnerable to various side channel attacks since the untrusted code and the enclave code share the same processor. These include memory access pattern attacks [25], cache-based side channels [26,27], branch shadowing attacks [28], etc. Several defenses have been proposed to mitigate those attacks, e.g., checking program execution time [29], data location randomization [30], using a commodity component of the Intel processor, Transactional Synchronization Extensions (TSX), to detect exceptions and interrupts during running an enclave [31], etc.

Accelerating SGX. Accelerating SGX is necessary for handling the ever-surging volume of cloud data. Intel has spent efforts on improving SGX performance in the upcoming version SGX2 [12]. The SGX can be accelerated by

---

[4] Note that the focus of this work is not the security of SGX itself, as we know that various new side-channel attacks on the SGX as well as the corresponding defenses have been actively investigated in the literature. Here we simply use SGX as a black box which is assumed to be secure.

Table 1. Time for each individual component during the RA process

enclave creation (server side)	0.06s
generating msg_0 (server side)	0.002s
Generating msg_1 (server side)	0.009s
Generating msg_2 (client side)	0.003s
Processing msg_2, generating msg_3 (server side)	0.27s
Processing msg_3 (client side)	1.18–1.7s

leveraging GPU [32], or implementing it in a more efficient platform [33], i.e., the PCIe ExpressFabric chips, with PCIe ExpressFabric working as a high-speed resource sharing network.

6 Implementation and Evaluation

6.1 Implementation

We implemented PoWIS in C. The server was implemented on a PC with SGX enabled (Intel Core i5-9400 2.9 GHz processor, 8 GB RAM, Windows 10, Intel SGXSDK version 2.7), and the client was implemented on another PC without SGX (Intel Core i5-6300 2.4 GHz processor, 8GB RAM, Windows 10). For efficiency, when the total number of file blocks exceeds a threshold (i.e., 460 [17]), the cloud server will always challenge a constant number of file blocks (i.e., 460 [17]); otherwise, the cloud server will check the entire file. OpenSSL [34] has been widely used for performing cryptographic computations, but Intel has omitted several potentially insecure operations, and only the specific SSL library adjusted by Intel [35] and compiled by an SGX processor, called *SGXSSL*, can be successfully linked and used by the SGX applications. Therefore, we used SGXSSL (based on OpenSSL-1.1.0d) for the server, and standard OpenSSL-1.1.1e for the client, respectively.

6.2 Performance Evaluation

We mainly evaluated the PoW process of PoWIS. We used 6 files for testing, the sizes of which range from 128 KB to 16 MB and the size of each file block is 4KB. We did not try too large file sizes, since once the file size exceeds 1.84 MB (i.e., $4KB \times 460$), the computation turns to be constant due to the use of spot checking. The PoW process of PoWIS has a few key components including the SGX Remote Attestation, the PoW proof generation, and the PoW proof verification. Since DEW [11] can be adapted to support PoWs over encrypted cloud data, we therefore compared PoWIS with DEW during the PoW process.

Remote Attestation (RA). In RA, the cloud server spends time on generating msg_0 and msg_1, processing msg_2, and generating msg_3. The client spends time

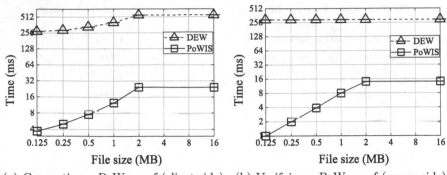

(a) Generating a PoW proof (client side)   (b) Verifying a PoW proof (server side)

Fig. 3. Proof generation and verification in the PoW process

on processing msg_0, msg_1, and msg_3 as well as generating msg_2. The experimental results are shown in Table 1.

We can observe that the most time-consuming operation in the server side is generating msg_3. By analyzing the source code of the RA in SGXSDK [36], we found that, the special *Quote* in msg_3 is generated through a series of function calls, which perform a few expensive operations, including the SGX processor carefully measuring the enclave, sealing the resulting valid *Report*, QE processing the *Report* by signing it with a private key, etc. The most time-consuming operation in the client side is processing msg_3, varying between 1.18s and 1.7s. This time is a little expensive because, *Quote* in msg_3 currently can only be validated through the online attestation service provided by Intel, and the resulting time is highly affected by network delay, server response delay, etc, i.e., this time is very unstable and strongly depends on where the client is located as well as the capability of the Intel attestation service. This should be improved as the SGX technology develops.

The PoW Proof Generation and Verification. The time for generating the PoW proof and verifying the PoW proof are shown in Fig. 3(a) and Fig. 3(b), respectively. The experimental results were averaged over 10 trials. We can observe that: 1) The time for generating/ verifying a PoW proof in PoWIS is approximately liner with the file size before the threshold (i.e., 1.84MB), but it remains constant after the threshold is reached. This is because, after the threshold is reached, the PoW check will be based on spot checking, which always checks 460 blocks, randomly selected from the entire file; 2) For a fixed file size, both the proof generation and the proof verification of PoWIS are more efficient than the DEW [11]. This is because, in PoWIS, the proof generation/ verification consists of lightweight hash operations and Merkle-tree computation, but in DEW [11], the proof generation/ verification contains expensive modular exponentiation operations over a multiplicative cyclic group. However, this does not imply that PoWIS is more efficient than DEW during the PoW process, since PoWIS has extra overhead in the Remote Attestation. The major advantage of PoWIS over

DEW is that, PoWIS does not require additional metadata (or "miniatures") to facilitate the PoW process, but DEW does, and the size of these metadata is $O(n)$, when n is the number of blocks in the file.

7 Related Work

7.1 Deduplication in Cloud Storage

Data deduplication has been used broadly in cloud storage for storage saving. The deduplication techniques can be roughly categorized into the server-side and the client-side deduplication, and the client-side deduplication is more advantageous due to its saving in both the storage and the bandwidth.

Message-Locked Encryption (MLE). To enable deduplication over encrypted data, different users should generate the same encryption key for duplicate data possessed individually. MLE has been designed for this purpose. Convergent Encryption (CE) [18] proposed by Douceur et al. can be used to derive the encryption key by hashing the file content, which is vulnerable to the brute-force attack [37]. To mitigate this attack, DupLESS [9] introduced an independent key server. Liu et al. [8] removed the independent key server at the cost of requiring users to synchronize username/ password in advance, which is impractical.

Proofs of Ownership (PoWs). In the client-side deduplication, a PoW protocol [7] can be used to prevent a malicious entity from claiming ownership of a file without really possessing it. Halevi et al. [7] proposed PoW protocols which rely on the Merkle-tree, under the assumption that the cloud server is fully trusted and can have access to the original file. Our work PoWIS removes this assumption and enables a PoW protocol for encrypted cloud data, in which the cloud server can only have access to the encrypted file but is still able to check whether the client possesses the original file. You et al. [11] proposed a PoW protocol specifically for the outsourced watermarked data, in which the untrusted cloud server can check whether the client possesses the original file even if it can only have access to the watermarked file.

7.2 Intel SGX in Cloud Computing

SGX [12] is an advanced security feature integrated into the Intel processors that can ensure both confidentiality and integrity of sensitive code and data even if the OS is compromised. SGX is particularly promising in cloud computing since a cloud server is typically an untrusted execution environment, and SGX has been supported in various cloud providers including Microsoft Azure [2]. Schuster et. al [38] proposed a MapReduce framework in the cloud which can allow users to run distributed MapReduce computations in the cloud without comprising data confidentiality as well as correctness of results by leveraging SGX. Pereira et al. relied on SGX to ensure use of audited software in an insecure environment [39]. Kurnikov et al. designed and implemented a TEE-based cloud key store (CKS) [40], facilitating key management securely. They implemented a proof of concept CKS using Intel SGX. Dang et al. [41] proposed a privacy-preserving server-side deduplication protocol that protects the confidentiality, the ownership as well as the equality information of the outsourced data.

8   Conclusion

This work identifies a novel conflict in traditional proofs of ownership protocols that the verifier (i.e., the cloud server) needs to have access to the original file, but the file accessible to the verifier is encrypted. To resolve this conflict, we design a novel PoW protocol for encrypted cloud data by leveraging Intel SGX (PoWIS), a security feature presenting in most of the cloud servers' processors. Security analysis and experimental evaluations justify that PoWIS is a secure PoW protocol for encrypted cloud data with a modest additional overhead.

References

1. Amazon simple storage service (2020). http://aws.amazon.com/cn/s3/
2. Microsoft azure (2020). http://www.windowsazure.cn/?fb=002
3. Meyer, D.T., Bolosky, W.J.: A study of practical deduplication. ACM Trans. Storage **7**(4), 1–1 (2012)
4. Dropbox (2019). https://www.dropbox.com/
5. Box (2019). https://www.box.com/
6. Google drive (2020). https://www.google.cn/intl/zh_cn/drive/
7. Halevi, S., Harnik, D., Pinkas, B., Shulman-Peleg, A.: Proofs of ownership in remote storage systems. In: ACM Conference on Computer and Communications Security, pp. 491–500. ACM (2011)
8. Liu, J., Asokan, N., Pinkas, B.: Secure deduplication of encrypted data without additional independent servers. In: Proceedings of the 22nd ACM SIGSAC Conference on Computer and Communications Security, pp. 874–885 (2015)
9. Bellare, M., Keelveedhi, S., Ristenpart, T.: DupLESS: server-aided encryption for deduplicated storage. In: USENIX Conference on Security, pp. 179–194 (2013)
10. Lei, L., Cai, Q., Chen, B., Lin, J.: Towards efficient re-encryption for secure client-side deduplication in public clouds. In: Lam, K.-Y., Chi, C.-H., Qing, S. (eds.) ICICS 2016. LNCS, vol. 9977, pp. 71–84. Springer, Cham (2016). https://doi.org/10.1007/978-3-319-50011-9_6
11. You, W., Chen, B., Liu, L., Jing, J.: Deduplication-friendly watermarking for multimedia data in public clouds. In: Chen, L., Li, N., Liang, K., Schneider, S. (eds.) European Symposium on Research in Computer Security (ESORICS), vol. 12308 (2020). https://doi.org/10.1007/978-3-030-58951-6_4
12. Intel software guard extensions (2020). https://software.intel.com
13. Chen, B., Curtmola, R., Ateniese, G., Burns,R.: Remote data checking for network coding-based distributed storage systems. In: Proceedings of the 2010 ACM Workshop on Cloud Computing Security Workshop, pp. 31–42. ACM (2010)
14. Chen, B., Curtmola, R.: Towards self-repairing replication-based storage systems using untrusted clouds. In: Proceedings of the Third ACM Conference on Data and Application Security and Privacy, pp. 377–388. ACM (2013)

15. Chen, B., Ammula, A.K., Curtmola, R.: Towards server-side repair for erasure coding-based distributed storage systems. In: Proceedings of the 5th ACM Conference on Data and Application Security and Privacy, pp. 281–288. ACM (2015)
16. Chen, B., Curtmola, R.: Remote data integrity checking with server-side repair. J. Comput. Secur. **25**(6), 537–584 (2017)
17. Ateniese, G., et al.: Provable data possession at untrusted stores. In: Proceedings of the 14th ACM Conference on Computer and Communications Security, pp. 598–609. ACM (2007)
18. Douceur, J.R., Adya, A., Bolosky,W.J., Dan, S., Theimer, M.: Reclaiming space from duplicate files in a serverless distributed file system. In: International Conference on Distributed Computing Systems, pp. 617–624 (2002)
19. Arm trustzone (2020). https://www.arm.com/products/silicon-ip-security
20. Attestation service for intel software guard extensions (2020). https://api.trustedservices.intel.com/documents/sgx-attestation-api-spec.pdf
21. Remote attestation in intel software guard extensions (2020). https://software.intel.com/content/www/us/en/develop/articles/code-sample-intel-software-guard-extensions-remote-attestation-end-to-end-example.html
22. Yu, S., Wang, C., Ren, K., Wenjing, L.: Achieving secure, scalable, and fine-grained data access control in cloud computing. In: INFOCOM 2010, pp. 1–9. IEEE (2010)
23. Wang, Q., Wang, C., Li, J., Ren, K., Lou, W.: Enabling public verifiability and data dynamics for storage security in cloud computing. In: Backes, M., Ning, P. (eds.) ESORICS 2009. LNCS, vol. 5789, pp. 355–370. Springer, Heidelberg (2009). https://doi.org/10.1007/978-3-642-04444-1_22
24. Harnik, D., Pinkas, B., Shulman-Peleg, A.: Side channels in cloud services: deduplication in cloud storage. IEEE Secur. Priv. **8**(6), 40–47 (2010)
25. Xu, Y., Cui, W., Peinado, M.: Controlled-channel attacks: deterministic side channels for untrusted operating systems. In: 2015 IEEE Symposium on Security and Privacy, pp. 640–656. IEEE (2015)
26. Moghimi, A., Irazoqui, G., Eisenbarth, T.: CacheZoom: how SGX amplifies the power of cache attacks. In: Fischer, W., Homma, N. (eds.) CHES 2017. LNCS, vol. 10529, pp. 69–90. Springer, Cham (2017). https://doi.org/10.1007/978-3-319-66787-4_4
27. Brasser, F., Müller, U., Dmitrienko, A., Kostiainen, K., Capkun, S., Sadeghi, A.-R.: Software grand exposure: {SGX} cache attacks are practical. In: 11th {USENIX} Workshop on Offensive Technologies ({WOOT} 17) (2017)
28. Lee, S., Shih, M.-W., Gera, P., Kim, T., Kim, H., Peinado, M.: Inferring fine-grained control flow inside {SGX} enclaves with branch shadowing. In: 26th {USENIX} Security Symposium ({USENIX} Security 17), pp. 557–574 (2017)
29. Chen, S., Zhang, X., Reiter, M.K., Zhang, Y.: Detecting privileged side-channel attacks in shielded execution with déjá vu. In: Proceedings of the 2017 ACM on Asia Conference on Computer and Communications Security, pp. 7–18 (2017)
30. Brasser, F., Capkun,S., Dmitrienko, A., Frassetto, T., Kostiainen, K., Sadeghi, A.-R.: Dr. SGX: automated and adjustable side-channel protection for SGX using data location randomization. In: Proceedings of the 35th Annual Computer Security Applications Conference, pp. 788–800 (2019)
31. Shih, M.W., Lee, S., Kim, T., Peinado, M.: T-SGX: eradicating controlled-channel attacks against enclave programs. In: Network & Distributed System Security Symposium (2017)

32. Jang, I., Tang, A., Kim, T., Sethumadhavan, S., Huh, J.: Heterogeneous isolated execution for commodity GPUS. In: Proceedings of the Twenty-Fourth International Conference on Architectural Support for Programming Languages and Operating Systems, pp. 455–468 (2019)

33. Zhu, J., et al.: Enabling privacy-preserving, compute-and data-intensive computing using heterogeneous trusted execution environment. arXiv preprint arXiv:1904.04782 (2019)

34. Openssl-cryptography and ssl/tls toolkit (2020). https://www.openssl.org/

35. Intel software guard extensions ssl (2020). https://github.com/intel/intel-sgx-ssl

36. Intel software guard extensions for linux os (2020). https://github.com/intel/linux-sgx

37. Known attacks towards convergent encryption (2013). https://tahoe-lafs.org/hacktahoelafs/drew_perttula.html

38. Schuster, F., et al.: VC3: trustworthy data analytics in the cloud using SGX. In: 2015 IEEE Symposium on Security and Privacy, pp. 38–54. IEEE (2015)

39. Pereira, L.W., et al.: Using intel SGX to enforce auditing of running software in insecure environments. In: 2018 IEEE International Conference on Cloud Computing Technology and Science (CloudCom), pp. 243–246. IEEE (2018)

40. Kurnikov, A., Paverd, A., Mannan, M., Asokan, N.: Keys in the clouds: auditable multi-device access to cryptographic credentials. In: Proceedings of the 13th International Conference on Availability, Reliability and Security, pp. 1–10 (2018)

41. Dang, H., Chang, E.-C.: Privacy-preserving data deduplication on trusted processors. In: 2017 IEEE 10th International Conference on Cloud Computing (CLOUD), pp. 66–73. IEEE (2017)

On the Verification of Signed Messages

Bowen Xu[1,2,3], Xin Xu[1,2,3], Quanwei Cai[1,2], Wei Wang[1,2],
and QiongXiao Wang[1,2,3](✉)

[1] State Key Laboratory of Information Security, Institute of Information
Engineering, Chinese Academy of Sciences, Beijing, China
{xubowen,xuxin,caiquanwei,wangwei,wangqiongxiao}@iie.ac.cn
[2] Data Assurance and Communication Security Research Center,
Chinese Academy of Sciences, Beijing, China
[3] School of Cyber Security, University of Chinese Academy of Sciences,
Beijing, China

Abstract. Signed messages are widely used in network security. A message is typically signed by the sender with semantically-secure signature algorithms, and then verified by any receiver which is configured with the sender's public key. A successfully-verified message ensures data origin authentication and data integrity. However, some known vulnerabilities or incidents indicate that this mechanism does not always take effect in the real-world systems; that is, even when the sender's private key is well protected, a message forged or modified by attackers, might still be successfully verified by receivers. This paper analyzes the implementations of digitally-signed message verification, and discusses possible weaknesses based on some publicly-disclosed vulnerabilities. This survey provides a guideline for the secure implementation of cryptographic protocols.

Keywords: Digital signature · Data integrity · Data origin authentication · Cryptographic implementation

1 Introduction

Digital signatures are widely used in network security, e.g., to ensure data origin authentication, data integrity and authentication. For a semantically-secure signature algorithm, only the entity owning the private key is able to generate the valid signature for a message, which is successfully verified using the corresponding public key. It is computationally impossible for any entity which does not own the private key, to generate a valid signature. Meanwhile, if any bit of the message is modified unintentionally or maliciously, the verification fails.

Typical signed messages include signed PDF documents, X.509 certificates in public key infrastructures, identity tokens in single sign-on protocols, access tokens for authorization frameworks, signed binaries of code signing, key

---

This work was supported partially by Cyber Security Program of National Key RD Plan of China (Grant No. 2017YFB0802100).

J. Zhou et al. (Eds.): ACNS 2020 Workshops, LNCS 12418, pp. 417–434, 2020.
https://doi.org/10.1007/978-3-030-61638-0_23

exchange messages of TLS, etc. In these different security applications of cryptography, a successfully-verified message means that the content of this message is certified by the signer, and it is not modified unintentionally or maliciously in the transmission.

However, this mechanism does not always take effect in the real-world systems. Vulnerabilities are reported in different steps. For example, CVE-2020-0601 [17] allows the adversaries to *arbitrarily* sign an X.509 certificate which will be successfully verified and accepted by some vulnerable versions of Windows operating systems (OSes). Attackers could exploit the signature verification vulnerabilities of PDF and XML documents to tamper with a signed document [18,20], and this document will be verified successfully by some PDF readers and XML libraries.

These attacks do not break the signature algorithms, but result from the careless and reckless implementations of cryptographic functions. Such vulnerabilities are logic errors, different from common software vulnerabilities such as buffer overflow, code injection, control flow hijacking, return-oriented programming, data-oriented attacks. Thus, the following questions appear when we analyze these vulnerabilities on the verification of signed messages: Which steps of the verification of signed messages are prone to such logic errors? What kinds of logic errors may exist in the verification of signed messages?

In this paper, we analyze the verification of signed messages, and discusses possible weaknesses based on some publicly-disclosed vulnerabilities. We survey the vulnerabilities related to algorithm identifiers, message formats, public keys, and message parsing. These discussions help to find vulnerabilities related to the verification of signed messages in network security solutions, and contribute to secure implementation of security applications of cryptography.

The remainder of this paper is organized as follows. Section 2 presents the background of signed messages in network security. Section 3 discusses the different ways to forge successfully-verified messages, followed by the learned lessons in Sect. 4. Section 5 concludes this paper.

2 Digital Signature and Verification

A semantically-secure signature algorithm is briefly explained as follows. A signer (or sender) holds a key pair, i.e., the private key sk and the public key pk. After generating a message m, the sender uses its private key to compute the signature $sig = Sign(m, sk)$. Usually m is firstly hashed into a message digest and then input to the digital signing.

After receiving a signed message $[m, sig]$, the receiver firstly finds the public key pk, and then verifies whether the signature matches the message or not. If this signed message is verified successfully, then the receiver parses m as the application-layer format specifies. The sender's public key is usually distributed as an X.509 certificate, which is also a message signed by the certification authority (CA) and verified by the receiver.

Next, we briefly describe some typical applications of signed messages in network security.

2.1   PDF Signature

Portable Document Format (PDF) is an electronic file format [10]. PDF provides PDF signature to ensure the integrity and authenticity of PDF files. To better understand the attack on PDF signature, the following introduces basic knowledge about PDF file structure and PDF signature.

PDF Structure: The structure of a PDF file is shown in Fig. 1.

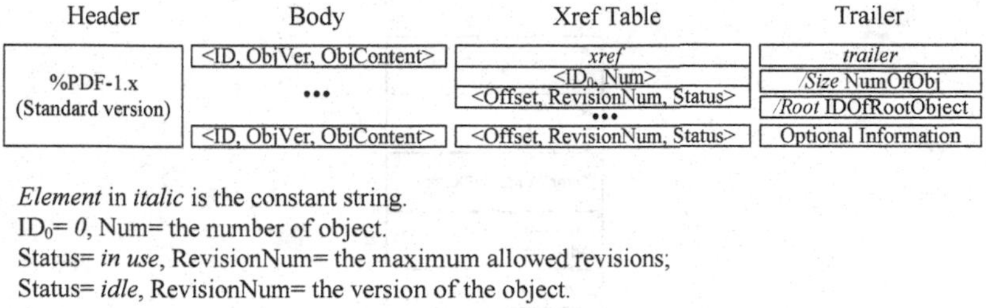

Header	Body	Xref Table	Trailer

	<ID, ObjVer, ObjContent>	*xref*	*trailer*
%PDF-1.x (Standard version)	•••	<ID$_0$, Num> <Offset, RevisionNum, Status> •••	/Size NumOfObj /Root IDOfRootObject
	<ID, ObjVer, ObjContent>	<Offset, RevisionNum, Status>	Optional Information

Element in *italic* is the constant string.
ID$_0$= *0*, Num= the number of object.
Status= *in use*, RevisionNum= the maximum allowed revisions;
Status= *idle*, RevisionNum= the version of the object.

Fig. 1. A brief structure of a PDF file

The PDF file is composed of four parts: Header, Body, Xref table, Trailer.

1. Header: The first line of a PDF file and indicates the version of the PDF specification used in the PDF.
2. Body: The main part in a PDF, including the objects of the text stream, images, other media elements, etc. The body section is used to hold all data that is displayed to the users.
3. Xref table: A cross-reference table indicates the byte offset from the start of the file for each object. The purpose of a cross-reference table is to allow random access to objects in a file without reading the entire PDF file to locate a specific object. An entry in the table corresponds to an object, and the length of an entry is 20 bytes.
4. Trailer: Trailer contains the byte offset of Xref table and the information about Catalog object which is the root object of Body. It is first processed when PDF viewers display a PDF file. Trailer ends with %%EOF.

Incremental Update: Incremental update is a feature of PDF. The PDF file is modified by adding a new body, Xref table, and Trailer after %%EOF without changing the original content and structure of the PDF file. Incremental updates improve the efficiency of PDF file generation when making a few changes to PDF.

PDF Signature: PDF files can be signed using incremental updates. The application creates the PDF signature with adding a new Body, new Xref table, and new Trailer to the original file. The new Body contains a new Catalog, a signature object, and some parameter objects related to PDF viewers when processing PDF files. The new Xref table contains the index of objects in the body that newly added.

The signature object is shown in Fig. 2. Some details have been excluded or abbreviated, specifically the signer name, signature creating time, etc. we mainly focus on /*Contents* entry and /*Byterange* entry.

Fig. 2. The simplified example of PDF signature object.

The /*Filter* entry and the /*SubFilter* entry specifies the handler used to process the data in the object. The /*Contents* entry contains the public key certificate, signed message digest and timestamp. The above information is collectively referred to as signature value. The /*ByteRange* entry is composed of two integer pairs and specifies the range for calculating the signature value. The integer pair [*a b*] specifies the first input for hash calculation in signature creation and validation which is before the /*Contents* entry. The integer pair [*c d*] specifies the second input for hash calculation which is after the /*Contents* entry.

When verifying the signature, PDF viewers calculate the value according to the range specified by /*ByteRange*, and compare the value with the signature value saved in /*Contents*.

2.2   XML Signature in SAML

SAML (Security Assertion Markup Language) is an XML-based standard data format that exchanges authentication and authorization data between identity providers and service providers [6]. SAML used XML signature to ensure the authenticity and integrity of the assertions. XML signature has much in common with PKCS7 but is more extensible and complex. For the same XML file, there are multiple implements of XML signature that conform to the standard.

XML Signature. The XML signature structure is shown as Fig. 3.

SignedInfo element contains a collection of reference elements.

CanonicalizationMethod and *SignatureMethod* elements in *SignedInfo* specify the algorithm used for canonicalization and signature.

Reference element includes the hash value and hash algorithm of the resource, and *URI* parameter in *Reference* element points to the signed element.

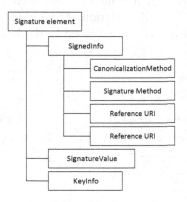

Fig. 3. XML Signature element structure

The XML signature standard [8] defines the rules for creating and verifying XML signatures. It allows the entire XML tree to be signed or only specific elements to be signed. According to the position of XML signature and signed data, XML signatures can be divided into three types (Fig. 4):

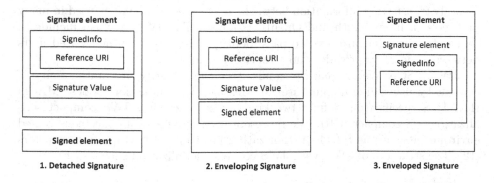

Fig. 4. Three types of XML signatures

1. Detached signature: The signature element is neither placed in the signed element nor as the parent element of the signed data.

2. Enveloping signature: The signature element is the parent element of the signed data.
3. Enveloped signature: The signed data is the parent element of the signature element.

XML Signature in SAML: Enveloped signature is used in SAML assertion [6]. The SAML assertion or its parent element is used as a reference to the signature element and the signed element is the parent element of the Signature. In the SOAP framework, SAML assertion is placed in the head of SOAP; in the REST framework, SAML assertion is placed in the Response element (Fig. 5).

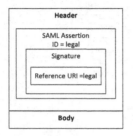
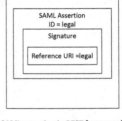

SAML assertion in SOAP framework   **SAML assertion in REST framework**

Fig. 5. The SAML assertion under SOAP Framework and REST Framework

2.3   JSON Web Signature

The JWT (JSON Web Token) is an Internet standard that defines a method for securely transferring information between two parties [13]. JWT is used in many protocols such as OAuth and OpenID-Connect. The JWT payload includes a series of claims that are used to pass identity messages of authenticated users between an identity provider and a service provider.

JWS (JSON Web Signature) guarantees the integrity and authenticity of content by using digital signatures or Message Authentication Codes (MACs) [11]. JWS specification defines two kinds of serializations. JWS compact serialization is a compact, URL-safe representation intended for space-constrained environments such as HTTP Authorization headers and URI query parameters [12]. The structure of JWT with JWS compact serialization shown in Fig. 6.

1. Header: Header contains attributes that related to JWT and parameters used to generate and verify JWT.
   - "alg": This parameter indicates the algorithm used to generate signatures or MACs. JWS support Message Authentications Code with symmetric key and digital signature with asymmetric key. This parameter is required in JWS Header.

Header	Payload	Signature

{
"alg" : "…"
"…" : "…"
}
	.	{
		claims
		}
			.	{
				Signature value
				}

Fig. 6. The structure of JSON Web Token with JSON Web Signature

- "jwk": This optional parameter is the public key used to verify JWT.
  JWT specification also defines some optional parameters in JWT Header that
  not be mentioned in this discussion.
2. Payload: Payload contains a series of claims that used to verify JWT. The
   data that the issuer wants to transmit is also stored in claims.
3. Signature: Signature contains the Base64URL encoded signature value. The
   signed message is Base64 URL encoded Header and Payload.

Header, payload, signature, use "." as the delimiter, and use Base64URL for
encoding.

2.4 Validation of Digital Certificate

In Public Key Infrastructure (PKI), a digital certificate is issued and signed by
an entity (Certificate Authority, CA) trusted by both parties in communication.
A certificate contains subject identity information, the information about public
key and the digital signature. The issuance of certificates can be multi-layered.
The uppermost CA acts as the root CA and uses its own private key to issue
certificates for lower-level CAs. The lowest-level CA uses the private key to issue
certificates for users. The intermediate-level CAs in this process are referred to
as the subordinate CA. The root CA has a self-signed certificate called "root
CA certificate", which contains the root CA's public key, identity information
and the signature calculated using the root CA's private key.

The root CA certificate, intermediate CA certificates, and user certificate
together form a certificate chain. When using a certificate, the receiver will verify
the certificate and the certificate chain. The verification process of the certificate
chain is as follows:

1. Obtain the certificate chain and verify each level of certificates in the certificate chain to ensure the integrity and validity of each certificate.
2. Securely obtain the root CA self-signed certificate which is generally preset
   by the manufacturer into the browser or operating system.
3. Verify the root CA certificate in the certificate chain. Since it is a self-signed
   certificate, verify its validity based on the obtained secure root CA certificate.

The digital certificate supports the use of OID to identify the signature algorithm used and the corresponding algorithm public parameters [5]. In the certificate, *subjectPublicKeyInfo* parameter contains the algorithm public parameters corresponding to the signature algorithm. Parameters can be identified by
OIDs (such as the OID of ECDSA-P384 parameters is 1.3.132.0.34). In addition,
parameters can also be displayed in *subjectPublicKeyInfo*.

Elliptic Curve Digital Signature Algorithm (ECDSA). The Elliptic Curve Digital Signature Algorithm (ECDSA) is a kind of digital signature algorithm accepted in 2000 as NIST standards [9].

ECDSA requires that the private/public key pairs used for digital signature generation and verification be generated with respect to a particular set of domain parameters. Domain parameters may be common to a group of users and may be public.

The domain parameters are (q, FR, a, b, G, n, h): q is the field size; FR is an indication of the basis used; a and b are two field elements that define the equation of the curve; G is a base point of prime order on the curve; n is the order of the point G; h is the cofactor. The signer's private key is x, and the public key $P = [x]G$. The signed message is m and the signature is the pair (r, s).

The ECDSA signature generation algorithm is shown as follows:

1. Calculate $e = Hash(m)$.
2. Let z be the leftmost bits of e.
3. Select a random integer k from $[1, n-1]$.
4. Calculate point $(x_1, y_1) = kG$.
5. Calculate $r = x_1 \bmod n$. If $r = 0$, select a new random integer k.
6. Calculate $s = k^{-1}(z + rd_A) \bmod n$. If $s = 0$, select a new random integer k.
7. The signature is the pair (r, s).

The ECDSA signature verification algorithm is shown as follows:

1. The receiver have the public key P, and verify P is valid curve point.
2. Verify that r and s are integers in $[1, n-1]$.
3. Calculate $e = Hash(m)$.
4. Let z be the leftmost bits of e.
5. Calculate $u_1 = zs^{-1} \bmod n$ and $u_2 = rs^{-1} \bmod n$.
6. Calculate the curve point $(x_1, y_1) = u_1 G + u_2 P$.
7. The signature is valid if $r \equiv x_1 \bmod n$.

2.5   Digital Signature in TLS Protocol

TLS (Transport Layer Security) protocol provides privacy and data integrity between two communicating applications [7]. TLS protocol is composed of two layers: The TLS Record Protocol and the TLS Handshake Protocol. The TLS Record Protocol is used for encapsulation of higher-level protocols. The TLS handshake protocol specifies the session negotiation process. The TLS Handshake protocol is shown as Fig. 7:

Hello messages are used to initialize a TLS connection, exchange encryption, hashing, compression algorithms, and random numbers used in subsequent connections, as well as information about the session. After sending *ServerHello* message to the client, the server sends its certificate in *ServerCertificate* message. If the *ServerCertificate* message does not contain enough data to allow the client to exchange a premaster secret such as use DHE and ECDHE as

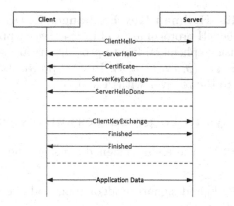

Fig. 7. An overview of TLS handshake.

the key agreement algorithm. The server sends *ServerKeyExchange* message to exchange the parameters. The *ServerKeyExchange* message is signed using the public key in Server Certificate.

When the client receives the messages from the server, the client first verifies the server certificate, then uses the public key to verify the *ServerKeyExchange* message and get the key agreement protocol message.

The client also generates the Key agreement protocol parameters. The parameters are encapsulated in *ClientKeyExchange* message and sent to the server. Then the client and server send *Finished* message and calculate the *premasterkey*.

Diffie-Hellman Key Exchange. Diffie-Hellman key exchange is a method of securely exchanging cryptographic keys over a public channel. DHE used in TLS protocol is a variety of Diffie-Hellman key exchange. To provide forward secrecy, DHE generate new key pairs for each session.

We use Alice and Bob to denote the two parties of communication. The domain parameters are (g, p) that have been agreed upon. The process of DH key exchange is as follows:

1. Alice generates a random a, and calculates $A = g^a \bmod p$.
2. Alice sends A to Bob.
3. Bob generates a random b, and calculates $B = g^b \bmod p$.
4. Bob sends B to Alice.
5. Alice calculates $k = B^a \bmod p$ and Bob calculates $k = A^b \bmod p$, k is the secret key.

In TLS protocol, the domain parameters are sent to the receiver with A and B.

Elliptic-Curve Diffie-Hellman Key Exchange. ECDH key agreement protocol is a variant of the DH protocol using elliptic-curve cryptography. ECDHE is a variant of ECDH using ephemeral key to provide forward secrecy. The domain parameters in ECDH are (p, a, b, G, n, h). In TLS protocol, the ECDH domain parameters are sent to the receiver with A and B.

3   Different Ways to Forge Successfully-Verified Messages

As mentioned in Sect. 2, on receiving a signed message, the receiver processes it as follows:

1. According to the adopted signature algorithm, find the sender's public key (or sometimes certificate);
2. Verify whether the signature matches the message or not, using the public key;
3. Parse the verified message into application-layer instructions.

Provided the signature algorithm is not broken, an adversary does not have attack opportunities in Step 2; that is, when the four inputs (i.e., the algorithm identifier, the public key, the message, and the signature) are correctly determined, the verification outputs correct results always. On the other hand, attacks could be launched in other steps by exploiting the algorithm identifier, the public key, the application-layer format, etc.

Next, we present different ways to forge successfully-verified messages. Firstly, the attackers might modify the algorithm identifier, so that they can generate a valid signature or the receiver does not verify the signature [1,3,4]. Alternative, the attackers might exploit the vulnerable steps of finding public keys, to deceive the receiver to use a manipulated public key [2,17]. Then, the attackers would be able to generate a valid signature corresponding to this public key, and the verification succeeds. Once more, the attackers might remove the signature in the message or delete some parameter in the signature element to mislead the receiver skip signature verification in Step 2 but accept the modified message [18,20]. Finally, the attackers might exploit vulnerabilities of the message parsing process, to inject some message parts which are parsed in Step 3 but not verified in Step 2, or to mislead the receiver to parse the whole message into different application-layer instructions.

3.1   Modified Algorithm Identifiers

As mentioned above, the receiver first finds the public key according to the signature algorithm (Step 1). If the attacker modifies the algorithm identifier, it is possible to mislead the receiver to process the signed message incorrectly, such as performing other cryptographic operations to verify the message, or skip the signature verification process.

In the implementation of some JWT libraries, the attacker can modify the algorithm identifier in the JWT Header to make the victim use the wrong cryptographic algorithm when verifying the JWT, or not to verify the signature.

Because some JWT libraries have vulnerabilities in their implementation, the victims that call these libraries for JWT verification will accept the forged JWT.

The verification API of some JWT libraries is as follows:

$$JWT.decode\ (string\ token, string\ verficationkey)$$

When the receiver calls the vulnerable JWT library to verify the JWT, it uses the *decode* function to decode and verify the JWT. The *token* parameter represents JWT, and the *verificationkey* parameter represents the key required for JWT verification. The verification API does not distinguish between the symmetric key used by MACs and the asymmetric key used by signature algorithms and does not have a parameter used to identity the algorithm corresponding to the key. Therefore, after receiving the *token* and *verificationkey*, the JWT library will parse the *verificationkey* string according to the "*alg*" parameter in JWT header. If the signature algorithm is the RSA algorithm, the JWT library will parse the *verificationkey* string into RSA public key to verify the signature. If the algorithm is the HMAC algorithm, the JWT library will directly use this string as a symmetric key to verify the MAC.

After obtaining the public key of the victim's program, the attacker can modify the algorithm identifier in "*alg*" parameter to make the JWT library incorrectly use the public key passed by the victim program [14], the forged JWT is shown as Fig. 8.

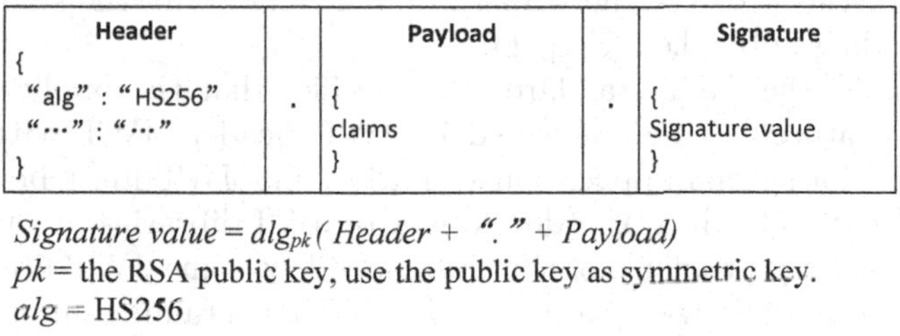

Header		Payload		Signature
{				{
"alg" : "HS256"	.	{	.	
"..." : "..."		claims		Signature value
}		}		}

Signature value = alg$_{pk}$(Header + "." + Payload)
pk = the RSA public key, use the public key as symmetric key.
alg = HS256

Fig. 8. A simplified example of a modified JWT.

In the implementation of *jwt.decode* function in the JWT-simple (version 0.3.0) [1], there is no mandatory use of the "algorithm" parameter. If the victim wishes to receive a JWT with RSA signature, but the attacker uses the RSA public key as the MACs symmetric key to create the MAC and modifies the "*alg*" parameter in JWT Header. Then the attacker sends the JWT with MAC to the victim. After receiving the JWT, the victim will use the RSA public key as the HMAC algorithm symmetric key to verify the JWT and accept the JWT modified by the attacker.

Another example is that the attacker uses the "none" algorithm to make the receiver bypass the signature verification process. JWT specification supports "none" algorithm that is used to sign the token. When using "none" algorithm,

JWT signature must be null and the receiver will not verify the signature when verifying the token. JWT specification points out that the JWS using "none" algorithm is called Unsecured JWS. The "none" algorithm must not be supported by default unless the application specified that it is acceptable for Unsecured JWS. However, some JWT implementations incorrectly supports the use of the "none" algorithm and are vulnerable to attacks.

The attacker intercepts a JWT and modifies the JWT by removing the JWT signature and change the signature algorithm to "none" algorithm. The victim will accept the forged JWT if the "none" algorithm is supported by default. Prime-jwt library (version prior to commit abb0d0479) is vulnerable to this attack [3]. The Xmidt cjwt library (version 1.0.1) processes the JWT signed with an unsupported algorithm as JWT using "none" algorithm [4]. For this vulnerability, the attacker can forge the JWT by changing the algorithm to an unsupported algorithm. In this case, the forged JWT can be accepted even if the "none" algorithm is disabled.

3.2   Fake or Manipulated Public Keys

The security of digital signature algorithms depends on the security of the private key. If the attacker obtains the private key, the attacker can forge any message. It is difficult to obtain the private key directly, but the attacker can forge or manipulate the public key used by the victim and use the private key corresponding to the fake public key to sign the message. This type of attack misleads the receiver to use the wrong public key to verify the signature in the process of finding public key (Step 1).

For example, the JWT standard [13] specifies that the public key used to verify the signature can be embedded in JWT Header. JWT with embedded key is suitable for special application scenarios, and JWT must be transmitted in a trusted channel. Since the developers of JWT libraries are not aware of the possible security problems of the embedded key, some JWT libraries do not restrict the use of the "jwk" parameter. If a JWT containing an embedded key is received, the JWT libraries trust the embedded key by default and use it to verify the JWT. The attacker modifies with the intercepted JWT, generates a new key pair, stores the public key in the "jwk" parameter in the JWT header, and then uses the private key to generate the signature. For the vulnerable JWT libraries, after receiving the modified JWT, it uses the embedded key to verify the JWT, and then it will accept the JWT modified by the attacker. This attack can be implemented in Cisco node-jose library (version before 0.11.0) [2].

In Windows operating system (Windows 10 version 1607/1709/1803/1903, Windows server 2016, Windows server 2019), there is an elliptic curve cryptographic digital certificate validation vulnerability [17]. The attacker can use this vulnerability to manipulate the public key used to verify the certificate and forge digital certificates.

A list of trusted root CA certificates is saved in the Windows operating system. When verifying the certificate chain, it first verifies the CA signature of all levels of certificates is correct, and then compare the root CA certificate with the certificates in the list of trusted root CA. If the root CA certificate is included in the list, then the certificate chain is considered to be trusted. The vulnerability appears in the comparison process between the root CA certificate and the corresponding certificate in the trusted certificate list. The Windows operating system judges whether the certificate is trusted by comparing the information in the certificate. When verifying the parameters related to the public key, only the public key is verified and the domain parameters are not verified, even if the domain parameters are present in the certificate. The attacker chooses a trusted root CA certificate whose the public key is p and the base point is G. After that the attacker chooses a random x, and calculates $p = [x]G'$. Then the attacker forges a self-signed root CA certificate that has the same public key p and different base point G'.

The Windows operating system considers the fake self-signed CA certificate as the trusted root CA certificate. In addition, another main factor for the success of the attack is that when verifying the CA digital signature, the Windows operating system uses the public key and the parameters in the self-signed root CA certificate to verify the signature. At this time, the public key is P, the base point is G', and the attacker holds the private key x, so the attacker can use the private key to sign any certificate, which is considered by the operating system to be issued by a trusted root CA Certificate.

3.3 Unverified-but-Accepted Messages

This kind of attack is launched based on modified messages. The attacker removes the signature value or deletes some parameter in the signature element, and then sends the forged message or file to the victim. This attack targets the second step (Step 2) of signed message processing. The attacker realizes the attack by manipulating inputs in the signature verification process.

If the signature value is removed or the signature element is modified, the verifier cannot obtain the correct inputs (signature and signed message) during the signature verification process. In implement of a semantically-secure signature algorithm, exception or error is thrown when verifying the signature of a modified message without signature value or signature element. However, due to the vulnerability in the implementation of signature verification, the modified message is accepted as the correct verified message. This kind of vulnerabilities appears in many applications and libraries. PDF signature and XML signature can be attacked in this way.

Attack XML Signature in SAML. Signature Exclusion Attack [20] relies on the logical vulnerability in the implementation of XML signature verification in SAML frameworks. It is simple to implement Signature Exclusion Attack. The attacker only needs to remove the signature element in the signed SAML assertion message. Some SAML frameworks with logic vulnerabilities will incorrectly accept modified signature messages. In JOSSO and the Java-based Eduserv framework (version before 2012), if the signature exists in the SAML assertion they will validate it. However, if the attacker removes the signature, both of them skip the validation step and accept the message without throwing any exception.

Attack PDF Signature. Universal Signature Forgery [18] against PDF signatures is a variant of Signature Exclusion Attack. Attackers' goal is to modify the PDF file while the PDF viewers still show the signature is correctly verified. Directly removed the references to the signature in PDF file cannot successfully implement the attack. Therefore, the attacker chooses to make the PDF viewers skip the signature verification by modifying the information in the signature element. The */ByteRange* entry which defines the signed content in the file. The attacker modifies the PDF file arbitrarily by removing the */ByteRange* entry or replacing its value to null. When the victim PDF viewer verify the signature, the viewer cannot access the signed message through */ByteRange* entry. In this case, the vulnerable PDF viewer default signature verification process has been completed without throwing an exception, and accepts and displays the modified PDF file. Adobe Acrobat Reader DC (version 2018.011), Adobe Reader XI (version 11.0.10) and PDF Editor 6 Pro (version 6.4.2/6.6.2) are vulnerable to this attack.

3.4   Parsed-but-not-Verified Message Parts

After receiving the signed message, the receiver verifies the signature (Step 2) and parsed the verified message into the application-layer instructions (Step 3). The signature verification process (Step 2) and the message parsing process (Step 3) are usually two separate modules. In some complex signature format messages such as signed PDF files and signed SAML assertions, the data processed by the signature verification module and the message processing module may be different. Due to the vulnerability in some implementation of the signature verification module, some parts of the message are parsed but not verified. Thus, the attacker can use the modified message to bypass the signature verification process to achieve the attack. Compared with above attacks, the signature has been correctly verified by the receiver in this attack.

XML Signature Wrapping (XSW) attack is first proposed by McIntosh and Austel in 2005 [16]. It described the process that the attacker inserting a malicious object into an XML signature document to attack the XML document. In the following research, variants of XSW attacks were used in various software attacks.

Signature Bypass in SAML. SAML standard supports complex SAML assertion formats and structures. The XML signature specified in the SAML standard is also complex. Therefore, the attacker can combine different SAML assertion structures and XML signature structures to forge SAML assertion messages such as inject malicious assertions in front of the original assertion or embed the original assertion in the malicious assertion. This kind of attack is called Refined

Signature Wrapping [20]. Because of the ID-based reference used in signature creation and validation, even if the position of the assertion changes, the original assertion can still be found and verified according to the ID in reference element in some SAML libraries. In this case, the modified message with injected evil assertion can still be successfully verified. The signature verification processing does not process the evil assertion. However, when parsing SAML assertions into the application-layer instructions, the message will be processed according to application logic. The malicious assertion inserted by the attacker is processed and accepted by the receiver. Attacker attacks SAML Framework or Providers by constructing different malicious messages. Many of them have the above vulnerabilities, such as IBM XS40, Higgins (version 1.x) which support Type1 SAML messages, and Guanxi, JOSSO which support Type2 SAML messages.

Signature Bypass in PDF. There are also vulnerabilities in PDF signature that allow the attacker to perform Signature Wrapping Attacks [18]. When creating a PDF signature, the content in /*Contents* entry will not be signed. The attacker can inject malicious content into /*Contents* entry to implement the attack. A mount of PDF viewers can be attacked in this way such as eXpert PDF 12 Ultimate (version12.0.20), Expert PDF Reader (version 9.0.180), Foxit Reader (version 9.1.0/9.2.0), etc [18]. By forging /*ByteRange* entry, the attacker control signature verification processing use the original data for signature verification. And by forging *Xref Table*, the content parsing processing can index the malicious objects injected by the attacker. The content processed by signature verification process and message parsing process are different. The malicious content injected by the attacker are accepted and displayed.

Such attacks can also be achieved by taking advantage of the incremental update feature of PDF files. The attacker uses incremental update to add new malicious content in the signed PDF file [18]. The /*ByteRange* entry in the PDF signature file does not change. Therefore, the victim PDF viewer verifies the original PDF file when verifying the signature, and processes all contents in the file including malicious contents injected by the attacker. Since the security issues brought by incremental updates have been realized by many PDF viewer developers, the attacker has to bypass the defense mechanisms of PDF viewers through some variants based on the attack. For example, by deleting the *Xref table* and *Trailer* in the incremental update content or adding the signature content to the new body, the PDF viewers are misled that the signed PDF file does not contain new incremental updating parts. When the PDF viewer processes the verified PDF file, it will think that the PDF file has no additional content, and use the original content for verification. However, due to the error-tolerant of the PDF viewer, when processing the contents of the PDF file, the PDF viewer will complete the missing structure in different ways and display the modified file without showing a warning. Attacker use this method attack Foxit Reader (version 9.1.0/9.2.0), PDF Editor 6 Pro (version 6.4.2/6.6.2), etc [18].

3.5   Misleading Message Parsing

Cross-protocol attacks [15,21] mislead the victims in the parse of signed messages after the successful verification. The verified message is generated and correctly signed by the signer in a specific context, and not modified by the attacker; however, it is sent in another context so that this message is parsed into different instructions. That is, for example, if a correctly-signed timestamp could be parsed as signed PDF documents, the innocent timestamp signing server would be exploited to sign malicious documents.

In the key exchange of TLS, the TLS server and client may choose DH or ECDH to finish the key negotiation. After negotiating the method of key exchange through unprotected messages with a client, the TLS server sends a signed DH or ECDH key exchange message along with its X.509 certificate. The client verifies the received certificate and the signed message, and sends its own key exchange message. Then, the server computes the session keys based on the received key exchange message and its own ephemeral private key, so does the client. These symmetric session keys are used for confidentiality and integrity of subsequent messages.

The cross-protocol attacker [15] impersonates the TLS server, by replaying a signed ECDH key exchange message as a DH one to the victim client. The attacker acts as a client to establishes TLS sessions with the impersonated TLS server by ECDH key exchange, while as a TLS server to establishes TLS sessions with the victim client by DH key exchange. Note that the ECDH key exchange message is replayed without any modification, so the verification by the victim client succeeds. As analyzed in [15], when secp384r1 is used and Explicit prime curve is supported, the probability is about $1.9 \cdot 10^{-8}$–$2.0 \cdot 10^{-8}$ that parsed as a valid DH key exchange message. Further, the probability is about 2^{-40} that it is valid and the ephemeral DH private key can be solved by the attacker easily.

4   The Lessons Learned from Known Attacks

We summarize the lessons learned from the above attacks as follows. These lessons provide some guidelines for the secure implementation of cryptographic protocols.

Modified Algorithm Identifiers. Either public-key cryptosystems or symmetric cryptosystems are adopted to provide data integrity and data origin authentication. When both digital signature algorithms and HMAC algorithms are supported in the implementation, the system must carefully configure the corresponding public and symmetric keys. Then, after recognizing the algorithm identifier, it finds the public key or the symmetric key correctly, to prevent the use of public keys as secret ones to verify HMACs.

In addition, when implementing cryptographic protocols in the real-world systems, we must support only semantically-secure algorithms. Insecure algorithms such as MD5 and RSA-512, shall be abandoned.

Fake or Manipulated Public Keys. Before verifying signed messages, the receivers need to find the correct public key. The public key shall come from some trusted storage of the system, or if the public key is obtained through insecure channels, typically as an X.509 certificate, it must be checked before used to verify signed messages.

Public parameters of the digital signature algorithm, shall be considered as parts of the public key; for example, the domain parameters of ECDSA and the prime modulus of Diffie-Hellman key exchange. However, such parameters may be neglected in the checking of public keys for some reasons. The neglecting of checking such public parameters may result in fake public keys.

Unverified-but-Accepted Messages. In the implementation of cryptographic protocols, the verification of signed messages is necessary but not an optional step. If multiple signatures are included, all signatures must be verified.

When signatures are absent in the messages, the verification shall fail explicitly. Unsigned messages are usually accepted for debugging and testing, but when the software is released, such messages must be rejected directly.

Parsed-but-not-Verified Message Parts. This vulnerability exists especially for messages with complex formats. In general, in order to ensure fault tolerance, the system is usually designed and implemented to parses not-well-formed messages, and some exceptions and errors are ignored in the message parsing process. However, this feature of fault tolerance is exploited to inject evil contents into a signed message, so that the verification succeeds because the inputs of the verification are correct (i.e., the injected parts are not input to the verification) but the injected evil contents are still parsed.

Therefore, when the system is processing a message requiring data integrity and data origin authentication, we suggest an additional step of strict format checking to detect such attacks. This additional step harms the fault tolerance of message parsing but improves the security of data integrity.

Misleading Message Parsing. In order to prevent the cross-protocol attackers from misleading the message parsing, the message type needs to be included in the signed message, to properly instruct the message parsing. There is no such a message type identifier in the key exchange messages of TLS. On the other hand, for example, JWT best current practices [19] recommend to explicitly include the "typ" parameter in a JWT, to eliminate the cross-JWT confusion.

5   Conclusions

Signed messages are widely used in network security. However, the real-world systems, even when the sender's private key is protected well, a message forged or modified by some attackers, might be still successfully verified by receivers. This paper surveys the implementation vulnerabilities in the verification of signed message, attempting to provide some guidelines for the secure implementation of cryptographic protocols.

References

1. Common vulnerabilities and exposures (cve): cve-2016-10555. https://cve.mitre. org/cgi-bin/cvename.cgi?name=CVE-2016-10555 (2016)
2. Common vulnerabilities and exposures (cve): cve-2018-0114. https://cve.mitre. org/cgi-bin/cvename.cgi?name=CVE-2018-0114 (2018)
3. Common vulnerabilities and exposures (cve): cve-2018-1000531. https://cve.mitre. org/cgi-bin/cvename.cgi?name=CVE-2018-1000531 (2018)
4. Common vulnerabilities and exposures (cve): cve-2019-19324. https://cve.mitre. org/cgi-bin/cvename.cgi?name=CVE-2019-19324 (2019)
5. Bassham, L., Polk, W.T., Housley, R.: Algorithms and identifiers for the internet X.509 public key infrastructure certificate and certificate revocation list (CRL) profile. RFC 3279, pp. 1–27 (2002)
6. Cantor, S., Moreh, J., Philpott, R., Maler, E.: Metadata for the oasis security assertion markup language (SAML) v2. 0 (2005)
7. Dierks, T., Rescorla, E.: The transport layer security (TLS) protocol version 1.2. RFC 5246, pp. 1–104 (2008)
8. Eastlake, D., Reagle, J., Solo, D., Hirsch, F., Roessler, T.: Xml-signature syntax and processing. In: W3C Recommendation, p. 12 (2002)
9. Gallagher, P.: Digital Signature Standard (DSS), vol. FIPS 186. Federal Information Processing Standards Publications (2013)
10. Adobe Systems Incorporated: Pdf reference: Version, vol. 1, p. 7 (2006)
11. Jones, M.B.: JSON web algorithms (JWA). RFC **7518**, 1–69 (2015)
12. Jones, M.B., Bradley, J., Sakimura, N.: JSON web signature (JWS). RFC **7515**, 1–59 (2015)
13. Jones, M.B., Bradley, J., Sakimura, N.: JSON web token (JWT). RFC **7519**, 1–30 (2015)
14. Maclean, T.: Critical vulnerabilities in JSON web token libraries. https://auth0. com/blog/critical-vulnerabilities-in-json-web-token-libraries/ (2015)
15. Mavrogiannopoulos, N., Vercauteren, F., Velichkov, V., Preneel, B.: A cross-protocol attack on the TLS protocol. In: The ACM Conference on Computer and Communications Security, pp. 62–72 (2012)
16. Mcintosh, M., Austel, P.: Xml signature element wrapping attacks and counter-measures. In: ACM Workshop on Secure Web Services (2005)
17. Microsoft: Cve-2020-0601—windows cryptoapi spoofing vulnerability. https:// portal.msrc.microsoft.com/en-US/security-guidance/advisory/CVE-2020-0601 (2020)
18. Mladenov, V., Mainka, C., Zu Selhausen, K.M., Grothe, M., Schwenk, J.: 1 trillion dollar refund: how to spoof PDF signatures. In: Proceedings of the 2019 ACM SIGSAC Conference on Computer and Communications Security, pp. 1–14 (2019)
19. Sheffer, Y., Hardt, D., Jones, M.B.: JSON web token best current practices. RFC **8725**, 1–13 (2020)
20. Somorovsky, J., Mayer, A., Schwenk, J., Kampmann, M., Jensen, M.: On breaking SAML: be whoever you want to be. In: Proceedings of the 21th USENIX Security Symposium, pp. 397–412 (2012)
21. Wagner, D., Schneier, B.: Analysis of the SSL 3.0 protocol (1999)

Applications and Developments of the Lattice Attack in Side Channel Attacks

Ziqiang Ma[1,3], Bingyu Li[2,3], Quanwei Cai[3(✉)], and Jun Yang[1]

[1] School of Information Engineering, Ningxia University, Yinchuan, China
{maziqiang,Dragon}@nxu.edu.cn
[2] School of Cyber Science and Technology, Beihang University, Beijing, China
libingyu@buaa.edu.cn
[3] State Key Laboratory of Information Security, Institute of Information Engineering, Chinese Academy of Sciences, Beijing, China
caiquanwei@iie.ac.cn

Abstract. Partial key exposure attacks have become a growing threat to the cryptographic system, as the side channel attacks can usually obtain the partial information easily, which makes the partial key exposure attacks much more practical. The lattice attack is the most common method to process the partial key information to recover the secret key. In this paper, we systematically analyse the developments of the lattice attacks and its use in side channel attacks. First, we divide the lattice attack into three categories based on the lattice construction. Then we investigate the lattice attacks on each algorithms and the way different side channel data is processed by. Finally, we summary the development trend of the lattice attack in side channel attacks.

Keywords: Lattice attack · Side channel attack · HNP · EHNP · Cryptographic algorithm · (EC)DSA · RSA

1 Introduction

The security of the cryptosystem relies on the security of the secret key. While the security of the secret key does not only relies on the computational complexity of the algorithm itself, i.e. the secret key cannot be retrieved through analysing the plaintext and the ciphertext with the algorithm. Also it needs to guarantee the secret key not being leaked from the system through any methods during the cryptographic computation. However, in real-world applications, the cryptosystem faces a variety of attacks so that the secret key is easy to leak, such as the hardware vulnerability attack [41,44], the software memory leak attack [37] and the side channel attack [36,45,70,71] and so on.

This work was supported by the Open Subject of the State Key Laboratory of Information Security, Institute of Information Engineering, Chinese Academy of Sciences (No. 2020-MS-08 and No. 2020-ZD-05).

J. Zhou et al. (Eds.): ACNS 2020 Workshops, LNCS 12418, pp. 435–452, 2020.
https://doi.org/10.1007/978-3-030-61638-0_24

Among lots of attack threats, side channel attacks take advantage of the various information leaked during the cryptographic computing to recover the secret key. The leaked information are obtained through the side channels such as timing [1,2,13,21], cache activities [1,71], electromagnetic fields [32], power [14, 57], ground electric potential [34] and acoustic emanations [35], etc. Compared with attacks by exploiting hardware or software vulnerabilities, side channel attacks can be launched even no software and hardware vulnerabilities exist in the target system. Moreover, the side channel information is generated along with the operation of the cryptosystem, which is difficult to eliminate. So the side channel attack is a serious and long-term threat to the cryptosystem.

From the side channels, the attacker only can obtain partial information about the key for most algorithm implementations [67]. Then the attacker requires to obtain a large amount of the partial information, consolidates and processes them to recover the whole secret key. This approach exploiting the partial information to recover the whole secret key is called the partial key exposure attack.

In 1998, Boneh presented several partial key exposure attacks on RSA in [19], requiring the knowledge of the least significant bits (LSBs) of the private exponent or the most significant bits (MSBs). they used Coppersmith's ideas [25] to exploit the data to recover the private key. After that, many improvements [16,18,30] are made to better use the partial information and reduce the constraints to recover the RSA private key. In 1996, Boneh and Venkatesan [20] proposed this type of attack on the Diffie-Hellman key exchange. They used the lattice attack to recover the secret key. Then the attack is extended to the DSA [53] and ECDSA [54]. Moreover, the partial information are not limited to LSB or MSB. More type of partial information from the side channels can be used to recover the DSA and ECDSA private keys, such as the position of the non-zero bits [31], length of the obtained chain [67], etc. Also the partial data processing methods are becoming more efficient.

With the continuous development and progress of the partial key exposure attacks, and their widely application to various cryptographic algorithms, the lattice attack technique has become the most effective method to recover the private key with the partial information. The lattice attack uses the partial key information and combines with the algorithm itself to construct a problem that can be solved by the lattice reduction algorithm, and then recovers the private key of the algorithm by solving the problem. The Hidden Number Problem [20] is a typical problem solved by the lattice reduction algorithm. This problem is used to attack various algorithms such as DSA [39], ECDSA [12,23] with different partial information. Another way is the Extended Hidden Number Problem which is a variant of the HNP problem. The EHNP problem [38] is proposed in 2007 and is used to construct more efficient lattice attacks [31]. Also, there are some other ways that do not used the HNP or EHNP problem. They directly use the obtained side channel information to construct the lattice and recover the private key with the lattice reduction algorithm.

Up to now, there is a little number of summary of lattice attack. In 2018, Anjali kumari [42] summarized the lattice attack methods of the DSA algorithm. Lu [48] summarized the progress of the Coppersmith's lattice-based method. However, no survey researches are focused on the lattice attack exploited in side channel attacks.

In this paper, we focus on the application and development of the lattice attack in side channel attacks. We study how the lattice attack method uses the side channel information to recover the complete algorithm private key, and the development of the lattice attack technology in processing the side channel information, so as to explore the future development and application direction of the lattice attacks.

First, we show the technological developments of the lattice attack over last 20 years. We illustrate the development of each case by dividing the lattice attack into three categories based on the construction methods of the lattice. Second, we investigate different lattice attacks on different algorithms. Because different algorithms have different structures, different lattices are constructed for recovering the private key. We demonstrate the improvement of the existing lattice construction method for different algorithms. Third, we study how to use the lattice attacks to process the obtained information from different side channels. Different forms of information need different methods to process, so attackers need to choose appropriate lattice attacks for different side channels. Finally, through analyzing the existing lattice attack technologies, we summarize its future development direction.

In summary, the main contributions of this paper are as follows:

- For the first time, we summarize and analyze the current developments of the lattice attack technology from three aspects: lattice attack technology itself, lattice attacks on different algorithms and lattice attacks for different side channels.
- We analyze the future directions of the lattice attack in side channel attacks.

The rest of this paper is organized as follows. Section 2 presents the preliminaries. Section 3 shows the development of the lattice attack technology itself. Section 4 provides lattice attacks on different algorithms. Section 5 shows lattice attacks for different side channels. Section 6 analyzes the future directions of the lattice attack. And, Sect. 7 draws the conclusion.

2   Preliminaries

In this section, we first present several cryptographic algorithms whose private key can be recovered using the lattice attacks with partial information, such as RSA, DSA and ECDSA. And then we introduce several effective side channel attacks obtaining the information about the private keys, including timing attack, cache attack, fault attack, power and electronic attacks.

2.1 Cryptographic Algorithms

In this section, we introduce the algorithms whose private key cannot be directly recovered from side channel information and need the lattice attacks.

RSA. The RSA public key cryptosystem can be briefly described as follows:

- large primes p, q, (generally considered of same bit size, i.e., $q < p < 2q$);
- let $N = pq$, $\phi(N) = (p-1)(q-1)$;
- e, d satisfy that $ed = 1 \bmod \phi(N)$;
- N, e are public keys and the plaintext $M \in \mathbb{Z}_N$ is encrypted as $C \equiv M^e$ (mod N);
- d is the private key and used to decrypt the ciphertext $C \in \mathbb{Z}_N$ as $M \equiv C^d$ (mod N).

The partial key exposure attack is to compute the private key d from partial information on d, and the public key (e, N).

DSA. DSA [52] is a digital signature algorithm standard published by American National Institute of Standards and Technology (NIST). DSA uses the multiplicative group in finite fields, and is described as follows: there exists large primes p and q satisfy that $q|p-1$. The multiplicative group on the finite field $\mathbb{F}_p$ has a generator g which order is q. The private key α of DSA is a random number satisfying $0 < \alpha < q$, while the corresponding public key is $y = g^\alpha \bmod p$. Given a hash function h, the DSA signature of a message m is computed as follows:

1. Select a random ephemeral key $0 < k < q$.
2. Compute $r = (g^k \bmod p) \bmod q$; if $r = 0$, then go back to the first step.
3. Compute $s = k^{-1}(h(m) + r \cdot \alpha) \bmod q$; if $s = 0$, then go back to the first step.

The pair (r, s) is the DSA signature of the message m. The modular exponentiation is the target of the attackers because it is vulnerable to the side channel attacks.

ECDSA. ECDSA [7,40] is the migration of the Digital Signature Algorithm (DSA) [52] from the multiplicative group of a finite field to the group of points on an elliptic curve.

Let E be an elliptic curve defined over a finite field $\mathbb{F}_p$ where p is prime. $G \in E$ is a fixed point of a large prime order q, that is G is the generator of the group of points of order q. These curve and point parameters are publicly known. The private key of ECDSA is an integer α that satisfies $0 < \alpha < q$, and the public key is the point $Q = \alpha G$. Given a hash function h, the ECDSA signature of a message m is computed as follows:

1. Select a random ephemeral key $0 < k < q$.

2. Compute the point $(x, y) = kG$, and let $r = x \bmod q$; if $r = 0$, then go back to the first step.
3. Compute $s = k^{-1}(h(m) + r \cdot \alpha) \bmod q$; if $s = 0$, then go back to the first step.

The pair (r, s) is the ECDSA signature of the message m. The scalar multiplication kG becomes the target of most attackers. The equation in the third step shows the private key can be computed if k is leaked. Even if only a portion of k is leaked, the private key can be recovered by lattice attacks.

2.2 Lattice

To solve the HNP problem, we need to use the knowledge of the lattice. Here we provide a briefly introduce to the lattice. For more detailed references on lattice we refer to the literature [55]. Consider the Euclidean space $\mathbb{R}^d$ and let $B = \{b_1, b_2, ..., b_r\}$ be a set of linearly independent vectors in $\mathbb{R}^d$. The set of vectors

$$L = L(B) = \{\sum_{i=1}^{r} n_i b_i \mid n_i \in \mathbb{Z}\}$$

is the **lattice** generated by B. The set B is called a basis of L, and L is spanned by B. The number r representing the number of vectors in B is the dimension or rank of $L(B)$. If $r = d$, the lattice $L(B)$ is a full-dimension lattice.

Hard Lattice Problems. Since the lattice is a set of vectors, it has a shortest non-zero vector, and the norm this vector is known as the first minima and denoted by $\lambda_1(L)$. That is, $\lambda_1(L) = \min\{\|u\| \mid 0 \neq u \in L\}$, where $\|u\|$ denotes the Euclidean norm of the vector u. The problem of finding a non-zero vector $v \in L$ with minimal norm is called the shortest vector problem (SVP). While for a lattice L and an arbitrary vector $v \in \mathbb{R}^d$, the problem of finding a lattice vector $u \in L$ of minimum distance from v is called the closest vector problem (CVP) similarly. In other words, finding a vector u satisfied $\|u\| = \min\{\|u - v\| \mid u \in L\}$.

2.3 Side Channel Attacks

Side channel attacks can exploit any information leaked during the cryptographic calculation, including timing [1,2,21,66], cache activities [1,71], electromagnetic fields [32], power [14,57] and so on. We briefly introduce the common used side channels to obtain the partial information about the private keys.

Power Attacks and Electromagnetic Attack. Side-channel power attacks have been extensively studied since their presentation by Kocher et al. Several techniques have been proposed to extract secret material analyzing the power consumption trace of a cryptographic device.

Simple power analysis (SPA) is one of them. SPA attacks exploit the existence of distinguishable power consumption patterns that reveal the sequence of operations or data processed by the target algorithm. Differential power analysis (DPA) is a statistical method to analyze the power consumption to identify data-dependent correlations. This approach takes multiple traces of two sets of data, then computes the difference of the average of these traces. Given enough traces, even tiny correlations can be seen, regardless of how much noise is in the system, since the noise will effectively cancel out during the averaging.

The electromagnetic attack is a closely related to the power attack, where the measured quantity is replaced with the time-resolved intensity of electromagnetic emission [32]. The electromagnetic attack measurements have to be performed close to the surface of the chip, and require significantly more effort, as compared to power analysis measurements.

Cache Attacks. Cache side-channel attacks, firstly proposed in 2002 [58], take advantage of the characteristic of the cache activity that accessing data from caches is much faster than from memory. Attackers exploit these time variations to deduce the operations of the target process and then infer the key information. Typical cache attacks contains the Evict+Time, Flush+Reload, Prime+Probe, Flush+Flush and Prime+Abort etc.

We use Flush+Flush [36] as an example. The Flush+Flush employs a spy process to monitor whether the specific memory lines have been accessed or not by the victim process. So this attack needs shared memory between the spy and the victim processes. It relies on the execution time of the `clflush` instruction, which is affected by whether the to-be-flushed data are cached or not. The execution time of `clflush` is shorter if the data are not cached and longer if the data are cached. So according to this time, the attackers determine the victim's cache activities. The execution of such an attack consists of three phases:

- **Flush:** The attacker uses the `clflush` instruction to flush the desired memory lines out from the caches.
- **Wait:** The attacker waits a moment while the victim is running.
- **Flush:** This phase detects whether the victim accesses the memory lines flushed in the first phase during the waiting time.

Fault Attacks. Fault injection attack was first introduced in 1997 by Boneh, Demillo and Lipton [17]. This type of attack is a serious threat for implementing cryptographic algorithms in practice.

Some of the most popular fault injection techniques include variations in supply voltage, clock frequency, temperature or the use of white light, X-ray and ion beams. The objectives of all these techniques is generally the same: corrupt the chip's behaviour.

To attack the cryptographic algorithms, the attacker induces some bytes error on the private key using the fault injection techniques and measure the output difference from the correct case when executing the algorithms. Then the attacker obtains some bits information about the private key through the measured difference. Finally, the attacker can use the partial key exposure technique to recover the whole private key.

Timing Attacks. The timing attack is the most common side channel attack with a long history. But it is rarely used to obtain the partial key information. Often the timing attack is launched in the remote scenario, because other types of side channel are hard to exploit.

The remote timing attack measures the total execution time of the algorithm. By the difference of the execution time, the attackers can extract some bits information of the private key. Then using the partial key exposure attack to recover the whole private key.

3   The Improvements of the Lattice Attacks

In this section, we introduce the lattice attack technology and its developments in detail. We first give the definition of the lattice attack and its attack steps. Then we divide the lattice attacks into several types, according to the way of constructing the lattice and the solving methods. For each type of lattice attacks, we fully analyse its technological development for the past years.

3.1   The Lattice Attack

The lattice attack is first proposed by Dan Boneh [20] in 1996 to attack the Diffie-Hellman Schemes with the most significant bits of the secret key known. Then the idea of using lattice to recover the private key is extended to many algorithms such as RSA, DSA, ECDSA and even the lattice-based ciphers. Broadly speaking, the lattice attack refers to the method of using lattice related theory to attack cryptographic algorithms. In this paper, the lattice attack specially refers to the method of using partial key information to recover the complete key by the lattice reduction algorithm. That is to say, we do not consider the lattice attacks on the NTRU and other lattice-based ciphers.

Generally, the lattice attack on the partial key information contains three steps. The first step is the problem transformation. In this step, the attacker analyzes the calculation formula of the encryption or signature and exploits the known partial information of the private key to transform the private key recovery problem into a problem that can be solved by a lattice reduction algorithm such as the HNP and EHNP problem. The second step is constructing the corresponding lattice. This step constructs the lattice with the partial key information and transforms the problem in the first step into the hard problems in the lattice such as CVP and SVP. The last step is to find the approximate solutions to the lattice hard problems. In this step the lattice reduction algorithm is used to solve the lattice hard problems. Then the private key is included in the result. Sometimes, the first and the second step are combined, that is directly using the partial key information to construct the lattice and the lattice hard problems.

Based on the type of the problem solving by the lattice reduction algorithm, we can divide the lattice attack into three categories: the HNP problem, the EHNP problem and other problems. Next we will elaborate the technology development on each type of lattice attacks.

3.2 HNP

The Hidden Number Problem (HNP) is first presented by Boneh and Venkatesan [20] in 1996. It is used to recover the secret key of Diffie-Hellman key exchange [20], DSA [39] and ECDSA [54], given some leaked consecutive bits of the ephemeral key. Given a prime number q and a positive l, and let $t_1, t_2, ..., t_d$ be randomly chosen, which are uniform and independent in $\mathbb{F}_q$. The HNP can be stated as follows: recovering an unknown number $\alpha \in \mathbb{F}_q$ such that the known number pairs (t_i, u_i) satisfy

$$v_i = |\alpha t_i - u_i|_q \le q/2^{l+1}, \quad 1 \le i \le d,$$

where $|\cdot|_q$ denotes the reduction modulo q into range $[-q/2, ..., q/2)$. If $|\alpha t - u|_q \le q/2^{l+1}$ is satisfied, the integer u represents the l most significant bits of αt which is defined as $MSB_l(\alpha t)$.

The HNP problem can be solved by the lattice basis reduction algorithm. The LLL [43] or BKZ [64] algorithm is used to solve the SVP problem, while Babai [10] algorithm or Enumeration technique is to solve the CVP problem.

Boneh and Venkatesan [20] initially investigated to use the partial information of the ephemeral key to construct an HNP problem and recovered the Diffie-Hellman private key by solving it using the lattice reduction algorithm. Howgrave-Graham and Smart [39] extended this work to recover the DSA private key by constructing an HNP instance from leaked LSBs and MSBs of the ephemeral key. Their attack is a heuristic approach to verify the availability of the partial key exposure attacks on DSA. Then Nguyen and Shparlinski [53] gave the rigorous theoretical proof that knowing the $l \ge 3$ LSBs, the $l + 1$ MSBs or any $2l$ consecutive bits of a certain number of ephemeral keys, was enough for recovering the DSA private key with the HNP problem. Further, they extended these results to ECDSA [54]. In 2013, Liu and Nguyen [47] provided a probabilistic attack based on enumeration techniques, where managed to find the secret key if they know 2 bits of 100 ephemeral keys. In 2019, more precisely in the work [3], the authors improve the upper bound under which it has at most one solution of the attack [60] by constructing the HNP problem. keys for 206 signatures is known.

The attack provided in [47] first reduces the problem of finding the secret key, to the hidden number problem (HNP) and then reduces HNP to a variant of CVP (called Bounded Decoded Distance problem : BDD).

3.3 EHNP

The Extended Hidden Number Problem (EHNP) introduced in [38] is a variant of the HNP and is stated as follows, which also can be used to recover the ECDSA private key [27,31]. Let N be a prime number. Given u congruences

$$\beta_i x + \sum_{j=1}^{l_i} a_{i,j} k_{i,j} \equiv c_i \mod N, \quad 1 \le i \le u,$$

where $k_{i,j}$ and x are unknown variables satisfying $0 \leq k_{i,j} \leq 2^{\varepsilon_{i,j}}$ and $0 < x < N, \beta_i, a_{i,j}, c_i, l_i$ and $\varepsilon_{i,j}$ are all known. The EHNP is to find the unknown x satisfying the conditions above. Similarly to the HNP, the EHNP can be transformed into a lattice problem and one can recover the secret x by solving a short vector problem in a given lattice.

EHNP mostly differs from HNP by the nature of the information given as input. Indeed, the information required to construct an instance of EHNP is not sequences of consecutive bits, but the positions of the non-zero coefficients in any representation of some integers. The authors in [38] first use the EHNP problem to recover the DSA private key. Then in 2016, Fan et al. [31] attacked the ECDSA and transformed the problem of recovering the secret key to the extended hidden number problem (EHNP) which was latter solved by the lattice reduction algorithm. In 2019, De Micheli [27] analyzed the construction of the lattice and optimized Fan's work to use less signatures to recover the ECDSA private key.

3.4   Others

RSA is different from the DSA because its security relies on the complex problem of large number factoring. Also their computational process are totally different. Therefore, the lattice construction to launch the partial key exposure attack of the RSA is different from that of DSA.

In 1996, Coppersmith [25] describes rigorous techniques to find small integer roots of polynomials in a single variable modulo n. This result can help the attacker with the knowledge of partial information of a secret to recover the remaining part by modeling as a univariate modular equation.

In 1998, Boneh, Durfee and Frankel studied how many bits of d need to be known to factor the RSA modulus N. The constraint was the upper bound on e, that had been $\sqrt{N}$. In 2000, Boneh and Durfee [18] improved Wiener's attack [68] and proposed the lattice based attack for the RSA cryptography.

In 2003, the idea of [19] has been improved by Blömer and May [16] where the bound on e was increased upto $N^{0.725}$. In 2005, Ernst et al. [30] use Coppersmith's technique and improved the results on known MSBs of d for small private exponent d and full size public exponent e. In 2008, Sarkar and Maitra [62] extended the work of [30] by guessing few bits of one prime. In 2010, Santanu Sarkar [63], proposed a variant of the idea presented in [30] to make the results more practical when some portion of Most Significant Bits (MSBs) of d are exposed and $d < N^{0.6875}$.

Later researches pay more attention on the vulnerabilities during the actual execution of RSA, in order to obtain the partial information and then based on the obtained information to construct appropriate lattice problem.

While, the Coppersmith's method also can be used to recover the ECDSA private key. BLAKE et al. [15] in 2002 present a key-recovery attack against the DSA based on the Coppersmith's method. While Draziotis et al. [29] in 2016 also investigate the Coppersmith's method to recover the ECDSA private key.

In addition, some works proposed lattice attacks with special methods. In 2003, Draziotis and Poulakis [28] exploited Lagrange's algorithm for the computation of a basis of a 2-dimensional lattice formed by two successive minima, to attack DSA and ECDSA with one or two signed messages given. In 2016, the attack on DSA described in [60] is based on a system of linear congruences of a particular form which has at most a unique solution below a certain bound, which can be computed efficiently.

4   Lattice Attacks on Different Cryptographic Algorithms

In this section, we investigate the lattice attack methods for different cryptographic algorithms. We already know that the lattice attack fall into several categories. Based that each cryptographic algorithm has its own structure, the attack methods on each algorithm are not the same. We present the lattice attacks for each algorithm and their effects.

4.1   RSA

For RSA encryption, because it exploits the complex of the large number factoring, the partial key exposure attacks often use the Coppersmith's method to construct the lattice problem to recover the private key.

In 1998, Boneh, Durfee and Frankel presented several partial key exposure attacks on RSA in [19]. They showed that the constraint was the upper bound on e, that had been $\sqrt{N}$, and a quarter of the least significant bits of d need to be known to factor the RSA modulus N. In 2000, Boneh and Durfee [18] improved Wiener's attack [68] and proposed the lattice based attack for the RSA cryptography.

In 2003, the idea of [19] has been improved by Blömer and May [16] where the bound on e was increased upto $N^{0.725}$. In 2005, Ernst et al. [30] use Coppersmith's technique and improved the results on known MSBs of d for small private exponent d and full size public exponent e. In 2008, Sarkar and Maitra [62] extended the work of [30] by guessing few bits of one prime. While in 2009, the work by Aono [8] improved the results of [30] when some portion of Least Significant Bits (LSBs) of d are exposed and $d < N^{0.5}$. In 2010, Santanu Sarkar [63], proposed a variant of the idea presented in [30] when some portion of Most Significant Bits (MSBs) of d are exposed and $d < N^{0.6875}$.

In 2019, Aldaya et al. [4] used the Coppersmith's method to process the real data from the side channel to recover the RSA private key, making the partial key exposure attack on RSA practically.

4.2   DSA

For DSA signature, attackers often construct the HNP or EHNP problem to recover the private key. Recall the expression that $s = k^{-1}(h(m) + r \cdot \alpha) \mod q$, if the attackers knew some bits of the ephemeral key k, they can construct the

HNP or EHNP problems and then solve them by lattice reduction algorithms. The private key is included in the results.

In 2001, Howgrave-Graham and Smart [39] gave the first attack on DSA using lattices. They have shown that if partial information on the ephemeral keys can be obtained for a certain number of signatures, the private key can be obtained using Babai's round-off (nearest point) algorithm. The attackers can use different partial information of the ephemeral key k to construct the lattice. The most used information is the LSBs of the ephemeral key to construct the HNP problem. Because in practise, this information is easy to obtain. Many works investigate how to use the LSBs to efficiently recover the private key with less signatures. Correspondingly, the MSBs of the ephemeral key also can be used to construct the HNP problem. More generally, arbitrarily continuous bits of the ephemeral can be used. For the EHNP problem, the partial information is some position information of the bits in the ephemeral key. This discrete information also is useful to recover the DSA private key.

4.3   ECDSA

For ECDSA signature, it structure is similar to the DSA. So the attack on ECDSA is also similar to the DSA. The used partial information for the lattice construction is also included the LSBs, MSBs and other information.

In 2009, Brumley and Hakala [22] recovered the LSBs of ECDSA ephemeral keys. They recovered a 160-bit ECDSA private key using the attack in [39] with $2,600$ signatures ($8K$ with noise). In 2011, Brumley and Tuveri [23] obtained the MSBs of the ephemeral keys through the timing attack and recovered the ECDSA private key over $8,000$ TLS handshakes. In 2014, Benger et al. [12] extended the technique in [53] to use a different length of leaked LSBs for each signature. They recovered the secret key of OpenSSL's ECDSA using about 200 signatures. Then in 2015, Van de Pol et al. [59] used all of the information leaked in the top half of the ephemeral keys to construct the HNP instance, allowing them to recover the secret key after observing only 14 signatures. In 2016, Allan et al. [6] improved the results in [59] by using a performance-degradation attack to amplify the side-channel to recover a 256-bit private key only need 6 signatures. Fan et al. [31] exploited the EHNP to reduce the number of signatures needed to 4. In 2017, Wang et al. [67] exploited the HNP to recover the ECDSA private key using 85 signatures with a few information. In 2019, Micheli et al. [27] updated the attack in [31] and only use 3 signatures to construct the EHNP to recover the ECDSA private key.

4.4   Others

The lattice attack is also useful to some other algorithms. In 1996, Boneh and Venkatesan [20] initially investigated to use the partial information of the ephemeral key to construct an HNP problem and recovered the private key of Diffie-Hellman by solving it using the lattice reduction algorithm. In 2017, Shani [65] used the HNP problem to attack the ECDH exchange protocol. In

2017, Zhang et al. [72] extended the attack in [54] to SM2 Digital Signature Algorithm (SM2-DSA), which is a Chinese version of ECDSA. Lattice attacks can also solve similar HNP instances to recover private keys for other signature schemes such as EPID in the presence of side channel vulnerabilities [26].

5   Applications of Lattice Attacks in Side Channel Attacks

With the development of side channel attack technology, the researches on the partial key exposure attack have shifted from theory to practical application. Researchers are more concerned about how to obtain the information about the key through the side channel and construct the appropriate lattice for private key recovery based on the obtained information. While, different side channels can obtain different data so that the lattice construction is different. Commonly used side channels to obtain the partial information include: the cache side channel, the power and electromagnetic side channel, fault injury and timing side channels.

5.1   Cache Attacks

As describe in Sect. 2, the cache attack is a very effective method software side channel attack. This attack requires very little capability of the attackers and is extremely easy to launch.

In 2007, the authors in [38] first suggested to use the cache side channel attack to obtain the partial key information to construct the EHNP problem to recover the DSA private key. After 2014, with the presence of the Flush+Reload attack, Benger et al. [12] obtained a different length of leaked LSBs. They recovered the ECDSA private key with the HNP problem. Then in 2015, Van de Pol et al. [59] used all of the information leaked from the cache side channel in the top half of the ephemeral keys to construct the HNP instance, allowing them to recover the secret key. Fan et al. [31] also used the Flush+Reload attack and transformed the problem of recovering the secret key to the extended hidden number problem (EHNP). In 2017, Wang et al. [67] exploited the HNP to recover the private key using a few information from the Flush+Reload attack. In 2019, [61] gives a cache side-channel based attack on ECDSA and DSA, modelling the problem using HNP. Aldaya et al. [4] proposed a methodology to analyze cryptographic software for traversal of known side-channel insecure code paths. They applied it to RSA key generation and use the Flush+Reload attack to obtain the side channel information.

5.2   Power and Electromagnetic Attacks

The power attack and the electromagnetic attack are similar due to the similar analytical methods, while the difference is only the measured quantity.

In 2008, Medwed et al. [49] used the template SPA attack to obtain the partial key information to construct the lattice attack to recover the ECDSA private key. In 2014, Aranha et al. [9] used the power attack on the ECDSA with the GLV/GLS implementation. In 2016, Genkin et al. [33] obtained the LSBs of the ECDSA signature on the mobile device with the power and electromagnetic attack, to recover the private key using the HNP problem. Belgarric et al. [11] also used the electromagnetic attack to obtain the LSBs of the ECDSA signature on the Android device. In 2017, Aldaya et al. [5] used the SPA attack to obtain the LSBs of the ECDSA signature and constructed the HNP problem to recover the private key. Zhang et al. [72] used the power attack on SM2 to obtain the LSBs, recovering the private key with HNP problem.

5.3   Fault Attacks

The fault attacks initiatively inject an error to the execution process, and analyse the difference with normal case to obtain the partial key information. This type of attack can not obtain a lot of bits.

In 2005, Naccache et al. [51] first used the fault injection attack to obtain the LSBs of the DSA on the smartcard and recovered the private key with the HNP. In 2012, Nguyen et al. [56] obtain the LSBs of DSA and RSA with this attack and using the HNP to recover the private key. In 2013, Liu et al. [46] extended the attack to the SM2 algorithm. In 2015, Cao et al. [24] use the differential fault attack on the ECDSA with the wNAF representation to get the LSBs of the ephemeral key. Then they recovered the private key with the HNP problem.

5.4   Timing Attacks

The timing attack is the oldest side channel but is still very effective. In 2011, Brumley et al. [23] presented the practical remote timing attack on ECDSA with the Montgomery Ladder implementation and construct the HNP problem to recover the private key. in 2015, Wong et al. [69] revisited Brumley's work and practically using the remote timing attack with the HNP problem to recover the ECDSA private key. In 2020, Moghimi et al. [50] exploited the timing attack to recover the ECDSA private key on the TPM constructing HNP problem with the obtained MSBs of the ephemeral key information.

6   Future Developments of Lattice Attacks

Up to now, we systematically analyse the improvements of the lattice attack in past years, and especially we have researched how the lattice attack is used to process the partial information obtained from the side channel attacks. In general, The development of lattice attacks has the following characteristics:

- From theoretical research to practical application research. The initial researches often focus on how to use partial information to recover the secret key theoretically. Then, the attention is turned to what kind of information we can really obtain, how to obtain the information effectively, and how to construct the appropriate lattice to fully use the obtained information.

- We divide the lattice attacks into three categories. While different lattice attack methods are applicable to different algorithms.
- the partial key exposure attacks now are already extended to various platforms and devices, not limited to the Intel platform.

Therefore, in the future, the development direction of lattice attack can be summarized as follows:

- **More practical.** We need to construct the lattice based on the type of data obtained from the side channels. Also we need to consider the effects of noise. Only in this way, the lattice attack can recover the private key of the real system.
- **More algorithm implementations.** So far, there are still many implementations not vulnerable to the actual attacks, such as the ECDSA with Montgomery Ladder. So there are a lot of implementations needed to construct actually attack to obtain some information in order to exploit appropriate lattice attacks to recover the secret key.
- **More application scenarios.** Different scenarios have different characteristics, which may influence the effect of the key recovery. Therefore, for different scenarios, corresponding changes need to be made to maximize the impact of the attack.
- **More efficient.** The efficiency contains two aspects. One side is to fully exploit the obtained partial information. That is the attacks need more efficient use of known data to construct lattices. On the other side, the private key can also be recovered effectively with very little data per on execution.

7   Conclusion

In this paper, we systematically analyse the developments of the lattice attacks and its use in side channel attacks. First, based on the lattice construction, we divide the lattice attack into three categories: HNP, EHNP, and others. Then we investigate the lattice attacks on each algorithms and the way side channel data is processed by the lattice attack. Finally, we summary the trend of the lattice attack in side channel attacks. The lattice attacks will be improved more efficient, practical, and have more application scenarios.

References

1. Acıiçmez, O., Koç, Ç.K.: Trace-driven cache attacks on AES (short paper). In: Ning, P., Qing, S., Li, N. (eds.) ICICS 2006. LNCS, vol. 4307, pp. 112–121. Springer, Heidelberg (2006). https://doi.org/10.1007/11935308_9
2. Acıiçmez, O., Schindler, W., Koç, Ç.K.: Improving Brumley and Boneh timing attack on unprotected SSL implementations. In: Proceedings of the 2005 ACM Conference on Computer and Communications Security (CCS), pp. 139–146 (2005)

3. Adamoudis, M., Draziotis, K.A., Poulakis, D.: Enhancing an attack to dsa schemes. Lecture Notes in Computer Science **11545**, 13–25 (2019)
4. Aldaya, A.C., García, C.P., Tapia, L.M.A., Brumley, B.B.: Cache-timing attacks on RSA key generation. IACR Trans. Cryptogr. Hardw. Embed. Syst. **4**, 213–242 (2019)
5. Aldaya, A.C., Sarmiento, A.C., Sánchez-Solano, S.: SPA vulnerabilities of the binary extended Euclidean algorithm. J. Cryptographic Eng. **7**(4), 273–285 (2017)
6. Allan, T., Brumley, B.B., Falkner, K., van de Pol, J., Yarom, Y.: Amplifying side channels through performance degradation. In: Proceedings of the 32nd Annual Conference on Computer Security Applications (ACSAC), pp. 422–435 (2016)
7. American National Standards Institute: ANSI X9.62-2005, Public Key Cryptography for the Financial Services Industry: The Elliptic Curve Digital Signature Algorithm (ECDSA) (2005)
8. Aono, Y.: A new lattice construction for partial key exposure attack for RSA. In: Jarecki, S., Tsudik, G. (eds.) PKC 2009. LNCS, vol. 5443, pp. 34–53. Springer, Heidelberg (2009). https://doi.org/10.1007/978-3-642-00468-1_3
9. Aranha, D.F., Fouque, P.-A., Gérard, B., Kammerer, J.-G., Tibouchi, M., Zapalowicz, J.-C.: GLV/GLS decomposition, power analysis, and attacks on ecdsa signatures with single-bit nonce bias. In: Sarkar, P., Iwata, T. (eds.) ASIACRYPT 2014. LNCS, vol. 8873, pp. 262–281. Springer, Heidelberg (2014). https://doi.org/10.1007/978-3-662-45611-8_14
10. Babai, L.: On Lovász' lattice reduction and the nearest lattice point problem. Combinatorica **6**(1), 1–13 (1986)
11. Belgarric, P., Fouque, P.-A., Macario-Rat, G., Tibouchi, M.: Side-channel analysis of Weierstrass and Koblitz curve ECDSA on android smartphones. In: Sako, K. (ed.) CT-RSA 2016. LNCS, vol. 9610, pp. 236–252. Springer, Cham (2016). https://doi.org/10.1007/978-3-319-29485-8_14
12. Benger, N., van de Pol, J., Smart, N.P., Yarom, Y.: "Ooh Aah... Just a Little Bit": a small amount of side channel can go a long way. In: Batina, L., Robshaw, M. (eds.) CHES 2014. LNCS, vol. 8731, pp. 75–92. Springer, Heidelberg (2014). https://doi.org/10.1007/978-3-662-44709-3_5
13. Bernstein, D.J.: Cache-timing attacks on AES. http://cr.yp.to/antiforgery/cachetiming-20050414.pdf (2005)
14. Bertoni, G., Zaccaria, V., Breveglieri, L., Monchiero, M., Palermo, G.: AES power attack based on induced cache miss and countermeasure. In: International Conference on Information Technology: Coding and Computing (ITCC), pp. 586–591 (2005)
15. Blake, I.F., Garefalakis, T.: On the security of the digital signature algorithm. Des. Codes Cryptogr. **26**(1–3), 87–96 (2002)
16. Blömer, J., May, A.: New partial key exposure attacks on RSA. In: Boneh, D. (ed.) CRYPTO 2003. LNCS, vol. 2729, pp. 27–43. Springer, Heidelberg (2003). https://doi.org/10.1007/978-3-540-45146-4_2
17. Boneh, D., DeMillo, R.A., Lipton, R.J.: On the importance of checking cryptographic protocols for faults. In: Fumy, W. (ed.) EUROCRYPT 1997. LNCS, vol. 1233, pp. 37–51. Springer, Heidelberg (1997). https://doi.org/10.1007/3-540-69053-0_4
18. Boneh, D., Durfee, G.: Cryptanalysis of RSA with private key d less than n/sup 0.292/. IEEE Trans. Inf. Theory **46**(4), 1339–1349 (2000)
19. Boneh, D., Durfee, G., Frankel, Y.: An attack on RSA given a small fraction of the private key bits. In: Ohta, K., Pei, D. (eds.) ASIACRYPT 1998. LNCS, vol. 1514, pp. 25–34. Springer, Heidelberg (1998). https://doi.org/10.1007/3-540-49649-1_3

20. Boneh, D., Venkatesan, R.: Hardness of computing the most significant bits of secret keys in Diffie-Hellman and related schemes. In: Koblitz, N. (ed.) CRYPTO 1996. LNCS, vol. 1109, pp. 129–142. Springer, Heidelberg (1996). https://doi.org/10.1007/3-540-68697-5_11

21. Bonneau, J., Mironov, I.: Cache-collision timing attacks against AES. In: Goubin, L., Matsui, M. (eds.) CHES 2006. LNCS, vol. 4249, pp. 201–215. Springer, Heidelberg (2006). https://doi.org/10.1007/11894063_16

22. Brumley, B.B., Hakala, R.M.: Cache-timing template attacks. In: Matsui, M. (ed.) ASIACRYPT 2009. LNCS, vol. 5912, pp. 667–684. Springer, Heidelberg (2009). https://doi.org/10.1007/978-3-642-10366-7_39

23. Brumley, B.B., Tuveri, N.: Remote timing attacks are still practical. In: Atluri, V., Diaz, C. (eds.) ESORICS 2011. LNCS, vol. 6879, pp. 355–371. Springer, Heidelberg (2011). https://doi.org/10.1007/978-3-642-23822-2_20

24. Cao, W., et al.: Two lattice-based differential fault attacks against ECDSA with wNAF algorithm. In: Kwon, S., Yun, A. (eds.) ICISC 2015. LNCS, vol. 9558, pp. 297–313. Springer, Cham (2016). https://doi.org/10.1007/978-3-319-30840-1_19

25. Coppersmith, D.: Finding a small root of a univariate modular equation. In: Maurer, U. (ed.) EUROCRYPT 1996. LNCS, vol. 1070, pp. 155–165. Springer, Heidelberg (1996). https://doi.org/10.1007/3-540-68339-9_14

26. Dall, F., et al.: CacheQuote: efficiently recovering long-term secrets of SGX EPID via cache attacks. IACR Trans. Cryptogr. Hardw. Embed. Syst. **2**, 171–191 (2018)

27. De Micheli, G., Piau, R., Pierrot, C.: A tale of three signatures: practical attack of ECDSA with WNAF. IACR Crypt. ePrint Arch. **2019**, 861 (2019)

28. Draziotis, K., Poulakis, D.: Lattice attacks on DSA schemes based on Lagrange's algorithm. In: Muntean, T., Poulakis, D., Rolland, R. (eds.) CAI 2013. LNCS, vol. 8080, pp. 119–131. Springer, Heidelberg (2013). https://doi.org/10.1007/978-3-642-40663-8_13

29. Draziotis, K.A.: (EC)DSA lattice attacks based on Coppersmith's method. Inf. Process. Lett. **116**(8), 541–545 (2016)

30. Ernst, M., Jochemsz, E., May, A., de Weger, B.: Partial key exposure attacks on RSA up to full size exponents. In: Cramer, R. (ed.) Partial key exposure attacks on RSA up to full size exponents. LNCS, vol. 3494, pp. 371–386. Springer, Heidelberg (2005). https://doi.org/10.1007/11426639_22

31. Fan, S., Wang, W., Cheng, Q.: Attacking OpenSSL implementation of ECDSA with a few signatures. In: Proceedings of the 2016 ACM SIGSAC Conference on Computer and Communications Security (CCS), pp. 1505–1515 (2016)

32. Genkin, D., Pachmanov, L., Pipman, I., Tromer, E.: Stealing keys from PCs using a radio: cheap electromagnetic attacks on windowed exponentiation. In: Güneysu, T., Handschuh, H. (eds.) CHES 2015. LNCS, vol. 9293, pp. 207–228. Springer, Heidelberg (2015). https://doi.org/10.1007/978-3-662-48324-4_11

33. Genkin, D., Pachmanov, L., Pipman, I., Tromer, E., Yarom, Y.: ECDSA key extraction from mobile devices via nonintrusive physical side channels. In: Proceedings of the 2016 ACM SIGSAC Conference on Computer and Communications Security, pp. 1626–1638 (2016)

34. Genkin, D., Pipman, I., Tromer, E.: Get your hands off my laptop: physical side-channel key-extraction attacks on PCs. In: Batina, L., Robshaw, M. (eds.) CHES 2014. LNCS, vol. 8731, pp. 242–260. Springer, Heidelberg (2014). https://doi.org/10.1007/978-3-662-44709-3_14

35. Genkin, D., Shamir, A., Tromer, E.: RSA key extraction via low-bandwidth acoustic cryptanalysis. In: Garay, J.A., Gennaro, R. (eds.) CRYPTO 2014. LNCS, vol. 8616, pp. 444–461. Springer, Heidelberg (2014). https://doi.org/10.1007/978-3-662-44371-2_25

36. Gruss, D., Maurice, C., Wagner, K., Mangard, S.: Flush+ Flush: a fast and stealthy cache attack. In: 13th International Conference on Detection of Intrusions and Malware, and Vulnerability Assessment, pp. 279–299 (2016)

37. Halderman, J., et al.: Lest we remember: cold boot attacks on encryption keys. In: 17th USENIX Security Symposium, pp. 45–60 (2008)

38. Hlaváč, M., Rosa, T.: Extended hidden number problem and its cryptanalytic applications. In: Biham, E., Youssef, A.M. (eds.) SAC 2006. LNCS, vol. 4356, pp. 114–133. Springer, Heidelberg (2007). https://doi.org/10.1007/978-3-540-74462-7_9

39. Howgrave-Graham, N.A., Smart, N.P.: Lattice attacks on digital signature schemes. Des. Codes Crypt. **23**(3), 283–290 (2001)

40. Johnson, D., Menezes, A., Vanstone, S.: The elliptic curve digital signature algorithm (ECDSA). Int. J. Inf. Secur. **1**(1), 36–63 (2001)

41. Kocher, P., et al.: Spectre attacks: exploiting speculative execution. In: 2019 IEEE Symposium on Security and Privacy (S& P), pp. 1–19 (2019)

42. Kumari, A., Roy, B.: A survey of lattice attack on digital signature algorithm. In: Proceedings of 3rd International Conference on Internet of Things and Connected Technologies (ICIoTCT) (2018)

43. Lenstra, A.K., Lenstra, H.W., Lovász, L.: Factoring polynomials with rational coefficients. Mathematische Annalen **261**(4), 515–534 (1982)

44. Lipp, M., et al.: Meltdown: reading kernel memory from user space. In: 27th USENIX Security Symposium, (USENIX Security), pp. 973–990 (2018)

45. Liu, F., Yarom, Y., Ge, Q., Heiser, G., Lee, R.B.: Last-level cache side-channel attacks are practical. In: IEEE Symposium on Security and Privacy, S&P 2015, pp. 605–622 (2015)

46. Liu, M., Chen, J., Li, H.: Partially known nonces and fault injection attacks on SM2 signature algorithm. In: Lin, D., Xu, S., Yung, M. (eds.) Inscrypt 2013. LNCS, vol. 8567, pp. 343–358. Springer, Cham (2014). https://doi.org/10.1007/978-3-319-12087-4_22

47. Liu, M., Nguyen, P.Q.: Solving BDD by enumeration: an update. In: Dawson, E. (ed.) CT-RSA 2013. LNCS, vol. 7779, pp. 293–309. Springer, Heidelberg (2013). https://doi.org/10.1007/978-3-642-36095-4_19

48. Lu, Y., Peng, L., Kunihiro, N.: Recent progress on Coppersmith's lattice-based method: a survey. In: Takagi, T., Wakayama, M., Tanaka, K., Kunihiro, N., Kimoto, K., Duong, D.H. (eds.) Mathematical Modelling for Next-Generation Cryptography. MI, vol. 29, pp. 297–312. Springer, Singapore (2018). https://doi.org/10.1007/978-981-10-5065-7_16

49. Medwed, M., Oswald, E.: Template attacks on ECDSA. In: Chung, K.-I., Sohn, K., Yung, M. (eds.) WISA 2008. LNCS, vol. 5379, pp. 14–27. Springer, Heidelberg (2009). https://doi.org/10.1007/978-3-642-00306-6_2

50. Moghimi, D., Sunar, B., Eisenbarth, T., Heninger, N.: TPM-FAIL: TPM meets timing and lattice attacks. arXiv: Cryptography and Security (2019)

51. Naccache, D., Nguyên, P.Q., Tunstall, M., Whelan, C.: Experimenting with faults, lattices and the DSA. In: Vaudenay, S. (ed.) PKC 2005. LNCS, vol. 3386, pp. 16–28. Springer, Heidelberg (2005). https://doi.org/10.1007/978-3-540-30580-4_3

52. National Institute of Standards and Technology: FIPS PUB 186-4 Digital Signature Standard (DSS), July 2013

53. Nguyen, P.Q., Shparlinski, I.E.: The insecurity of the digital signature algorithm with partially known nonces. J. Cryptology **15**(3), 151–176 (2002)
54. Nguyen, P.Q., Shparlinski, I.E.: The insecurity of the elliptic curve digital signature algorithm with partially known nonces. Des. Codes Crypt. **30**(2), 201–217 (2003)
55. Nguyen, P.Q., Stern, J.: Lattice reduction in cryptology: an update. In: Bosma, W. (ed.) ANTS 2000. LNCS, vol. 1838, pp. 85–112. Springer, Heidelberg (2000). https://doi.org/10.1007/10722028_4
56. Nguyen, P.Q., Tibouchi, M.: Lattice-based fault attacks on signatures. In: Joye, M., Tunstall, M. (eds.) Fault Analysis in Cryptography, pp. 201–220. Springer, Heidelberg (2012). https://doi.org/10.1007/978-3-642-29656-7_12
57. Oren, Y., Shamir, A.: How not to protect PCs from power analysis. Rump Session, CRYPTO (2006)
58. Page, D.: Theoretical use of cache memory as a cryptanalytic side-channel. IACR Cryptology ePrint Arch. **2002**, 169 (2002)
59. van de Pol, J., Smart, N.P., Yarom, Y.: Just a little bit more. In: The Cryptographers' Track at the RSA Conference (CT-RSA), pp. 3–21 (2015)
60. Poulakis, D.: New lattice attacks on DSA schemes. J. Math. Cryptology **10**(2), 135–144 (2016)
61. Ryan, K.: Return of the hidden number problem. a widespread and novel key extraction attack on ECDSA and DSA. IACR Trans. Cryptogr. Hardw. Embed. Syst. **2019**(1), 146–168 (2019)
62. Sarkar, S., Maitra, S.: Improved partial key exposure attacks on RSA by guessing a few bits of one of the prime factors. In: Lee, P.J., Cheon, J.H. (eds.) ICISC 2008. LNCS, vol. 5461, pp. 37–51. Springer, Heidelberg (2009). https://doi.org/10.1007/978-3-642-00730-9_3
63. Sarkar, S., Sen Gupta, S., Maitra, S.: Partial key exposure attack on RSA – improvements for limited lattice dimensions. In: Gong, G., Gupta, K.C. (eds.) INDOCRYPT 2010. LNCS, vol. 6498, pp. 2–16. Springer, Heidelberg (2010). https://doi.org/10.1007/978-3-642-17401-8_2
64. Schnorr, C.P., Euchner, M.: Lattice basis reduction: improved practical algorithms and solving subset sum problems. Math. Program. **66**(1), 181–199 (1994)
65. Shani, B.: On the bit security of elliptic curve Diffie–Hellman. In: Fehr, S. (ed.) PKC 2017. LNCS, vol. 10174, pp. 361–387. Springer, Heidelberg (2017). https://doi.org/10.1007/978-3-662-54365-8_15
66. Tromer, E., Osvik, D.A., Shamir, A.: Efficient cache attacks on AES, and countermeasures. J. Cryptology **23**(1), 37–71 (2010)
67. Wang, W., Fan, S.: Attacking OpenSSL ECDSA with a small amount of side-channel information. Sci. Chin. Inf. Sci. **61**(3), 032105:1–032105:14 (2017)
68. Wiener, M.J.: Cryptanalysis of short RSA secret exponents. IEEE Trans. Inf. Theory **36**(3), 553–558 (1990)
69. Wong, D.: Timing and lattice attacks on a remote ECDSA openssl server: how practical are they really? IACR Cryptol. ePrint Arch. 839 (2015)
70. Yarom, Y., Benger, N.: Recovering OpenSSL ECDSA nonces using the FLUSH+RELOAD cache side-channel attack. IACR Cryptol. ePrint Arch. p. 140 (2014)
71. Yarom, Y., Falkner, K.: Flush+Reload: a high resolution, low noise, L3 cache side-channel attack. In: Proceedings of the 23rd USENIX Conference on Security Symposium, pp. 719–732 (2014)
72. Zhang, K., et al.: Practical partial-nonce-exposure attack on ECC algorithm. In: 2017 13th International Conference on Computational Intelligence and Security (CIS), pp. 248–252 (2017)

Exploring the Security of Certificate Transparency in the Wild

Bingyu Li[1,4(✉)], Fengjun Li[2], Ziqiang Ma[3,4], and Qianhong Wu[1,5]

[1] School of Cyber Science and Technology, Beihang University, Beijing 100191, China
{libingyu,qianhong.wu}@buaa.edu.cn
[2] Department of Electrical Engineering and Computer Science,
The University of Kansas, Lawrence, USA
fli@ku.edu
[3] School of Information Engineering, Ningxia University, Yinchuan, China
maziqiang@nxu.edu.cn
[4] State Key Laboratory of Information Security, Institute of Information
Engineering, Chinese Academy of Sciences, Beijing 100093, China
[5] Hangzhou Innovation Institute, Beihang University, Hangzhou, China

Abstract. Certificate Transparency (CT) is proposed to detect fraudulent certificates and improve the accountability of CAs. CT as an open auditing and monitoring system is based on the idea that all CA-issued certificates are logged in a publicly accessible log server, and that CT-compliant browsers only accept publicly recorded certificates. The purpose of CT is to make all TLS server certificates issued by the CA publicly visible; once a fraudulent certificate is publicly published, it can be discovered by the domain name owner. In practice, the CT can achieve its intended purpose only when the three components (i.e., log server, monitor, and auditor) of the CT cooperate and work correctly and effectively. Compared with traditional PKI systems, the CT framework does not rely on a single trusted party, but as a distributed system that distributes trust guarantees to many CAs, log servers, auditors, and monitors. In this paper, we study the interaction among log servers, monitors, auditors, CAs, domain owners (or websites), browsers, and other components in practice, and then analyze the security impact of each component on the CT. We explore the security of CT framework in practice from multiple perspectives, and find that each component has many security vulnerabilities. Thus, the attackers might first exploit the vulnerability to disable the CT and then launch an attack using fraudulent certificates. The overall security guarantees of CT are jeopardized due to the weak protections of any components.

Keywords: Certificate Transparency (CT) · Fraudulent certificate · Trust management

This work was partially supported by National Natural Science Foundation of China (No. 62002011), Open Project of the State Key Laboratory of Information Security, Institute of Information Engineering, Chinese Academy of Sciences (No. 2020-ZD-05, No. 2020-MS-08), NSF CNS-1422206, DGE-1565570, NSA Science of Security Initiative H98230-18-D-0009, and the Ripple University Blockchain Research Initiative.

J. Zhou et al. (Eds.): ACNS 2020 Workshops, LNCS 12418, pp. 453–470, 2020.
https://doi.org/10.1007/978-3-030-61638-0_25

1   Introduction

Public Key Infrastructure (PKI) uses certificates to establish and transmit trust on the Internet [8]. By 2020, there are more than 2.3 billion valid certificates on the Internet [41], which are widely used for confidentiality, authentication, data integrity, etc. The certification authority (CA) is responsible for issuing a certificate, which is used for binding users' identity and public key. So it is usually assumed that the CA is completely reliable. However, in recent years, a series of security incidents [7,12,24,32,43,44] have shown that accredited CAs may issue fraudulent certificates due to compromised or deceived. The fraudulent certificate binds a domain name to a key pair held by man-in-the-middle (MitM) attackers, instead of the legitimate website. Thus, attacks using fraudulent certificates can launch MitM or impersonation attacks without any warning against targets such as websites, national core devices or user networks. Numerous fraudulent certificates weaken the trust provided by PKI system and result in serious threat to the compromising or deceiving of PKI.

Traditional PKI system lacks the mechanism of finding fraudulent certificate. The fraudulent certificate usually takes a long time to be detected (from weeks to months). In addition, browsers' trust in accredited CAs are undifferentiated, and any of the CA's security problems may harm the entire Internet ecosystem. Therefore, the attack surface of fraudulent certificates on the network is long-term and extensive.

Certificate transparency (CT) [26] is proposed to timely detect the fraudulent certificates and enhance the accountability of CAs. CT as an open auditing and monitoring system, the basic idea is to record all certificates issued by the CA in a publicly accessible log server, and clients (e.g., browsers) only accept such publicly issued certificates. CT has been widely adopted by CAs, websites, browsers and TLS software, including Chrome [19], Apple platforms [3], Mozilla Firefox/NSS [33], OpenSSL [36], Nginx [34] and Microsoft AD Certificate Service [31]. Its purpose is to make all TLS server certificates issued by the CA publicly visible and subject to public monitoring and auditing. Once a fraudulent certificate is published via CT log, it can be detected by the domain owner. Therefore, CT introduces the following three new components: (a) Log server, being used to record certificates submitted by the CA or domain owner, etc.; (b) Monitor, obtaining all certificates recorded in the log regularly to help find suspicious (or fraudulent) certificates; (c) Auditor, verifying that the log server behavior is correct.

Compared with the traditional PKI system, the CT framework does not rely on a single trusted party, but as a distributed system, it distributes trust security to CAs, log servers, auditors and monitors [11,25,26]. The CT requires that certificates signed by the CA be recorded in publicly-visible logs, and then the domain owner can monitor suspicious certificates issued for its domain. In particular, a certificate is submitted by the CA or website to the log server, which responds with a signed certificate timestamp (SCT), as a promise for the certificate to be publicly-visible in the logs. Then, the certificate is sent along with SCTs in TLS handshakes to the browser; otherwise, a CT-compliant browser rejects the certificate. The log server is only responsible for recording the certificate, but not for checking whether the certificate is signed with the domain owner's authorization or not. Meanwhile, the latter work mainly depends on the monitor. Finally, based on SCTs and signed tree heads (STHs) issued by log servers, auditors ensure the correct behaviors of log servers; that is, certificates are append-only in the logs, and a log server provides consistent views to different parties.

In an ideal state, the components and each link of CT achieve the security via redundant and digital signature [26, 27]. First of all, log server, CA and domain owner depend on the digital signatures of certificate and SCTs, and the public keys of the signers are publicly known or pre-installed in the verifiers. Secondly, the behavior consistency of log server is audited by auditor and monitor. The interaction security between log server and other components, including browser, auditor and monitor, is designed with the fault tolerance of redundant auditors. These interactions also rely on digital signatures, including SCT or/and STH, and the public keys are publicly known. Auditor and monitor provide security services to browsers and domain owners through mutual interaction and redundant to help detect fraudulent certificates or incorrect behavior of the log servers. In summary, among these components, the public keys of the signers are publicly known and it is assumed that at least one of the numerous auditors and monitors is secure and reliable. Therefore, they will seldom suffer from MitM attack exploiting fraudulent certificate.

In practice, only the three components of CT work correctly and effectively, then it can achieve the expected goal. There are a variety of reasons that can cause an attacker to exploit a fraudulent certificate to launch a MitM or impersonation attack without triggering any alarm in the CT. For example, the log server does not record the certificate to the public log within the maximum merge delay (MMD), auditor fails to detect the incorrect behavior of the log, or monitor fails to reliably detect fraudulent certificates from the log server in a timely manner, etc. The longer the fraudulent certificates stay undetected in the system (or CT logs), the more the damage they may cause to the PKI ecosystem. Therefore, these factors such as the correctness of CT log behavior, the quality of certificate monitoring server, and the granularity and timeliness of audit, will all affect the overall security enhancement by the CT framework in practice.

In this paper, we investigate the security configuration of each component in the CT framework and the mutual security influence among them in practice. We find that, compared with the security design, these components are not significantly more immune to the security vulnerabilities. Therefore, the attacker could first launch MitM or distributed denial of service attack (DDoS) attacks on one or more of the CT components to manipulate the certificate monitor and/or audit results. Then, when a fraudulent certificate is exploited in the MitM attacks on any ordinary website which supports CT, the domain owner still can not detect this fraudulent certificate because the attackers would conceal the certificate in the manipulated search result, or force the browser not to perform CT policy checks, etc. Note that, in this attack scenario as explained above, CAs, log servers, monitors, and auditors have malicious behavior due to their own vulnerabilities or defects, while the domain owners and CT-compliant browsers will accept the fraudulent certificate without receiving any warning from the CT mechanism.

Contribution. We shed light on the security design of each component of the CT framework, and disclose that if any of the components are not well protected and configured, the attackers could still exploit fraudulent certificates to launch MitM attacks on an ordinary website, without trigger any alerts in the CT. Then, we comprehensively analyze the security impact of each CT component on other components in practice, including the log server, monitor, and auditor, and find that any one of them could have various security issues that directly or indirectly affect the security of other components, and ultimately affect the effectiveness of CT. So the overall security guarantees of CT is jeopardized due to the weak protections of any components. Finally, we discuss several improvements to enhance the reliability of CT framework.

The remainder is organized as follows. The CT framework, the security design of each component in the CT and its deployment in practice are described in Sect. 2. Section 3 studies the security of CT components on the Internet and analyzes the mutual security influence of each CT component in practice, and Sect. 4 proposes several potential countermeasures to improve the reliability of CT. Section 5 surveys the related works and Sect. 6 draws the conclusions.

2   The Components of Certificate Transparency

In this section, we first describe the CT framework. Then, we analyze the security design of each component in the CT framework, and finally show the deployment of CT in practice.

2.1   The CT Framework

CT scheme is proposed to resist fraudulent certificate which binds a domain name to a key pair held by MitM attacker. As shown in Fig. 1, compared with the traditional PKI system, the CT framework introduces new component and enhances the functions of the traditional PKI system, so that the CT can achieve the expected purpose.

CA. Compared with the CA in traditional PKI system, a CA supports the CT by adding the following steps. The CA signs the certificate and submits it to the log server to obtain the SCT. Alternatively, before signing the certificate, the CA creates a precertificate that binds the same data but in a different format from the final certificate. The precertificate is then submitted to return an SCT. Finally, the SCT is embedded as a certificate extension when the certificate is issued. According to the CT policy, a certificate may be submitted to multiple log servers to obtain multiple SCTs.

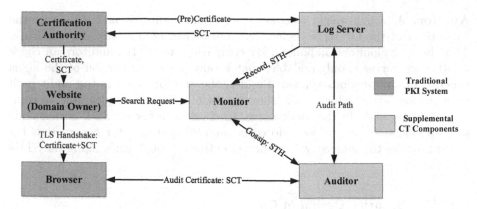

Fig. 1. The framework of Certificate Transparency

Website. Sometimes, it needs to submit its own certificate to the log server to obtain SCT. Then, in the TLS handshake, the SCT is sent to the website along with the certificate via a TLS extension (e.g., OCSP stapling) or certificate extension. Finally, domain name owner needs to periodically query all certificates issued for its domain name from monitor, so as to monitor suspicious certificates and detect the fraudulent certificate.

Browser. Compared with the browser in traditional PKI systems, a CT-compliant browser is enhanced with the following functions. In TLS handshakes, the browser verifies the certificate and SCTs based on the pre-installed public keys of CAs and approved log servers. If the CT policy is not met (e.g., without enough valid SCTs), the browser will reject the certificate. In addition, the browser can also periodically send each SCT to the auditor to check whether it corresponds to a certain certificate entry in the public logs.

Log Server. Log server is responsible for recording the certificate and returning SCT as the promise to make the certificate be publicly-visible in the logs within the maximal merge delay (MMD). Certificates are recorded in the log in the form of a Merkle hash tree, which is convenient for auditing. and the log server periodically signs the root node of the tree, called signed tree head (STH).

Monitor. Monitor is responsible for regularly and continuously monitoring suspicious certificates from public logs. Monitor obtains all the records from the monitored log set, parses the certificates and checks the certificates of interest. The logs are publicly visible, and anyone can act as monitor to obtain certificate from these logs, monitor suspicious certificate and find fraudulent certificate. log servers are publicly-accessible, and any individual or third-party can act as monitor, querying certificates for domain name of interest and monitoring suspicious certificates.

Auditor. As a lightweight software component, auditor is used to ensure the correctness of the log server behavior. Auditor can be a standalone service, a TLS client or monitor component. By comparing two STHs, auditor can check whether log server is only addable, that is, any particular version of the log is superset of any previous version. Besides, the auditor requests the audit path from the log server, which is the shortest list of additional nodes used to compute the root node in the Merkle tree, to check whether an SCT corresponds to a specific entry in the log. Moreover, auditor and monitor ensure that log server provides the same view for different entities through exchanging the STHs periodically.

2.2 The Security Design of CT

The CT framework is different from the traditional PKI system in that it does not rely on a single trusted party, but distributes trustworthiness among CAs, log servers, auditors, and monitors [11,25,26]. These components establish distributed trust through message exchange, verification, auditing, and monitoring. Based on the CT framework, we analyze the interactions and connections between different components and investigate the security design of each link.

Log Server - CA, WebSite, Browser. Over these components, certificates are signed by CAs, and then verified by log servers, websites, and browsers. Meanwhile, SCTs are signed by log servers, and verified by CAs, websites, and browsers [27]. The vendors of browsers evaluate the certification practice of CAs and log servers, and maintain the public certificate trust list (CTL) and log list for global users. The public keys of these CAs and log servers are pre-install to browsers (e.g., Chrome). The domain name owner chooses the CA to issue the certificate, and the CA further chooses the log server to record the certificate. Therefore, the public key of the CA and the log server shall be known in advance (i.e., publicly-known, pre-install by out-of-band means). The transfer of trust between these components depends on the authentication of the signer's public key and the correctness of the component's behavior.

Monitor - Log Server, Domain Owner. The incorrect behavior of the CA (e.g., issuing fraudulent certificates) is recorded by the log server and discovered by the monitor by monitoring the fraudulent certificates in the log. The monitor servers provide certificate search services to the domain name owner via the TLS/HTTPS session. Therefore, this link depends on the authenticity of the monitor server's public key and the quality of the monitor's service.

Auditor - Log Server, Monitor, Browser. As mentioned above, in order to ensure the correct behavior of the log server, the auditor will periodically request STHs from the log server. To verify the signed STHs, the log server's public keys are pre-installed in the auditors. Besides, the auditors sometimes even exchange

STHs with the monitors to ensure that the same view is provided to different entities, which is guaranteed by the redundancy of the monitors and auditors.

In addition, browsers periodically send the SCTs to auditors, who get the audit paths from log servers to ensure that the corresponding certificate is recorded in the public log. The audit path is verified by the SCT and the STH which are signed by the log server, and the public keys of log servers are pre-installed in the auditors. This verification is also redundant, because massive and independent browsers will send SCTs to different auditors.

2.3 CT in Practice

CT has been widely deployed on the Internet [39]. In July 2020, we created a list of 93 accessible logs by collecting the information from the log list maintained by Google [18], and the websites of CA companies, third-party monitors and auditors. Then, using the get-roots command of log servers [26], we obtain the list of root CAs accepted by each log. In total, these logs support 596 unique CAs, covering almost all the mainstream CA (e.g., Let's Encrypt, DigiCert, GeoTrust, GoDaddy, Comodo, and GlobalSign) [6,38]. By July 2020, there were 8.196 billion certificates in these 93 public logs. As of February 2018, at least 60% of HTTPS connections support the CT[39]. Moreover, Chrome browser and Apple platform have been staring the mandatory enforcement of CT policies since Jun 2018. Certificates used by the website servers that do not meet CT policies will no longer be accept by Chrome and Apple platform. By July 2020, there are 41 approved logs in Chrome [19], and 59 in Apple platform [3].

There are maturely deployed third-party monitor servers on the Internet. They can obtain records from logs, parse certificate and provide certificate query and monitoring services for users. To our best knowledge, there are 6 mainstream third-party monitors on the Internet, namely crt.sh, SSLMate, Censys, Google Monitor, Facebook Monitor, and Entrust CT Search Tool. There are also some CT auditors have been deployed on the Internet, such as Edgecombe [13] and Merkle Town [6]. They audit the running state of log servers by verifying STHs and execute Gossip verification along with each other. The CT-over-DNS scheme [16] is integrated into the browser (e.g., Chrome) to help the latter to implement CT audit function.

3 Certificate Transparency on the Internet

In practice, there are hundreds of log servers, multiple monitors and auditors deployed on the Internet. They run independently, redundant and cooperate with each other to ensure the effective work of CT. In practice, the implementation of each CT component may face various challenges, including internal policy influences or the impact caused by external component interactions, etc. Any problem of them will lead to security problems of the whole framework of CT and ultimately affect the application effect of CT.

In this section, we study the security of the CT components on the Internet, to analyze the strength of CT in practice. We have collected a list of log servers, monitors and auditors that are operating normally on the Internet and providing external services by the end of July 2020. We analyze and summarize the security impact of the interaction between different components, following the framework of CT described in Sect. 2, including the number of certificates covered by these components, the scope of CA supported, the log list monitored, and the policy and deployment of CT by the mainstream platform. In particular, we investigate the security vulnerabilities of each component, based on the implementations of the security designs in practice.

3.1   Website and CA

Website and CA are the security enhancement targets of CT. In practice, any website may be attacked by fraudulent certificate and any CA may be forced to issue fraudulent certificate. This is consistent with the threat model and hypothesis as the CT scheme [17,26]. The policies of websites and CAs for CT will also directly influence the deployment of CT, including the accepted log servers and the supported SCT delivery methods, etc.

Next, we will find whether the security guarantee of CT (i.e., the CA-signed TLS server certificate in TLS handshakes is publicly visible to the domain owner) is well supported by other components or not.

3.2   Log

As the core of CT framework, log server is responsible for recording all accepted certificate, responding the corresponding SCT, providing public accessible interface, supporting third-party or individual to act as monitor for certificate monitoring, and accepting auditor to audit the correctness of log serve's behavior. Therefore, the parameter configuration, internal and external policies and running quality of log servers will affect multiple components of CT and mass CT-enable devices.

We created a list of public logs in July 2020. It includes a total of 93 logs collected from the list maintained by Google and third-party monitors. Based on this log list, we analyze the challenges and potential impacts of the deployment of the log server in practice.

List of Accepted CA. Mainstream browsers and platforms pre-install a number of root CAs that they trust by default, called mainstream CAs. There are 174 in Apple macOS, 307 root CA certificates in Microsoft Windows, and 144 in Mozilla NSS by July 2020. The union consists of 341 root CAs. Meanwhile, each log holds an accept list of CAs and accepts only the certificates issued by these CAs [28]. The CA list accepted by log server will directly influence CAs, websites and mass clients.

For example, using the *get-roots* command [26], we obtain the list of root CAs accepted by each log. The 93 public logs accept 596 unique root CA certificates in total, among which 337 belong to mainstream CAs. While 4 mainstream CAs are not accepted by any regular log, which means that CT can not cover all certificates deployed in the network. On the one hand, these CAs are excluded from the CT framework, so any fraudulent certificates issued by them will not be detected by monitors. On the other hand, the certificates issued by these CAs, will be rejected by Chrome always, but acceptable to browsers that currently do not support CT such as Mozilla Firefox and Microsoft Edge.

CT Log Policy. With the widespread application and deployment of CT, more and more certificates are submitted to log servers. For example, using the *get-sth* command [26], we obtain the STHs for each log, to explore the amount of records in public logs. Until July 2020, 8.196 billion certificates are recorded in 93 public logs, at an average growth of 82.6 million records per day. The massive and fast-growing certificates increase the long-term operation and operational burden of log server operators. In addition, the massive and expired certificates in the log server also add extra burden to the third-part monitors and auditors, seriously affecting monitoring and auditing efficiency [28].

In order to solve this problem, researchers propose a partitioned log server based on the validity of certificate to limit the range of received certificates (e.g., the log server *Argon2020* only accepts certificates that are valid until 2020 [21]). This gives the operator the right to shut down the log server after a specified date without any impact to any CT-compliant software, since all certificates recorded by the logging server have expired normally. While, for early non-partitioned log servers, operators plan to freeze these servers within a limit time and no longer receive new certificates [20,22]. However, this also may leads to some issues: as mentioned above, the early system of Apple platform directly on the accepted log list into the system source code. Therefore, the log list cannot be updated online in time. Once the accepted log server stops working, CA can only submit the newly issued certificate to other log servers, which can not be verified by some Apple platform.

Key Update for the Log Server. The private key of log server is mainly used for digital signature of STH and SCT. The public key is used to verify signature by CAs, monitors, auditors and browsers, and it is publicly-known or pre-install in CT-compliant software. Therefore, these components may be affected if the log server's key needs to be updated due to leakage or expiration. The number of CA, monitor and auditor deployed on the Internet is limited (tens or hundreds). These components can be updated in a secure and controlled manner, such as manually by out-of-band means.

However, there may be various problems in the key update of the log server for a large number of client devices (e.g., browsers). These massive client devices are deployed around the world, and different platforms adopt different key update methods. For example, the Chrome browser regularly visits the CT official website to obtain the latest approved log server list. While, the early Apple platform (e.g., iOS 11.0, watchOS 4.0, tvOS 11.0, and macOS 10.13) pre-installs the list of approved log servers in the platform source code, which made it impossible for the device to update the log server information independently from the platform [22]. This may cause potential security threats to users who fail to update or refuse to update the operating system version: the SCT issued for a fraudulent certificate through the leaked private key of log server will still be verified by the client.

Summary. The number of certificates recorded by the log server is increasing rapidly, and the requirement for access and auditing is also increasing. These increments increase the storage, computing, network bandwidth, and maintenance costs of log servers. In addition, there is a deviation between the CA list accepted by the log server and trusted by the mainstream platform, which makes it impossible for the CT to fully cover all CAs and realize ecological supervision of TLS certificates. Finally, the operation plan of the log server and the CT policy of each CT-compliant software may influence and conflict with each other. Furthermore, this may cause legitimate certificates to be unacceptable by the CT-compliant software, while the fraudulent certificates cannot be detected.

3.3   Monitor

Monitor plays a key role in monitoring fraudulent certificate. The service quality of monitor will directly determine the effectiveness of CT, and further affect the promotion and deployment of CT. If there is a security vulnerability in monitor's implementation, an attacker can exploit this vulnerability to circumvent monitor's monitoring of fraudulent certificates. Therefore, if there is a fraudulent certificate which is issued by the publicly-trusted CA, meets the CT policy, is verified by the browser, but cannot be detected by the monitor and is "invisible" to the legitimate domain name owner. An attacker can use the fraudulent certificate to launch a MitM attack or impersonation attack on the target. The security and reliability problems of monitor will directly affect the security effect of CT framework: in TLS/HTTPS ecosystem, certificates conforming to CT policy should be more trustworthy.

The implementation of monitoring technology in the certificate transparency system is essentially to establish a fraudulent certificate monitoring system, to ensure that all valid certificate sets related to the monitored domain name can be securely, reliably and timely fed back to the legitimate domain name owners. To achieve the CT target, we believe that monitoring services should meet the following requirements: (a) it should be able to monitor all valid certificate sets related to the target domain name in the log servers in a timely and reliable manner; (b) it should be able to securely and completely feed back the complete and valid certificate set monitored to the domain name owner; (c) it should have certain fault tolerance, comprehensive and fast security measurement means and be able to identify and repair faults and resist malicious attacks.

In practice, there are many factors that determine the service quality of monitor, including monitoring policies, interface rules, and so on. Some studies [27, 28] have shown that CT monitor, which provides certificate query and fraudulent certificate monitoring service on the Internet, has obvious defects in terms of reliability and timeliness and exists hidden danger of being attacked. Therefore, monitors can not provide users timely and complete certificate set of monitored domain name.

We studied the CT policies and security configurations of monitors in the Internet, to analyze the strength of this component in practice. In particular, we analyze 6 popular third-party monitors, namely crt.sh, SSLMate, Censys, Google Monitor, Facebook Monitor, and Entrust. We analyzed the list of logs they monitor, the ability to monitor certificates, and the security configuration of the external service interface, to explore the possible problems with monitor services in practice.

Handling Massive Amounts of Certificates. We combine the CT policies of mainstream CT applications such as Google and Apple to investigate various types of log sets that monitor can monitor, including the maximal set (i.e., all regular logs) and the minimal set (e.g., minimum set of logs for the certificates compliant with the Chrome CT policy, as of July 2020, there are 13 log servers in this set). However, monitoring the minimal set still consumes huge storage space and network bandwidth. There are billions certificates in these logs by 2020, the amount increases at a daily growth of millions records. Massive certificates have brought great challenges to the timely processing of monitor. In fact, even some third-party monitors (e.g., crt.sh, Censys, and SSLMate) have to keep lots of fetched-but-unprocessed (pre)certificates in backlogs [28].

Parsing Multiple Domain Name Types. We use multiple types of domain name test sets to test the monitoring quality of monitors. Test types include parent domain name (i.e., C.B), subdomain name (i.e., D.C.B.A), and wildcard domain name (i.e., *.B.A) of specified domain name (e.g., C.B.A), as well as domain names containing special symbols (e.g., '_', '*', '?', etc.), and also internationalized domain names (IDNs), etc. We find that each monitor may handle these types of domain names differently, resulting in a different set of certificates being queried. Moreover, almost all monitors may be missing some certificates. We found that each monitor may handle these types of domain names differently, resulting in different sets of queried certificates. Almost all monitors may be missing some certificates. In particular, Google Monitor admitted to us that they had problems with the handling of certificates containing '_' in domain names in their previous software programs, resulting in missing such certificates in the query results. The format of certificate and domain name is diversified and the binding relationship is complex, which increases the difficulty and unpredictability for correct monitor [37].

TLS/HTTPS Configurations of the Monitor Servers. We also conducted the TLS/HTTPS configurations analysis on all 6 monitors, including the Protocol-related configuration (e.g., TLS version, HTTPS redirection, and HSTS) and Certificate-related configuration (e.g., HPKP, Expect-CT, CAA, and Revocation), by using the protocol analyzer of Wireshark and the network security analysis tool. While, none of these monitors on the Internet is perfectly deployed with TLS/HTTPS configurations [27]. Compared with ordinary domain name websites, they do not achieve obvious security enhancement and the generated potential TLS MitM vulnerability will seriously threaten the overall security of CT framework.

Summary. In practice, there are many factors that affect and determine the quality of monitor's service. Currently, mainstream monitors on the Internet have various problems in terms of reliability, timeliness, and security. Such as, delayed processing, interface limitation, unclear policies, etc. Problems in any of the above links may lead to the existence of a fraudulent certificate "invisible" to the domain name owner, which can then be used to launch attacks on legitimate websites.

3.4   Auditor

Auditor plays a key role in auditing log sever behavior. The service quality of auditor will directly determine the reliability of CT. If there is a security vulnerability in auditor's implementation, an attacker can exploit this vulnerability to avoid auditor's auditing of malicious log server. Therefore, if there is a fraudulent certificate which is issued by the publicly-trusted CA, meets the CT policy, is verified by the browser, but the malicious log server has not recorded it and the auditor has not detected this illegal behavior, and is "invisible" to the legitimate domain name owner. An attacker can use the fraudulent certificate to launch a MitM attack or impersonation attack on the target.

The implementation of auditor technology in certificate transparency system is essentially to establish a malicious log server auditing system on the Internet, to ensure that the audited log server meets the consistency and existence proof. To achieve the CT target, we believe that auditing services should meet the following requirements: (a) it should be able to perform security audits on the behavior of the log server in a timely and reliable manner; (b) it should be able to securely and efficiently provide the SCT audit path for the browser, to ensure that the certificate (or SCT) is recorded in public logs.

In practice, there are many factors that determine the service quality of auditor, including deployment mode and location (i.e., independent third-party server or integrated in the browser), coverage scope, frequency of detection, and robustness, etc. Therefore, in practice, the implementation of auditor faces many challenges. For example, (a) Privacy. Privacy leakage happens when browsers access auditor services. An SCT audit path request includes the identifier of the validated certificate, so the log server or auditor server knows the website that the client is visiting [14]. (b) Security. The existing auditor implementation methods cannot effectively check all STH and SCT in use. If it cannot effectively verify whether an SCT has been appended to the log, it may be used by attackers to launch attacks on websites. (c) Performance. If the browser wants to obtain the audit path of an SCT, it needs to additionally access a third-party (i.e., auditor server or log server) during the TLS establishment process. If the extra cost is too large, it will seriously affect the performance of client network connection, affect the user experience, and thus affect the promotion and deployment of auditor.

Summary. There are very few third-party auditors (e.g., Edgecombe and Merkle Town) deployed on the Internet. They typically audit the running status of log servers, by performing gossip validation of STHs with each other. However, there is no third-party auditor that provides users with SCT audit services, and while Chrome integrates the CT-over-DNS scheme, it is not enabled by default. In practice, there are many influencing factors that need to be considered when implementing an auditor, including privacy protection, security, reliability, and performance efficiency. If these problems cannot be properly resolved, it will greatly limit the application and deployment of the auditor in practice.

3.5   Browser

As the certificate verifier, the browser needs to be as the main body to participate to check whether the certificate meets the CT policy. These checks include the signature validity, quantity and existence proof of SCT, so as to alleviate the security threat brought by the fraudulent certificate. Therefore, as the beneficiary of CT framework, the support policy of browser and other client directly influences the promotion and deployment of CT. We combined the Chromium source code to analyze and summarize the browser's CT policies from the following points. In practice, these CT policies may affect the deployment and security of CT.

Trust Anchor. This includes a list of trusted root CA certificates and a list of approved log servers. The former determines which CAs issued certificates can be accepted, and also indicates that these CAs must comply with CT policies. The latter defines at least which log server the certificates issued by these CAs must be submitted to. As we mentioned in Sect. 3.2, there are 4 mainstream CAs that are not accepted by any regular log. This may result in a valid certificate issued by a CA that the browser trusts, but does not support the CT policy and thus is not accepted by the browser [28]. Moreover, as mentioned above, the way that the browsers update the approved log server list also affects many components of CT, including the running status of the log server, the accepted CA list, etc. [22]. It even cause log servers to overwork for a long time.

SCT Policy. The browser's requirements for the number and source of SCT will affect the scope of the log servers where CAs submit certificates [3,21,28]. This may further potentially affect the range of monitoring log server list of monitor. In addition, the browser's requirements for the SCT delivery method (i.e., TLS extension or certificate extension) will affect the application of CT by CAs and a large number of website servers [2,35,38]. Finally, the browser's verification policy for SCT will also affect the effect of CT. For example, browser developers often "soft-fail" by deciding to trust certificates when the list of approved log servers cannot be updated, so as not to rest their perceived reliability on the shoulders of a disparate set of third-party log servers. Soft-failing when latest log list is unavailable may at first appear to be an innocuous trade-off for usability, but in practice it has surprisingly extensive implications on the security of the CT as well as the PKI system [29]. Any attacker who can block a victim's access to specific domains (e.g., an attacker on the same wireless network) could leverage soft-failures to effectively turn off the victim's SCT checking.

Interactions with Auditor. The browser needs to interact with the auditor to complete the existence check of the SCT (i.e., a particular certificate has been appended to the log). Therefore, the browser's SCT checking policy, including validation methods, frequency, etc., will affect the deployment of the auditor. This may also further determine the audit scope and reliability of the auditor. In addition, as mentioned above, the browser performs the SCT checking through the auditor, which may affect the performance of the TLS connection and leak private information such as the website visited by the user.

Summary. As the certificate verifier, the browser's support policy for CT will directly determine the deployment of core components of CT such as log servers, auditor, etc. Then, judging from the existing actual deployment, there are certain deviations in the CT policy between the browsers and the CT components, including the list of supported CAs, the method of performing SCT verification, etc. These deviations may be exploited by attackers to evade CT detection of fraudulent certificates, and then be used to launch attacks on websites.

4   Feasible Suggestions

The problems existing in the practical application of CT components make CT possible to suffer from various attacks, which seriously endanger the overall security of CT. Our analysis shows that these CT components lack uniform and standardized implementation standards and are not robust. As a distributed security enhancement mechanism, no component of CT should not be assumed by default as fully trustworthy [28]. From these considerations, we propose to design countermeasures to improve the security of CT.

Formulate Security, Unified and Standardized CT Implementation Standards. The deviation between the new components introduced by CT and the original system of PKI leads to the possibility that CT security enhancement cannot completely cover the PKI ecological environment. For example, the scope of support of CA, the client's implementation policy for CT (e.g., approved log servers, update mechanism, implementation level, etc.). Establishing a unified and standardized implementation standard and data set will not limit the principles of CT distributed security design, but it can effectively reduce the degradation attacks caused by the deviation of each component.

Implement Security Measures for CT Services. CT auditor and monitor are respectively used, to audit log behavior and find fraudulent certificates. Therefore, similar audit mechanism should be implemented to detect the misbehavior or problematic behavior of CT auditor and monitors, especially on service reliability [28]. By integrating the resources and functions of the publicly deployed auditors and monitors on the Internet, the online regular status evaluation mechanism can be implemented to realize mutual supervision and redundancy between them. For example, by regularly exchanging data (e.g., SCTs, STHs, certificates), or requesting services based on the same domain name test set, testing their quality, and realizing automated error cause analysis and reporting.

Certificate Transparency as a Service. With the rapidly increase of certificates in logs and the widespread use of CT on the clients, it is difficult for a monitor or a auditor to have enough resources and capabilities to handle massive CT service requests. Incapable of addressing this challenge leads to several issues [28], such as erroneous certificate processing, delayed incident recovery, and also prevents the instantiation of the auditor function, etc., which might lead to delayed or failed detection of fraudulent certificates.

Therefore, certificate transparency, as a public security infrastructure, should provide "certificate transparency as a service (CTaaS)", certificate monitoring and auditing services to the outside world [10,28]. CTaaS can be implemented based on cloud computing platform, so as to achieve dynamic resource allocation, unified and continuous service capability [28]. This can effectively mitigate the impact of single point failure and limited resources on CT services.

5   Related Work

CT Deployment. The deployments of CT on the Internet are investigated from various perspectives. Stark et al. [39] completed a comprehensive study of CT deployment across the Internet, including compliance, user experience, and potential risk. Nykvist et al. [35] studied the adoption of CT in Alexa Top-1M websites and evaluated the performance of SCT delivery methods. Scheitle et al. [38] analyzed the server-side deployment of CT, and discussed the subdomain information leakage caused by the certificates in public logs. B. Li et al. conducted systematic in-depth research and analysis on CT monitor from the perspectives of reliability [28] and TLS/HTTPS configurations [27] respectively. Gustafsson et al. [23] characterized 11 public logs and highlight the differences of certificates they record. Amann et al. [2] finished a large-scale study on the adoption of various TLS/HTTPS security enhancements, including CT, HPKP, HSTS, CAA, SCSV downgrade prevention and DANE.

CT Extensions. Following the basic CT framework, several designs were proposed to improve the security and/or performance. Matsumoto et al. [30] studied the incentives of parities in the PKI system to deploy log-based enhancement schemes, and proposed the deployment status filters to detect the deployment status of a domain against the downgrade attacks. Dowling et al. [11] defined four security properties of logging schemes, and formally proved that CT implements these security properties. An efficient gossip protocol was proposed to detect several types of log inconsistencies [5]. Eskandarian et al. [14] proposed to audit a CT log without exposing user privacy by zero-knowledge proofs, and with the support of non-public subdomains by commitments with binding and hiding properties. Dahlberg et al. [10] proposed a verifiable light-weight monitoring, which enabled users to verify the correctness of the certificate notification from monitors. Tomescu et al. [40] introduced an append-only authenticated dictionary to construct logs, to provide efficient append-only proofs and lookup proofs.

TLS Certificate on the Internet. The certificates in public logs help to understand the TLS/HTTPS ecosystem. Gasser et al. [15] used the certificates in CT logs to investigate the violations of the baseline requirements for the certificate issuance [4]. Cui et al. [9] analyzed multiple attributes of forged certificates in the wild, such as preferences, causes, and attributes. Aertsen et al. [1] exploited the data obtained from several CT logs to study the certificate services of Let's Encrypt adopted in different organizations, hosts and domains. Vander-Sloot et al. [42] attempted to present a complete view of the certificates in the wild, by integrating the certificates in logs with data from passive measurement, active scanning, and search engines.

6   Conclusion

In this paper, we analyze the overall CT framework and its components. We find that, to achieve the design goal of CT, CT components themselves need to formulate reasonable policies and implement them correctly, and each component must ensure that it is more secure and reliable than regular TLS sessions when exchanging information. Then, we analyze the security design of each component of the CT framework and its impact on other components in practice. The analysis results show that each component faces various challenges in the implementation process, and its own policies and implementation methods can influence other components to different degrees. If the CT components cannot be deployed in a unified, coordinated, security and reasonably manner, an attacker may launch an attack on any component. This makes CT unable to achieve its intended purpose and thus conceals the fraudulent certificates exploited in the MitM attacks on the target websites. Therefore, the overall security guarantees of CT is jeopardized due to the weak protections of any components.

References

1. Aertsen, M., Korczynski, M., Moura, G., et al.: No domain left behind: is let's encrypt democratizing encryption? In: 2nd ANRW (2017)

2. Amann, J., Gasser, O., Scheitle, Q., et al.: Mission accomplished? HTTPS security after DigiNotar. In: 17th IMC (2017)
3. Apple Inc: Certificate transparency in Apple (2018). https://support.apple.com/en-us/HT205280
4. CA/Browser Forum: Baseline requirements for the issuance and management of publicly-trusted certificates, version 1.6.1 (2018). https://cabforum.org/baseline-requirements-documents/
5. Chuat, L., Szalachowski, P., Perrig, A., et al.: Efficient gossip protocols for verifying the consistency of certificate logs. In: 3rd IEEE CNS (2015)
6. Cloudflare Inc: Explore the certificate transparency ecosystem (2018). https://ct.cloudflare.com/
7. Comodo Group Inc: Comodo report of incident (2011). https://www.comodo.com/Comodo-Fraud-Incident-2011-03-23.html
8. Cooper, D., Santesson, S., et al.: IETF RFC 5280 - Internet X.509 public key infrastructure certificate and certificate revocation list (CRL) profile (2008)
9. Cui, M., Cao, Z., Xiong, G.: How is the forged certificates in the wild: practice on large-scale SSL usage measurement and analysis. In: Shi, Y., et al. (eds.) ICCS 2018. LNCS, vol. 10862, pp. 654–667. Springer, Cham (2018). https://doi.org/10.1007/978-3-319-93713-7_62
10. Dahlberg, R., Pulls, T.: Verifiable light-weight monitoring for certificate transparency logs. In: Gruschka, N. (ed.) NordSec 2018. LNCS, vol. 11252, pp. 171–183. Springer, Cham (2018). https://doi.org/10.1007/978-3-030-03638-6_11
11. Dowling, B., Günther, F., Herath, U., Stebila, D.: Secure logging schemes and certificate transparency. In: Askoxylakis, I., Ioannidis, S., Katsikas, S., Meadows, C. (eds.) ESORICS 2016. LNCS, vol. 9879, pp. 140–158. Springer, Cham (2016). https://doi.org/10.1007/978-3-319-45741-3_8
12. Eckersley, P.: A Syrian man-in-the-middle attack against Facebook (2011). https://www.eff.org/deeplinks/2011/05/syrian-man-middle-against-facebook
13. Edgecombe, G.: Certificate transparency monitor (2018). https://ct.grahamedgecombe.com/
14. Eskandarian, S., Messeri, E., Bonneau, J., et al.: Certificate transparency with privacy. In: 17th PETS (2017)
15. Gasser, O., Hof, B., Helm, M., Korczynski, M., Holz, R., Carle, G.: In log we trust: revealing poor security practices with certificate transparency logs and internet measurements. In: Beverly, R., Smaragdakis, G., Feldmann, A. (eds.) PAM 2018. LNCS, vol. 10771, pp. 173–185. Springer, Cham (2018). https://doi.org/10.1007/978-3-319-76481-8_13
16. Google Inc: Certificate transparency over DNS (2016). https://github.com/google/certificate-transparency-rfcs/blob/master/dns/draft-ct-over-dns.md
17. Google Inc: Certificate transparency (2018). http://www.certificate-transparency.org/
18. Google Inc: Known logs (2018). http://www.certificate-transparency.org/known-logs
19. Google Inc: Certificate transparency enforcement in google chrome (2020). https://groups.google.com/a/chromium.org/forum/#!msg/ct-policy/wHILiYf31DE/iMFmpMEkAQAJ
20. Google Inc: Changing the roots of the non-temporally-sharded Google Logs (2020). https://groups.google.com/a/chromium.org/g/ct-policy/c/iOg8Jqc0XxU?pli=1
21. Google Inc: Chromium certificate transparency policy (2020). https://github.com/chromium/ct-policy

22. Google Inc: Continued Operation of Logs with Planned Turn Down Dates (2020). https://groups.google.com/a/chromium.org/g/ct-policy/c/i1NFmE7txNE?pli=1

23. Gustafsson, J., Overier, G., Arlitt, M., Carlsson, N.: A first look at the CT landscape: certificate transparency logs in practice. In: Kaafar, M.A., Uhlig, S., Amann, J. (eds.) PAM 2017. LNCS, vol. 10176, pp. 87–99. Springer, Cham (2017). https://doi.org/10.1007/978-3-319-54328-4_7

24. Heather Adkins: An update on attempted man-in-the-middle attacks (2011). https://security.googleblog.com/2011/08/update-on-attempted-man in-middle html

25. Kent, S.: IETF Draft - Attack and Threat Model for Certificate Transparency (2018)

26. Laurie, B., Langley, A., et al.: IETF RFC 6962 - Certificate transparency (2013)

27. Li, B., Chu, D., Lin, J., et al.: The weakest link of certificate transparency: exploring the TLS/HTTPS configurations of third-party monitors. In: 18th IEEE TrustCom (2019)

28. Li, B., Lin, J., Li, F., et al.: Certificate transparency in the wild: exploring the reliability of monitors. In: 26th AMC CCS (2019)

29. Liu, Y., Tome, W., Zhang, L.: An end-to-end measurement of certificate revocation in the web's PKI. In: 15th IMC (2015)

30. Matsumoto, S., Szalachowski, P., Perrig, A.: Deployment challenges in log-based PKI enhancements. In: 8th EuroSec (2015)

31. Microsoft Inc: Certificate transparency in Microsoft (2018). https://blogs.msdn.microsoft.com/azuresecurity/2018/04/25/certificate-transparency/

32. Morton, B.: More Google fraudulent certificates (2014). https://www.entrust.com/google-fraudulent-certificates/

33. Mozilla: Certificate transparency in Mozilla (2018). https://wiki.mozilla.org/PKI:CT

34. Nginx: Certificate transparency in Nginx (2018). http://www.certificate-transparency.org/resources-for-site-owners/nginx

35. Nykvist, C., Sjöström, L., Gustafsson, J., Carlsson, N.: Server-side adoption of certificate transparency. In: Beverly, R., Smaragdakis, G., Feldmann, A. (eds.) PAM 2018. LNCS, vol. 10771, pp. 186–199. Springer, Cham (2018). https://doi.org/10.1007/978-3-319-76481-8_14

36. OpenSSL: Certificate transparency in OpenSSL (2018). https://www.openssl.org/docs/man1.1.0/crypto/ct.html

37. Opsmate Inc: How Cert Spotter Parses 255 Million Certificates (2020). https://sslmate.com/blog/post/how_certspotter_parses_255_million_certificates

38. Scheitle, Q., Gasser, O., Nolte, T., et al.: The rise of certificate transparency and its implications on the Internet ecosystem. In: 18th IMC (2018)

39. Stark, E., Sleevi, R., Muminovic, R., et al.: Does certificate transparency break the web? Measuring adoption and error rate. In: 40th IEEE S&P (2019)

40. Tomescu, A., Bhupatiraju, V., Papadopoulos, D., et al.: Transparency logs via append-only authenticated dictionaries. In: 26th ACM CCS (2019)

41. University of Michigan: Censys (2018). https://censys.io/

42. VanderSloot, B., Amann, J., et al.: Towards a complete view of the certificate ecosystem. In: 16th IMC (2016)

43. Wikipedia: Flame (malware) (2017). https://en.wikipedia.org/wiki/Flame_(malware)

44. Wilson, K.: Distrusting new CNNIC certificates (2015). https://blog.mozilla.org/security/2015/04/02/distrusting-new-cnnic-certificates/

SecMT – Security in Mobile Technologies

DaVinci: Android App Analysis Beyond Frida via Dynamic System Call Instrumentation

Alexander Druffel[(✉)] and Kris Heid

Fraunhofer Institute for Secure Information Technology, Darmstadt, Germany
{alexander.druffel,kris.heid}@sit.fraunhofer.de

Abstract. Today there are billions of mobile Android devices and the corresponding app stores contain millions of different apps. Due to their access to personal data and their commonly closed source nature, program analysis remains the only instrument to analyze app behavior and protect user data. At the same time, many measures for hardening apps have been developed to make analysis more difficult and to hide the inner workings of applications, making dynamic analysis a time-consuming task. We propose *DaVinci*, an Android kernel module for system call hooking, which allows a fully transparent and scalable dynamic analysis. *DaVinci* comes with preconfigured high level profiles to easily analyze the low level system calls. *DaVinci* works even on hardened apps without manual adjustments where common tools like Frida fail or require exhausting reverse engineering. We evaluate our approach against state-of-the-art hardening measures in a custom app as well as several hardened real-world examples and find that we successfully overcome all protection measures even when other tools fail. Our framework will be open-sourced and made available to the research and security communities.

Keywords: Android · Hooking · Program analysis · Kernel · Rootkit · Instrumentation

1 Introduction

In the current market for mobile devices, Android remains the most popular operating system with over 85% market share in 2020 [13]. Thus, the number of apps in the largest Android app store (Google Play Store) is also steadily growing. Due to the sensitive data that smartphones come into contact with during their everyday usage and the fact that apps in the Play store are distributed without access to the source code, users can be at risk through malicious or vulnerable code in the apps. Google conducts basic behavioral analysis of all uploaded apps to prevent such malware from entering their store. However, the exact nature of the analysis is kept secret and prior work has shown successful methods of hiding malicious code from analysis [6]. Even if apps do not contain known malware, they can exhibit undesired behavior, such as collecting and

© Springer Nature Switzerland AG 2020
J. Zhou et al. (Eds.): ACNS 2020 Workshops, LNCS 12418, pp. 473–489, 2020.
https://doi.org/10.1007/978-3-030-61638-0_26

sending personal data without the user's explicit consent. Google added a permission system to Android as a first privacy protection measure, allowing users to grant or restrict access to protected resources such as location data or the camera. Over the years, permission granularity has continuously improved, such that explicit consent is now required during access to the resource at runtime. While it provides an overview of the resources that an app accesses, it does not provide any information on exactly what happens with the acquired data and whether privacy is violated. For example, a navigation app has a legitimate reason to access location data and connect to the internet, but users may not want their location data to be shared with the developer or third parties.

Static and dynamic code analysis are techniques to understand what an app does besides what is presented to the user. These methods are used to identify hidden code and vulnerabilities in apps. The results can be useful for end users to protect their privacy, as well as companies who might want to generate white or black lists of applications to protect their data. In addition, antivirus companies and researchers use the same techniques to analyze applications or potential malware.

While static code analysis works by disassembling the program and analyzing the recovered code, reconstructing control flow graphs and data dependencies, dynamic analysis manipulates function calls and system interaction of an app during runtime. Both methods offer complementary results, and depending on the task and app, one or both are appropriate. Some apps, such as online banking apps, streaming apps with protected content, games with anti-cheating protection, or malware, often contain various measures to prevent static and dynamic analysis to protect their code or assets. In banking apps, code obfuscation is implemented to protect the user and to prevent fraud. Apps with copyrighted content, such as streaming apps, use these measures to prevent the extraction of the copyrighted material to prevent piracy. Game developers want to prevent cheating, and malware apps often use obfuscation to hide their malicious behavior and remain undetected for as long as possible. That presents analysts with the problem that analysis of those apps consumes significantly more resources and time.

In addition, although most Android apps contain only Java bytecode, some apps also include native libraries written in C or C++ that are loaded at runtime via the Java Native Interface (JNI). This effectively breaks many analysis frameworks that only consider the Java bytecode and do not provide functionality to analyze the native code, as hiding functionality in native code is an easy and effective strategy to defeat those frameworks.

This leads to a perpetual arms race between the developers of app protection frameworks who try to make reverse engineering as difficult as possible and the developers of program analysis tools who try to provide insight into even the most protected apps.

In this work, we try to stop the arms race and propose a barely detectable dynamic analysis method. We propose a configurable kernel module for selectively hooking and manipulating system calls. We offer a comfortable interface to remotely control and configure the kernel module and custom hooks or load reconfigured profiles. Using a kernel module for dynamic analysis, removes obvious side channels and hides our approach well. Other dynamic analysis tools are much easier detectable by anti-analysis libraries and require manual adjustments by the analyst for each analysis target. *DaVinci* is therefore well suited for large-scale automated analysis, as we will demonstrate a generic bypass of all anti-dynamic-analysis measures we found in the wild.

We include features for tracing, hooking and blocking system calls in a reconfigurable and workflow-oriented manner that speeds up dynamic analysis of apps and is designed to work with hardened applications. Despite efforts to harden current Android versions by restricting available system calls using the seccomp feature of the kernel, the vast majority of system calls is still available to applications, and they remain the only way of interacting with the system, meaning that restriction for security reasons can limit features, which results in a conflict of interest for manufacturers. Some processes are sandboxed and therefore further restricted, with renderer threads in web browsers being a prominent example, but Android applications in general have a broad variety of system calls to interact with the system.

We are aware that kernel modules on Linux are not new, but are quite uncommon in Android and there exist no publications in the area of dynamic analysis via kernel modules on Android.

We would like to emphasize that while our tool is capable of analyzing hardened applications in detail, it does not pose any risk to users and our results should not be seen as a vulnerability of the Android system or the analyzed apps. It is not suitable as a hacking tool as it requires root privileges and, depending on the Android version, even a customized kernel build.

In Sect. 2 we list related approaches and highlight our improvements in contrast. Section 3 shows the working principle and features of DaVinci. Section 4 evaluates our design against hardened apps, malware and a customized root-detection app. This section also shows scenarios, where state-of-the-art tools like Frida fail or would require complex workarounds as well as a performance comparison discussion. Finally, we give a short conclusion and an outlook on future work.

2 Related Work

Dynamic app analysis is still an effective approach to program analysis that complements static analysis methods well. In the 12 years since the first Android release, many approaches have been proposed and implemented [4]. Due to the Java Native Interface (JNI), Android applications, which normally consist of Java bytecode, can load shared-object libraries at runtime and move functionality into native code. This bypasses many existing approaches working on bytecode.

Most dynamic analysis tools, such as debuggers and tracers, use the `ptrace` system call to implement process instrumentation. Classic dynamic analysis approaches such as debugging can be slow and difficult to set up generically, since they usually require manual analysis of each target application to find relevant breakpoint locations. However, many modern operating systems limit the use of ptrace to improve integrity, and there are also many anti-debugging techniques for detecting ptrace within applications themselves.

The Xposed [14] framework takes a different approach. Xposed injects itself into applications by modifying the zygote process from which all apps are forked, and overlays functions and symbols with custom ones. It includes an interface to write modules with custom code, making it very extensible. This allows generic hooking of Java functions. A drawback of this approach is that it only operates on function granularity, which can be too coarse for analysis, and native code is not considered either.

Compared to Xposed, the dynamic analysis toolkit Frida [7] has fewer limitations. It allows instrumentation of native code and Java byte-code but is also limited to basic block granularity. Also, system calls can only be intercepted at the wrapper function level, like at the *libc* and Java runtime. This means that Frida's interception can be bypassed with inline assembly system calls, which is a problem because analysts need to be able to intercept all system interactions.

CopperDroid [22] and CuckooDroid [5] take a potentially more powerful sandbox based approach. Both works use an Android emulator to implement a sandbox for dynamic analysis. We note that CuckooDroid, since it uses the Xposed framework internally, inherits its constraints.

The use of emulators generally provides good access, monitoring and interception possibilities. However, it is relatively easy for apps to detect the emulation [20] and possibly obfuscate their behavior.

To overcome the limitations of previous approaches, we propose implementing analysis in the kernel space, transparent to applications. There are many kernel space tracing and filtering tools such as Kprobes [8], eBPF [9] or LTTng [10], but they do not offer arbitrary system call manipulation, which is essential since we need to hide data that discloses our analysis to the application. A kernel module for macOS, especially targeting malware detection, is presented in [19]. This approach traces system calls and through pattern analysis similar to [15], the kernel module succeeds in reliably detecting malware with a low false negative rate. Since this approach aims to detect malware patterns without defending against them, it lacks instrumentation functionality. In [18], the authors used a similar approach to implement a debugger without using ptrace, by implementing the features in a kernel module. Their goal was to defeat debugger-detection and provide an easier user experience than traditional debuggers. One notable difference to our approach is that it is not able to be automated for applications without symbols. For example intercepting a certain system call only works on the libc function layer and not on inline assembly, which requires manual analysis. It also does not fully work on ARM, as some of the uprobes features it relies upon are not available on ARM.

The kernel module for dynamic binary translation of kernel code presented in [16] allows kernel code instrumentation and could therefore be used for an approach similar to ours. However, at this time, it is only a proposed framework, the code is not maintained and it does not implement our use case, which is scalable and dynamically reconfigurable system call instrumentation for application analysis.

2.1 Contribution

In contrast to related approaches, we see two main novel contributions in DaVinci:

1. Dynamic application analysis from kernel space, which is hardly detectable by the analyzed app, even with commercial hardening solutions.
2. Compared to other kernel space analysis tools, we offer a more powerful hooking interface that not only traces system calls, but also allows arbitrary manipulation.

3 Overview of DaVinci

Our approach circumvents the aforementioned limitations of other dynamic analysis frameworks by working on a different analysis layer. We change the system call table and dispatch into custom functions and therefore can intercept all system calls made by all processes. To achieve this, we have developed a kernel module that locates the system call table and overwrites the function pointers of the system calls we are interested in with pointers to the functions of the kernel module. We implement filtering, logging and manipulation of parameters and return values. This technique is commonly used in rootkits to hide their presence and activity [1,3], and we use the same approach to hide our analysis tool (Fig. 1).

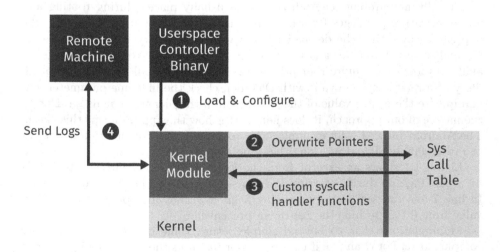

Fig. 1. High level overview of our architecture

3.1   Non-invasive Instrumentation

Because this approach hooks the system calls made by all processes on the entire system, we must first filter out all calls that were not made by our target application. To have a reliable filter, we take advantage of the fact that each app installed on an Android system is assigned a new Linux user id and all processes that are spawned in the application life cycle are bound to that user id. This way we can verify the user id of the calling process for each system call and dispatch to the original handler if it does not come from the target app. While android allows developers to specify a shared user id for multiple of their apps, this does not cause problems for DaVinci, as these apps can also run in the same process and in the same JVM, therefore making it the same target for all intents and purposes. Some system calls are invoked at a very high rate and usually most do not come from the target app. Therefore, it is important to keep the common case runtime overhead low. For this reason, user ids are always filtered as the first step. For relevant system calls, the occurrence, the parameters and return value can be logged in a configurable logging measure. We implemented logging to a file, to the kernel message buffer, and over a custom in-module network stack to a remote server, with the last option being the least detectable.

3.2   System Call Hooking

For some dynamic analysis tasks, it can be useful to change the result of a system call based on a condition. Our approach can actively change and manipulate parameters and results of system calls, thereby break integrity assumptions made by application developers. This feature is missing on most other kernel-space instrumentation approaches. For example, some apps try to detect if they are running on a rooted device, and one of the measures to detect this is to look for a program called *su*(switch user) in the usual program folders. The *su* program is normally not present on Android and is usually placed during rooting and allows elevating privileges from a normal user to the root user. Therefore, the app can assume that the device is rooted when the binary is found. However, an analyst might want to analyze such an app from their rooted device to use analysis tools that require root privileges. The analyst could now intercept all filesystem related system calls with DaVinci, check the filename parameter and manipulate the return value of the system call if the filename equals su. Due to the nature of our approach, it does not matter how the app performs this check. The Android Java API, for example File.exists(), the libc function access() or raw assembly all end up using the same system calls.

Listing 1.1 shows an excerpt from the log of filesystem related system calls by a banking app during startup. We can see how it searches for the su binary. In line 7 one can see that our hooking framework has manipulated the return value from 0 to 2 to hide the /sbin/su present file.

Manipulations that go beyond simple return value overrides require more complex logic. For example, if the app under test uses the system call getdents

Listing 1.1. Excerpt of system calls of the Commerzbank app

```
1   LOG: openat(dfd:64 pathname:"/property_contexts" flags:256) = −2
2   [...]
3   LOG: newfstatat(dfd:64 pathname:"/vendor" flags:256) = 0
4   HOOK: newfstatat(dfd:64 pathname:"/sbin/su" flags:0) = 2
5   [...]
6   HOOK: newfstatat(dfd:64 pathname:"/vendor/xbin/su" flags:0) = 2
7   HOOK: newfstatat(dfd:64 pathname:"/sbin/su" flags:0) = 2 <− 0
8   HOOK: newfstatat(dfd:64 pathname:"/system/sbin/su" flags:0) = 2
9   [...]
10  HOOK: newfstatat(dfd:64 pathname:"/vendor/xbin/su" flags:0) = 2
```

to get all directory entries and search these for the su binary, we need to manipulate the buffer into which the directory entries are written.

To speed up the dynamic analysis workflow, we designed DaVinci for dynamic reconfiguration at runtime. There are several options, with a configuration program running in userspace being the simplest. The program communicates with the kernel module via an exposed kernel device. Alternatively, DaVinci can be configured via its hidden network stack. Since we have not implemented any kind of configuration verification, any party could change the configuration. Therefore, we strongly advise against using DaVinci outside a trusted lab environment.

3.3 High Level Common Analysis Profiles

Since there are a lot of system calls on Linux that can reveal the existence of a file, it would be cumbersome to hook each one individually every time. Therefore, we have created profiles that summarize common manipulation goals for analysis into profiles. They consist of a single setting in our module, for example to hide a particular file described by name, and sets up hooks for all system calls that interact with the file system, including checks and manipulations to hide any result or side effect of a system call that would reveal the existence of the file. We deemed this useful and necessary because hiding a file requires a total of 45 system calls to be hooked to intercept every possible system call for this fairly common analysis goal. Since many rooting and emulator detection approaches look for specific files, this should speed up analysis considerably.

We included profiles for the following common tasks:

− Transparently disable filesystem modifications
− Hiding specific files
− Create a virtual filesystem overlay
− Filter network traffic.

Filesystem overlays can be used to provide custom files such as known-good configuration and device property files, which are commonly checked in anti analysis code. To do this, we hook every system call that takes a filename and replace the path with a specifiable one if it matches, so the analyst only needs to place a known-good file somewhere on the device.

Unlike other tools that isolate programs into filesystem or network namespaces to secure the system, our tool can offer a common environment for apps to trigger code paths behind environmental checks. For example, if an application tries to write a file and terminates if the write fails, our toolkit can manipulate the system call to prevent the actual change from happening, but give the program a return value indicating a successful write. Further work could expand to dynamic virtual files that exist purely in kernel memory, for cases where the app is trying to verify that the data was actually written.

As our target user base are application analysts, DaVinci can be integrated with other common dynamic analysis tools like Frida or XPosed if the application under test implements advanced anti-analysis techniques to bypass their way of intercepting system interaction. This would enable to use the mature plugin-base of these tools without the need to re-implement the needed features as kernel driver code in C, which has a high complexity and might be time-consuming.

4   Evaluation

To evaluate our approach, we verify that DaVinci is not detected by commercially hardened applications and common malware evasion techniques. In addition, we highlight real world targets where other tools such as Frida are unable to bypass protection measures, while DaVinci is successful, which underlines our contribution. We evaluate our approach on a real device, as well as on an emulator, both running Android 10, the most recent version available during evaluation. To further evaluate with known behavior, we developed a testing app that implements all previously mentioned techniques for detecting if it is running on a legitimate device without being analyzed. We started by evaluating the effectiveness by testing 14 hardened apps from the Google Play Store.

In the next step, we extended the open-source root-detection app RootBeer [12] with a multitude of additional checks, including anti-debugging, anti-root, anti-emulator and anti-hooking code to evaluate if our kernel module manages to hide its presence.

Finally, we analyzed six malware samples to look for more common malware anti-analysis patterns. The numbers were chosen as each app required manual analysis to confirm our results and to help develop profiles for common analysis goals, laying the foundation for a future comprehensive large-scale analysis. We explain the process for two hardened apps and one malware sample in more detail to demonstrate the capabilities of our approach and highlight the workflow. As a last step, we discuss the performance overhead introduced by our method in contrast to other approaches.

4.1   Hardened Apps from the Store

We found a variety of different obfuscators, application packers, anti-debugging and anti-emulator measures, as well as VM detection measures, in mobile

Table 1. Test apps with detected measures (- = not detected)

No.	App & Version	Obfuscator	Packer	Anti-analysis
1	de.brillux.brilluxapp-3.2.2	-	dxmerge	properties
2	com.commerzbank.mobilebanking-1.0.0	Arxan	Promon	API, properties
3	com.commerzbank.photoTAN-7.1.16	llvm 3.5	Promon	-
4	**com.commerzbank.msb-2.3.0**	Arxan	-	API, properties
5	com.secneo.guard-1.0	SecNeo	Bangcle	ARM-only
6	com.phone.calller.locator-2.2.2	-	Jiagu	-
7	com.readdle.spark-5.0.1	DexGuard, llvm 3.5	-	Invalid classes, properties
8	com.sand.airdroid-4.1.0.4	-	DexProtector	properties
9	de.datev.smartlogin-2.0.4	-	-	API, properties
10	com.dring.juice.cocktail.simulator.relax-4.0	Unknown	Tencent Protect	ARM-only, properties
11	com.tgelec.kidssmartwatch-1.0.0	-	Ijiami, upx	ARM-only, properties
12	com.nineton.best.line-1.8.3	llvm 3.5	Jiagu	-
13	com.hawsoft.mobile.speechtrans-1.4.5	llvm 3.6.1	Jiagu	-
14	**com.supercell.clashofclans-13.180.8**	-	-	ARM-only, properties

applications. The initial analysis was performed using an open source hardening-measures identifier called APKiD [2], which gives a first overview over the hardening measures taken. We used this to filter a larger set of apps for samples with unique combinations of hardening measures. We selected a unique combination of detected code obfuscators, packers and detected anti-analysis techniques to get samples from the most popular hardening frameworks. A list of which is shown in Table 1. We do note that this list is not comprehensive and serves as a proof of concept and a more comprehensive analysis of a large scale sample set of applications is left as future work. We focus on hardened applications, since this is the use case where our approach offers functionality beyond that of existing tools. During analysis, we were able to overcome the protection mechanisms from all tested apps.

We assume that the apps do not implement different levels of protection, and once the application starts and performs its tasks rather than exiting, we have overcome the protection measures. Since we do not have access to the source code we have to make this assumption. Nevertheless, it would be theoretically possible to have a multi-stage anti-analysis detection mechanism and that certain features are step by step enabled with increasing anti-analysis test stages for more critical components. For example: reading the balance of a bank account may be less secured than actual transactions. However, we can not check this claim without source code access, and we also consider this unlikely for a legitimate application.

In the following, we will for brevity pick two sample apps for a more in depth example. We discuss the mechanisms used and how they were overcome with DaVinci. The methods are similar for other hardening frameworks.

Finance: Commerzbank App. To get an idea of the measures taken by the app, we first enable logging of all system calls for the app and run it. During startup, we see an error message informing us that the app detected an untrustworthy environment and is refusing to continue running. We observed in our system call log that the app uses the openat call to read several device property files and uses the *newfstatat* system call at multiple candidate locations to look for a su binary. Since we run our analysis on a rooted device, the app eventually checks the correct location of su and shows the error message. In the next step we configured DaVinci to modify the return code of *newfstatat* if the filename matches su. Restarting the app with this hook enabled results in the successful start of the app, like shown in Fig. 2. With this, we consider the anti-root mechanisms of the app defeated. This hook can easily be activated through loading the "hide files" profile described in Sect. 3.3. This includes hooks for all system calls with interact with the file system and filter out results and side channels for the presence of su binaries. Therefore, just enabling this profile enables execution and further analysis of the application.

To compare our approach with Frida as an example of a userspace based analysis toolkit, we also tried to circumvent the root detection using many publicly available Frida scripts that claimed such functionality, but found that the application was especially hardened against Frida and kept crashing during start up when Frida was enabled, even when no script was loaded.

With manual static analysis we found out that the app implemented its own signal handlers for breakpoints as anti-debugging measure, which breaks the analysis foundation of Frida, as Frida uses ptrace to hook onto processes and interact with them. So to analyze this app with Frida, manual reverse engineering and customization is necessary to defeat these specific Anti-Frida methods. This is an example of the anti-debugging arms race we explained in Sect. 1.

Mobile 3D Games: Clash of Clans. Another example we discuss in more detail is *Clash of Clans*, a very popular 3D game for Android. We chose this example because it is protected and offers special challenges, as it only ships the ARM version of its native libraries and does not run in any of the ARM emulators we tested, presumably because of performance reasons and missing 3D cross-architecture acceleration. It also uses many system calls and we can see the real world performance overhead of our analysis. Again, we first traced all system calls of the application and found checks for debuggers and su binaries in the log. One challenge we encountered was that certain system calls are used so frequently in this game, namely read and write, that logging them to the kernel buffer crashed the device. This means that we need to consider overhead here and not log unnecessary calls or choose to log over the network, instead of the kernel message log. The anti-debugger checks were defeated trivially, as we did not rely on debugging measures and the root detection was defeated in the same way as explained in the previous example. We found that we were able to bypass the anti analysis checks and progress to the actual game without a perceivable performance penalty. When trying to achieve the same with Frida, we found

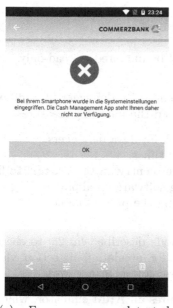

(a) Error screen: detected rooted device

(b) Successful login screen after activating DaVinci

Fig. 2. The Commerzbank app on a rooted device

that the app also contains measures to detect Frida. This time the app tried to connect to the Unix socket that Frida uses internally for communication between the analysis client and the Frida daemon. Again, manual reverse engineering is required to patch or hook those anti-analysis measures, hindering scalability of automated analysis based on Frida on hardened apps.

4.2 Anti-analysis Testapp

Finally, we built our own app to implement all anti-analysis checks we found and test our hooks. We based our app on RootBeer [12], an open source app for android that checks if the device is rooted. We extended the list of implemented root detection checks and implemented additional anti-debugging measures as described in the following list. As a result, the modified RootBeer app should contain most state of the art hardening measures against dynamic analysis condensed into one app. DaVinci is able to successfully hide from all checks in the app with our preconfigured profiles.

Detecting Root. Many hardened apps are designed to not run on rooted smartphones or custom roms and use these or similar measures.

– Existence of *Magisk*, *SuperSU*, *Luckypatcher* or other common ROM/Root Manager apps.

- Test-keys tag in the kernel signature.
- Developer properties such as ro.debuggable=1.
- Existence of su or busybox binaries.
- Writable file system partitions that should be mounted as read-only.

Detecting Debuggers. To detect the presence of a debugger like gdb or the Android Studio Java debugger, we implemented the following measures:

- *Debug.isDebuggerConnected()* API to check for Java debuggers.
- Using ptrace on our own process multiple times.
- Checking /proc/self/status for a non-zero entry on the TracerPid field.
- Defining a SIGTRAP handler and executing software breakpoints.
- Reading /proc/self/cmdline and verifying the process name.

Detecting Emulators. We use most methods described in [23] to check the runtime environment. Advanced techniques for emulation detection via side channels are currently out of scope and will remain as future work.

- Using a native library in ARM. This requires an ARM emulator, which significantly slows down analysis.
- Checking if there are traces of qemu, e.g. the kernel device /sys/qemu_trace, and the file /system/bin/qemud, since it is the default Android Studio ARM emulator.
- Checking if the CPU info contains Goldfish, the name of the official Android emulator.
- Checking for hardware-specific values like described in [20]: ethernet interfaces, product and device name, phone properties (IMEI, SIM, Number, Voicemail number and mobile carrier).

Detecting Hooking Frameworks. The following methods are implemented to check for the presence of the most common hooking frameworks:

- Checking loaded libraries under */proc/self/maps* for common tools. e.g. Frida-agent-32.so.
- Scanning the mapped memory pages for known strings and values from hooking frameworks. Frida for example loads the v8 JavaScript engine into the memory space, which is identifiable by the strings in the code.
- Scanning the list of installed apps for hooking tools.

Detecting Runtime Modifications. A common technique for defeating anti-debugging techniques is to unpack the application and simply remove the code and then package the app again. To harden our app against this, we implemented the following measures.

- Verification of the signature of the running app to see if it matches the one in the package manager.

– Continuous checksum generation of the code to detect modifications or breakpoints during runtime.

Most of the anti-analysis techniques we have found are trivially bypassed
with DaVinci, since they rely on system call results. We do not use `ptrace`,
which defeats self-ptracing and debugger detection measures. We do not cause
differences in the memory layout of the program, as Frida would, and therefore
scanning memory pages and loaded libraries does not detect DaVinci. We do
not install a custom app, like XPosed would, therefore scanning installed apps
does not reveal our toolkit. We do not manipulate the app, which means that
integrity verification measures can not reveal the analysis.

Popular hardened apps having special checks against Frida is most likely
based on the fact that Frida is one of the most popular tools for dynamic analysis on Android and our approach only existed in our lab environment. If our
approach becomes more popular and widespread, application developers could
try to specifically harden against DaVinci too. The options for this are however limited, as we will discuss now by proposing different techniques by which
DaVinci can be detected from userspace.

One theoretical measure would be to use proceedings in rootkit detection
from userspace, like [21] or [17]. These approaches either rely on information
that is not exposed to the userspace anymore or require *a priori* knowledge
to measure timing data on the system prior to enabling the hooks in DaVinci
to successfully detect it, which can be circumvented by the analyst by loading
DaVinci before starting the app under test. In general, most userspace based
rootkit detection approaches rely on either timing side channels or data supplied
by the kernel, which makes such approaches either dependent on gathering prior
data, as Android devices vary greatly in hardware and performance metrics, or
on system calls, which could always be manipulated by us. We note that this
might require a one-time cost of implementing the correct response to a new
heuristic to detect kernel modifications or runtime details that DaVinci doesn't
handle yet.

We did not implement these techniques and leave this area for further
research, as the authors did not make their tools publicly available and the
scenario does not apply to our use case, as previous measurements have to be
made to detect changes at runtime and in our case we always load the analysis
before starting the app.

Another measure an app developer could take is to use Google's SafetyNet
Attestation API, which provides developers a fresh, signed assessment of the
device integrity from the Google Playstore Services itself at runtime. Intercepting and manipulating this result would not be sufficient, as we are unable to
forge the cryptographic signature. However, our analysis toolkit does not need
to change the result, as our full analysis setup passes the SafetyNet test on
Android 10. Because SafetyNet's internals are kept secret by Google, we assume
that it is overly careful to avoid creating false negative reports, and that the
rooting tool we use is not detected. Many newer rooting frameworks manage
to achieve this through means of union mounting the system partition to leave

the original system partition unchanged [11], allowing us to analyze apps on a rooted Android device with a custom kernel booted, DaVinci loaded and the SafetyNet API reporting a fully trustworthy device. We mention here that using Xposed causes SafetyNet to consider the device untrustworthy, as the zygote file on the system partition gets modified. In order to work around a SafetyNet result that indicates our analysis framework as untrustworthy, another approach is required. For example patching out the check in the app itself or use in-app hooking or debugging to change behavior after the result is received.

4.3   Malware

We analyzed some malware samples from the Android Malware Genome Project [24] to test the stability of our approach and learn about potential further techniques that apps might use. The Genome Project was chosen, since it contains an exhaustive list of malware, also used in previous research. However, it is currently not maintained and samples are a few years old, which leaves a more broad analysis on more recent samples as future work. Table 2 shows the six randomly chosen malware samples and the hardening measures detected by APKiD. Since manual analysis is required to confirm our findings, we could not analyze all samples and decided to randomly pick six, but we quickly realized that the behavior is often very similar.

Again, as an example to demonstrate the capabilities of DaVinci, we have analyzed malware app 1 and will discuss the results in more detail. The procedure for the other malware samples was quite similar, and we were able to identify the behavior of all samples using our toolkit. We initially enabled the *no-filesystem-modification* and *no-network-communication* hooking profiles to minimize the risk of compromising our device and invalidating further results. In the logs, we observe that the malware attempts to contact a command and control server. The malware attempts to transmit a device fingerprint, consisting of unique device identification values such as the IMEI, local time, location, language and device model to the server. Additionally, the app searches for its own process details in `/proc/self`. Without network connection, no further actions can be observed because blocking requests are used in the malware. To verify our observation, we use static reverse engineering methods to analyze the malware. We find the properties to be passed, in addition we find binaries to root the device, along with a tool for taking screenshots and one for installing and removing apps. No further hardening against dynamic analysis was detected, except the Java API check to find debuggers, which resulted in the `/proc/self` access.

As we can see, DaVinci provides adequate protection against persistence and botnet code, as well as analysis capabilities for malware.

Table 2. Malware with detected measures (- = not detected)

No.	SHA256 start	Obfuscator	Packer	Anti-analysis
1	04f9634fe910	-	APKProtect	properties
2	05e8e162979c	-	APKProtect	properties
3	049a64f049d9	-	Qihoo 360	properties
4	040f1be49973	-	Bangcle	-
5	04a22268aad7	llvm	Baidu	API
6	06ed56758a7c	-	APKProtect	-

4.4 Performance Evaluation

Since measuring precise performance overhead for kernel code is significantly more complex than in userspace, we confine our performance evaluation to an informal discussion. One reason for this is the need to consider kernel thread scheduling, which introduces a variability of results that is difficult to control. And since DaVinci is a framework, actual overhead is highly dependent on the runtime of the used hooks and the frequency of the hooked system call. Loading the kernel module and not tracing anything induces zero overhead. When intercepting a system call, the general overhead for the rest of the processes is limited as only one additional indirect branch is performed on the fast path. The hooked function compares the user id of the process with the configuration and jumps to the original handler. Due to branch prediction, this induces only a minimal overhead, as the instructions for the branch are already prefetched. For the application under test, our approach has a significantly smaller overhead than Frida, as our hooks are implemented in C and not in interpreted JavaScript. We found that our approach is stable, if logging is either done over the network or rate limited for the kernel message buffer. Otherwise, system crashes have been observed when logging without rate limiting of high-frequency system calls, like `read` and `write`, which occurred thousands of times per second on some applications. Our experimental evaluation confirmed our intuition, as the system remained responsive and no perceivable difference was found when using the applications under test. Since our approach is intended for software analysts and not day-to-day usage, a performance overhead beneath the perceivable threshold is most likely acceptable, as most of the time in analysis is often spent developing custom analysis code and evaluating the results and runtime is only a small factor.

5 Conclusion and Future Work

In this work, we have presented DaVinci, a novel approach for dynamic android app analysis, which allows fast and scalable analysis where existing approaches have severe limitations or require tedious manual analysis. The presented tool allows for dynamic system call instrumentation and reconfiguration while analyzing the whole process, meaning all code is considered. In contrast to existing userspace based tools, system calls can no longer be hidden from the analysis and anti-debugging measures are not effective. We have shown, that our approach works well for several classes of hardened apps, including banking, anti cheating and malware. Additionally, we have evaluated DaVinci against several state-of-the-art anti-analysis checks. With these results, we also show that detecting our approach is barely possible. We see three promising topics for future research: detailed inter process communication analysis, high level behavior reconstruction from system call behavior and improved virtual environment modeling, for example in the filesystem. Analysis of the inter process communication would be helpful to for example detect confused deputy attacks and find connections to different apps to extend analysis to. For this, the Android IPC system (Android Intents), which use the `ioctl` system call on the `/dev/binder` device with serialized Java data, would need to be analyzed in depth, including target analysis and monitoring which apps receive the messages. Decoding of the data of `Intents` has shown itself to be a complex problem. CopperDroid [22] explored this direction and could be a valuable addition to this toolkit. Custom hooking logic based on different IPC messages could be very valuable in modeling the system and analyzing interactions between app families. This can be generalized into recovery of high-level behavior from system call traces. This would allow to further accelerate the analysis process for apps. Regarding the virtual environment, it would be helpful to not only be able to block modifications to the filesystem, but also allow writes to files without actual filesystem modifications, for example in purely virtual files that live in kernel memory and only exist in the context of the analysis. With this, an app could interact more and may progress into deeper code paths without the dangers of allowing file system access to untrusted code. We plan to open-source DaVinci soon.

References

1. Android platform based linux kernel rootkit. http://www.phrack.org/issues/68/6.html
2. Apkid github. https://github.com/rednaga/APKiD
3. Bypassing integrity checking systems. http://phrack.org/issues/51/9.html#article
4. Collection of android security related resources. https://github.com/ashishb/android-security-awesome
5. Cuckoodroid. https://github.com/idanr1986/cuckoodroid-2.0
6. Dissecting the android bouncer. https://jon.oberheide.org/files/summercon12-bouncer.pdf
7. Frida binary instrumentation toolkit. https://frida.re
8. Kernel debugging with kprobes. https://www.ibm.com/developerworks/library/l-kprobes/index.html
9. Kernel tracing with ebpf - unlocking god mode on linux. https://media.ccc.de/v/35c3-9532-kernel_tracing_with_ebpf
10. Lttng. https://lttng.org/
11. Magisk. https://github.com/topjohnwu/Magisk

12. Rootbeer. https://github.com/scottyab/rootbeer
13. Smartphone market share (2020). https://www.idc.com/promo/smartphone-market-share/os
14. Xposed framework. https://repo.xposed.info/
15. Borek, M.: Intrusion detection system for android: linux kernel system calls analysis. G2 pro gradu, diplomity, Aalto University (2017). http://urn.fi/URN:NBN:fi:aalto-201709046813
16. Feiner, P., Brown, A.D., Goel, A.: Comprehensive kernel instrumentation via dynamic binary translation. SIGARCH CAN **40**(1), 135–146 (2012). https://doi.org/10.1145/2189750.2150992
17. Wampler, D., Graham, J.: A method for detecting linux kernel module rootkits. In: Craiger, P., Shenoi, S. (eds.) DigitalForensics 2007. ITIFIP, vol. 242, pp. 107–116. Springer, New York (2007). https://doi.org/10.1007/978-0-387-73742-3_7
18. Holl, T., Klocke, P., Franzen, F., Kirsch, J.: Kernel-assisted debugging of linux applications. In: 2nd Reversing and Offensive-oriented Trends Symposium 2018 (ROOTS), November 2018
19. Mieghem, V.V.: Detecting malicious behaviour using system calls. Master thesis, TU Delft (2016). http://resolver.tudelft.nl/uuid:c71c85bc-d742-449b-88e7-33e172392ec2
20. Petsas, T., Voyatzis, G., Athanasopoulos, E., Polychronakis, M., Ioannidis, S.: Rage against the virtual machine: hindering dynamic analysis of android malware. In: EuroSec. Association for Computing Machinery, New York (2014). https://doi.org/10.1145/2592791.2592796
21. Singh, B., Evtyushkin, D., Elwell, J., Riley, R., Cervesato, I.: On the detection of kernel-level rootkits using hardware performance counters. In: Proceedings of the 2017 ACM on Asia Conference on Computer and Communications Security, ASIA CCS 2017, pp. 483–493. Association for Computing Machinery, New York (2017). https://doi.org/10.1145/3052973.3052999
22. Tam, K., Khan, S.J., Fattori, A., Cavallaro, L.: CopperDroid: automatic reconstruction of android malware behaviors. In: NDSS (2015)
23. Vidas, T., Christin, N.: Evading android runtime analysis via sandbox detection. In: ASIA CCS, pp. 447–458. Association for Computing Machinery, New York (2014). https://doi.org/10.1145/2590296.2590325
24. Zhou, Y., Jiang, X.: Dissecting android malware: characterization and evolution. In: IEEE Symposium on Security and Privacy, vol. 4, pp. 95–109, May 2012. https://doi.org/10.1109/SP.2012.16

MobHide: App-Level Runtime Data Anonymization on Mobile

Davide Caputo⬧, Luca Verderame⬧, and Alessio Merlo(✉)⬧

DIBRIS - University of Genova, Via Dodecaneso, 35, 16146 Genova, Italy
{davide.caputo,luca.verderame,alessio}@dibris.unige.it

Abstract. Developers of mobile apps gather a lot of user's personal information at runtime by exploiting third-party analytics libraries, without keeping the owner (i.e., the user) of such information in the loop. We argue that this is somehow paradoxical. To overcome this limitation, in this paper, we discuss a methodology (i.e., MobHide), allowing the user to choose a different privacy level for each app installed on her device. According to the user's preferences, MobHide anonymizes the data collected by the analytics libraries before sending them to the app developers, through a fruitful combination of data anonymization techniques. More in detail, the methodology enables to i) analyze all the network traffic generated by the invocation of analytics libraries, ii) anonymize the personal and device data using a *generalization technique*, and the events related to the user's behavior by exploiting *local differential privacy*, and iii) send the anonymized data to the developers.

We empirically assessed the viability of the approach on Android, by implementing the methodology as an Android app, i.e., HideDroid, that relies on the VPN service provided by Google to intercept all network requests. Our preliminary experiments - carried out on a real app (i.e., Duolingo) - are promising, and suggest that runtime data anonymization on mobile is feasible nowadays, as it negligibly impacts the app performance.

Keywords: Android privacy · Analytics libraries · Data anonymization

1 Introduction

In mid-2020 the number of available mobile applications (hereafter, apps) is growing towards 4.5 millions[1] (i.e., 2.56 M Android apps and 1.86 M iOS apps). This fact suggests that the competition among app developers to rise to (or stay

---

[1] https://www.statista.com/statistics/276623/number-of-apps-available-in-leading-app-stores/.

This work was partially funded by the Horizon 2020 project "Strategic Programs for Advanced Research and Technology in Europe" (SPARTA).

J. Zhou et al. (Eds.): ACNS 2020 Workshops, LNCS 12418, pp. 490–507, 2020.
https://doi.org/10.1007/978-3-030-61638-0_27

on) top is always more fierce, as they need to keep building apps that fully meet the user's expectation. To this aim, app developers need to receive continuous feedback on the way users interact with their apps. To achieve such result, they actually keep monitoring both the user's activities and the status of the device in order to *i)* track errors and crashes in the app, *ii)* understand the tastes of the user, and *iii)* deliver personalized advertisements, products or functionalities, in order to maximize the user's experience.

Such monitoring activity is currently carried out at runtime by exploiting *third-party analytics libraries* that enable the collection of information regarding the user's behavior. In detail, such libraries are made of a set of API that allows collecting the user-generated events (e.g., the set of the most visited pages or the history of purchases), and several details about the user herself and the device (e.g., the IMEI number, the OS version, and the GPS location). Developers can include such libraries in the app and invoke their API methods in the app code to log a meaningful event or information. Currently, the most widespread analytics libraries [3,23] are Facebook Analytics[2] and Google Firebase Analytics[3].

However, the adoption of analytics libraries raised serious concerns regarding the user's privacy [14,17] for several reasons. First, as analytics libraries are embedded in the app, they share the app privileges and get access to its resources. Furthermore, analytics libraries do not enforce any privacy-preserving mechanism, as discussed in [11,17,20]. Finally, the user has no control over them: although she can grant or deny the permission to collect personal data, she cannot choose the data to track nor apply any anonymization techniques to her data collected by the analytics libraries. Paradoxically, this means that the management of some user's personal information is devoted to the app developers rather than the user, which is the legal owner. This "status quo" currently maximizes the utility of data (for app developers) at the expense of the user's privacy. To this aim, we argue that the user must be kept in the loop and be free to choose the trade-off between utility and privacy of her own data, before they are delivered to any third-party.

Currently, this problem is gaining momentum, as researchers recently proposed some solutions to try mitigating the privacy issues of third-party libraries at large, and to anonymize the collected personal data. For instance, Zhang et al. [24] proposed a solution allowing the developer to anonymize the collected information according to differential privacy techniques. However, the approach is still developer-centric, i.e., the developer chooses both the anonymization strategy and its configuration. Liu et al. [17] designed an Android app able to intercept and block all the API related to analytics libraries, while Razaghpanah et al. [19] developed an app able to block the network requests that contain personal information. However, both solutions follow an "all or nothing" approach: all personal data are exported in their original form (i.e., maximizing the utility of data), or none of them is exported at all (i.e., maximizing the user's privacy). As data anonymization can be modeled as an optimization problem, where the

---

[2] https://developers.facebook.com/docs/graph-api/reference/application/activities/.
[3] https://firebase.google.com/docs/analytics/get-started.

aim is to find the optimal balance between data privacy and utility, previous approaches need to be extended further. As a last remark, it is also worth pointing out that the implementation of all the proposed solutions is strongly invasive (i.e., it requires either the adoption of a customized OS, the mandatory presence of root permissions, or the modification of the app logic), and could hardly be adopted in the wild.

Contributions of the Paper. This paper presents a novel, user-centric methodology, called **MobHide**, that allows the per-app anonymization of collected personal data according to a privacy level chosen by the user. In a nutshell, the idea is to collect all the network traffic generated by the invocation of API calls belonging to analytics libraries, and extract the exported data. Then, the next step is anonymizing the personal and device data using a generalization technique, and the data related to the user's behavior using an approach based on the concept of *local differential privacy*, in a way that preserves as much data semantics as possible. Finally, the anonymized data are sent to the expected recipients by mimicking the original network calls.

To prove the effectiveness and the feasibility of MobHide, we implemented the methodology in an Android app called **HideDroid**, and we used it to anonymize the data collected by a real Android app with more than 100M downloads (i.e., Duolingo). HideDroid relies on standard Android APIs to build a VPN-Client that successfully intercepts the network traffic generated by the app with a minimal configuration (i.e., by installing the app certificate). Furthermore, we integrated a transparent repackaging mechanism for the installed apps that do not alter the app behavior, to overcome the network restrictions imposed by the most recent Android OS versions.

Structure of the Paper. The rest of the paper is organized as follows: Sect. 2 introduces the functionalities of analytics libraries, and some basic concepts on data anonymization, while Sect. 3 defines the MobHide methodology. Section 4 presents the HideDroid prototype implementation on Android. Section 5 shows and discusses the usage of our approach on a real app. Section 6 presents the current state of the art, Sect. 7 discusses the limitation of our proposal, while Sect. 8 concludes the paper and points out some extensions of this work.

2   Background

2.1   Notes on Analytics Libraries

Analytics libraries allow to log user's events and device properties during the app execution. There exist several providers of mobile analytics libraries [3]. Among them, Firebase Analytics, Facebook Analytics, and Flurry are largely the most adopted ones [23].

Analytics libraries are composed by two parts, namely i) a Software Developer Kit (SDK) that can be included by developers in the app, and ii) a backend system - usually located in the Cloud - that allows the same developers to track and analyze the collected data through proper control dashboards. The SDK allows the developer to log and monitor either a pre-defined set of standard events or define properly customized events. In general, standard events are common to all apps, and are automatically collected by the SDK and sent to the analytics backend without any further configuration. Examples of such events are "app installation, "app open", and "app close". A custom event is defined by the developer to track app-specific activities. The event is typically represented in a key-value format (e.g., JSON) and sent to the backend by invoking a proper SDK API - typically named logEvent. Also, the event often contains some metadata [4].

2.2 Data Anonymization

Data Anonymization (DA) is the process of protecting private or sensitive information by erasing or encrypting identifiers that explicitly connect an individual to some data. For instance, such a process is of paramount importance when companies share data about their users with third parties for analytics or marketing analysis [12]. State of the art DA techniques can be divided into *perturbative* and *non-perturbative*, depending on the kind of data to protect. One of the most widespread *non-perturbative* technique, especially for the multidimensional data (e.g., relational databases), is generalization [21].

Generalization. A piece of information describing an entity (e.g., a user) can be represented by a set of attributes that give details about its features (e.g., gender, date of birth, address). In the original data, where each value is as much specific as possible, each attribute is considered to be in the most specific domain. Generalization techniques consist of replacing the specific value of a set of attributes with a more general one, preserving as much data semantics as possible.

In detail, given an attribute A of a table T, we can define a **domain generalization hierarchy** (DGH) for A as a set of n functions $f_h : h = 0, ..., n-1$ such that:

$$A_0 \xrightarrow{f_0} A_1 \xrightarrow{f_1} ... \xrightarrow{f_{n-1}} A_n \tag{1}$$

For example, Fig. 1 depicts a set $Z0$ of actual ZIP codes. In such a case, we can define a generalization function f_0 that strips the first rightmost digit to represent a larger geographical area. To make $Z1$ less informative, we can iterate the process and define f_1 and f_2 to strip other digits from the ZIP codes until the most general domain Zn is reached, i.e., where all zip codes are mapped to a singleton value. It is trivial to notice that the more generalization functions are invoked on the original data, the higher is the obtained privacy (and the lower is the data utility), as heterogeneous data are transformed into an always more reduced set of general values.

Generalization techniques are suitable only for semantically independent multidimensional data (e.g., the tuple of a relational database table), but they do not work properly to anonymize sequences of semantically related data. Therefore, they can be used to anonymize the attributes of a single event logged by

$$Z0 = \{16124, 16129, \xrightarrow{f_0} Z1 = \{1612^*, 1614^*\} \xrightarrow{f_1} Z2 = \{161^{**}\} \xrightarrow{f_2} \cdots \xrightarrow{f_{n-1}} ZN = \{^{*****}\}$$
$$16145, 16148\}$$

Fig. 1. A sample domain generalization hierarchy (DGH) for ZIP values.

analytics libraries only. To anonymize a sequences of logged (and semantically related) events, we leverage Differential Privacy [13] techniques.

Differential Privacy. In a nutshell, Differential Privacy (DP) applies a perturbation function to a set of related data, e.g., a sequence of events, by using a random noise to alter the original distribution according to a ratio parameter, defined a priori.

There are two main models for defining DP problems: *centralized* and *local* model. In the *centralized model*, the data are sent to a trusted entity (e.g., an analytics company) that applies DP algorithms and then shares the anonymized dataset with an untrusted third-party client. On the contrary, the *local model* assumes all external entities and communication channels as untrusted. In such a situation, local DP techniques aim at performing the data perturbation locally before releasing any dataset to an external party. In our scenario, we consider the user as the sole owner of its data, and we trust neither the advertising company nor the developer. To this aim, the local DP model is suitable to anonymize sequences of events logged by analytics libraries.

In a *local model*, we can define a sequence of n events such as $e_1, e_2, ..., e_n$ where e_i defines the $i - th$ event. We can assume that all possible values of these events belong to E. A local DP solution can be defined as a perturbation function R that takes as input a sequence of events (i.e., e_i) and outputs another sequence of events (i.e., z_i) different from the previous one. For example, a perturbation function can be a function that adds some noise to the data or replace some events according to a probability defined a priori. The resulting data, i.e., $z_i = R(e_i)$, can be sent to the destination server (e.g., the analytics server). The interested reader can find more details on local DP techniques in [13].

3   The MobHide methodology

The **MobHide** methodology allows the user to choose a different *privacy level* for any app installed on the device. The idea is to dynamically analyze the app behavior at runtime and anonymize the actual exported data. In principle, we could leverage static analysis techniques, by following, e.g., the techniques we applied in [8], to locate and instrument the methods that invoke analytics libraries APIs. Nonetheless, instrumentation leads to high customization of the app code, requires the systematic repackaging of any app, as well as to deal with potentially obfuscated code [7]. Therefore, MobHide leverages runtime monitoring of any app according to the following steps: i) intercept all data exported by the app through the invocation of API calls belonging to analytics libraries, ii) anonymize data therein by applying the generalization and local DP techniques previously discussed, and iii) send the anonymized data to the backend by mimicking the original network calls. Figure 2 provides a high-level view of the workflow.

In detail, the first step is carried out by the *Privacy Detector* module, which intercepts and filters the traffic that comes from the apps. For each network request belonging to an analytics library API, the module stores it in a buffer repository (*Event Buffer*) and drops the original communication (step 2). Otherwise, the connection is transparently forwarded (step 3).

The *Data Anonymizer* module carries out the anonymization procedure. Periodically, this module pulls the data from the *Event Buffer* (step 4) and applies the anonymization strategy according to the selected app privacy level (step 5) and data generalization hierarchies (step 6). Finally, the anonymized data is sent to the *Data Sender* module (step 7) that forwards them to the expected recipients (step 8). The rest of this section details the different modules and the MobHide anonymization strategies.

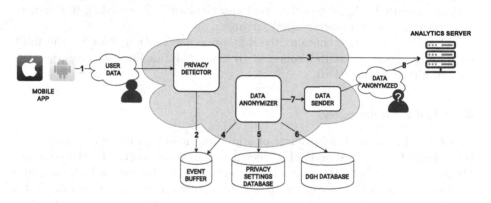

Fig. 2. MobHide - high-level workflow.

3.1 Privacy Detector

The **Privacy Detector** inspects all network traffic coming from the apps selected by the user (Step 1 in Fig. 2). The module parses both encrypted and plain-text traffic according to i) the domain name and ii) the content of the request itself.

In detail, if the domain name belongs to a set of well-known analytic libraries (e.g., `graph.facebook.com` is related to Facebook Analytics, and `app-measurement.com` to Firebase Analytics), the corresponding request is immediately stored in the *Event Buffer*, and the original communication is dropped. If the domain name is not sufficient or unknown, the *Privacy Detector* analyzes the data within the request to identify the parameters and the value most commonly used by analytics libraries. The most common attributes are obtained by the official documentation of the analytics library[4,5,6].

Finally, the rest of the network traffic is forwarded to the expected recipients without any further change.

3.2 Privacy Settings Database and DGH Database

MobHide relies on two databases to store the settings defined by the user and the configuration rules for the anonymization strategy.

The privacy level chosen by the user for each app is stored within the *Privacy Settings Database*, and it contains the per-app privacy level defined by the user and thus enables the use of a fine-grained anonymization strategy to each of the apps. The privacy level is mapped into four different values, i.e. NONE, LOW, MEDIUM, HIGH. If an app is set to NONE, its traffic will be excluded by the anonymization process. On the contrary, the maximum privacy level HIGH leads to execute both the generalization and the local DP according to the more restrictive (i.e., privacy-preserving) settings.

The *DGH Database* contains the domain generalization rules for the most common personal attributes collected by the analytics libraries (e.g., gender, date of birth, and location).

3.3 Data Anonymizer

The *Data Anonymizer* is in charge of applying the anonymization strategies on the collected data. As described in Sect. 2.1, the data collected by the analytics libraries includes both the user's in-app actions (i.e., the user's behavior) and information about the user or the device. To deal with such heterogeneous data, the Data Anonymizer builds an anonymization pipeline based on both data generalization and differential privacy techniques.

User's and Device Data Anonymization. To anonymize the information regarding the user and the device, the Data Anonymizer adopts a procedure based on data generalization [21]. The *Data Anonymizer* scans each network request to detect and extract all exporting data. For each attribute, the module looks up for a generalization rule in the *DGH Database*. If a match is found, the value is generalized according to the privacy level. In detail, each increment in the privacy value (i.e., from LOW to HIGH) implies the application of an extra generalization function of the DGH. In case a match is not found, the Data Anonymizer relies on the following heuristics:

- If the attribute is a **string**, the generalization replaces the last p elements with a generic value $'*'$. The value of p depends on the privacy level, and it is defined as follow:

---

[4] https://firebase.google.com/docs/analytics/get-started.

[5] https://developers.facebook.com/docs/graph-api/reference/application/activities/.

[6] https://developer.yahoo.com/flurry/docs/.

$$p = \frac{stringLength * selectedPrivacyLevel}{\#PrivacyLevels - 1} \tag{2}$$

where *stringLength* is the string length, *#PrivacyLevels* is the number of available privacy levels (i.e., 4), and *selectedPrivacyLevel* is the privacy level selected by the user (i.e., NONE=0, LOW=1, MEDIUM=2, HIGH=3).

– If the attribute in a **number**, the generalization rounds the value to the p most significant digits. The value of p is computed as:

$$p = \frac{\#digits * selectedPrivacyLevel}{\#PrivacyLevels - 1} \tag{3}$$

where *#digits* is the number of digits while the other values are defined in the same way as discussed above.

Anonymization of the User's Behavior. To anonymize the user behavior modeled as a set of related events generated as a consequence of a user action, the Data Anonymizer adopts a heuristic based on local Differential Privacy and the concept of local data perturbation. This heuristic enables the anonymization of the user behavior while preserving structured data for the developer.

The local data perturbation process aims to modify the original behavior distribution by either (i) **removing** intercepted events, (ii) **replacing** events, or (iii) **injecting** crafted events. To do so, the Data Anonymizer relies on a threshold value defined as follows:

$$Threshold_{action} = 1 - \frac{selectedPrivacyLevel}{\#action + 1} \tag{4}$$

where

$$action \in [\texttt{inject}, \texttt{remove}, \texttt{replace}]$$

The Data Anonymizer assigns to each intercepted event three pseudo-random numbers (ranging from 0 to 1) that represent the probability of executing one of the three perturbation actions (i.e., inject, remove, replace). Then, the perturbation action is executed only if the corresponding probability is higher than the threshold.

Anonymization Pipeline. The complete procedure for the data anonymization follows the algorithm described in Algorithm 1. For each event stored in the *Event Buffer* (row 3), the algorithm computes the three pseudo-random numbers: $Pr_{inj}, Pr_{rem}, Pr_{rep}$ (rows 4–6).

If the Pr_{inj} is higher than the threshold, the *Data Anonymizer* module builds a new generalized event taken from the pool of the supported event types. If the Pr_{rep} is greater than the threshold (row 11), the module replaces the original event with another valid one. Then, it generalizes the attributes of the replacing event (following the rules described above). Otherwise, the *Data Anonymizer* module checks whether to remove the original event or generalize it. In all three previous cases, the modified event is added to the set of anonymized data (rows 8–9, 12–14, and 17–20), which are returned at the end of the pipeline (row 22).

Algorithm 1. Data Anonymization Pipeline

Input: $eventBuffer, selectedPrivacyLevel$
Output: $anonymizedEvents$
1: Initialize $anonymizedEvents \leftarrow$ list()
2: Initialize $Threshold_{action} \leftarrow 1 - (selectedPrivacyLevel/4)$
3: **for each** $event$ in $eventBuffer$ **do**
4:     $Pr_{inj} \leftarrow$ rand()
5:     $Pr_{rem} \leftarrow$ rand()
6:     $Pr_{rep} \leftarrow$ rand()
7:     **if** $Pr_{inj} > Threshold_{action}$ **then**
8:         $newGenEvent \leftarrow$ generateNewGenEvent($selectedPrivacyLevel$)
9:         $anonymizedEvents$.add($newGenEvent$)
10:    **end if**
11:    **if** $Pr_{rep} > Threshold_{action}$ **then**
12:        $replEvent \leftarrow$ replaceEvent($event$)
13:        $replGenEvent.attributes \leftarrow$ generalizeEvent($replEvent.attributes$,
                        $selectedPrivacyLevel$)
14:        $anonymizedEvents$.add($replGenEvent$)
15:    **else if** $Pr_{rem} > Threshold_{action}$ **then**
16:        deleteEvent($event$)
17:    **else**
18:        $originalGenEvent \leftarrow$ generalizeEvent($event.attributes$,
                        $selectedPrivacyLevel$)
19:        $anonymizedEvents$.add($originalGenEvent$)
20:    **end if**
21: **end for**
22: **return** $anonymizedEvents$

3.4   Data Sender

The *Data Sender* module is in charge of forwarding the anonymized data returned by the Data Anonymizer pipeline (step 7) to the analytics backends. To do so, the module mimics the original calls dropped by the Privacy Detector by encapsulating each anonymized data instead of the original plain data (step 8).

4   Implementing MobHide on Android

We empirically assessed the feasibility of MobHide on Android by developing a prototype implementation, called HideDroid, and testing it on a real app.

HideDroid leverages the Android VPN API[7] to capture and analyze the network traffic generated by the apps installed on the device. The app includes a Couchbase Lite[8] NoSql database to implement the *Event Buffer* and two SQLite databases to store the privacy settings and the generalization hierarchies, respectively.

HideDroid Setup. The execution of HideDroid begins by determining the runtime environment, i.e., the OS version and the presence of root permissions. HideDroid implements a transparent SSL/HTTPS proxy [5] to intercept both plain and encrypted network traffic. To this aim, the app generates a self-signed CA and requires the permission to install it in the user's CA store. If the device has root permissions, HideDroid also requires the permission to install the certificate within the system CA store.

App Privacy Configuration. The HideDroid interface allows the user to view all the apps installed on the device, and select a different privacy level for each app, as shown in Fig. 3. Privacy levels are stored in the *Privacy Setting Database*. For each selected app with privacy level higher than NONE, HideDroid checks if the app requires an additional setup to be intercepted by the *Privacy Detector*. It is worth pointing out that this extra step is required only if the Android version is ≥ 7.0, and the user does not have root permissions, due to the current restriction imposed by the OS [1]. Indeed, if the Android OS version is <7.0, or if the user accepts the installation of the HideDroid CA in the system CA store, the *Privacy Detector* can intercept the app network traffic without any further customization.

The additional setup step is an *app repackaging* phase, in which proper network configurations are added to the app, without affecting the original app logic. More in details, the repackaging phase is composed of four steps in which HideDroid:

1. unpacks the app using Apktool[9];
2. adds a new network security configuration file[10] to the app, in order to force the usage of the user certificate store (Listing 1.1);
3. modifies the Android manifest file to enable the use of the new network configuration;
4. re-installs the configured app using the INSTALL_PACKAGES permission.

At the end of this phase, HideDroid is able to intercept and anonymize the data collected by the analytics libraries.

---

[7] https://developer.android.com/reference/android/net/VpnService.
[8] https://docs.couchbase.com/couchbase-lite/current/java-android.html.
[9] https://github.com/iBotPeaches/Apktool.
[10] https://developer.android.com/training/articles/security-config.

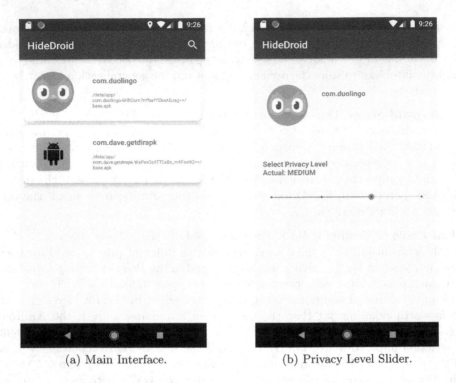

(a) Main Interface. (b) Privacy Level Slider.

Fig. 3. Screenshots from the HideDroid prototype.

5 Empirical Assessment

We evaluated the viability of MobHide by executing HideDroid on a real application. After reversing and analyzing a set of most downloaded apps equipped with analytics libraries, we selected Duolingo[11] as a relevant use case for several reasons: first, Duolingo adopts four of the most widespread analytics libraries (i.e., Google Firebase Analytics, Google Crashlitics, Facebook Analytics, and Adjust); furthermore, it requires 30 permissions that can be used to extract information regarding the user and the device (Table 1); finally, it has more than 100M downloads worldwide.

We carried out the experiment on a Huawei P10 device equipped with Android 9.0, an Octa-core (4×2.4 GHz Cortex-A73 & 4×1.8 GHz Cortex-A53), and 4 GB of RAM. Since the experiment involves an Android version ≥ 7.0, the Duolingo app has been repackaged (see Sect. 4). An actual user manually tested the app for two hours, in order to push the invocation of a relevant number of API calls belonging to analytics libraries. During the testing phase, HideDroid captured all network traffic generated by Duolingo, and anonymized the data according to the MobHide strategies described in Sect. 3.

---

[11] https://play.google.com/store/apps/details?id=com.duolingo&hl=en.

Listing 1.1. The `network_security_config.xml` file injected by HideDroid.

```
<?xml version="1.0" encoding="utf-8"?>
<base-config cleartextTrafficPermitted="true">
    <trust-anchors>
        <certificates src="system" />
        <certificates src="user" />
    </trust-anchors>
</base-config>
```

Table 1. Permissions required by Duolingo.

Permissions	
ACCESS_NETWORK_STATE	BADGE_COUNT_WRITE
AUTHENTICATE_ACCOUNTS	BADGE_COUNT_READ
FOREGROUND_SERVICE	PROVIDER_INSERT_BADGE
GET_ACCOUNTS	BROADCAST_BADGE
INTERNET	WRITE
READ_APP_BADGE	READ
READ_EXTERNAL_STORAGE	WRITE_SETTINGS
RECEIVE_BOOT_COMPLETED	READ_SETTINGS
RECORD_AUDIO	UPDATE_BADGE
VIBRATE	WRITE_SETTINGS
WAKE_LOCK	READ_SETTINGS
WRITE_EXTERNAL_STORAGE	CHANGE_BADGE
UPDATE_COUNT	UPDATE_SHORTCUT
BILLING	READ_SETTINGS
RECEIVE	BIND_GET_INSTALL_REFERRER_SERVICE

We analyzed the network traffic generated by the advertising libraries. Regarding the user's and device profiling, the `model of device`, the `network latency`, the `username`, and the `free space on disk` are the most captured information. Also, the app collected a set of events that describes the user's behavior. Examples of such events include `app_open`, `app_install`, and `learning_reason_tap`. During the two-hours experiment, HideDroid collected 123 events belonging to 39 different classes. Figure 4 summarizes the frequency of each captured event, while Listing 1.2 shows a subset of actual personal data collected by Duolingo and exported to the analytics backend.

We tested all the available privacy levels on Duolingo, in order to evaluate the anonymization capabilities of HideDroid. As described in Sect. 3, MobHide performs two types of anonymization for personal and device information and for user's events, respectively. Listing 1.3 shows an example of the data anonymized after applying a generalization technique with the privacy level set to HIGH to the original data showed in Listing 1.2: note that all the string values have been converted to a sequence of * (e.g., "client_id"), while the integer parameters have been rounded to the most meaningful digit (e.g., "memory_maximum").

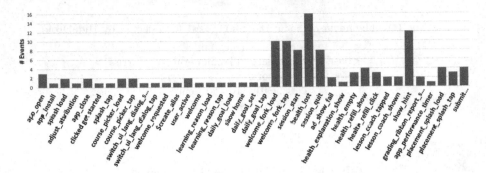

Fig. 4. Distribution of the user's events collected by Duolingo during the two-hours experiment.

```
...
" event_type ":  " app_open ",
" event_timestamp": 1591880722000,
" client   ":  {
      " client_id   ":  " android−excess "
},
" attributes ":  {
      " memory_maximum ": 268435456,
      " memory_class ": 96,
      " memory_system_available ": 2669375488,
      " data_saver ":  " enabled ",
      " memory_class_large ": 256,
      " $screen_height ": 1794,
      " $app_release ": 951,
      " memory_system_total ": 3156844544,
      " screen_width ": 411,
      " $carrier   ":  " Android ",
      " Client  ":  " Duodroid ",
      " orientation  ":  " portrait  ",
      " mp_lib ":  " android ",
      ...
```

```
...
" event_type ":  " app_open ",
" event_timestamp ": 1591880722000,
" client   ":  {
      " client_id   ":  "*************"
},
" attributes ":  {
      " memory_maximum ": 200000000,
      " memory_class ": 90,
      " memory_system_available ": 2000000000,
      " data_saver ":  " undefined ",
      " memory_class_large ": 200,
      " $screen_height ":  1000,
      " $app_release ": 900,
      " memory_system_total ": 3000000000,
      " screen_width ": 400,
      " $carrier   ":  " undefined ",
      " Client  ":  " undefined ",
      " orientation  ":  " undefined ",
      " mp_lib ":  " undefined ",
      ...
```

Listing 1.2. Example of event collected by Duolingo.

Listing 1.3. Example of anonymized event with privacy level HIGH.

Figure 5 shows the distributions of the anonymized event frequencies for each levels of privacy (i.e., NONE, LOW, MEDIUM, HIGH). It is worth noticing that each privacy level has its own specific distribution pattern. To prove that the distributions are actually different from each other, we computed the KL_Divergence [15] (i.e., D_{KL}) which allows measuring the *distance* between two distributions. A high value of D_{KL} suggests that the two distributions are very different, while $D_{KL} = 0$ indicates that two distributions are identical. We calculated D_{KL} between the original event distribution and each anonymized distribution. The results are reported in Table 2.

Table 2. Parameters and metrics of the HideDroid anonymization phase.

Privacy	TH	$\# \, Inj_{Ev}$	$\# \, Rem_{Ev}$	$\# \, Rep_{Ev}$	$\# \, Tot_{Ev}$	D_{KL}	Ex. Time
LOW	0.75	24	35	28	140	0.11	0.416
MEDIUM	0.5	62	61	66	190	0.28	0.352
HIGH	0.25	94	93	98	223	0.38	0.419

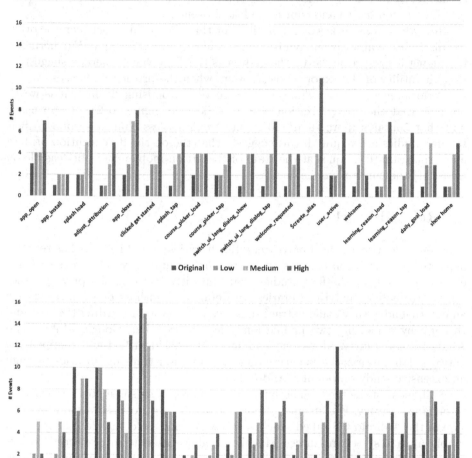

Fig. 5. Comparison of the different event distributions generated by HideDroid, according to the selected privacy level.

Such a table summarizes the results of the anonymization phase on the set of events for each privacy level. In detail, the first column indicates the privacy level (i.e., Privacy), while columns 2 to 6 describe the parameters and the metrics for the local DP, i.e., the $Threshold_{action}$ (i.e., TH), the number of injected, removed and replaced (i.e., $\# \ Inj_{Ev}$, $\# \ Rem_{Ev}$ and $\# \ Rep_{Ev}$ respectively) events, the number of total events (i.e., $\# \ Tot_{Ev}$). Column 7 contains the value of the KL-Divergence, while the last columns contain the execution time (i.e., Ex. Time) required to anonymize the list of events.

Regarding D_{KL}, it is worth pointing out that the distance between the original distribution and the anonymized ones is always greater than 0. Furthermore, the higher is the privacy level, the greater is the D_{KL} value, thereby suggesting that the utility of the exported data lowers when the privacy level rises.

Performance (i.e., Ex. Time) is likewise very promising. In fact, it is worth noticing that the anonymization of a data flow belonging to 2 h of app usage and that contains more than 120 events, requires less than a second. Albeit further studies are required, this suggests that the on-the-fly execution of data anonymization techniques at the state of the art on mobile could be feasible on (most of) the current mobile devices.

6   Related Work

The wide adoption of third-party analytics libraries in mobile apps has recently attracted the attention of the security research community. The work of Chen et al. [11] is one of the first studies that explicitly focus on the privacy issues related to mobile analytics libraries. In detail, the authors demonstrated how an external adversary could extract sensitive information regarding the user and the app by exploiting two mobile analytics services, i.e., Google Mobile App Analytics and Flurry. Moreover, Vallina et al. [22] identified and mapped the network domains associated with mobile ads and user tracking libraries through an extensive study on popular Android apps.

Still, most of the research activity focus on proposing some novel approaches to enhance privacy. For instance, Beresford et al. [10] proposed a modified version of the Android OS called MockDroid, which allows to "mock" the access of mobile apps to system resources. MockDroid allows users to revoke access to specific resources at run-time, encouraging the same users to take into consideration a trade-off between functionality and personal information disclosure.

Zhang et al. [25] proposed PRIVAID, a methodology to apply differential privacy anonymization to the user events collected by mobile apps. The tool replaced the original analytics API with a custom implementation that collects the generated event and applies DP techniques. The anonymization strategy is configured directly by the app developer, which can reconstruct at least a good approximation of the distribution of the original events.

The authors in [19] proposed an Android app called Lumen Privacy Monitor that analyzes network traffic on mobile devices. This app aims to alert the user if an app collects and sends personally identifiable information (e.g., IMEI, MAC,

Phone Number). The application allows the user to block requests to a specific endpoint. To do that, Lumen Privacy Monitor asks for all the Android permissions in order to collect the user data and perform the lookup in the network requests.

Unfortunately, the above solutions do not provide proper data anonymization, thereby proposing either block-or-allow strategies or approaches that enable the reconstruction of the original data by a third-party (e.g., the app developer). Also, most of them require invasive modifications of the apps or the OS (e.g., custom OS and root permissions), and can very hardly be adopted in the wild.

To the best of our knowledge, MobHide is the first proposal that allows the user to choose a per-app privacy level and, at the same time, granting the possibility to export anonymized data. Furthermore, our prototype HideDroid has been designed to ensure minimal invasiveness on the mobile device.

7   Discussion and Future Developments

This work aims to demonstrate the feasibility of runtime anonymization of personal data exported by mobile apps and the viability of allowing users to choose a level of privacy for each installed app. Nonetheless, both our methodology (i.e., MobHide) and implementation (i.e., HideDroid) have some limitations.

In the current definition, the MobHide methodology adopts basic - yet effective - DA techniques on the collected data. Still, an extensive evaluation of the type of data transmitted by third-party analytics libraries could unveil complex structures (e.g., multidimensional data, time-series, transaction data, ...). To this aim, other - more complex - DA techniques, such as k-anonymity [21], l-diversity [18] or t-closeness [16], must be taken into consideration and implemented in HideDroid.

Moreover, the traffic recognition capabilities of MobHide are based on a predefined mapping between the hosts and the corresponding analytics services. If an app sends data to an unknown host, MobHide tries to recognize whether the request belongs to an analytic service, according to a keyword-based heuristic (e.g., if the word "event" is contained in the network request). However, such a technique could introduce some false positives, leading to potential app malfunctioning if the request contains data related to the logic of the app. Also in this case, an extensive analysis of such heuristic in the wild will allow evaluating its reliability. In case of low reliability, the adoption of ML-based network recognition techniques [22] could be taken into consideration.

Regarding the limitations of the prototype implementation, HideDroid has been designed to minimize the impact on the target apps. Indeed, we developed the tool with the aim to reduce as much as possible the app customization, and, therefore, we rely on app repackaging only on devices equipped with Android geq 7.0 and without root permissions. However, the repackaging process may fail against system apps or apps with anti-repackaging mechanisms in place. Also, the presence of certificate-pinning mechanisms applied to the network traffic of analytics libraries could interfere with the ability of HideDroid to analyze and anonymize the corresponding data.

To overcome the above technical limitations, we plan to evaluate the usage of DroidPlugin [2] or VirtualApp [6] virtual environments that provide the ability to intercept the network traffic without the need of any app customization.

8 Conclusion

In this paper, we introduced MobHide, the first "user-centric" methodology for the per-app anonymization of the data collected by third-party analytics libraries. Furthermore, we proposed HideDroid, a prototype implementation for Android that has been tested on a real-world app with more than 100M downloads.

This work is a first step towards balancing between data utility and user privacy in mobile ecosystems, demonstrating the feasibility of introducing data anonymization locally, i.e., directly on the mobile device without the need for an external trusted party.

Albeit promising, the results suggest that an extensive assessment campaign is needed to tune the proposed anonymization pipeline. As a first step in this direction, we intend to include the support of other third-party libraries and generalization heuristics, and to use Trusted Execution Environment (TEE) technologies [9] to protect the confidentiality and integrity of the collected data. Finally, we plan to release HideDroid on the Google Play Store by the end of 2020.

References

1. Android 7.0 news. https://developer.android.com/about/versions/nougat/android-7.0#network_security_config. Accessed 27 May 2020
2. Droidplugin. https://github.com/DroidPluginTeam/DroidPlugin. Accessed 27 May 2020
3. Exodus privacy. https://reports.exodus-privacy.eu.org/en/trackers/stats/. Accessed 27 May 2020
4. Firebase log event. https://firebase.google.com/docs/reference/android/com/google/firebase/analytics/FirebaseAnalytics.Event. Accessed 27 May 2020
5. Transparent proxy TLS. https://docs.mitmproxy.org/stable/concepts-modes/. Accessed 27 May 2020
6. VirtualApp. https://github.com/asLody/VirtualApp. Accessed 27 May 2020
7. Aonzo, S., Georgiu, G.C., Verderame, L., Merlo, A.: Obfuscapk: an open-source black-box obfuscation tool for android apps. SoftwareX **11**, 100403 (2020). https://doi.org/10.1016/j.softx.2020.100403, http://www.sciencedirect.com/science/article/pii/S2352711019302791
8. Armando, A., Costa, G., Merlo, A., Verderame, L.: Enabling BYOD through secure meta-market, pp. 219–230 (2014). https://doi.org/10.1145/2627393.2627410
9. Armando, A., Merlo, A., Verderame, L.: Trusted host-based card emulation. In: 2015 International Conference on High Performance Computing & Simulation (HPCS), pp. 221–228. IEEE (2015)

10. Beresford, A.R., Rice, A., Skehin, N., Sohan, R.: MockDroid: trading privacy for application functionality on smartphones. In: Proceedings of the 12th Workshop on Mobile Computing Systems and Applications, HotMobile 2011. Association for Computing Machinery, New York (2011)
11. Chen, T., Ullah, I., Kaafar, M.A., Boreli, R.: Information leakage through mobile analytics services. In: Proceedings of the 15th Workshop on Mobile Computing Systems and Applications (2014)
12. Cormode, G., Srivastava, D.: Anonymized data: generation, models, usage. In: Proceedings of the 2009 ACM SIGMOD International Conference on Management of data (2009)
13. Dwork, C., Roth, A., et al.: The algorithmic foundations of differential privacy. Found. Trends® Theor. Comput. Sci. 9(3–4), 211–407 (2014)
14. He, Y., Yang, X., Hu, B., Wang, W.: Dynamic privacy leakage analysis of android third-party libraries. J. Inf. Secur. Appl. 46, 259–270 (2019)
15. Kullback, S.: Information Theory and Statistics. Courier Corporation, North Chelmsford (1997)
16. Li, N., Li, T., Venkatasubramanian, S.: t-Closeness: privacy beyond k-anonymity and l-diversity. In: 2007 IEEE 23rd International Conference on Data Engineering. IEEE (2007)
17. Liu, X., Liu, J., Zhu, S., Wang, W., Zhang, X.: Privacy risk analysis and mitigation of analytics libraries in the android ecosystem. IEEE Trans. Mob. Comput. 19(5), 1184–1199 (2020)
18. Machanavajjhala, A., Kifer, D., Gehrke, J., Venkitasubramaniam, M.: L-diversity: privacy beyond k-anonymity. ACM Trans. Knowl. Discov. Data (TKDD) 1(1), 3 (2007)
19. Razaghpanah, A., et al.: Apps, trackers, privacy, and regulators: a global study of the mobile tracking ecosystem (2018)
20. Stevens, R., Gibler, C., Crussell, J., Erickson, J., Chen, H.: Investigating user privacy in android ad libraries
21. Sweeney, L.: Achieving k-anonymity privacy protection using generalization and suppression. Int. J. Uncertainty Fuzziness Knowl. Based Syst. 10(05), 571–588 (2002)
22. Vallina-Rodriguez, N., et al.: Tracking the trackers: towards understanding the mobile advertising and tracking ecosystem. arXiv preprint arXiv:1609.07190 (2016)
23. Verderame, L., Caputo, D., Romdhana, A., Merlo, A.: On the (un)reliability of privacy policies in android apps. In: Proceedings of the IEEE International Joint Conference on Neural Networks (IJCNN 2020), Glasgow, UK, July 2020
24. Zhang, H., Hao, Y., Latif, S., Bassily, R., Rountev, A.: A study of event frequency profiling with differential privacy. In: Proceedings of the 29th International Conference on Compiler Construction, CC 2020. Association for Computing Machinery, New York (2020)
25. Zhang, H., Latif, S., Bassily, R., Rountev, A.: Privaid: Differentially-private event frequency analysis for google analytics in android apps

Evaluation of the Adoption and Privacy Risks of Google Prompts

Christos Avraam[1]([✉]) and Elias Athanasopoulos[2]

[1] School of Electronics and Computer Science, University of Southampton,
Southampton, UK
ca2u19@soton.ac.uk
[2] Department of Computer Science, University of Cyprus, Nicosia, Cyprus
eliasathan@cs.ucy.ac.cy

Abstract. Internet services struggle with implementing better techniques for making authentication easier for the end-user by balancing those traits without sacrificing their security or privacy. One very recent such technology is Google Prompts, where users can authenticate by merely tapping a prompt to their mobile phone. In this paper, we attempt to understand how Google Prompts work and the extent to which current users adopt them. To this end, we build a collection system for estimating, using a completely transparent methodology, the fraction of users that have enabled Google Prompts in their accounts. Our collection system can infer the adoption of Google Prompts in the wild. Most importantly, we can use the system for performing a preliminary study of the privacy implications of Google Prompts.

Keywords: Authentication · Privacy · Measurements

1 Introduction

2-Step Verification Phone Prompts (most commonly abbreviated to Google Prompts) [5] is a mobile-based authentication method and was introduced relatively recently by Google. With Google Prompts enabled, a user needs to only enter their email for authenticating with Google and then complete a *Yes/No* notification prompt received on their phone. If the user selects the option *Yes*, they automatically gain access to the account; otherwise, the authentication process gets canceled and blocked. Since 79% of the human population between ages 18–44 carry their mobile phones 22 h a day [21], an unauthorized person (attacker) who does not possess the mobile device cannot gain access to the account. As previously explained, a user can either opt-in for an entirely password-less authentication experience or even combine it with another security factor from Google's weaponry to form a more traditional and convenient 2FA mechanism. By selecting the latter and more commonly with the combination of a text-based password, the user is required to enter it before receiving the Google Prompt explicitly. Essentially, this means they trade off performance and

© Springer Nature Switzerland AG 2020
J. Zhou et al. (Eds.): ACNS 2020 Workshops, LNCS 12418, pp. 508–522, 2020.
https://doi.org/10.1007/978-3-030-61638-0_28

usability for additional security. These two modes (a) password-less authentication and (b) 2FA-mixed are deeply integrated with currently available Google services and allow users to easily switch from mode to mode or entirely turn off Google Prompts and rely upon traditional authentication.

Although Google Prompts seems like a real-life problem solver and 2SV adoption seems exponential, according to Google [14], the actual user adoption, through not just enabling Google Prompts but also for its wide variety of authentication methods, is still questionable. It is also questionable how this system behaves under an adversarial setting. Precisely, we show how an attacker can carefully issue silent probes to Google Prompts enabled accounts for receiving back signals about their geographical location. Since the user's privacy is considered a top priority aspect, we need to perform a proper vulnerability assessment. In this paper, we build a collection system for assessing the *current* use of Google Prompts in the wild. Our system can perform all measurements without violating users' privacy or *disturbing* them by any means. The measurement methodology is entirely transparent, i.e., users are not affected by our probes. Building such a collection system allows us to infer how Google Prompts are integrated with the current authentication mechanisms offered by Google as well.

In this paper, we make the following contributions.

1. We review Google Prompts, a fairly recent 2FA technology introduced by Google. Our main goal is to understand how Google Prompts are integrated into the current authentication system of Google.
2. Towards realizing this understanding, we design and implement a collection system that estimates how many users who have a Google account, have enabled Google Prompts. All measurements are carried out ethically without affecting the security and privacy of the analyzed users. All measurements are stored entirely anonymized.
3. Based on our experimental findings, we make a preliminary assessment of the privacy risks introduced by Google Prompts. Towards this, we suggest possible attack methodologies, where an adversary can carefully issue silent probes to Google Prompts enabled accounts for receiving back signals about their geographical location.

2   Google Prompts

Google has developed a mobile-based 2-Step Verification (2SV) method to enhance the process of accessing Google services. By enabling this authentication method as the default, the sign-in process goes as follows: the users after they input their email, they receive a notification prompt on a preconfigured trusted device, such as a smartphone. On that prompt, they can tap *Yes* to allow sign-in (see Fig. 6) and gain access to the service immediately or *No* to deny/block the sign-in process. Since its primary function is sending a prompt on a device, for future reference, we will refer to it as *Google Prompts*. The default configuration of Google Prompts is to outsource authentication to it, transforming authentication into an entirely password-less experience. Google Prompts removes the

Fig. 1. Google Prompt as it is being received on the user's pre-configured device. By tapping *Yes*, it allows immediate access to the service otherwise *No* it blocks the unauthorized access.

need for remembering passwords or tokens, as it only requires the user's email address. It is considered more user-friendly and faster for the average user than other 2SV and 2-Factor Authentication (2FA) methods [8]. For instance, one-time codes received via SMS or the Google Authenticator app, not only require password input but also to transfer/copy them into Google's sign-in page manually. The prompt may also include details of the device/client initiating the authentication request: (a) Operating System, (b) current timestamp, and (c) the location if it could be determined.

It is important to note that with the default configuration if a user for some reason has no internet access or even physical access to their trusted device, they have the option to select alternative authentication methods from the Google's available security features (e.g., text-based password, Google Authenticator app, SMS token). Illustratively, when the user has selected to enter their password instead of sending the prompt, in the next authentication session, the previously selected method (in this case, the password) is again *optionally* requested by default (Fig. 1).

Besides the above mode, there is another configuration where Google Prompts is used as a second factor (2FA) to trade-off speed with additional security. If this mode is enabled, the user enters compulsory their password or any other of the available Google's security factors. Then the Google Prompt is also *required* to be answered in order for the signing-in process to complete.

Moreover, when someone attempts an authentication for the first time on a new entity (e.g., the user is authenticating with Google using a new laptop), an extra step is added. A number appears on the browser, and if the device holder selects *Yes* to approve sign-in, the user has to select one of the three given numbers on the phone to match it. Otherwise, if the wrong number is selected, the authentication process gets canceled, regardless of the previous step selection.

Finally, depending on the operating system of the user's device (IOS/Android), compatibility requirements are slightly different. Android devices must keep Google Play Services up to date and have enabled screen-lock. In iPhones, screen-lock is already enabled because Touch ID requires it, and it is also necessary to have the Google Search app pre-installed since it delivers the prompts. Screen-lock is a core requirement, since it prohibits unlocked phones, accessible by anyone, to confirm Google Prompts.

2.1   Research Challenges

Assessing Google prompt's user adoption, was a challenging task since it was required to construct a collection system that can infer if a given e-mail account is associated with Google Prompts (black-box evalution). We needed to evade Google's defense mechanisms or at least deal with them in a proper manner. By resolving such issues, we can conclude to a better understanding of how exactly this new 2SV variant works. In this part, we review the significant difficulties we had to overcome.

Fig. 2. Indication that Google Prompts are disabled with three possible error messages. Most imporrntantly, the under analysis account does not receive any prompts. For case C, it occurred explicitly when the routing was made through Tor.

Request Rate. When a single entity issues about 5 to 6 consecutive requests on a given day for one account, Google Prompts gets disabled. Instead of sending a prompt on the preconfigured trusted device, as we have already discussed, a corresponding error message (see Fig. 2 case A) appears on the browser that issued the request, and a password is required in order to sign-in. Therefore, each account should be tested only *once*. In addition to this limitation, we lessen the number of emails we can analyze per day, due to we should not be intrusive to the server itself. Google Prompts can also be disabled in cases where the users cannot use, reach (see Fig. 2 case B), or lost their device. For such cases, Google recommends to its clients to take specific actions [3] in order to resolve any issues.

CAPTCHAs. The combination of performing automated procedures in the Google API and assessing different accounts using one client had as a result of the service to project CAPTCHAs [22,23] after just a few requests. Therefore, we needed to perform all tests as cultivated/humanly as possible and in a more distributed fashion. We route all of our traffic through the anonymizing network service TOR [12], so we can send all requests using several exit nodes with different geolocations. Interestingly enough, using TOR gives us two notable benefits. Firstly, different exit nodes will issue requests that in most of the times will not be blocked by CAPTCHAs. Secondly, and most important, assuming the account under test has enabled Google Prompts, Google will refuse to send the prompt to the user under some under investigation circumstances (will be discussed further in Sect. 5). Instead, Google will issue a unique message that *prompts are disabled* for the particular account and requests for the user's password. The above case scenario allows us to infer if Google Prompts are enabled without actually annoying or disturbing *any* user. The received message for this particular case is depicted in Fig. 2; notice the case *C)*.

Fail Validation Page. As we have previously mentioned, there is a second configuration/mode where Google Prompts are used as a second factor. In this mode, for the authentication to be successful, the user's password is compulsory and entered before the validation with the phone prompt. Since we do not know the user's password to proceed further, we cannot examine and measure this configuration. Therefore we cannot differentiate between Password-only configurations and Password&Google Prompts configurations. However, we have noticed that we can deduce whether a user is using this particular mode by invoking the reminder-password process (Forget password? - see Fig. 5b).

Upon initiating this process, Google attempts to validate the user's identity before allowing them to reset their password. The options presented to the user are last remembered passwords, sending an SMS to the user's device, and using another email address (previously defined). If the configuration we mentioned earlier, is enabled, one of the reminder-password validation options involves sending a prompt to the user's pre-configured device; otherwise, it is not an option. This deduction was confirmed by enabling/disabling this configuration for a multiple of our owned test accounts and consequently checking all options presented to the user.

A significant drawback to this approach is that Google only allows the password-reminder process to occur when the device issuing the request has already been successfully authenticated in the past. In other cases, Google prohibits the password-reminder process and returns a *Fail Validation Block Page*, which we have not yet found a successful way to bypass it (Fig. 3).

Fig. 3. *Fail Validation Block Page.* The above page may be displayed during the Password Reminder process and blocks the collection system from continuing forward.

3 Research Methodology

3.1 Dataset

According to Forbes [16], on the 9th of September 2014, almost 5 million Gmail addresses paired with passwords were leaked and published online on a Bitcoin Security forum. As well as other websites, Google announced about the leaked accounts and suggested that its clients take action to increase their account's security by adding extra verification layers [9]. Therefore, we assume that these emails should be enhanced with additional security measures. We apprehend this dataset with only the email addresses and storing each of them in our database to be checked. Some of its entries were not adhering to a correct email format, and we exclude those using an email regular expression. Also, some duplicates existed, which we excluded since we must check each email only once.

3.2 Collection System

The collection system is designed for a single purpose, to experimentally measure how many users with a Google Account have set Google Prompts as their default authentication method. It can navigate effectively through the whole authentication process and, depending on each account security configuration, follows a different evaluation path. The system comprises two major components: the interface, written in Python, and an evaluation script, written in JavaScript.

The interface initially creates and connects to an SQLite database (see Sect. 3.1) and retrieves a specified amount of not yet analyzed email addresses. To achieve automation, we implement this component based on the Selenium WebDriver [2]. Selenium uses a browser-specific web driver which sends commands (sent in Selenese, or via a Client API) to an actual browser to fetch its results. However, any attempt performed by automated means was blocked by

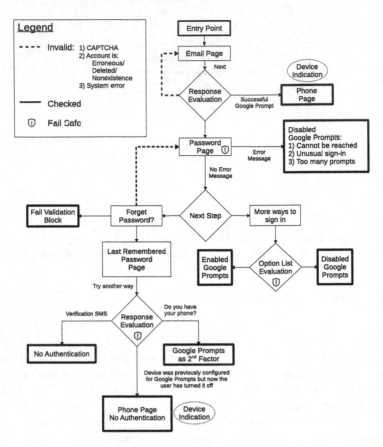

Fig. 4. Evaluation Decision Tree used by the collection system. The different states and their interconnections allow us to effectively understand how Google Prompts are realized and, using this understanding, to proceed and perform actual measurements related to the adoption of Google Prompts in the wild. Notice, that Google Prompts can be enabled in several ways, such as for *password-less authentication* (see states *Response Evaluation, Password Page* and their derived ones), as well as the second factor in 2FA (see states *Forget Password?, More ways to sign-in* and their derived ones).

CAPTCHA and to remain under the radar without issuing too many requests from the same hosts, as explained in Sect. 2.1, we use a proxy which redirects all network traffic through Tor. For each distinct email address, we create a new TOR circuit by utilizing the Stem Controller [4], and we record the current IP address of that TOR exit node. Before that, we ensure that it has a different address than the previously analyzed email; otherwise, we send a signal *NEWNYM* to create another TOR circuit. Since TOR exit nodes are located worldwide, the messages and texts displayed are in different languages; so, we used the URL parameter "hl = en-GB" to always display text in English

(a) *More ways to sign-in.* The user can gain access to the service through alternative means than the password. The available options are presented in a list and could be either enabled or disabled.

(b) *Reminder Password.* The user can recover their account through a series of sequential steps where they must prove their identity. The steps displayed are depended on the account's security configurations.

Fig. 5. Additional steps/options a user can perform on the Google's sign-in page

in the progression of being appropriately evaluated by the system. The Selenium handler is suited better for sites that use browser detection (i.e., Google), since it ensures cross-browser consistency and has more options than other more lightweight equivalents, such as CasperJS [7]. One of these options is selecting between multiple browser drivers, e.g., Firefox and Chrome. We chose the Firefox driver (geckodriver) since it allows disabling specific parameters, such as Cookies and History trackers, which helped us to disguise Selenium further. Also, in the progression of making the whole process more similar to a real-time authentication attempt by an ordinary user, we emit random delays (time sleeps) between each execution of the Selenium commands that interact with the browser.

Next in line, the system enters the email address to the Google sign-in page, automatically clicks the button *Next* to receive the response. Here we perform most of the processing using the evaluation script component, which scans the HTML document for specific tags to determine its next move. We have constructed an *evaluation decision tree*, which we depict in Fig. 4, and based on that, we reach a verdict regarding the default authentication method the user has set. In essence, in Fig. 4, rectangle nodes represent distinct pages in the Google Authentication system, whereas those emphasized in bold indicate the inferred authentication method for each valid account, which we mark as *Checked*. On the other hand, dotted lines mean that the account was marked as *Invalid* due to one ore more of the following reasons: 1) response contains a CAPTCHA (some instances may still occur for yet unknown reasons), 2) the email account under testing is either erroneous, deleted, or does not exist, 3) a system/network error occurred. Additionally, nodes with dotted circles can indicate the type of the user's device, which is considered a privacy leak and will be discussed further in Sect. 5. Recall that a user can decide to use Google Prompts in two modes (see Sect. 2). For inferring the alternative authentication option change-up we invoke the *More ways to sign* (see Fig. 5a) process. On the other hand, for deducing the second mode (see Sect. 2.1), we invoke the *Reminder Password* (see Fig. 5b) process as well.

Moreover, one significant enhancement we added to our collection system was the implementation of Fail Safes. They have an active role in ensuring that the system is running smoothly without any interruptions. They are located strategically in specific points in the EDT to maintain a debug log, which indicates necessary specific system changes (new/modified JavaScript elements) and to handle possible exceptions due to network or driver failure. Finally, after each email analysis, we store the Status (Checked/Invalid/Null), Exit IP Address, Current Time, Authentication method, and a Debug Log in our database.

3.3   Ethics

Before starting our research, we had to confirm that our approach does not annoy or affect the owner of the account in any case. We did this by replicating our experiments on various Google accounts created by us for this purpose. Generally, if we do not reroute our script through TOR and when Google prompts is the default authentication method, the user usually receives the notification on his trusted device. However, if we do reroute through TOR, in most cases, Google Prompts are disabled, as explained in Sect. 2.1. Then the process terminates, and as a result, the user is never notified by the service for an authentication attempt. At the same time, we count this in our evaluation as a Google Prompt authentication.

The number of active registered users in Google is over 425 million [1], and the service receives over 106 million requests per month, which is over 3.5 million requests per day. In order not to be intrusive to the service, we apply a limit of an average of 1000 requests per day. Thus, the number of requests we issue per day is about 0,028% of the total daily requests it receives, and in any case, it can not be considered intrusive.

Furthermore, as far as the collecting data is concerned, we do not store any privacy-related information of the user (e.g., images, phone numbers), and all other information is anonymized. We only store data that we categorized as observations on which method of authentication a user has set as default. After that, we use this data to store counters which represent our measurements.

4 Results

4.1 Initial Evaluation

Our initial evaluation consisted only of the password-less configuration mode. Therefore inferring if a particular Google account is using this mode, requires only a single request with the e-mail address as the sole input. We initially analysed 30,319 Google accounts from our dataset of which 27,286 (90.00%) were valid (*Checked*). The others were *Invalid* for reasons described in Sect. 3.2.

Table 1. The number of Google accounts, where Google Prompts are enabled in password-less mode only.

Result		Checked accounts	
		Total	Percentage
Google Prompts	Successful	3	0.01%
	Disabled	1,024	3.75%
Unknown cases		26,259	96.24%
Total		27,286	100.00%

Out of the valid accounts, we conclude that 1,027 (3,76%) of Google users, grouped as *Google Prompts* in Table 1, have Google Prompts enabled with the password-less configuration method. In the 3.75% of the cases, Google Prompts were disabled (password was requested instead with an error message) for the reasons we discussed in Sect. 2.1 and displayed the Fig. 2. Since Google does not show the error message for an account that has not configured Google Prompts *in any mode*, we can filter out all of those accounts. More importantly, the accounts mentioned above *do not receive* an actual prompt, while we perform the measurements, and our method is relatively transparent. Nevertheless, in the sporadic three cases (0.01%), Google displayed a message indicating that it successfully sent the prompt. We are thoroughly discussing the reason behind this in Sect. 5.

For the remainder accounts, 26,259 (96.24%), there was no error message, and only the password form was presented. Since our collection system could not proceed further, at first, we assumed that these cases were not having an enhanced authentication mechanism enabled and *relied only on password*. However, we were wrong in our assumption, and more accurate measurements are depicted below.

4.2 Final Evaluation

We later discovered there are additional ways to deduce whether an account has Google Prompts enabled. In particular, a user can:

- Enable Google Prompts with the first configuration (password-less) but chooses to use the password (e.g., because their device is inaccessible during authentication). In the next authentication session, a password form is used as default but is *optional* since the option for more ways to sign in is still enabled (sign in only with the prompt).
- Enable Google Prompts as a second factor (second configuration). The password is *compulsory*, and to complete the authentication the prompt must be accepted (tap *Yes*) as well. To deduce this configuration of Google Prompts, our collection system must interfere with the password-reminder process (see Sect. 2.1).

Both these states are presented in Fig. 4 and in the Table 2 under *More ways to sign in* and *Forget Password - 2nd Factor*) paths, accordingly.

Table 2. More accurate measurements obtained with the inclusion of the second configuration mode of Google Prompts and the additional cases of the first one. We observe that the number of Google Prompts accounts almost doubled (6.76%).

Authentication		Checked accounts	
		Total	Percentage
Google Prompt	Successful	13	0.05%
	Disabled	1129	4.17%
More ways to sign in	Enabled	7	0.03%
	Disabled	440	1.62%
Forget Password	2nd Factor	242	0.89%
	No authentication	1670	6.17%
	Fail Validation Block	23585	87.07%
Total		27086	100.00%

In this evaluation, we analyzed an additional amount of 30,014 Google accounts (distinct from the previous evaluation) from our dataset, of which 27,086 (90.24%) were valid (*Checked*). The others were *Invalid* for reasons described in Sect. 3.2. For the cases which have Google Prompts enabled in both configuration modes (1st mode: *Google Prompt* and *More ways to sign in*, 2nd mode: *Forget Password - 2nd Factor*) we have a total of 1831 (6.76%) accounts, of which Google Prompts were enabled in either of the two configuration modes. It is a small percentage, but it is almost double the previous estimate in our initial evaluation. In addition, notice that the Fail Validation Block section which covers a large percentage of our results. Similarly, as the previous evaluation (*Unknown Cases*), we were not able to navigate further to discover whether they were using Google Prompts as a second factor or have not set an authentication at all (see Sect. 2.1).

In summary of both evaluations, we can conclude that our collection system can successfully infer that 2858 (5,25%) accounts have adopted Google Prompts out of the total of 54372 valid Google accounts we checked.

5   Privacy Leaks

While measuring the adoption of Google Prompts in the wild, we tried to be as stealthy as possible to avoid users' annoyance. We performed all the measurements in such a way that they will not be receiving the actual prompts. Nevertheless, there was *still* a tiny fraction of Google Prompts received by users (about 16 in more than 50,000 valid accounts), which we could not mitigate further due to the black-box evaluation. We stress here that for those few successful Google Prompts, we did not further analyze if the prompts were answered positively. Security implications are out of the scope of this paper. Still, in such cases, if the targeted user accidentally confirmed the prompt, our collection system or generally an attacker can freely access the corresponding account. Therefore a possible attack scenario is to send phishing emails to the victims (real-time) to manipulate them to accept the prompt. Beyond security, it is also essential to emphasize the protection of the user's privacy. Thus we focused here on finding possible privacy violations.

As we have previously mentioned in Sect. 2, location tracking is part of the Google Prompts authentication, but we do not know at what extend it is being utilized. For that reason, we tried to investigate the variables enabling the successful reception on the user's device for that small percentage of users we have found. Recall that our collection system leverages exit nodes that are distributed across the globe, and in each email analyzation, we switched from node to node. Since the location was the primary variable change, successfully sent prompts are indicating a common signal between the triggering node (i.e., the TOR exit node) and the under analysis account. For instance, a TOR exit node that is closely (geographically) located to the user may successfully trigger a Google Prompt, which in turn can reveal the user's location. On the other hand, a Google Prompt that fails to be delivered indicates that the user is likely *not* geographically close to the particular node. As a result, determined attackers can orchestrate probes from different TOR exit nodes to infer the areas where the victim user (targeted Google account) is not currently located. Sequentially, they might discover the actual location by the process of elimination. Conducting a study to demonstrate such issues is beyond the scope of this paper, and is likely beyond the common sense of ethical research.

Of course, we understand that the location is not the only crucial factor here. Nevertheless, we alert the reader that at this point, Google Prompts, as designed, may be potentially used for extracting other private information as well. For example, our collection system during email analyzation was able to view data such as device brands and operating systems, user's first names, and profile pictures if they were previously set. In Fig. 6, which is the default HTML response the client receives when the user has enabled Google Prompts, we can see the illustration of these examples. The above information can be obtained in the final pages with the indication of *Device Indication* in Fig. 4.

6 Related Work

2FA hardens authentication for protecting users with stolen credentials; however, its efficacy is still questionable [19]. Initially, 2FA was a promising defense layer against simple, but highly effective attacks, such as phishing [11]. Nevertheless, today we are aware of advanced attacks that can bypass 2FA by *phishing* the second factor, aswell [13]. Despite the shortcomings of 2FA, researchers seek to invent and propose new 2FA-based systems that utilize second factors that can be reasonably user-friendly by requiring little or no user interaction. For instance, Sound-proof [17] uses as a second factor the proximity of the user's phone to the authenticating device. At the same time, Wi-Sign [20] leverages perturbations in the WiFi signals incurred due to the hand motion while signing. In this paper, we do not assess the effectiveness of or exploring attacks that can bypass 2FA. Still, we investigate the mechanics of Google Prompts, a very new 2FA system offered by Google. To this aspect, this paper is closer to a similar study about quantifying the adoption of 2FA [18]. In this particular study, the researchers found out that 6.39% of about 100,000 email accounts of Google had enabled the 2-Step Verification method. Acemyan et al. [6] compare the usability, efficiency, effectiveness, and satisfaction measures among four of Google's 2FA mechanisms. Included in that set is Google Prompts which they found is more usable than the authenticator app.

As far as other 2FA measurements are concerned, Weir et al. [15] performed a user case study asking e-banking customers to rate different 2FA methods

Fig. 6. Default HTML response the client receives when Google Prompts are enabled. We can see some information that can be linked to the user (first name, profile picture, device operating system and brand)

regarding security, quality, and convenience. Overall, they found that users preferred usability above all and did not see the need for additional security. Ganson et al. asked mobile banking users to rate a single-factor and two 2FA schemes for telephone banking [24]. They found that the average user took 20 more seconds to complete each 2FA process than the single-factor one, and 2FA appears to users as a more secure solution but less easy-to-use. In a similar study, De Cristofaro et al. asked by various 2FA-familiar users to rate the usability of the three most popular 2FA solutions with different forms, that is, email or SMS sent to the user, a mobile app used an authenticator and a hardware token that produces OTP codes [10]. They observed that people who use 2FA for work prefer the mobile app option, while those who use it for personal and financial reasons prefer sending a text.

7 Conclusion

In this paper, we review and analyze Google Prompts, a recently enabled authentication mechanism by Google. Towards realizing our understanding, we developed the first collection system that can estimate how many users across the world have adopted Google Prompts. We have analyzed more than 60,000 email accounts, of which more than 50,000 were valid Google accounts. Out of the valid accounts, we have successfully inferred that 2858 (5,25%) accounts had Google Prompts enabled in either of its two configuration modes. However, due to the many obstacles we faced since the evaluation was black-box based, we could not determine with certainty the authentication method used for a large percentage of our results. Moreover, we showed how an attacker could carefully issue silent probes to Google users for receiving back signals about their geographical location.

References

1. Gmail now has 425 million active users. http://www.theverge.com/2012/6/28/3123643/gmail-425-million-total-users
2. Selenium. https://www.seleniumhq.org/
3. Sign in faster with 2-step verification phone prompts. https://support.google.com/accounts/answer/7026266?co=GENIE.Platform%3DAndroid&hl=en
4. Stem docs. https://stem.torproject.org/
5. Sign in faster with 2-Step Verification phone prompts (2019)
6. Acemyan, C.Z., Kortum, P., Xiong, J., Wallach, D.S.: 2FA might be secure, but it's not usable: a summative usability assessment of Google's two-factor authentication (2FA) methods. In: Proceedings of the Human Factors and Ergonomics Society Annual Meeting, vol. 62, pp. 1141–1145. SAGE Publications, Los Angeles (2018)
7. Agarwal, R.: Choosing automated testing frameworks - phantomjs / casperjs vs selenium (2015). https://www.algoworks.com/blog/choosing-your-automated-testing-frameworks-phantomjscasperjs-vs-selenium/
8. Bisson, D.: Two-factor authentication (2FA) versus two-step verification (2SV) (2016). https://www.grahamcluley.com/factor-authentication-2fa-versus-step-verification-2sv/

9. Google Security Blog: Cleaning up after password dumps. http:// googleonlinesecurity.blogspot.gr/2014/09/cleaning-up-after-password-dumps. html

10. De Cristofaro, E., Du, H., Freudiger, J., Norcie, G.: A comparative usability study of two-factor authentication. arXiv preprint arXiv:1309.5344 (2013)

11. Dhamija, R., Tygar, J.D., Hearst, M.: Why phishing works. In: Proceedings of the SIGCHI Conference on Human Factors in Computing Systems, pp. 581–590 (2006)

12. Dingledine, R., Mathewson, N., Syverson, P.: Tor: the second-generation onion router. In: Proceedings of the 13th Conference on USENIX Security Symposium - Volume 13, SSYM (2004)

13. Gelernter, N., Kalma, S., Magnezi, B., Porcilan, H.: The password reset MitM attack. In: 2017 IEEE Symposium on Security and Privacy (SP), pp. 251–267. IEEE (2017)

14. Grosse, E., Upadhyay, M.: Authentication at scale. IEEE Secur. Priv. **11**(1), 15–22 (2012)

15. Gunson, N., Marshall, D., Morton, H., Jack, M.: User perceptions of security and usability of single-factor and two-factor authentication in automated telephone banking. Comput. Secur. **30**(4), 208–220 (2011)

16. Hill, K.: Google says not to worry about 5 million Gmail passwords leaked. http://www.forbes.com/sites/kashmirhill/2014/09/11/google-says-not-to-worry-about-5-million-gmail-passwords-leaked/

17. Karapanos, N., Marforio, C., Soriente, C., Capkun, S.: Sound-proof: usable two-factor authentication based on ambient sound. In: 24th {USENIX} Security Symposium ({USENIX} Security 2015), pp. 483–498 (2015)

18. Petsas, T., Tsirantonakis, G., Athanasopoulos, E., Ioannidis, S.: Two-factor authentication: is the world ready?: quantifying 2FA adoption. In: Proceedings of the Eighth European Workshop on System Security, EuroSec 2015, pp. 4:1–4:7. ACM, New York (2015)

19. Schneier, B.: Two-factor authentication: too little, too late. Commun. ACM **48**(4), 136 (2005)

20. Shah, S.W., Kanhere, S.S.: Wi-sign: device-free second factor user authentication. In: Proceedings of the 15th EAI International Conference on Mobile and Ubiquitous Systems: Computing, Networking and Services, MobiQuitous 2018, New York, NY, USA, pp. 135–144. Association for Computing Machinery (2018)

21. Stadd, A.: 79% of people 18–44 have their smartphones with them 22 hours a day, 2 April 2013. https://www.adweek.com/digital/smartphones/

22. C. M. University. Captcha: Telling humans and computers apart automatically 2000–2010. http://www.captcha.net/

23. von Ahn, L., Blum, M., Hopper, N.J., Langford, J.: CAPTCHA: using hard AI problems for security. In: Biham, E. (ed.) EUROCRYPT 2003. LNCS, vol. 2656, pp. 294–311. Springer, Heidelberg (2003). https://doi.org/10.1007/3-540-39200-9_18

24. Weir, C.S., Douglas, G., Richardson, T., Jack, M.: Usable security: user preferences for authentication methods in eBanking and the effects of experience. Interact. Comput. **22**(3), 153–164 (2010)

On the Evolution of Security Issues
in Android App Versions

Anatoli Kalysch[✉], Joschua Schilling, and Tilo Müller

Friedrich-Alexander University Erlangen-Nürnberg (FAU), Erlangen, Germany
{anatoli.kalysch,joschua.schilling}@fau.de, tilo.mueller@cs.fau.de

Abstract. Since its launch in 2008, the Android platform has seen a lot of development and improvements to this day. Android developer studios had to refine their understanding and available codebases considerably in the past decade since Android's conception. For example, they had to handle monumental changes in the OS, like the introduction of ART or the continually evolving permission system. With this study, we look into the code-base of 1,250 apps from 57 different development studios and analyze the evolution of security-related issues in past versions of an app. To analyze a total of 11,002 APKs, we build on popular vulnerability assessment tools like QARK and drozer and extend them with our own security checks. We discover that the attack surface of an app usually grows over time, including issues that are open for a long time or remain unclosed. Considering the false positive rate of automated vulnerability scanners like QARK or drozer, the total number of vulnerabilities in an app must be taken with care, but nevertheless our study substantiates that the number of security issues typically grows with code complexity and size, rather than shrinking over time.

Keywords: App security · Mobile security · IPC · UI security

1 Introduction

Android has experienced a fair amount of vulnerability research, continually uncovering new vulnerabilities and helping to make the Android ecosystem more secure and robust over the past decade. To keep up with these developments, each Android major release required developer studios to commit a substantial amount of resources to adapt their existing code base, purge it from legacy code, rewrite parts of their app that use deprecated library calls, and stay up-to-date with new platform features, like security-related functionality. Contrary to expectations that a strengthened Android platform would strengthen the security of apps over time, we show that the number of security-related issues inside an app typically grows over time, from one version to another.

One reason is the use of out-dated third-party code that was made obsolete by Android, as was the case with Android's extension of the cryptographic API, or libraries that are not supported anymore by the original developer [4,31].

© Springer Nature Switzerland AG 2020
J. Zhou et al. (Eds.): ACNS 2020 Workshops, LNCS 12418, pp. 523–541, 2020.
https://doi.org/10.1007/978-3-030-61638-0_29

Previous studies concerned with code reuse even suggest that Google's code samples[1] are sometimes reused in apps, code samples that are not necessarily kept up to date, and will lead to vulnerabilities if left unattended between new Android releases [9].

To substantiate our claim, we create a dataset of the top Development Studios (DS) being active in Google Play and assess the situation of security related issues in their apps. By extending the automated vulnerability scanners QARK and drozer with our own implementations, we create a semi-automated system that facilitates our study. By separating our dataset into apps from different DS, we want to gain insights into how DS handle improvements in Android's security mechanisms differently, and whether they maintain apps that show better security conciseness than the average case. Previous studies on the evolution of security in Android app versions, e.g., by Taylor et al. [28] and by Gao et al. [8], did not take the programmers or DS behind apps into account.

Contribution. In detail, our paper makes the following contributions:

- We present an overview of security issues in Android apps, grouped by the DS behind it. To analyze the evolution of issues in different versions of the same app, we create a timeline for each app, analyzing 11,002 apps in total.
- We provide an overview of "trending categories" of app vulnerabilities growing over the lifetime of an app. For example, we find that IPC vulnerabilities are typically increasing with new app versions, resulting in 1135 flagged components per app on average, while network and cryptography-based issues appear roughly the same at a smaller scale with only 406 components being affected in 369 apps.
- Analyzing our dataset, we assess the amount of third-party-introduced security issues, as opposed to security issues stemming directly from DS code. Conducting cross-app observations of the same DS, we are able to assess the vulnerability reuse, which hints at code reuse between different apps from the same developer, e.g., we discover 141 unique security issues that affect 52 DS over 525 apps in the Android GSM internal library.

2 Background

This section describes basic information helpful to understand the rest of the paper. Readers familiar with automated vulnerability scanners on Android (Sect. 2.1), or with the top ten mobile vulnerability categories suggested by the Open Web Application Security Project (OWASP) [18] (Sect. 2.2) introduced in Sect. 1 may safely skip these sections.

---

[1] https://github.com/googlesamples, accessed on 05.06.2020.

2.1   Vulnerability Scanners

The Quick Android Review Kit, or QARK[2], is a static analysis tool developed by LinkedIn Research, which allows to scan APK files for a wide range of known potential vulnerabilities. The methodology is a static off-device analysis.

Drozer[3] is a security assessment framework for Android apps. Contrary to QARK it follows a dynamic on-device analysis methodology, and supports the analysis of environmental interactions of the application with the device it's installed on, e.g., active changes to the Android Runtime (ART), network interactions, other apps' IPC endpoints and the underlying OS.

2.2   Considered Vulnerabilities

Like any other system Android was victim to several vulnerabilities from diverse categories since its introduction in the late 2000s. In our case we will be relying on the OWASP [19] mobile vulnerability taxonomy to assess which categories we include in our analysis, since they summarize the top threats endangering the mobile ecosystem, and additionally developer guidelines on how to test and mitigate them.

UI Security. Clickjacking and accessibility (a11y) services can be both used to mount UI-based attacks tricking the user to provide personally identifiable information (PII) to the wrong application or even stealthily manipulating the Android device and other apps [7].

IPC. Wrong use of Android's IPC can yield PII and secrets transmitted between apps on the same device. If Android's IPC is used incorrectly or protected insufficiently an attacker might even get access to another app's resources. The Open Web Application Security Project (OWASP) cites Improper Platform Usage, which includes IPC-based vulnerabilities, as the top risk category for mobile applications [18].

Network Communication. We consider in the network communication category the vulnerabilities related to the communication with the apps backend, or a third-parties backend. Apps should adhere on modern authentication and cryptographic standards for network communication, lest they fall victim to an attacker on the same network [18].

Cryptography. User data protection, especially PII protection, is a key feature to prevent malware from gaining insights to use in social engineering attacks or in case of banking information to abuse for banking fraud [18]. In regards to cryptography the use of modern ciphers and sensible key management needs to be enforced [18].

---

[2] https://github.com/linkedin/qark, accessed on 09.05.2020.
[3] https://labs.mwrinfosecurity.com/tools/drozer/, accessed on 05.05.2020.

3   Approach

The goal of our study is to investigate Android vulnerabilities in Google Play published apps, maintained by the same developer studios. The *purpose* is (i) to discover which vulnerabilities are the most common occurring and which components are the most at risk, (ii) to what extent code reuse in DS apps is also reusing vulnerabilities, and (iii) whether vulnerabilities are increasing over the lifetime of an application or progressively getting fixed. The *context* of our study is a dataset of 57 Android DS and their applications, described closer in Sect. 3.1 and the vulnerability analysis described in Sect. 3.2. With our study we thereby address the following research questions:

- How do security findings evolve through the life-time of an app? This question aims to provide insights into the evolution of security issues of an app. These findings could help security researchers to narrow down potential flaws in apps depending on their update cycles and previous security finding evolution.
- Are the security issues located in developer written code or in third-party libraries? Answering this research questions will shed light into the awareness of developers who include vulnerable third-party code into their projects.
- How many security issues are introduced through reused code? Code reuse is quite common in software development, however, it brings about additional maintenance overhead.
- Which types of security issues are most common in experienced developer studios? We strive to provide a categorical overview of which components and which issues have the highest chance to appear even in the work of professional developers. This vulnerability study provides invaluable insights to both, app developers and security researchers, on which vulnerabilities should receive more attention.

3.1   Dataset Creation

We operate on a newly created dataset of over 57 DS. The DS all have a public website promoting the studio's apps and additionally have a presence in the Google Play Store, which we used as a source to download the initial app versions. Some studios had different publishers; hence the developer accounts on Google Play could also differ, but as long as the app was listed as primarily developed by the DS, we matched the app to the studio in our dataset. To obtain past versions of the apps, we used apkpure [1].

The initial aggregation from Google Play yielded 1,250 apps from 57 different studios. We focused on the most downloaded apps on the Google Play Store and the studio's most downloaded apps. On average, each app was downloaded 6.5 Mil. times. The average number of versions per app was 11.0 with a new app version being released every 136 days days. All apps and their versions resulted in a dataset of 11,002 apps.

3.2   Vulnerability Analysis

For the vulnerability analysis, we follow a hybrid approach, first performing a static analysis with QARK, followed by a manual UI, input-method editor (IME), and a11y analysis, and concluding with a dynamic IPC vulnerability analysis with drozer. These three processes and the following report creation per app are depicted in Fig. 1. Due to the preferred focus of this study on improper use of Android's security features, IPC, and network interaction, QARK was chosen for static vulnerability assessments, based on the study of Ranganath and Mitra [20] who investigated the trade-offs of different vulnerability assessment tools. A static-only analysis is not enough and needs to be assisted by a supplementary dynamic analysis, especially to include assessing the app's UI interaction and improving the IPC testing methodologies. While several tools are available [10, 26, 27], we chose drozer due to its lightweight nature and ease of extendability and extended its IPC fuzzing capabilities with an improved version of a Template-based Intent Fuzzer [14] for Activities, Services and BroadcastReceivers.

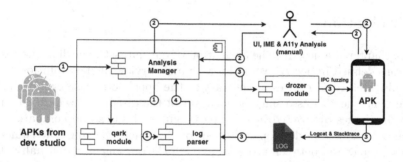

Fig. 1. The three analysis processes overseen by the analysis manager module. Denoted by ① is the initial static analysis process, disassembling the app and conducting a vulnerability analysis with QARK. ② represents the manual UI, IME and a11y analyses performed in parallel dynamically on a dedicated Android device. Following, denoted by ③, is the dynamic IPC analysis conducted after ②. Lastly, after the log parser module transferred the vulnerability analysis results, the analysis manager consolidates all results into a report.

For our dynamic approaches, we focused on Android versions 6.0 to 9.0. The last available Android version distribution data[4] places 16.9% devices using Android 6, 19.2% using Android 7, 28.3% using Android 8 and 10.4% using Android 9. Remaining devices used even older Android versions at that time.

Vulnerability assessment tools rely on constant development and addition of the vulnerabilities they scan for in apps. One major issue we encountered, is

---

[4] Last update by Google was on March 10, 2019 https://developer.android.com/about/dashboards/.

that several other approaches suggested in recent years for Android vulnerability tracking were either not supported for the latest Android versions or have never been extended with new capabilities. Other vulnerabilities have been fixed by the Android Open Source Project developers and were not applicable anymore. Keeping this in mind we decided on recent vulnerabilities that focus on errors in the apps development and do not constitute a vulnerability in the Android OS itself. The vulnerabilities we test for can be avoided during or post-development, and countermeasures are well known [18]. In detail, we extend our vulnerability assessments with the IPC fuzzing methodology from the Template-based Intent Fuzzer [14] and the UI, a11y, and input method editor testing methodologies from Kalysch et al. [13]. We additionally make modifications to the report creation in QARK, to ensure all reports include a unique identifier for the same vulnerability types to make the analysis easier. The IPC fuzzing approach distinguished itself through the comparison with other available open-source IPC fuzzing approaches for Android [14]. The UI testing methodologies test for major issues with the UI, IME and a11y subsystems on Android. These subsystems represent crucial interfaces where Android's sandboxing model can be subverted [13].

4   Evaluation

In this chapter, we describe the evaluation of our dataset regarding the research questions defined in Sect. 3. We start with an overview of the evolution of security vulnerability categories in contrast to the apps' code-base evolution. Then we shift our view to assessing the location of the discovered security issues by discerning issues discovered in third-party vulnerabilities and comparing them to issues discovered in developer written code, further assessing how vulnerabilities are propagated between projects, and which components are usually at risk. Lastly, we take a look at the most common security issues discovered and derive trends of which vulnerabilities appear in the apps in our dataset.

4.1   Vulnerability and Code-Base Evolution

In this section, we look at the development of vulnerabilities over time and compare it to the apps' growing code-base. For every app in our dataset, we conduct a lifetime study of all available versions of this app from apkpure [1], resulting in a consolidated dataset of all versions of 11,002. After analyzing all the app versions with our vulnerability assessment pipelines in QARK and drozer, we compare the numbers of detected issues for the vulnerability categories IPC, cryptography, and network.

Although we have 11.0 versions for apps on average, this number can differ between apps, and the number of different vulnerabilities occurring will also vary considerably, so we need to perform a normalization process. First, we cast the different versions to an interval of 0 to 1, with zero being the first version, and one the last. By doing the same for the vulnerability categories IPC, cryptography, and network, we can graph the resulting trends of whether a particular vulnerability category increases in time or not, which is visualized in Fig. 2. Note that this trend analysis only presents an increase over the published versions and does not provide information about the nominal occurrence of vulnerabilities.

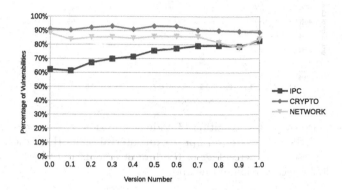

Fig. 2. This figure shows the probabilistic occurrence of vulnerabilities in different versions of the same app. We mapped the versions of an app to an interval of [0..1] on the X-Axis, and the mean percentage of vulnerabilities encountered on the Y-Axis.

Interestingly, the IPC security issues seem to increase over time, while the network and cryptography issues seem to decrease slightly. This development may be attributed to new IPC components being included over time, usually through additional functionality, e.g., sharing mechanisms. On the other hand, network and cryptography mechanisms will probably not be affected by new functionality in a meaningful way, and are thus becoming slightly more secure as old vulnerabilities are uncovered and fixed. Clearly, IPC-related security issues are a trend that is increasing over the lifespan of an application, with vulnerable interfaces increasing over time.

Similarly, we observe the development of an apps code size over time, which is plotted in Fig. 3. We perform the same normalization process as before for the versions of an app and use the largest code-base in the app's evolution as the 100% mark on the Y-Axis. This creates a comparison of the overall code size of an app and allows us to compare the trends that show when the code size of an app starts to grow and shrink during its lifetime.

Curiously, an apps code-base does not seem to increase with each incremental version. While the code size continually increases during the first versions of an app, it then begins to fluctuate between increasing and decreasing with each subsequential update. This development might be an indicator that the app has reached maturity, and fewer new features are introduced, while instead, the code-base is streamlined.

Comparing both figures reveals that the decreasing code-base coincides with the decreasing cryptography and especially network vulnerabilities. Interestingly, for the IPC category, the probability of security issues increases with a growing code-base. While the rising probability can also be seen for the other

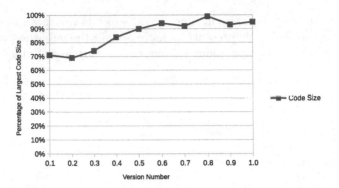

Fig. 3. This figure shows the evolution of code size in different versions of the same app. We mapped the versions of an app to an interval of [0..1] on the X-Axis. For the Y-Axis, we present the percentage of the largest amount of code as 100% and the amount of code for each version of this app.

categories, the increase is much less. Our findings thus support the notion that with an increase in the code-base, the probability for bugs and thus vulnerabilities increases.

4.2   Developer Code vs. Third-Party Vulnerabilities

To shed light on the vulnerable code location, we analyzed the third-party libraries in each application and the core developer packages. Third-party libraries often offer outsourced functionality not directly related to the apps actual use case, e.g., ad support, social media interaction, analytics, and legacy support for older platforms. In our dataset, third-party libraries were responsible for at least 80.7% of overall vulnerabilities detected in the applications, thus having a significant impact on the security of an app as a whole. Table 1 provides an overview of the top 10 common vulnerable third-party library packages that were frequently flagged during testing. Since they affect a large number of developer studios, we assume that developers trust third party code, especially if it is from a renowned source. The table shows, which unique security issues were flagged in how many faulty components during analysis, and how many development studios were affected.

4.3   Most Common Security Issues

The analysis of the most common security issues in our dataset yielded insights into currently disregarded attack scenarios, as well as possibly missed vulnerabilities. For example, the percentages of vulnerable apps to our UI, IME, and a11y-based attacks suggest a disregard for this attack scenario, while the revelations from our IPC fuzzing suggest missing testing methods.

Table 1. This table shows different well-known third-party libraries that were flagged during testing with security issues. We combined the detected issues into unique security issues and sorted the table according to the faulty component's number of affected developers.

Library name	Faulty components	Unique security issues	Affected DS	Affected apps
Android GMS internal	97	141	52	525
Facebook SDK	36	92	42	508
Android GMS common	19	19	56	975
StartApp	19	60	5	40
Android GMS measurements	15	16	31	136
Amazon SDK	12	32	17	116
Moat Analytics	12	31	15	97
Appnext	12	33	4	34
Android GMS ads	11	42	49	639
Android GMS gcm	11	17	28	307
Pushwoosh API	11	22	2	4
Android GMS analytics	9	9	25	197
Alipay SDK	8	21	3	26
Fyber	8	22	6	28
Apache HTTP Client	8	8	7	10

(1) UI, IME, and A11y Vulnerabilities. We analyzed the initial 57 DS (1,250 apps) to find vulnerabilities against UI-based Overlays [7], malicious third-party keyboards [13], screen recordings [13], and a11y-based attacks [13]. Testing the 1,250 apps provided a good trade-off, as it allowed us to make statistically significant statements while keeping the manual overhead manageable, as we needed to input the credentials manually for each app. Since most of the applications were from the game category, a11y events leaking any in-game data were mostly deactivated. However, that proved to be not the case for in-app purchases and login fields in the apps. They were providing enough a11y events to sniff confidential information, e.g., passwords, and even leaked the login window coordinates, needed to execute the UI overlay-based password sniffing.

Two apps had their own implementation of Android's keyboard, which rendered IME-based attacks useless against a minuscule percentage of apps. While this is an improvement in terms of security, their in-app keyboard proved to be vulnerable against a11y-based sniffing attacks, and screen recordings. A possible countermeasure against the screen recording attack is FLAG_SECURE. We encountered 14 apps that used this flag to secure their screen's content. However, FLAG_SECURE does not protect the keyboard, thus allowing attackers to extract typed in credentials despite explicitly setting this flag (Table 2).

Table 2. Out of 1,250 apps 1,027 had a login screen, either for an account with the app development studio or third-party, e.g., Facebook and Google. A close examination revealed most of these accounts being vulnerable to at least one UI-based attack, thereby compromising user credentials or even credit card information in case of in-app purchases.

Downloads	Apps with a login	Percentage of logins vulnerable against			
		Android overlays	A11y events	Screen records	Malicious IMEs
50+ Mio.	64	100%	96.88%	90.63%	100%
10+ Mio.	119	100%	100%	100%	98.32%
1+ Mio.	385	100%	100%	100%	100%
500+ Tsd.	128	100%	100%	100%	100%
100+ Tsd.	162	100%	100%	100%	100%
50+ Tsd.	36	100%	100%	100%	100%
10+ Tsd.	133	100%	100%	100%	100%
Summary	1,027	100%	99.54%	98.66%	99.76%

(2) IPC Vulnerabilities. Aside from the UI-related vulnerabilities, the most common issue we encountered was Android IPC-related. The most common vulnerability in this regard was the pending Intent. Pending intents are used to encapsulate another intent object, thereby allowing another application to execute the inner Intent as if it were from the original application. This misinterpretation effectively allows another app to use the same permissions and identity of the executing app because this can lead to unwanted access to app resources, access to hardware depending on dangerous permissions, and access to an apps execution context. This issue affected 3345 components in 1131 different apps. In the same category of IPC vulnerabilities fall the empty pending intent instances that affect 488 components in 417 apps, and sticky broadcasts that are affecting 274 components in 231 apps.

Sticky broadcasts pose a vulnerability because custom permissions can not secure them. Thus any application may access, remove, or modify them – even the Google Developers guidelines advise against their use starting API level 21 [2]. Since other applications can remove sticky intents, developers should not trust them to persist. All another app needs to modify or remove sticky broadcasts is the BROADCAST_STICKY permission, which is classified as normal and therefore, might be used by any application without explicit approval by the user.

Another major IPC issue were exported components with inadequate error handling. Out of the 1,250 apps, 2603 components were inadequately protected through permissions in 1135 apps, ultimately leading 377 of these apps to have at least one crash during our fuzz testing. Apps with a higher number of exported components did not necessarily show more crashes than apps with a lesser number.

However, exposing more parts of an app increases its attack surface and, therefore, the number of possible entry points accessible from outside the app. This entry point explosion leads to a higher risk for unsafe source code being executable from outside the app's scope.

Whenever key-value-mappings were left out, or null references were assigned to the Intents, it was more likely that a `NullpointerExceptions` was raised by the receiving component, which was responsible for two-thirds of the crashes. However, in case all expected mappings were assigned correctly, but the format of the data stored in the mappings was modified instead, it was more likely that the payload passed the extraction step without any errors. This left a higher chance of discovering interesting bugs in deeper levels of the components' execution paths and resulted in more advanced exception types like `ClassNotFoundExceptions`, `ClassCastExceptions` or `IllegalArgumentExceptions`.

(3) Network and WebView-Based Vulnerabilities. The detected network vulnerabilities focused on wrong certificate usage and broken session management. We found trusted server checks always returning `true` (406 components in 369 apps), `SSLSession` objects not checked through the `HostnameVeriefier` (270 components in 233 apps), unsafe implementations of the `SSLError` handler (161 components in 107 apps), and instances where all hostnames were explicitly allowed (109 components in 108 apps). Altogether, these issues affected 550 apps, making this issue quite pressing for nearly half of our dataset. These issues reveal a deeper problem with how certificates and host verification are handled by developers, in the worst-case facilitating spoofing attacks where an allegedly verified host is an attacker.

WebViews, while useful additions to the Android UI arsenal, introduced an enormous interface directly into an app's context. In our dataset, issues with WebViews were highly prominent: WebViews were running unprotected in an app's context with Javascript enabled, meaning they had access to an app's permissions, resources, and execution context. While these issues affected 12,170 different components in 1128 apps, they become much graver if coupled with the networking vulnerabilities detailed above since an attacker could include their Javascript code in a spoofed host's website.

(4) Cryptography Vulnerabilities. While regarding the cryptography issues, we discovered two distinct categories. For one, several issues were the instantiation of outdated ciphers or ciphers with weak parameters, e.g., the use of the Electronic codebook (ECB). After we an analysis of the afflicted apps we discovered, that most cases were a result of ECB being used as the default for cipher instantiations if no explicit cipher was chosen. For example, the popular cryptographic Android library Spongycastle[5] automatically uses ECB mode whenever only the transformation algorithm, for example, DES or AES, is specified, but no cipher mode is given.

---

[5] https://github.com/rtyley/spongycastle, accessed on 09.04.2020.

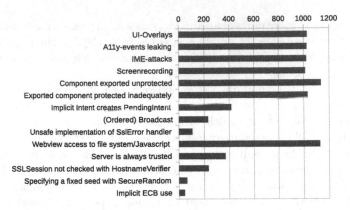

Fig. 4. This figure presents an overview of the affected apps and the security issues we detected during our screening procedures.

Random numbers often play a critical role as they are needed for the ad-hoc creation of encryption keys. The class `java.util.Random`[6] generates pseudo-random numbers based on a 48-bit seed, which is modified via a linear congruential formula. Javas popular `Math.random()` method is based on this class and therefore, should not be used for cryptographic purposes [5]. Instead `java.util.SecureRandom`[7] offers a true random number generator for use in cryptography. However, `SecureRandom` can only return truly random numbers when no predictable seed is used. In the context of true random generators setting a fixed Seed eludes the purpose of `SecureRandom` as long as no truly random seed is passed and therefore, should not be used. Thus random generators should not be called with `setSeed` if their results are used in cryptography. QARK detected a total of 104 uses of `setSeed` or `generateSeed` together with `SecureRandom` that belong to 64 different applications.

To summarize the detected vulnerabilities and their occurrence in our dataset, we refer to Fig. 4. Based on the overwhelming number of UI-based findings, we can assume that this attack vector is currently not considered for the DS attacker model. Further, the IPC-based findings appear to be a more significant issue seeing that roughly three-quarters of all apps had an issue belonging to this category. Network and cryptography issues appear to be less prevalent in our dataset.

4.4 Vulnerability Reuse Between Different Projects

We assess the code reuse with specific focus on the detected vulnerabilities in our dataset. To that end we correlate the detected vulnerabilities in apps from the

---

[6] https://docs.oracle.com/javase/10/docs/api/java/util/Random.html, accessed on 17.04.2020.

[7] https://docs.oracle.com/javase/10/docs/api/java/security/SecureRandom.html, accessed on 17.04.2020.

same development studio. Note, that a direct correlation of crashed components in these apps is not possible due to Android Studios default ProGuard obfuscation process which obfuscates the class, function, and most identifier names in developer written code.

We instead focus on identifying the same vulnerabilities in apps and assessing a studios predisposition towards certain vulnerability categories. As can be seen in the previous Sect. 4.3, most UI vulnerabilities were shared among all apps in our dataset, meaning IPC, network and cryptography issues are a better fit to assess any correlations between the apps and development studios. These are summarized for the DS in Table 3, including an overview of how many DS were actually affected throughout their apps with a certain vulnerability, as well as the variance, of how many vulnerable components were detected per app on average. To spot the most significant vulnerabilities in the data set that can be best attributed towards a specific author, only components not belonging to external packages are considered.

Generally a lower number of affected DS show a higher correlation with the affected DS, also a high variance between the frequency numbers of different authors are better for correlation, as they allow to separate DS more clearly. A high number of affected DS shows a very common vulnerability, that seems to be shared throughout development studios.

Table 3. In this table we group selected vulnerabilities from affected DS. Aside from the percentage of affected developers we also display the variance of how many app components were on average vulnerable per app. A high variance thus suggests, that different DS had very different numbers of vulnerable components per app.

Issue	Affected DS	Variance
(netw.) Webview access to file system/Javascript	40 (66.67%)	652.97
(IPC) Component exported unprotected	36 (60.00%)	50.47
(IPC) Implicit Intent creates PendingIntent	19 (31.67%)	50.47
(cryp.) Implicit ECB use	5 (8.33%)	17.98
(netw.) Unsafe implementation of SslError handler	5 (8.33%)	37.14
(IPC) Exported component protected inadequately	3 (5.00%)	10.86
(netw.) Server is always trusted	2 (3.33%)	69.47
(cryp.) Specifying a fixed seed with SecureRandom	2 (3.33%)	0.03
(IPC) (Ordered) Broadcast	2 (3.33%)	10.13
(netw.) SSLSession objects not checked (HostnameVerifier)	1 (1.67%)	17.98

High variance numbers suggest major differences in the vulnerable components per DS app. This means that these issues have a different impact between different DS in our dataset and offer insights, that some authors have bigger issue of dealing with these vulnerabilities, similar to those vulnerabilities that affect only a small number of DS with high variance.

To take a closer look at the vulnerability behaviour for each DS, we inspect the percentage of that developer's apps affected by the selected issue compared to the total number of apps of the selected developer. Also, that specific security issue has to be in a similar way contained in every affected application of the developer. This means that the frequency of the selected vulnerability should be approximately the same for each affected application of the selected developer. To measure whether the frequency of a vulnerability within the application set of a certain development studio is constant, the variance of the issue occurrence count of each app can be utilized. A lower frequency variance within the developers as well as a high percentage of affected apps within a developer indicate high correlation throughout the apps of a developer, as they have similar features and are therefore more specific for a selected user.

A few examples of vulnerabilities occurring in specific studios are, e.g., the hostname verification issues where servers are always trusted. Taking a look at the two DS affected we can see major differences in the implementation: While one studio had similar issue numbers for hostname verification issues throughout the apps, the other had major fluctuations in these specific security issues. This suggests a high level of code reuse on the one studio.

In another case the constant appearance of the same amount of security issues in the IPC category led us to discover a DS internal SDK which they used throughout roughly half of their app projects. Judging by the detected unprotected components the SDK was developed at one point to enable easier communication handling with core app features and apps from the same developer. Since this internal SDK was reused between apps it posed an extremely lucrative point of entry for attackers as well, since it contained several unprotected components that could be abused as entry points into the app.

5   Discussion

After inspecting the results, a key recommendation is to include vulnerability scanning and app fuzzing approaches into the CI/CD pipeline of an app development project. This would already allow developers to check their apps for the most common vulnerabilities and create a safer environment. However, the inclusion of vulnerability scanners comes at a price.

For one, it is the limited scope. No single scanner supports all known vulnerabilities or testing methodologies, meaning to get decent coverage, several scanning and assessment tools have to be employed in tandem. This requires developers to understand the trade-offs and limitations of each tool and imposes a significant overhead on top of regular project work. Once tools are included, however, there is no guarantee for future support and incremental work to keep updated with new developments.

On the other hand, there seems to be no mutual consent on how to communicate or classify vulnerabilities or place them in a severity category.

While in research, some Android vulnerability studies define their own taxonomies [16,21,22] they seem not widely used. Usually, vulnerability scanners either define their own, e.g., QARK, rely on industry taxonomies like OWASP, or leave it to the authors of the vulnerability submodules to communicate the vulnerability.

All of this is making the prioritization of the detected vulnerabilities harder and requires specific domain knowledge and experience to resolve detected issues. We thereby question the usability of the naive inclusion of vulnerability scanners into project development pipelines. The reason why a particular code fragment or behavior is flagged as vulnerability and how to resolve this issue is what the vulnerability scanner needs to communicate understandably. Ideally, developers should be able to understand the output in its human-readable format. However, in our case, the interpretation of vulnerability messages required a deep understanding of the vulnerability already or domain-specific knowledge of, e.g., cryptographic ciphers, to correctly address the issue.

Threats to Validity. As with most empirical studies, the here presented results might not apply to other platforms. Android has a vast scope of changes introduced to the system from a developer perspective; other platforms might have a slower pace in development.

Another threat to validity is the reliance on automated vulnerability scanners. As with most approaches, there is a chance for false positives, meaning not all the detected vulnerabilities might be exploitable. The actual exploitation of these vulnerabilities would, in most cases, require a deeper understanding of the app's internal logic and pose a considerable manual overhead. To mitigate this, we relied on additional dynamic analysis in the form of IPC fuzzing and on purely dynamic analysis for UI vulnerabilities.

6   Related Work

In this Section we discuss related works in the vulnerability study area and additionally differentiate our own contributions from previous work. So far, we conducted a developer studio focused vulnerability study, to assess whether vulnerabilities are reused in different projects and to what extent. Our results allow to predict vulnerabilities of an application by utilizing a database of previously detected vulnerabilities in previously published apps by the same developer studios. Conceptually closest to us is the work of Scandariato et al. [25] and Jiminez et al. [12]. Scandariato et al., who developed an automated approach to predict vulnerable classes, base the vulnerability assumptions on software complexity metrics computed for each class in the apps Dalvik bytecode instead of our authorship based approach. Jiminez et al. manually check the vulnerabilities reported to the National Vulnerability Database between 2008 and 2014 to create a complexity overview for different Android functionality. This allows them to predict the areas where vulnerabilities might arise in an Android project.

Taylor et al. [28] also looked at vulnerabilities in apps at the beginning and end of a two year period with vulnerability scanners and came to the conclusion, that number of vulnerabilities increases as well as the number of permitted resources the app has access to. While some of the premises of both studies are similar, e.g., tracking vulnerabilities in Android apps over a period of time, we have a broader scope of considered vulnerabilities, and a focus on DS. In a similar fashion, Gao et al. [8] conduct a vulnerability study on randomly chosen 28,564 consecutive app releases, relying on the Androbugs Framework for vulnerability analysis. Our study differs through the different focus groups, Android apps in their study and DS in ours, and the additionally introduced tests we conducted beyond the vulnerability scanning with automated screening procedures.

General vulnerability studies without a focus on DS, and have been conducted as well. Notable regarding our scope are especially Enck [6] and Linares et al. [16]. Enck conducted a study of 1,100 apps from Google Play discovering flaws especially in the platform usage of the studied apps. Linares et al. analyzed 660 vulnerabilities, including their inner workings in the Android OS, to identify the components most at risk and provide guidelines on how to better secure the OS and improve app security.

Some vulnerability studies for Android apps focus on a subset of vulnerabilities regarded in our scope. These subsets of vulnerabilities also do not contain our focus on the development organization that is responsible for the maintenance of the app, and do not assess the time it takes to fix the app after a vulnerability was made public. Wei et al. [30], Li et al. [15] and Sadeghi et al. [23] focus on IPC vulnerabilities, which is covered in broader scope through our dynamic drozer module. Chin et al. [3], and Sasnauskas et al. [24] conducted studies on IPC vulnerabilities to test their fuzzing implementation, however, they were much more limited in their scope and dataset, and do not focus on DS. The Android IPC robustness study of Maji et al. [17], who strongly relied on a null intent fuzzer and generated sets of valid and semi-valid intents also falls under the same limitations.

Wang et al. [29] and Egele et al. [5] regard several misuse vulnerabilities which are also a subscope of our paper, albeit with a different focus than our study. Liu et al. Wang et al. focus on apps that save private data on publicly accessible storage. Egele et al. focus on cryptographic APIs on Android and their frequent (88% of apps) misuse. Cryptographic API misuse is also a subscope of this paper. Our findings reflect a better understanding for cryptography on the developer side, however, which can be explained by our focus on DS, i.e., proficient software developers.

Jang et al. [11] analyzed accessibility features of Microsoft Windows, Ubuntu Linux, iOS and Android. They found vulnerabilities related to these features in all regarded OS, and proposed improvements. Fratantonio et al. [7] presented a security assessment of Android's UI and uncovered design flaws and several innovative attacks which combine the use of UI-elements and a11y services. In addition, they describe overlay-based attacks that can be used to bootstrap the activation of an a11y service. Kalysch et al. [13] focus on a11y-based attacks and conduct a vulnerability study of 1100 Google Play apps.

7 Conclusion

In this paper, we performed a study on app DS, focusing on vulnerability reuse between different apps and on the vulnerability evolution of these applications. Our analysis showed that DS have severe blind spots for UI security, endangering users, mainly if their apps include in-app purchases. We further discovered that the category *IPC* is usually the most endangered, with over 1135 apps having at least one IPC related security issue. Analyzing the evolution of security issues in an app, we discovered that the number for IPC-based security issues generally increases with each subsequent app version, contrary to network and cryptography-related vulnerabilities, which stay mostly the same. However, many vulnerabilities are introduced due to third-party library code, and less so through developer code.

References

1. APKpure Inc.: APKpure (2014). https://apkpure.com. Accessed 13 Mar 2020
2. Burns, J.: Mobile application security on Android. In: Black Hat 2009 (2009)
3. Chin, E., Felt, A.P., Greenwood, K., Wagner, D.: Analyzing inter-application communication in Android. In: Proceedings of the 9th International Conference on Mobile Systems, Applications, and Services, pp. 239–252. ACM (2011)
4. Clark, S., Frei, S., Blaze, M., Smith, J.: Familiarity breeds contempt: the honeymoon effect and the role of legacy code in zero-day vulnerabilities. In: Proceedings of the 26th Annual Computer Security Applications Conference, pp. 251–260 (2010)
5. Egele, M., Brumley, D., Fratantonio, Y., Kruegel, C.: An empirical study of cryptographic misuse in Android applications. In: Proceedings of the 2013 ACM SIGSAC Conference on Computer & Communications Security, pp. 73–84 (2013)
6. Enck, W., Octeau, D., McDaniel, P.D., Chaudhuri, S.: A study of Android application security. In: USENIX Security Symposium, vol. 2, p. 2 (2011)
7. Fratantonio, Y., Qian, C., Chung, S.P., Lee, W.: Cloak and dagger: from two permissions to complete control of the UI feedback loop. In: 2017 IEEE Symposium on Security and Privacy (SP), pp. 1041–1057. IEEE (2017)
8. Gao, J., Li, L., Kong, P., Bissyandé, T.F., Klein, J.: Understanding the evolution of Android app vulnerabilities. IEEE Trans. Reliab. (2019)
9. Hanna, S., Huang, L., Wu, E., Li, S., Chen, C., Song, D.: Juxtapp: a scalable system for detecting code reuse among Android applications. In: Flegel, U., Markatos, E., Robertson, W. (eds.) DIMVA 2012. LNCS, vol. 7591, pp. 62–81. Springer, Heidelberg (2013). https://doi.org/10.1007/978-3-642-37300-8_4
10. Hay, R., Tripp, O., Pistoia, M.: Dynamic detection of inter-application communication vulnerabilities in Android. In: Proceedings of the 2015 International Symposium on Software Testing and Analysis, pp. 118–128. ACM (2015)
11. Jang, Y., Song, C., Chung, S.P., Wang, T., Lee, W.: A11y attacks: exploiting accessibility in operating systems. In: Proceedings of the 2014 ACM SIGSAC Conference on Computer and Communications Security, pp. 103–115. ACM (2014)
12. Jimenez, M., Papadakis, M., Bissyandé, T.F., Klein, J.: Profiling Android vulnerabilities. In: 2016 IEEE International Conference on Software Quality, Reliability and Security (QRS), pp. 222–229. IEEE (2016)

13. Kalysch, A., Bove, D., Müller, T.: How Android's UI security is undermined by accessibility. In: Proceedings of the 2nd Reversing and Offensive-Oriented Trends Symposium, pp. 1–10 (2018)
14. Kalysch, A., Deutel, M., Müller, T.: Template-based Android inter process communication fuzzing. In: Proceedings of the 12th International Conference on Availability, Reliability and Security. ACM (2020). https://fau1-files.cs.fau.de/public/ publications/Template_based_Android_Inter_Process_Communication_Fuzzing.pdf
15. Li, L., et al.: IccTA: detecting inter-component privacy leaks in Android apps. In: Proceedings of the 37th International Conference on Software Engineering-Volume 1, pp. 280–291. IEEE Press (2015)
16. Linares-Vásquez, M., Bavota, G., Escobar-Velásquez, C.: An empirical study on Android-related vulnerabilities. In: 2017 IEEE/ACM 14th International Conference on Mining Software Repositories (MSR), pp. 2–13. IEEE (2017)
17. Maji, A.K., Arshad, F.A., Bagchi, S., Rellermeyer, J.S.: An empirical study of the robustness of inter-component communication in Android. In: 2012 42nd Annual IEEE/IFIP International Conference on Dependable Systems and Networks (DSN), pp. 1–12. IEEE (2012)
18. OWASP Foundation: Mobile top 10 (2016). https://www.owasp.org/index.php/ Mobile_Top_10_2016-Top_10. Accessed 22 June 2020
19. OWASP Foundation: Owasp mobile security project (2017). https://www.owasp. org/index.php/OWASP_Mobile_Security_Project. Accessed 22 June 2020
20. Ranganath, V.P., Mitra, J.: Are free Android app security analysis tools effective in detecting known vulnerabilities? arXiv preprint arXiv:1806.09059 (2018)
21. Rangwala, M., Zhang, P., Zou, X., Li, F.: A taxonomy of privilege escalation attacks in Android applications. Int. J. Secure. Network. 9(1), 40–55 (2014)
22. Sadeghi, A., Bagheri, H., Garcia, J., Malek, S.: A taxonomy and qualitative comparison of program analysis techniques for security assessment of Android software. IEEE Trans. Software Eng. 43(6), 492–530 (2016)
23. Sadeghi, A., Bagheri, H., Malek, S.: Analysis of Android inter-app security vulnerabilities using covert. In: Proceedings of the 37th International Conference on Software Engineering-Volume 2, pp. 725–728. IEEE Press (2015)
24. Sasnauskas, R., Regehr, J.: Intent fuzzer: crafting intents of death. In: Proceedings of the 2014 Joint International Workshop on Dynamic Analysis (WODA) and Software and System Performance Testing, Debugging, and Analytics (PERTEA), pp. 1–5. ACM (2014)
25. Scandariato, R., Walden, J.: Predicting vulnerable classes in an Android application. In: Proceedings of the 4th International Workshop on Security Measurements and Metrics, pp. 11–16 (2012)
26. Schütte, J., Fedler, R., Titze, D.: ConDroid: targeted dynamic analysis of Android applications. In: 2015 IEEE 29th International Conference on Advanced Information Networking and Applications, pp. 571–578. IEEE (2015)
27. Sounthiraraj, D., Sahs, J., Greenwood, G., Lin, Z., Khan, L.: SMV-HUNTER: large scale, automated detection of SSL/TLS man-in-the-middle vulnerabilities in Android apps. In: Proceedings of the 21st Annual Network and Distributed System Security Symposium (NDSS 2014). Citeseer (2014)
28. Taylor, V.F., Martinovic, I.: To update or not to update: insights from a two-year study of Android app evolution. In: Proceedings of the 2017 ACM on Asia Conference on Computer and Communications Security, pp. 45–57 (2017)
29. Wang, H., et al.: Vulnerability assessment of OAuth implementations in Android applications. In: Proceedings of the 31st Annual Computer Security Applications Conference, pp. 61–70 (2015)

30. Wei, F., Roy, S., Ou, X., et al.: Amandroid: a precise and general inter-component data flow analysis framework for security vetting of Android apps. In: Proceedings of the 2014 ACM SIGSAC Conference on Computer and Communications Security, pp. 1329–1341. ACM (2014)
31. Xia, P., Matsushita, M., Yoshida, N., Inoue, K.: Studying reuse of out-dated third-party code in open source projects. Inf. Media Technol. **9**(2), 155–161 (2014)

SiMLA – Security in Machine Learning and Its Applications

Unsupervised Labelling of Stolen Handwritten Digit Embeddings with Density Matching

Thomas Thebaud[1,2](✉) , Gaël Le Lan[2] , and Anthony Larcher[1]

[1] LIUM - Le Mans University, 72085 Le Mans, France
{thomas.thebaud,anthony.larcher}@univ-lemans.fr
[2] Orange Labs, 35510 Cesson-Sevigne, France
{thomas.thebaud,gael.lelan}@orange.com
https://lium.univ-lemans.fr/

Abstract. Biometrics authentication is now widely deployed, and from that omnipresence comes the necessity to protect private data. Recent studies proved touchscreen handwritten digits to be a reliable biometrics. We set a threat model based on that biometrics: in the event of theft of unlabelled embeddings of handwritten digits, we propose a labelling method inspired by recent unsupervised translation algorithms. Provided a set of unlabelled embeddings known to have been produced by a Long Short Term Memory Recurrent Neural Network (LSTM RNN), we demonstrate that inferring their labels is possible. The proposed approach involves label-wise clustering of the embeddings and label identification of each group by matching their distribution to the label-relative classes of a comparison hand-crafted labeled set of embeddings. Cluster labelling is done through a two steps process including a genetic algorithm that finds the N-best matching hypotheses before a fine-tuning of those N-candidates. The proposed method was able to infer the correct labels on 100 randomised runs on different dataset splits.

Keywords: Label inference · Handwritten digits · Density matching · Privacy · Long Short Term Memory · Recurrent Neural Network · Genetic search

1 Introduction

The widespread use of biometrics for authentication [11] brings personal data in the center of security systems. Most recent biometric systems [11] encode biometric data, such as gait sequences [14], voice recording [19], faces images [15], fingerprints [23] or handwritten digits [13,20,21], into high dimensional representations commonly named embeddings. Encoding is done through trained classifiers such as Convolutional Neural Networks [15,23] for physiologic biometrics or Recurrent Neural Networks [13,14] for behavioural ones. Those embeddings are then used for authentication: new embeddings are compared with the ones

© Springer Nature Switzerland AG 2020
J. Zhou et al. (Eds.): ACNS 2020 Workshops, LNCS 12418, pp. 545–563, 2020.
https://doi.org/10.1007/978-3-030-61638-0_30

recorded during enrollment, to determine if the user accessing the system is the same. When stored and transferred between devices, embeddings are subject to theft and represent a possible breach in a system's security. However, unlabelled embeddings alone are not enough to apply commonly known attacks by reconstruction [2,5,15] and labels are required. To label those stolen embeddings we propose to match to a hand-crafted set of labelled embeddings, using unsupervised techniques. The task of unsupervised matching of embeddings has already been vastly explored for machine translation [6]. Most common methods involve Adversarial training [3], Normalisation flow [24], Wasserstein distances [9], Procrustes analysis [9], Principal Component Analysis [10] and Stochastic optimisations [10].

In this paper, we examine the threat of an unlabelled embedding database theft, all embeddings being extracted from handwritten digits in the context of a One-Time-Password authentication system [21]. The embeddings are computed from handwritten digits, thus contain information about writer identity and digit value. This paper focuses on digit value (label) retrieval, which to our opinion is the first problem to address in this attack scenario. The embeddings are computed from handwritten digits, the number of classes is known to be 10, and we make the hypothesis that the feature extractor is known to be based on LSTMs (standard architecture for that kind of sequence data [13]).

Due to the small number of classes and the simple nature of the data, we suppose that an attacker can find another database of raw handwritten digits, create his own classifier and compute his own set of embeddings for labelling purposes. Inspired by various unsupervised bilingual translation methods [6,9,10,24], we investigate whether it is possible to compute the optimal transformation between the stolen set of unlabelled embeddings and the comparison set of labelled embeddings to infer the labels of the stolen embeddings. Being able to label stolen embeddings and map them to a known space (the output space of the attacker's classifier), pose a security risk into biometric systems [2,5]. Mai et al. [15] showed that original face images can be reconstructed from face embeddings, using the black-box feature extractor that was used to compute them. Here we only use unlabelled embeddings to get the transformation from their proper space to the output space of a known feature extractor and then guess their labels.

In this paper, our contributions are:

- Inferring labels (digit values) of unknown handwritten digits embeddings by comparing the statistical distributions of their clusters.
- The combination of unsupervised translation methods for label inference from an attack perspective.
- The successful labelling of those embeddings and the estimation of a transfer function to map them into a known space.

In Sect. 2, we expose related works about embedding matching and their limits. Section 3 presents the proposed attack scenario. Section 4 details the proposed method to infer the stolen embeddings labels. In Sect. 5, we present the data, the feature extractor architecture and the pre-processing steps. Finally,

Sect. 6 presents the experimental work, before Sect. 7 concludes and presents our future works.

2 Related Work

2.1 Template Reconstruction Attacks

Biometric recognition systems compute templates from physiological or behavioural characteristics by using neural networks which are often referred to as feature extractors. The resulting templates are then used for authentication purpose. Cappelli et al. [2], Galbally et al. [5] and Mai et al. [15] respectively proposed critics of the current biometric templates by showing that fingerprints, iris and faces templates can be reconstructed using neural networks.

Here we focus on the deep face template reconstruction [15]. Having access to real deep face templates and the black-box feature extractor, the authors generate artificial faces from noise vectors thanks to a generative adversarial network [7]. Artificial deep face templates are then computed from those artificial faces thanks to the feature extractor. Artificial face and template pairs are used to train a neighborly de-convolutional network (NbNet) that infers the inverse function of the feature extractor, i.e., compute the generated artificial face images from the artificial face templates. Finally they use that NbNet network to compute real face images from the real face templates. Their work shows that face images can be retrieved from stolen face templates and a black box feature extractor.

Our work differs from the work of Mai et al. [15] as we deal with *unlabelled* stolen templates of *handwritten digits* and assume to know the architecture of the feature extractor (without any knowledge of the weights of the network). We aim to find the digit values (labels) of unlabelled templates, further called *embeddings* for coherence with the unsupervised machine translation literature cited in this paper. We propose to find the labels of stolen embeddings by matching their space to the output space of a known, hand-crafted, comparison feature extractor (here a LSTM RNN), using a transfer function. Once the transfer function is found, that known RNN feature extractor could then serve as a black-box feature extractor, to perform an attack similar to the one described in [15].

2.2 Unsupervised Translation for Embedding Matching

The scope of this paper is to find the labels of stolen biometric embeddings by matching their distribution to the one of labelled embeddings. Unsupervised machine translation aims at achieving a bilingual translation by matching word embeddings from a language with word embeddings of another, without knowing the corresponding labels. The closeness of both problems leads us to explore unsupervised translation literature.

For unsupervised machine translation, the success of the algorithm is highly dependent on the initialisation [9,10]. However, most of unsupervised translation methods either use a few labelled examples or the first thousands most frequent words in each language. The initialisation strategies based on that are not suitable for our problem. Our problem involves a lower number of classes but with multiple samples for each class. For that reason, most initialisation approaches discussed hereafter cannot be directly implemented.

Grave et al. [9] propose a method to match high dimensional word embeddings from two different lexicons, using Procrustes Analysis [8] and Wasserstein distance [22] with a stochastic optimisation of a rotation matrix. They achieve state of the art performance using the 2000 most frequent words of each language to initialise the matrix. The translation of this initialisation to our task is not directly applicable as we do not have information about the most frequent digits. However, we keep the idea of using Procrustes analysis to find an optimal rotation for a given combination.

Still for unsupervised machine translation, Hoshen and Wolf [10] use Principal Component Analysis to efficiently initialise their algorithm with the 5000 most frequent words of each language. Their algorithm computes the optimal rotation from a given permutation matrix, and finds the optimal permutation matrix according to that rotation. Thanks to the high number of classes (5000) compared to the low number of dimensions (50 after PCA), switching two classes in the permutation matrix only induces small variations in the rotation matrix, so their algorithm can do a step-by-step search. However, due to the low number of classes (10 digits) in our problem, we cannot apply the step-by-step search. Indeed, a permutation error would induce a much more important variation of the rotation matrix. However, we propose to initialise with a global PCA on the data to align both spaces and reduce the number of dimensions before further computing.

Zhou et al. [24] match word embeddings by modeling each one as its own gaussian distribution and fitting Gaussian Mixture Models [17] to each set of words. The transfer function is then trained by minimizing the distance between GMMs. Note that they also use a few identical words in both languages to add a weak similarity constraint to their search. As we want to find the transformation function without any example, we cannot apply that exact method. However we keep the idea of modeling the statistic distribution of embeddings with GMMs and the concept of normalising flow [18] to map the transfer function between the unlabelled embeddings space and a known space.

3   Proposed Attack Scenario

We want to label a set U of stolen unlabelled embeddings. We suppose that those embeddings have been produced on a touchscreen biometric system [21], for authentication by handwritten digits, as illustrated in Fig. 1.

The U set is composed of N unlabelled embeddings of dimension D, resulting from the penultimate layer of a LSTM classifier designed to process 2D stroke sequences taken from handwritten digits from 0 to 9. For the purpose of this paper, the number N of embeddings depends on the size of the considered dataset.

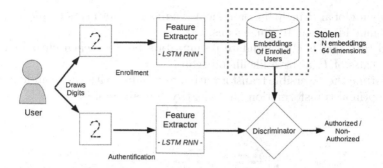

Fig. 1. Illustration of the stolen embeddings, in a touchscreen biometric system for handwritten digits. During enrollment, few examples of each digit are drawn by an user, then computed into embeddings by the F.E and stored. To authenticate, the user draws a digit or a sequence of digits, computed into embeddings by the same F.E and compared to the stocked embeddings by the discriminator.

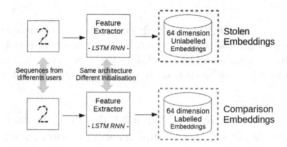

Fig. 2. Illustration of the differences between the stolen, unlabelled embeddings and the comparison, labelled embeddings.

We suppose an attacker able to find or provide its own data. This data can be used to produce a labelled set of statistically comparable embeddings. To simulate that scenario, we train a second LSTM classifier with a disjoint set of 2D sequences, taken from different users, as illustrated in Fig. 2. Those labelled embeddings will be referred to as the L set. To exploit the stolen embeddings, we propose a method to transfer them into a known, labelled space, namely the output space of the second LSTM classifier. The optimal transformation between the two spaces (i.e. the permutation matrix between unlabelled classes of U and labelled classes of L) can be used to label the stolen embeddings. Those notions of permutation and optimal transformation between two spaces are linked in most of unsupervised translation works [6,9,10], and we manipulate both in our proposed method.

The method we propose follows 4 steps, as illustrated in Fig. 3:

1. Cluster the embeddings of U in 10 clusters, expecting each cluster to correspond to a class (i.e. a digit value).

2. Apply a global Principal Component Analysis to both sets U and L, projecting embeddings on 10 dimensions;
3. Find the most likely candidate permutation between each cluster of U and each class of L, using a likelihood score.
4. Fine-tune the reversible transformation associated with each candidate to get the optimal transformation, and identify the labels of U.

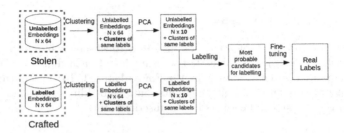

Fig. 3. Illustration of our labelling method: embeddings are clustered and PCA projected, then clusters of both sets are compared to find the most probables permutations candidates, and fine-tuning select the candidate that associate clusters of same labels. Knowing the labels of the crafted set, we infer the labels of the stolen set.

Our main contributions, related to step 3 (labelling), are detailed in Sects. 4.2 and 4.3. The steps of clustering and dimension reduction that are necessary to achieve good performance are later described in Sect. 5.3.

4   Labelling

To effectively consider the U set as labelled, we need to find the labels of each one of its clusters. The U set is considered labelled when each of its ten clusters is paired with a class from L corresponding to a digit value. To represent a possible match between clusters of U and labels of L, we use a permutation matrix $P = (p_{ij})_{i,j \in [\![0,9]\!]^2}$, a bi-stochastic matrix composed of 0 and 1, where $p_{ij} = 1$ means the ith cluster is labelled as class j (e.g. digit value j). This section introduces three contributions. First we propose to apply a Procrustes analysis [8] between the cluster centers of U and the class centers of L, in order to approximate the optimal transformation between both sets. Second, we propose a scoring method to evaluate the success of the optimal transformation for a given permutation. Third, we search through the space of all possible permutations to find the best candidates, according to our scoring method. Finally, we fine-tune the best candidates to re-rank them and find the ultimate optimal permutation.

4.1   Optimal Rotation for a Given Permutation

Search for Transfer Function as a Rotation. Mikolov et al. (2013) [16] pointed out that the transformation between the word-embedding spaces of two languages can be well mapped by a linear transformation, so a multiplication matrix and a bias matrix. Each sets being centered, we can ignore the bias matrix. Each embedding being length-normalised, the multiplication matrix should have a determinant of module 1 and after applying the PCA, the embeddings of both sets are projected into two orthogonal spaces.

We consider that the transfer function between spaces of embeddings is a rotation, which will be verified in Sect. 6.

Procrustes Analysis. Considering that the transfer function is a rotation, it can be found by a Procrustes analysis that computes a linear transformation between two sets of matched points $U \in \mathbb{R}^{N \times D}$ and $L \in \mathbb{R}^{N \times D}$. In case the match between the two sets is known (i.e., which point of U corresponds to which point of L), the linear transformation W can be simply recovered by solving the least square problem:

$$\min_{W \in \mathbb{R}^{D \times D}} \|UW - L\|_2^2 \tag{1}$$

Here we use the 10 centers of the unlabelled clusters as C_U, the 10 centers of the labelled classes as C_L and the match is given by the permutation matrix P. As in Grave et al. (2018) [9], we compute for a given permutation matrix P the solution to the Eq. 2.

$$\min_{W \in \mathbb{R}^{D \times D}} \|C_U W - PC_L\|_2^2 \tag{2}$$

Procrustes analysis presents a simple solution to that problem. Let the square matrix $M \in \mathbb{R}^{D \times D}$ be:

$$M = C_U^t . PC_L \tag{3}$$

M can be decomposed in singular values as:

$$M = X \times \Sigma \times Y^* \backslash (X, Y^*) \in (\mathbb{R}^{D \times D})^2 \tag{4}$$

Then the W rotation matrix solution to the Eq. 2 is defined as:

$$W = X.Y^* \tag{5}$$

Evaluation of a Given Rotation. To select the most probable permutation between the two sets, we have to find a reliable heuristic that evaluates its corresponding rotation, without knowing the labels of one of the sets. We assume that the statistical distribution of each cluster of embeddings is different enough to distinguish it from the others, and thus find its label.

Modeling of the Embeddings Distribution with Gaussian Mixture Models. The statistical distribution of embedding from each set is approximated by a multivariate Gaussian Mixture Model (GMM). The number of components in the GMM is chosen via Bayesian Information Criterion [1]. We do not impose priors, means or co-variances to the models, and use full co-variances matrices.

Global Log-Likelihood Scoring. To measure the distance between a set of embeddings and a GMM, we propose to use the global log-likelihood.

Let the GMM of the labelled set L be $GMM_L = \{(p_i, \mu_i, \Sigma_i) \in (]0,1[\times\mathbb{R}^D \times \mathbb{R}^{D\times D})\backslash i \in [\![1,K]\!]\}$, p_i, μ_i and Σ_i being respectively the prior, mean and co-variance of the ith gaussian, with $\sum_{i=1}^{K} p_i = 1$. Let $U = \{u \in \mathbb{R}^D\}$ be the set of unlabelled embeddings, and $W \in \mathbb{R}^{D\times D}$ the given rotation matrix, then $U_W = \{u_W = W.u\backslash u \in U\}$ is the set of projected unlabelled embeddings.

The log-likelihood between a projected embedding u_W and a Gaussian i is:

$$\log\mathcal{N}(u_W|\mu_i,\Sigma_i) = -\frac{1}{2}(K\log 2\pi + \log|\Sigma_i| + (u_W - \mu_i)^T\Sigma_i^{-1}(u_W - \mu_i)) \quad (6)$$

The log-likelihood between a projected embedding u_W and the model GMM_L is then defined as the log of the average of the likelihood with each Gaussian, weighted by the priors $P = \{p_i \in \mathbb{R}\}$:

$$\log\mathcal{N}_{GMM_L}(u_W) = \log\sum_{i=1}^{K} p_i\mathcal{N}(u_W|\mu_i,\Sigma_i) \quad (7)$$

$$= \log\sum_{i=1}^{K} \exp(\log(p_i) + \log\mathcal{N}(u_W|\mu_i,\Sigma_i))$$

Finally, the global log-likelihood score of the set X_W is set as the average of the individual log-likelihood scores:

$$Score(U_W, GMM_L) = \frac{1}{Card(U_W)}\sum_{u_W \in U_W}\log\mathcal{N}_{GMM_L}(u_W) \quad (8)$$

Here the $Score(U_W, GMM_L)$ function is defined as the likelihood score between the GMM of a set of embeddings L and a set of embeddings U projected by a W rotation matrix. If the transformation W is confirmed to be a rotation, then W is invertible and its inverse is W^t. Thus, we can define this score for the reversed rotation, between embeddings L projected by a rotation W^t and a GMM fitted to a set U: $Score(L_{W^t}, GMM_U)$.

We propose to take the maximum of the two options, evaluating in a single score the likelihood of a transformation and its reverse:

$$Score(U, L, W) = max(Score(U_W, GMM_L), Score(L_{W^t}, GMM_U)) \quad (9)$$

A higher score means a better matching between sets, so by taking the maximum we use the best of both comparisons. For the rest of the article, we used the opposite global log-likelihood score ($-Score(U, L, W)$) as the function to minimize.

4.2   Genetic Search

For any given permutation, we can compute the associated optimal rotation and evaluate its ability to statistically align both datasets. To find the candidates that minimize the score described above, we explore the space of the possible permutations $P \in [\![0,1]\!]^{10 \times 10}$. To find the global best rotation, we need to try all possibles $10! = 3628800$ permutations. To limit the number of tested permutations, we choose to use a genetic algorithm [4] to find the fittest permutations. The genetic algorithm considers each permutation as a chromosome, and gets the best candidates through merging and mutations without scoring every possible permutation. We propose to represent chromosomes as ordered sequences of 10 digits instead of matrices of zeros and ones:

$$C = \{c_i \in [\![0,9]\!] \setminus i \in [\![0,9]\!]\} \tag{10}$$

Each element from a chromosome represents the link between a cluster of unlabelled data and a labelled class. c_i being the value of the i_{th} element means that the unlabelled cluster c_i is linked to the labelled class i (each cluster is linked to a unique other class).

$$\forall i,j \in [\![0,9]\!]^2, i \neq j \Leftrightarrow c_i \neq c_j \tag{11}$$

4.3   Fine-Tuning

Rotations are approximated using the center of each cluster and thus might not be as precise as if every embedding was used. As a result, the best candidate permutation found by the genetic search might not always be the genuine one. To refine and re-rank the k-best candidate permutations, we propose a stochastic optimisation. The candidate with the best score after fine-tuning is expected to give the true labels.

Our fine-tuning is inspired by [24], which uses gradient descent to find the optimal rotation matrix a comparable statistical alignment problem, using two weak constraints during training (orthogonality and unitary determinant). For each k-best permutation candidate, we fine-tune W with the Adam stochastic optimisation method [12] to minimize the global log-likelihood score.

Losses. To fine-tune each matrix W to minimize the global log-likelihood score while keeping their rotation properties, we combine three loss functions:

1. Loss 1: The global log-likelihood score $-Score(U, L, W)$
2. Loss 2: The absolute log of the determinant of W: $|\log(\det W)|$
3. Loss 3: The difference $u_i - (W^t \times W \times u_i)$

The first loss fits the matrix W to the optimum transformation between the two sets of embeddings. The second targets a determinant of 1, and the third insures that W is orthogonal. The last two guarantee that W stays a rotation matrix. The global loss is a non-pondered sum of the three losses.

After a few dozens of epochs, the losses are stabilized, and we get W^*, the fine-tuned version of W. Once each instance of W^* is scored with global log likely-hood score, the one with the minimum score is the best candidate, the permutation associated giving the searched labels.

5   Data and Preprocessing

5.1   Data

The data is taken from two different datasets described in: Tolosana et al. (2018) [21] and Tolosana et al. (2019) [20], both produced by the University of Madrid, containing data from respectively 217 and 93 users. The first set contains 8460 stroke sequences of variable length (mean = 31.9, std = 13.1, max = 164), in 2 dimensions, representing digits drawings from 0 to 9. The second contains 7430 sequences of variable length (mean = 33.9, std = 13.2, max = 125). In total, it results in 16350 sequences, with an equal proportion (a tenth) of each digit. Those sequences are divided into 4 sets of equal digit proportion, each set containing the sequences of a randomized quarter of the total number of users. Those sets will then be referred as: **Train U**, **Test U**, **Train L** and **Test L**.

Both *Train* sets are used to train the classifiers and the *Test* sets to evaluate their performances. The embeddings used for unsupervised matching in the rest of the paper are produced by passing the sequences from the *Test* sets through the classifiers.

In order to multiply the experiments with the same original data, we randomly split in 4 parts the set of users in 100 different ways, to get 100 different simulations. Sets of users are always composed of 77 to 78 users, and each set contains 3450 to 4560 sequences (mean = 4079.35) with each digit having the same number of examples.

5.2   Architecture of the Networks

The architecture of the feature extractor, assumed to be known by the attacker, is a Long Short-Term Memory (LSTM) RNN. We train thus two classifiers with an input in 2 dimensions and a hidden state vector of $D = 64$ dimensions. The last hidden-layer is passed through a fully connected layer of dimension 10 and an a softmax function to predict the digit value.

Both networks are trained with both *Train* sets using Cross Entropy Loss as the objective function to predict the digit associated with each sequence. The training stops when each network has a precision of 96% on its *Test* set. Both networks have the same architecture but a different, random initialisation of their parameters. 64-dimension embeddings are then extracted from the penultimate layer of each network for all digits from the respective *Test* set.

The set *Test L* is processed by the first network to produce a set of *Labelled* embeddings referred to as *L set*, while the set *Test U* is processed through the second network to produce a set of *Unlabelled* embeddings referred to as *U set*. All produced sets are composed of 3450 to 4560 embeddings (average of 4079.35) in 64 dimensions, with each class having the same number of examples.

5.3   Preprocessing

Normalisation. For each set, all embeddings are length-normalised, centered as in *Grave et al. (2018)* [9] and length-normalised again.

Clustering. The networks being trained to be classifiers, we assume they project the original sequences in a vector space were borders can be drawn between same-label classes. Thus, we should be able to split the data in class-related clusters. To assert this point, we propose to use the K-means clustering algorithm to split the unlabelled set in ten clusters. For further purposes, the groups formed by same-label embeddings of L set will be referred as classes, as opposed to the clusters of U.

Principal Component Analysis. We propose to initiate our method with principal component analysis, as in Hoshen and Wolf [10]. We propose $D = 10$, so the number of dimensions do not exceed the number of distinct matched points used to compute the Procrutes rotation matrix. For the rest of the paper, we work with the 10-dimension PCA-reduced embeddings for both sets. We compute the means of each cluster of U and each class of L after the PCA, so we end up with 2×10 average embeddings representing the centers of the clusters and classes.

6   Experiments

Firstly, each following experiment is carried out with the same dataset split, and results are presented for that example dataset split. Secondly, we carry out the same experiment over the 100 pairs of sets produced in Sect. 5, to provide reproducible and precise experiments.

6.1   Clustering

We split the unlabelled embeddings in 10 clusters with the K-means algorithm. The result of this clustering is in the Table 1. We measured the cohesion of the clusters relative to the original labels of the embeddings. We found a cohesion of $\frac{3792}{4000} = 0.948$ after the clustering, meaning 94,80% of the embeddings can be grouped together by a clustering.

For a better precision, we measure the clustering cohesion for every set of embeddings over the 100 different split of data. The global cohesion was between 92.26% and 96.04% (mean = 94.45%). This is an acceptable cohesion, knowing that the originally trained classifier got a 96% of accuracy over the test set.

Table 1. Embeddings of each label and their associated cluster number after K-means clustering

Label\Cluster	0	1	2	3	4	5	6	7	8	9	Σ
0	0	12	4	4	9	1	4	3	**363**	0	400
1	0	1	**395**	4	0	0	0	0	0	0	400
2	**394**	0	2	1	0	3	0	0	0	0	400
3	0	0	0	0	1	1	0	**392**	0	6	400
4	1	0	7	**375**	0	4	13	0	0	0	400
5	0	0	0	1	14	0	0	4	1	**380**	400
6	0	**382**	0	0	0	1	0	0	14	3	400
7	6	0	4	0	2	**380**	6	0	1	1	400
8	0	4	7	0	**350**	1	2	2	30	4	400
9	0	6	1	6	2	0	**381**	0	3	1	400
Maximum:	394	382	395	375	350	380	381	392	363	380	3792

This confirms that our unlabelled embeddings can be split in label-wise clusters. This also means that when we have 100% accuracy on the clusters labelling, an average of 94.45% of the individual embeddings will be correctly labelled.

6.2 Principal Component Analysis

Each set of embeddings from the 100 splits is projected in $P = 10$ dimensions using PCA. The total ratio of explained variance is between 80,4% and 88,2% (mean = 84,9%).

6.3 Rotation

To prove that the relation between the two sets of embeddings can be well mapped as a rotation, we suppose the labels of both sets to be known, just for the purpose of this experiment. We apply Procrustes analysis on the centers of the label-wise clusters of both sets to compute the optimal rotation W between the two sets. Then we project every embedding of the unlabelled set with W. For each projected embedding, we measure the nearest labelled cluster center, the projection being considered as successful if that nearest cluster has the same label as the original embedding. The Table 2 presents the results of that association. This experimentation shows 94.31% accuracy, meaning 4,103 out of 4,350 embeddings from the unlabelled set were associated with the right cluster. When reproducing this experiment with every pairs of sets from the 100 splits we observe 92.44% and 95.86% accuracy (mean = 94.50%). From there, we can consider that the transformation between the two spaces can be well approximated as a rotation, as thus confirm that if we get the right permutation, over 92% of the embeddings will be correctly labelled. We are therefore looking for the optimal rotation between the Labelled space and the Unlabelled one. Thus, as said in Subsect. 4.1, the transfer function between the spaces of both sets of embeddings is considered a rotation.

Table 2. Embeddings projected with optimal rotation: label by nearest cluster

Label\Nearest cluster	0	1	2	3	4	5	6	7	8	9
0	**402**	0	1	0	13	1	14	0	1	3
1	0	**412**	1	0	19	0	2	1	0	0
2	0	0	**429**	0	1	1	1	3	0	0
3	1	0	0	**417**	0	3	2	3	7	2
4	3	3	1	0	**402**	0	0	4	5	17
5	1	0	0	4	3	**401**	10	9	7	0
6	7	0	0	3	0	4	**420**	0	0	1
7	1	2	2	0	4	1	0	**425**	0	0
8	14	6	3	2	1	15	2	2	**386**	4
9	0	1	0	1	21	1	1	1	0	**409**

6.4 Reliability of the Global Log-Likelihood Score

To test the reliability of that score function we use every one of the 10! combinations to compute the 10! rotations associated, and measure the score of the rotated set for each of them. The genuine permutation is supposed to obtain the lowest score. We group all permutations by their number of correct matches and plot them on Fig. 4 with the corresponding scores. The first column is only the expected permutation, and the others are the scores of permutations with 2 to 10 mismatches. The second graphic is a zoom on the lower part of the first one. The figure shows that the genuine permutation only obtains the third lowest score. The score depends on the GMM and since the GMM initialisation is random, the score is slightly different each time. After running this experiment 10 times on this particular dataset split to smooth the variations due to the GMM initialisation, the genuine permutation is always observed between the 1st and the 6th rank. Over all the candidate permutations, the global log-likelihood score gives the genuine permutation one of the lowest scores. Therefore, we have to not only consider the candidate with the lowest score, but a list of the k candidates with the lowest scores, to be sure to have the genuine candidate among them. That is why we have to fine-tune the rotations in order to re-rank the k-best permutations.

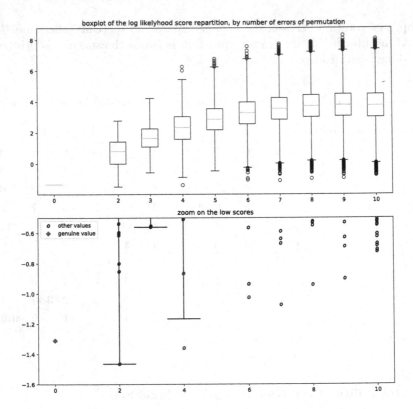

Fig. 4. Box plot of the global log likelihood score of every embedding, as a function of the number of errors.

6.5   Genetic Search

We are searching through all possible permutations using chromosomes consisting of ordered sequences of 10 naturals numbers (see Eq. 10). Each element represents the link between a cluster of unlabelled data and a digit class.

A Initialisation The search is initialised with 150 Chromosomes and each of them is evaluated by computing its rotation matrix and their score as explained in Subsect. 4.

B Selection The 20 chromosomes with the lowest score are selected.

C Merging Two chromosomes from the 20 selected are randomly taken, and merged to create a new one. The common elements stay the same while the elements that are different are randomly selected from one or the other. If the new chromosome has not been seen yet, it is added to the list, and an other merge is done until reaching the 100 more chromosomes.

D Mutation One of the 20 selected chromosomes is randomly selected. 2 to 10 elements of that chromosome are randomly selected and then rotated to obtain a new, mutated chromosome. If the new chromosome have not been seen yet, it is added to the list, and an other mutation is done until reaching the 50 more chromosomes.

E End of the Main Loop Finally, after getting a list of 170 chromosomes, the score of each is evaluated, and the algorithm get back to step B: the selection. It loops over until the 20 selected chromosomes stabilise and stay the same 100 loops in a row. The output is the list of those $k = 20$ selected chromosomes

We use the genetic search to find the 20 best permutations according to the global log-likelihood score. An experiment takes around 55 loop each to be completed, so around 10^4 permutations are evaluated over the 3.6×10^6 possible ones. At the end of the search, the genuine combination is part of the $k = 20$ best candidates. An example of the score for each one of the 20 best candidates is presented in Table 3.

Table 3. Example of a table of the scores for the first 20 candidates after a genetic search. *genuine candidate.

Rank	Candidates										Score
1	0	4	2	3	1	5	6	7	8	9	**−1.465**
2	8	1	2	3	4	6	5	7	0	9	−1.360
3*	0	1	2	3	4	5	6	7	8	9	−1.310
4	8	0	2	3	6	7	5	1	4	9	−1.074
5	8	7	2	3	4	6	5	1	0	9	−1.025
6	8	1	2	3	7	6	5	4	0	9	−0.937
7	7	1	2	3	4	6	5	0	8	9	−0.867
8	0	1	2	3	4	6	5	7	8	9	−0.853
9	0	1	2	3	4	8	5	7	6	9	−0.559
10	0	2	4	3	1	5	6	7	8	9	−0.553
11	0	7	2	3	4	6	5	1	8	9	−0.509
12	0	2	7	3	1	5	6	4	8	9	−0.461
13	0	7	2	3	4	5	6	1	8	9	−0.457
14	6	0	2	3	8	7	5	1	4	9	−0.403
15	7	6	8	9	5	1	4	0	2	3	−0.386
16	0	5	2	3	6	7	1	8	4	9	−0.364
17	0	1	2	3	4	5	8	7	6	9	−0.361
18	6	0	2	3	4	7	5	1	8	9	−0.355
19	0	4	7	3	1	5	6	2	8	9	−0.331
20	8	1	2	3	4	0	5	7	6	9	−0.305

For the given example, the genuine candidate, [0 1 2 3 4 5 6 7 8 9], is not the best one selected. It is ranked third. Thus fine tuning is required, in

Subsect. 6.6. To present more consistent results, we run this genetic search over the 100 splits of data and registered the rank of the genuine permutation for each pair of sets. The genuine candidate is ranked first 62 times out of 100, note that it is also ranked 20th once. Figure 5 presents an histogram of the ranks obtained for each dataset split.

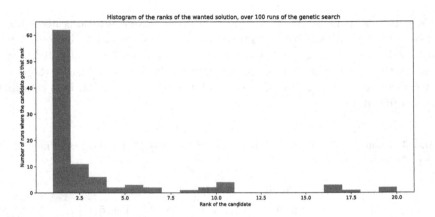

Fig. 5. Histogram of the ranks of the wanted solution after a genetic search.

6.6   Fine Tuning

The genetic search gave us a quick reliable way to find a set of good candidates, we now target to find the absolute best permutation by fine tuning each candidate, using the fine-tuning algorithm Sect. 4.3.

For each candidate permutation, the fine-tuning rotation matrix is initialised with the one previously computed using Procrustes analysis on the centers. Each candidate rotation matrix is fine-tuned for 200 epochs with the configuration detailed in Subsect. 6.6. The global log-likelihood of the statistical alignment is computed again afterwards. Table 4 corresponds to the same experiment as Table 3 but after applying fine-tuning.

The genuine candidate effectively got the best score, while the previous best candidate moved back to rank 5. For this example, the permutation that matches the cluster of i with the label i ($\forall i \in [\![0, 9]\!]$) is selected and the clusters are correctly labelled.

To present more consistent results, we run the proposed fine-tuning over the 100 splits of data and register the rank of the genuine solution for each pair of sets. **The genuine solution is ranked first every time.** Before fine-tuning, the average score on the 20 selected candidates is -1.910 while the average score of the genuine candidate is -2.325, for an average rank of 3.27. After fine-tuning, the average score on the 20 selected candidates became -4.453 while the average score of the genuine candidate went down to -5.042, for an average rank of 1.00

Table 4. Table of the scores for the first 20 candidates after fine-tuning. *genuine candidate

Updated Rank	Previous Rank	Candidates										Updated score	Previous score
1*	3	0	1	2	3	4	5	6	7	8	9	−5.914	−1.310
2	9	0	1	2	3	4	8	5	7	6	9	−5.827	−0.559
3	6	8	1	2	3	7	6	5	4	0	9	−5.770	−0.937
4	2	8	1	2	3	4	6	5	7	0	9	−5.603	−1.360
5	1	0	4	2	3	1	5	6	7	8	9	−5.602	−1.465
6	10	0	2	4	3	1	5	6	7	8	9	−5.420	−0.553
7	13	0	7	2	3	4	5	6	1	8	9	−5.335	−0.457
8	20	8	1	2	3	4	0	5	7	6	9	−5.334	−0.305
9	17	0	1	2	3	4	5	8	7	6	9	−5.322	−0.361
10	7	7	1	2	3	4	6	5	0	8	9	−5.269	−0.867
11	5	8	7	2	3	4	6	5	1	0	9	−5.219	−1.025
12	12	0	2	7	3	1	5	6	4	8	9	−5.043	−0.461
13	19	0	4	7	3	1	5	6	2	8	9	−5.026	−0.331
14	15	7	6	8	9	5	1	4	0	2	3	−4.999	−0.386
15	8	0	1	2	3	4	6	5	7	8	9	−4.985	−0.853
16	4	8	0	2	3	6	7	5	1	4	9	−4.775	−1.074
17	14	6	0	2	3	8	7	5	1	4	9	−4.731	−0.403
18	18	6	0	2	3	4	7	5	1	8	9	−4.727	−0.355
19	16	0	5	2	3	6	7	1	8	4	9	−4.687	−0.364
20	11	0	7	2	3	4	6	5	1	8	9	−4.622	−0.509

7   Conclusion - Future Work

This paper presents a statistical alignment method for high dimensional unlabelled embeddings of handwritten digits, in the event of a theft. Our method is inspired by unsupervised bilingual translation and reconstruction of biometric templates literature. We aim to find the digit value (label) of each embedding. Provided a set of unlabelled embeddings produced by a LSTM RNN, we train a comparison RNN with the same architecture to produce hand-crafted comparison labelled embeddings.

We proposed to label the stolen embeddings by matching their clusters to the label-wise classes of the comparison embeddings. The labelling consists in a genetic search through all possible permutations between clusters and classes to find the 20 candidates with the lowest global log-likelihood score. Each of those candidates is fine-tuned and the fine-tuned candidate with the lowest score is expected to represent the genuine permutation.

We have applied this method on 100 different distinct splits of the original dataset. Our experiment showed that after the genetic search, the genuine candidate got an average rank of 3,27, and got ranked first every time after fine tuning. Thus the proposed method proved to be a reliable way to recover most labels of the stolen handwritten digits embeddings (without further exploitation we report a 94.45% average accuracy over the labeling of the individual embeddings due to the clustering cohesion).

Future work will be dedicated to the relaxation of the constraints (higher number of classes, unknown network architecture, other biometrics) and the reconstruction of the signals. Overall, our work highlight the importance of personal data protection, especially embeddings from biometric systems, and open perspectives for further threat models analysis and associated defenses.

References

1. Akaike, H.: A new look at the statistical identification model. IEEE Trans. Autom. Control **19**, 716 (1974)
2. Cappelli, R., Maio, D., Lumini, A., Maltoni, D.: Fingerprint image reconstruction from standard templates. IEEE Trans. Pattern Anal. Mach. Intell. **29**(9), 1489–1503 (2007)
3. Conneau, A., Lample, G., Ranzato, M.A., Denoyer, L., Jégou, H.: Word translation without parallel data. arXiv preprint arXiv:1710.04087 (2017)
4. Forrest, S.: Genetic algorithms: principles of natural selection applied to computation. Science **261**(5123), 872–878 (1993)
5. Galbally, J., Ross, A., Gomez-Barrero, M., Fierrez, J., Ortega-Garcia, J.: Iris image reconstruction from binary templates: an efficient probabilistic approach based on genetic algorithms. Comput. Vis. Image Underst. **117**(10), 1512–1525 (2013)
6. Glavas, G., Litschko, R., Ruder, S., Vulic, I.: How to (properly) evaluate cross-lingual word embeddings: on strong baselines, comparative analyses, and some misconceptions. arXiv preprint arXiv:1902.00508 (2019)
7. Goodfellow, I., et al.: Generative adversarial nets. In: Advances in Neural Information Processing Systems, pp. 2672–2680 (2014)
8. Gower, J.C.: Generalized Procrustes analysis. Psychometrika **40**(1), 33–51 (1975). https://doi.org/10.1007/BF02291478
9. Grave, E., Joulin, A., Berthet, Q.: Unsupervised alignment of embeddings with Wasserstein Procrustes. arXiv preprint arXiv:1805.11222 (2018)
10. Hoshen, Y., Wolf, L.: Non-adversarial unsupervised word translation. arXiv preprint arXiv:1801.06126 (2018)
11. Jain, A.K., Nandakumar, K., Nagar, A.: Biometric template security. EURASIP J. Adv. Signal Process. **2008**, 1–17 (2008)
12. Kingma, D.P., Ba, J.: Adam: a method for stochastic optimization. arXiv preprint arXiv:1412.6980 (2014)
13. Le Lan, G., Frey, V.: Securing smartphone handwritten pin codes with recurrent neural networks. In: ICASSP 2019–2019 IEEE International Conference on Acoustics, Speech and Signal Processing (ICASSP), pp. 2612–2616. IEEE (2019)
14. Lee, L., Grimson, W.E.L.: Gait analysis for recognition and classification. In: Proceedings of Fifth IEEE International Conference on Automatic Face Gesture Recognition, pp. 155–162. IEEE (2002)

15. Mai, G., Cao, K., Yuen, P.C., Jain, A.K.: On the reconstruction of face images from deep face templates. IEEE Trans. Pattern Anal. Mach. Intell. **41**(5), 1188–1202 (2018)
16. Mikolov, T., Chen, K., Corrado, G., Dean, J.: Efficient estimation of word representations in vector space. arXiv preprint arXiv:1301.3781 (2013)
17. Reynolds, D.A.: Gaussian mixture models. In: Encyclopedia of Biometrics, vol. 741 (2009)
18. Rezende, D.J., Mohamed, S.: Variational inference with normalizing flows. arXiv preprint arXiv:1505.05770 (2015)
19. Snyder, D., Garcia-Romero, D., Sell, G., Povey, D., Khudanpur, S.: X-vectors: robust DNN embeddings for speaker recognition. In: 2018 IEEE International Conference on Acoustics, Speech and Signal Processing (ICASSP), pp. 5329–5333. IEEE (2018)
20. Tolosana, R., Vera-Rodriguez, R., Fierrez, J.: BioTouchPass: handwritten passwords for touchscreen biometrics. IEEE Trans. Mob. Comput. **19**(7), 1532–1543 (2019)
21. Tolosana, R., Vera-Rodriguez, R., Fierrez, J., Ortega-Garcia, J.: Incorporating touch biometrics to mobile one-time passwords: exploration of digits. In: The IEEE Conference on Computer Vision and Pattern Recognition (CVPR) Workshops, June 2018
22. Vallender, S.S.: Calculation of the Wasserstein distance between probability distributions on the line. Theory Probab. Appl. **18**(4), 784–786 (1974)
23. Yang, W., Wang, S., Hu, J., Zheng, G., Valli, C.: Security and accuracy of fingerprint-based biometrics: a review. Symmetry **11**(2), 141 (2019)
24. Zhou, C., Ma, X., Wang, D., Neubig, G.: Density matching for bilingual word embedding. arXiv preprint arXiv:1904.02343 (2019)

Minority Reports Defense: Defending Against Adversarial Patches

Michael McCoyd[1]([✉]) [iD], Won Park[1,2] [iD], Steven Chen[1], Neil Shah[1],
Ryan Roggenkemper[1], Minjune Hwang[1] [iD], Jason Xinyu Liu[1] [iD],
and David Wagner[1]

[1] University of California, Berkeley, Berkeley, CA 94720, USA
{mmccoyd,daw}@cs.berkeley.com,
{scchen,neilshah430,rroggenkemper,mjhwang,xinyuliu}@berkeley.edu
[2] University of Michigan, Ann Arbor, MI 48109, USA
wonpark@umich.edu

Abstract. Deep learning image classification is widely used yet is vulnerable to adversarial attack, which can change the computer classification without changing how humans classify the image. This is possible even if the attacker changes just a small patch of the image. We propose a defense against patch attacks based on partially occluding the image around each candidate patch location, so that a few occlusions each completely hide the patch. We demonstrate on CIFAR-10, Fashion MNIST, and MNIST that our defense provides certified security against patch attacks of a certain size. For CIFAR-10 and a 5×5 patch, we can provide certify accuracy for 43.8% of images, at a cost of only 1.6% in clean image accuracy compared to the architecture we defend or a cost of 0.1% compared to our training of that architecture, and a 0.1% false positive rate.

Keywords: Adversarial machine learning · Adversarial patch · Partial occlusions ensemble defense

1 Introduction

Deep learning image classification is widely used yet is vulnerable to adversarial attack, which can change the computer classification without changing how humans classify the image. An attacker with knowledge of a neural network model can construct, from any normal image x, an *adversarial example* x^* that looks to humans like x but that the model classifies differently from the normal image [SZS+14], [GSS15, HJN+11, CW17].

Recently, researchers have proposed the *adversarial patch* attack [BMR+17, KZG18], where the attacker changes just a limited rectangular region of the image, for example, by placing a sticker over a road sign or other object. Others have expanded on the vulnerability to this type of attack [EEF+17, TRG19, XZL+19]. In this paper, we propose a defense against this attack.

© Springer Nature Switzerland AG 2020
J. Zhou et al. (Eds.): ACNS 2020 Workshops, LNCS 12418, pp. 564–582, 2020.
https://doi.org/10.1007/978-3-030-61638-0_31

The idea of our defense is to occlude part of the image and then classify the occluded image. First, we train a classifier that properly classifies occluded images. Then, if we knew the location of the adversarial patch, we could occlude that region of the image (e.g., overwriting it with a uniform grey rectangle) and apply the classifier to the occluded image. This would defend against patch attacks, as the attacker's contribution is completely overwritten and the input to the classifier (the occluded image) cannot be affected by the attacker in any way.

In practice, we do not know the location of the adversarial patch, so a more sophisticated defense is needed. Our approach works by occluding an area larger than the maximum patch size and striding the occlude area across the image, making an occluded prediction at each stride. We then analyze the classifier's predictions on these occluded images. If the occlusion region is sufficiently larger than the adversarial patch, several of the occluded images will completely obscure the adversarial patch and thus the classifier's prediction on those images will be unaffected by the adversary and should match the correct label. Thus, we expect the correct label to appear multiple times among the predictions from occluded images. We show how to use this redundancy to detect adversarial patch attacks. We call our scheme the minority reports defense because no matter where the patch is located, there will always be a minority of predictions that cannot be influenced by the attacker and vote for the correct label.

Figure 1 illustrates our defense. We take the input image (Fig. 1a) and construct a grid of partially occluded images (Fig. 1b) with occlusions at different locations, chosen so that any attack will be occluded in a cluster of several predictions. We then apply the classifier to each occluded image to obtain a grid of predictions. When under attack, we can expect most predictions to differ from the true label, but there will always be a cluster of locations where the adversarial patch is fully obscured, and thus the labels are all expected to agree with the true label; in Fig. 1, the 3rd and 4th images in the 4th row obscure the adversarial patch and thus vote for the true label. Our defense analyzes the grid of predicted labels to detect this pattern. If there is a cluster of predictions that all match each other but are in the minority for the prediction grid overall, then this suggests an attack. Figure 2 visualizes the prediction grid for a benign image (on the left) and a malicious image containing an undefended adversarial patch (on the right).

We evaluate our scheme on the CIFAR-10 [KH09], Fashion MNIST [XRV17] and MNIST [LBBH98] datasets with a stride of one. We show that our defense does not harm accuracy much. We also evaluate its security against adaptive attacks. In particular, we show how to bound the success of any possible attack on a given image, and using this, we are able to demonstrate certified security for a large fraction of images. In particular, we are able to prove a security theorem: for a large fraction of images in the validation set, we can prove that no patch attack will succeed, no matter where the patch is placed or how the patch is modified, so long as the size of the patch is limited. In summary, our contributions in this paper are:

Truck

(a) An attack image: a picture of a dog with a malicious 5 × 5 sticker that causes a standard model to classify it as a truck.

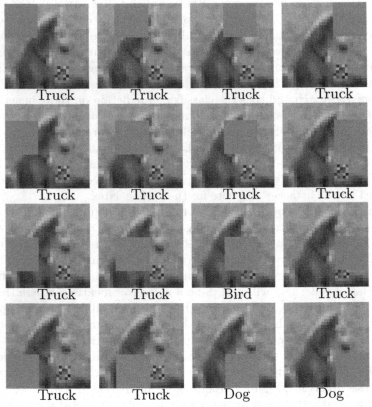

(b) We occlude part of the image with a grey square, then classify these occluded images. Here the 3rd and 4th predictions in the 4th row will be unaffected by this attack. Our actual defense ensures that any attack will be fully occluded by a 3 × 3 grid of predictions, instead of the 1 × 2 grid shown here.

Fig. 1. Our scheme works by occluding different portions of the image and analyzing the predictions made by the classifier on these occluded images.

– We quantify the vulnerability of undefended networks for Fashion MNIST and MNIST against patch attacks with patches of different sizes (Sect. 2.2).

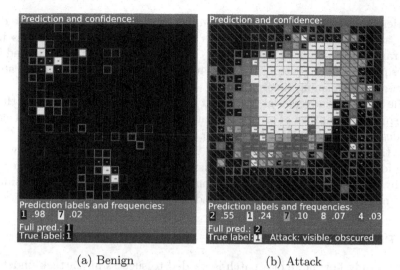

(a) Benign   (b) Attack

Fig. 2. Prediction grids for a benign image (left) and an undefended attack image (right). Each cell in the grid is colored based on the classifier's prediction when fed an image obscured at that position in the grid. A cluster of identical minority predictions, as seen in the right image, suggests an attack. In the attack image on the right, green hashes mark the nine predictions where the adversarial patch was fully occluded.

- We propose a novel method for detecting patch attacks, based on differently occluded views of the input image (Sect. 3).
- We provide a worst-case analysis of security against adaptive attacks for CIFAR-10, Fashion MNIST, and MNIST (Sect. 4 and Sect. 6).

2   Patch Attack

Patch attacks [BMR+17] work by replacing a small part of the image with something of the attacker's choosing, e.g., by placing a small sticker on an object or road sign. Figure 1a shows a patch attack. Patch attacks represent a practical method of executing an attack in the physical world. Digital images can be manipulated throughout the entire scene they present, yet this is impractical in a physical, not digital, scene. It is far more practical to add an attacker-controlled object to part of the scene.

As a simple, non-malicious example, it is not uncommon to see stickers on road signs in the real world, without preventing humans from understanding the signs or prompting the patch's immediate removal.

2.1   Attack Model

We assume the attacker knows everything the defender knows: the architecture, weights, training data, and algorithm of all models and methods used by the defender. The attacker may place a 'compact' patch anywhere within the digital image and arbitrarily modify all pixels within the patch to any values in the pixel range. For simplicity, we restrict the attacker to a patch contained in an $n \times n$ square area for some n, n being a measure of the attacker's lack of stealth, and 'compact' meaning square.

The size of the adversarial patch that can be defended against can be thought of as similar to the size of an adversarial example L2 perturbation that can be defended against. Certainly, the attacker could make a larger change, but at some point, the change either becomes very obvious or changes the meaning of the image for humans. Thus crossing the fussy boundary from being an adversarial, stealthy, attack to being an image of something completely different to humans – thus no longer adversarial as described in Sect. 1.

2.2   Patch Sizes

We first study how large of a patch is needed to successfully attack undefended Fashion MNIST and MNIST. We test multiple patch sizes and measure the attacker's success rate for each patch size.

Setup. We conduct a targeted attack against standard Fashion MNIST and MNIST models from Sect. 6. We attack the first 300 validation images for Fashion MNIST and the first 100 validation images for MNIST. We report the fraction of images for which we can successfully mount a patch attack. For each image, we select a target label by choosing randomly among the classes that are least likely, according to the softmax outputs of the classifier (namely, we find the least likely class, identify all classes whose confidence is within 0.1% of the least likely, and select the target class uniformly at random among this set). That target is used for all attacks on that image. For each base image and its chosen target class, we enumerate all possible patch positions and try at each position to find an attack patch at that position.

Attack Algorithm. To generate patch attacks, we iterate over all possible locations for the patch and use a projected gradient descent (PGD) attack for each location. We consider the attack a success if we find any location where we can place a patch that changes the model's prediction to the target label. The resulting adversarial patch is specific to one specific image and one specific location.

The standard PGD attack uses a constant step size, but we found it was more effective to use a schedule that varies the step size among iterations. In our experiments, a cyclic learning rate was more effective than a constant step size or an exponential decay rate, so we used it in all experiments. We used a cyclic learning rate with ten steps per cycle, with step sizes from 0.002 to 0.3, for a maximum of 150 steps. We stopped early at the end of a cycle if the attack achieved confidence 0.6 or higher for the target class, or if the confidence had not improved by at least 0.002 in the last 20 steps from the best so far. For each image, we attacked in parallel across all possible patch locations.

Results. For our MNIST model, a 6×6 patch is large enough to attack 45% of the images successfully. The success rate for 4×4 patches was 19%, and for 8×8 patches, 80%. When an image can be attacked, there are often many possible locations where an adversarial patch can be placed: for a 6×6 patch, out of all images where a patch attack is possible, there were, on average, 41 different positions where the patch can be placed.

For our Fashion MNIST model, the success rate for patch attacks was as follows: 4×4 patch: 27% success, 5×5 patch: 50% success, 6×6 patch: 60% success.

These results indicate that, on MNIST, an attacker needs to control a 6×6 patch to have close to a 50% chance of success, while a 5×5 patch is large enough for Fashion MNIST, occupying 5% and 3% of the images respectively.

We use 5×5 patches for CIFAR-10, Fashion MNIST and MNIST, as that size is used by recent work [CNA+20].

3   Our Defense

The basic idea of the minority reports defense is to occlude part of the image and classify the resulting image. If the occlusion completely covers the adversarial patch, then the attacker will be unable to influence the classifier's prediction. We don't know where the adversarial patch might be located, so we stride the occlusion area across the image. Because we use an occlusion area sufficiently larger than the adversarial patch, no matter where the adversarial patch is placed, there should be a cluster of occlusion positions that all yield the same prediction.

3.1   Occlusion Training

As our defense will internally use partial occlusions of the image it is given, we train, or retrain, with occluded images. Each time an image is presented in training, a randomly placed $n \times n$ square is occluded, and the model receives the occluded image. This is similar to cutout training from Devries et al. [DT17], who used occlusion as a regularizer. The difference in our training is that the occlusion is the size we will use in our defense. We also internally provide the model an additional input of a sparsity mask that indicates which pixels are occluded.

For instance, the input to an MNIST model is an image, with dimensions $28 \times 28 \times 1$, and a mask, with dimensions $28 \times 28 \times 1$. The image has its normal channels, and the mask has one channel. In the mask, a 0 indicates an occluded position, and a 1 a non-occluded position.

If a model already predicts accurately with a random partial occlusion of the size we use, there is no need to retrain or modify it, it can just be wrapped in our defense as described in the following sections.

To better handle the missing pixels, we modify the architectures we test by replacing convolutions with sparsity invariant convolutions [USS+17]. If the mask indicates no occlusions, the sparsity invariant convolutions behave as normal convolutions, but when occlusions are indicated, the occluded pixels are handled better.

Training on occluded images appears to have only a small change on the accuracy of the inner model on non-occluded images, see Sect. A.

3.2   Creating a Prediction Grid

At evaluation time, our defense's first step is to generate a *prediction grid* as follows. We describe the simpler case of low-resolution images here, leaving the larger stride for higher resolution images to Sect. 5. For defending MNIST images against a 5×5 adversarial patch, we use a 7×7 occlusion region. We slide the 7×7 occlusion region over the 28×28 image with a stride of one pixel, yielding 26×26 possible locations for the occlusion region. This ensures any patch is covered by nine occlude areas, even a patch at the image edge, $26 = (28 - (7 - 1)) + 2 + 2$. The prediction grid is a 26×26 array that records, for each location, the classifier's output. At each location, we mask out the corresponding occlusion region of the image, classify the occluded image, obtain the confidence scores from the classifier's softmax layer and record that in the corresponding cell of the prediction grid. Cell (i, j) of the prediction grid contains the confidence scores for all 10 classes when the pixels in the square $(i-2, j-2), \ldots, (i+5, j+5)$ of the image are masked out.

We visualize the pattern of occlusions in Fig. 1b, though with a large stride for illustration. A stride of one on MNIST produces prediction grids such as Fig. 2 and Fig. 3a and 3c.

If the image contains an adversarial patch centered at location (i, j), then obscuring at each of the 9 locations centered at $(i - 1, j - 1), \ldots, (i + 1, j + 1)$ yields nine images where the adversarial patch has been completely overwritten, and the predictions in those cells of the prediction grid are completely unaffected by the attacker. If the classifier is sufficiently accurate on occluded images, we can hope that all of those 9 predictions match the true label. Thus, within the prediction grid, we can expect to see a 3×3 region where the predictions are uninfluenced by the attacker and (hopefully) all agree with each other. Our defense takes advantage of this fact.

3.3   Detection

In a benign image, typically, every cell in the prediction grid predicts for the same label. In contrast, in a malicious image, we expect there will be a 3×3 region in the prediction grid (where the adversarial patch is obscured) that predicts a single label and some or all of the rest of the prediction grid will have a different prediction. We use this to detect attacks.

In our simplest defense, we look at all 3×3 regions in the prediction grid that vote unanimously for the same label (i.e., all 9 cells yield the same classification). If there are two different labels that both have a 3×3 unanimous vote, then we raise an alarm and treat this as a malicious image.

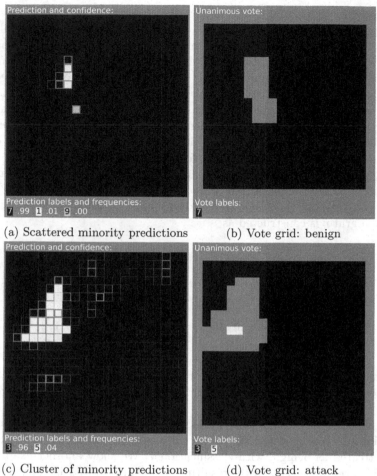

(a) Scattered minority predictions   (b) Vote grid: benign

(c) Cluster of minority predictions   (d) Vote grid: attack

Fig. 3. In (a) and (c), we show the prediction grids for two benign images. (b) and (d) show the corresponding vote grids. We must decide if the minority votes (yellow) are benign errors or what remains of the truth after an attack has influenced the other predictions. Unanimous voting classifies the top example as benign and the bottom as an attack. (Color figure online)

Equivalently, we categorize each 3×3 region within the prediction grid as either unanimously voting for a class (if all 9 cells in that region vote for that class) or abstaining (if they don't all agree). We construct a 24×24 *voting grid* recording these votes. If the voting grid consists of solely a single class and abstentions, then we treat the image as benign, and we use that class as the final prediction of our scheme. Otherwise, if the voting grid contains more than one class, we treat it as malicious.

The idea behind this defense is twofold. First, in a benign image, we expect it to be rare for any 3×3 region in the prediction grid to vote unanimously for an incorrect class: that would require the classifier to be consistently wrong on 9 occluded images. Therefore, the voting grid for benign images will likely contain only the correct class and abstentions. Second, for a malicious image, no matter where the adversarial patch is placed, there will be a 3×3 region in the prediction grid that is uninfluenced by the attack and thus can be expected to vote unanimously for the true class. This means that the voting grid for malicious images will likely contain the correct class at least once. This places the attacker in an impossible bind: if the attack causes any other class to appear in the voting grid, the attack will be detected, but if it does not, then our scheme will classify the image correctly. Either way, the defender wins.

We can formulate our defense mathematically as follows. Let x denote an image, $m_{i,j}$ denote the mask that occludes pixels in $[i-2, i+5] \times [j-2, j+5]$, and $x \odot m_{i,j}$ denote the result of masking image x with mask $m_{i,j}$. Then the prediction grid p is constructed as

$$p_{i,j} = C(x \odot m_{i,j}, m_{i,j}), \tag{1}$$

where the classifier C outputs a vector of confidence scores. The voting grid is defined as

$$v_{i,j} = \begin{cases} c & \text{if } c = \arg\max_{c'} p_{i+u,j+v,c'} \; \forall u, v \in \{0, 1, 2\} \\ \llcorner & \text{otherwise.} \end{cases} \tag{2}$$

If there exists a single class c such that $v_{i,j} = c$ or $v_{i,j} = \llcorner$ for all i, j, then our scheme treats the image as benign and outputs the class c; otherwise, our scheme treats the image as malicious.

We illustrate how the defense works with two examples. For instance, if the prediction grid is as shown in Fig. 3a, then it yields the voting grid in Fig. 3b. This will be treated as benign, with classification 7. We show another example of a prediction grid in Fig. 3c and the resulting voting grid in Fig. 3d. This image will be treated as malicious, and our scheme will decline to classify it. In particular, it is possible that the true label is 5, but an adversarial patch was placed in the upper-left that caused most of the classifications to be shifted to 3, except for a few cases where the patch was partly or wholly obscured. It is, of course, also possible that the image was benign, and a cluster of classification errors caused this pattern, which is the case here.

3.4   Visualization

To give some intuition, we visualize a few sample prediction grids in Fig. 4. The 26×26 prediction grid is displayed as a Hinton diagram with 26×26 squares. The color of each square indicates which class had the highest confidence at that location in the prediction grid (i.e., the class predicted by the classifier). The size of each square is proportional to the confidence of that class.

We show a representative example from each of four different common cases that we have seen:

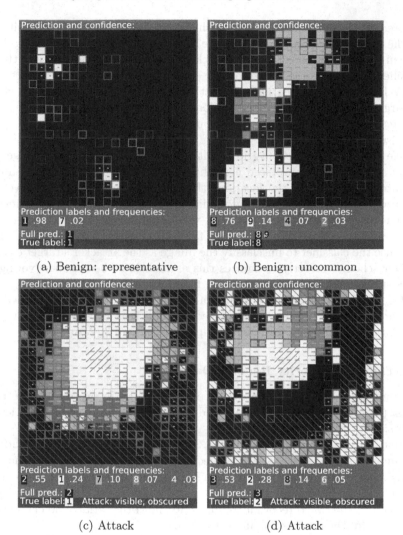

(a) Benign: representative   (b) Benign: uncommon

(c) Attack   (d) Attack

Fig. 4. Representative prediction grids for benign and undefended attack MNIST images. Color indicates the arg max label for that occlusion position, and confidence is indicated by how much of the square is filled. We show at the bottom of each figure a legend indicating which class each color corresponds to and its frequency in the prediction grid; we also show the top prediction and confidence if no pixels are occluded. For attack images, green hashes show the 3×3 grid of predictions that completely occlude the attack; red hashes show the predictions that do not occlude the attack at all. The hashes are not part of our defense, merely an aid for the reader. (The short orange bars are from a detection method that compares with the non-occluded prediction.) (Color figure online)

(a) Most benign images have a prediction grid that predicts all for the same label or has just scattered minority predictions and looks like case (a). The predictions almost always agree with the true label for almost all positions of the occlusion region. However, there are a few locations that, when occluded, cause classification errors (non-black squares). These will be correctly classified and treated as benign by our scheme.

(b) A few benign images have prediction grids that are noisier and contain large clusters of incorrect predictions in the prediction grid. These will be (incorrectly) categorized as malicious by our scheme, i.e., they will cause a false positive.

(c) We show the prediction grid resulting from a typical attack image, with an adversarial patch placed near the center of the image. The green cross-hatching represents the locations that completely occlude the adversarial patch. Those locations in the prediction grid, as well as some other locations in a broader ring around this, vote unanimously for the true label (1). Occlusion regions placed elsewhere fail to occlude the adversarial patch and cause the classifier to misclassify the image as the attacker's target class (2). Our scheme correctly recognizes this as malicious, because the voting grid contains both unanimous votes for 1 and for 2.

(d) Other attack images have even more noise outside the fully occluded area. These, too, are correctly recognized as malicious because the voting grid contains unanimous votes for multiple labels, here 3, 2, and 6.

3.5   The Full Minority Reports Defense

We found that the above defense can be improved by incorporating two refinements: (a) using soft agreement instead of hard unanimity, and (b) tolerating outliers.

First, instead of checking whether a 3×3 region in the prediction grid votes unanimously for the same label, we check whether the confidence for that label averaged over the region exceeds some threshold. For instance, with a 90% threshold, if the confidence scores for class c within that 3×3 region average to 0.9 or larger, then we'd record a vote for c in the voting grid; if no class exceeds the threshold, then we record an abstention.

Second, when computing the average, we discard the lowest score before computing the average. This allows us to tolerate a single outlier when checking for agreement in a 3×3 region.

Mathematically, we fix a threshold τ, and then form the voting grid as

$$
v_{i,j} = \begin{cases} c & \text{if } \operatorname{avg}(\{p_{i+u,j+v,c} \ \forall u, v \in \{0, 1, 2\}\}) \geq \tau \\ \llcorner & \text{otherwise.} \end{cases} \tag{3}
$$

Here we define $\operatorname{avg}(S)$ to be the average of $S \setminus \{\min S\}$, i.e., the average of all but the lowest score in the multiset S.

The threshold τ is a hyper-parameter that can be used to control the trade-off between false positives and false negatives. Increasing τ reduces the number of false positives, but also risks failing to detect some attacks; decreasing τ increases detection power, at the cost of increasing the false positive rate.

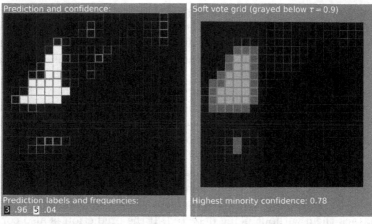

(a) Cluster of minority predictions   (b) Vote grid: benign

Fig. 5. Our full defense on the benign prediction grid from Fig. 3c, with $\tau = 0.9$ classifying as benign (b). A sticker under any of the nonvoting areas would be undetected. A sticker in the lower right, when occluded, would leave in (a) the confident remains of the original prediction, and be classified as an attack.

The size of the occlusion region is another hyper-parameter of our defense. In our experiments, we always chose an occlusion region that is two pixels larger than the largest adversarial patch we seek to defend. Thus our occlusion region will be 7×7, and we provide certified results against adversarial patches up to 5×5 in size.

We visualize the operation of our final defense in Fig. 5.

4   Security Evaluation

One benefit of our design is that it enables us to guarantee the security of our scheme on some images. This provides a stronger result than evaluating against a specific adaptive attack. Were we to rely on evaluation against some adaptive attack, an adversary might be smarter than our adaptive attack and achieve a higher attack success rate. Instead, our certified result provides a guarantee that can not be beaten by any adaptive attack. We describe our certified security analysis in this section.

The core observation is: if the adversarial patch is completely occluded, then the adversary cannot have any influence on the prediction made by the classifier on the corresponding occluded image. For certified security, we make a very conservative assumption: we assume that the adversary might be able to completely control the classifier's prediction for all other occluded images (i.e., where the patch is only partly occluded or is not occluded at all). This assumption lets us make a worst-case analysis of whether the classification of a particular image could change in the presence of an adversarial patch of a particular size.

Notice that wherever the sticker is placed, there will be a 3×3 grid in the prediction grid that is unaffected by the sticker. (This is because with a stride of one, we use an occlusion region that is 2 pixels larger than the maximum possible sticker size.) It follows that there will be some cell in the voting grid that is not changed by the sticker.

If the voting grid for an image x is completely filled with votes for a single class c, with no abstentions, then any image x' that differs by introduction of a single sticker will either be classified by our defense as class c or will be detected by our defense as malicious. (This follows because at least one element of the voting grid is unaffected by the sticker, so at least one element of the voting grid for x' will vote for c. If no other class appears in the voting grid, then our defense will classify x' as class c; if some other class appears, then our defense will treat x' as malicious.) Thus, such images can be certified safe—there is no way to attack them without being detected. If the prediction is also correct, we classify the image as certified accurate.

In contrast, if the voting grid has even one region that does not vote or votes as the attacker would like, then our conservative analysis is forced to assume that it might be possible to attack the image: the attacker can place a sticker at that location, potentially changing all the other regions' votes, and thereby escape detection.

We evaluate the security of our scheme by measuring the fraction of images that can be certified safe and certified accurate, according to the conservative analysis above.

5   Higher Resolution Images

For higher resolution images, increasing the stride and pixel size of the occlude area lets us manage the cost of the prediction grid. For a patch of size $p \times p$ pixels and a stride of s pixels, an occlude area of $(p + 2s) \times (p + 2s)$ produces nine full occlusions of any patch, if the patch is aligned to our stride grid. This mirrors what we have done with a stride of one. To account for patches not aligned to our stride grid, we increase our occlude by one stride less one pixel. Thus our occlude area is $(p + 3s - 1) \times (p + 3s - 1)$ pixels, for $s > 1$.

As an example, for CIFAR-10, we evaluate against a 5×5 attack patch, covering 2.4% of the image. For that, we occlude a 7×7 area, covering 4.8% of the image. With a stride of one, our prediction grid is 30×30.

If CIFAR-10 had ten times the resolution, 320×320, then the comparable sized attack patch would be 50×50 pixels, the same 2.4% of the image. For a stride of ten, our occlude area would be $(50+3\times10-1)\times(50+3\times10-1) = 79\times79$, or 6.1% of the image, more than before. Our prediction grid would be the same 30×30 size. However, we would be making predictions with more of the image occluded.

If occluding a larger percentage of the image was an issue, a 40×40 patch would allow a 69×69 occlude area. The predictions for the grid would thus have 4.7% of the image occluded, similar to before, with an expectation of comparable accuracy.

6 Experiments

We evaluate the effectiveness of our defense by measuring the clean accuracy (the images that when unmodified are classified correctly by class and as benign) and the certified accuracy (the images that when unmodified are classified correctly by class and as benign and where any attack – targeted or un-targeted – will either not change the classification or will be detected).

Data and Models. We evaluate our defense on standard convolutional architectures, trained with data augmentation and random 90/10 train/validation splits. For CIFAR-10, we use SimpNet's 600K parameter version [HRF+18] trained for 700 epochs, though we do not yet reproduce all details of their training; for Fashion MNIST, a VGG-16 model [SZ14] trained for 50 epochs; for MNIST, the Deotte model [Deo18], with 40% dropout and batch normalization and 45 epochs. These serve as an inner model in our architecture.

Method. We measure the clean and the certified accuracy on the 5000 or 6000 validation images. We perform multiple trials, using a different random 90/10 train/validation split for each trial. For each dataset, we perform $n = 4$ trials. The standard deviation is relatively low (for clean and certified accuracy they are CIFAR-10: 0.2–0.8% 0.5–1.1%, Fashion MNIST: 0.2–0.4% 0.2–0.6%, MNIST: 0.0–0.1% 0.1–0.5%). We report results for different points in the tradeoff between clean and certified accuracy, and we compare with recent related work using Interval Bounds Propagation (IBP) [CNA+20].

Results. Our results, Table 1, show that our defense achieves relatively high clean and certified accuracy and outperforms the previous state of the art.

For CIFAR-10, we achieve a clean accuracy of 92.4%, and 43.8% of images can be certified accurate (no matter where a sticker is placed, the resulting image will either be classified correctly or the attack will be detected) for 5×5 stickers. Our clean accuracy is 1.6% below that reported in the literature for the architecture we defend. It is only 0.1% below the accuracy we achieve with that architecture when evaluated on non-occluded images.

This is significantly better than recent work by Chiang et al. [CNA+20], which achieves clean accuracy of 47.8% and certified accuracy of 30.3% for CIFAR-10 against 5×5 stickers.

For MNIST, we achieve a clean accuracy of 99.4%, and 64.2% of images can be certified accurate for 5×5 stickers. This is again significantly better than recent work [CNA+20]: the error rate on clean images is more than an order of magnitude lower, and the certified accuracy is slightly higher.

Our measurement of certified accuracy is based on conservative assumptions. We suspect that many images that we cannot certify accurate are in fact secure against attack, even though we cannot prove it. Thus, the number certified accurate represents a conservative lower bound on the true robustness of our scheme.

Table 1. The clean accuracy and certified accuracy of our defense (MR) vs. the previous state of the art (IBP) on all three datasets, for a 5 × 5 adversarial patch. We report
the false positive rate of our defense in the third column; it is also included in the clean
and certified accuracy. We report the literature reported accuracy of our inner model
architectures in the fourth column. We report the accuracy our inner model achieves
on non-occluded clean images in the fifth column.

| Dataset | Defense | F.P | Accuracy | | | |
			Lit.	Inner	Clean	Cert.
CIFAR-10	IBP [CNA+20]				47.8%	30.3%
	MR (Our)	19.9%	94.0%	92.5%	78.8%	77.6%
		3.3%			90.6%	62.1%
		0.2%			**92.4%**	**43.8%**
Fashion	MR	12.9%		93.8%	85.4%	84.3%
		1.4%			93.0%	69.4%
		0.1%			93.9%	42.0%
MNIST	IBP [CNA+20]				92.9%	62.0%
	MR	4.8%	99.6%	99.6%	95.1%	94.9%
		0.7%			99.0%	75.8%
		0.2%			**99.4%**	**64.2%**

Discussion. Our experiments show that by choosing a high τ, we can achieve
clean accuracy that is very close to the accuracy of our inner model on non-
occluded images. With a lower τ we can achieve a higher certified accuracy at
the cost of a lower clean accuracy.

For CIFAR-10, the architecture we used is reported to have an accuracy
of 94.0% when trained appropriately. We did not replicate all aspects of the
authors' training procedure and achieved only 92.5%. Once we replicate their
full training procedure, we expect our CIFAR-10 results would also improve.

We did an ablation study where we omitted the occlude training, and found
that the occlude training is essential: Without it, the defense is extremely ineffective.

7   Limitations

Multiple patches would not be easy to handle with this approach, though they
may also draw more attention to the attack. The simple extension would be all
combinations of multiple occlude areas. For two patches, this would mean two
occlude areas and a 4D prediction grid. That would be prohibitive in compute
cost, and the multiple occludes would likely degrade accuracy.

Two patches might be present because the image is actually a binocular
image. This would be straightforward to handle if the image came from a true

physical scene and the parallax shift was not much. Widening the occlude area slightly would cover the two views of the same physical adversarial patch object.

The evaluation time cost of our defense is the size of the prediction grid, as for each occluded prediction, we predict on a new occluded image. It is possible lower layer convolutional results could be reused, but there would be a complexity cost, and we have not investigated this. For CIFAR-10 with a 5×5 patch, this is 900 times the evaluation cost of the original model. For a 320×320 pixel image, 50×50 patch, and stride 10, this is also 900 times the cost. We have not found any real difference in the time to train an occlude trained model than a normally trained one.

Our certified accuracy depends on the occluded accuracy of the architecture we defend. We have not examined datasets with lower top-1 accuracy, such as the 1000 class ImageNet. The more occluded predictions that are different, the more voting areas will not vote unanimously, causing the image to be vulnerable to attack.

Our defense is only effective against patches of irregular or unknown shape if they are bounded by the shape(s) we expect, of which one $n \times n$ shape is the most practical.

8 Related Work

In earlier work, Hayes proposes a defense against sticker attacks using inpainting of a suspected sticker region to remove the sticker from the image [Hay18]. This is similar to our defense. However, Hayes uses a heuristic to identify the region to inpaint (based on unusually dense regions within the saliency map), so any attack that fools the heuristic could defeat their defense. One could use inpainting in our scheme instead of occlusion, and it is possible this might improve accuracy, though our work can be viewed as showing that simple occlusion suffices to get strong results. Naseer et al. propose a defense against sticker attacks by smoothing high-frequency image details to remove the sticker [NKP18]. They limit accuracy loss by using windows that overlap by a third, but their windows are smaller than the attack patch. Chiang et al. broke both of these defenses [CNA+20], so neither is effective against adaptive attacks; in contrast, we guarantee security against adaptive attack.

Wu et al. defend against adversarial patches with adversarial training [WTV20]. The primary advantage of our approach is that it provides certified security.

Chiang et al. study certified security against patch attacks using interval bounds propagation [CNA+20]. As discussed above, our defense achieves significantly better certified accuracy on both MNIST and CIFAR than their scheme. They also examine how their defense generalizes to other shapes of stickers and how to achieve security against L_0-bounded attacks, topics that we have not examined.

Zhang et al. limit the effect of a patch by clipping logits in a bag of features classifier and provide certified results [ZYMW20]. Comparing our results with theirs is difficult as they use the higher resolution ImageNet dataset. They have higher robustness to attack but a larger cost to clean accuracy.

9   Conclusion

We propose the minority reports defense, a network architecture designed specially to be robust against patch attacks. We show experimentally that it is successful at defending against these attacks for a significant fraction of images.

Acknowledgments. This work was supported by generous gifts from Google and Futurewei, by the Hewlett Foundation through the Center for Long-term Cybersecurity, and by Intel through the ISTC for Secure Computing.

A   Effects of Occlude Training

Our defense requires the inner model to handle occluded images well. To assess the effect of this requirement, we trained models with and without occlusions for all three inner-model architectures.

Training on occluded images appears to have only a small change on the accuracy of the inner model on non-occluded images, see Table 2. The change is, at worst, the standard deviation of our measurements. Note from Table 1 that the clean accuracy of our defense might have either a small or no drop from the accuracy of our inner-model.

Table 2. The effect of training on occluded images, on the inner model's accuracy on non-occluded images. We show the difference (last column) and the standard deviation ($n = 4$).

Dataset	Type of training images		Δ
	Non-occluded	Occluded	
CIFAR-10	$92.5 \pm 0.3\%$	$92.5 \pm 0.2\%$	-0.0%
Fashion	$94.1 \pm 0.4\%$	$93.8 \pm 0.3\%$	-0.3%
MNIST	$99.58 \pm 0.08\%$	$99.63 \pm 0.33\%$	$+0.05\%$

Note that this does not measure the accuracy of our defense as a whole. Our defense feeds the inner model occluded images at test time, and accuracy on occluded images is slightly lower than on non-occluded images.

B   Defense Details

The inner models are standard convolutional architectures modified to handle partially occluded data by the use of sparse convolutional layers that we created. The inner model returns a normal logit prediction for the dataset classes.

C   Model Details

MNIST We used the Deotte model with layer descriptions ([32C3-32C3-32C5S2] - [64C3-64C3-64C5S2] - 128).

References

[BMR+17] Brown, T., Mane, D., Roy, A., Abadi, M., Gilmer, J.: Adversarial patch (2017). arXiv:1712.09665

[CNA+20] Chiang, P.-y., Ni, R., Abdelkader, A., Zhu, C., Studor, C., Goldstein, T.: Certified defenses for adversarial patches. In: ICLR (2020)

[CW17] Carlini, N., Wagner, D.: Towards evaluating the robustness of neural networks. In: Security and Privacy (2017). arXiv:1608.04644 [cs.CR]

[Deo18] Deotte, C.: How to choose CNN Architecture MNIST (2018). https://www.kaggle.com/cdeotte/how-to-choose-cnn-architecture-mnist

[DT17] Devries, T., Taylor, G.W.: Improved regularization of convolutional neural networks with cutout (2017). arXiv:1708.04552 [cs.CV]

[EEF+17] Eykholt, K., et al.: Robust physical-world attacks on deep learning models (2017). arXiv:1707.08945

[GSS15] Goodfellow, I.J., Shlens, J., Szegedy, C.: Explaining and harnessing adversarial examples. In: ICLR (2015). arXiv:1412.6572 [stat.ML]

[Hay18] Hayes, J.: On visible adversarial perturbations & digital watermarking. In: The IEEE Conference on Computer Vision and Pattern Recognition (CVPR) Workshops, June 2018

[HJN+11] Huang, L., Joseph, A.D., Nelson, B., Rubinstein, B.I.P., Tygar, J.D.: Adversarial machine learning (2011)

[HRF+18] HasanPour, S.H., Rouhani, M., Fayyaz, M., Sabokrou, M., Adeli, E.: Towards principled design of deep convolutional networks: introducing simpnet. CoRR, abs/1802.06205 (2018)

[KH09] Krizhevsky, A., Hinton, G.: Learning multiple layers of features from tiny images (2009)

[KZG18] Karmon, D., Zoran, D., Goldberg, Y.: Lavan: localized and visible adversarial noise. CoRR, abs/1801.02608 (2018)

[LBBH98] LeCun, Y., Bottou, L., Bengio, Y., Haffner, P.: Gradient-based learning applied to document recognition. Proc. IEEE **86**(11), 2278–2324 (1998)

[NKP18] Naseer, M., Khan, S., Porikli, F.: Local gradients smoothing: defense against localized adversarial attacks. CoRR, abs/1807.01216 (2018)

[SZ14] Simonyan, K., Zisserman, A.: Very deep convolutional networks for large-scale image recognition (2014). arxiv:1409.1556

[SZS+14] Szegedy, C., et al.: Intriguing properties of neural networks. In: ICLR (2014). arXiv:1312.6199 [cs.CV]

[TRG19] Thys, S., Van Ranst, W., Goedemé, T.: Fooling automated surveillance cameras: adversarial patches to attack person detection (2019). arXiv:1904.08653

[USS+17] Uhrig, J., Schneider, N., Schneider, L., Franke, U., Brox, T., Geiger, A.: Sparsity invariant CNNs (2017). arXiv:1708.06500 [cs.CV]

[WTV20] Wu, T., Tong, L., Vorobeychik, Y.: Defending against physically realizable attacks on image classification. In: ICLR (2020)

[XRV17] Xiao, H., Rasul, K., Vollgraf, R.: Fashion-MNIST: a novel image dataset for benchmarking machine learning algorithms. CoRR, abs/1708.07747 (2017)

[XZL+19] Xu, K., et al.: Adversarial T-shirt! Evading person detectors in a physical world (2019). arXiv:1910.11099

[ZYMW20] Zhang, Z., Yuan, B., McCoyd, M., Wagner, D.: Clipped BagNet: defending against sticker attacks with clipped bag-of-features. In: DLS (2020)

Author Index